A MEDITERRANEAN SOCIETY

PUBLISHED UNDER THE AUSPICES OF THE

GUSTAVE E. VON GRUNEBAUM CENTER
FOR NEAR EASTERN STUDIES
UNIVERSITY OF CALIFORNIA,
LOS ANGELES

S. D. GOITEIN

A Mediterranean Society

THE JEWISH COMMUNITIES OF THE ARAB WORLD
AS PORTRAYED IN THE DOCUMENTS OF THE CAIRO GENIZA

VOLUME IV

Daily Life

UNIVERSITY OF CALIFORNIA PRESS
Berkeley · Los Angeles · London · 1983

University of California Press
Berkeley and Los Angeles, California

University of California Press, Ltd.
London, England

First Paperback Printing 1999

Goitein, S. D., 1900–
A Mediterranean society : the Jewish communities of the Arab world as portrayed in the documents of Cairo Geniza / S. D. Goitein.
p. cm.
Originally published: Berkeley : University of California Press, 1967–c1993.
Includes bibliographical references and indexes.
Contents: v. 1. Economic foundations – v. 2. The community – v. 3. The family – v. 4. Daily life – v. 5. The individual.
ISBN 0-520-04869-5 (cl. : alk. paper)
ISBN 0-520-22161-3 (pbk. : alk. paper)
1. Jews–Islamic Empire–Civilization. 2. Islamic Empire–Civilization. 3. Cairo Genizah. I. Title.
DS135.L4G65 1999
956′.004924–dc21 99-36039
CIP

Printed in the United States of America

08 07 06 05 04 03 02 01 00 99
10 9 8 7 6 5 4 3 2 1

The paper used in this publication meets the minimum requirements of ANSI/NISO Z39.48-1984 (R 1997) (*Permanence of Paper*). ♾

Contents of Volumes I through V

NOTE: The title originally planned for Chapter X, The Mediterranean Mind, was relinquished to avoid the erroneous impression that the personality emerging from the Geniza documents is regarded as representative of a hypothetical human type common to the Mediterranean area.

Contents

Preface

The history of material civilization, of the things surrounding man day in day out and requiring his attention willy-nilly, has become a special branch of medievalist research. Called *Sachkultur* in German, culture as expressed in matter, it forms part and parcel of social history, since the relationship between man and object is apt to reveal much about man himself (for a note on *Sachkultur* see p. 270). Generations of students of classical antiquity have worked on this subject. With regard to the Middle Ages, however, when the emphasis was on religion and on all that was connected with it in one way or another, it was felt that material civilization had been somewhat neglected or, at least, had not been treated specifically and systematically enough, and that the time had come to remedy the situation.

I had a similar experience with my study of the letters and documents of the so-called Cairo Geniza, materials that originated mostly among Jews living in the Muslim countries of the Mediterranean area (and along the India route) during the tenth through the thirteenth centuries. Planning to draw a comprehensive picture of the society encountered in that marvelous treasure trove of manuscripts, I described its economic foundations and its communal and family life in the first three volumes of this work. I intended to conclude with a portrait of the individual—his physical environment and spiritual world. The idea was to give the latter the lion's share and to keep the former as brief as feasible.

Yet, the more my work progressed, the more doubtful it became that the proportion was right, that it reflected faithfully what really occupied the mind of the Geniza person. His letters deal almost exclusively with practical matters and physical objects. It should not be argued that the vast majority of writings preserved in the Geniza were books (or, rather, remnants of books), which might reflect a society predominantly interested in learning. Most of these writings were either professional and specialist texts as in our own libraries, or biblical and liturgical ones used at the synogogue service, or for popular study, "adult courses," which also were a kind of worship.

One should not jump to the conclusion (as some are apparently inclined to do) that medieval man was not really as religious and spiritual as had been assumed. It is a complex question, about which more must be said in the concluding part of this study. Suffice it to state here that God is mentioned in Geniza letters as frequently as the dollar is elsewhere; that the Geniza person's day, week, and year were punctuated and regulated by religion; and that it also provided him with well-integrated beliefs and moral principles, which were conducive to good mental health, albeit not always honored by compliance. Add to it that not only Jews, but also medieval Muslims and Eastern Christians, knew that their station in society depended largely on the particular sect, denomination, rite, or "school" to which they belonged. In short, religion was present everywhere, but one gets the impression that, with the exception of the few really pious and God-possessed, religion formed the frame rather than the content of the daily existence.

Consequently, if we wish to know the Geniza person's life, we must stroll with him through his beloved native town, which was his *waṭan*, or home (the town, not a country or state with constantly changing borders); we must visit his house, which, together with everything in it, differed so completely from ours. His clothing, especially his outerwear, received his meticulous attention, for it identified him, it showed the world who he was; the jewelry of the womenfolk was a matter of utmost concern for a variety of reasons, in particular as a means of protection of female economic independence; mounts, like clothing, could be status symbols, somehow similar to our cars. For the pleasures of the table the Geniza is not a good source; for, unlike ourselves, but almost like our grandparents, the Geniza people regarded speaking about food as bad manners. My chapter about the subject is, I am afraid, somewhat lopsided with emphasis on bread and wine, the basic diet of ancient and early medieval common man.

The study of material civilization became for me a real voyage of discovery. Originally, it was forced upon me by the necessity of trying to identify the countless objects mentioned in the Geniza, and to understand their place in life and their value in money and prestige. This undertaking required much toil, but was unavoidable; for without knowing what people were talking about, it was hazardous to assess their psyche and attitudes.

My labors were well rewarded. Every object seemed to tell a story or at least to pose a problem. The minutiae of daily life often reflected great historical processes or intricate situations. During the high-strung and bigoted Late Middle Ages, we are told, men regarded themselves as citizens of the quarters into which they had separated themselves with their own kind. In Fatimid and early Ayyubid times houses of Muslims, Christians, and Jews bordered on one another and, as the Geniza shows, their inhabitants felt themselves strongly as belonging to the larger unit, the town. Tables, chairs, and beds were in use by the ancient Egyptians, Israelites, Greeks, and Romans, but had totally disappeared by the middle of the eleventh century together with the concepts of dining room or bedroom. This tremendous change might have been attributable partly to the progressive deforestation of the area with the resulting shortage of timber and partly to its domination by a race of desert dwellers and pastoral peoples, who made use of textiles instead of wood for comfort. As in spiritual matters, by the turn of the eleventh century the heritage of Late Antiquity had either been digested in the Middle East or relinquished. The fantastic development of textiles with their precious fabrics and gorgeous colors for seating, bedding, carpets, and hangings (as well as for clothing, of course) was due to these changes.

The familiar process of the seeping down of luxurious ways of the ruling class to lower layers of the society is often to be observed in our documents. Textiles that had once been the prerogative of the Sassanid kings of Persia and their successors, the Abbasid caliphs, became almost a convention for middle-class brides, naturally, in cheap varieties or imitations. The very architecture of the house and the arrangement of the furnishings in it seem to have followed royal examples. "A house without a large hall is not a house." The spacious *majlis*, literally, sitting room, which provided a gathering place for the extended family and its friends, seems to have been modeled, both in its relative size and in the distribution of seating facilities, carpets, and hangings, on the archetype of a caliphal palace. The colorful pillows and cushions, "destined to give the house the look of a garden," as well as the equally gay covers of the benches on which one was seated, occupied a prominent place in the trousseau of any bride with some means.

Another instance of seeping down was the adoption by the general populace of a custom cherished by an elite circle, in the process of which its original significance got lost. In the thirteenth century and later, Arabic manuscript illustrations show persons, high and low, female and male, wearing decorative stripes on the upper part of their sleeves, embroidered with writing, imitations of writing, or otherwise. This custom is well documented in the Geniza, so much so that a large order for clothing indicates for each type whether or not it should have writing. One is reminded of poetry-loving Baghdad of the early Abbasid period, when verses with allusive content were attached by sophisticated ladies to their sleeves, a practice followed by the eccentric eleventh-century poet Wallada of Cordova, Spain, who used her own audacious creations for the purpose. Such practices may ultimately have had their origin in remote antiquity: kings and chieftains wore a bracelet around the upper arm, seat of human strength and valor.

Even a small object could have a long history. Soap was used for washing clothes; the human body was cleaned with an alkaloid substance, which, as we learn from a literary source, was recommended to the Arab conquerors by the more sophisticated Persians. In the Geniza, the receptacle containing this substance is regularly included in trousseau lists. (It had to be tightly closed lest the scented material lose its fragrance.) The substance itself was already used in classical antiquity and is also known from the Talmud, that vast repository of postbiblical Jewish writings. The Talmud is often quoted in this volume because it demonstrates the large extent to which the material civilization of the Greeks and Romans had been absorbed by the Middle East before the advent of Islam.

In the course of the thirty years or so during which I have studied the life of the Geniza people, I have somehow come to know the subjects about which they talked when they came together. In this volume, a representative portion of them is communicated to the reader in the numerous summaries and translations, partial or full, provided in the text and appendixes. In problematic cases more than one example is given in order to enable the reader to judge for himself. In the very process of discussing an object, its identity, use, and significance become revealed.

I cannot produce any illustrations because by their very nature the Geniza documents contain none. The quotations are my illustrations. Throughout this volume, however, the reader is referred to comparative pictorial material in many different types of publications, general or specialist. Students of Islamic art and architecture are rightly alert to the risk of relating illustrations or still extant objects to terms or descriptions found in literary sources. But details preserved in a primary, not literary, source, as is the case with the documentary Geniza, may be a welcome addition to our understanding of Islamic artifacts. A distinguishd student of Islamic art wrote, after having read my section on jewelry: "It is really art history come to life."

Another matter is involved. My lamented friend, Richard Ettinghausen, whose untimely death is an irreparable loss for me, as it has been for Islamic scholarship at large, impressed on me again and again: "Be as precise and detailed as possible; you cannot know what will be of interest for the readers. Let the Geniza speak for itself and prepare the avenues which may guide future research." I faithfully followed his advice, but only up to a certain point. For I am confident that the topics treated in this volume will be taken up by scholars specifically engaged in the study of material civilization, as has already been done so successfully by Moshe Gil for housing and Yedida K. Stillman for clothing (see Abbreviations). I tried to keep this book within the limits of its stated purpose: a chapter of social history.

A word must be said about the Arabic language used in the Geniza documents. This medieval Arabic is neither the written classical language nor the modern vernacular, but something in between. Despite the admirable work done in Arabic lexicography both by medieval Muslim authors and modern scholars it became soon clear to me that the vocabulary of the Geniza documents was only imperfectly registered elsewhere. This was natural. The letters and documents of the Cairo Geniza were written mostly by members of the middle class; just as the medieval chronicler had little opportunity to pay attention to that segment of mankind, so the lexicographer, lacking sufficient written sources describing those people, was not in a position to leave us complete lists of the things used by them in daily life.

In order to avoid misunderstanding, I hasten to add that Middle Arabic, as that medieval Arabic is now called, was spoken by Muslims, Christians, and Jews alike. Jews wrote it mostly in Hebrew characters, which they had learned in school, and also used Hebrew phrases when speaking about matters of religion, in blessings, titles, and the like, and, of course, in quotations from the Bible and postbiblical literature. But *things* were always expressed in Arabic. Even in letters and documents written in the Hebrew language, objects went by their Arabic terms, and for a very simple reason: they were the terms one had to use when going to the bazaar to buy and to sell. The conclusion of subsection B, pp. 193–200, shows that, in Fatimid times, Jewish clothing did not differ essentially from that of the general population.

How, then, was one to go about knowing the things with which the Geniza people lived? One had to resort to the method already adopted by the ancient commentators of Alexandria, namely, "explaining Homer through Homer," collecting as many instances as feasible of the occurrence of an object and noting whatever one could learn about its use, price, relationship to other objects mentioned together with it, and so forth.

This type of research is known as philology. I am well aware of the fact that nowadays nothing more disparaging could be said of a historian than that he is a philologist. But we are doing spadework here, and this cannot be done without a spade.

Another matter is, of course, how much of this labor should be shared by the user of this book. The reader is the author's guest. He should be at the table, being served, not stand with him in the kitchen watching him cook. But I must reiterate that my endeavor is to let the reader listen to the Geniza people's talk. By participating in the process of inquiry into the meaning of a term, one becomes familiar with the object itself.

My original plan was to include the material presented here in the first volume of this book. The sections herein on the city, domestic architecture, and socioeconomic aspects of housing were already typed by the middle of the 1970s. But I soon realized that I had not done enough homework and that the significance of the things of daily life would become more apparent after the social aspects, namely, communal and family life, had been treated. Thus, Horace's *nonumque prematur in annum* (let it be kept quiet till the ninth year) was more than fully observed. I do not regret the delay. Not only has my factual knowledge largely expanded during this long period, but my education, I mean my understanding of and feeling for social phenomena and processes, has been much enhanced through my contact with contemporary scholarship. Thus I hope that the late appearance of this volume has benefited it, although I am only too well aware of its shortcomings.

ACKNOWLEDGMENTS

As in the previous volumes, it is my pleasant duty to express my sincere thanks to the librarians and staffs of the libraries whose manuscripts have been used. Unlike the previous volumes, this one did not necessitate new visits. All material had been collected in the preceding decades, although the process of deciphering and identifying went on unabated. But whenever I take a photostat into my hands I feel how much I owe to the guardians of those treasures, who toiled so much to preserve and ready them for the use of the student.

I wish to reiterate here my appreciation of the assistance received from the late Egyptian archaeologist, Ahmad Fakhri, whose guidance on the subjects treated in this volume was most valuable. I am grateful to Professor Bernard Lewis and Professor Eva Baer for their useful observations. I am particularly indebted to Dr. Marilyn

Jenkins of the Metropolitan Museum, New York, who read the extensive section on jewelry and took the trouble to write detailed observations on it, which were most informative. My new assistant, Paula Sanders, a gifted and conscientious young scholar, contributed much to the smooth progress of my work. And, as with the preceding volume, Sandra S. Lafferty's painstaking and beautiful typing was a great help. I regard it as a stroke of luck that Mrs. Teresa Joseph, who had edited the first three volumes of this work, was able to watch over the preparation of this volume as well. I am confident that the reader will join me in my feelings of gratitude for the fruits of her labor.

Last, but not least, my deep-felt thanks go to Dr. Harry Woolf, the director, and to the faculty of the Institute for Advanced Study, Princeton, as well as to Dr. Harry Starr, the president, and to the board of the Luscius N. Littauer Foundation for their continuous support of the Geniza project.

I cannot conclude this Preface without commemorating my former student and later collaborator of many years in the work of the Geniza, Dr. Gershon Weiss, professor of Hebrew at Temple University, Philadelphia. He, a sturdy young man of forty-six, a father of three, died of cancer on October 15, 1981. Besides being a meticulous and sedulous scholar, he was a wonderful human being, beloved and esteemed by many. His memory will be cherished by all who have known him.

May 1983 S. D. GOITEIN
The Institute for Advanced Study
School of Historical Studies
Princeton, New Jersey

Abbreviations

The abbreviations listed in *Med. Soc.*, I, xix–xxiv; II, xv–xvi; and III, xix–xxi, are used also in this volume.

Additional abbreviations, not used in volumes I–III:

Abraham Maimonides *The Highways to Perfection*	Abraham Maimonides, *The Highways to Perfection*, vol. II, ed. and trans. Samuel Rosenblatt. Baltimore, 1938.
Abu-Lughod, *City Victorious*	Janet L. Abu-Lughod, *Cairo, 1001 Years of the City Victorious.* Princeton, 1971.
Alf Layla	*Alf layla wa-layla* (The Arabian Nights), standard edition of Būlāq, A.H. 1252/A.D. 1836/7, and its reprints.
Ashtor, *Social and Economic History*	*E. Ashtor, A Social and Economic History of the Near East in the Middle Ages.* Berkeley and Los Angeles, 1976.
Barthélemy, *Dictionnaire arabe-français*	A. Barthélemy, *Dictionnaire arabe-français, Dialectes de Syrie.* Paris, 1935.
BEOIF Damas	*Bulletin d'Études Orientales, Institut français de Damas.*
BIFAO	*Bulletin de l'Institut Français d'Archéologie Orientale* (Cairo).
Brandenburg, *Islamische Baukunst*	Dietrich Brandenburg, *Islamische Baukunst in Egypt.* Berlin, 1966.
Bresc-Goitein, *Inventaire dotal*	Henry Bresc and S. D. Goitein, "Un inventaire dotal des Juifs

	Siciliens [1479]," *Mélanges d'Archéologie et d'Histoire*, École Française de Rome 82 (1970), 903–917.
Briggs, "The Saracenic House"	M. S. Briggs, "The Saracenic House," *Burlington Magazine*, 38 (1921), 228–238, 289–301.
Brown, *Madina*	L. Carl Brown, ed., *From Madina to Metropolis*. Princeton, 1973.
Colloque 1969	Arab Republic of Egypt, Ministry of Culture, General Egyptian Book Organisation, *Colloque International sur l'Histoire du Caire*. Cairo, n.d.
Dimand, *Muhammadan Art*	M. S. Dimand, *A Handbook of Muhammadan Art*. New York, 1947.
Dozy, *Vêtements*	R. Dozy, *Dictionnaire détaillé des noms des vêtements chez les Arabes*. Amsterdam, 1845.
ENA New Series 48	This mark replaces JTS Geniza Misc. See *Med. Soc.*, I, xxiii, 502.
Ennen, *Europäische Stadt*	Edith Ennen, *Die Europäische Stadt*, Göttingen, 1975. Trans. Natalie Fryde, *The Medieval Town*. Amsterdam and New York, 1979. In cases of doubt consult the original.
Erdmann, *Oriental Carpets*	Kurt Erdmann, *Seven Hundred Years of Oriental Carpets*, ed. Hanna Erdmann, trans. May H. Beattie and Hildegard Herzog. London, 1970.
Ettinghausen, *Arab Painting*	Richard Ettinghausen, *Arab Painting*. Cleveland, Ohio, 1962.
Eudel, *Bijoux*	Paul Eudel, *Bijoux de l'Afrique du Nord*. Paris, 1906.

Eudel, *Orfèverie*	Paul Eudel, *L'Orfèverie algérienne et tunisienne*. Algiers, 1902.
Fahd, *Couleurs*	T. Fahd, "Genèse et causes des couleurs d'après l'agriculture nabatienne," *Fritz Meier Jubilee Volume*, ed. Richard Gramlich. Wiesbaden, 1974. Pp. 78–95.
Fraenkel, *Aramäische Fremdwörter*	Siegmund Fraenkel, *Die aramäischen Fremdwörter im Arabischen*. Leiden, 1886.
Friedman, *Marriage*	M. A. Friedman, *Jewish Marriage in Palestine: A Cairo Geniza Study*, Tel Aviv and New York. Vol. I, 1980, Vol. II, 1981. The numbers refer to the texts in Vol. II. Cf. *Med. Soc.*, III, ix, xx.
Gil, *Foundations*	Moshe Gil, *Documents of the Jewish Pious Foundations from the Cairo Geniza*. Leiden, 1976.
Gil, "Maintenance"	M. Gil, "Maintenance, Building Operations, and Repairs in the Houses of the Qodesh in Fustat: A Geniza Study," *JESHO*, 14 (1971), 136–195.
Goitein, *Palestinian Jewry*	S. D. Goitein, *Palestinian Jewry in Early Islamic and Crusader Times* (Heb.). Jerusalem, 1980.
Goitein, "The Synagogue and Its Furnishings"	S. D. Goitein, "The Synagogue Building and Its Furnishings according to the Records of the Cairo Geniza" (Heb.), *Eretz-Israel*, 7 (1964), 81–97.
Golombek-Gervers, "Tiraz Fabrics"	Lisa Golombek and Veronika Gervers, "Tiraz Fabrics in the Royal Ontario Museum," in *Studies in Textile History in Memory of Harold B. Burnham*, ed. Veronika Gervers, Toronto, 1977. Pp. 82–125.

Grabar-Nordenfalk, *Early Medieval Painting*	André Grabar and Carl Nordenfalk, *Early Medieval Painting from the Fourth to the Eleventh Century*. New York, 1957.
Grabar, "A Manuscript of the *Maqāmāt* of Ḥarīrī"	Oleg Grabar, "A Newly Discovered Illustrated Manuscript of the *Maqāmāt* of Ḥarīrī," *Ars Orientalis*, 5 (1963), 97–109.
Harksen, *Frau im Mittelalter*	S. Harksen, *Die Frau im Mittelalter*. Leipzig, 1974.
Herzfeld, *Geschichte der Stadt Samarra*	E. Herzfeld, *Geschichte der Stadt Samarra*. Hamburg, 1948.
Higgins, *Greek and Roman Jewellery*	R. A. Higgins, *Greek and Roman Jewellery*. London, 1961.
Holmes, *Daily Living*	U. T. Holmes, *Daily Living in the Twelfth Century*, based on the observations of Alexander Neckam in London and Paris. Madison, Wisc. 1962.
HUC Geniza	Hebrew Union College, Cincinnati, Ohio, Geniza MSS.
Ibn Ẓahīra, *Faḍā'il*	Ibn Ẓahīra, *Al-Faḍā'il al-bāhira fī maḥāsin Miṣr wal-Qāhira*, ed. Muṣṭafā al-Saqqā and Kāmel al-Muhandis. Cairo, 1969.
Ibn al-Zubayr, *Dhakhā'ir*	Ibn al-Zubayr, *Kitāb al-Dhakhā'ir wal-Tuḥaf*. Kuwait, 1959.
Idris, "Vie économique en Occident Musulman"	Hady Roger Idris, "Contribution a l'étude de la vie économique en Occident musulman médiéval," in *Mélanges le Tourneau*. Aix-en-Provence, 1973. Vol. II, pp. 75–87.
IJMES	*International Journal of Middle East Studies*
JARCE	*Journal of the American Research Center in Egypt*

Jenkins, *Fatimid Jewelry*	Marilyn Jenkins, "Fatimid Jewelry: Its Sub-types and Influences," *Kunst des Orients*, accepted for publication.
Johnson, *Persian and Arabic Dictionary*	F. Johnson, *Persian, Arabic and English Dictionary*, 2 vols. London, 1852.
Kafih, *Jewish Life in San a*	Joseph Kafih (Qāfeḥ), *Jewish Life in Sanʿa* (Heb.). Jerusalem, 1961.
Keene-Jenkins, "Djawhar"	M. Keene and M. Jenkins, "Djawhar," *EI^2*, *Supplement*, 1982, pp. 250–262.
Kiener, *Kleidung*	Franz Kiener, *Kleidung, Mode und Mensch*. Munich and Basel, 1956.
Krauss, *Griechische und lateinische Lehnwörter*	S. Krauss, *Griechische und lateinische Lehnwörter in Talmud, Midrasch und Targum*. Berlin, Vol. I (Grammar), 1898; Vol. II (Glossary), 1899. Only the Glossary is quoted.
Kühnel-Bellinger, *Tiraz Fabrics*	Ernst Kühnel, *The Textile Museum: Catalogue of Dated Tiraz Fabrics*. Technical Analysis by Louisa Bellinger. Washington, D.C., 1952.
Lane, *Arabian Society*	E. W. Lane, *Arabian Society in the Middle Ages*. London, 1883.
Marzouk, *Textile Industry in Alexandria*	Muhammad Abdelaziz Marzouk, *History of Textile Industry in Alexandria*. Alexandria, 1955.
Migeon, *Art musulman*	Gaston Migeon, *Manuel d'art musulman*. Paris, 1927.
Miskimin et al., *The Medieval City*	Harry A. Miskimin, David Herlihy, A. L. Udovitch, eds., *The Medieval City*. New Haven, 1977.

Morabia, "Noms de couleur"	Alfred Morabia, "Recherches sur quelques noms de couleur en arabe classique," *Studia Islamica*, 19 (1963), 61–99.
Nadwa 1969	*al-Nadwah al-Dawlīyah li-Tārīkh al-Qāhira, Cairo, 1969*. 3 vols. Dār al-Kutub. Cairo, 1970–.
O'Dea, *Social History of Lighting*	William T. O'Dea, *The Social History of Lighting*. London, 1958.
Qāfeḥ	*See* Kafih, *Jewish Life in Sanʿa*
Qasīmī, *Métiers damascains*	M. S. al-Qasimy. *Dictionnaire des métiers damascains*. 2 vols. Paris, 1960.
Pauty, *Palais et maisons*	Edmund Pauty, *Les palais et les maisons d'époque Musulmane au Caire*. Cairo, 1932.
Ransom, *Couches*	Caroline L. Ransom, *Studies in Ancient Furniture; Couches and Beds of the Greeks, Etruscans and Romans*. Chicago, 1905.
Rathjens, *Sanʿa*	Carl Rathjens, *Jewish Domestic Architecture in Sanʿa, Yemen*. Jerusalem, 1957.
Reuther, "Qaʿa"	O. Reuther, "Die Qaʿa," *Jahrbuch der Asiatischen Kunst*, II/2. Leipzig, 1925.
Reuther, *Wohnhaus in Baghdad*	Oscar Reuther, *Das Wohnhaus in Bagdad und anderen Städten des Irak*. Berlin, 1910.
Revault-Maury, *Palais et maisons*	J. Revault and B. Maury, *Palais et maisons du Caire du XIVe au XVIIIe siècle*. Paris, 1975.
Rice, *Islamic Art*	D. T. Rice, *Islamic Art*. London, 1965.
Richards, *Arabic Doc.*	D. S. Richards, "Arabic Documents from the Karaite Community in Cairo," *JESHO*, 15 (1972), 105–162.

Richards, *Karaite Doc.*	Photos of Karaite Documents put at my disposal by D. S. Richards of the University of Cambridge.
Richter, *Furniture*	Gisela M. A. Richter, *Ancient Furniture. A History of Greek, Etruscan, and Roman Furniture.* Oxford, 1926.
Robertson, *Greek and Roman Architecture*	D. S. Robertson, *A Handbook of Greek and Roman Architecture,* Cambridge, 1929.
Roden, *Middle Eastern Food*	Claudia Roden, *A Book of Middle Eastern Food.* New York, N.Y., 1972.
Sadan, *Mobilier*	J. Sadan, *Le Mobilier au Proche Orient médiéval.* Leiden, 1976.
Serjeant, *Islamic Textiles*	R. B. Serjeant, *Islamic Textiles.* Beirut, 1972. This book was published first as a series of articles, see *Med. Soc.*, I, xxv.
Stillman, "Female Attire"	Y. K. Stillman, "Female Attire in Medieval Egypt according to the Trousseau Lists and Cognate Material from the Cairo Geniza." Ph.D. diss., University of Pennsylvania. Philadelphia, 1972.
Stillman, *Palestinian Costume and Jewelry*	Y. K. Stillman, *Palestinian Costume and Jewelry.* Albuquerque, N. Mex., 1979.
Stillman, "Wardrobe"	Y. Stillman, "The Wardrobe of a Jewish Bride in Medieval Egypt," in *Folklore Research Center Studies.* Vol. 4, ed. Dov Noy and Issachar Ben-Ami. Jerusalem, 1974.
Studies in [the] Geniza and Sepharadi Heritage, 1981	*Studies in [the] Geniza and Sepharadi Heritage, 1981,* presented to Shelomo Dov Goitein, ed. Shelomo Morag and Issachar Ben-Ami, with the assistance of

	Norman A. Stillman. Jerusalem, 1981. (In Hebrew.)
Studies in Judaism and Islam, 1981	*Studies in Judaism and Islam, 1981*, presented to Shelomo D. Goitein, ed. Shelomo Morag, Issachar Ben-Ami, Norman A. Stillman. Jerusalem, 1981.
Wehr, *Modern Written Arabic*	Hans Wehr, *A Dictionary of Modern Written Arabic*, ed. J. Milton Cowan. Ithaca, 1961.
Weibel, *Two Thousand Years of Textiles*	Adele Coulin Weibel, *Two Thousand Years of Textiles; The Figured Textiles of Europe and the Near East*. New York, 1952.
Wiet, *Cairo*	Gaston Wiet, *Cairo: City of Art and Commerce*, trans. Seymour Feiler. Norman, 1964.
Wiet, *Objets en cuivre*	Gaston Wiet, *Catalogue General du Musée Arabe du Caire. Objets en cuivre*. Cairo, 1932.
Wiet, "Tapis"	Gaston Wiet, "Tapis Égyptiens," *Arabica*, 6 (1959), 1–24.

Words in double brackets [[ ]] are translations of words crossed out in the original.

A MEDITERRANEAN SOCIETY

Map of Medieval Egypt

CHAPTER IX

Daily Life Housing, Clothing, Food, and Mounts

A. THE HOME

1. *The City*

The medieval Islamic city.—The people speaking to us through the Geniza documents lived in cities and towns, large and small. Only a few possessed orchards, vineyards, fields, and cattle, but, as a rule, they did not look after them in person.[1] They represented an intrinsically urban population. Consequently, all that is reported about them in these four volumes concerns city life. In this subsection the city is studied as a place of habitation in the narrower sense of the word, and even in this respect, much of the relevant Geniza material is more conveniently treated under the subsequent headings of "Domestic Architecture" and "Socioeconomic Aspects of Housing." Now that the medieval city, European, Mediterranean, and Islamic, is a main concern of historical research, some general observations about urbanism as illustrated by the Geniza papers seem to be appropriate.

The Geniza world comprised cities from Samarkand, Central Asia, and the port cities of India and Indonesia in the east, to Seville, Spain, and Sijilmāsa, Morocco, in the west; from Aden, Arabia, in the south, to Constantinople, the capital of Byzantium, in the north. The maritime cities of the northern shores of the Mediterranean, such as Narbonne, Marseilles, Genoa, Pisa, and Venice, were well known, but, until the end of the twelfth century, not visited.[2] Sporadic information about faraway places, such as Rouen, the capital of Normandy in northern France, or Kiev, the capital of the present-day Ukraine in southern Russia, is occasionally found in the Geniza.[3] Family names derived from towns in Iraq, and especially Iran, including little-known places, are extremely frequent, but they testify to the continuous movement westward of the ninth and tenth centuries.[4] In the eleventh century we still—or should we say: again—find merchants from Iraq and Iran active and also settling in the Mediterranean area. But practically no travelers moving in the opposite direction have left records, or are mentioned, in the Geniza papers. The eastward movement turned to the India route via Upper Egypt and the Red Sea.[5]

There was continuous coming and going between Egypt and the port cities of Spain, Sicily, Tunisia, and Libya in the west, and the towns of Palestine and Greater Syria in the east. Our main information about urban life is derived from Egypt itself and, in particular, its ancient Islamic capital, Fustat (Old Cairo), where the Geniza papers were found. All in all, it is the Islamic city of the Middle Ages which is reflected in our documents.

As far as I know, the Swiss Arabist Adam Mez made the first comparative study of the "Muhammedan" city, as he called it, in a paper published in 1912.[6] Mez did not wish to imply that there existed a uniform type of Islamic city or that it was Islam that created it. Quite the contrary. He differentiates among four original types of town: Arabian (characterized by its multistoried buildings and narrow streets, and represented by the towns of South Arabia, Mecca, and Fustat[7]), Hellenistic-Mediterranean, Mesopotamian, and Iranian. To them was added from the third Islamic century a fifth type, the spacious imperial garden city, realized, for instance, in the Fatimid foundation of Cairo. In general, Mez emphasizes that the fully developed Islamic city represented a reemergence of the ancient Near Eastern city. Mez's main purpose was to show what the Muslims themselves said, or omitted to say, about their multifarious urban conglomerations; his interest was not theoretical. I have summarized his paper because certain aspects of the problem which have been vividly discussed of late, such as the question of continuity or new creation and the role of religion versus local tradition, were already broached in that early treatment of the subject, which shows that they are inherent in its very nature.

A comprehensive and systematic survey of recent research done in this field is contained in a study by the German geographer Eugen Wirth entitled "The Oriental City: A Survey Based on Recent Publications on Material Civilization."[8] By "Oriental" Wirth means the medieval Islamic city, which he, like Mez, regards as a continuation of the ancient Near Eastern city, remodeled by the Hellenistic-Roman imprint. According to him, Islam as such had little influence on its formation. He says, when through conquest mosques were converted into churches, or churches into mosques, the character of the cities concerned did not change. The really new creation of the medieval Near Eastern city was the bazaar, according to him an absolutely novel and unique topographic and socioeconomic phenomenon, to which he dedicated a most extensive study, both descriptive and speculative.[9]

An entirely different type of summary of all that is known about the Islamic city is represented in Oleg Grabar's chapter "Cities and Citizens" in the magnificent volume *The World of Islam*, edited by Bernard Lewis. As the title indicates, the approach of the eminent art historian and Islamist is sociological, but it is so in the widest sense of the word, inclusive of the physical, economic, political, religious, and cultural aspects involved. The author's personal stance and original contribution to the problems discussed are clearly indicated.[10]

The Islamic city seemingly differed from both the Greek-Roman and the medieval European cities by its lack of a municipal organization. The historian is bound to try to explain this seeming difference and to inquire what, instead, kept Islamic urban society together and how did the individual resident relate, legally and emotionally, to the town in which he lived. In search for answers to these questions many other aspects of city life must be considered.

French scholars have been leading in the research on Islamic urbanism through the painstaking study of individual cities on one hand and by attempts at generalization and characterization on the other. Outstanding examples of the first type are Jean Sauvaget's classic on Aleppo, Syria (historical and archaeological), Roger Le Tourneau's work on Fez and the cities of North Africa in general (socioeconomic), and André Raymond's quantitative and demographic studies on Cairo of the eighteenth century, which also shed light on the previous history of the city.[11]

Impressed by the religious fervor prevailing in the cities of North Africa during the first half of this century and the manifold corporative formations found in them, French scholars, and above all the former doyen of French Islamists, Louis Massignon, projected this image into the past. They concluded that Islamic religion created the character of the medieval Middle Eastern town, including its physical layout, whereas guilds of artisans and merchants, as well as brotherhoods of scholars and mystics, provided the nuclei that kept society from falling apart. The interdisciplinary *entretien* on the

Islamic, mainly the Maghrebi, city held in 1958 at the Sixième Section d'Ecole Pratique des Hautes Etudes, Sorbonne, under the chairmanship of Fernand Braudel, represents a stimulating and many-sided exposition of these concepts.[12]

More recent research by Claude Cahen, the present doyen of French historians of Islam, and many others have qualified and questioned those assumptions. A modest share in this development is also attributable to Geniza research, which has demonstrated that commerce and industry in those times and places were based on free cooperation and partnerships on the one hand and government control on the other.[13] Discussions on the medieval city of the Middle East are now being held on an international plane.

The proceedings of several conferences dedicated to the subject have already appeared in print. The Oxford colloquium of summer 1965, presided over by Albert H. Hourani and S. M. Stern, forcefully indicated that a revision of many views on the character and development of the Islamic city was taking place. The Berkeley symposium of October 1966, organized by Ira M. Lapidus, conceived of the Islamic city as a link between the ancient and the modern Middle East. The Princeton conference of April 1970, chaired by L. Carl Brown, although mainly concerned with contemporary developments, tried to define the structure of the "traditional," that is, medieval, Muslim city, and its adaptability to modern needs. The Cambridge Colloquium on the Islamic City, held in July 1976 under the chairmanship of R. B. Serjeant, the most ambitious one convened thus far (five full days), tried to encompass the topic in all its different aspects.[14]

The Jerusalem colloquium of French and Israeli scholars, The Near Eastern City from the Fourth to the Fifteenth Century, convened in April 1975, as well as the Dumbarton Oaks symposium, Urban Societies in the Mediterranean World, held under the direction of David Herlihy in spring 1976, linked Byzantine, Islamic, and Western urbanism. The Robert S. Lopez Jubilee Volume, edited by D. Herlihy, H. Miskimin, and A. Udovitch, is of similar scope. This tendency to learn by contrast is particularly pronounced in the volume *Comparing Cities* edited by Sylvia Thrupp, which contains contributions on the medieval cities of the Near East. Michael E. Bonine's "Urban Studies in the Middle East" summarizes the state of the art.[15]

The multitude of speakers and writers on the subject seems to indicate that many points are still controversial and in need of further study. To illustrate this state of affairs I cite two French scholars discussing this topic in *The Cambridge History of Islam*. Both refer to the generally accepted view that Islam is essentially an urban civilization, meaning that a Muslim can live a full religious life only in a town. The geographer X. de Planhol writes: "The urban ideal of Islam created no forms, no urban structure. . . . It replaced the solidarity of a collective community [as in classical antiquity] with an anomalous disorganized heap of disparate quarters and elements. By a really very remarkable paradox, this religion endowed with the ideal of urban life produced the very negation of urban order."[16]

In the same volume, Claude Cahen has this to say:

> The town as such is unknown in Islamic law. It does not possess the individuality either of the ancient city or of the Western commune of the later Middle Ages. However, this distinction must not be misinterpreted or attributed to Islam. The Muslim town naturally took its place in continuity with the town of late antiquity, which, against the background of empires that became more and more centralized, had lost almost all autonomy: and the European communes came into being in under-organized states, a thing, which, by comparison, the medieval Muslim world had never been. Generally speaking, true urban autonomies would have been unthinkable in that world, but . . . it does not follow that the towns formed amorphous and passive communities.[17]

In reality, it appears to me that these contradicting statements are matters of approach and evaluation rather than of substance and facts. A certain consensus on the general nature of the medieval Near Eastern cities seems to have emerged. The medieval Islamic city was a place where one lived, not a corporation to which one belonged. There were town dwellers, but no citizens in the legal sense of the word, for there did not exist a municipality that made laws and under whose jurisdiction one could come. It was not, however, Islam that destroyed the corporate institutions of the Greeks and Romans. These had decayed or disappeared long before the Arab conquest. Obviously, in later antiquity, the cities had become too big for the primitive democratic institutions developed in classical times. The management of these unwieldy conglomerations had to be entrusted to managers, to administrators appointed by the government. The assertion that, in early Islam, corporate life found a refuge in the guilds of artisans and merchants, although reiterated with strong emphasis by some scholars, cannot be upheld, for these guilds, as far as this term may be applied to them at all, developed only during the Late Middle Ages. In the cities of Syria and Iraq, rudiments of urban autonomy are discernible, particularly in the formation of local militia forces. Yet these beginnings were limited in time and place and did not develop into enduring institutions. The role of the ulama, or religious scholars, as a cohesive force within the urban amalgam is still being much discussed (see below). Despite their organizational weakness, however, the Islamic cities represented effective social realities. As seats of the government or of its representatives they guaranteed relative security; as local markets or international emporiums they provided economic opportunities; and with their mosques and madrasas, their churches, synagogues, and schools, their bathhouses and other amenities they contained all a man needed for leading a religious and cultured life. It is true: cities as such did not make laws. But neither, as a rule, did the medieval Muslim governments. Yet both were most tangible factors in everyone's life.

It was in this environment that the Geniza people, those inveterate city dwellers, were found. Urban life is necessarily reflected in everything they wrote.

Capitals and port cities.—In rural societies the towns grew out of the land. Their growth was mostly slow and intermittent. In Arabic Islam, a society originally of long-distance traders and bedouins, the process was reversed. The cities preceded the countryside, so to speak. They were founded and filled with populace immediately after, or even in the course of, the conquest and formed the nuclei of Arabization. There, Arabic and Islam were soon predominant, whereas in the countryside it took hundreds of years for the religion, the language, and the social traditions of the conquerors to be assimilated. Consequently, it was natural that the capital of a country or district be identified in terms of the region that it dominated. The region, as it were, was subsumed in its capital.

Throughout the Geniza papers, Fustat is called Miṣr (Egypt, probably pronounced Maṣr then as now). Only in legal documents is Fusṭāṭ Miṣr (Fustat of Egypt) used to differentiate it from the newly founded sister city Cairo.[18] Damascus is referred to as Shām (Land of the North, Syria), but often also by its old name Dimashq,[19] certainly because Syria contained other ancient cities conquered and immediately occupied by the Arabs after the conquest. In diyār Ḥalab wa-diyār Anṭākiyā (Aleppo and Antioch [both in northern Syria] with their surroundings) the district is defined by its capital city.[20] Palermo, the capital of Sicily, is usually called Ṣiqillīya, Sicily (often spelled with *s*), occasionally Madīnat Ṣiqillīya, The City of Sicily, sometimes shortened to al-Madīna, The City (which the uninitiated reader of Geniza letters should not take as Medina in Arabia), whereas Balarm, the Arabic equivalent of Palermo, is nearly absent.[21]

In Roman times, provincial capitals, such as Caesarea of Palestine, Alexandria of Egypt, and Carthage of the province of Africa, were situated on the seashore, where they could be easily reached from Rome, the center of the world. Under Islam, the cities chosen or founded as capitals—Fustat, Ramle of Palestine, Damascus, and Qayrawān of Tunisia—were situated inland, where they were safe from surprise attacks of the Byzantine and other Christian navies. The main ports of a country, such as Alexandria, Tyre on the Lebanese coast, or al-Mahdiyya, Tunisia, were regarded as frontier fortresses. Alexandria is often referred to in the Geniza letters as *al-thaghr*, the frontier fortress, and not by its name.

It would be wrong to assume that Alexandria, the Mediterranean port, was the pivot of commerce, and that Fustat, originally the capital of the country, derived its riches from its function as seat of the administration. The unmistakable testimony of hundreds of Geniza letters proves that Fustat, the Arab inland city, was also the commercial and financial center of the country, on which Alexandria, the originally Greek maritime town, was economically dependent in every respect. Fustat was the emporium of the region, where all the goods were hoarded. For consignments destined to be sent overseas, customs had to be paid first and foremost in Fustat, and no goods could pass through its gate to the sea at Alexandria without being accompanied by the receipts for the dues issued in the capital. Even commodities from Mediterranean countries, which were imported by way of Alexandria, had to be obtained from Fustat, when they became scarce in the former city. Foreign currency from places with which Alexandria entertained a lively commerce, was regularly acquired by Alexandrians in Fustat. Everyday commodities, such as shoes and clothing, implements for silversmithing or parchment and even ink, were ordered for Alexandria in the capital, "for here," as several letters from Alexandria emphasize, "nothing is to be had." To be sure, Alexandria, like other places, had its local industries, such as its world-renowned mats, which were popular everywhere, its *maqṭaʿ* textiles, exported as far as India, and its pens, cut from the reeds of the lake of Maryūṭ. It seems that it also served as the international entrepot and bourse of the silk trade.[22]

The situation was similar in Ifrīqiya (present-day Tunisia) and Palestine. Goods were sent to Qayrawān via its port al-Mahdiyya, but as a rule, the consignments were not opened there; customs were paid in the capital. The great merchants lived in Qayrawān, their agents stayed in al-Mahdiyya. Wheat was cheapest in the capital, where it was stored. In times of scarcity one turned there. Naturally, at the arrival of ship convoys fairs were held in the port city, but one relied on the bazaar of Qayrawān for the winter season, when the sea was closed and the overland traffic from Morocco to Egypt passed through the city. In Palestine, commerce, the dispensation of justice, and communal life were concentrated in Ramle, the administrative inland capital. Its nearest ports, Jaffa and Caesarea, rarely occur in the Geniza papers. The eastern shores of the Mediterranean, however, had an ancient tradition of kingly maritime cities. Thus the Geniza clearly shows that Tyre, then—as in antiquity—the mightiest town on that coast, although serving Damascus as seaport, was not dependent on the Syrian capital.[23]

Alexandria and Fustat differed also in the composition and character of their populations. Both cities were full of foreigners. But the difference seems to have been that those who had reached the capital intended to remain there for good, whereas those staying behind in Alexandria either had not yet made up their minds or were resolved to return home *baʿd qaḍā al-ḥawā'ij*, after having attained their economic goals. It perhaps explains why we find fierce clashes between the foreigners and the local people in Alexandria, but not in Fustat. Moreover, at least as far as the Jewish community is concerned, the lower classes of Alexandria seem to have been stronger and more vociferous than those in the capital. They were an unruly crowd, always dissatisfied with their leadership and making trouble which led to the interference of the Muslim authorities. These, too, with few exceptions (and in contrast with those in Fustat) had a bad name in the Geniza, and the mob of the port city was a ceaseless nuisance and menace.

The presence of numerous visitors from Christian countries with their different social notions was not without influence. Drinking bouts accompanied by music, anathema to both Islam and traditional Judaism, are reported from Alexandria. Rūmī, that is, Italian or Greek, wine was preferred there to the local brand. In view of the differences in the life-styles of the two cities, Alexandrians might not always have felt comfortable in the capital. When a woman in Alexandria learned that her brother, a widower living in Qalyūb, a small town north of Cairo, was about to marry a girl from there (and not, as she had feared, from Fustat) "she was happy that you did not become involved with people from Miṣr" (as reported in a letter to him).[24] Conversely, a divorcée from Fustat, who became engaged to a divorced man from Alexandria, stipulated that the couple would live in the capital and that she was prepared to accompany him on his visits to his family in Alexandria, but for not more than one month per year. A month, she obviously felt, was the maximum she could stand.[25]

The great cities and "the Province."—Besides the inland capitals and their port cities many other urban conglomerations occur in the Geniza records. For towns situated on the trade routes of the Mediterranean, see *Med. Soc.*, I, 211–214. In Egypt, the number of large, medium, and small towns, that have left their trace in the Geniza documents is considerable (see Index, s.v. *Egypt, places in*). Special attention is drawn to the meritorious paper by Norman Golb on the places of settlement of Jews in medieval Egypt, where repeated references are also made to Muslim and pre-Islamic sources.[26] Individual traits of the various localities and population shifts occurring in such places are recognizable, as may be concluded from the examples of a middle-sized and two smaller local communities discussed in *Med. Soc.*, II, 44–51.

It is remarkable that all places outside the capital and Alexandria, including such towns as Damietta, the Mediterranean port on the eastern arm of the Nile, which was a main entrepot for trade with the Syro-Palestinian coast, and al-Maḥalla al-Kubrā, a provincial capital and industrial center, were subsumed under the untranslatable term *rīf*, the Province. In the language of the Geniza letters *dakhal*, coming home, meant returning to Fustat-Cairo or Alexandria from a visit to towns of the Rīf; *kharaj*, leaving, meant the opposite. No doubt, rīf originally meant countryside, farmland, and *rīfī* means the peasant as opposed to the townsman.[27] The extension of the term to denote towns other than Cairo andAlexandria betrays a unique attachment to the great city.[28]

This attitude had practical consequences. Marriage contracts stipulated that the husband was not permitted to exchange the city for another place except with the consent of his wife. In one letter we read that a woman could not bear "life in the Rīf" although she was married in the provincial capital al-Maḥalla. She escaped to Cairo, but her husband declared that at most he was able to manage to make living in Damietta, where he offered to move with his recalcitrant wife.[29] A defaulting debtor would abscond from the city and try to hide in one of the provincial communities, wherefore we find a circular from a Nagid addressed to "all the judges and muqaddams in the Rīf" to catch him.[30] Exigencies of business or office forced many a Cairene or Alexandrian man to take up his domicile temporarily in a smaller town, and bitter complaints about the "wrongs" suffered there, about the "Sodom and Gomorrha" endured from its uncouth people, may be read in the Geniza letters.[31] Under these circumstances it is not surprising that a member of the urban jeunesse dorée appointed to posts in the Rīf, again and again forsook them and returned to the city.[32] Community officials implored their superiors to transfer them to the capital (in order, of course, to continue their education . . .), and businessmen would come to the conclusion that after all it was wiser to stay home in the city than to seek profit in the Rīf. The idea of being forced to pass a holiday "outside" was particularly abhorred.[33]

An incessant exodus from the Rīf to the cities can be observed in the Geniza documents. It is illustrated by the large number of persons bearing family names derived from small, even the smallest, villages in the Egyptian countryside. The lists of the receivers of bread, clothing, and other help from the community of Fustat are full of such names. But some of the influential families in the capital also originated in the Rīf. These migrations will occupy us again.[34]

Despite this contrast, or even tension, between city and Rīf, it is precisely in the Geniza papers that we see the importance of the smaller towns. There was a tendency to move not only from the Rīf to the cities but also in the opposite direction. Persons bearing the family names of Miṣrī, Iskandarānī, ʿAsqalānī, Qudsī, or Dimashqī, that is, originating from Fustat, Alexandria, Ascalon, Jerusalem, or Damascus, are encountered in the small towns of Egypt. In fact, we find there people from all over the Mediterranean, including Byzantium and France. Edith Ennen, in her recent book on the European town in the Middle Ages, devotes a special section to the importance of the small towns in medieval Europe.[35]

In more than one respect the small towns were of vital economic importance for the people who left us their records in the Geniza. Flax and indigo, the staple exports of Egypt, were partly processed where they were grown and needed supervision at the source. The manufacture of cheese, the main foodstuff after bread, was preferably done where the best sheep were bred, and its processing had to be supervised, since it was subject to ritual taboos. Jews, although to a lesser degree than Christians, were widely active as tax-farmers, and as such had to live in small towns or even villages in order to collect the taxes in person. They were also employed by the government in the Rīf in other capacities.[36] Jewish physicians and apothecaries seem to have been ubiquitous in the Rīf.[37] The economic strength of the Rīf is demonstrated by the fact that it was regularly visited by traveling merchants and agents to sell their textiles, especially silk, and other wares, and by persons soliciting funds for works of public or private philanthropy.

Cairo and Fustat.—Still, the majority of the data on urban life refers to the capital, and in what follows, where no remark to the contrary is made, Fustat is meant. Fustat—not Cairo—for although the two cities were only about two miles apart, the people lived more or less distinctly separate lives. The marriage contract of a wealthy bride from the year 1156 stipulates: "She will live in Fustat [called, of course, Miṣr in the document] to the exclusion of Cairo." No reason is given for this condition, but it demonstrates how strongly the contrast was felt almost two hundred years after the foundation of the imperial city. Similarly, in 1248, a man "from Cairo" repudiates his wife, who was "from Miṣrayim" (Heb., Fustat).[38] The Maghrebi Muslim traveler Ibn Saᶜīd, who visited Egypt in the 1240s, describes the people of Fustat as soft-spoken and far friendlier than those of Cairo and expresses his astonishment that there should be such a difference between two adjacent cities.[39] The reason for the contrast probably was the fact that Fustat was dominated by an easygoing middle class, whereas Cairo lived under the shadow of a stiff court. Originally, Cairo "was the seat of the caliphate and no one lived there except the caliph, his troops, his entourage, and those whom he honored to be near to him."[40] There is, indeed, documentary evidence that the Fatimid court physicians, higher government officials, and other persons somehow connected with the court lived there. When a Jewish government official was fired from his post he was ordered to leave Cairo and to take up residence in Fustat.[41] Maṣlī'aḥ Gaon, the head of the Palestinian yeshiva, who moved to Egypt in 1127, bore the titles Jalāl al-Mulk and Tāj al-Riyāsa (The Luster of the Empire and The Crown of the Leadership). His titles, together with the robes of honor bestowed on him according to an Arabic Geniza letter, indicate that he, as head of the Jewish community, belonged to the caliph's retinue. We find that he and some of the scholars attached to him did live in Cairo. Others had houses both in Cairo and in Fustat.[42]

Paradoxically, Cairo, especially in Fatimid times, is represented in the Geniza mostly not by the upper crust, for which it was renowned, but by a social layer that both materially and spiritually was poorer than many a community in a provincial town. The houses and dowries mentioned in the documents are often of low value, the documents themselves are not rarely of poor quality and signed by persons whose handwriting betrays them as having had little practice in writing. This section of the population worked as menials, such as water carriers, or consisted of destitute persons who had come to the city seeking help. The persons connected with the court presumably corresponded in Arabic characters, wherefore they had no reason to discard their letters in the Geniza chamber, or they left their Hebrew writings in their own synagogue, which has long since disappeared.[43]

The fire set on Fustat in 1168 by the Fatimid vizier Shāwar did not do permanent harm to the city, at least not to the section where most of the Jews were found. For another three-quarters of a century there is a steady flow of Geniza documents. Maimonides, though a physician to the Ayyubid court, lived in Fustat and had to commute every day to the Sultan's palace in Cairo, a nuisance woefully described by him in one of his letters. His son, the Nagid Abraham (1186–1237), who, like his father, was a physician in attendance, also lived in Fustat, which is proved by direct references to his home there and by a little note inquiring whether he would spend a weekend in Cairo. By the middle of the thirteenth century, however, the majority of the Jewish population of the capital must have been concentrated in Cairo, and the correspondence of Abraham Maimonides' great-grandson, the Nagid Joshua (1310–1355) shows the Fustat community in full decay.[44]

Topographic features.—The capital of Egypt is, of course, one of the most studied cities of the Islamic world. Minute descriptions by medieval Muslim scholars are invaluable, and their modern successors, Egyptian and Western, have continued their work. The flood of literature on the occasion of Cairo's millenary (969–1969) is indicative of this situation.[45] As far as Fustat, or Old Cairo, is concerned, excavations were carried out there at the beginning of this century and again during the last decade or so and still are going on.[46] Ultimately it will be necessary to collect the rich topographic material dispersed in the Geniza documents and to coordinate it with the information to be gained from medieval sources and modern research. This task is outside the scope of this book. The short topographic notes that follow aim at social rather than archaeological aspects of the city's history.

The nucleus of Fustat was formed by a Byzantine fortress, situated on the eastern bank of the Nile and called the Fortress of the Greeks or, more frequently, the Fortress of the Candles. The Christian and Jewish elements remained preponderant in this, the pre-Islamic, section of the city, and time-honored churches, some of which are still extant, as well as the two main synagogues, were found there. The place had entirely lost its military function. Some of the towers of the fortress were used as apartments and workshops and were owned in part by the synagogues as pious foundations. The Islamic city, founded at the time of the conquest (A.D. 641), surrounded the Fortress of the Greeks on the north, east, and south, and later, when the Nile silted up, also on the west. It was laid out according to the tribes, clans, and groups that composed the conquering army. A section assigned to such a group was called *khuṭṭ* (pronounced thus by the Geniza people), literally, line.[47] The area reserved for the high command and its guards, comprised a part of the Fortress of the Greeks and extended northeastward to the newly founded mosque of ʿAmr, the conqueror. It was called Ahl al-Rāya, those around the Standard, or al-Rāya for short. Our documents reveal the interesting fact that six hundred years after the Muslim conquest, the main quarters were still called by the names of those ancient Arab groups, such as Banāna, Banū Wā'il, Khawlān, Mahra, Tujīb, Waʿlān, but were inhabited, among others, by Jews. In Fatimid times we also find Christians and Jews living in al-Rāya, the original center of the Muslim city.[48]

The topographic terminology in the Geniza documents is rather fluid, which seems to indicate that in practice the borders between the various parts of the city cannot have been too strict. George Scanlon has come to a similar conclusion on archaeological evidence. The term "khuṭṭ" was still used for the ancient tribal sectors of the city, but could be applied also to an area of limited extent such as The Old Spinnery.[49] The word designating a quarter today, *ḥāra*, could refer not only to a large district, such as the Mamṣūṣa, one of the quarters of Fustat most frequently mentioned in the Geniza documents, or the even larger Mahra, a tribal sector, but also to a small place, described as a covered alley, to a prison, or to a little mosque. The two terms are found together in a document from al-Maḥalla, speaking of *khuṭṭ ḥārat al-Yahūd*, District of the Jewish Quarter (where Christians also lived).[50] The word generally designating a block, or segment of a street, *ṣuqʿ* (often spelled with *s*) could also be applied to larger urban districts, such as the Fortress of the Candles, the Mamṣūṣa, or the Great Bazaar.[51] Its derivative, *taṣqīʿ*, designated a public record that listed revenue from houses in a certain district. In the Geniza it meant rent paid by the tenants living in houses that were communal property. The term was no doubt borrowed from the Fatimid administration where it designated a cadastre of houses for the purpose of taxation and police supervision, as is known from Mamluk times.[52] In Alexandria, but occasionally also elsewhere, a quarter was called *nāḥiya*, in modern times an administrative unit approximately the size of a county.[53] As far as we can tell by our documents, it must have been more common in Alexandria to call a neighborhood by name without the addition of a descriptive appellative.[54]

Special mention must be made of the term *rabʿ*, which is as evasive in meaning as it is frequent. Despite its pronunciation in the Geniza papers as *rubʿ*, the word is not the classical *rubʿ*, fourth, quarter, but *rab*ʿ, area, residence. Documentary and literary evidence taken together indicate that it represented the smallest subdivision of the ṣuqʿ, the urban district; rubʿ designated a large building, a compound, or a "block" under the care of the *ṣāḥib al-rub*ʿ, a combination of doorkeeper and neighborhood police officer, the one official with whom the local population was in daily contact. The blocks containing "compounds of the poor" or "compounds of the Jerusalemites," that is, pious foundations benefiting those people, were also called rubʿ. In other words, here again a term of the government administration was taken over by the pious foundations.[55] It is indicative of the fluidity of the terms that the ṣāḥib al-rubʿ is also styled *ḥāmi 'l-ḥāra*, or guard of the quarter.[56] I assume that the *darrāb*, or guard of the *darb* (alley, street), was not much different. This short report about a squabble between a Karaite stranger and a local Rabbanite illustrates the character of his office.

I inform you, my lords, the illustrious elders, that this morning, early in the day, Shabbetay, the Rūmī, [from Byzantium], came to the house of Joseph, the Rūmī, and knocked on the door of his house, while Abu 'l-Faraj, the Son of the Weigher,[57] was standing at the gate of the alley, knocking and saying to Shabbetay: You ʿĀnānī [Karaite],[58] go to the darrāb and have him open the alley for the elder Abū Thābit who wishes to go to the. . . .[59] Then, as was reported, he uttered a strong curse, whereupon Shabbetay said to him something in Rūmī [Greek], which he [Abu 'l-Faraj] did not understand. He thought that Shabbetay had cursed him and exclaimed: "This one has cursed the government, the religious scholars, and the leaders of the community." [The elders of the Karaite congregation are asked to take action].[60]

The term "darrāb," noted thus far only from Spain during the later Middle Ages, occurs here in this report and elsewhere in the Geniza as early as the twelfth century.[61] As the passage shows, the darrāb had to lock the gate of the alley overnight. But at the same time it appears from this story that not all inhabitants lived in places protected in this way. It tallies with a responsum by Maimon, father of Moses Maimonides, written in the third quarter of the twelfth century, which states that the markets of Fustat were not closed at night. Yet that practice must have been fairly general in Fustat, at least in earlier centuries, for in a description of the festival of Epiphany from the year 941, in which all parts of the population took part, it is mentioned as something exceptional that during that particular night the gates of the streets were not closed. One is reminded also of the order of the caliph al-Ḥākim to keep the markets open and brightly lit at night. To be sure, there is a difference between keeping a bazaar street or hall locked overnight and doing the same with a residential alley or a compound.[62]

Zoning.—Was there a marked division of the city into residential, commercial, and industrial areas? A partial answer to this question is given in the subsections on craftsmen and business localities, *Med. Soc.*, I, 83–84, 193–195. The wide dispersion over the city of the ubiquitous druggists or perfumers is described in *Med. Soc.*, II, 263–264, where their Square, the Murabbaʿa, is characterized as a social center second in importance only to the synagogue. As is well known from the works of medieval Muslim antiquarians and richly illustrated in the Geniza, many streets, bazaars, halls, and "houses" were named for a certain branch of commerce, an industry, or a product. It is true not only for Fustat but also for other cities, for example, Damascus. In addition, the Geniza reveals that this concentration of the various branches of economy in separate districts was by no means complete. Mills and presses (of oil and wine) seem to have been common in residential areas.[63]

Similarly, there must have been some districts that were exclusively or predominantly residential, and others that were essentially reserved for economic activities. In many cases the neighboring houses forming the object of deeds of transfer are described as the houses of private persons. When there is a shop in a house it is expressly stated. We find high-priced houses, clearly serving as living quarters, bordering on busy bazaars; stores are often topped by an *ʿulūw*, that is, one or several stories used as domiciles.[64] We find a physician in the street of the wax makers, another in that of the horseshoers, and a judge in the bazaar of the perfumers.[65] A sugar workshop belonging to a physician is expressly described also as known as his domicile (*sukn*, which could hardly mean his office).[66] Conversely, a petition addressed to the vizier Ibn al-Sallār al-Malik al-ʿĀdil (Dec. 1150) with regard to the estate of a *tājir*, or prominent merchant, emphatically makes a distinction between the family's *maṭbakh*, (sugar) factory, and sukn, living quarters.[67] An interesting but fragmentary letter says: "People who had been living in their properties give them up. When you sell the house, they will convert it into a workshop (*maʿmal*)."[68]

Eugen Wirth, in his previously mentioned basic study on the bazaar, comes to the conclusion that the characteristic arrangement of the traditional Middle Eastern city was the strict separation of residential quarters from those destined for economic activities, with the latter situated in the middle of town, the combination forming an organic whole. With this creation the medieval Islamic town preceded by centuries what we know in modern times as Downtown.[69]

As the Geniza documents of the tenth through the thirteenth centuries prove, this process of separation and concentration was in progress during the High Middle Ages, but by no means complete. Since the testimony of the documents is sometimes ambiguous, I wish the reader to share with me the interpretation of some of them. The first seven examples, all from the tenth or early eleventh century, are taken from the pre-Islamic nucleus of Fustat, the Fortress of the Rūm (Romans, meaning Greeks) or of the Candles.

In the deed of gift from summer 959, that is, ten years before the conquest of Egypt by the Fatimids, a father gives to his firstborn son two adjacent stores and two adjacent houses. The twin stores were bordered by two other stores, one belonging to a church, the church itself, and a street. The twin houses were bordered by two private homes, a lane, and by "the mills in the Market of the Greeks."[70] Slightly earlier, a father gave to a married daughter a house surrounded by the homes of two Christian neighbors, the property of a Muslim woman, and a non-Jewish house of worship (not the one mentioned in the preceding deed).[71] In a mortgage deed of spring 969 (the year of the Fatimid takeover) the property concerned was situated opposite the Bū Sargā (St. Sergius) Church, one neighboring house belonged to a Jew, another was described as "known as the house of Mr. Goldsmith," and the description of the third is lost.[72] In July 1004 a man sold to a representative of merchants, a man from northern Palestine, one-third of a house, which third he had inherited from his father. It bordered on property of an ophthalmologist, *kaḥḥāl*, of two Jews, one of whom bore a Persian name, and a Christian called Ben Masīḥ, son of Jesus. The price of that third was 70 Muʿizzī dinars (which means almost new; the caliph al-Muʿizz died in 975), making a total of 210 gold pieces, a large amount. All these examples show that the neighborhood was comparatively prestigious.[73]

A different picture emerges from a deed of sale of 9/24 shares in a house, which a man had inherited from his wife, written a few years later (1009/10). The neighborhood was known as The Wool Hall, *qaysāriyyat al-ṣūf*,[74] and the house was surrounded by properties named after a wax maker, a seller (and probably also preparer) of raisins, a belt maker, a (Christian) manufacturer of glass, and a woman defined solely by the name, not the occupation, of her husband. The house had three small inner courts. This architectural feature, however, should not induce us (as it has excavators) to assume that the house served exclusively as living quarters. As discussed later, the *qāʿa*, or ground floor with an inner court, was largely used for industrial and commercial undertakings.[75] The buyer of the shares was a money changer. The seller's name is eaten away (parchment is highly cherished by rodents), and of the price only 1/2 (dinar) has remained. But this one-half proves that the amount was small; otherwise, a round sum would have been stipulated.[76] A report of administrations of Jewish communal buildings referring to a slightly earlier period notes the construction of an apartment on the top of two stores near the synagogue.[77] Two shops and two storerooms formed part of a building consisting of several apartments that belonged to pious foundations in the early eleventh century.[78] But we also find an exceptionally valuable property in a residential section of the Fortress of the Greeks described in detail in a document written around 1130.[79]

Thus it appears that the ancient Byzantine nucleus of Fustat comprised residential sections that were fairly homogeneous, whereas the industrial and commercial areas were of mixed character, including some living quarters. The fact that the Christians, former rulers of the country, were wealthier than the Jews explains why they were the first to move out to the new, Muslim town; they were replaced by Jews, wherefore we find, in three of the examples above, Jews possessing properties in the immediate vicinity of Christian houses of worship.

Low-priced houses with both domiciles and stores were common outside the Greek fortress too, even in the Great Market bordering it. In Jan./Feb. 1139 a woman there sold to another one-quarter of a house for 14 1/2 dinars (total value of house, 58). The neighboring properties were remarkably diversified: a small house; a store in ruins; a newly build *funduq*, or caravanserai; and a tower of the Roman fortress, which belonged to "the Jewish synagogue." Besides the two doors of its stores (possibly workshops) "its door," that is, the one leading to the living quarters, is specifically mentioned.[80] A few years earlier a widow sells in the same neighborhood, the Mamṣūṣa, which is described as containing or partly overlapping the Great Market, one-sixth of a house with an upper floor, and two stores, each of which faced a different street, for 11 dinars (total value, 66).[81] There are other examples.[82]

The same district, however, harbored high-priced homes that contained no stores and were surrounded by other homes or open space. The Great Market and the Mamṣūṣa formed parts of the Tujīb district, which was bordered on the east by the Fortress of the Greeks. Tujīb was one of the more prominent Arab clans to settle in Fustat immediately after the conquest. They belonged to the royal tribe of Kinda. Their leader Muʿāwiya b. Ḥudayj was one who cantoned Fustat out for its settlement by the conquerors, and it was he who was given the honor of bringing in person the great news of the fall of Alexandria, the capital of Byzantine Egypt, to the caliph

Omar. Ḥudayjī Street, repeatedly mentioned in the Geniza papers, was named after his father. The Tujīb were also notorious for starting the first civil war in Islam, which led to the assassination of the third caliph, Othman. ("When the caliph ascended the pulpit to address the people assembled in the mosque, a man from the Tujīb of Fustat, clad in a yellow silk robe, stood up, cursed the caliph, and chided him for his bad government.") The Tujīb vigorously took part in the conquest of North Africa, bringing immense booty home to Fustat, and later they were prominent in Spain. We may imagine, threfore, that the Tujīb district of Fustat originally was purely Arab and probably also very luxurious. Because of the proximity of the Fortress of the Greeks, however, it was infiltrated by Christians and Jews, so that by the fifth Islamic century it presented a completely mixed picture, both with regard to the composition of its population and the juxtaposition of residential and predominantly commercial neighborhoods.[83]

Houses with twin stores and upper apartments, their boundaries, and prices have already been discussed. In the Tujīb quarter are numerous examples of high-priced and prestigious residences, many forming compounds of several buildings. In 1139 a Jew sells to another one-half of a house in the Mamṣūṣa (spelled here Muṣāṣa) which they had built in partnership, for 300 dinars, making the total house worth 600 dinars, one of the highest prices for a house mentioned in the Geniza. Unfortunately, the document does not spell out the boundaries, because the building was "famous."[84] On August 25, 1151, a physician gives to his son a large house newly erected by him in the same quarter, as we learn from an Arabic document written by a Muslim notary. It bordered on the house of a mason, a ruin belonging to a Muslim pious foundation, a zareba, or cattle pen, belonging to a qadi, and on the House of Ibn al-ʿAjamī, Son of the Persian, who could have been a Muslim, Christian, or Jew.[85] In 1156 Sulayman, son of the late Abū Zikrī Kohen, a representative of merchants in Fustat and a prominent India trader, bought for one of his two stepsisters one-eighth of a house in the same district, namely, in the Street of the Wine Dealers, *nabbādhūn*, in the neighborhood of the *suwayqat al-wazīr*, Little Market of the Vizier, well known from Arabic sources. The price of that share was 50 dinars (total value, 400 dinars). But the Muslim historians seemingly were reluctant to perpetuate the name of a street of wine dealers, although a traveler from the conservative Maghreb noted with dissatisfaction that—despite the censure of the Koran—wine was sold openly in the capital of Egypt.[86]

Later in the century a compound of four houses, two ruins, and a cattle pen, bordering on Ḥudayjī Street, formed the object of a settlement among a man, his mother, and his sister. One of the neighbors was a Christian government official bearing the titles Pride of the State and Trustee of the Government, another was a Jewish sugar merchant, and the third was a Jewish pious foundation. The property also contained a ruin with three storerooms. In the same neighborhood the family possessed part of a house consisting of a ground floor and nine upper apartments.[87] Nahray b. Nissīm, the well-known merchant banker and communal leader (d. 1096), was partner in a house also bordering on Ḥudayjī Street.[88] His younger contemporary, the India trader Abu 'l-Barakāt b. Joseph Lebdī, possessed a house in the Mamṣūṣa, half of which was given, after his death, to his daughter at her marriage (1146).[89] It should be noted that the Karaites, who were then the more affluent members of the Jewish community, had their synagogue in that district.[90]

In Byzantine Constantinople, Steven Runciman tells us, the slums of the poor jostled against the palaces of the rich.[91] In Fustat, as the analysis of documents from two main districts, the Fortress of the Greeks and the Tujīb, shows, the look of the city was somewhat different. There were residential neighborhoods with houses of high value, but they did not form large, independent quarters; they were more like islands surrounded by a network of bazaars and streets with houses consisting of twin stores topped by domestic structures and generally of low price. Even an area of suburban character, such as the Jazīra, or Island of the Nile (known today as Rōḍa, Garden), is represented in the Geniza by store-top homes: one house was worth approximately 660 dinars; another house, bounded by the palace of the late vizier Ibn Killis and other prestigious homes (one situated in an orchard), comprised also a building of two shops bordering on an open space. Another property on the Jazīra was mortgaged against a debt of 50 dinars.[92]

Documents related to other cities, naturally limited in number, seem to reflect similar traits. Three deeds—two of sale (one dated 1040, the other slightly later) and one, a gift (1050)—show us a large house in Qayrawān, Tunisia, the upper story of which was sold for 295 dinars, and another house whose upper story was given by a notable to his half sister, surrounded by residences, some Muslim, some Jewish.[93] A mansion in Damascus belonging to two brothers, one of whom was a government official, bordered on a number of domestic buildings (and one ruin), and was situated "on the East Gate [of the city] in the quarter, ḥāra, known as the House of Quzmān." In the same quarter, however, a place belonging to a pious foundation was occupied by a potter.[94] Two neighboring

Damascene houses, one large and one small, which formed "the end of the Market of the Jews and faced the Market of the Laborers," sold for the considerable sum of 280 ʿAzīzī dinars. The document was written at the end of the tenth or the beginning of the eleventh century and in Hebrew, wherefore it is difficult to identify the Arabic names of the markets. The Market of the Laborers was probably a place where workers available for hire were stationed, as were porters according to a Geniza document. We see, though, that a commercial section of Damascus could comprise quite valuable properties.[95] The same mixture of residential and commercial applies to a house in the immediate vicinity of the Great Synagogue in Damascus established around 1090, as a *waqf*, or charitable foundation, in favor of that house of worship.[96] On its southern and eastern boundaries the synagogue was adjacent to shops and storerooms.[97]

Damascus, like Cairo, had its fashionable suburbs. We read about an orchard with a house in the Ḥammūriyya village near Damascus, part of which was made a charitable foundation by a physician. From a Muslim document it appears that a Jew acquired a considerable tract of land in that neighborhood as early as 922.[98]

The general picture emerging from the data seems to indicate that in the times and places concerned the division of a city into residential and commercial areas was not regulated by statute. In practice some sort of zoning was achieved by private initiative, by the protection that Islamic (and Jewish) law granted a proprietor against any changes effected by a neighbor which might prove harmful to his own property.

A characteristic example, taken from a legal inquiry submitted to the Nagid Abraham Maimonides (d. 1237), vividly illustrates the problem. A dyer converted a house in a residential neighborhood, *diyār al-sukna*, into a workshop, the smoke of which caused grave nuisance to his neighbor. The latter sold his house; the new proprietor let it fall into disrepair and sold it as a ruin. The third landlord renovated the place and complained about the smoke which made it impossible for him "to hang his linen or wool clothing." The dyer moved his furnace from the wall he shared with his neighbor to the one facing the lane, but the smoke still proved to be damaging. Although the dyer had converted his house into a workshop fifteen years before the neighboring house was acquired by its new proprietor, Abraham Maimonides decided in favor of the latter, for "damage has no claim based on undisturbed possession." If it could be proved that one of the former proprietors had waived his rights, the complaint would be dismissed. Islamic law rules similarly. The case shows, that the protection of the property rights of the individual proprietor was not a complete safeguard for preserving the residential character of a quarter.[99]

Zoning is also involved where restrictions concerning the choice of a domicile are imposed on the members of a religion, sect, clan, or social group. In this respect, too, the situation in the High Middle Ages was far more fluid than in later times. The detailed discussion of this problem in *Med. Soc.*, II, 289–293, shows that Jewish houses bordered on those belonging to and occupied by Christians or Muslims, or both, that Christians and Muslims lived in Jewish houses and vice versa, and that properties were held in partnership by members of the three religions. Jews as a rule lived in a limited number of neighborhoods, but none was exclusively Jewish. There is no reason to assume that the situation was different with regard to other sections of the population. On the contrary. By the very injunctions of their religion Jews were forced to concentrate in certain neighborhoods. Since they were not permitted to ride on Sabbaths and religious holidays, they had to live within walking distance from their synagogues. Moreover, Judaism stresses, more emphatically than Islam, the importance of daily attendance at communal worship.

Finally, Jewish (and certainly also Christian) women disliked sharing houses with Muslims because with such neighbors the Islamic purdah affected them too. To avoid the inconvenience for their womenfolk, Jewish authorities promulgated statutes from time to time prohibiting the sale or lease of parts of houses to Muslims. Two letters addressed to Moses Maimonides emphasized that restrictions like these considerably reduced the value of Jewish properties. A recently discovered letter to the Nagid Abraham, Maimonides' son, illustrates an opposite situation: apartment houses inhabited exclusively by Jews were difficult to come by and therefore were expensive. The rent in such a house was beyond the financial capacity of an unhappy husband whose wife had the right to choose the couple's domicile; she insisted on renting a floor in a house without undesirable neighbors. Meanwhile, she had left the family home of the husband, to which, as usual, she had been brought first, and was staying with her brother. The writer asks whether the young wife could now be forced by court decision to be content with an apartment in a house inhabited at least partly by Jews. All this shows that the seclusion of Jews (and other minority groups, as far as it existed) was self-imposed and not dictated by an oppressive government.[100]"

Ruins.—An additional factor adversely affected the homogeneous character of neighborhoods: the mass of neglected buildings that fell into decay. After years, the sites could be used for purposes quite different from those served by the original structures. The abundance of references to ruins in the writings of the Muslim historians of the fourteenth and fifteenth centuries might induce the belief that they reflect the general decline marking the Late Middle Ages. But ruins appear in the Geniza documents of the eleventh and twelfth centuries as frequently as in the pages of an Ibn Duqmāq or al-Maqrīzī. High-priced neighborhoods no less than poor environments were dotted with them. The data also concern cities besides Fustat, such as Damascus and Jerusalem. It is noteworthy that the Maghrebi traveler Ibn Saʿīd, in the passage referred to above, note 36, observed that there were many ruins in Fustat, but states at the same time that a revival had taken place owing to the influx of the military.

Ruins were repeatedly mentioned as adjoining, facing, or being in the vicinity of inhabited buildings, either as being bequeathed or sold together with them, or, to the contrary, expressly excluded from a transaction. In July 1156, a government official bequeathed to his younger sister, the widow of "a merchant in the House of Exchange," one-half of the house in which he lived together with one-half of a ruin adjoining it. The property was situated in the Fortress of the Greeks between the two synagogues and opposite the women's bathhouse known as the Bath of the Cook. The two synagogues were connected by the often mentioned Milk Alley, *zuqāq al-laban*, probably named thus because milk, which was subject to a religious taboo, was sold there to members of the community. In any case, it was a much frequented place. One-half of a house in the prestigious Ḥudayjī Street was sold in 1143/4 by its proprietor and occupant for 75 dinars. He had to declare in court that the ruin adjoining it was not his and consequently was not included in the sale. Another ruin in that street has been noted before.[101] At approximately the same time the wife of the judge Nathan b. Samuel willed to him one-half of the house in which they lived together with a ruin facing it.[102]

The number of transactions in which ruins are noted as bordering buildings, even new ones, is astounding, when one considers that only a minority of documents dealing with houses care to indicate their boundaries.[103] Ruins were purchased, given as a gift, and, of course, rebuilt. A well-known banker, a public figure in Fustat around 1090, bought two ruins bordering on the Mamṣūṣa and gave them as a gift to a person whose relationship to him is not evident from the only partly preserved Muslim document.[104] A letter from Ramle, Palestine, reports that the president of the Jewish high court (which had his seat in that town, then the administrative capital of the country) was absent and in Jerusalem, where he had purchased a ruin adjoining his house and supervised its rebuilding in person (ca. 1045).[105] It is also not surprising that ruins, partly or totally, were taken away from their proprietors in a high-handed fashion.[106] Finally, parts of buildings described as *kharāba*, or ruin, were used, for instance, as storerooms, perhaps even as dwellings; at least the revenue lists of the charitable foundations note rents paid for such properties.[107] A long document deals with whether the proprietor of a ruin was entitled to dispose of his rubbish there.[108] The very practice of describing houses in a deed of sale as being "built up" seems to point to the fact that they often changed hands after having fallen into decay.[109] Contracts of lease for protracted periods where the rent is waived on condition that the tenant repairs or rebuilds a structure were commonplace. Consequently, it is not surprising that we find references to a house built on the ruins of another one. This is a passage from the letter of a widow in reply to a suggestion that she sell her house and buy a new one about whose quality she had doubts:

> The old house in the Maḥras [quarter] used to bring [rent] 60 dinars, and there is nothing wrong with it except the neighborhood. I do not know what would be the price today, whether it has gone up or down. However, its foundations are excellent and its structure is solid, and people say that beneath it is a *qāʿa* [ground floor] and beneath its pillars are other pillars. I shall pursue this matter until I have certainty about the purchase of the new house, so that I shall have a place where I can put my head down, for in this house I cannot live any longer.

The widow lived in the old house and derived her sustenance from apartments leased. The house constructed on the ruins of another was in good shape, but the neighborhood had become insecure—developments only too familiar to us.[110]

The socioeconomic causes of the proliferation of ruins in the medieval Middle Eastern city, as demonstrated by the Geniza papers, are discussed in A, 3, below. Its legal and psychological aspects are touched on here. Both Islamic and Jewish law deeply respected the property rights of an individual. He could do with it as he liked, even neglect it totally, provided he did not cause damage to his neighbor. Here, a psychological factor comes into play. The constant sight of desolation presented by ruined houses apparently did not annoy excessively the people who lived there. Otherwise, means would probably have been found to mend the situation. Perhaps the reason for this attitude is to be found in a certain degree of otherworldliness, which was not offended by these constant reminders of human decay and transitoriness.

Unoccupied premises.—One may ask whether the ubiquity of ruins was directly connected with the vexing problem of unoccupied premises mentioned in private correspondence as well as in the reports of charitable foundations. Empty houses or apartments could be listed by the government as having no proprietor and consequently as subject to confiscation. Action by the interested party to avert a takeover cost money.

A scholarly person from Byzantium or Western Europe, who was installed by his absentee Egyptian relatives as "gatekeeper" of their house, explains in a beautifully written Hebrew letter why he was unable to leave the house: the tenants might move out, the house would remain empty and then be seized by the government, "as is the practice here"; this would subject his relatives to heavy expenses. A woman in a family house in a provincial town north of Cairo asks her sister in Fustat to return together with her family; otherwise, Ghuzz, or Turkomans, would be billeted in the house, or the place would be taken by the government altogether. The passage deserves translation:

> Please come. The house is in bad shape and unoccupied, and I am afraid, it might be taken by the government [*nazl*, which could also mean billeting], for the finance director [*ṣāḥib al-dīwān*] lives on our side in the house of Joseph; he has become an old man [*shaykh*, might also mean important person], who takes walks across the roofs [and knows well what goes on in the houses]. The Ghuzz might take it and I cannot say a word. Imagine! Ibn al-Sarūjī [family name derived from Sarūj, a town in northwestern Mesopotamia, today Sürüç] has sold his house because of the Ghuzz. I implore you by God, quench my yearning and come. Let us live all together in one place.[111]

Complaints about unused premises in houses belonging to an individual are found ("three months she received rent, four—the apartment was not occupied"), as is the stipulation in contracts that a person receives the rights on the rent of a story in a house, but will not be indemnified if the place remains vacant.[112]

Entries in the accounts of charitable foundations note vacant premises as early as the first half of the eleventh century, when the community possessed only a few houses and the exodus from Fustat to Cairo had hardly begun, if at all. A revenue list of the year 1043, the first completely preserved, concludes with items introduced by the phrase "Unoccupied this month." An eighth-century Arabic papyrus listing the income of a church describes two out of six houses as vacant. All this clearly shows that such occurrences were common.[113] A communal account from the year 1164 notes: "Messengers to the government in matters of the unoccupied house in the Tujīb quarter—6 1/2 dirhems." The content of the message no doubt was that the vacancy was only temporary.[114] A similar, but more costly item from an account for the year 1184, "For the vacancy of the story held in partnership with the judge up to the end of the month of Nisan—16," is squeezed in between one expenditure on school fees for a poor boy and another on the purchase of a garment for a widow. These payments to the government for unoccupied premises were clearly quite regular features and needed no special comment.[115] The enigmatic "Vacancy—1/2" in an account for 1183 probably was hush money for a Muslim gatekeeper.[116]

These references in the Geniza to empty apartments or houses and others like them are not necessarily symptoms of a decline in population. A decline is palpably felt when we notice a *sudden* increase in the number of uninhabited premises, so many that the charitable foundations found it expedient to draw up lists of them and of premises still occupied. It happened in 1201, when the devastating famine and great plague played havoc among the population, a blow from which Fustat never recovered.[117]

The obligatory report to the government of unoccupied premises was not solely a matter of finance, namely, that they were deserted and therefore fiscal property. It was a security measure. When the vizier al-Ma'mūn in 1124 ordered the heads of the police of the twin capital to register the names of all the inhabitants and not to permit them to move from one house to another without his authorization, he was not interested in statistics (religious Muslims and Jews shun fixed numbers), but did so because he dreaded the infiltration of terrorists from the secessionist sect of the Assassins.[118] Vacant premises were a threat to public security. Therefore, the structures concerned had to be boarded up and a report sent to the authorities.[119]

Another deadly visitation by famine and plague, and a complete breakdown of public order occurred in Egypt during the dreadful years 1063–1072. E. Ashtor, who assumes a general decline in the urban population of Egypt by the end of the eleventh century, ascribes it partly to that disaster and partly to general socioeconomic conditions.[120] The Geniza does not reflect that change, perhaps to a certain degree because no dated documents of the pious foundations have been found for the years 1060–1090, which in itself may be an indication of some disarray in their administration.[121] In any case, the phenomenon of unoccupied premises in the Geniza cannot be compared in importance with that of dilapidated buildings and ruins.

Semipublic buildings and other landmarks.—Besides homes, stores, and workshops, a wide variety of other urban structures are mentioned in the Geniza whose functions are more or less self-evident, but whose legal character is usually not clearly defined. The term "semipublic" may be appropriate, inasmuch as the buildings served the public but were owned by an individual or a charitable foundation, or were leased from the government by a private entrepreneur.

In the first place, mention must be made of the *dār wakāla*, the house of a *wakīl al-tujjār*, or representative of merchants, which could serve as a warehouse, bourse, bank, seat of public notaries, mailing address, or all these functions together, depending on the importance of the individual wakīl. The proprietors of a wakāla were of widely differing provenance. One could be an illustrious qadi, or a man from the Egyptian Rīf, or the son of a Jewish immigrant from Spain. In Fatimid and early Ayyubid times these wakālas, like family firms, were of short duration—two, at most three generations—and did not leave a mark on the look of the city. The time of the great khāns, as the wakālas were later called, began in the thirteenth century.[122]

The various "houses" named after a commodity, such as jewelry, silk, carpets, threads, sugar, rice, oil, vinegar, saffron, almonds, or apples—all occurring both in the Geniza and in the works of the Muslim historians—served similar purposes, but some functioned also as toll stations. The term "house" in this connection is perhaps best translated as "bazaar."[123]

One example should serve as an illustration. The *dār al-jawhar*, the Jewelry House, was situated in the vicinity of the Mosque of ʿAmr, the oldest "cathedral" mosque in the capital (still extant). In the Geniza it appears first as the place where the merchant prince Joseph Ibn ʿAwkal (active ca. 990–1030) had his office, although his overseas correspondence shows him mainly handling commodities of large volume like flax and Oriental spices.[124] Nahray b. Nissīm, while still in Tunisia (ca. 1050 or earlier), asks a friend in Fustat to buy for him in the dār al-jawhar inexpensive unsorted pearls, *nathr*, at a price of 1 dinar for approximately 3 dirhems (9.475 grams); these pearls, he writes, were in demand by Spanish merchants visiting the Tunisian markets.[125] When Nahray as a young man was himself in Egypt (we find him there first in 1045), his senior partner in Tunisia writes to him: "You, brother, take your seat in the Jewelry House on every market day which might occur and buy for our partnership everything noted in the letter of Barhūn" (their common mentor, a relative).[126] After Nahray had settled in Egypt and had become an esteemed citizen, he was asked to assist two Muslim merchants from Barqa, eastern Libya, in selling their wares in the dār al-jawhar, especially their *kharaz*, or beads, cheap trinkets which were sold in units of tens of thousands of pieces.[127] Later in the century, another type of costume jewelry, also sold in large quantities, was manufactured in the Jewelry House by a man from Spain.[128]

The Geniza references to the dār al-jawhar are incomplete and for good reasons. We never read there about what must have been its most important business: dealings in costly jewelry, scores of which are known to us from the trousseaus of brides and similar sources. Orders for the precious consignments and notifications about their dispatch were not entrusted to paper. They might be read by the secret police, who was always feared and who might pass the information on to even less desirable elements.

Still, what we have is enough to show us the dār al-jawhar as a place of many-sided commercial and industrial activities. From sporadic references by Muslim historians can be gleaned some architectural details. It had an eastern and a western gate and an eastern and a western *saqīfa*, or roofed passage. An open space, into which several routes ushered, was on its eastern boundary.[129]

The often mentioned *dār mānak* requires special consideration. In a report about the massacre of merchants from Amalfi, southern Italy, in the year 996 it is described as being located near the *ṣināʿa*, the customs house of Fustat.[130] In the Geniza it appears as the toll station for a great variety of articles of export and of transit trade, in particular, large-volume items such as flax and Oriental spices.[131] I take the strange word *mānak* as Greek *monach(os)*, monk, and the place as a continuation of the pre-Fatimid Market of the Greeks, mentioned before.[132] The Byzantines and Italians came to Fustat for buying those commodities, and it would be natural for the place to be named after a Christian who had farmed its revenue. A monk could be prominent in international trade, just as were qadis and Jewish religious scholars. A notorious finance minister under the Fatimids was a monk.[133] The dār mānak, like the Market of the Greeks, was no longer in existence when the Muslim topographers described Fustat.[134]

Money could be changed, promissory notes written, and other financial transactions made in a dār wakāla, or one of the commodity "houses." Two places in Fustat were especially devoted to such activities, the House of Blessing, *dār al-baraka*, and the House of

Exchange or of Money Changing, *dār al-ṣarf*. The former was located in the Street of the Coppersmiths in the immediate vicinity of the cathedral mosque of ʿAmr—a propinquity of temple and money changers familiar to readers of the New Testament. Paul Casanova, the meritorious author of a book on the topography of medieval Fustat, read *brkh* as *birka*, pool. But the reading *baraka*, blessings, is established by *al-dār al-mubāraka*, The Blessed House, in Alexandria,[135] and, to the best of my knowledge, no pool was found in the Street of the Coppersmiths of Fustat. "God's blessing makes rich" (Proverbs 10:22), and fixed sums of coins, as traded in that house, were exposed to the evil eye and in need of particular protection from Heaven. The dār al-baraka appears in the Geniza frequently as an address, for example (in Arabic characters), "To the office of Joseph, the Kohen, House of Blessings, Coppersmiths" or as a place where one obtained sealed purses with fixed sums, which could be traded without being examined by an assayer.[136]

The dār al-ṣarf, literally, the house of Money Changing, must have been so well known that it served as an address without any additional topographical identification. On the reverse side of two letters sent there from Jerusalem shortly after 1051 the recipient made detailed notes about a large-scale governmental act of confiscation or fine imposed on the Jewish community, possibly in connection with the murder of the two Tustarī brothers.[137] This data, as well as that given in *Med. Soc.*, I, 238–239, seem to indicate that the place had a semiofficial status. It was not merely a hall where certified money changers had their seat. It might well have been that the Fatimid government received and made payments through "the big merchants of the House of Exchange." One Geniza letter is addressed to the Square of Money Changing, *murabbaʿat al-ṣarf*, but it is doubtful that the Square and the House were identical.[138] Muslim topographers, who wrote long after the Fatimid period, mention neither. Most probably the dār al-ṣarf was later known by another name, or, rather, was transferred to Cairo.

The caliphal mint, *dār al-ḍarb*, so often mentioned in the Geniza, seems to be absent from Casanova's *Reconstitution* of Fustat. Here the reason is obvious. Since the accession of Saladin, money was coined in the residential city of Cairo. Many people worked in the mint of Fustat, in various capacities, and under different arrangements. Because of its celebrity there was no need to indicate its location or to describe its appearance.[139]

Various structures, known from the Geniza as the scenes of intense commercial and industrial activity, seem to have been remnants from antiquity. Life in the *ṣaffayn*, the Two Rows, or the

Colonnade, is described in *Med. Soc.*, I, 194. To this should be added that this colonnade led directly to the venerated Bū Sargā (St. Sergius) Church in the Fortress of the Greeks. This colonnade is no longer mentioned in Geniza texts from Ayyubid times or by the Muslim topographers.[140]

The Qālūs market for flax, then the main export article of Egypt, as well as for other voluminous commodities, betrayed its pre-Islamic origin not only by its name but also by a Greek inscription on one of its gates, whose meaning was still known to the Arabs (*kalōs*, welcome!). "Half a small house in the Qālūs" is repeatedly noted as belonging to a Jewish charitable foundation. This market must have contained considerable areas of open space. One-twelfth of a *misṭāḥ*, or site for spreading materials dyed or tanned, in the Qālūs cost 10 dinars in October 1138, making the total of the site 120 dinars, a large sum for such a facility.[141]

The Greek derivative qaysāriyya has penetrated the Arabic language as an appellative noun meaning market hall. But in a number of Geniza texts it still is a proper name for one particular compound, as brought home by combinations such as "in the Colonnade and in the Qaysāriyya, namely in the Carpet House," and other references.[142] The original qaysāriyya of Fustat and those under the name of a (present or former) proprietor appear in the Geniza as places for the manufacturing and sale of clothing, carpets, and wool fabrics.[143]

Finally, the term "funduq," in modern Arabic, hotel, had preserved in Geniza times much of its pre-Islamic connotation of hospice for travelers and lodgings for the needy, as Greek *pandocheion*, from which it is derived. One funduq was situated between the two synagogues in the Fortress of the Greeks and another one, named The Small, was in the Great Market. Whether it was identical with the New Funduq, also noted in the lists of the charitable foundations, cannot be decided yet. I assume that they had been private homes donated to the Jewish community, and were then converted into buildings befitting their new function. I have come to this conclusion because the structural details applied to them are the same as those applying to residential quarters.[144] Funduqs first appear in the second half of the twelfth century. Before then, the needy and the travelers were put up within the synagogue precincts.[145]

Funduqs in the sense of caravanserai, that is, structures providing lodgings for traveling merchants upstairs and shelter for their pack animals as well as storerooms for their goods on the ground floor, are mentioned throughout the Geniza but seem to have become recognized landmarks only in the thirteenth century. Here, too, we find specialization according to the commodities traded, such as funduqs for traders in raisins, honey, hides, or mats. But they are rare, and cannot be compared with the Houses so often referred to in the Geniza which did not furnish lodgings. The all-comprising caravanserais belong to the Ayyubid and Mamluk periods.[146]

A Geniza document from the beginning of the eleventh century mentions two Jewish abattoirs, one in the market at the Bathhouse of the Mice and one in the Great Market.[147] Both markets were busy places,[148] but no doubt the abattoirs were situated in side streets. Ibn Duqmāq, the Muslim topographer, knows of only one "store serving as slaughterhouse of the Jews," namely, near the Little Market of the Jews and the block of the pious foundation for the Jerusalemites. That store was on a street leading to the Tujīb quarter, which, we remember, encompassed the Great Market. It is noteworthy that according to Ibn Duqmāq, a qadi, who was an overseer of the government finances, and Coptic notables had their residences precisely in the neighborhood of that slaughterhouse.[149] No general conclusions should be drawn from these bits of information. It is not excluded that the Jews, because of their taboos with regard to meat, were granted special privileges, or that the abattoirs had been there before the neighborhood was built up.

Besides buildings defined by their function, mention must be made of a structure that by its very appearance must have dominated the look of the capital of Egypt: the saqīfa, portico, or roofed passage. About eighty passages, often leading through or underneath buildings, even mosques, or adorning their fronts, are mentioned by Ibn Duqmāq, and the Geniza mentions others that he does not.[150] The Geniza also mentions *sābāṭ*, which denotes a similar structure, in a document in which a story built over it forms part of a marriage gift, in a letter by a Maghrebi living in Cairo (not Fustat), around 1110, giving Ṣabaṭ (thus) Ibn Ayyūb as his address, and in a letter of a Muslim captive in Nablus, Palestine, which is addressed to a sābāṭ in Cairo.[151] A number of mosques are described as *muʿallaq*, suspended, and the Muʿallaqa Church is still a landmark of Old Cairo.[152] In a Geniza letter a Jew introduces himself as "the Joseph from under the Muʿallaqa," that is, who had his store in the passage beneath the church—a concrete example of the economic foundations of a religious institution.[153]

Structures serving public health, such as bathhouses and hospitals, are discussed in *Med. Soc. V*, A, 2. (in preparation). Education was housed in the homes of the teachers, in rented premises, or in the compounds of the houses of worship.

Looking back on what has been said here on zoning and semi-public buildings one arrives at the conclusion that the medieval Islamic city possessed all the elements that later led to the formation of that unique phenomenon, the compact Grand Bazaar, stretching from one end of a city to the other. In the Middle Ages these elements were still disjointed, functionally and geographically. It was the great monarchies of Ottoman Turkey, Iran, and, Morocco, and the flourishing times of the sixteenth and early seventeenth centuries which completed what an earlier period had prepared.[154]

The House of God as the gathering place for the people.—The observation has been made that the medieval Islamic city lacked a central public square, comparable with the Greek agora or the Roman forum, because it did not possess the democratic institutions that required a large open space for communal assemblies. This reasoning misses the point. The Muslims were "brothers through their religion" (Koran 9:11, 33:5); the constituent element of their polity was their faith. Consequently the natural place for their public gatherings was the mosque. The same held true, and perhaps with even stronger force, for the houses of worship of Christians and Jews within Islam.

The Friday mosque, that is, the cathedral mosque of a city, or the main mosque of a quarter in a large city, proclaimed this purpose in its very architecture. It was of large dimensions in itself, and, in addition, possessed a spacious court, so that the entire male population of a city or a representative part of it could assemble there at one time.

The people attending communal prayer were by no means a passive crowd following the recitation of the leader of the service, or silently listening to the person occupying the pulpit, whether he was a caliph, a governor, or a professional preacher. As the example on p. 00 illustrates, the mosque was the place where the assembled could give vent to their grievances, and, of course, where the rulers or popular leaders tried to create public opinion. Because of the paucity of other means of communications, the mosque was also the place for public announcements.

Moreover, with its shady colonnades and other structures adjoining it, the mosque formed an extended compound, sufficient to harbor all the public, religious, and cultural activities with which the community was concerned. Here, as in the temples of antiquity, the public treasury was kept; fiscal arrangements, such as the farming out of taxes, could be made; the qadis administered justice there (when they did not do so in their houses); and *muftīs*, or legal experts, could be consulted in the precincts. Notaries served the public in drawing up their contracts or copying their letters. As we have seen, mosques, like churches and synagogues, were often situated in the midst of lively commercial neighborhoods; it is natural: where there are people, there is business. It should be noted that the use of church premises for secular purposes was by no means unknown in medieval Western Europe. Edith Ennen emphasizes that well into the thirteenth century the urban public bodies of many Italian cities held their meetings in the churches (or the palaces of the bishops).[155]

Finally, in Islam, as in Judaism, study is a prime religious duty. Before the eleventh century, when special buildings, richly endowed by foundations, began to be dedicated to higher education, the mosque was the natural place for study and instruction. Masters and students of all "Islamic" subjects (to which also belonged knowledge of the Arabic language) could be found there, forming circles of different size and duration. Learning was fostered by libraries housed in the premises of the mosques, some of which have become renowned for their treasures. And despite the development of buildings and institutions of Muslim higher education, the mosque, like the synagogue, never ceased to serve as a house of study, especially on a more popular level (which nowadays would be labeled as adult education). I recall vividly a visit to a mosque in Bursa, Turkey, some time before the sunset prayer, when I observed ordinary people from the neighborhood listening to an exposition of a sacred text, occasionally addressing the reader with a remark or a question. A few days before I had been present in a small synagogue in Jerusalem between the afternoon and evening prayer, where Yemenites, mostly craftsmen, recited the Mishna (the basic source of Jewish Oral Law) in unison, thus concluding, or interrupting, their day's work. In both cases, I was struck by the impression that for these people the House of God was theirs; it was the meeting place of the community.[156]

Naturally, the Geniza is not a source for the role of the mosque in Islam.[157] But it was necessary to include here these few remarks in order to put the mosque's place in Islamic urbanism into proper focus. All that has been said about life in the synagogue, in *Med. Soc.*, II, 155–170, applies, *mutatis mutandis*, and in far larger dimensions, to the mosque, both to the cathedral Friday mosque and to the more modest, but socially not less vital, street or neighborhood mosque, which catered to a limited number of parishioners. The Friday noon service in the cathedral mosque endowed the participants with the feeling of belonging to a great urban, and beyond this, ecumenical community and provided opportunities for the discussion of public affairs. The neighborhood mosque took care of the individual and probably discharged welfare services for the needy of the parish, although this latter point requires further research.[158]

The synagogue, as pictured in the Geniza papers, served all these purposes, the "great" or main synagogue in a city like Fustat serving also as the seat of the rabbinical judiciary as well as the center for the charitable activities of the community. The courtyard of the main synagogue, that of the Jerusalemites in Fustat, must have been roomy enough for accommodating any overflow during services, discussion lectures, and other events. There are many indirect references to the synagogue court, but no details of measurements. In the thirteenth-century synagogue of Aleppo, Syria, the court occupied a ground as large as the building. In Fustat, with its far more benign climate, the court might have been even larger.[159]

In short, since religion represented the social framework of a medieval Islamic city, religious buildings were its most conspicuous architectural creations. It was true with regard to the Muslim majority as well as the minority groups, with the differences inherent in the limitations imposed on the latter.[160]

The presence of the government. Security and sanitation.—No imposing government building, conspicuous by its location or structure, appears in the Geniza documents relating to Fustat during the Fatimid period. Nor have the Muslim topographers much to offer in this respect. An ancient building named Government House had ceased to function as such long before the eleventh century and had been partly dismantled. It is not mentioned in the Geniza.[161] The imperial palaces and their barracks were in the newly built city of Cairo; they served the court and the army. The civil population of Fustat had nothing to do there. This changed in Ayyubid times, when the citadel, *qalʿa*, of the capital was constructed on the Muqaṭṭam mountain in order to defend the city and partly also to centralize the various branches of government. Summons and visits to the qalʿa now make their appearance in the Geniza, sometimes with unpleasant consequences for the persons concerned.[162] A building named *dīwān*, government office, is occasionally mentioned, but only very rarely and without any hint to its appearance or location. It is not even clear that the sparse references concern the same building. Had the dīwān been conspicuous, it would have formed a landmark and lent its name to its neighborhood. But both the Geniza and the Muslim topographers are silent on this point.[163]

All in all, there seems to have been little direct contact between the populace and the government and, consequently, not much need for public buildings. The taxes were usually farmed out and collected in the markets and so-called houses, where the relevant transactions were made. The Nile harbors of Fustat and Cairo, respectively the Arsenal, *al-ṣināʿa*, and the customs house al-Maqs, served international trade and they, of course, recur frequently.[164] Busy government offices, such as that in charge of the poll tax, or the one supervising inheritances must have had their own premises, possibly even more than one each, but they are always referred to by function, never by location.[165] I conclude that they cannot have been buildings of distinction. I assume the government used for its offices some of the many houses that had come into its possession by confiscation or otherwise, for instance, estates whose heirs could not be located or were disqualified (e.g., according to Muslim law, a daughter could never inherit more than one-half of her father's possessions). This surmise seems to be confirmed, positively, by the consensus of the Geniza documents and the Muslim topographers with regard to all those houses and other semipublic structures discussed above on the one hand, and their silence on government offices on the other.

A number of buildings, designated as *ḥabs*, prison, *maḥbas*, house of detention, or *maḥras*, guardhouse or barracks, or indiscriminately by all three terms, appear both in the Geniza and Muslim sources as landmarks, which lent their names to their neighborhoods. These structures are all named after a person, such as the repeatedly mentioned ḥabs, maḥbas, or maḥras Bunāna (or Bunān, both female), the maḥras ʿAmmār, and the maḥras al-Sāriya.[166] Thus it seems that in these cases, too, private homes that had come into the government's possession it used for the purposes indicated by those designations.[167]

The word ḥabs, however, also means pious foundation. Therefore the word should be taken as meaning prison or police station only where one or two of the other terms is also used.[168] When we read in a document from Oct./Nov. 1117 about "the market known as the ḥabs [here twice written *ḥubs*] of Yūnus [Jonah, Muslim form], which is presently under the jurisdiction of the Ministry of the Friday and Neighborhood Mosques," most likely a pious foundation is meant.[169]

Although government was not conspicuous by public buildings of distinction, it was present in the city in many other ways. In the absence of a municipality, it supplied all aspects of city administration then in existence.

Overall security, entrusted to the police, regular and mounted, has been dealt with before.[170] In addition, the individual quarters, streets, or compounds benefited from special protection, for which a monthly payment, called *ḥars*, or *ḥirāsa*, guard, watch, had to be paid. (I paid ḥirāsa in Jerusalem until 1938.) The protection was both stationary and mobile, and there might have been changes in this respect during the Geniza period. Permanent protection was represented by the *ḥāmi 'l-ḥāra* or the *darrāb*, the guards for a quarter or a block, and, especially, the ṣāḥib al-rubʿ, the gatekeeper of a compound, three terms that were probably interchangeable.[171] The night watchmen, *ṭawwāfūn*, those who make the round, as their title indicates, were ambulant. There is definite information that Jews, too, could be employed as night watchmen, which was a job like any other. Consequently it would appear that this service was organized by the neighborhood concerned. The difference is reflected in the bookkeeping of the community. The ḥirāsa was a monthly payment incumbent on a building; therefore it is listed regularly in the accounts of the real estate owned by the pious foundations. The emoluments of the night watchmen were a matter of agreement between them and the community; they appear in the lists of beneficiaries receiving cash and loaves of bread and are recorded from the middle of the eleventh through the beginning of the thirteenth century. No doubt the watchmen also received bonuses from the individual inhabitants of a neighborhood; we have a chance example to this effect from a provincial town.[172]

The communal accounts contain numerous details about the cost of the ḥirāsa, but the amounts listed cannot be related to the value of the buildings protected, for they were sums paid either for all houses under the administration of the official concerned or for special cases, the circumstances of which are not revealed. But it is evident that the sums were moderate.[173]

Properties outside the town limits needed protection of the Arab or Berber clan that wielded authority in the area concerned. This imposition, called *khifāra*, it seems had to be paid in advance. In an account for the year 1182/3 regarding the orchard of the holy shrine of Dammūh southwest of Fustat, 30 dirhems are listed as having been delivered for the year 1183/4. The recipient was definitely the head of the clan, and the actual watchman, *khafīr*, was compensated with a "gift" of only 3 dirhems.[174]

Similar to the fee for security, another payment, called dust [garbage] removal, is listed regularly as required from a landlord. I counted about fifty of them in the reports of administrators of charitable foundations. Naturally, the sums paid varied widely according to the size of the buildings, the interval between removals, and special circumstances such as repairs, so frequently carried out. The amounts noted for single buildings range from 1/2 to 16 dirhems (or more).[175] But when we read in one monthly account that 1/2 dirhem was paid for garbage disposal from each of three different houses, or that 3 1/2 dirhems were charged for both a synagogue and a funduq, standard dues for this service seem to have been in force.[176] The regularity of payments for garbage removal, which are sometimes accompanied by a fine or tip, discreetly called *juʿl*, consideration, gives the impression that payment was not left up to the landlords. An eighth-century qadi is reported as having made a monthly round of the Muslim charitable foundations, and, when he found that a manager was remiss in paying up, ordered him to be flogged.[177] When Maimonides writes a note in his own hand to the administrator of the holy shrine of Dammūh, sending him 40 dirhems "for what is still due for garbage removal," one learns that the man had taken an advance for paying the due for that service in time.[178] Just as the proprietor of a house was responsible for the upkeep of the street bordering on it (as will be seen presently), so was he obliged to keep it clean. Among other such items, a communal account notes "dust removal from above the gate of the synagogue of the Palestinians, from the building itself, and the place in front of the synagogue."[179]

Another sanitary measure, the installation, cleaning, and maintenance of subterranean pipes, was no doubt also supervised by the government. When one account notes *ʿamal qanāt*, construction of a water conduit, in three different buildings owned by the community, such action would hardly have been taken at one time (since the community usually was short of funds), had it not been ordered from above.[180] The cleaning and maintenance of those clay pipes, which drained used water and other waste to cesspools or to the Nile, commonly appear in the accounts of the charitable foundations. It had to be regulated by a central authority or the system could not have worked. Excavations in Fustat and nearby localities have uncovered sophisticated water supply and sewage networks. George Scanlon's detailed description exemplifies how intricate they were.[181]

In countries where the non-Muslim population was exposed to particularly oppressive treatment, such as Morocco, Yemen, and Bukhara in Central Asia, the Jewish communities were forced at times to supply men who would serve as cleaners of the cesspools of a city. In Yemen this imposition was still enforced at the beginning of this century, or, rather, was reinstated when the Turks evacuated the country during World War I. I started my research among

Yemenites about ten years later and learned quite a bit about that new hardship. At the beginning, men from prestigious families volunteered for the job, so that the persons who would be doing it permanently should not feel humiliated. Among the hundreds of manual occupations performed by Jews according to the Geniza no trace of a cesspool cleaner could be discovered; had one existed, he would have appeared in the lists of the poor receiving bread and other handouts from the community. Payments for the cleaning of the qanāts are noted as such, not as given to specified persons doing the job. Thus it is evident that this operation was under the inspection of the government, which employed the men, probably through a contract with an entrepreneur.[182]

Along with the monthly payment for security, the ḥirāsa, another monthly due, called *ḥikr*, an Aramaic loanword meaning rent, had to be paid for houses in the Fortress of the Greeks and its environs. The Fortress had been taken by assault (at least, so goes the theory), wherefore by right of conquest its ground belonged to the Muslims, that is, the government, or, as a Hebrew document says, "to the King."[183] Only the originally Byzantine part of the city (or what was regarded as such) was subject to the ground rent. One building could be situated partly inside and partly outside the ḥikr zone. When one-eighth of the sugar factory of the Lebdis (once a renowned family of India traders) was sold around 1230 for 136 1/2 dinars (making the total value of the property 1,092 dinars), it was expressly stated that for the entrance hall ḥikr had to be paid to the Ministry of the Charitable Foundations, whereas the rest of the plot was free and not subject to that due. The factory was outside the Fortress of the Greeks, but not far away from it.[184] In view of this complicated situation one understands why, in later Mamluk times, this tax fell into desuetude.[185]

In the Geniza documents, however, the ḥikr is very much in evidence. Wills, deeds of gift, contracts of sale or rent had occasion to make mention of it, and in the communal accounts it is ubiquitous.[186] For "a small house" in the Fortress of the Greeks, sold for 20 dinars in 1124, a monthly ground rent of 1 qīrāṭ had to be paid, a total of 12 qīrāts, or 1/2 dinar, per year. Thus the yearly ground rent represented one-fortieth of the value of the property.[187] Several accounts from the year 1183/4, which register the revenue from rents for buildings belonging to charitable foundations and the ḥikr paid, show the latter amounting to eight through ten percent of the former. Should both series of payments refer to the same houses, which is almost certain, the ground rent in 1183/4 would have been far larger than in 1124, for rents, as shown presently, were comparatively low in those days. The houses donated to charitable foundations had probably deteriorated while the ground rent remained the same.[188] It would explain why, early in the thirteenth century, the community would pay the ground rent for the poor, who, being unable to afford it, probably would have lost their habitations. For the Muslim year 615, which began on March 30, 1218, the payment was 1,005 qīrāts, that is, about eighty-three times as much as paid in 1124 for one house. The relevant order of payment is written in the Nagid Abraham Maimonides' own hand, which underlined the urgency of the matter.[189]

In deeds of gift it is repeatedly stated that the ground rent would be paid by the donor or a third party, as when a woman who had donated the house in which she lived "to the poor" gave an adjacent small house to another woman, probably her housekeeper, free of ḥikr, since this due was included in that paid to a charitable foundation for the larger house.[190] Or, a father gives to his daughter an upper floor in his house on condition that if she preferred to live elsewhere, she would receive the rent, and he or his heirs would pay the ground rent.[191] In leases for prolonged periods one preferred to have the tenant pay the ḥikr.[192] All these examples show that this tax was an imposition very much felt by the people concerned. Like other taxes it was most probably farmed out.[193]

In many cases the government, either referred to as *sulṭān*, or represented by one of its ministries (such as that of the pious foundations of the Muslims or that of the mosques) owned not only the ground, but also part of or the entire property. Jews, like other inhabitants, could be coproprietors of such a place or could lease it. A father in despair over his profligate son even played with the idea of donating his house to the (Jewish) poor or . . . the government. Thus one had the government as close neighbor everywhere in the city.[194]

The erection of a building probably required a license, although none is found or referred to in the Geniza. But the government provided surveyors, *muhandiz* (later, as today, spelled with *s*), who supervised the correct demarcation of boundaries between properties in the city and whose expert judgment was sought whenever a dispute over an alleged encroachment arose. In a document dated 1136, two surveyors, expressly described as "generously made available by the government," inspected a tilting house that caused damage to an opposite building.[195] In a communal account of April 1184 Salīm the surveyor receives 8 1/2 dirhems, in another, written exactly fifty years later (April 1234), the unnamed surveyor gets 10 dirhems, and in a third account, written ca. 1240, the fee is 9 1/2 dirhems. The fact that this service, which was provided by the government, was remunerated with approximately the same sum over such a long period of time proves that it was a well-established institution.[196]

Any transfer of urban property was taxed and had to be certified by a Muslim authority. No wonder, therefore, that numerous fragments of deeds of gift or sale written by a Muslim notary have been found in the Geniza. The ends of the documents, as many as are preserved, are cosigned by one or several Muslims whose handwriting betrays them, too, as professional *ʿudūl*, or adjuncts of a qadi. I searched for a dīwān or other type of central office that would have assembled the information contained in these documents, thus creating a public record of urban properties, but in vain. Although I have not found in the Geniza any reference to such a cadastre, I have little doubt that one was compiled, and perhaps on more than one occasion, for the extremely detailed topographical information about Fustat (and Cairo) from Muslim sources, which largely tallies with the data of the Geniza, cannot have been entirely the work of interested individuals. It must have been based on archival material. I have already mentioned the order given in 1124 by the vizier al-Ma'mūn to the heads of the police in Cairo and Fustat to register all inhabitants of the capital, street by street and quarter by quarter. It would be worthwhile to inquire whether or not the topographical information provided by an Ibn Saʿīd al-Maghribi, Ibn Duqmāq, or Maqrīzī shows us Fustat mainly as it was in the first quarter of the twelfth century.[197]

In a letter from Sicily, either from its capital Palermo, or from Mazara, a port on its southwestern tip, the writer, an immigrant from Tunisia, says: "I have already entered my name in the *qānūn* [register, from Greek *kanōn*] and am about to buy a house." The writer hardly refers here to a cadastre recording urban property. He means, rather, that he, a non-Muslim, had already registered as a *qāṭin*, or permanent resident, and would now pay his poll tax in Sicily instead of Tunisia. Sicily, as the Greek derivative indicates, might have been a special case.[198]

The reader may wonder how the government could assure the payment of the conveyance tax when it had no central office supervising and registering all transactions in urban property. The answer is simple. No one could make a claim in court without producing a Muslim document properly issued by ʿudūl approved by the government. This legal situation is reflected in many Geniza sources. And just as a government surveyor would assist the Jewish courts in deciding matters connected with the architectural aspects of a building, thus a Muslim notary, "great in the art of the notariate," would confirm property rights by authoritative interpretation of a conveyance document submitted to him.[199]

The cost of the upkeep of streets devolved on the properties bordering on them. The repairs were carried out under the supervision of the ṣāḥib al-rubʿ, the gatekeeper of a block or compound, or the proprietors themselves. This state of affairs is evident from entries in communal accounts, such as "through the ṣāḥib al-rubʿ for the repair of the street [at the synagogue—4 dirhems]," "to Sulaymān—1 dirhem for the repair of the street at the al-Azraq house," "to the mason for work on the street of the compound of the Jerusalemites—3 1/2 [dirhems]."[200] Correspondingly, properties had certain rights on the street on which they were situated. In a document from June/July 1301, the elders of the Karaite community in Cairo leased to a merchant who had rented a store in the vicinity, for 6 dirhems per year, the right of way through a gate of the street at their synagogue. At that time, as is stated in the document, the synagogue itself was closed by government order. It was a period of persecutions of the non-Muslims, when their houses of worship were made inaccessible to them. The hope expressed in the document, "may it soon be reopened," came true.[201]

In the preceding pages the presence of the government in a city has been described as experienced by the common people. The officials representing government, the amīr, or governor, the wālī, or head of the police, the qadi, the muḥtasib, or superintendent of the market, and the host of clerks in general are discussed in *Med. Soc.*, II, 345–373, to the extent that the Geniza mentions their activities. There it is also emphasized that, as in the Middle Ages in general, the functions of the various officials were not always clearly defined and divided among them, and the muḥtasib, the official who, according to the textbooks, should be expected more than anyone else to represent the government to the populace, is all but absent from the Geniza papers during the Fatimid period. It is perhaps natural that the man in the street had little occasion to refer to the members of the upper echelon of officialdom. The sulṭān, government at large, however, was continuously present. Without it, no city life was possible, which was felt only too acutely when it was absent, when its authority broke down, a catastrophe experienced by the urban population in Fatimid times more than once.[202]

The individual and his hometown.—This topic is an extremely delicate one, difficult in itself and made even more complicated by the nature of our sources. The more extended letters in the Geniza were written by overseas traders who were mostly foreigners or new settlers in the cities from where they wrote. The second largest group of letter writers were scholars, who, like the academics of our own time, moved, or were moved around from one town to another. Moreover, during the two hundred and fifty years of the Geniza period, conditions changed, and so did the general mood, but this change is perceivable in the tone of the letters rather than in particular statements. Finally, the period of Fatimid and early Ayyubid rule, during which most of the Geniza papers were written, was distinct from the later Middle Ages, which furnished most of the material to the authors who have so admirably described the attitudes of the medieval Mediterranean man to his city. Any difference of emphasis or presentation which might be discovered in the subsequent pages as compared with previous descriptions should be understood not as a revision of former findings but rather as the reflection of a different period.[203]

Modern man speaks of his native city, the place where *he* was born. In Geniza times, a man's house was "the inheritance of his fathers" (1 Kings 21:3), the town where his father and mother were laid to rest. A merchant from Jerusalem angrily left his native city after having suffered serious losses there and settled in Egypt. His friends admonished him to return—not because Jerusalem was the holy city, but because it contained the tombs of his father and mother.[204] A Jerusalem pilgrim from the Maghreb had been impeded from reaching the goal of his journey first by the struggle between the Fatimids and the Seljuks and the general insecurity of the roads, second, by the civil war over the caliphal succession, which led to the siege of Alexandria where he happened to stay, and, finally, by the advent of the Crusaders. Notwithstanding these adversities, which were aggravated by a prolonged illness, he assures his relatives that he would tarry until the Egyptian army would have expelled the Crusaders. But, he adds, after having "seen" Jerusalem, he was resolved to return to his hometown, *waṭan*, and "the inheritance of his fathers."[205]

Using the same phrase, an ascetic who had settled in Jerusalem in order to "mourn" its desolation and "to tear himself away from the world," speaks of his intention to return (where to, is not preserved).[206] The term *waṭan* has been translated here as home*town* (and not homeland which it could mean, too), for the intention of the writer was to return to the place where his family lived. Similarly, when the Nagid Mevōrākh traveled from the Egyptian capital to another city (it seems, Alexandria), a communal official, writing to him, expresses regrets that the addressee had to separate from "his dear waṭan and his beloved son."[207] Or when Nahray, in his old age, left Alexandria for Malīj in the Nile Delta and then for Fustat, his home, a cousin, anxiously inquiring about his well-being, writes, "May God never separate you and me from our waṭans."[208]

The notion that a man's waṭan was his city rather than his country finds its expression in the blessing "may God keep her," "may God guard her" (the city is conceived as a female being), and similar wishes, which in the Geniza letters, as in Arabic literary texts, are regularly attached to the names of towns, but, in the Geniza, at least, never to those of countries. Countries were political complexes, often changing their borders and characters, cities were units of life.

Such blessings usually appear in addresses, but often also in the text of a letter, for example, "I happened to be in Labla [Spain], may God protect her";[209] or even in a legal document: thus a contract of partnership is concluded "in the city of Fez [Morocco], may God keep her."[210] In this connection, the Geniza writers sometimes use Hebrew phrases, even in an Arabic context, as when a man from Jerba, Tunisia, writes "to Cairo, may God shield her King and herself, Amen."[211] The most remarkable Hebrew example of attachment to one's city is found in the biblical phrase "May the Most High establish her forever," used exclusively with regard to the Holy City of Jerusalem, but applied in a letter to the name of the Egyptian capital, where the writer resided.[212]

In later centuries it became customary in Jewish letters to attach the blessing to the Holy Congregation in a certain city, not to the name of the city itself. This change reflects, of course, the deterioration of relations among the various religious communities. This alienation became extreme where oppression proved to be unbearable. I remember how shocked I was when I first read in a letter (many others in the same vein were to follow): "From X [a town in Yemen], may it be destroyed and laid waste, to Jerusalem, may it be built and established forever." I was shocked because it was the 1920s, but not surprised. It was the way in which one spoke of the city of an enemy in an Islamic ambiance. The highly cultivated Muslim traveler Ibn Jubayr writes, "Acre, may God destroy it," because, at the time of the writing (1183), that Palestinian city (Akko) was in the hands of the Crusaders.[213] Nothing of the kind is found in the papers of Ibn Jubayr's contemporaries, the Geniza people. They heeded the admonition of the Prophet Jeremiah addressed to the Judean captives in Babylonia: "Pray for the welfare of the city to which I [God is speaking] have exiled you . . . for her welfare is yours."[214]

In most Geniza letters the blessing refers to the city of the recipient or to one mentioned, not to the writer's own place. It is, so to say, the *idea* of the city, namely, the benefits any city bestows on its inhabitants, which makes it worthy of God's protection. The term "waṭan" originally designated a place where a man's family was indigenous and he himself was born. But in the mobile Islamic society waṭan came to mean also one's adopted city. Thus, Nahray and his cousin were Tunisians who had settled in Egypt, one in Alexandria, the other in Fustat. But in the letter cited, the cousin speaks of their waṭans.[215] It tallies with Arabic literary usage. The renowned Maghrebi historian Ibn Saʿīd, quoting a source contemporary to Nahray, says of the Fatimids that they "took Cairo as their waṭan," meaning, their seat and new home (as opposed to their original home, the Muslim West, from which Ibn Saʿīd himself hailed).[216]

This expansion of the linguistic usage betrays a change in social attitudes. The ancient Arabs despised the populace they conquered, who could identify themselves only by their place of habitation, and not, like their overlords, by a noble lineage. But that paragon of Arab virtues, al-Aḥnaf, the leader of the Tamīm tribe in the newly founded city of Baṣra, was reported to have said: "An Azdī [a member of the rival tribe] of Baṣra is dearer to me than a Tamīmī of Kūfa." The urban community had become (or was on the way to becoming) a reality of greater concern than the bonds of lineage.[217]

"Throughout the Middle Ages cities grew solely through influx from their environment." This statement, made by Edith Ennen with regard to Europe, certainly could be applied to a large extent to the capital of Egypt.[218] Many of the illustrious men of Islamic letters ornating Cairo-Fustat derived their family names from smaller towns in Egypt such as al-Subkī, al-Qalqashandī, and al-Shaʿrānī, and were actually born there, but it is not surprising that ordinary Jewish persons with the same family names left their records in the Geniza.[219] The number of Jewish inhabitants of Fustat named after obscure localities in the Egyptian Rīf is surprising; some of them were paupers, but others were not.[220] Smaller towns, such as Damīra or Damsīs, provided men who rose to riches and to influential positions in the Fustat community.[221] The Mediterranean port Damietta gave its name to at least ten families or persons in Fustat differing from one another by origin (Kohens, or "simple" Jews), socioeconomic position (schoolmasters, physicians, India traders, divines) and, of course, the periods in which they were active. Often it is difficult to decide whether a person was a newcomer to the capital or the son of one. Thus, in a document from June 1087, Abu 'l-Ḥusayn al-Tinnīsī (from the Mediterranean port Tinnīs) appears as a well-established representative of merchants in Fustat, but in an earlier letter, showing him in a similar capacity, he is referred to with his full name as Abu 'l-Ḥusayn Aaron, son of Yeshuʿā al-Tinnīsī.[222] Naturally, the same ambiguity prevailed with regard to persons from countries other than Egypt. In his early years in Egypt Nahray b. Nissīm of Qayrawān was identified as al-Maghribī, but in the vast majority of cases this epithet was omitted, because Nahray had become a permanent resident of Fustat. The same happened with the often mentioned ʿArūs b. Joseph, in some letters called al-Mahdawī (from the Tunisian port al-Mahdiyya), but mostly appears without that epithet. Much research will be necessary before it can be established with even approximate likelihood whether the majority of the Jewish inhabitants of the Egyptian capital represented in Geniza papers were indigenous, or had adopted it as their home. My impression is that the percentage of newcomers or their children was exceedingly high. One wonders how such circumstances might have affected a man's attitude to his town.

In ancient Israel, where the citizens were mostly "Ackerbürger," farmers organized in small urban settlements surrounded by walls, the town was one's "mother" (2 Samuel 20:19), the relationship was natural and, as a rule, indissoluble. In the mobile and mercantile world of the Geniza times, the connection of a man with his town should be rather compared with the bond of marriage. Marriage may be dissolved by divorce, and Muslims, Jews, and even the Christians of Egypt often took recourse to this expediency.[223] Similarly, many Geniza letters speak of the writer's intention to forsake his hometown or report about such a step.[224] But once a marriage is successful, it might become a stronger bond than that created by filial piety. The strong attachment of the Geniza man to his waṭan, whether in the sense of native city or a place chosen for permanent residence, has been illustrated above in various ways. In a written source like the Geniza these feelings are most vigorously expressed when the writer is away from home and is longing to return.

"Yearning after one's home," *al-ḥanīn ila 'l-waṭan*, was a great topic in ancient Arabic poetry. Al-Jāḥiẓ, the renowned creator of the Arabic essay (d. 869), dedicated a special study to this genre.[225] Gustave von Grunebaum evaluated it for the modern reader.[226] The verses written by the unhappy Jewish doctor from Alexandria who practiced his art in Qūṣ, Upper Egypt (cited in Med. Soc., II, 259) may give an idea of that type of poetry.[227]

It is noteworthy, however, that medieval Muslim writers recognize a man's attachment to his hometown as an important sociological factor. The geographer Yāqūt, in describing the town of

Zughar (the biblical Zoar) on the southern tip of the Dead Sea, expresses astonishment that anyone could live there given its murderous climate. His answer is one word: waṭan, love of one's native city. The Geniza letters show that, in the eleventh century at least, there was another good reason for Zughar's existence: it was an entrepot of the trade between North Arabia and the Mediterranean.[228] Ibn Jubayr reports that Muslims returned to Tyre, Lebanon, although that city was in Christian hands at the time and therefore due to be destroyed. He explains their blameworthy action by man's natural attachment to his hometown.[229]

The same motive is found even in official documents. A *dhimmī*, or non-Muslim from Alexandria, had been forced by the adversities of the time to leave his cherished city, his parents and brothers, and to settle in a place where he had commercial dealings with a government office (which one is not said). Now, he writes, "he has been repeatedly visited by remembrance of his hometown and longing after it," wherefore he respectfully asks that his affairs be settled so that he might return to Alexandria.[230] Similarly, a Muslim baker petitions the caliph's vizier to permit him to pay a debt in installments so that he may be able "to remain in his native city, his waṭan."[231]

The attachment to one's city is most patently manifested in the concern for one's compatriots. *Baladiyya* in modern Arabic means municipality, but in the Geniza letters it designates the feelings and care for the inhabitants of one's town. In a highly interesting document from 1122 an aged man from Tripoli turns over his possessions to a relative from the same city living in Fustat who, in return, would take care of him until his death. He trusted the man because of "the common bonds of family and city."[232] A Jewish dignitary from the Maghreb, in asking the Egyptian Jewish authorities to inquire about the death of a Maghrebi merchant, who was murdered on his way to Yemen, adds: "He is also my co-citizen, *baladīnā*, and I am particularly concerned about him."[233] Such feelings were by no means confined to the members of one's own religion.[234]

While away from home, baladīs stuck together: Maghrebis (meaning mostly persons from Qayrawān and its port city al-Mahdiyya) in Alexandria and Fustat or wherever we find them; newcomers from Hebron and Ghaza in Ascalon; people from Tiberias in Acre; people from Aleppo in al-Maḥalla; and groups of pilgrims from Tyre and Tiberias fighting one another in Ramle. Beyond these examples, where compatriots are expressly mentioned as groups, a major part of the Geniza correspondence reflects the same situation, inasmuch as overseas trade was largely organized in the form of business between the inhabitants of a city and expatriots from the same city living abroad. "I did not sell any of the bales that have arrived from Tripoli, Syria. This can be done solely in the presence of merchants from the city of origin, and there were none here," writes a representative of merchants in Alexandria.[235]

It has often been said that in the traditional Islamic city a man was attached to his quarter or otherwise close surroundings, not to his city as such. This might have been true with regard to later times. In the Geniza I cannot find that attitude. A study of the topographic features of Fustat proves that the many quarters and districts mentioned in the Geniza were not clearly separated from one another; there was much overlapping and seemingly no strict division.[236] The various religions and denominations or sects formed distinct groups, but social separation among them was far less rigid than in the later Middle Ages. Similar observations have been made with regard to Europe.[237] The division of a city into separate administrative units indicates the ever stronger bureaucratic rule of military elites, as was apparent in the Mamluk state and perfected under the Ottomans. It seems, also, that the population of the capital of Egypt under the Fatimids was considerably smaller than under the Ayyubids and early Mamluks, when the twin cities were united into one large complex with much new space encircled by a wall and defended by a fortress. In short, Fustat was then still a manageable entity, a place where one could feel that one belonged.

The question of ghettoes for the members of minority groups is discussed in *Med. Soc.*, II, 289, where it is shown in detail that in classical Geniza times Muslims, Christians, and Jews lived in close proximity. There were predominantly Jewish neighborhoods, especially in the vicinity of synagogues, an arrangement made almost necessary by the practice of daily attendance at the public service. Occasionally a contract stipulates or mentions that the property transferred might be alienated solely to a Jew. A newly identified Geniza document, in which one party renounces its right of preemption to another, formulates this condition thus: "They may sell the nine and a half shares of the house acquired to any Jew they wish." The house was situated in the Bīr Jabr quarter of Alexandria, which harbored the synagogue of the Iraqians of that city, but was contiguous with the house of a *qissīs*, or Christian clergyman.[238]

In discussing the question of marital habitation, the Talmud states that a husband could not force his wife to follow him from a middle-sized town to a big city, "because life in big cities is hard." According to the medieval commentators the reason for this statement was the congestion and unhealthiness of cities, whereas smaller towns with their gardens and green plots around the houses furnished fresh air. In the Geniza this statement was repeated with regard to Jerusalem, which was much smaller than Fustat.[239] I have not yet encountered outspoken complaints about the unhealthiness of Fustat, but the Geniza is replete with stories about illness, and the frequent invitations to places in the Rīf (addressed also to children) seem to show that one was aware of the physical hazards of city life. It should be noted, however, that Fustat-Cairo was not devoid of parks and gardens and other open spaces where one could enjoy fresh air.[240]

Life in a big city, then as in medieval Florence or in our own time, was expensive, and not everyone could afford to live there.[241] It was also a difficult place for a chaste man who was staying there without a wife.[242] In general, however, complaints about one's town are surprisingly rare. One cursed the bad times, never one's place of domicile.[243]

If, as the Talmud has it, life in big cities is hard, life in villages, or in the tents of nomads, according to the same source, is no life at all.[244] Al-Shaʿrānī, the great Muslim mystic, opens his two-volume autobiography with thanks to God "for my 'exodus,' by the Prophet's blessing, from the countryside to Cairo, for God's transplanting me from the region of hardship and ignorance to the city of gentleness and knowledge."[245] Similarly, the Geniza man knew well what the city meant for him. It afforded him a measure of security and opportunities for gaining a livelihood; it supplied his religious and other cultural requisites and even some amenities. Above all, he was an eminently social being. "Good company or death" is an ancient Near Eastern maxim. The Geniza man found life in the familiar and variegated ambiance of the city.[246]

2. *Domestic Architecture*

General character—"Three things set a man at ease: a beautiful home; a comely wife; and fine clothing." This Hebrew saying is cited in the Talmud as a general truth, not as the personal opinion of a scholar. The home comes first, because a man should build a house before taking a wife.[1] Seen from the point of view of women, this piece of popular wisdom from Late Antiquity expresses the same idea: "A woman prefers colorful rooms and colorful garments to choice food."[2] The emphasis is on beauty. A person's happiness is largely conditioned by the look of his immediate and constant environment. Hence the advice: "Save on food and drink, and lavish on your home."[3]

This attitude is borne out by the very numerous details about domestic architecture which, in various contexts, make their appearance in the Geniza. These bits of information enable us to form an idea of the type of home regarded as desirable in those days. In modern times people tried to make their premises convenient and pleasing by an appropriate choice of furnishings and furniture. The architect seen at work in the Geniza papers seems to have striven mainly for the creation of inner space, of roominess. He tried to bring the expanse of the sky into the interior of the house. It was achieved first and foremost by the general layout of a dwelling. Whether on the ground floor or in the upper stories, there was one very large social room, the *majlis,* tentatively translated by me as living room; the numerous other rooms were small and very small; they are often noted as "belonging" to the majlis. Structural items, such as wall cabinets, and ornate recesses and niches fulfilled the purposes of armoires and even bedsteads. Easily movable objects served instead of fixed pieces of heavy furniture. And the inner court, often beautified by a fountain, sometimes even by a garden, brought God's wide world—sky, water, and plants—into the space created by man.

Mobility within the house conditioned the rhythm of life. Despite the rich architectural nomenclature of the Geniza and contemporary Muslim documents we would look there in vain for such terms as dining room or bedroom. In winter one slept in a small closet, which could easily be warmed by a brazier; in summer one sought relief from the heat in the spacious living room with its ventilation shaft, which brought the cool north wind from the roof into the interior of the various floors. The meals were taken where it was appropriate in accordance with the circumstances. There were no fixed tables surrounded by chairs; food was brought in from the kitchen on trays and put on movable low stools. Thus, whether resting or being with other people, one could enjoy either roominess or intimacy. But the emphasis was on space.

As the Geniza shows—and this aspect is its intrinsic contribution—the High Middle Ages was a period of transition for the history of domestic architecture as it was in so many other respects. The main constituents of the traditional Egyptian Arab house were already in the making. The heritage of Late Antiquity, so far as it was not absorbed in the new developments, had by now been discarded. The famous Coptic Budge papyrus of Columbia University, which was written in early Islamic times, still lists as main parts of a house the dining room and the bedroom, using Greek terms.[4] Similarly, Hebrew Midrashic literature, which continued to be written well into the Islamic period, also using Greek words, constantly refers to these structural elements, which had disappeared from the Geniza documents and were replaced by an entirely different concept of a home.[5] As shown further on in this subsection, however, some of the more characteristic elements of the traditional Egyptian house clearly developed only in the thirteenth century or later and are practically absent from the "classical" Geniza. Moreover, the terminology of the Geniza is largely different from later usage, and the change, most likely, was not merely a question of language. It is unavoidable, therefore, that I bother readers with a few architectural terms; their indulgence is craved in advance. Without the identification of terms one does not get a clear picture of how the home of a middle-class family looked in Fatimid and Ayyubid times. And we cannot understand those people well without knowing something about their physical environment, which was so important to them. As far as possible, the information to be derived from the Geniza is related to what is known about the traditional urban house in Egypt and, in particular, to the results of excavations carried out in the area of ancient Fustat.

Geniza evidence, archaeology, and the traditional Egyptian house.—Private and commercial correspondence occasionally contains telling and illustrative references to the structural and social aspects of housing in the Geniza period. A person traveling or moving to a city asks a friend to look for an apartment or a home and describes what kind of dwelling he has in mind; and we have answers to queries of this type. Notes on the need of repairs in houses and the expenditure on them form a not infrequent topic in both family and business letters. Then there are reports about special events connected with houses, for instance, accidents caused by structural defects, or the damage or devastation resulting from earthquakes. With regard to cities for which we have no legal documents, such as Mosul, Iraq, detailed references in letters are particularly welcome.

Our main source, naturally, is the information to be gathered from legal documents and accounts. Deeds of sale hold the highest rank in this category, side by side with notes and drafts made for that purpose by court clerks or judges. The Geniza contains a considerable number of such deeds written by Muslim notaries in Arabic script. In most cases, they tell us about houses, or parts of houses, acquired by Jews from other Jews, or from Christians or Muslims. There are also some items in which the two contracting partners are Muslims; we may assume the property concerned was later acquired by a Jew who received all the documents related to it, including that item.

By far most deeds of sale preserved are written in Hebrew characters and in a mixture of Arabic, Aramaic, and Hebrew legal parlance. The form of such a deed, abstracted from a number of actual examples, has been published by G. Weiss and supplied with an English translation.[6] An old and most detailed collection of Muslim forms for contracts of sale, the *Shurūṭ* of Ṭaḥāwī (ca. 853–933), edited by Jeanette A. Wakin, deals mainly with houses. The enormous diversity of cases reflected in those forms proves how much experience had already been accumulated in these matters in the third Islamic century.[7] Naturally, we are concerned here with the descriptive details of a document rather than with its legal aspects, but often the two are closely interconnected. To give an idea of the type of information to be derived from this source, I enumerate the main elements normally found in a Geniza deed for the purchase of a house.

1. Exact location of the property, often elaborately described according to town, district, streets, and lanes.

2. Its name, normally identified by the present proprietor, often plus that of a former, but better-known, proprietor or occupant. Occasionally, a house was known under a byname, such as "the garden house," or, "the house with the palm tree."

3. Its characteristic parts. Most contracts confine themselves to the main architectural features, which give a general idea of the type of building sold. But some contain numerous details, leading the reader from the entrance door through all the corridors, courtyards, and rooms up to the roof, or, rather, roofs, which enables us to gain a complete picture of a place. Some deeds, both Muslim and Jewish, contain the disappointing remark that, because of the "fame" of the building, no description or indication of its boundaries or other features is necessary.[8]

4. The boundaries, mostly indicated by the names of streets or public buildings and of persons to whom the adjacent houses belonged. From the sociological point of view, these details are often very precious. Muslim deeds preserved in the Geniza list the borders in the order of south-north-east-west, starting with south, and many Jewish records follow that custom. The sequence east-west-south-north and other sequences starting with east are equally frequent in Jewish deeds, at least in those of the tenth and early eleventh centuries. One remembers, of course, that south, the direction of Mecca, was sacred to the Muslims, and east, to the Jews and Christians, but both systems go back to pre-Islamic usages.[9]

5. Details about proprietors and proprietorship. More often

than not, only a part of a house was sold. In this case it was normally stated whether this share was all, or only a fraction, of the seller's property, and who the other proprietors were; also, whether the house was "common and undivided," that is, whether the share sold was a percentage of its total value or represented an actual part of the house. If the latter, this part, as well as its location and relationship to other parts, was described. But it was the exception rather than the rule. Normally, a house was evaluated as consisting of twenty-four nominal shares and the purchase consisted in the acquisition of a certain number of them.[10]

6. The price. In addition to the amount, the type of money received or to be paid is always exactly indicated. If the price was not delivered in full at the transaction, details about payment of the balance naturally would be given together with any conditions attached to it, for example, that the seller was permitted to live in the house until the balance was settled. Occasionally, the deed states whether or not the price included a commission for the real estate broker or any special bonus.[11]

7. Special conditions. In regular contracts, it is always stated, often with an enormous display of legal verbiage, that no conditions whatsoever were attached to the sale, that the seller had reserved for himself no rights, that the buyer might do with his newly acquired property whatever a proprietor is allowed to do, and that the entire property with all its appurtenances, rights, and privileges had been transferred. Here again, and often in fine detail, the parts of the building and the materials used for its construction are listed, but clearly these lengthy enumerations were taken from formularies rather than from actual descriptions provided by the parties. Still, the very fact that these stereotyped specifications differ so much from one document to another proves that they were not entirely divorced from reality. In this part it would also be stated whether the plot was included in the transfer or whether it belonged to the government or to any other public authority, and what the amount was of the "lease" to be paid for it. Special conditions normally consisted of privileges granted to the seller or his family, especially the right to buy the house back, in which case, of course, the necessary specifications had to be given. Or, a relative of the seller would renounce the right of preemption in case part of a family property was alienated.

Deeds of gifts, wills, and donations of houses for philanthropic and religious purposes contain many of the elements found in deeds of sale. Sales are in principle unconditional, whereas it lies in the nature of gifts and wills to have conditions attached. Often the considerations guiding the donor are stated or are evident by implication. For all these reasons, documents of this type compel strong human interest.

Contracts of lease, whether made out by Muslim or Jewish notaries, usually contain only short descriptions of the property concerned and cannot be compared in this respect with deeds of sale. They do show us how much people were prepared and able to spend on their living quarters. In addition to the essential stipulations concerning the duration of the rent and the amount and terms of payment, contracts of lease sometimes contain special conditions, for example, whether the tenant is allowed to sublet the premises, or who bears the cost of repairs.

Court records about disputes over houses and settlements made in such matters are another and most valuable source of information. As may be expected, an endless variety of situations is reflected in records of this type. Partitions agreed upon by relatives or partners, claims arising from allegedly unpaid rent, or the pledging of a property as a collateral are more common cases. There are others, more specific and complicated ones, such as a dossier about property first confiscated by a rapacious governor and subsequently encroached upon by a greedy relative; inspection by judges and government experts of a house tilting over the street and damaging the opposite building; or the submission of a long series of documents to a court in order to prove a title of rights.

Unfortunately, most of the documents pertaining to the groups described have come down to us in an incomplete state. In particular, the deeds of sale, being of large size by their very nature, have suffered much from the clipping off of parts and otherwise. Not a single one of those written in Arabic characters has been preserved in its entirety.

The situation is more satisfactory with regard to an extremely precious group of records for the history of housing, namely, the accounts of the administration of buildings belonging to pious foundations or the community. Such accounts usually were written on paper of comparatively small size, as was used for the notes of judges (approximately 7.5 × 5.5 inches) with both sides of a leaf fully covered with writing. Thus there existed no inducement for clipping. Moreover, and most important, these accounts were disposed of in the Geniza not very long after they had been drawn up, for they contained reports about revenue and expenditure for short periods, often only for a few months, and there was no purpose in preserving them. Consequently, they did not suffer from reuse and from climatic and other damaging agencies. The accounts include information about the cost of maintenance and repairs, the occupancy of houses, and, in particular, the rents actually paid for individual apartments or rooms.[12]

No such accounts have been found with regard to houses belonging to private persons. We have some elaborate receipts of rents for more highly prized property, made out by Muslim notaries. Some casual notes about wages of masons and other workmen, as well as expenditure on materials, also have turned up. It seems, however, that the Geniza people did not keep regular account books on the revenue from, and maintenance of, houses belonging to them and rented out in part or in their entirety.

References to houses are found in marriage contracts, for brides frequently were given shares in one or several houses as part of their dowry. These references, however, are mostly short and of a general nature. The transfer of the property itself had to be ratified in a proper deed made out by a certified notary.

Comparatively few Arabic papyri refer to houses. They originated in provincial towns and contain little descriptive material.[13] The deeds preserved in the archive of the Karaite community of Cairo, so well described in D. S. Richards's meritorious article on the subject, are of great value. Only documents about houses built not later than the thirteenth century are considered in this book.[14]

Excavations were carried out in the area of ancient Fustat by Aly Bahgat and Albert Gabriel in the years 1912 through 1920, described by them in a volume published soon afterward.[15] Gabriel summarized the results with respect to domestic architecture in a separate publication.[16] In the 1960s work was resumed by the Egyptian Department of Antiquities under the direction of the late Gamal Meḥrez, who also paid special attention to the problems of habitation.[17] At approximately the same time systematic excavations were undertaken by George T. Scanlon, who was joined later by Wladyslaw Kubiak. Reports about their work appeared in several volumes of the *Journal of the American Research Center in Egypt*, where reference is made to other papers by these authors connected with their findings.[18]

For several reasons, the results of the Fustat excavations are not as helpful for the interpretation and testing of the Geniza documents as one might expect. Fustat was not a city suddenly destroyed and quickly covered with lava and debris, and later with earth, like Pompeii. It was given up in the course of many centuries. People moving from Fustat to Cairo or elsewhere took everything of value with them; the dilapidated houses were slowly dismantled, and the stones and other building materials were carried away and used for other structures. What remained were the foundations of buildings or, rather, the rest of them, and their interpretation is often dubious. The situation is more favorable with regard to the elaborate canal system (or, rather, systems) of the city. Scanlon's diggings were very instructive in this respect.

Second, as Scanlon has emphasized, the most central, populous, and important parts of ancient Fustat cannot be reached by excavations owing to the building up of that area from the mid-eighteenth century to the present day.[19] The section unearthed is "somewhere in the area where al-ʿAskar and Qaṭā'iʿ [two suburbs founded around 760 and 870, respectively] conjoined."[20] The network of streets uncovered, with its lack of clearly identifiable thoroughfares, betrays the suburban character of the neighborhoods. Those suburbs were situated on hard, rocky ground far away from the Nile, whereas Fustat itself bordered on the river (before its shores partly silted up). The drainage system uncovered by the excavators consisted of channels connecting one or several houses with a cesspool, which had to be emptied from time to time. The Geniza, however, mentions work on a drainpipe leading from a new house to the Nile (ca. 1037).[21] This item tallies with a treatise on health care by Ibn Riḍwān, a famous Cairene physician (998–1061), where he says about Fustat: "Their lavatories empty into the Nile and sometimes obstruct the flow of the water. Thus they drink water mixed with that putrid matter."[22] The difference between the two systems was not merely technical. Conducting drainage to the Nile necessitated centralized direction and supervision to a far higher degree than required by a system of local cesspools.

Finally, as Albert Gabriel himself observed, there is a blatant discrepancy between the findings of excavators and the descriptions of Fustat by competent observers visiting the city during the Fatimid period and earlier who speak about houses four, five, seven, and eight stories high.[23] In an often quoted passage the distinguished Persian author Nāṣir-i-Khosraw says that from afar the city looked like a mountain, because it contained buildings between seven and fourteen stories high. Considering the flimsy foundations he unearthed, Gabriel doubted whether most of the houses comprised more than one story. Therefore, tentatively, Gabriel weighs the possibility, made a certainty by later findings, that the parts of the city excavated by him and Aly Bahgat were different from those represented in the descriptions of medieval travelers.

The late A. Lézine, in a study on the persistence of pre-Islamic traditions in the domestic architecture of Muslim Egypt, accepts the testimony of such renowned medieval writers as Iṣṭakhrī, Ibn

Ḥawqal, al-Muqaddasī, and Nāṣir-i-Khosraw, and concludes that Arab tribesmen from South Arabia built their houses in Fustat in the manner they were accustomed to in their native country, namely, in the form of multistoried *immeubles-tours*.[24] Anyone who has seen pictures of a city such as Shibām in the Hadramaut, South Arabia, with its mountainlike high houses closely adjacent to one another, can imagine how the original, Arab, part of Fustat might have appeared to the admiring looks of medieval Islamic travelers. This matter is taken up again in the discussion of types of houses represented in the Geniza.[25]

Next to the results of excavations it is the traditional Egyptian house, as it developed in Mamluk and Ottoman times and still was commonly in use during the first half of the nineteenth century, which must be taken into consideration for the study of the data of the Geniza. The most lucid, exact, and complete description of the Cairene house, as it looked around 1830, and the most easily accessible to the general reader, is contained in E. W. Lane's *Account of the Manners and Customs of the Modern Egyptians*, first published in 1836, and available today in inexpensive editions. Each detail in the house is illustrated by a painstakingly executed engraving ("which I have made, not to embellish the pages, but merely to explain the text"), and its Arabic term is provided and discussed.[26]

E. W. Lane was preceded by the magnificent *Description de l'Égypte*, the result of the scholarly work accompanying Napoleon's expedition to Egypt, and succeeded by David Roberts's artistic lithographs.[27] From the vast scientific and technical literature on the subject I should like to mention those that I found particularly useful for the purpose of this volume. Edmond Pauty described houses and palaces of medieval and Ottoman Cairo actually preserved, at least in part, until his time, and, in a separate publication, the admirable woodcarvings that formed a most prominent element of inner decoration.[28] Martin S. Briggs's study "The Saracenic House," amplified in his book *Muhammedan Architecture in Egypt and Palestine*, forms an excellent introduction to the specific properties of Cairene dwellings.[29] The houses of Rosetta, a town, which, during the fifteenth through the eighteenth centuries, had replaced Alexandria as the main Mediterranean port of Egypt, have attracted the special attention of students of domestic architecture, beginning with members of Napoleon's expedition. The various studies on this subject have been integrated in a joint publication by A. Lézine and Abdel Tawwab.[30] Dietrich Brandenburg's German book on the Islamic art of building in Egypt contains a fairly complete summary of the research done on domestic architecture.[31] Oscar Reuther's detailed study of traditional housing in Iraq, which is so different from the Egyptian, is extremely valuable because of its minute details, profuse illustrations, exact terminology, and constant comparison with Egypt. Reuther has also dedicated a special study to the central part of the traditional Egyptian house, the *qāʿa*.[32] The same structure is the subject of a fascinating paper by the architect and town planner Hassan Fathi, which, although mainly concerned with the application of past experience to future planning, is also an eye-opener for the historian.[33] *Palais et maisons du Caire du XIVe au XVIIIe siècle*, by J. Revault and B. Maury (Paris, 1975) is a most important contribution to the history of the traditional Cairene house.[34]

Types of houses.—From all that has been said on the preceding pages it is evident that more than one type of house is represented in the Geniza papers. Before trying to discuss them we must explore how the very idea of "house" was expressed in Arabic and Hebrew, the two languages mainly used in that source.

The Arabic word generally used for house was *dār*, literally, enclosure, properly called thus because it could comprise several buildings. The Hebrew equivalent *ḥāṣēr*, originally, courtyard, conveys the same idea, namely, that of a central court around which the buildings would cluster.[35] A document mentions "the building standing *in* the dār"; others, one referring to Fustat, another to Damascus, speak of a dār within a dār; and an eighth-century papyrus lists "a shop in the dār of the church." The term included more than the built-up parts.[36]

Frequently, a house is defined as the large, comprehensive or complete dār, as when a Christian sells to a Jew 1 2/3 out of 24 shares in such a property, of which the latter already possessed 4 shares. We find this usage both in Egypt and in Tunisia. The upper floor of such a "large house" in Qayrawān, given by a husband to his wife in February 1040, cost 295 dinars.[37]

Then, too, our documents frequently describe a building as a *duwayra*, or small house. One such house, situated between the two synagogues of Old Cairo, was sold in May 1124 for the low price of 20 dinars. Another one, "located at the corner of the Street of the Furriers and the Little Market of the Tanners" in Aleppo, Syria, was estimated as having a value of only 30 dinars "because of the slump in the prices of real estate" around 1100, that is, when the Crusaders were not far away. A third one, though, a garden house on the Nile, was rented in July 1137 for 8 1/4 dinars per year, which presupposes that the property itself was worth about 170 dinars. This price tallies with that of another duwayra with a garden, which in 1233/4 was worth 160 dinars. In general, we should not imagine a duwayra as being exceedingly small. Even the one sold for 20 dinars comprised two upper floors, each containing a separate apartment, as well as a *mustaraqa*, or loggia. The garden house on the Nile had an inner court with a fountain, a living room on the ground floor, and several apartments on the upper story.[38] Along with duwayra (which may be rendered by French *maisonette* or German *Häuschen*) the sources speak also of *al-dār al-saghīra*, the small house, especially when an adjacent large house is mentioned in the context. But this expression seems to be a matter of style rather than of typology.[39]

In view of this usage of the term "a small house" we might expect a regular dār to have been quite a composite architectural creation. There is, therefore, nothing strange in a letter addressed to one dār within another.[40] Great houses could break up and form a whole lane or quarter, as we find in two documents from Damascus from the year 1094: "The dār which he built in the dār of Quzmān which is in the dār known as the Sulphur Lane," and "the stable in the city of Damascus, at the East Gate, in the quarter, ḥāra, known as the dār of Quzmān."[41] This comprehensive meaning associated with the word dār explains why it was applied to large compounds serving administrative and commercial purposes, as shown above,[42] and also why Arabic lacks a word for palace. The palace of a caliph, sultan, or vizier, whatever its dimensions, would simply be called dār.

The common Semitic word for house, *bayt*, which is used in this sense in Egypt today, has two different applications in the Geniza. As a technical term, it denotes a room in both Arabic and Hebrew, and there is no difference with regard to this usage between the capital of Egypt, a provincial town, Jerusalem, or Damascus.[43] In the figurative sense, in expressing notions such as "the lady of the house," or "household expenses," bayt may stand for house, or, rather, family. Thus one would speak of dār bayt, the house of the family of so-and-so.[44]

Finally, *manzil*, dwelling, so common as a term for house in the Arabic papyri, and *sukn*, residence, have in the Geniza the more specific meaning of living quarters, the room or rooms actually occupied by a person or a family, as opposed to dār, which denotes a structure or compound. Words meaning place are used similarly. Attention to these shades of meaning is required for a proper understanding of the texts related to housing.[45]

The vast difference in price of properties changing hands at one time and place (ranging from 20 to 800 dinars) confirms the assumption that houses differed not only in size and quality, but also in their type and function.[46]

The *bazaar house*, consisting of two stores topped by one or more upper floors, has been copiously referred to in the preceding subsection. Our sources also mention twin stores without upper apartments.[47] It seems, however, that the twin stores were constructed in such a way that they were able to bear at least one additional floor. Thus we find that one generation of administrators of a pious foundation purchased two stores, and the next one added an upper apartment.[48] It is noteworthy that a house in Amalfi, Italy, sold in 970 for 70 solidi, also contained two shops.[49] Two obviously were needed for providing the space required for a proper residence. E. W. Lane notes that in houses of this type the living quarters usually were reached by a separate entrance. The same is noted in a Geniza document. That the merchants or craftsmen operating those stores did not necessarily live in the same house, but rented their business premises, is indeed evident from many documents speaking about the rent of stores.[50]

From the bazaar house, which mostly served smaller enterprises, must be differentiated the *Nile-bank house*. The Persian traveler Nāṣir-i-Khosraw and other visitors pointed out, as a characteristic trait of Fustat, that goods were unloaded from the Nile boats at the very doorsteps of the shops. In a Geniza document written by a Muslim notary a foreign Jew purchases shares in a property from a Christian, which bordered on a Muslim house "with stores looking on the embarkation place known as that of The Falcons, adjacent to the *qaysāriyya* of ʿAbd al-ʿAzīz [also a Muslim], in which clothes are sold." Here, the stores are called *ḥawānīt*, originally designating a structure of larger measures (not *dakākīn*, retail shops, as usual); the word is in the plural, not dual; and the property forming the object of the transaction was a "comprehensive" one, situated in a prestigious section of the Rāya quarter, originally the center of the new Arab city. These Nile-bank houses should be compared with the great mercantile mansions, as found in many other medieval cities, where the transport of goods was mainly done by water.[51]

The multistoried houses which, "according to hearsay" (as Muqaddasi remarks), could accommodate up to two hundred people, are represented in the Geniza by only one example, a house consisting of one ground floor and nine upper stories, partly owned by a Jew.[52] The word for story, used by both the Geniza documents and the Arab and Persian travelers describing Fustat, is *ṭabaqa*, which, in the Geniza, at least, designates not only an upper floor but also an apartment forming a part of it.[53] Jews did not live in those fortress houses which harbored the large clans of which the Arab tribes settling in Fustat had been composed. When the tribal system dissolved (already noted by Ibn Ḥawqal who visited the town in the middle of the tenth century), those oversized houses became obsolete. But the testimony of the early Muslim travelers, strengthened by the casual reference in the Geniza document, which presupposes the existence of such huge buildings as something common, should not be easily discarded. Paula Sanders drew my attention to a pertinent story recorded by the Fatimid historian Ibn Zūlāq (d. 996). A boy who was destined to become an eminent scholar fell from the eighth story of a building, of which four stories "were in the open sky" (that is, were surrounded by buildings four or less stories high) and four near the ground. The boy plunged into an open well full of water. He was badly crippled, but because of the water miraculously escaped death. In view of these and other realistic details in the account, the story bears the stamp of truth. It happened prior to the conquest of Egypt by the Fatimids.[54]

The types of houses which mainly occupy us are the family house, that is, one built around a central court, and the apartment house, which usually consisted of three or more stories, as evidenced by actual documents and by the use of the terms "middle" and "upper floors." Here the question arises, whether the apartment house was originally planned for the purpose of renting out, like the *insulae* of Roman and Late Antiquity, or was converted into such a structure by changes made in a family home. The late Egyptian archaeologist Ahmed Fakhri, who read the first draft of this chapter and wrote valuable notes on it, insisted that medieval Egypt knew no insulae. The evidence of the Geniza is not unequivocal in this respect. Still, when we read, for instance, that two partners (not relatives) built a new house worth the extraordinarily high sum of 600 dinars, one wonders whether such a building was not conceived from the beginning as a commercial enterprise.[55]

The house in the provincial capital of al-Maḥalla described in the document translated at the end of this subsection consisted of three floors (to which a fourth could be added), but it certainly had no inner open court, since one of the coproprietors retained the right to hang his laundry on the roof. Clearly, this provincial town house from the year 1121 already showed characteristics later fully developed in the houses of Rosetta.[56]

Finally, it is worthy of note that a semirural Delta house like that in Minyat Ghamr, consisting of an unpaved court and three rooms, was occupied by Jews, intrinsically urban people.[57]

Front and entrance.—In the following description of a dār, as it appears in the Geniza papers, we adopt the procedure of the deeds of sale, leading the reader from the doorway through the interior up to the roof and concluding with some special features, as well as details requiring further research.

The walls encircling a house did not necessarily encompass the whole plot on which it stood. References to open spaces outside a house and settlements made with regard to them are found in our documents.[58] Walls were often shared with adjacent houses, which gave rise to lawsuits or agreements, when structural changes threatened to increase the load borne by a wall.[59] In a narrow street, a tilting house could damage the front of an opposite building, and when a house possessed a *saqīfa*, or portico, its breadth, protruding into the street (in one case 1 1/6 cubits) was fixed by ordinance.[60] The front of a house facing the street was called its face, *wajh*, and in one instance we read that "the large wajh" of a house was built in one year and the rest two years later. It tallies with the observation of the Baghdadian physician ʿAbd al-Laṭīf that Egyptian architects would finish each section of a house completely before starting another so that people could move in immediately and use it. The Geniza report precedes ʿAbd al-Laṭīf by about two hundred years.[61]

Descriptions of entrances in the Geniza documents are very explicit and profuse. Since the excavations have not furnished sufficient data for this architectural feature, and since the portal, this symbol of hospitality, was as important in Islam as it was in antiquity, some details about it may be welcome. The entrance to a larger house normally had an arched gateway with two door leaves (described as dark brown in one case), and when there were two gateways, one would be arched and the other rectangular. Smaller houses and those in provincial towns would have a rectangular gate.[62] Houses bordering on several streets or lanes would have two or three entrances, in one case there were four, one doorway leading into a caravansary erected by a Christian neighbor.[63] In a house situated in a business center, there could be three doors opening to the main street, two of which served the shops, and one the private quarters.[64] We read, albeit rarely, about a special gate leading to a stable, either directly or through an alley inside the dār.[65] For reasons not easily evident, a house would have two doorways on the same street, one opening as usual, into a corridor, and the other directly into the inner court, or qāʿa.[66]

Any larger compound seems to have had a *bāb al-sirr*, or secret door, "an entrance to a convenient secret passage, connecting the house directly with the street and thus allowing the master to escape from justice, vengeance, or assassination, or, conversely, according to the best authorities, to enable a paramour to enter the *ḥarīm* [or women's quarters]." I should point out that I have frequently found the "secret door" in Geniza documents, but it is never referred to as being used for specific purposes.[67] It seems that the term should be understood merely as secondary entrance, not necessarily as women's entrance. Doorways to the women's galleries of synagogues (and most probably also of churches which possessed the same structural detail) were designated by the same term but also by *bāb al-nisā*, women's entrance.[68] Both in private and in public buildings the secret door opened out to a street different from that approached through the main doorway.

An entrance door was equipped with a "ring," presumably of iron or brass, serving as a knocker. "I stood there all the time, knocking the rings, while the neighbors looked on, but he feigned not to hear."[69] In one instance, we read about a bell. "The burglars broke the street door. When they entered up to the bell door at the domicile of the judge and broke it, we heard the noise." This account seems to indicate that in buildings inhabited by several families, bells, perhaps of different sounds, were attached to the doors of the apartments.[70] The locks of the doors were made of wood.[71]

Above the doorway and jutting out from the wall, sometimes occupying the whole breadth of the house, was the bay window, a kind of alcove allowing the inhabitants to comfortably observe what was going on in the street. This arrangement, a bay window above the main entrance, is still beautifully visible in the Sinnārī mansion, famed as the seat of the scientists accompanying Napoleon on his Egyptian expedition. The window balcony is usually referred to in the Arabic Geniza texts by the Persian term *rawshan*, and in Hebrew documents by *gezozṭrā*, derived from the Greek *exostra*. I suspect that the strange Arabic word *ʿaskar*, used in this sense in several documents written by Muslim notaries, has the same Greek origin. The window balcony was an important part of the house, and the right of preserving its view was safeguarded in the contracts. Some houses had more than one.[72] In one case we read about a rawshan protruding menacingly from the wall of a building under construction, frightening the people walking beneath it. Even propping it up was no remedy for the nuisance caused. When the authorities (*al-rayyis*) demanded its "lowering," the proprietor claimed that it would endanger the entire building. Another case, illustrated by three court records, concerned bay windows of two confronting houses which touched each other. (I saw just such an arrangement in the *alfama*, or Old City, of Lisbon, Portugal). When both houses fell into disrepair and, after many years, one of them was rebuilt, witnesses testified that the alcove of the original house had protruded from the wall by about one cubit.[73] The window balcony was not necessarily part of a room. It could be constructed in the middle of a flight of stairs, as in a three-story house in the provincial town of al-Maḥalla belonging to two partners, wherefore it had to be stated whose property it was.[74] The wooden latticework that screened the inhabitants of a house from the view of persons outside, never absent from a traditional Muslim house, has not yet been found mentioned in a Geniza document, but perhaps there was no occasion to refer to it.

Besides a window balcony, a house could have regular windows looking on the street. That window was called *ṭāqa*, again a Persian term. A deed from Old Cairo mentions a bay window and regular windows together as being on the front side of a house, but a document from Damascus, describing the mansion of a prominent family, speaks of ṭāqas in a general way.[75] E. W. Lane reports that even at the beginning of the nineteenth century no windowpanes were used in Cairo. A communal account from the year 1181 notes that the replacement of a glass window cost 1 dirhem. It seems, however, that the reference is to a synagogue rather than to one of the houses belonging to the pious foundations of the community.[76]

The front of a house could feature an "opening for the wind," which was not meant to serve as a window, and, if submitted to structural changes, would give rise to lawsuits.[77] A prisoner escaped through such an air hole, which suggests that usually it was placed high above the ground.[78] It was found also in upper floors, as in a document from the year 1285, where the living room in an upper apartment had both windows and an "opening for the wind" in the wall opposite the entrance. The widely held view that the medieval Egyptian town house received its light exclusively from the inner court is not born out by our documents. Thus a settlement after marital strife ended in an agreement that the wife would live in an apartment looking on the inner court, and the husband's parents and his sisters would occupy a separate apartment on another floor looking on the street.[79]

Opening the entrance door, one normally faced a *dihlīz*, a corridor, or hallway. The descriptions also speak of hallways in the plural, or of a second hallway following the first. It shows that the entrance passage, wherever feasible, formed a turn, in order not to allow the visitor a look into the interior.[80] In better houses, the dihlīz would be paved with marble and contain one or two built-in benches, called *maṣṭaba*, a word familiar to visitors to the country of the Nile as the designation for tombs of the ancient Egyptian kings.[81] These benches served the gatekeepers. In one house, the kitchen and the rest room are described as being "in the dihlīz"—an exceptional feature; in another, a place for water jugs was attached to it, which is reasonable, since drinking water was brought from the Nile by water carriers, who would dispose of their load at the doorway.[82] According to the circumstances, the staircase leading to the upper floors was found in the entrance passage, a practical arrangement, since it facilitated the partition of a house into several tenancies. We find this arrangement both in a small house and in a large building containing six apartments upstairs, but, as shown in the following, it was by no means general.[83]

The qāʿa, or main floor.—From the hallway one entered (occasionally through a second, double door)[84] the qāʿa, literally, the ground floor. The term has acquired in the course of time, and even within the Geniza period itself, so many different facets of meanings that a short discussion of its use in the Geniza documents is imperative. There, qāʿa could denote three different things: (1) The ground floor in general, as opposed to the *ʿalw*, the upper part, which comprised all structures above the ground floor, whether they consisted of a number of floors and apartments, or of a single room. When used in this sense, qāʿa would be identical with *sufl*, the lower part. (2) A courtyard including the majlis, or living room, and all the other buildings surrounding it. Thus, in one and the same legal document, a tenant would be spoken of as having rented "the two qāʿas," namely, the two courtyards including the buildings belonging to them, and "the qāʿa," which then would mean the ground floor in its entirety.[85] (3) The courtyard proper as opposed to the built-up sections of the dār. This usage is intended when we read that a child fell from the arcade "into the qāʿa," or that a certain number of people were in the living room "and in the qāʿa even more."[86]

The court normally was open to the sky. It could be large enough to comprise a garden: "He planted six trees in a garden in his house *in* the qāʿa" (ca. 1100).[87] On the other hand, one deed dealing with the transfer of a new house, describes it as having "a small qāʿa *with a decorative ceiling*, a living room with two columns, as well as an upper floor" (1157).[88] With regard to a house in al-Maḥalla we learn about the qāʿa "of the middle floor," described as "suspended," meaning "to be reached by steps" (1121).[89] It foreshadows the final development of the term to designate the reception hall of the traditional Egyptian house.[90]

I mentioned above a house with two qāʿas. Such references are found in Geniza documents either without further specification[91] or with, as when the first court is described as the lower one, or the second and smaller one is called "the women's qāʿa" (the latter appears in two houses in Alexandria mentioned in documents dated 1132 and 1194, respectively). A Hebrew deed, dated 1010, describes a house bordering on that of a Christian glassmaker as having three small qāʿas.[92]

Except for the two examples from Alexandria, I have not found the term *ḥurmiyya*, women's qāʿa or apartment, elsewhere in documents from the "classical" Geniza period. This should not be ascribed to the fact that the separation of the sexes was not as strict in Judaism as in Islam. Houses frequently changed hands between members of the different religious communities, and in the numerous documents from Fustat written by Muslim notaries no such division is visible. Besides, in the first case referring to Alexandria (1132), a Jew rented the house from a Christian, and the place itself bordered on the property of a Christian clergyman and that of a Mr. Kohen. Thus one might wonder whether Alexandria, the Hellenistic and Byzantine capital of Egypt, might have preserved some Hellenic custom or, at least, nomenclature; I am referring to the *gynaikonitis*, the Greek women's apartment. The strict division of a home into male and female sections perhaps became common under the influence of the Mamluk and Turkish military aristocracies, who kept real harems and were imitated in this custom by the high bourgeoisie. The only document from Fustat which I remember as having a women's qāʿa concerns a house newly erected by a Jewish physician and given by him to his son in 1345.[93]

The living room, its interior, and accessory chambers.—Before trying to discuss the manifold uses to which a qāʿa could be put, I describe its parts in the order they appear in the more elaborate documents, which reflects the degree of attention paid to the various details by a visitor or a prospective buyer or tenant. Naturally, the size of the inner court, if it was particularly large or small, would be noted. Measurements, unfortunately, are never given.[94]

Invariably, the first item mentioned in the description of a qāʿa was its majlis, literally, sitting room, but better rendered in English as living room, for there the social life of the family, with or without its guests or customers, took place. The two columns of the portico leading into the majlis, traces of which excavators have found in most houses, are referred to, and, when they were of marble, it would be expressly stated.[95] With regard to a qāʿa with two living rooms, a detailed description of both is given. Both had several folding doors of carved wood. Doors of carved wood were so common that the documents stated expressly when they were plain.

Decorative wall hangings probably were the first item that drew the attention of a visitor to a majlis in a well-to-do home.[96]

In the qāʿa mentioned, both rooms had on the wall opposite the entrance, a "wind catcher," or ventilation shaft, the floor and walls of which were of marble. This contrivance, which was intended to carry fresh air from above the roof into the inner parts of a house (both ground floor and upper apartments), must have been rather wide at its lower end, because people slept there to enjoy the cool north wind of the night brought down by the wind catcher. For reasons of privacy, in both majlises the wind catchers had folding doors with carved decorations, and in one there was a gilded washbasin nearby, certainly for the ablutions required after a night's rest. The first majlis is described as longish, its walls covered with marble and its ceiling painted in oil "according to the Syrian fashion," a luxury already castigated by the Prophet Jeremiah (22:14). The decoration of the second reception room consisted only of marble of different colors covering the prestigious *ṣadr*, that is, the wall opposite the entrance.[97] In the majlis of other houses was a marble *fisqiyya*, or basin with a fountain, a feature otherwise noted in the Geniza documents with regard to the courtyard, but found regularly inside the living room in later Middle Eastern homes.[98]

Another cooling device, the *shādirwān*, an inclined flagstone, over which water flows into a basin, is specifically noted as belonging to a house.[99]

An idea of the size of a majlis in a large house is vividly shown in a letter reporting that on a festive occasion 400 persons were gathered together "in the majlis and in the qāʿa even more." Another indication of the huge crowd assembled there was the allegation that thirty particularly large candles and two hundred of ordinary size illuminated the place in addition to thirty oil lamps and twenty chandeliers.[100]

The majlis occupied the main part not only of the ground floor but also of the upper apartments. One or several large social rooms, connected with a number of small chambers, characterized the house as described in documents referring to the Fatimid and Ayyubid periods.[101]

In the more detailed documents, the majlis is described as adjoined by two or more accessory rooms. The vestibule, or *kumm*, literally, sleeve, mostly appears in the dual, and it is almost certainly the name of the two small, narrow rooms appearing in A. Gabriel's plans on both sides of what he calls "salle," which, together with the portico before it, actually represents the majlis. The same arrangement is still visible in the Dardīr mansion of Cairo, the most ancient private building in that city still partly preserved. In Yemen, *kummāh* is the name of a small inner chamber up to the present day. In the house with the two living rooms the larger one had two passages of carved wood, each of which had a door leading to an adjacent vestibule. Elsewhere it is expressly stated that the vestibules had no doors. The combination of a living room and two vestibules was so common that documents speak about a majlis with *its* two vestibules. This floor plan probably was inherited from Late Antiquity.[102]

Another type of accessory room, and referred to even more frequently than kumm, was the *khizāna*, which we render as closet, because, like its English equivalent, it has the double meaning of both a private room and a cupboard. The following examples lead to the conclusion that it could have been of considerable dimensions. A congregation intended to convert the khizāna of its synagogue into an open gallery with columns but refrained from doing so because the walls dividing it from the main hall were too thick. A plaintiff visited the chief Muslim judge in his khizāna in the sultan's palace, which could be translated here as office. A woman was handed her bill of divorce in the presence of three men while sitting in a room described by this term. A letter written by Nahray in 1050 refers to "the khizāna in which I used to sleep." When a report about an earthquake in Mosul states that the entire house was destroyed with the exception of the khizāna and part of another room, it is evident that the former represented a valuable portion of the building. Finally, a rent of 12 dirhems per month, by no means a negligible sum, was paid to a brother for a khizāna in a house that the latter had received from his father as a gift. One or several khizānas were found on the ground floor and also in the upper apartments.[103]

The two types of accessory rooms, rendered here by vestibule and closet, respectively, must have been of clearly distinctive structure, since the documents often mention them side by side, and not only documents on the transfer of houses. Thus, an old widow, complaining that her rent for an upper apartment in a building belonging to the community was raised from 2 to 3-1/2 dirhems, points out that her place was poor, having neither a kumm nor a khizāna (ca. 1230).[104]

I am not sure that I did not see the term "khizāna" applied also to a shelf in the recess of a wall in documents from Fatimid and early Ayyubid times. The specific word designating that structure and still in use, *khūristān* (derived from the Persian), does appear in the description of a "little house" from the year 1124, repeatedly mentioned here, and is found in other documents from the twelfth century.[105] A larger room could have such a shelf in each of its four walls. Some khūristāns had doors of carved wood; others had no doors at all.[106]

The most characteristic part of the traditional Egyptian house, the *īwān*, or *līwān*, a vaulted room, often several stories high and open on one side to a central covered floor, is absent from the Geniza documents preceding the advent of the Mamluk period (1250). The īwān, as Ahmed Fikri emphasized, was transplanted from Mesopotamia to Egypt during the Ayyubid period, and it takes time, of course, until a new house, through sale, gift, or rent, makes its appearance in a document.[107] Moreover, the introduction of those proud, princely vaults into Egypt marked the rise of a military aristocracy, which was reared by the Ayyubids and took over the country under the Mamluks. The bourgeoisie emulated the condottieres. But the adoption of those newfangled, costly structures was a slow process.

These changes are reflected in our documents. A Karaite deed of sale from the year 1260 first minutely describes a large house with several upper apartments and then adds: "The structures [on the ground floor] have been removed with the exception of the gate of the house, the majlis, and the washroom; likewise the upper rooms on the front of the house have been replaced by a newly erected īwān, which now faces the aforementioned majlis on the ground floor (qāʿa), and a special entrance has been constructed leading to three upper apartments."[108]

We see here how things developed. Instead of two living rooms facing each other, an īwān was built opposite the existing majlis, but the layout remained the same as in the mansion of Fustat described before, where a large majlis was situated opposite a smaller one.[109] The same arrangement, an īwān facing a majlis, was found in the newly erected house that in September 1345 a Jewish physician gave to his son. Here we also find the *dūrqāʿa*, that part of the inner floor where one slips off one's shoes, which is one step lower than the rooms, an architectural detail that remained ubiquitous well into the nineteenth century.[110] In order that the new house be really "complete" (as it is called in the document), the Jewish doctor provided "a women's qāʿa" for his son's house, the only such occurrence known to me from Fustat.[111]

One of the more common features of the qāʿa, and in larger houses, also of the upper apartments, was the *ṣuffa*, from which is derived the English word sofa. Our documents enable us to follow the interesting history of this structure. It was originally a roofed bench or bower in front of a house or a mosque. The Egyptian architect took it into the house, first to the court and later into the rooms, and slowly changed its function. Its final development in the traditional Egyptian house is described by E. W. Lane: "A shelf of marble or of common stone, about four feet high, supported by two or more arches, or by a single arch, under which are placed utensils in ordinary use, such as perfuming vessels and the basin and ewer which are used for washing before and after meals; waterbottles, etc. are placed upon [that is, on the roof of] the ṣuffah." In the High Middle Ages this development was not yet completed. Two and even four ṣuffas were in one place, and when we read about one on an upper floor which "looked on the lane," or another, whose "ceiling was painted with oil," it seems that a ṣuffa still served also as a bench.[112]

Another type of bench was the *sidillā* (the Latin *sedilia*, originally the plural of *sedile*, a seat; in English, *sedilia* is a specific set of seats in a church reserved for clergymen when not officiating). With regard to the traditional Egyptian house it has been described as "a platform of stone, about half a foot high . . . or a recess, of which the floor is similarly elevated and nearly equal in width and depth, with a mattress and cushions laid against one or two or each of its sides." In a document written about 1120, a sidillā faced the visitor when entering the uppermost floor. In another house a sidillā with marble columns stood in front of the living room of the ground floor. A third document describes its location thus: "The water closet is adjacent to the sidillā which is situated opposite to the entrance to this qāʿa. This sidillā is also adjoining a door through which one obtains access from the qāʿa to its kitchen." A "small sidillā" was adjacent to the kitchen in a fourth house. This placement induces us to assume that, unlike more modern use, repose during the day rather than social intercourse or nightly rest was the purpose of this architectural feature.[113]

The water basin and fountain of the qāʿa or the majlis were there to delight the eye and to refresh the air. The qāʿa regularly had also a well providing water for cleaning purposes. In all descriptions of houses the well is prominently mentioned. (Drinking water was brought from the Nile by carriers.) Upstairs tenants had to obtain right of access to the qāʿa for the purpose of drawing water.[114]

In Alexandria even a modest house had both a well and a cistern, and both, their repairs, or the brackishness or disappearance of their water are mentioned in letters. Water was partly provided by the Nile during the month of its overflow by means of the canal that connected the city with the river. When the Nile was low, the water supply of Alexandria was in trouble.[115]

The placement of the well determined also that of the kitchen and the rest room usually situated in the qāʿa or in the entrance hall. It has already been remarked that the notion that even the houses of the rich had no kitchen is entirely unfounded. In any larger house, both were also found on upper floors, and we read about three upper apartments or a loggia, each of which had its separate washroom, commonplace for us, but very remarkable for those days. The five terms used in English—washroom, water closet, bathroom, restroom, and convenience—are all represented in the Arabic of the Geniza, in addition to the pre-Islamic Hebrew "room with a seat," although probably no fixed seat was provided. In the house of a well-to-do family the floor of the washroom was entirely paved with marble and was topped by a copula with stucco work. The student of Arabic and Hebrew literatures is reminded of the superb satire of the Persian Arabic poet Hamadhānī, successfully imitated by the Spanish Hebrew poet al-Ḥarīzī, in which a rich merchant is ridiculed for bragging about his wonderful home, wife, and other possessions, climaxing his boasts by showing his guests his ultramodern bathroom with its glazed tiles.[116]

The uses of the qāʿa.—Our survey of the various components of a qāʿa and of their purposes leads to the conclusion that the qāʿa as a whole served as the common link between the inhabitants of the rooms upstairs and between them and the outer world. Often, however, we also find parties who had their living quarters in the qāʿa, for example, in a house rented by a Muslim from a Jew. It was almost the rule in buildings belonging to pious foundations, about which we have much information. In private homes, too, as the family expanded, sections of the qāʿa were converted into separate apartments. Whether the term *majlis ḥayrī*, or enclosed living room, which evokes the desert castles of the Umayyads described as *ḥayr*, has anything to do with such arrangements is not evident from the documents.[117]

Many qāʿas served as premises for commercial and industrial undertakings, or as schoolrooms, and one wonders whether at least some of the houses concerned were not planned in advance to fulfill those functions. Foreign merchants would rent a qāʿa to a store their goods, which would involve conducting a great deal of business there. The item "for the qāʿa" in accounts simply stands for storage or rent.[118] The "returning of the qāʿas" designates the end of the business season.[119] Local people, too, would use or rent a qāʿa as a store. "He bought from him the complete Bible codex together with other things which he bought from him in the qāʿa which he and his son kept for selling and buying pharmaceuticals."[120] In particular, qāʿas contained workshops, so much so that *qāʿat ḥarīr* would designate not only the place where silk was manufactured, but also the company that was engaged in this industry. *Al-qāʿatayn* in the same context refers to two companies working in the same field.[121] Because of the frequent use of qāʿas for industrial purposes, contracts of lease would contain a condition like this one: "No workshop requiring a fireplace in the qāʿa, such as used in the production of rosewater, litharge, or arsenic, is permitted."[122] Ground floors serving as schoolrooms were commonplace.[123] We remember that qāʿas sometimes were very large. One of the most famed buildings of Cairo, the hospital of the Mamluk sultan Qalāwūn, was converted from a qāʿa without changing its structure, as the Muslim historian reporting the fact expressly states. "He left the qāʿa as it was and made it into a hospital."[124]

The upper floors.—Turning to the ʿalw, the structures above the ground floor, we meet with an ambiguity in nomenclature similar to the one incurred with respect to the qāʿa. An upper floor or story is called ṭabaqa, and where we read about a middle or uppermost ṭabaqas this meaning is assured; otherwise, however, the word may denote an upstairs apartment. Thus, the house with nine ṭabaqas mentioned before was hardly one with nine upper stories, but one with nine apartments on an unspecified number of floors.[125] For a house with six "habitations," *masākin*, in the part above the ground floor we have two fragmentary documents, one, written around 1095, in which the proprietor confirms having sold one-twelfth of it (the original document had been lost), and another where his stepson gives a quarter of the total to his paternal sister in June 1131. The place is succinctly described as having loggias, columns, a wooden staircase, and a wooden parapet (around the roof), as well as two gates, one of which opened on the street opposite the Ḥujja mosque.[126]

A fuller description of a house with six upper habitations is translated at the end of this subsection. Two apartments on the second floor and one on the third had been part of the original building. Three additional apartments, one of them consisting of two lighter structures, were erected on the different roofs.[127] An uppermost floor of a house in the Fortress of the Candles, the object of a contract of lease written by the clerk Ḥalfōn b. Manasse (1100–1138), comprised at least three different levels. It consisted of a large living room with a stalactite (or "beehive") vault, "connected with the columns"; another large room over which a loggia was built; a room, bayt, to be reached by the main staircase; and another "small story", *ṭubayqa*, "situated in the passage," *majāz*, "of this floor," containing the "service room," *mustakhdam*, a pantry, or whatever that may mean, the kitchen, and the washroom. There was also a sidillā bench and a ṣuffa facing each other. Thus we see that even in the most ancient part of Fustat an uppermost story could have been of a rather composite structure.[128]

The feature that one floor consisted of different levels remained alive in the traditional Egyptian house. "The apartments are generally of different heights, so that a person has to ascend or descend one, two, or more steps to pass from one chamber to another adjoining it."[129] The same was true of the Jewish house of Sanʿa, Yemen, which was of the Mediterranean type and entirely different from the Arab fortress house indigenous to that country. Carl Rathjens, that keen observer of material civilization, emphasizes that this way of structuring upper floors was intentional, planned in advance, and not the result of piecemeal building during different periods.[130] The height of a room was conditioned by its function. A spacious majlis had to be lofty, the small adjacent rooms would have looked odd if they had been of the same height. As mentioned the physician ʿAbd al-Laṭif, the visitor from Baghdad, observed that the Egyptian architect planned the entire building in advance, and that he erected its different parts in accordance with the needs and wishes of the proprietor.[131]

This arrangement of the upper floors, which interrelated a room with the ones beneath and above it, had legal effects. A house was divided not only horizontally but also vertically, as attested by documents from the tenth through the thirteenth centuries for both Fustat and other cities. The marital documents from Damascus from the year 933 relate that a groom possessed rooms on the ground floor and an upper floor, forming one-sixth of the value of the total building; that a bride received from her parents, in addition to a trousseau worth 260 dinars, one room in each of the ground and middle floors estimated as representing one-eighth of the value of the house; the other proprietors, bordering on her share, are listed.[132] A bride in very modest circumstances, whose outfit was worth only 30 dinars, brought in "the majlis at the entrance of the house with its cabinet and upper floor and the right to build on top of it whatever she liked"; the relevant document is from the second part of the eleventh century.[133] Of particular interest is a deed of sale written in 1088 by a Muslim notary, where parts of a second floor exempted from the sale are described as being "above the entrance hall, the straw storeroom, and the vault west of the southern room of the qāʿa."[134] In a question addressed to Maimonides from Alexandria in, or shortly after, 1194, two upper stories are defined as "being above the secret passage and the kitchen that is in it."[135] Finally, a draft of a document in which one notable leases to another one-half of a garden house in spring 1229, thirty-two lines are devoted to legal parlance, whereas the object itself is described simply as "the qāʿa with its upper apartments, forming a unit which can be locked." The structural relationship with the other half of the house is not defined.[136] All in all, it appears from our documents that a residential building, whether serving one family or different parties, normally had up to three stories, on the top of which one or more apartments, some made of lighter materials, could be added.[137]

Two types of light superstructures occur in our documents again and again. The first is the *ṭārma*, which should by no means be identified with the Iraqian structure bearing this name, a kind of portico or peristyle, often referred to in studies on Islamic architecture.[138] In Egypt, the ṭārma was "a room made of timber," according to a competent Muslim historian, which tallies with Maimonides' note that it was the name of the cabin in (or perhaps rather upon) a boat.[139] In the Geniza documents it is a wooden structure on top of a ṭabaqa and serves as a complete dwelling place. The following quotations are illustrative. A settlement between relatives made in 1133 stipulates: "Abu 'l-Faḍl will live in the empty ṭārma of the house, while the ṭabaqa beneath it will be occupied by his niece." In a letter written in January 1148, a son in Old Cairo complains to his father traveling on the route to India: "Life in the ṭārma is unpleasant because of the toil of ascending staircases and the noise of the mortars"—a reference to the women preparing meals on the roofs extending from their ṭabaqas. Thirteenth-century deposition in court states that the uppermost ṭabaqa of a certain house and the ṭārma above it were property of the community. Rents for a ṭārma are repeatedly noted in communal accounts.[140]

Unlike the ṭārma, which always appears in the singular, normally several structures (sometimes up to five, or even seven) called *khuṣṣ*, plural *akhṣāṣ*, are found in one house. Khuṣṣ was originally a hut made of reeds or similar material, and one Geniza document speaks indeed of "mats of khuṣṣ on the roofs of the rooms," referring to dwelling places. The accounts of pious foundations, however, often list revenue from rents of rooms described as khuṣṣ and mention akhṣāṣ donated to the community. Private proprietors, too, would let rooms of this description. In view of all this, we must assume that these structures were of a somewhat more stable character than mere shanties. The great al-Afḍal, the actual ruler of Egypt during the years 1094–1121, built his palace on a site formerly occupied by akhṣāṣ.[141]

The loggia and similar structures.—An architectural element rarely absent from any detailed description of a house, but not yet found by me in any source outside the Geniza documents, was the mustaraqa, a kind of loggia or belvedere, mostly overlooking the inner court. It seems to have had a function similar to that of the *maqʿad* (meaning place where one sits) in the traditional Egyptian house. The maqʿad has been described as a "room generally elevated about eight or ten feet above the ground floor, having an open front, with two or more arches and a low railing." In the Middle Ages such a structure was called mustaraqa, the filched one, meaning taken away from the space of one of the upper stories. It was mostly open to the north, and, when used as a place of habitation, was screened off by a wooden lattice.[142] This strange architectural term has its counterpart in South Arabian usage.[143] A few quotations clarify the mustaraqa's location. "Opposite the entrance to the qāʿa there is a door leading to its kitchen and to its women's qāʿa, as well as to a staircase made of stone, on which one ascends to the roof of the women's qāʿa and to the mustaraqa which belongs to it."[144] "The house also comprises a kitchen and two mustaraqas, which overlook the court of its qāʿa."[145] "The house has two adjacent mustaraqas, one giving a view on the entrance door and the other on the qāʿa."[146] The variety of locations explains perhaps why we read in one deed of an "inside mustaraqa."[147] One description speaks of mustaraqas in the plural (not the dual), and another situates one between two upper stories.[148] In one legal deed a mustaraqa is rented out together with the qāʿa; in another it is combined with an upper floor; a third states that it was added to the second floor; and we also find one above a third floor. In houses belonging to pious foundations the rental of a mustaraqa alone, no doubt partly screened off by some lighter construction, was commonplace (as from the eleventh century).[149]

The *riwāq* (a Persian word), or arcade, must have been an important structure in Syrian houses, since it is mentioned in documents from both Damascus and Tyre as having remained common property after other parts of the homes concerned had been divided between partners.[150] In Egypt it appears once as facing the street, in a letter as above a courtyard, and is even mentioned as a structure within a majlis. It strengthens Creswell's surmise that the Azhar mosque possessed lateral riwāqs from the outset.[151]

The *mashraqa* seems to have been a veranda facing east on an upper floor, where one enjoyed warmth in winter and where the wheat was kept to protect it from dampness, and perhaps also from thieves. In one document the mashraqa looked onto the street and possessed a separate washroom. A letter referring to it reports that burglars succeeded in breaking in and taking away two waybas, which is over fifty pounds. The mashraqa is noted also as part of a house in Damascus.[152] Another space on an upper floor specifically mentioned as an appurtenance was the *mafrash*, a place to hang laundry, or to spread fruits for drying, a right referred to also in an agreement between two partners.[153]

Staircases and roofs.—The communication between the floors was made by staircases constructed mostly of stone, partly also of wood, both mentioned together in a document, occasionally also of baked bricks. The excavator of Fustat, A. Gabriel, concluded from the scant remnants that the staircases were never treated in a monumental way. Frequently reference is made to "staircases on arches of stone," and, in one letter, the landing of a staircase was large enough to accommodate four men and one woman. In apartment houses, small or large, the staircase was in the first corridor, the one near the main doorway; in a family mansion it was in the innermost part of the house, to be reached through a door opposite the entrance to the qāʿa. We hear also about one or two staircases connecting two houses. Repairs of one or more steps were a regular item in the expenditure accounts for buildings belonging to the community. A father writing home expresses concern that the children may incur harm while going up the staircases. He mentions it in his letter and reiterates his fear in a postscript.[154]

When the rooms and apartments of a house were of different height, our documents speak of roofs in the plural.[155]

In private homes roofs were flat, and, when a neighbor was able to prove that they provided a view into his own premises, had to be walled in. But with regard to a smaller town we have read about a person walking on the roofs of several houses. A wooden railing around the opening of the staircase is mentioned. Part of a roof often formed an important appurtenance to an upper floor. Gable roofs were normally constructed only above larger and public buildings such as synagogues.[156]

Storage rooms.—Before bank safes were invented, a man's valuables were mostly kept in his house. Gold, silver, and precious stones could be buried in the earth or concealed in walls or ceilings, but other objects had to be kept in regular repositories. The *maṭmūra*, literally, "the buried, underground room," seems not to have had a fixed location. When, as in an account of October 1230, a maṭmūra harbors 117 jugs of wine, clearly a cellar is referred to. But when, in a court record from September 1093, a man accuses his brother of having removed from the maṭmūra of the family Arabic books on medicine, reams of paper, fifty pounds of mercury, and gold coins, one would rather assume that this maṭmūra was built in a hidden corner of the maze of rooms on a ground floor, or even on an upper story, or between stories (as in Yemenite houses). Such a "treasure room" is a regular feature in the stereotyped descriptions of houses found in deeds of transfer.[157]

A compartment named *kandūj* makes its appearance in the documents from the first half of the twelfth century. It is described as fixed on top of a closet, a wall cupboard, a kitchen, or a staircase, or accessible from two adjacent rooms. In a deed of gift of half a house, written around 1140, the giver stipulated that the kandūj would be open on the recipient's side, as long as he remained in possession of his half, but if he alienated it, the compartment would revert to the exclusive use of the original proprietor. A Karaite document from the year 1260 notes as many as seven such structures in one single, albeit spacious, building.[158]

The regular storeroom, *makhzan*, must have been open to the air, since in houses belonging to charitable foundations, and even in private homes, it frequently served also as a human habitation. In a deed from Tyre the makhzan was beneath the majlis, or living room; in Damietta, the Egyptian seaport, a makhzan was located in a dihlīz, or entrance hall. (A jug containing a thousand gold pieces was discovered there and, of course, confiscated by the government.) In a house in the al-Mamṣūṣa quarter of Fustat, converted into workshops, each side of the dihlīz had a makhzan whose ceiling was made of palm trunks and acacia wood. A makhzan could also form a separate building. The word seems to be most common in connection with funduqs, or caravansaries, where the merchants stayed upstairs, and their goods were stored in the rooms beneath their living quarters.[159]

Stables and other isolated structures.—Stables to shelter riding animals and their fodder were less common than one might expect. One took a taxi instead of keeping a car, I mean, mules and donkeys for hire were available at reasonable prices. Moreover, the distances within the living space of the Geniza people were moderate. Well-to-do families possessed buildings serving solely as stables or having upper floors used as living quarters (probably for attendants). Such arrangements spared the families concerned the nuisance of flies and other inconveniences connected with the proximity of animals.[160]

An isolated structure frequently occurring in the Geniza documents and Arabic papyri was the *qaṣr*, which literally means castle (both derived from Latin *castrum*, fort), but which was anything but a building of that description. In accounts of charitable foundations from the years 1037–1043 it denotes rooms of poor quality for which monthly rents of 3–4 dirhems were paid.[161] Three twelfth-century documents speak of "the qaṣr on the ground floor," in one case described as "known as the stable."[162] In a fragment of a deed of gifts one border of a house was formed by "the site with the two qaṣrs." E. W. Lane, in his translation of the *Arabian Nights*, supplies the following definition: "Pavilion, piece of building, or set of apartments, isolated, or only connected with another piece of building on one side; or an upper room, generally isolated or nearly so." Thus the salient feature of a qaṣr seems to have been its total or partial isolation, which required walls stronger than those common to regular rooms. Hence the name castle.[163]

Belvederes and gardens.—A *manẓar*, literally, "a place from which one looks," or belvedere, on the top floor served as an audience hall of the ruler of Aden, South Arabia, in 1198. A *manẓara*, or rather *munayẓara*, "little belvedere," in Mosul, Iraq, described as being adjacent to a majlis, or living room, was destroyed by an earthquake in 1237. Manẓaras are frequently mentioned as used by Fatimid caliphs. A *ghurfa*, or loggia on an upper floor, was added to a house with a garden in Alexandria, which a Jew rented from a Christian in November 1132; another served as a guest room and storeroom in the small town of Qalyūb a hundred years later. One wonders whether these terms refer to a belvedere overlooking a garden, so beautifully illustrated in a Ḥarīrī manuscript published by Oleg Grabar. The ghurfa or lodging for travelers in a synagogue was also on an upper floor.[164]

A building known as the garden house, a garden house on the Nile, and a garden with a qāʿa have already been mentioned.[165] In a deed of sale from December 1088 the garden is mentioned expressly as a part of the property, and a real estate broker notes in his diary of 1233/4 that he bought one-fourth of "the little house and the garden" for 40 dinars.[166] A letter addressed to Maimonides vividly describes the nuisance caused by a date palm in the courtyard of a Jewish house, which leaned over the street and endangered a nearby mosque and Muslim houses during strong winds. Moreover, children in the street, pelting the tree in order to get its sweet dates, filled the courtyard with stones and other missiles. The proprietor had refrained from removing the nuisance because of the biblical prohibition of cutting down a fruit tree (Deuteronomy 20:19). A compound known as "the house with the palm tree" was sold in 1285. In the provincial towns of Minyat Ghamr and Bilbays one and two *sidr*, or ziziphus trees, respectively, decorated the court of a house. The orchards providing income for pious foundations, as far as we are able to ascertain, were all situated outside the precincts of the city.[167]

The *miẓalla*, a pavilion, or wooden structure in a courtyard, or outside a house, is often mentioned in the Geniza documents. Thus far, however, it has been found only in connection with the Jewish Feast of Tabernacles and only as situated in the court of a synagogue, not in that of a private home. Such miẓallas, as in later times, might have ornated the shores of the Khalīj, the Nile canal which traversed the city.[168]

Conclusions.—The material presented leaves the reader with the impression that not one house was like another. Probably true, but the basic principles in the structure of a habitation were followed with surprising uniformity. The general characteristics set forth at the opening of this subsection are vindicated. The polarity of individualism and conformity to be observed in so many aspects of the medieval civilization of the Near East was conspicuous also in its domestic architecture.[169]

Each section of the house had one dominant large room adjoined by two or more smaller adjuncts, thus providing both conviviality and privacy. Benches or divans, to be covered with upholstery, built in or placed along the walls, as well as sideboards in the recesses of the walls, together with the use of light furniture made the rooms both spacious and easily convertible. A central court, either open to the sky, or, especially in later times, covered, or both, an open court, and a central reception hall linked the various parts of the house and served many other purposes. Finally, wherever means were available, buildings were planned so that they could be expanded, or that a smaller house could be erected adjacent to a larger one, or that several structures would form one extended compound. It was done in order to keep a growing extended family together; probably also with the intent that the rent from the apartments not needed for the family should form a source of income for its members, especially its women.

With few exceptions, the dwellings described thus far were owned or occupied by people of the middle class or by the poorer sections of the population. Yet the types and numbers of rooms and their many appendages, such as loggias, kitchens, washrooms, and smaller accessories, betray a highly developed type of urban habitation.

The rich heritage embodied in the domestic architecture revealed by the Cairo Geniza is manifested also by the large number of architectural terms of foreign origin: Aramaic, Greek, Latin, and especially Persian, which are exceedingly numerous. It does not necessarily mean that the architectural features designated by Persian terms were all imported from the East. In early Islamic times the cities of Egypt and North Africa, depleted of their Greek inhabitants, formed a colonial area for the southwest Asian bourgeoisie, an influx that became even mightier in the wake of migrations during the third and fourth centuries of Islam.[170] It may well be that the immigrants used Persian terms to denote structures that had been in existence in Egypt long before their arrival, perhaps changing some of the details in accordance with what they had been accustomed to in their country of origin. Thus the bay window, the closed balcony projecting over the street, generally referred to by the Persian word rawshan, is designated also by a Greek term in both its Arabic and Hebrew forms. Projecting balconies had been the object of taxation (and prohibition) in classical Athens.[171] The wind catcher, the ventilation shaft designated by a Persian word, seems to have been in use in Egypt in Pharaonic times.[172] It must be remembered, too, that several of those foreign terms had become parts of Arabic speech long before the Geniza period.

Closed balconies were as conspicuous in the Coptic quarter of Old Cairo (ancient Fustat), or a Jewish street in Baghdad, as in the Muslim thoroughfares of Cairo.[173] Their regular occurrence in Geniza descriptions of houses, where they are mentioned with terms derived from both Greek and Persian, points to a joint Mediterranean–Near Eastern tradition, well preceding Islam. The general layout of the home in Geniza times with its inner court and dominant large hall adjoined by two smaller rooms has a long prehistory in Greek and Hellenistic domestic architecture. There, matters are rather diversified and complicated.[174] As represented in the Geniza, however, the Mediterranean house of the High Middle Ages seems to have attained a high degree of integration and standardization.[175]

Three houses as described in documents: A mansion in Fustat.—This example of the full description of a house is taken from a document dealing with a property consisting of three houses and two ruins. The house is described as large and situated in a blind alley between the Old Spinnery and the Mahra quarter, both mentioned here before.[176] A description of the entire compound is included in my edition of the document.[177]

The large house has an arched doorway closed by two dark-brown door leaves. Through it one enters a corridor paved with marble in which there are two benches. From the aforementioned corridor one enters a second corridor, through which one comes to a large qāʿa, or ground floor, comprising two living rooms, facing one another with folding doors fastened on them, the cross boards and outsides of which are carved.

One of the two living rooms is longish, its walls are of marble and it has two passages of carved wood, each of which has a door leading to an adjacent cabinet. The reception hall has on its "front" (i.e., the wall opposite the entrance) a "wind catcher," or ventilation shaft, whose floor and walls are of marble. In front of the ventilation shaft there is a gilded washbasin. The reception hall is encircled by a gilded cornice. On the aforementioned ventilation shaft there are folding doors, the cross boards and outsides of which are carved. The ceiling of the room is painted in oil according to the Syrian fashion.

The second living room, which faces the first one described before, has folding doors on its entrance, and on its front a ventilation shaft with folding doors, all of whose cross boards and outsides are carved. The "front" is of marble in different colors.

The ground floor has two ṣuffas, or covered benches, facing each other, with marble walls and ceilings painted in oil.

In the open court of the qāʿa, there is a fountain of marble, and the entire court of this qāʿa, both its floor and its walls, are covered with marble. There are also various closets with doors, whose cross boards and outsides are of carved wood.

The qāʿa includes a kitchen, as well as two loggias, which look on the open court of the ground floor, and each of which one reaches by a staircase of stone.

The floor of the washroom belonging to the qāʿa is entirely paved with marble and is topped by a copula of carved gypsum. The qāʿa has a secret door which belongs to it and which opens on the place known as al-Ḥudayjī Street. The court of this qāʿa is topped by a gallery of carved gypsum.

A rectangular door belongs to the upper floor of this qāʿa; through it one enters a small corridor with a staircase of stone which enables one to reach an upper floor comprising three apartments adjoining one another. Each of these apartments has a ceiling of *naqī* wood and doors fastened on the closets belonging to it as well as a separate washroom, and other appurtenances and rights.

Above all this there is a roof with a parapet and a wooden railing around the staircase which leads to the upper floor. The house possesses also canalization pipes which belong exclusively to it and other appurtenances and rights.

The house is delimited by four boundaries. First, to the south, the lane from which it is entered and on which its doorway opens. Second, to the north, the house known as that of Abu 'l-Thanā, son of Barakāt, son of ʿAmmār, the Jew, the sugar merchant, which is entered from al-Ḥudayjī Lane. Third, to the east, the ruin which belongs to the house. The ruin consists of an open space and three storerooms. Fourth, to the west, the house known as that of Ibn al-Kardūsh, the Christian, and their [thus!] partners.

The upper floors of a Cairene house.—The house was situated in the Zuwayla quarter of Cairo, facing the main thoroughfare, and was known as the house with the palm tree. It was sold by two brothers and three sisters, all Jewish, to a Mamluk emir. The siblings sold the house most probably because they had inherited it from their father or mother at a time when they themselves already had their own domiciles. Thus, although the sale took place in November 1285, the building probably was erected in Ayyubid times. The price of 9,000 *nuqra* dirhems, corresponding at that time to about 450 gold pieces, proves that the property was a very substantial building.

Since the text of the document describing the transaction has not yet been edited, I provide the Arabic terms in cases of doubt.[178]

[Line 17] In the aforementioned first corridor (of the ground floor) there is a staircase made of stone by way of which one reaches three upper apartments.

[18] One of these has a main door (*bāb zimām*), serving two apartments (ṭabaqa) facing each other. The larger one has a main door at the entrance to its living room (*majlis*), which has a ceiling of *naqī* wood. Its doors and those of its adjoining cabinet are plain [that is, are not made of carved wood], its floor is covered with [19] marble. In the majlis are three wall cupboards with carved doors. In the wall opposite the entrance are windows (*ṭāqāt*) and an opening for the wind. The central part of the inner court (*dūrqāʿa*) of the apartment is paved with tuff gravel. There is also a covered bench (ṣuffa) which looks on the lane. The apartment has closets, a restroom, a kitchen, and other appurtenances [20] and rights.

On the aforementioned staircase one goes up to the third apartment, whose main door is composed of double doors, leading to a corridor with windows for looking out (*ṭāqāt lil-muṭṭaliʿ*), a restroom, a majlis without doors, [21] a *dūrqāʿa*, closets, and a loggia with rights, which one reaches by way of an upper floor (*ṭābiq*).

Further on, one ascends on the same staircase to the roofs (*suṭūḥ*) elevated above all this, which comprise several terraces (*asṭiḥa*), [22] on one of which is a newly built apartment with a majlis having appurtenances and rights. There are also two light structures (*ṭārma*) [seemingly counted as one apartment], and on one of the terraces is a third apartment.

A three-story house in a provincial town.—The document translated below was written in al-Maḥalla, an important town in the Nile Delta, in Feb./March 1121. It represents an agreement between two partners in a house, a Jew "from the Land of the Romans," that is, from Western Europe or Byzantium, and a convert to Judaism, no doubt a former Christian, who was forced to leave his native country because of his change of religion. The two probably had come to Egypt together and ran a workshop or store on the ground floor, which therefore remained common, undivided property.[179]

"This testimony was given before us, we, the witnesses signing beneath this document. Thus it was: There appeared before us Mr. Yeshūʿā [Salvation], son of Mr. Yeshūʿā from the land of the Romans, and Mr. Abraham, the proselyte, son of Mr. Moses, and declared: "We have reached the following agreement, out of our free will, with regard to the house belonging to us in the Qālū.[180]

Its *qāʿa*, or ground floor, which has two doors, one in the East and one in the West, two entrance halls, a large, covered bench (*ṣuffa*), and a closet, will belong to us in common, to each an equal share.

The middle story, which is above it [consisting of], a 'suspended' *qāʿa* [i.e., one to be reached by a staircase] with two columns, four benches facing each other, six double doors, and a main door leading to the large landing, from which one enters a small room, a kitchen, a restroom, and a cabinet(?)[181] belongs, with all its rights, to the aforementioned Mr. Abraham, the proselyte.

Above this, there is a third story, with two belvederes (*ghurfatayn*) having a Ma'mūnī[182] and with a bay window on the staircase, possessed by Mr. Yeshūʿā, to the exclusion of the above-mentioned Abraham.

Thus, of these two, Abraham and Yeshūʿā, Abraham possesses the apartments which are above the ground floor, to the exclusion of his partner Yeshūʿā, and Yeshūʿā possesses the third upper story to the exclusion of Abraham.

When Abraham has washing day and hangs his laundry above Yeshūʿā's upper story, the latter will not prohibit it, nor the storing of six irdabb of wheat together with what belongs to them[183] with Yeshūʿā, as far as the upper story is able to bear them.

The two have consented and reached a total agreement, etc.[184]

When any part of the apartments of the qāʿa, possessed by Abraham, the proselyte, crumbles down, he alone will be held to make the necessary repairs. Likewise, when any part of the third upper story, belonging to Yeshūʿā, crumbles down into that qāʿa, Yeshūʿā will be held to repair it, to the exclusion of Abraham.

Should Yeshūʿā wish to build a fourth story above his third, and there will be any damage in the ground floor qāʿa (*al-sufl al-qāʿa*), Yeshūʿā will be held to repair it, to the exclusion of Abraham; for he will have *made a change* by his adding to the building, and *whosoever makes a change is at a disadvantage*."[185]

(There follow the usual legal phrases concluding a document, and the date: "*the month of Adar II of the year 1432 according to the era used by us here in the town of al-Maḥalla the Great, which is situated on the Nile.*")

The document is signed by three men with a good, scholarly handwriting.

3. Socioeconomic Aspects of Housing

Ownership.—The preceding study of domestic architecture necessarily touched upon many matters exemplifying what a house meant for its inhabitants and what type of life it presupposed or was able to sustain. This section is specifically devoted to these topics and discusses also the more technical aspects of urban dwelling.

Housing, as reflected in the Geniza, displays a polarity characteristic of a society that was enterprising, mercantile, and mobile, and, at the same time, tradition bound and clannish. Ideally, and very often actually, various branches of an extended family lived in one house, and frequently adjacent houses were in the possession of relatives or of one person. Occasionally, marriages between cousins or other close relatives were concluded in order to reunite properties which had become divided through the process of inheritance. In short, housing was organized so as to secure the coherence of the extended family.[1]

On the other hand, numerous documents tell about young couples living in rented premises or otherwise away from the family. As a rule, a house was treated as a monetary unit. At transactions, such as gifts, sales, or bequests, usually it was not divided physically, but according to nominal shares. These shares frequently changed hands. Partnerships with outsiders, even members of another religion, were common. The right of preemption, intended to keep aliens out, was often waived or disregarded. The tension between these two opposing tendencies of family cohesion and mobility gave rise to the many contracts, lawsuits, and settlements with regard to houses that are recorded in the Geniza papers.

With few exceptions, documents, whether issued by Muslim or by Jewish authorities, describe the houses concerned as being "held in joint, undivided ownership."[2] This means that the parts of a house which formed the object of a contract were units of account, not real segments of a building. A house was divided into twenty-four nominal shares, a division modeled on the twenty-four qīrāṭs, or parts, of the dinar, the same division adopted in the apportioning of an inheritance in Islamic law. The shares transferred by sale or gift could be very small. In a carefully executed Arabic deed, a husband acquired for his wife 1/48 of a house from her brother. In the year of famine 1200, a woman sold 1/48 of a house for 12 dinars. Shares of 1/18, 1/16, 1/9, or 1/8 were commonplace.[3] Yet, the majority of the transactions recorded concerned portions of a house amounting to 1/6, 1/4, or more, which means that they normally were large enough to form separate residences. In any case, we see that the institution of partnership, which in those days dominated commerce, finance, industry, and employment, also prevailed in the ownership of houses.[4]

Urban property was an important form of investment. A physician owned, in addition to 2/3 of one house, which also served as his domicile, shares of 1/2, 1/3, and 1/8 in other houses, two of which were facing, and the two others were side by side.[5] A woman married for the second time possessed in full the house in which she lived with her first husband, as well as a ruin opposite it, and, in addition, held shares of 1/4 and 1/8 in houses in other parts of town.[6] A Tunisian merchant who lived in Alexandria possessed two houses in Fustat, the income from which, after deduction of the costs of maintenance, was regularly remitted to him.[7] When the widow of an India trader acquires 1/6 of two shops, the total value of which exceeded 300 dinars, one can hardly see in this step anything other than a means of investment. The same applies to the father-in-law of this woman, also an India trader, who bought a large house worth 500 dinars, letting most of it to others, while purchasing, approximately at the same time, half of another for 300 dinars, and retaining the former proprietor of that half as a tenant.[8] When a bride receives from her parents shares in a house, more often than not the circumstances prove that the property given did serve as a source of income rather than as the residence of the young couple, see *Med. Soc.*, III, 519, s.v. "Residence."

When a house was occupied by a number of parties, the actual division of the premises and the conditions entailed by it had to be agreed upon. The contract concerning the three-story house in the provincial town of al-Maḥalla, translated above, may serve as an example for so comprehensive an agreement. A document in which a party is permitted to enter the premises of another once a month for inspecting the drainage pipe illustrates special arrangements necessary for peaceful relations between occupants.[9] When parts of a house were rented to a third party, the distribution of the income from that source had to be regulated as well.[10]

Relatives who were on good terms with one another would not make any formal settlements nor reserve for themselves any parts of the common property. Such a situation referring to the families of three cousins is described in a letter submitted to Moses Maimonides.[11] Naturally, the legal inquiry became necessary only when the three began to quarrel. There was even a more ingenious type of arrangement: In order to give all partners the opportunity of enjoying, at least temporarily, the amenities of the best section of a house, relatives would rotate year by year from one floor, or one part of the house, to the other. An agreement of this type is mentioned in another question submitted to Maimonides, and we have an actual contract to this effect from the city of Tyre on the Lebanese coast made in, or around 1196. Strange as the arrangement may appear to us, it shows how much care was taken to avoid squabbles between members of a family who were joint owners of a house. We read about bitter and prolonged lawsuits over similar matters. One magnificently written Hebrew fragment, written around 1000, describes the vicissitudes of a contention about the use of the main hall of a house. One entrance was walled up; on another a board was nailed and the rights of the parties were defined. When one of the relatives tried to obtain the removal of that board by bribing a Muslim judge, Shemarya, then the *rav*, or highest religious authority of the Jewish community, was approached, the results of which are not preserved.[12]

Examples of precautionary measures taken for the same purpose abound in the Geniza. A merchant embarking on a journey overseas leaves to his daughter, as a gift, one-eighth of his house, two maidservants, and everything found in the *manzil*, room or suite of rooms, occupied by her. This manzil, however, and that inhabited by her brother are expressly described as being the property of the father.[13] The following, somewhat complicated case is particularly noteworthy. A man married a widow who brought in as her marriage portion one-sixth of a house. She shared this house with the children of her late husband and a Muslim partner. The new couple moved into a *ṭabaqa*, or apartment, on an upper floor. The husband was afraid that the other partners might claim that the living quarters actually occupied by him represented more than one-sixth of the total value of the house. Therefore, his wife stood security with her share in the property for all claims on rent which might be raised against her husband.[14] A similar case, where the actual occupation by the member of a family exceeded a nominal sixth, with the consequence that a partial rent was paid by him to his relatives, is reported below.[15]

Income from real estate was regarded by great merchants as an investment inferior to that derived from commerce. This attitude is understandable in view of the facts discussed presently, namely, that rents were low and repairs expensive. For the rank and file of the middle class, however, urban property, which could be easily supervised, seems to have formed the favorite choice for securing a steady flow of revenue, true especially for women, who, with the exception of the poor, normally did not earn money by work.

Perhaps one-half, if not the majority, of the proprietors of houses appearing in the Geniza were women. Fathers and mothers would give their daughters one or several houses or, more frequently, shares in them, at the time of their marriage, or at any other time, in order to ensure their economic security and independence. A husband would leave his wife real estate as payment of what he owed her as deferred installment of the marriage gift. When a childless old woman, among other things, left to her nephews a *new* house, she had probably acquired it not long before her death because she regarded it as the safest form of preserving her savings. Gold, silver, or jewelry could be stolen. The house was registered with the authorities.[16]

The possession of real estate was a necessity also for the pursuit of regular economic activities. If one wished to contract a loan, one had to have a house, which could serve as collateral. This situation is particularly well illustrated in a document dated March 969. A few months earlier a woman and her husband had borrowed 50 dinars from a physician and had mortgaged for this loan a house which she had inherited from her father. In March 969, the couple needed that house, presumably for taking an additional loan from someone else. Therefore, they pledged to the physician another house, adjacent to the first and most probably given to her as part of her marriage portion.[17] It stands to reason that the value of a house given as collateral usually was higher than the sum taken as a loan. A glassmaker pledged his house, which had already changed owner three times, for a loan of only 10 dinars, an amount found only exceptionally as the price of a house in the capital of Egypt.[18]

There is no need to emphasize that the most common incentives for the building or acquisition of a home were family adherence and social status. Houses had no numbers in those days. They bore the names of their proprietors, and often also (or solely) that of a previous owner, if it was he who had made the house "famous." "Oh my house, you concealer [Ar. *sātir*] of my deficiencies," says an all-Arabic maxim; the term *mastūr*, respectable, which occupies us later, has much to do with the proprietorship of a home.[19] A man built a new house not so much for himself as with the intention of providing a shelter for his progeny. The father's house, like the mother's womb, was a son's natural frame of growth. He brought there his own wife so that she, too, should become one with the body of the family.

Prices, sales, and gifts of houses.—An examination of the prices of houses seems to reveal a certain degree of standardization and division into distinct groups, as shown in Appendix A, which presents the relevant information from the Geniza with regard to houses in towns. In the villages, as the papyri from the Egyptian Library published by Adolf Grohmann disclose, one could have a complete house for less than 1 dinar, and prices of 4 to 5 dinars were commonplace. An Arabic fragment from the caves of Murabbaʿāt on the Dead Sea, edited by the same author, concerns the sale of a house for 1 dinar. In the Geniza, similar cases are exceptional and obscured by complicated circumstances, as when a man had to pledge 3/4 of a house and 1/2 of a ruin belonging to him against a debt of 6 dinars which he owed to an orphan. Presumably his house also was more like a ruin. The name of the place where these properties were situated has not been preserved.[20]

For smaller provincial towns, such as Ṣahrajt, Malīj, and Ushmunayn, houses worth 10, 11, 12, and 17 dinars, respectively, have been attested in the Geniza records and in a papyrus from the Egyptian Library. In 998, in one small place in the Nile Delta, al-Banā, near the town of Fāqūs, a woman sold one-twelfth of a house to her son-in-law for 3 1/2 dinars, which makes a total value of 42 dinars.

The most modest houses in the capital cost between 20 and 40 dinars. Prices of 20, 36, and 40 dinars have been found twice, and if we include the few documents from the Mamluk period (the second half of the thirteenth and the fourteenth centuries), the sum of 500 *nuqra* silver, whose actual value corresponded at that time to approximately 25 dinars, has twice been ascertained. Prices of these amounts perhaps were standard for modest habitations.[21]

The two groups, of houses worth around 60 and 120 dinars, respectively, are represented in the Geniza by a large number of documents. These groups seem to comprise houses occupied by the broad mass of the lower and middle classes, for example, craftsmen, schoolmasters, and local shopkeepers.

A merchant engaged in international trade or a physician would buy for himself a home worth 200 or 300 dinars or more. Residences in this range of prices are attested not only for Egypt but also for Qayrawān, Tunisia, Palermo, Sicily, and Seleucia-Silifke, Asia Minor (which, at that time, was a Byzantine town and not inhabited by Muslims). The upper crust of society—government officials and the like—would live in houses worth 600 to 800 dinars, and we are fortunate in possessing a most detailed description of a house costing 729 dinars. The details given in Appendix A show that specific circumstances prevailed in many cases of sales. Attention should be paid to this fact by anyone undertaking to evaluate the prices listed there.

An important feature of the transfer of houses was the right frequently given to the seller and to his heirs to buy the sold property back when they were able and willing to do so. The periods stipulated for repurchase, although sometimes short (in one case only seven months), were usually of considerable length, amounting to four, five, ten, and even twelve years. It indicates that houses, or parts of them, were often sold only as a last resort in situations of extreme need, as when a debtor was unable to pay back a loan.[22]

In all cases in which the right of redemption was extended for several years, the seller continued to live in his place and paid rent to the buyer. Arrangements of this legal character are foreseen in the Talmud and are commonplace in Islamic law.[23] When, in such circumstances, the rent was exorbitant, veiled interest was clearly implied, but not always, as the Geniza proves. In a deed from Alexandria, dated 1103, two Jewish partners bought half a house for 60 dinars and granted the Muslim seller the right to live in it for ten years against a yearly rent of 3 dinars. Until the end of that period he had the right to buy his half back. If he was unable to do so, the buyers would sell their share but return to him any amount in excess of the 60 dinars originally paid by him. A yearly rent worth 5 percent of the value of a property was modest, and the additional stipulation that any profit accruing from the sale would revert to the original proprietor shows that the buyers must have had a reason for extending help to the Muslim, who bore the honorific title The Venerable.

The element of consideration was present also when Abraham Maimonides, the Nagid, or Head, of the Jewish community of Egypt, was granted in 1213/4 the right to repurchase the *burj*, a tower in the ancient Byzantine fortress of Fustat, for 60 dinars over a period of five years, or, when, in 1246, two plus one out of twenty-four shares of a property near the Great Bazaar, purchased for a total of 42 dinars, were given the same privilege for a duration of three years. In both instances the rent was waived, so that one gets the impression that the purchase was in reality a loan with collateral but without interest. When, however, in 1229, a dyer, the son of a dyer, conceded a similar privilege to a fellow artisan (who, like his father, practiced the same craft) for four years, but imposed on him a yearly rent of 66 dirhems for half a house worth 430 dirhems, it was a clear case of veiled interest. In addition, the seller-tenant had to pay the government tax, the watchmen, and for garbage removal—all duties normally incumbent on the proprietor—making a total of about 16 percent of the value of the property to be paid per year. The transactions described in *Med. Soc.*, I, 384, sec. 65 (twelve years, and about 16 percent, Bilbays 1239) and III, 329 (1123/4) were of a similar character. In a fragmentary contract, written by the prominent judge Immanuel b. Yehiel (ca. 1231-1279), the seller-renter of a mill in Ḥudayjī Street pays all the dues on the building and also for the necessary repairs, but will be reimbursed for all these expenses at the time of the repurchase.[24]

Gifts of houses are recorded in the Geniza as frequently as sales. The beneficiaries normally were sons or daughters or grandchildren, or other relatives, mostly sisters.[25] The category of relatives included maidservants, who legally were slaves. Thus a woman on her deathbed freed her two slave girls and gave them a part of one house as a place to live and a part of another as a source of maintenance for the rest of their lives.[26] There were, however, many other types of gifts, especially those illustrating that houses fulfilled in those days to a large extent the role life insurance does today. An old woman gave to a trustworthy person the upper floor of a house against the obligation to supply her with food and clothing during her lifetime.[27] A man, obviously a widower, made a gift of a small house to a woman on condition that she look after him until his death.[28] One house in one case and two houses in another were given to women, with the stipulation that they provide the donors with proper funeral attire and a fine burial. In that society the greatest luxury a man permitted himself in life was—to die.[29]

Religious or charitable institutions were frequently the recipients of gifts of houses. One would donate the whole or part of a house for the upkeep or lighting of a synagogue, for the poor in general, or for specified groups, such as the poor, the scholars of Jerusalem, or the copying of a Torah scroll or the education of orphan boys. *Waqf* or *ṣadaqa*, as pious foundations were called in Arabic, *heqdēsh*, or more frequently, *qōdesh*, as they were named in Hebrew, played a significant role in the disposition of houses. The waqfs of the princes and military leaders are known to us from Muslim literature and also through inscriptions and documents, especially from the Mamluk period. The Geniza shows us how the common people acted in these matters.[30]

Donating a property in its entirety was certainly regarded as particularly meritorious. Thus, one document tells us about a man who had inherited half a house from his mother, and, before dedicating it to the two synagogues of Fustat, purchased the remaining half for that purpose.[31] Very frequently, however, only part of a house, such as one-third or one-quarter, would be turned over to a pious foundation, even when the donor owned the entire property. Since income from houses was derived from rent, it must have been a common practice for a family house to be occupied partly by members of the family, or the donor himself, and partly by tenants. This parceling of a house into some sections devoted to pious purposes and others given to various relatives or other persons is well illustrated by the deathbed declaration of a woman made in November 1006, in which she willed one-sixth of her house to each of the two synagogues of Fustat and another three-sixths to a brother, a niece, and a girl (in order to enable her to marry). The value of one-twelfth had already been spent for repairs, and the remaining twelfth was earmarked for the transportation of the testator's body to Palestine for interment in the Holy City. In or around 1161 a woman donated one-quarter of a house, which she held in partnership with another proprietor, "to the poor" and one-sixth to a person not described as her relative. In a court record dated 1186, a woman shares with other tenants a house which she had donated to a pious foundation, paying rent to the latter for the premises occupied by her. People must have been accustomed to being crowded together with others in the same house.[32]

The transfer of a property took place in two stages: the first when the sale, gift, or settlement was made before a court or a notary assisted by at least one witness, and the second when the property was registered in the name of the new proprietor with the Muslim and normally also the Jewish authorities. In the first act, all the deeds relating to the object, "both Arabic and Hebrew," were handed over to the new proprietor and the promise was given that it would be properly registered. This procedure is evident in numerous documents. When the house sold was located in another city the buyer had to confirm that he had inspected it.[33] Since registration with the government authorities was obligatory, one wonders why the parties were eager to obtain also a "Hebrew deed" with regard to the transfer of a property and often made the actual transaction before a Jewish court. The answer seems to be that a husband used as security his possessions for the sums due his wife at his death or in the case of divorce. Marriages and divorces were under the jurisdiction of the communal courts. Consequently, the latter had to be consulted where property changes affecting the security of the wife were involved. A story illustrates the situation: One evening the proprietor of part of a sugar factory made an agreement with a prospective buyer to sell him his share. Next day, when they came to the court to ratify their deal, the judges sent two witnesses to the proprietor's wife asking her whether she was prepared to lift her rights on that share in the factory. When she refused, the agreement was canceled.[34]

In Muslim documents, especially late ones, room was left for transactions subsequent to the first transfer of a property. A huge, but much damaged Arabic deed from July 1317 contains at least eight additional entries regarding parts of the property concerned or its entirety. The Karaite deeds, all of which were written by Muslim notaries, exhibit the same usage.[35]

A tax on the transfer of the ownership of houses is referred to in a letter complaining about the extortions of a tax farmer who claimed that many people had executed the transfers before a Jewish court without registering them with the government.[36] A deed from December 1132 concerns a house, half of which was sold for 117 dinars "free of all charges," meaning perhaps that the value of the property was 120 dinars and that a tax in the amount of 3 dinars had been paid by the seller. This sum may represent, at least in part, also a remuneration for an agent. It is, however, more likely that with "charges," as common in business accounts, payments to the government are intended. A similar transfer tax of something around 3 percent is noted in a court record written on June 22, 1145. The price of the property, a house in the al-Mamṣūṣa quarter, was 123 dinars, "the charges," 3 7/12 dinars ("one-third and one-fourth"), and the payment to the agent, 4 1/2 dinars. The court record is translated in Appendix A.[37]

The services of a real estate broker must have been engaged frequently, for we even read about a *simsār al-yahūd*, a broker specializing in a Jewish neighborhood.[38] A brokerage fee amounting to about 7 percent of the price of a property is noted in January 1139. Pages from the account book of a real estate agent, dated 1233-1236, have been found. He bought and sold houses and orchards, and sometimes repaired the former before selling them. Since a bull and a ewe also figure in his accounts, he probably lived in a small town.[39]

Entering a newly acquired property was a festive occasion, on which one received congratulations, such as "may God grant blessings through it." This wish is to be understood in light of the belief, shared by both Jews and Muslims, that new houses (and wives) acted as auguries, that is, if one was successful after having been blessed with the possession of them, one would continue to be so all one's life.[40]

Renting of premises.—In medieval Egypt an astonishingly large section of the population lived in rented houses. Varying reasons accounted for this socioeconomic phenomenon. Distinguished travelers and, in particular, the more important traders, loathed staying in caravanserais, the medieval motels. Long before one arrived in a city one would ask a friend to rent an apartment, and often the sojourn in a foreign town or country would extend over many months or years. We read of both Nāṣir-i-Khosraw, the Persian poet and theologian, who stayed in Cairo during the years 1046-1049, and the Spanish Hebrew poet Judah ha-Levi, who visited Alexandria in the concluding months of 1140, that they lived in rented apartments.[41]

Two passages from Geniza letters, one, a request to rent a place, and the other, a report about an apartment rented, show what types of domicile were desired. A Tunisian merchant, before setting out from Alexandria to the capital, writes to his business correspondent: "Please rent me an apartment, a clean place, even if the rent be high. I do not care. I like a clean place. Choose it wherever you like and lock it. May God prolong your life." Obviously this man had had bad experiences in previous similar situations.[42] In a letter from Fustat, the writer, after having expressed regret that the addressee had not accepted his offer to put him up as long as he wished, reports about the apartment chosen: "The place is near the 'House of Ibn Rajā' [a well-known *wakāla*, or caravanserai], before one comes to the entrance of Ibn Rajā's portico. It is an upper story in the rear section of the house. No one else lives on the same floor. The people living beneath that apartment are foreigners who keep to themselves. They do not ask questions about anyone and nothing you say would be heard or known. The only trouble is—that they are women." Here the letter ends abruptly. The writer must have had second thoughts about the propriety or desirability of such neighbors.[43] When a merchant had a house in Alexandria and an "upper floor" in Fustat, the latter might well have been rented. In view of the bad times, he asked a business friend to sublet the Fustat apartment.[44]

The great mobility of the Mediterranean populace, described in *Med. Soc.*, I, 42–70, explains why many families were forced to make use of rented apartments. Nahray b. Nissīm, the Qayrawanese merchant and scholar, was active in Egypt from 1045 on. In 1066 he still lived in a sixth of a house which belonged to the family of his Egyptian wife, and was prepared to pay a dinar per month for rooms occupied by him in excess of this sixth.[45] In between these two dates he wrote, in a postscript added to a letter of another Tunisian: "I took a *qāʿa* [ground floor] in the Fortress of the Candles and shall move there on the first of next month—may God make the move a success—albeit that it is not so fine a place as my present one—I informed you about the reason of the change in a former letter."[46] Later in life, a house he owned in partnership with another was a landmark in the city, and he possessed, in addition, a house in Alexandria and one in Jerusalem.[47] A community official wishing to move from the Egyptian countryside to the capital asks a colleague to help him out with a temporary shelter for two months until he found an apartment, adding the biblical verse (Exodus 23:9): "You know how a stranger feels."[48]

Furthermore, although young couples were expected to live with the husband's parents, we also find the opposite tendency, the desire to break away from the extended family and all the limitations it imposed on those living together. The detailed stipulations about prospective changes in the residence of the newly married, so commonly found in Jewish (and Muslim) marriage contracts are an indication of the frequency of such occurrences. Young couples, as the Geniza documents prove, often had to be content with a rented apartment.[49] Inheritance was another and more frequent cause of renting. When a property was split into units too small for a comfortable residence, heirs wishing to remain or to move into a house affected by partition had to pay rent to those who had become coproprietors.

Last, but not least, large sections of the population were poor and unable to acquire homes for themselves. The enormous development of the institution of pious foundations, that is, the donation of houses for charitable purposes, described in *Med. Soc.*, II, 112–121, presupposes the existence of an extensive clientele in need of housing. It must have been common practice to let part of a family home, as is evident from references in letters, from documents, and the practice of donating only part of a house to a pious foundation.[50] Moreover, renting an apartment house seems also to have been a form of commercial undertaking. In December 1032, a Muslim rented from a Jew a house in Khawlān quarter of Fustat with the right to sublet. This house consisted of two apartments on the ground floor, two on the upper floor, and three light constructions (*akhṣāṣ*), each forming a separate habitation. It sounds as if, from the outset, the house was rented as a source of income rather than a place to live. The acquisition of real estate as a source of income from its rent to be used for the support of orphans was commonplace.[51]

The duration of a renting period was short, sometimes only six months, but mostly one lunar year.[52] The start of the period in Muḥarram, the first month of the Muslim year, is attested, but was by no means general (as it was in later times).[53] Some contracts were made for two years. A person who lived in his brother's house for more than thirty years renewed the contract every second year.[54] Longer periods of rent, such as four years, were exceptional and owed to specific circumstances; thus the administrator of the property of the mosques in the Egyptian capital let a garden house on the Nile for that period. Even in this instance, payment was made at the end of each month, which was the usual procedure in most cases. Twice a quarter of a house was let to relatives for the five years; in one instance, for a monthly rent of 1 1/2 dirhems, in another, for a *rubāʿī*, or 1/4 dinar, about 9–10 dirhems.[55]

Arrears, naturally, did occur, especially among poorer tenants, but to a lesser degree than one would expect. Hence the strong contractual warning, even in an agreement with a relative, to pay at the end of every month "without procrastination and excuses." At certain times it seems to have been customary to set four months as the ultimate limit for the accumulation of debts from the monthly rents.[56]

When the rent was paid in advance, a certain discount was granted. An Adenese merchant advanced in 1186 100 dirhems for an apartment on an upper floor, for which he presumably would have had to pay 10 dirhems per month if he had paid in installments. An advance payment of 6 3/4 dinars for a place used as a reservoir of rose oil during two years also gives the impression of being the result of a reduction.[57]

The rates of rent are richly documented in the Geniza texts. Detailed accounts of revenue from houses owned by pious foundations enable us to study the development of the rates of rent during two hundred years (1040–1250 approximately), and there are many details to be learned on the subject from sundry documents referring to residences owned by private persons. We must bear in mind that the lists of communal revenues record actual payments. Since arrears occurred, the sums given do not always represent the total rent. Yet the information contained in these accounts is so abundant and variegated that, with a certain measure of circumspection, one is able to determine the full amounts of the average rents stipulated. Second, one would expect houses given to pious foundations to be in such a state that only the poorest would choose to live in them. It was true, however, only with respect to some houses, in particular those which served many parties, mostly single or old people, who occupied only one room each. In general, the amounts of rents discernible in documents concerning communal houses did not differ substantially from those of privately owned ones. Therefore these two sources of information may be regarded as complementary and used accordingly.[58]

In Appendix B are analyzed representative accounts of pious foundations from the eleventh, twelfth, and thirteenth centuries. A comparison of that material with sources dealing with houses belonging to private proprietors leads to these conclusions: People in very modest circumstances paid for their living quarters 4–6 dirhems per month, approximately 60 a year, which corresponded to about 1 1/2 dinars. The Geniza has preserved a lease for an apartment belonging to the community for 5 dirhems per month, and one of an entire private house in a provincial town for 6 dirhems. In the latter case the tenant also had to pay the night watchmen.[59] In a query addressed to Maimonides, a quarter of a house (*dār*) is let for 1 1/2 dirhems, which presupposes a total of about 5 dirhems, since one had to pay relatively more for a part than for an entire property.[60] An Arabic papyrus gives 1 1/6 dinars as a yearly rent, also in a provincial town, but from the ninth century.[61] The rent of 1/6 dinar per month, or 2 dinars a year, also belongs here.[62]

Another, even poorer, group is conspicuous in the lists discussed, those who paid an average rent of 2 1/2 dirhems per month. The frequent occurrence of the names of women in this category induces us to assume that these premises were mostly occupied by single persons and not by families. In a letter to a communal authority, a woman complains that her rent was raised from 2 to 3 1/2 dirhems, although the place was very modest and shared by her only with her son who was away all the day at work. A 1/4 dinar as the yearly rent of a house belonging to the Jewish community of Ascalon, Palestine, during a period of about fifteen years is entirely exceptional. No doubt the tenant made repairs in the house, in recognition of which he was granted this token payment for an extended period.[63] The lower middle class spent 9–12 dirhems, or 1/4–1/3 dinars, per month on rent, which equals 3–4 dinars a year. Instances of this are found in the lists in Appendix B. A yearly rent of 3 dinars with regard to Alexandria 1103 and an advance payment of 100 dirhems representing a yearly rent of the same amount for Fustat 1186 have been discussed earlier.[64] An India trader, while away, leased a house to his brother for 12 dirhems a month, approximately 4 dinars per year, a sum paid for a complete house in Fustat according to a fragmentary contract in Arabic characters.[65] A *khizāna*, or closet, which was rented for 12 dirhems a month from a brother, also belongs to this category. A store in the Market of the Sellers of Seed, which could serve also as living quarters, cost 15 dirhems in 1143/4.[66]

Half a dinar per month, or 6 dinars per year, must have been estimated as a reasonable rent for a decent middle-class home. We find this sum stipulated in a marriage contract which fixes 50 dinars as a fine for default in fulfillment of any of the conditions of the contract—a very high sum for a fine.[67] An entire house with a garden could be had for 5 dinars per year in Alexandria 1132, and in the same city, in 1165, a house was let for 9 dinars for two years, which corresponds to a yearly rent of approximately the same amount. A house in Jerusalem was rented for 5–6 dinars around 1060. A garden house on the Nile in Fustat was let in 1137 for 8 dinars and half of another garden house cost 300 dirhems per year in 1229, which also represents a yearly rent of approximately 8 dinars.[68] A similar sum can be calculated as the rent for an apartment from a lawsuit submitted to Maimonides.[69]

More opulent merchants would occupy premises costing a dinar or more per month. The India trader whose purchases of houses have been mentioned above, rented for himself a ground floor consisting of two qāʿas and costing 1 1/6 dinars per month, although he himself was traveling all the time, and another India trader leased his house in Barqa, Libya, for two years for 40 dinars, which is approximately the same.[70] Nahray b. Nissim, as we have seen, was prepared to pay 1 dinar a month for the part of a house which he sought to occupy in addition to the share belonging to him, and in one account he actually paid 30 dinars for two and a half years rent.[71] The rent for a ground floor of a large house in Alexandria cost 40 dirhems per month in 1194, which corresponds at least to a dinar.[72] Rents of 5–11 dinars per month, as recorded for Cairo by the Persian traveler Nāṣir-i-Khosraw, have not yet been traced in the Geniza records. The Persian perhaps was accompanied by several wives and concubines and a retinue of servants, wherefore he needed premises of a type never dreamt of by persons in more modest circumstances.[73] Even an amir (military commander or nobleman) paid only 34 1/2 dirhems per month for a qāʿa he occupied, according to a Geniza document.[74]

The foregoing seems to indicate that the amounts of the rents remained remarkably steady during the eleventh through the thirteenth centuries, although we are able to observe actual or attempted raises in the payments of individual occupants. One case where we have two contracts relating to the same property, but separated by an interval of forty-four years, is particularly instructive. In 1076, a man who already possessed one-quarter of the compound in question (consisting of a large and a small house) rented the remaining three-quarters for 4 1/2 dinars. In 1120, half the property was let to the husband of the sister of the proprietress;

the sister owned the other half. In both cases the social circumstances of the rent were the same: The tenant acquired full occupancy of the place. The payment in 1120 was 7 qīrāṭs per month, that is, 84 qīrāṭs or 3 1/2 dinars for half the property per year, which would equal 5 1/4 for three-quarters. The difference of 3/4 dinars in the amounts of the rent is fully accounted for by the fact that the lower sum was an advance payment for the entire year. Again we see that a rent of 6–7 dinars per year for a whole residence was commonplace among middle-class people.[75]

The ratio between the value of a house and the rent paid for it can be established with certainty only with regard to properties where the relevant data are available in full. A house in Fustat was sold in 1102 for 500 dinars and brought a total of 30 dinars rent per year, which included taxes paid by the tenants. Half a house in Alexandria cost 60 dinars in 1103, and the rent for that half was 3 dinars. Thus, the yearly rent was 6 percent of the price of the house in the first case and 5 percent in the second.[76] That ratio might indeed be inferred from our findings regarding the prices of house and the amounts of rents in general. The reason for the relatively low rents most probably rests in the availability of living space, whereas the relatively higher cost of houses might have had its cause in the cost of repairs and in the limited opportunities of investment, for which urban property was one of the most avidly coveted objects.

Income from houses, that is, rent, was one of the most common constituents of the dowry given to a bride. Various documents show us how this arrangement worked in practice. In a betrothal agreement, a daughter receives the uppermost floor of a house; if she preferred to live elsewhere, she would receive the rent, but her father and his heirs were responsible for the payment of the ground rent and the watchmen.[77] In another document, a woman is given the rent from a middle floor with the proviso that if the place remained vacant, it was her loss.[78] The fragment of a marriage contract from Alexandria contains the condition that if one of two sisters sharing a house chose to live in another place, she could rent her share only to her sister.[79]

Such restrictions are natural and common. In a letter, a tenant is warned not to sublet a part of the premises leased to him, especially not to Jews, who made too much use of stoves and of the kitchen which would ruin the house. In a strongly worded note a young man is ordered to vacate the apartment let to his father and to remove his belongings by noon, for the place was let to his father, not to him.[80] A contract for the lease of a qāʿa for two years stipulates that the lessee was not permitted to install anything for the production of rose water or for the use of litharge or arsenic, or for other operations requiring the use of fire.[81] Of a different type was a restriction imposed by a landlady quoted as saying: "No unmarried person shall live in my house, in particular, no stranger."[82]

The number of persons living in one house could be considerable. The communal House of the Glassmaker housed between ten and fifteen tenants at different times. One hundred and fifty years earlier, ten people were found in another house belonging to the community.[83] There is no reason to assume that apartment houses belonging to private persons were less populated. When a Muslim rented a house comprising seven habitations with the right to sublet it, and paid only half a dinar rent per month, we may assume that the space occupied by the subtenants was rather limited.[84] Yet overcrowding was regarded as an offense and liable to give rise to a lawsuit. A legal question submitted to Maimonides deals with this problem. Two sisters sold the ground floor of their house, which represented two-thirds of the property, while they lived with their husbands and their children on the upper floors. The buyer lived in that house for eighteen years and married off his daughters and sons, purchasing for them living quarters elsewhere. After his death, the widow let her children with their families live with her, so that they could derive income from the apartments given to them by their late father. Instead of one couple, about fifteen persons now occupied the ground floor, causing damage to the lavatories (in the plural!), the water supply, and the building in general, "which had become like a caravanserai." The two sisters requested that the widow be ordered to turn out her sons and daughters and their families. Maimonides rejected the claim for the purely formal reason that the inhabitants of the ground floor did not trespass on the premises of the upper floors. On the opposite side, if the number of the occupants of the upper floors had considerably increased, it would have been judged an offense. The master's decision proves perhaps that such occurrences were not very frequent and did not represent a general nuisance, in which case he perhaps would have adopted a more pragmatic attitude. Living space was plentiful in Fustat. As a rule, only the quarters of the poor were crowded.[85]

Durability and maintenance.—Mosques, but no palaces or houses, have survived from the period studied in these pages. Should we conclude from this that human habitations were of ephemeral construction? What do the Geniza documents reveal to us about the lifetime of a house in those days? In 1004, a man acquired one-third of a house of which he already possessed two-thirds, probably through inheritance. That house could hardly have been very new at the time. Twenty years later, in 1024/5, his daughter claimed the place as an inheritance from her father.[86] A property consisting of two houses was let in 1076 and again in 1120, and the circumstances of the first lease indicate that the buildings must have been in existence a considerable time before that date.[87] "The house of the maker of wooden locks" in the Mikā'īl Lane in the Fortress of the Greeks, is mentioned as a boundary (and as the property of two brothers who had inherited it from their father) in a document from July 959 and again in 965, and half of it was given as part of a marriage portion to the bride of a prominent communal leader in September 1037. This house had been in existence for at least eighty years, but most probably for many more, before it served as part of a dowry.[88] Communal records refer to certain properties during periods over a hundred years and, naturally, such places had been owned by the families of the donors for a long time before they were given away. The testimony of the pious foundations about the duration of houses owned by them is indeed most impressive, although it is not always unequivocal.[89]

The history of a house is recorded in the documents describing the transactions related to it. Since the Geniza is not an archive, it has not preserved a complete dossier of deeds, but describes one that was submitted to a rabbinical court, no doubt, in a lawsuit. The original proprietor of the house concerned was the amir Iftikhār al-Dawla (Pride of the Realm) Mubārak (Blessed, a personal name) al-Afḍal (The most Noble) al-Juyūshī (i.e., belonging to the retinue of the viceroy of Egypt Badr al-Jamālī, Amīr al-Juyūsh, Commander of the Armies, 1074–1094). Iftikhār sold a part of his house to a *qissīs*, or Christian clergyman, of the Melkite denomination, and another part was given, or willed, by him to his daughter Sarwat (Cypress).[90] The clergyman sold his share to another Melkite Christian, who gave or left it to his daughter Banīna (Little Girl). The two girls, the daughter of the amir and that of the Christian, sold their shares, amounting to the entire house, to a Jewish notable, known also from another document as The Illustrious Persian Head Physician, who acquired them for himself and his wife Sitt Aʿdāhā (Mistress over her Enemies).[91] There was an additional transaction (recorded in a Hebrew document), namely, between the two spouses, through which the wife became the owner of the entire property. In the end, she sold the house to her son-in-law Abu 'l-Karam (The Distinguished), party to a contract from the years 1128 and 1129.[92] Abu 'l-Karam, whose property rights obviously had been contested by somebody, submitted the entire dossier to the court. Besides the documents written by Muslim notaries, there were two entries in Hebrew script on one of those official papers, and two "Hebrew documents" issued by Jewish authorities. As the court record notes, all documents were written on parchment. Thirty years or so might have lapsed between the first and the last transactions recorded in the dossier.[93]

Another chain of transfers of a property among members of the three monotheistic religions must be described as a bogus procedure. A Jacobite patriarch sold a ruin to a Muslim, who, on the same day and for the same price, sold it to a Karaite Jew through a Karaite real estate agent.[94] I assume that after the patriarch Michael had sold a church (which became the synagogue of the Iraqians) and other valuable Christian property to Jews during the reign of Aḥmad Ibn Ṭulūn (868–884),[95] a ban or curse was pronounced on any patriarch selling church property to Jews. In order to circumvent that prohibition, the Jacobite patriarch arranged that fake sale to a Muslim. I wonder whether this surmise is confirmed by any direct statement in a Christian source.

The complete life story of a house is presented in a deed from April 1260, which bears eight additional entries from the years 1265 through 1324. At the time of the sale recorded in 1260 the house must already have existed for a considerable time, since the deed notes radical changes made in the original building. The front was converted into an *īwān* facing the living room. It required a complete remodeling of the upper apartments, since the iwān is an open hall up to three stories high; consequently, the upper part of the house facing the street was, at the time of the sale, in repair. On the other hand, three new upper apartments had been added, to be reached now not through the house, but by a staircase erected in the entrance hall.[96]

The original proprietor, the Karaite banker Abu 'l-Faraj b. Abi 'l-Saʿīd (Salvation, Son of Auspicious) of the noble Ibn al-Khāzin (Treasurer) family, is known from a Karaite memorial list, where he is eulogized as one "who led the congregation in prayer, whose house was open for learned discussion, study, and hospitality, and who did works of philanthropy and charity, and was God-fearing."[97] The purchaser, an ophthalmologist from a Karaite family of physicians named al-Kirmānī,[98] sold half the house in three transactions within six years after he had acquired it. The purchasers were Karaite Jews: four and three out of twenty-four shares were acquired by one, and five by another. The total price for twelve shares, or half the house, was 1,350 nuqra dirhems, which, in 1265/6, had an exchange value of about 67 1/2 dinars, so that the total price of the house was approximately 135 dinars, the normal price for a middle-class residence partly under repair.[99]

The Karaite Luṭf Allah (God's Benevolence), who had acquired five shares in 1266, donated them to the poor of his community only eight years later, in 1274, but retained for himself the administration of the charity throughout his lifetime.[100] What happened to the other four and three shares sold in 1265 and 1266, respectively, is not noted in the document.

Sixty-four years after the original purchase, the eye doctor al-Kirmānī, who had retained for himself half the building, died, and his two sons and heirs, made these dispositions: one, Maḥāsin (Virtues, not: Muḥāsin),[101] sold his shares to the official in care of the pious foundations of the Karaites, and the other, the physician Abu 'l-Bishr (Good Tidings) donated his quarter with the provision that his wife be the beneficiary during her lifetime.[102] Both brothers are mentioned in the memorial list of the Kirmānī family.[103]

The house probably served the charitable purpose to which most (and probably all) of it had been dedicated for many years. In any case, the deed telling its story weathered eight hundred years of the history of a Cairene community experiencing many vicissitudes.[104]

The durability, structural changes, and sequence of proprietors of a house are particularly well illustrated in a deed containing dated entries for one hundred years, March 1436 through May 1535. Entries from April 1438 represent an agreement between two parties, each of whom had acquired half the building, which, naturally, must have been in existence for some time. A hundred years later, in 1535, Sara, a Karaite woman, sells half the house to two other Karaite women, one of whom was named Esther, both biblical names. The history of the house did not end there. It was donated for the benefit of the poor, as is proved by the fact that its deed is in the possession of the Karaite community in Cairo.[105]

The material presented on the preceding pages should make us reluctant to assume that the private houses of the medieval capital of Egypt were poorly constructed. How then can one explain the existence of the many ruins which were so conspicuous in medieval Fustat?[106] Its main cause, perhaps, was the joint ownership of houses, which was common in those days. With one or several partners who were unable or unwilling to bear the cost of repairs, or who were out of the country and could be reached only with difficulty or not at all, the property was neglected until it fell into ever more decay. Moreover, repairs were costly. The average wage of a mason was 5 dirhems per day, the rent of a modest apartment for a month. If the proprietor did not need the place for himself, there was no great urge for expenditure on its upkeep. It was more profitable to sell it, even as a ruin, than to repair it in order to lease it to others. Furthermore, the climate of Lower Egypt, where precipitation is rare, does not require much protection against rain. If, however, the damage done by one or two strong downpours is not immediately repaired, decay quickly sets in. Finally, superstition might have been responsible for many a ruin. Houses were looked upon as omens. When something inauspicious such as an untimely or unnatural death happened in a house, it was considered as being haunted and ill-omened, *mayshūm*, and was abandoned. Such occurrences, known from Islamic sources, are rare in Geniza documents.[107]

Trying now to form some idea about the cost of maintenance, we find that even an old house was supposed to bring substantial revenue over and above the cost of its upkeep. Dedicating a house for the illumination of the two synagogues of Fustat, the donor stipulated that the upkeep of the property had precedence over the intrinsic purpose for which the gift was made.[108] We should not attribute too much importance to a statement in a question submitted to Maimonides, according to which most of the rent of an apartment occupied during the thirty years was spent on repairs. For it was reported that the tenant, the brother of the proprietor, purposely damaged the place to force the latter to cede it to him.[109] In a document from July 1150, a perfumer undertakes the renovation of a ground floor and a loggia for 40 dinars in return for which he was entitled to occupy those localities for eight years, which presupposes a rent of 5 dinars per year. The house belonged to "Wuḥsha's daughter's daughter" and was situated in the Zuwayla quarter of Cairo in the Street of the Slavs, *saqāliba*. A ṭabaqa, an apartment or part of an upper floor, "the one adjacent to the house of the Christians," in a Jewish communal building was restored for a cost of 30 dinars, while, at the time of the writing of the report, the ground floor beneath it was completely occupied, bringing revenue.[110] A rent of 3/4 dinars per month or 9 per year was waived for 16 months against structural changes or repairs carried out in a building belonging to a pious foundation according to an agreement made in 1156.[111] A tenant in a house worth 500 dinars spent the equivalent of ten months' rent on supports costing 280 dirhems with the subsequent approval of the proprietor, who had been abroad during the period.[112]

Records of more expensive repairs are found throughout. For instance, in a will made in 1006, a woman notes that one-twelfth of the price of her house had gone for the purchase of beams for strengthening its structure.[113] In 1103, a court permitted the use of

50 out of 74 dinars left to two minor orphans for the repair of a house belonging to them, since otherwise it would have disintegrated.[114] The revenue from the compound of the Jerusalemites in Fustat was 118 dirhems per month, but the administrator who had farmed that revenue presented a bill of 209 3/4 dirhems for repairs in July 1151.[115]

These examples, widely varying, of course, in accordance with the degree of disrepair of the building concerned and other circumstances, bring home the fact that the structures of the time needed constant surveillance and that people went to great lengths in order to keep their properties in good shape. The best illustration of our problem is perhaps to be found in a large communal account dated December 1, 1164. It shows that repairs made in the course of six months in 21 houses totaled 922 1/2 dirhems, and that the revenue from these houses and a number of others belonging to the community amounted to 3,683 dirhems for the same period. Thus we see that the community spent about one-quarter of its revenue from houses on their upkeep. In view of the comparatively long period concerned, this situation may be regarded as typical.[116]

The Geniza documents abound in details about materials used, workmen employed, and structural changes effected. They are indeed a first-rate source for the history of the Mediterranean building industry of the High Middle Ages. Attention is drawn to *Med. Soc.*, I, 112-113, and, in particular, to the meritorious study on the subject by Moshe Gil, which presents the Geniza findings related to the houses of pious foundations systematically and discusses them through constant comparison with ancient Egyptian, Roman, and Byzantine, as well as medieval and modern Egyptian archaeological and literary material.[117]

Bricks, usually sold by the thousands, floor tiles made of limestone, black and "yellow" (sandy) clay soil, lime, gypsum, Nile mud, pebbles, straw, ashes, and water were the basic materials regularly listed as transported to a site of building operations. Besides the master builder, who was also the bricklayer, a whole array of specialists were occupied with the preparation of mortar, cement, and plaster, or whitewashed the rooms, while others installed or repaired the clay pipes for water supply and drainage. Stones are not listed at the regular building operations. Private homes, as a rule, were not made of stone.[118] When the synagogue of the Palestinians, like the other houses of worship of Christians and Jews, was demolished in 1013 or so, the Muslim authorities sold its bricks and timber (which action, by the way, testifies to the durability of these materials). When, however, the building was rebuilt in or around

1039/40, a structure that lasted until the end of the nineteenth century, its main features were stone foundations and stone (or marble) columns.[119] The account notes an expenditure of 11 1/2 dinars for "Heliopolis stone" (stones taken from ancient Egyptian ruins), hewn blocks, small used dressed stones, and broken stones, but 76 1/2 dinars for one large and seventeen regular columns. It stands to reason that large sections of the original stone walls were reused at the renovation.[120]

Timber was indispensable in the form of logs for supports or crossbeams in ceilings on the one hand, and in that of planks in doors, screens, and surfaces on the other. Carved woodwork was one of the main ornaments of buildings, both private and public. The supports were expensive, since they were usually made of fir, pine, or elm (or ash) trees, which mostly had to be imported.[121] The local woods: acacia, (the Egyptian) sycamore, palm trunks and leaves, naturally, were regularly used. The construction of ceilings was achieved by covering the crossbeams with palm sticks or reeds, on which flock (waste cotton) and dried bushes were fastened with nails and then overlaid with planks and plaster.[122] Since Egypt is a country where timber is scarce, the rich development of carved woodwork probably was due to foreign influence. With regard to the painted wooden ceilings, "Syrian fashion" is expressly mentioned.[123]

The floors, and often parts of the walls in rooms, corridors, and courts, were covered with limestone tiles or marble flagstones. Those marble layers were removable and regarded as valuable possessions. In a complicated settlement regarding an inheritance, made in summer 1156, two beneficiaries forego rights worth 30 and 50 dinars against "a share in the marble" of a house involved.[124]

In Egypt limestone and marble were more easily available than timber. The wide use of those fire-resistant materials had the additional advantage of making the houses safer against the danger of conflagration. Fire damage is practically absent from the Geniza records. In a letter sent from Salonica, Greece, around 1090, the writer, among many other matters, expresses regret to have heard that a common acquaintance in Fustat had perished with his family in flames.[125] In the memorial lists, however, where often are indicated the circumstances of a death by accident, such as the collapse of a house, no instance of a death by fire has been encountered. In a contract of sale from August 1174 one-fourth of a private home ruined by fire is sold for 6 dinars.[126] But it is the only case known to me, and may very well have been that one of the victims of the notorious burning of Fustat of December 1168, purposely initiated by Shāwar, the Fatimid vizier.[127]

Besides the protection by appropriate materials, the scarcity of fires, as apparent in the Geniza documents, might have had its cause in the simple fact that people used fire far less than we do. One did not eat much warm food; the hot climate did not require it, and the fuel, wood, was expensive. Cooked meals were brought home from the bazaar. When Jews were said to use fire in the house more than others, the reason is to be found in their many culinary taboos, which made it difficult for the husband to find warm kosher food on the street (even though Jews were prominent in the food industry). People were also reluctant to lease premises for industrial activities requiring the use of fire.[128]

Labor, as the accounts for the upkeep of communal buildings show, was, as a rule, more costly than the materials. The emoluments of the various groups of workmen engaged in building operations are discussed in *Med. Soc.*, I, 94-97: long-standing traditions must have prevailed in those matters.[129] It is also noteworthy that work on one specific job was not always done consecutively, but was interrupted by shorter or longer periods, when nothing was done. Repairs in the Ben Pinhas house (mentioned as from ca. 1160 through ca. 1230) carried out in October-November 1215, required eight days altogether, but were interrupted once for two days, once for five days, and twice for two weeks. Lack of funds could hardly have been responsible for these irregularities, since the administrators of public buildings used to cover expenses on one place with the revenue from others. More likely the skilled labor needed was not always available, which would also explain its relative costliness.[130]

Appraisal.—A highly developed urban civilization, based on age-old local experience blended with foreign traditions, and expressed in orderly procedures, seems to emerge from an examination of the socioeconomic conditions of housing as revealed by the Geniza documents. There was a wide gap between the lowest and highest prices of houses and amounts of rents. But in both prices and rents the differences were gradual, as is to be expected in a well-integrated society not torn apart by extreme contrasts. To be sure, the Geniza has little to tell about the very rich. But they were far away. Their mansions were found not in Fustat but in the residential city of Cairo. They belonged to another world. The ordinary citizen did not expect to get as housing anything comparable to that enjoyed by the "great ones."[131]

Since the living quarters of the nuclear families belonging to an extended one were often united in one house—either originally planned so, or created by the process of inheritance—people were accustomed to a building sheltering a number of households. A natural development of this was the practice of selling or leasing parts of one's house to others and sharing it with strangers. Good neighborly, family-like relations could develop.[132] Whether buildings were originally constructed so as to serve as apartment houses is not evident with absolute certainty from the Geniza, although it is likely. Bazaar houses seem to have been intended for lease.

The communal accounts show that tenants often remained in their premises for a long time. There is no reason to assume that the matter was different in respect to private properties. Contracts of rent were normally concluded for one year. The same practice prevailed in business partnerships, but we know that these relationships were continued for years and sometimes transmitted from father to son. Popular wisdom, expressed in Aramaic and Arabic maxims, dissuaded frequent moving from one place to another. Even a rented apartment should become one's enduring home.[133]

4. Furnishings of the Home

The interior: The wife's domain.—The husband provided a home, the wife its furnishings. He took care of the shelter; she made it habitable and pleasant. It would not be farfetched to say that the colorful clothing and sparkling jewelry of the urban woman also formed part of the furnishings, for when she was out on the street she covered herself. So all the beautiful things she wore not only enhanced her own good looks but helped to beautify her home, attracting the attention of the women and children in the house and brightening the eyes of the husband and other male relatives and regular visitors.

Lists of trousseaus are the main source of our knowledge of the furnishings found in a house during the "classical" Geniza period (mainly through thirteenth centuries). In addition to her jewelry and clothing a bride brought in sitting and sleeping facilities, draperies, hangings, and decorative covers of furnishings, inlaid or plain chests and trunks (which served instead of modern cupboards and wardrobes), objects used for lighting, deodorizing, washing, and cleaning, and, of course, kitchen utensils, and sometimes tableware.

Each household was unique. No two outfits were identical. The dowry brought in was the outcome of negotiations carried on for months, if not years, between the two families. Since many, if not most, of the objects in a home were heirlooms, or gifts passed from the household of parents to that of their children, much depended on the circumstances. We find a well-to-do bride with no draperies at all—one of the more costly items of the trousseau; we can only guess the reason: perhaps the family into which she married had been one of merchants dealing in such articles. A very rich bride possessed only a scant selection of copper vessels; perhaps her future mother-in-law had a kitchen full of pots and pans and was happy to get rid of some of them. In view of the possibilities, only a comprehensive examination of all the Geniza trousseau lists is apt to supply a reliable and detailed picture of the interior of a house.

Here, however, we incur certain difficulties, partly discussed in *Med. Soc.*, III, 126–128. Under certain circumstances, the objects brought in by the wife had to be returned to her at the termination of the marriage. Consequently, they had to be of durable material. It excluded, for instance, china and other pottery, glass vessels, and mats, all of which were commonly used in daily life but occur only rarely in trousseau lists. Another difficulty inherent in this source of information, namely, the inflation of prices in honor of bride and groom and their families, is less formidable than it might appear. Many marriage contracts state expressly that the prices are real, "a dinar is worth a dinar"; it enables us to check the prices in other documents lacking that remark or written in places and times where it was customary to enter into the contract double or other multiple of the actual value.

All the prices listed in marriage contracts are approximate for they are mostly given in full dinars, which means in round sums, as compared with business correspondence, where, in accounts of hundreds of dinars, fractions of one twenty-fourth, one seventy-second, and even smaller are noted. For the purpose of this section, however, round sums provide sufficient information, since they show the approximate value of an object in relation to the total outfit in general and to the particular category to which it belongs (e.g., Bedding, Hangings, Copper).

Besides marriage contracts and cognate material (settlements after marital strife or lists of objects returned to a woman after the termination of her marriage), wills and, in particular, inventories of estates form an important source of information on our topic. They enable us to identify the male aspects of the interior, including such items as workbench and trade tools. Only a limited number of inventories, however, have been preserved and, as a rule, they note only objects of special value. A Rūmī (Byzantine) bedstead is listed in the inventory of the belongings of a scribe (probably from Byzantium), because bedsteads were not common in Egypt (see below, nn. 36–39). But other sleeping facilities, often very expensive and regularly included in trousseau lists, are rarely to be found in inventories of estates. In short, without the sources provided from the female side we would not have been able to form an idea of the look of the interior of a home in the Geniza society.

Of course, occasional references in business and family correspondence also contribute to our knowledge of the furnishings of a home. Much of that material has gone into the section "The Main Industries," *Med. Soc.*, I, 99–116. The reader may use that section to complement what follows.

The discussion of domestic architecture has shown that, unlike the *majlis*, the sitting, that is, living room or reception hall, the other rooms of the house are described in the Geniza documents according to their size and situation in the buildings or to the specific materials of which they were constructed, but not with regard to their function (such as dining room, bedroom, study, office). Depending on the seasons of the year and other circumstances, they could serve different purposes at different times and occasions. Consequently, in trying to describe the objects usually found in a house, one may succeed in identifying the functions they fulfilled, but, with obvious exceptions (majlis and kitchen), not be able to pinpoint their exact location.

The very process of identification is fraught with difficulties, and only the vastness of the Geniza material enables us to check and recheck a term until its meaning is established with certainty. The casual reader who takes a certain word to mean one thing may find on closer examination that it designates different objects; one term may reveal itself as having several meanings. *Ṣadr*, front, the word for the wall opposite the main entrance of a room and its most prestigious side, also designates the carpet that covers that wall or is spread out before it, and elsewhere something entirely different: a brass or copper tray to carry cups for use at meals. The *milʿaqa* is the tureen ladle, but the word also designated the tiny spoons of silver or gold used by the woman of the house to stir and mix her perfumes and makeup, as well as an ornament in the form of a spoon which served as a safety pin to keep the loose garment of a woman together, comparable to the Roman *fibula*.

Things being so, a discussion of some Arabic terms for household effects is unavoidable. I hope also that the linguistic and historic clarification will enable the object itself and its "seat in life" to be visualized. Students of Islamic art and archaeology may wish to use the descriptions provided in this section to identify objects now in museums or private collections.

Seating and bedding.—Chairs and tables, as we use these words, were unknown in the Geniza homes. During the tenth and the eleventh centuries, bedsteads are still mentioned, albeit sporadically, but that went entirely out of fashion later. The functions fulfilled by these pieces of furniture in our world were satisfied in those days and regions in other ways. By the Middle Ages the Mediterranean area had become scarce of good wood but was renowned for its manufacture of textiles. When the *martaba*, a kind of sofa, literally meaning step, was item number one in the list of furnishings brought in by a bride, the reference is not to the material of which the elevation on which one sat or slept was made (wood, wickerwork, bricks, mortar), but to the precious fabrics and their fillings with which it was covered and heightened. The furnishings spread on the ground were pile carpets or mattresses of varying heights. Whoever could afford it, even the poorest of the poor, tried to be comfortable while seated or reclining by using heaps of textiles.

The absence of chairs, tables, and beds should not be taken as an indication of a primitive state of material civilization. Everyone knows today that the ancient Egyptians possessed these pieces of furniture in the most refined shapes and embellished by costly veneers and inlays. The Bible reader is reminded of the "great" woman from the village of Shunem who suggested to her husband the construction of a small roof chamber for the Prophet Elisha, a frequent guest, and to "put there for him a bed, a table, a chair, and a lamp" (II Kings 4:10). Thus, what was regarded as prerequisite even for a casual visitor by a peasant woman in ancient Israel was next to absent from the houses of the thoroughly urbanized people of Geniza times. Not only the progressive depletion of the area of fine timber, but also a change in taste must have been responsible for this development. It was not primitiveness, but a different concept of what was desirable in the look of a home which accounted for the absence of heavy furniture. The spaciousness of the main hall, created by the builder, was enhanced by its relative emptiness.

The furnishings that served for nightly rest could be used for seating during the day. But the Geniza sources clearly indicate that, wherever possible, the two functions were kept apart. Every middle-class bride brought in one or, more frequently, several martabas, and at least one *firāsh*. Martaba means literally a place onto which one steps up. In numerous documents it is described as consisting of several pieces (two to six), *qiṭaʿ*, which should not be translated as cushions, for along with the qiṭaʿ cushions are regularly enumerated. Thus, the martaba consisted of sofa sections on which one sat and cushions and bolsters of different makes to enhance comfort. In many cases a *misnad* or *masnad*, support, also a piece of textile with a filling, served as a back or otherwise as a prop.[1]

In contrast, firāsh is derived from a root meaning spreading out, laying on the ground. It was a furnishing on which one rested in stretched-out position; nowhere does it consist of more than one piece; saying of a man that he was *fī firāshih(i)* meant that he was confined to bed.

A distinction was made between cushion and pillow. As with us, several terms and types were in use. But since the term most commonly mentioned in the Geniza was *mikhadda*, literally, a place on which to put the cheek (*khadd*), the specific idea of sleeping pillow was expressed by the strange but frequent phrase *mikhadda lil-khadd*, a cheek-pillow for the cheek, namely, during sleep. Arabic *al-mikhadda* became Spanish *almohada* in this double sense: *consultar con la almohada* means taking pillow counsel (sleeping on it), but *dar la almohada* is the ceremonial assignment of a seat of honor to the spouse of a Spanish grandee at her first reception by the Queen, which may be compared with the cushions accommodating the guests in an Arab living room. In at least six instances a bride possesses, in addition to a number of costly cushions, four less expensive cheek-pillows for the cheek, obviously one pair to be used by the spouses while the other pair was laundered.[2]

Similar to, but different from, the martaba was the *majlis*, or seat (the same word as that for the main room in the house, the sitting or living room).[3] All documents in which it occurs are dated or datable in the first half of the eleventh century. The majlis was made of Ṭabarī, a sumptuous heavy silk shot with gold threads originally manufactured in Ṭabaristān in northern Iran. It had once been a prerogative first of the Sassanian kings of Persia and then of the caliphal court of Baghdad, but later became popular all over the world, from India to the Muslim West and was imitated everywhere.[4] The majlis was an expensive furnishing; a new one is listed at 80 dinars, and another, consisting of two parts of imported and two others of locally manufactured Ṭabarī, was evaluated at 50 dinars. The majlis, like the martaba, occasionally had a support or back.[5]

People in modest circumstances had to be content with a *maṭraḥ*. This word, from which are derived English mattress and its Italian, French, and German equivalents, had a checkered history. In modern Arabic it has the general meaning of place, locality, seat (in a theater), but in classical Arabic it designated a furnishing similar to the martaba.[6] In the Geniza documents it forms part of the bedding (see below), but as its prices and use show, it must have been a mattress of good size and height so that in households with limited means it could replace the martaba. Like the firāsh it was always made of one piece. A bride in modest circumstances brought in one maṭraḥ and one firāsh, or two maṭraḥs, each accompanied by one or two pairs of cushions.[7]

Another kind of sofa, mentioned in the trousseau lists of middle-class or well-to-do brides along with martabas, and in those of poorer women instead of them, was the *ṭarrāha*, derived from the same root as maṭraḥ and meaning to throw or lay down. In the classical dictionaries it is described as "a square firāsh on which one sits," but the object referred to in the Geniza documents had to be oblong, since, like the martaba, it could consist of several sections (three to five).[8] Since the materials of which it was made were often the same as those of the martaba, but the prices far lower, it must have been shorter and flatter; it is often listed together with other items of bedding and, in better-off houses, probably served mainly as a bed, whereas poorer people had to use it also as a sofa. I translate ṭarrāḥa as daybed.

Returning to the main piece of furnishing of the living room, the martaba, it is noteworthy that at least three martabas or their substitutes (majlis, ṭarrāḥa) were brought in by middle-class brides, one piece outstripping all the others in quality and price. For instance, Abraham, the Son of the Scholar, a merchant banker, serving later also as judge, received at his marriage in January 1050 a martaba of Byzantine brocade, worth 30 dinars, and two others of Ṭabaristān silk, each worth half that price. Milāḥ, the Fairest of the Fair, an upper middle-class bride, brought in at her marriage in November 1059 a similar combination, the brocade martaba costing 40 dinars and the two local Ṭabarīs 10 each.[9] About a hundred years later, in October 1155, a lower middle-class bride had a martaba of Byzantine brocade worth 14 dinars, another of Dabīqī linen worth 5, and a third one of imitation Ṭabarī silk worth 3 dinars.[10] In between, around 1100, in a trousseau list mostly providing the prices of groups, not of the individual articles, the sitting facilities are headed again by a martaba of Byzantine brocade consisting of five parts, followed by two genuine Ṭabaristāns, and one green Ṭabarī manufactured in Ramle (Palestine).[11] Even a poor bride had three martabas, worth 5, 3, and 2 dinars, the first having four sections.[12] Prices of 40, 50, and even 60 dinars for the showpiece of the house, the main martaba, mostly made of (Byzantine) brocade, were not uncommon. A brocade martaba was the prerogative of a high government official.[13]

It is not difficult to understand why such arrangements were made. The best martaba, often comprising five or six sections, that is, a very long piece of furnishing, was placed against the wall opposite the main entrance of the living room which was regarded as its ṣadr, or prestigious front.[14] That martaba formed a kind of dais for the leading members of the family and honored guests. It had to be long, for unexpected VIPs had to be accommodated there. Most likely it was also higher than the other martabas, for the marked differences in price prove that much more material went into it.

Concerning the divans placed on the side walls, two contrasting tastes seem to have existed side by side. In the documents of 1050, 1059, and ca. 1100 discussed above, and others, "two Ṭabaristāns" are noted. A well-to-do Karaite bride, married in the fall of 1117, brought in a five-piece Ṭabaristān costing 40 dinars together with two ṭarrāḥas valued together at 15 dinars. A similar distribution, a five-piece brocade martaba valued at 20 dinars with two Ṭabarī maṭraḥs costing a total of 5 dinars, appear in a lower middle-class ketubba of 1125, and one martaba for 40 dinars and two ṭarrāḥas, each worth 15 dinars, are recorded in summer 1156.[15] The arrangement of the main divan flanked by two counter pieces corresponds to the predilection for pairs and the sense of symmetry characteristic of a taste revealed by Islamic art. The same applies to other furnishings of the home, as is noted subsequently. In the list of 1155 and often elsewhere, however, each of the martabas is made of different material, such as Byzantine brocade, Iranian silk, or its imitations, or Egyptian linen, or others, and, wherever noted, also of widely differing colors. Individual taste or specific circumstances must have been at work in these matters rather than a marked development in the style of the interior, for the relevant Geniza data of the eleventh and twelfth centuries, that is, the Fatimid and early Ayyubid periods, in general display a remarkable degree of continuity and uniformity.

A complete change occurred in the thirteenth century, especially the beginning of the Mamluk period, its second part. The wife no longer provided the living room equipment, and her contribution even for the bedding proper was so scanty as to be symbolic. This change was not confined to the poorer sections of the population but is discernible also in the trousseau lists of well-to-do brides.[16] The rising, but still modest, importance of the economic role of the wife in the Late Middle Ages, discussed in *Med. Soc.*, III, 132–135, was hardly responsible for this development. A change of attitude must have occurred. Sometime in the course of the thirteenth century it must have become customary for the husband to have the obligation to provide sitting and sleeping facilities, the main furnishings of a home. But this change, in the main, lies outside the classical Geniza period.

Next to the divans and sofas, and perhaps even more so, it was the colorful cushions and bolsters that enlivened the interior of a home.

They occupy more space in the seating and bedding section of the trousseau lists than any other single item. There were different types. Many came with a martaba or its alternative, that is, they were included in the price of the main price and probably were of the same fabric and color. For instance, a bride brings in "a blue Dabīqī martaba with its cushions and a pomegranate-colored martaba with its cushions,"[17] another "a Ṭabaristān daybed, ṭarrāha, with its cushions, costing 10 dinars,"[18] a third, "a silken martaba with its support [back] and cushions, worth 10 dinars,"[19] a fourth, "a borax-colored martaba with its cushions,"[20] and so forth. In these instances and in numerous others like them the number of cushions is not specified. An ancient Karaite marriage contract states expressly when martabas are not accompanied by cushions. Conversely, a husband's receipt of the outfit of his wife lists a martaba with the cushion(s) especially made for it.[21]

Most of the cushions are listed separately, though, and are usually described by color, material, or specific embellishment. This group is discussed next. The "pillows for the cheek," that is, for sleep, are characterized as such and are listed with their numbers but without any further details.

I have always been puzzled by the prominence of cushions in the outfits of a bride. They were, of course, an intrinsic part of the seating and sleeping facilities, but their full function was revealed to me when I came upon a passage in Abu 'l-Qāsim's *Ḥikāya*, a delightful eleventh-century satire on the society of the time. He writes that a house full of cushions looks like a ground covered with flowers. One type of cushion in the Geniza is indeed called "garden pillow." The ardent desire for color of a population living in a mostly gray-brown landscape could find easiest satisfaction in the interior of a home through numerous pieces of furnishings of limited size but most diversified looks. Compare with this the look of a modern living room as presented in the *Architectural Digest: The International Magazine for Fine Interior Design*, September 1978. The photo shows a large window, and, beneath it, a mighty sofa consisting of three sections, and covered with six sizable cushions, all in the same discreet and subdued pale beige. As the accompanying article explains, the emphasis is on the panorama, on the outside. The proliferation of cushions in modern living rooms is described in the same article as influenced by Near Eastern taste.[22]

Abu 'l-Qāsim's *Ḥikāya* enlightens us also on another aspect of those ubiquitous objects. I had always assumed that the relevant items noted in trousseau lists referred to the pillow *cases*. When one reads, however, in an ancient marriage contract describing the exhibition of a bride's outfit, "two crates, and on top of them fifteen silken cushions—100 dinars; two chests, and on top of them eighteen cushions—20 dinars," it is evident that these were complete cushions with their fillings. One does not need two crates for storing fifteen silk pillow slips.[23] Details in the *Ḥikāya* prove that the type of filling could contribute much to the value of a pillow.[24]

Wherever colors are noted—and there is a fantastic range of them—each piece, without exception, has only one color.[25] It seems strange, for they loved to wear contrasting colors, and the same tendency is discernible in hangings. Of course, many cushions are embellished: borders, probably of different material, noted especially for cushions of Egyptian linen, whether of the Dabīqī or the Tinnīsī type;[26] badges with inscriptions;[27] ornamental stripes;[28] fringes or tassels;[29] pieces in different colors (on fine Tinnīsī linen), if my translation of the frequent term *mulawwan* is correct;[30] gold threads or gilded borders (on pomegranate-colored Tinnīsī);[31] figures of birds. (Textiles with figures of animals, such as elephants, lions, or horses, are mentioned in Arabic literature and have actually been preserved. The Geniza people had hangings decorated with lions, but preferred to sleep on pillows with birds, probably doves.)[32]

Yet it is hard to believe that the cushions, so carefully noted in the trousseau lists together with their prices, were all pieces of one color. These lists were legal documents; the clerks intended not to describe the objects but to identify them; for this purpose it was sufficient to note the dominant color and, if necessary, also the material and an additional embellishment. For the same reason the trousseau lists do not indicate the shape. Quadrangular, oblong pieces probably were the norm. Round and long cushions are mentioned in a letter because the writer was specifically interested in them. This letter and other Geniza papers defining cushions as round were written around 1200 and slightly later.[33] The *miswara*, mentioned in earlier documents alongside mikhadda, the regular term, and the "support" (for the back), probably was of that description; it is also found in an Arabic literary source.[34] The idiosyncrasies of clerks writing the marriage contracts were no doubt responsible for another puzzle, namely, that important trousseau lists, especially of the eleventh century, never identify cushions by color.[35]

Bedsteads, *sarīr*, as the Geniza clearly shows, must still have been widely used during the tenth century, but they went out of fashion in the course of the eleventh. In ancient ketubbas, or marriage contracts, brides in modest circumstances occasionally brought in bedsteads of ebony wood, *sa'sam*, that precious dark hardwood which was imported from India and other warm countries and had been used for the same purpose in antiquity.[36] We are justified in assuming that such a costly piece of furniture was acquired when the families had seen better days and was a much used and wornout heirloom given to the bride. In an early Karaite ketubba a sarīr cost 10 dinars, in another, together with two chests, the same price, and in a similar document from Yemen even less.[37] But a bedstead inlaid with ivory (as was customary in ancient Egypt, Israel, and Rome) and equipped with a mattress of Tinnīsī linen cost 50 dinars, approximately one-tenth the value of the entire dowry presented to a bride in 1059. Another bedstead inlaid with ivory heads the list of sleeping furnishings in a ketubba of 1039.[38] When a copyist (one of the worst-paid occupations) possessed a Byzantine bedstead, it is likely that it was a heirloom, he brought from his native country.[39] I do not remember having seen a bedstead listed in a document from the last third of the eleventh century or later.

A "tripartite sleeping bench," *dakka* (or *dikka*), worth 10 dinars is noted in a fragmentary trousseau list. Since dakka also designates a cupboard for keeping the kitchen copper or a druggist's containers, three chests of equal size over which a mattress was laid must be intended here.[40] The bedding outfit of a rich bride is headed by a dakka of teak, a precious Indian timber (used also as building material), accompanied by two mattresses of "triple-thread" (see n. 44) and two others of Sicilian material)—a common combination—and cost, together with two items lost, 100 dinars.[41] Another bride (of the eleventh century, like the two preceding ones) had a white Tinnīsī linen dakka with two mattresses.[42] All this shows that in those early days one or several chests long enough to serve as bench and bed were occasionally brought in by a bride, of course, together with other sleeping equipment.[43]

The disappearance of bedsteads in the later part of the eleventh century should not be taken to mean that bedding was simple. It was, in fact, elaborate, and it is not easy to find one's way through the mass of information on it in the Geniza.

The basic sleeping equipment was the firāsh. The usual translation as mattress is misleading since it was often made of costly material: Sicilian or Spanish silk (the former being the fabric most frequently mentioned in the ketubbas of the eleventh century), Dabīqī linen, or *muthallath*, "triple-thread" fabric, or twill, an article of export from Egypt.[44] Two Sicilian firāshes and a Ṭabarī pad laid over them cost 10 dinars in 1050.[45] Slightly earlier, a pair of Sicilian and another one of Dabīqī stuff, together with a pad, were evaluated at 15 dinars.[46] Yemenite firāshes and other Yemenite bedding equipment begin to appear in the twelfth century, an indication that the Islamic (and Jewish) international trade had swung from the Mediterranean to the India route.[47]

Often, a maṭraḥ, usually translated as mattress, or a tarrāḥa, a daybed, substituted for a firāsh. By far the majority of maṭraḥs were made of locally manufactured Ṭabarī, the popular fabric.[48] Its standard price, mostly including two pillows, fluctuated between 4 and 5 dinars. But a modest maṭraḥ with its pillows could be had for 1 dinar, as could a firāsh of similar quality.[49] A white Dabīqī maṭraḥ with two blue pillows was priced at 12 dinars, but was probably worth only half that amount.[50] Since in carefully executed marriage contracts brides brought in both a maṭraḥ and a firāsh, in which cases the former was more costly than the latter, the two words should not be taken as different terms for the same object. The different materials also tell a story: I have not yet come across a firāsh made of Ṭabarī, nor a maṭrah made of Sicilian silk. There is little doubt that these furnishing differed also in shape.[51]

The ṭarrāḥa, or daybed, came somewhere between the martaba sofa and the maṭraḥ mattress. Like the latter, it if often noted together with sleeping equipment, but like the former it could consist of several sections and was mostly made of precious fabrics, genuine Ṭabaristān and brocades of different provenance leading the list. Fine reeds and leather were also among the materials of which a ṭarrāḥa was made and might have been used for it exclusively. Since the ṭarrāḥa is listed with the other types of seating and bedding, martaba, maṭraḥ, and firāsh, it must have had a distinctive appearance differentiating it from them.[52]

Over the bed mattress was laid a pad, called *bardaʿa,* mostly made of Ṭabarī; in well-to-do households the bardaʿa could be of brocade or fine linen. The word bardaʿa commonly designates the pad beneath the pack saddle on the back of a donkey, which, up to the present day, is woven in gay colors. A similar arrangement, a pad with decorative borders visible above the mattress and bedstead, seems to have been used by the ancient Greeks.[53]

The covers for nightly rest were as variegated as the beds. Our sources clearly distinguish among six types, one, the *liḥāf,* serving exclusively as blanket, the others used also for other purposes. The liḥāf never appears in pairs, although pairs of beds (firāsh) were very common in the trousseau lists.[54] A wealthy bride marrying in the year 995 had three beds but only one liḥāf.[55] Besides its natural function of keeping the body warm during sleep, the single liḥāf brought in by a bride probably had a ceremonial connotation. During the day it was not displayed, and must certainly have been stored in a closet or trunk. At night it covered the conjugal bed. This would explain its sumptuousness, suggestive of the bridal canopy, as well as the regular listing of other covers in the marriage contracts. A variety of precious fabrics—Byzantine and Maghrebi brocade and siglaton damask being the most favored ones—went into their manufacture. In the middle of the twelfth century a new material, exclusively connected with the liḥāf, makes its appearance. It was named Saqlābī, Slav, probably after an official in charge of the caliphal wardrobe. ("Basil" served in this capacity in 1141, see *Med. Soc.*, I, 147.) Slav slaves were the confidants of the Fatimid caliphs. The general who conquered Egypt for them was a Slav. Naming a textile after a caliph or a high official was not unusual. What is interesting is that the Saqlābī was used, as far as I can see, solely for the liḥāf, another indication of the special significance of this furnishing.[56]

Four types of nightly covers that served as outer garments during the day are discussed in subsection B, below. Here it is necessary to emphasize that in many trousseau lists each of these pieces of clothing is described as "for sleep." I take it to mean, then, that the *ridā*, coat, *mulā'a*, cloak, *malḥafa*, wrap, or *īzār*, mantle had the form of the garment worn during the day but was destined to serve exclusively as cover during the night. When any of these four garments is listed under bedding, and not under clothing, it stands to reason that it served nightly rest, even where it is not labeled "for sleep." In many Greek, Roman, and medieval illustrations persons appear lying on their beds in clothing identical with or similar to that worn on the street. It means not necessarily that they did not change but that the night cover was not, or not much, different in make from regular clothing. One contribution of the Geniza papers to the history of wearing apparel is beyond doubt: of those medieval people whoever had the means changed for the night. A poor scholar from Jerusalem complains: "My cover for night, day, and Sabbath is all the same." It was normal for the three to be different.[57]

One high-priced item of sleeping equipment frequently noted in the Geniza eluded me for a long time: the *muzarra*, the buttoned one, known from literary sources as a bag held together by clamps fastened to buttons (buttonholes had not yet been invented).[58] Only when I encountered this passage in a legal declaration of a mother, "the sleeping equipment of my daughter consists of a muzarra, a pad, a mattress, and two cushions," did it become clear beyond doubt that this precious article represented a kind of dressing gown, which was used also as a cover for nightly rest.[59] Should it designate a sleeping bag? Such a contrivance is known to me from contemporary Yemen and also from a medieval illustration, although one far from the Genzia scene (it is found in the prayer book of the German emperor Henry II, before 1014), where a man sleeps on a mattress, entirely enveloped in what seems to be a bag covering his head and fastened with a clamp.[60] In Europe that cover might have represented a garment with a hood worn also in the daytime; in the Geniza it is always listed with bedding, and as made of brocade or heavy silk fabric. It served perhaps as cover during winter. In Egypt the Geniza people often complain about cold, never about heat.[61]

The bedding outfit was completed by an awning, called *killa,* as in Aramaic and Hebrew before. The word has the double meaning of mosquito net and canopy. Mosquito nets were in common use in pre-Islamic and Islamic times and the word has retained this meaning up to the present day in both Arabic and Hebrew.[62] The killa as decorative canopy, however, as common as it was in the outfits of well-to-do brides during the eleventh century, completely disappears from the trousseau lists of the twelfth. In the two cases in which I noted a similar furnishing, one from the year 1143 and another from approximately the same time (at "the rich bride"), two different terms were used, which shows that the decorative canopy had become entirely exceptional. Like the pre-Islamic bedstead the canopy had gone out of fashion.[63]

The canopy was mostly made of *sharb,* or fine linen, emerald and other shades of green being the preferred colors, followed by white, sky blue, pomegranate, blue, yellow, and red. In three cases a sharb canopy cost 50 dinars. In one of them, it is described as being plain, without patterns, *muṣmat,* from which one may conclude that the killa cloth was normally decorated with geometrical, floral, or other designs.[64] Canopies were repeatedly imported to Egypt from Tunisia, among them a blue one described as *qābisiyya,* manufactured in Gabes.[65] One wonders whether Tunisia, which was more thoroughly romanized than Egypt, retained that Roman luxury longer than the country of the Nile. However, in the trousseau list of a Jewish bride from Palermo, Sicily, from the year 1479 (still written in Arabic), a canopy headed the list. The editor remarks that every Sicilian bride of that time got one. In this matter, East and West had parted company.[66]

Draperies, carpets, mats, and hides.—Sofas and cushions imparted to the interior of a house its characteristic appearance. So did curtains and hangings.

Curtains, *sutūr* (sing. *sitr,* literally, cover), formed so profuse and costly an item in the outfits even of middle-class brides that one wonders what purposes they served. They did not cover the windows as our curtains usually do. The windows were protected from the sun and the eyes of neighbors or riders on the street by screens made of cheap wood or similar light material. Window curtains, especially when made of the heavy goods mentioned in the Geniza for curtains, would have been utterly impractical. They would have robbed the rooms of ventilation, so vital in a hot country.

Descriptions of houses, preserved in the Geniza and translated above, pp. 79–81, always emphasized it when a room had a door and specified the type. We may therefore conclude that many rooms did not have doors. Only when the main room of an apartment lacked this equipment is it expressly stated.[67] It is safe to assume, then, that curtains often replaced doors, serving as portieres. They were common among the Greeks and Romans, as proved by such archaeological evidence as the many bronze rings for curtains found during the excavations at the Agora of Athens and other sites, as well as by frequent references in literature ("they have curtains at the entries to their bedchambers"), and reliefs portraying that usage.[68]

Illustrations in Arabic books provide similar information. As described above, the majlis, or main room of a house, often opened into two accessory rooms.[69] One painting shows such openings covered with two pairs of curtains. Another painting shows only one curtain on each entrance, each matching the other.[70]

The recesses in walls which served as cupboards or bookcases are listed sometimes as having doors and sometimes as having none.[71] Roman bookcases were protected by doors, but occasionally also by a curtain.[72] The Holy Ark containing the Tora scrolls was covered with a single green curtain in the Synagogue of the Iraqians in 1080, and with a pair of curtains in that of the Palestinians in 1075.[73] That ceremonial object had a specific function, comparable with the curtain at the entrance to the Holiest of the Holy in the Temple of Jerusalem and later in front of the altar in Byzantine and Coptic churches.

The late Veronika Gervers, in "An Early Christian Curtain in the Royal Ontario Museum," discussed in detail the function and historical development of curtains in early medieval synagogues and churches, as well as in Muslim palaces.[74]

I do not remember seeing an Arab illustration of a bookcase with a curtain but suspect they had some. In the beautiful picture of a library from an al-Ḥarīrī manuscript preserved in the Bibliothèque Nationale, Paris, one sees an open bookcase without doors, but crowned on each side with decorative spandrels, behind which, in other illustrations, curtains were suspended.[75] Arabic literary sources seem to imply, however, that bookcases, even in private homes, had doors which could be locked and which occasionally bore eloquent inscriptions encouraging the visitors to make good use of the treasures they concealed. The Geniza has preserved such an inscription, executed in huge Hebrew letters, certainly destined to be engraved in wood—if not to be embroidered on a curtain.[76]

Curtains fulfilled a great variety of other functions in the medieval Mediterranean–Near Eastern home. We cover our walls with durable paperhangings, they decorated them with carpetlike textiles, which could be exchanged from time to time, especially on festive occasions. Moreover, curtains were hung up across a room to be used as a divider for privacy, or, when not needed for this purpose, to be pulled up to leave the room as spacious as its measurements permitted. When entering the large reception hall or living room, one faced a curtain. The master of the house and his company were seated behind the curtain against the wall farthest from the entrance door. Then the curtain was drawn, and the scene was ready for a petition to be submitted to a governor, a case to be brought before a cadi, or simply a reception, followed by a festive meal. The illustrators of Arabic books have left us pictures of such scenes, always carefully depicting the curtain, either pulled up to the ceiling and knotted, or drawn aside and floating in the draft caused by cross ventilation. In the house of Maimonides the usher was termed "keeper of the curtain."[77]

Arabic literature is replete with stories about the use of curtains as decoration, perhaps the most famous being the description of the reception of a Byzantine embassy at the caliphal court of Baghdad in 917. The palace was bedecked with 38,000 curtains and wall covers, some ornamented with the figures of horses, elephants, and lions, others with gorgeous Arabic script; still others were imported from China, Armenia, or Egypt; and the rest were old pieces taken from the storehouses of the caliph's six predecessors. The number was probably exaggerated, but the many details furnished by the narrators, on this and other occasions, drive home the decisive role of the curtain for interior decoration.[78]

Against this background the data of the Geniza become meaningful. Curtains appear in the trousseau lists mostly in pairs, but often also as single pieces (expressly designated as such: *fard*), and, where details are supplied, the latter are more costly and longer than the former. In a list from the year 1028 a bride had a pair made of Maghrebi brocade costing 20 dinars, a single one of Dabīqī linen with Tustarī bands worth 15 dinars, and two pairs of Bahnasī make totaling 25 dinars.[79] Around 1075 or so Nahray b. Nissim ordered (probably for the wedding of his daughter, mentioned in his correspondence) two curtains of "good" Bahnasī, seven cubits long, and one of the same material, but of "high quality" and of a length of nine or ten cubits.[80] Of particular interest is the trousseau of a wealthy Karaite bride from the year 1117. She had eight "fresh" (which I take to mean new) Bahnasī curtains, costing a total of 40 dinars, a single curtain, the description of which is lost, a chameleon-colored single worth 6 dinars, and a Wāsiṭī (see below) of 8 dinars, described as *ṣadr*, or central piece, that decorating the wall opposite the main entrance or serving as a divider in front of it.[81] The daughter of the India trader who became engaged in December 1146, had a brocade ṣadr with two "sidepieces," totaling 30 dinars (and this in a list where "every dinar" was "worth a dinar").[82] Ten years later, the two sidepieces appear again in the draft of a marriage contract written by Mevōrākh b. Nathan, and together with the ṣadr, in a list written by the same scribe.[83] When a bride has three curtains or one or two pairs plus one single, as found in eleventh-century ketubbas, probably the same arrangement was intended.[84] This combination of one central and two sidepieces will be encountered again in the study of carpets.

The most popular fabric for curtains, evident from the Geniza, was the Bahnasī, so called after al-Bahnasā, a town about 200 kilometers south of Cairo and once the capital of a flax-growing district (see *Med. Soc.*, I, 456). Al-Bahnasā was renowned for its textile industry, which was not confined to the manufacture of linen cloth. In the exceptional instance that I have found in the Geniza in which a Bahnasī is defined by its material, it was made of wool.[85] (The Islamic Museum of Cairo possesses a multicolored piece of wool showing a human head surrounded by little hares [not: hairs!] and bearing the inscription: Al-Bahnasā.[86]) One bride had two pairs of Bahnasī, each six cubits long and ornamented with figures of lions.[87] Al-Bahnasā was famous for its tapestry. No wonder, then, that as early as 956 a Jewish bride in faraway Damascus possessed a valuable pair of Bahnasī curtains.[88]

Maghrebi brocade and silk, or silk without a description of its provenance, made up the second largest and most valuable group of materials for curtains. In documents from 1028 and 1030, a pair of Maghrebi brocade curtains cost 20 dinars, the highest price recorded.[89] The inventory of an estate drawn up on order of Moses Maimonides in April 1172 notes three used curtains of Maghrebi brocade, each approximately five and a half cubits long and three cubits broad, and having blue ornamental bands lined with white (the curtains themselves might have been red, as noted elsewhere for Maghrebi silk).[90] Where given at all, measurements were included in inventories or orders but not in trousseau lists. An eleventh-century merchant from al-Mahdiyya, Tunisia, orders in Egypt curtains ten or less spans wide and fifteen or less long. The size of these pieces and the relation between their breadth and length were approximately the same as those of the curtains listed in the inventory just mentioned.[91]

Fine Dabīqī linen and the heavy damask internationally known as siglaton were third and fourth in frequency—but not in price—as materials, for curtains. Pairs of siglatons and Dabīqīs are noted as worth 15 dinars, and once a pair of siglatons together with a single Dabīqī cost 25 dinars. The popular Bahnasī could be had for 5 dinars per pair and less. Woolen curtains were rare.[92]

In Karaite documents brides bring in single curtains made of costly materials named after two cities in souther Iraq, Wāsiṭ and Qurqūb. The rich Karaites were mostly immigrants from Iran and Iraq. No wonder that they cherished fabrics known to them from their native countries which were used to adorn the palaces of the caliphs. "Kingly" curtains, Khusrawānī (from Khusraw, the Arabic name for the kings of Persia), adorned the houses of wealthy people. I do not believe that the term simply means sumptuous, for, if it did, it would not have been used in a long list specifying the types of gifts presented to a Byzantine emperor nor would it have been mentioned in a Geniza marriage contract along with other curtains made of siglaton and Bahnasī. The Khusrawānī probably was a piece embroidered with medallions of crowned heads, like the one in a story about the patricidal caliph al-Muntaṣir. One night his throne happened to be put on such a carpet between the medallions of two rulers who, like him, had murdered their fathers and were punished with premature death. That ominous portent soon came true.[93]

A person praying at home stood facing a wall so that the mind should not be distracted by any objects. But what should one do when the wall itself was *manqūsh*, covered with stucco work, or beautified with curtains replete with figures? When asked this question, Moses Maimonides replied that it was indeed a nuisance, since figures certainly were apt to attract the prayer's attention. The use of decorative hangings was so widespread, however, that the master did not attempt to discourage it. He advised the questioner to do what he himself did: to close his eyes while praying.[94]

The wall paintings with motifs from Greek mythology in the private homes of Pompei, the biblical stories illuminating the synagogue of Dura-Europos, and the Coptic tapestries so richly represented in our museums are by now so familiar to lovers of art that the covering of walls with artistic hangings in medieval Mediterranean and Near Eastern homes must appear to everyone as the continuation of an ancient tradition. With regard to the religious scenes once filling the walls of the Romanesque churches of the West, a competent observer has aptly remarked that they formed part of the very architecture of the building by conveying its function to the spectator. In the Geniza, other than some reference to animal figures, no details are provided concerning the illustrative elements of wall hangings. As known from contemporary Islamic tapestry preserved, the figures must have been purely decorative, satisfying the craving for beauty and, one should perhaps add, sumptuousness, but not for religious indoctrination.[95]

Since draperies served largely as interior decoration of a home, it is not surprising to find that people tried to borrow some for special occasions. The note translated below betrays in its humorous vein, enhanced by highfalutin Hebrew phrases (italicized), the mood of the revelry for which the draperies were requested.

> "*All those who know* my lady, *the righteous and most excellent dowager, and take refuge under the shadow of her wings* say that she lends out hangings or curtains, in so far as they are available and easy to spare, so that people can decorate their homes with them. May I ask you kindly to grant me this favor? If, however, for any reason you cannot do it this time, please let me know. *And Peace. May the well being of your excellency increase steadily.*
>
> If the elder Abu 'l-Maḥāsin—*may his Creator preserve him*—has arrived, let him show me his face. *And Peace.*"

The postscript is an invitation to a relative of the "dowager."[96] One may wonder why the bride was supposed to supply the draperies. The reason, I assume, is that the curtains were originally part of the bedding outfit. They were to serve as dividers of a room shared by husband and wife in common, providing privacy for her. This explains why wealthy brides and others rich in bedding furnishings often bring in only one pair of curtains.[97] In a carefully written list from the provincial town of Malīj, a poor bride has besides the four traditional pillows only a pair of curtains "for the arch," meaning hung up as a divider (and not as a wall cover). It obviously was regarded as a basic necessity. But, as often happens, the original custom of the bride bringing in curtains for the purpose of privacy was expanded in the course of time to include all their other uses.[98]

The Geniza has preserved placards in superb Hebrew script of large size containing verses from the Bible. Since the materials on which they were written are not of durable quality, and there are no holes for hanging them up, these placards obviously served as models for an embroidery on a wall hanging or an inscription to be carved in wood. The texts express trust in God, prayers for guidance and forgiveness, blessings, and messianic expectations.[99] One placard is decorated with floral designs. Tuliplike patterns, alternating in direction (top up, top down, turning right, turning left) and colors (black, red) are placed between two lines of Hebrew script. The text reads: "Blessed shall you be when you arrive, and blessed when you leave" (Deuteronomy 28:6). This placard was not written by hand; it was a medieval print, which could be bought in the bazaar, to be placed or pasted on an appropriate spot when dear guests were expected.[100]

Carpets, with rare exceptions, were not part of the bridal outfit. Details about them occur occasionally in private or business correspondence. But Jews did not participate in the wholesale trade of this commodity, which was probably monopolized by merchants from nations that manufactured carpets, such as Persians or Armenians. No Jewish *anmāṭī*, or carpet dealer, has turned up thus far.[101] The largest quantity of carpets ordered in a Geniza letter seen by me was six pairs.[102] Jewish craftsmen occasionally entered into a partnership for work in the Carpet House of Fustat, and a Jewish *kātib*, or government official, who must have been well-to-do, was employed there.[103] But dealings in carpets were definitely a sideline, and a very minor one at that. Yet the spare information on the subject contained in the Geniza is not without interest.

There was no absolute dividing line between carpets, bedding, and hangings. When a poor bride who married in Tyre, Lebanon, in 1054, had a cover, a carpet (*ṭunfusa*), and seven Ṭabari pillows, worth a total of 3 1/2 dinars, the ṭunfusa served as her bedding.[104] A furnishing with the same name and certainly serving the same purpose is listed as worth 1 dinar in the marriage contract of another poor woman from the same century.[105] The terms probably described a pile carpet of small dimensions, as borne out by repeated references in Arabic literature to one person sitting on a ṭunfusa, or by a Geniza story of a wife pilfering one (together with other easily movable objects) from her husband's house, or by another of a woman giving one to a pawnbroker together with a gold ring against a loan of only 3 dinars.[106] When the estate of a coppersmith included three old ṭunfusas and that of a foreigner, two, described as prayer carpets, it is likely that the pieces concerned were of modest size.[107] A ṭunfusa could serve as a wall hanging. According to a report about the treasures of the viceroy al-Malik al-Afḍal, murdered in 1121, "four thousand carpets and wall covers in the style of ṭunfusas" were removed from his house. Less affluent people might have used a ṭunfusa alternately for seating, bedding, and hanging, as the occasion demanded. They did not walk on carpets with their shoes on.[108]

A business letter sent from Aden, South Arabia, to India around 1140 describes a ṭunfusa as decorated with the signs of the zodiac circle. The zodiac was a favorite ornament of the mosaic floors of Byzantine churches and of synagogues contemporary with them, and decorates the bottom of a copper basin encrusted with silver made for a ruler of Yemen in 1295. The casual way in which the item is mentioned in that letter seems to show that a carpet with a zodiac medallion in its center must not have been extraordinary in those days.[109]

The flexibility of terms for what we call carpet reflects the variety of uses for the same textile. This is beautifully illustrated by comparing two inventories of the synagogues of the Palestinians and Iraqians in Fustat from the years 1159 and 1201 with two others from the eleventh century. In the later documents a section is devoted to the *anmāṭ*, the term from which anmāṭī, carpet dealer, is derived. The passage in the 1159 inventory says: "The anmāṭ for the two synagogues: Three for the Tora scrolls, decorated with gold threads 'mixed' with niello; one smaller one, of the same type, for the scroll of the readings from the Prophets; two red ones 'mixed' with gold threads; twenty-two namaṭs made of brocade and siglaton; one for rotation;[110] and nine others, partly old and partly worn-out; a piece of cotton woven with cotton, twenty cubits long."[111]

The twenty-two namaṭs were the carpets covering the floor of the synagogues, as proved by comparison with an inventory from the year 1075, where mats of different descriptions do the same service (see below). The two red namaṭs decorated with gold threads formed the hangings on the holy arks in the two synagogues, described as "curtains" in the eleventh-century documents.[112] Finally, the namaṭs for the Tora scrolls (not "worn" by them, as is customary today, but put over them as a cover when they were taken out of the ark) were artistically decorated but otherwise of the same material (brocade or siglaton) as the floor carpets and were therefore called by the same name.

The inventory from which the translated passage is taken was written in 1159, when a new beadle took over. We may assume that it was made also because some or many of the possessions of the synagogues had been lost during the terrible period of internecine wars and anarchy experienced by Egypt in the 1150s.[113] The assumption is even safer with regard to the list of the anmāṭ found in the two synagogues in October 1201. A low Nile caused famine, followed by epidemics and a complete breakdown of the public order.[114] It is possible that the inventory, of which only the part on the anmāṭ is completely preserved, was compiled before everything was hidden away in a safe place.

The list has some interest for our purpose. Each textile is called namaṭ and is defined by its dominant color (red, three times, orange, twice, wine-colored, yellow, black, and so on) or by its make, *ʿattābī*, tabby, listed five times. Six of the twenty-four pieces were decorated with gold threads or "mixed" (gold and other threads), which means that they served as covers or hangings. Of the namaṭs covering the floor one is described as "made in the House," namely, the Carpet House of Fustat, that is, locally manufactured, and not imported as most others, and another as "a physician's carpet," *namaṭ ṭabībī*.[115]

What a doctor's carpet looked like may be inferred from the estate of a physician which comprised three large pieces, one "a middle piece" (see below), white with blue borders, twenty-two cubits long, and two others, one of red silk, twenty-seven cubits long, and another, a red one, eighteen cubits long. A successful physician had to seat many visitors (as both Maimonides and Judah ha-Levi, the Spanish Hebrew poet, who were physicians, emphasize in their letters), and silk was perhaps favored because it could be cleaned more easily than other textiles.[116]

The description of the distribution of martabas and sutūr, the seating facilities in the living room, and the hangings on its walls has shown that the wall opposite the main entrance took pride of place, while the side walls were less prestigious.[117] Ernst Herzfeld's reconstruction of the arrangement of carpets in the audience hall of the Sassanian kings and later the Abbasid caliphs shows a similar pattern, imitated, as the Geniza finds suggest, in private homes. Under or in front of the seat of the ruler a large "front" or middle piece, sometimes called ṣadr, was spread out, bordered on its right and left side (as seen from the entrance) by two runners, mostly referred to as *muṣallā*, prayer carpet. The prayer carpet, as Herzfeld explains, originally showed a long row of praying men, represented by the arches of the prayer niches. After a reception at the caliph's court, muṣallās were cut into pieces, each showing a single prayer niche, which were distributed to particularly honored guests. A single piece became the Muslim prayer carpet, as it is known up to the present day.[118]

Prayer carpets were ordered, and, in one case, even preserved in an estate, in pairs, which reflects their role as runners alongside the borders of a larger carpet.[119] In both an order and an inventory, prayer carpets appear together with runners: "Two fine runners, newly made, each twenty-four cubits long; four fine white prayer carpets; two dark blue; two green; and two red ones."[120] "A Spanish runner, curtailed, a small runner, a prayer carpet, and a piece of a runner."[121] The runners, like the caliphal prayer carpets, must have been patterned in such a way that they lent themselves easily to parceling.

I take the textile ṣadr to be the cover of the wall opposite the entrance hall because one trousseau list refers to it expressly as ṣadr hangings. But since there was no strict distinction between floor and wall covers, the term might also have been used in the Geniza documents, as in earlier Arabic literature, for the central carpet, called "middle piece" in the estate of the physician mentioned earlier. The same holds true for the *mijnab*, or side piece, which, in literary sources, fulfills the same function as prayer carpets and runners.[122]

The carpet arrangement of a room was completed by an *ʿataba*, literally, doorsill, threshold, but not to be translated as doormat. It was a longish, but small, piece laid between the entrance door and the central carpet to protect the edge of the carpet, or was laid anywhere between carpets for the same purpose, as was the "bridge" in central Europe. The word was also used for mats having that purpose.[123]

The general terms for carpeting a room were derived from the roots that designated seating and bedding: *farsh*, which is a collective, and *busuṭ*, the plural of *bisāṭ*, rug. One would praise a synagogue for the beauty of its carpeting, farsh.[124] An account lists the carpeting of the two aisles of the women's gallery as *farshayn*.[125] A letter from Alexandria accuses a dignitary of having appropriated the books and busuṭ of a synagogue.[126] The singular, bisāṭ, however, is not very common in the Geniza writings, but it does occur, together with some other terms and types still in use today. "Of the carpets you have, send me the red Armenian rug, *bisāṭ*, and the *zarbiyya*, which is new."[127] A Spanish rug, costing 33 quarter dinars, was sent around 1050 to Egypt along with three, manufactured in Demona, Sicily.[128] In an ancient trousseau list a Karaite bride had a brocade martaba with a brocade rug of red and amber color (or perhaps: one red and one amber), which might have served as cover.[129] The bisāṭ never appears in pairs.[130] The zarbiyya, found in the Koran and today the common word for rug in Morocco, is very rare in the Geniza. One, sent from Tunisia to Egypt in 1048, cost approximately 1 dinar.[131]

More popular was the *ḥanbal*, today in Morocco a specific type of rug made of coarse wool with alternating bands of pile and solid (flat) weave. The business woman Wuhsha (on her see *Med. Soc.*, III,

346–352) had a pair of woolen ḥanbals costing 3 dinars; a husband who was asked by his wife to buy one for her in Fustat suggests to her that she had better make the choice herself; and a merchant writing from Alexandria who had given orders to buy for him a number of textiles in the capital adds, on second thought, "Leave the ḥanbal until I come." Ḥanbals had different patterns; therefore the purchaser preferred to make the choice himself.[132]

Floor covers made of textiles had to compete with those made of reeds or rushes. In a hot region the latter had many advantages over the former, especially if they were the product of fine workmanship. Mats were often made to order, and letters sent to and from Alexandria, the main manufacturing center in Egypt for that commodity, are replete with information. Even mats needed in a household in faraway Qayrawān, Tunisia, would not be bought in Alexandria ready-made.[133] The reason is self-evident. One wished to cover the floor as completely as possible "from wall to wall". In addition to the main mat or mats one had to have an entrance piece and sidepieces, as with carpets, but even more so with mats because their edges were more vulnerable. Here is an order sent from the capital to Alexandria around 1140:

[Abu 'l-Ḥasan's brother showed me a pair] of fine ʿAzīzī[134] mats. I am asking you now to be so kind as to order for me a pair exactly like that one, eleven cubits long over a breadth of six and a half[135] cubits, so that each one will be three and a quarter cubits wide. The entrance piece: five cubits over two less a quarter. The sidepiece should be single [not a pair, as usual] and of the same model [as the main mats], four cubits long and three and a half wide.[136] They all should be of eighty "houses."[137] Ask his brother Abu 'l-Ḥasan; he will show you the craftsman. Their make should be perfect. He should not leave much of a border. The borders should be as dense as the middle, approximately one cubit; otherwise their make will not be proper. And have him work at his leisure. I wish to have them, God willing, for the Passover holiday.[138]

To obtain a single piece for a room (and not a pair with extras, as the writer of the passage translated) one had to be particularly explicit: "The place is eleven cubits long, twice as long as the thread attached to this letter, plus one cubit, and five cubits wide, less two finger breadths, exactly like the length of this thread, when it is stretched out well. [These measurements are provided] so that the mat should not be ruffled."[139]

At the end the writer apologizes for troubling the recipient with an order for a one-piece mat, which was so much more difficult to adjust to a room than a number of pieces. A large hall, especially one with columns, like the synagogue of the Palestinians, needed many smaller mats. According to an inventory from 1075, it possessed thirty-eight large mats and twenty-five ʿatabas and round pieces.[140] In those early days even the floor of the Azhar, the imperial mosque founded by the Fatimids, was covered with a variety of mats: no carpets are mentioned in an inventory from the Muslim year 400 (began on August 25, 1009), preserved by the historian al-Maqrīzī. Moses Maimonides in his Code of Law (preface dated 1176/7) states that the synagogues in Muslim Spain, the Maghreb, Iraq, and the Holy Land provided mats for sitting, whereas in Christian countries one sat on chairs.[141]

Next to mats manufactured in Alexandria, the ʿAbbādānī, named after the city of ʿAbbādān in southernmost Iran, is the variety that occurs most frequently in the Geniza. (Today it is Abadan, site of the largest oil refinery in the world).[142] Like Ṭabaristān textiles, ʿAbbādānī mats were copied everywhere and became such a trademark that the traveler Muqaddasi, who visited Egypt in or around 985, mentions "ʿAbbādānī and mats" among the commodities produced in that country.[143] Mats were manufactured in many places in Egypt, which is natural, since it was a furnishing needed in every home.[144]

The ʿAbbādānī was stronger and more durable than regular mats, and a good one should have a design.[145] Therefore it was included occasionally, albeit rarely, in the outfit of a bride. A pair of ʿAbbādānīs formed part of the belongings of a deceased young woman in 1063. It was evaluated as being worth 1 dinar in Tyre 1079, but double that in a trousseau list written about two hundred years later.[146] Mats were regularly traded in pairs, even when made to order (see the first order translated above); a woman removing furnishings from her husband's house to that of her brother was careful to take a pair.[147] When only one was found in the apartment of a deceased person, the clerk made note of it: "A small ʿAbbādānī mat, single."[148] The inventory of the al-Azhar mosque mentioned above notes "plaited" mats as different from the ʿAbbādānī. According to the Geniza the plaited ones were of inferior quality.[149]

Sāmān, a fine reed cultivated in the Jordan valley, is referred to as material for the ṭarrāḥa, or daybed. In an old Karaite marriage contract a bride has a pair of sāmān mats, the only such occurrence noted by me.[150] Sāmān should not be confused with *samār*, a common Egyptian rush still used for the manufacture of mats. Around 1060, samār mats were ordered in Alexandria to be shipped to Jerusalem "for the cemetery," that is, for a building there. Paula Sanders drew my attention to a pre-fatimid source speaking of "a sheykh sitting on a lined sāmān mat." I have never seen a reference to any mat with a lining.[151]

In a letter sent from Tripoli, Libya, to Nahray b. Nissīm in Egypt he was requested to buy for the writer "two matching pairs of mats as floor cover."[152] Should we infer from this wording that they used mats as wall hangings (as many people do today)? There can be no doubt that they did, for medieval Arabic has a special word for such a mat, which, however, has not yet turned up in the Geniza.[153] In any case, a pair of mats could be valuable enough to be sent as a present to a prominent communal figure.[154]

Hides, or leather mats, *anṭāʿ*, (sing. *naṭʿ*) loom large in the Geniza because they served as prime covers for consignments going overseas. Their use as household furnishing, however, namely, as a tablecloth or as a spread beneath the dining tray or for other purposes, probably was less widespread than assumed in *Med. Soc.*, I, 111, bottom. When writing that volume I was still immersed in collecting letters on the India trade. In that correspondence household items were kept apart from goods, and hides clearly belonged to the first category. "A good Abyssinian leather mat" would be sent from Aden as a gift to a merchant from the Mediterranean area sojourning on the Malabar coast of India.[155] An object of the same type, costing 2 dinars, was dispatched from Aden to that merchant together with a mat from Berbera, Somalia, and the zodiac carpet mentioned above.[156] One ordered a *faylam*, a sheet of dressed leather used as tablecloth, from Nahrawāra in the Indian province of Gujarāt for use in Aden, or thanked for a hide, cushions, and a sari or napkin (*fūṭa*) from India.[157]

The combination of hide and cushions just mentioned might have been fortuitous, but in two marriage contracts and in an inventory the hide appears in connection with bedding. At her second marriage a widow brought in as bedding a "mattress" (firāsh), six pillows, a bedstead, and a hide, of a total value of 9 dinars.[158] In a trousseau list written in the Egyptian townlet of Damsīs in 1083, a hide worth 1 dinar is followed by seven pillows totaling the same price.[159] An inventory of textiles and household goods concludes with "a large new hide, 40 [dirhems], and pillows [no number], also new, 25."[160] One wonders whether in these cases furs serving as covers or carpets or both were intended. Such use is natural and common. Are not carpets a human invention substituting for furs? It is only surprising that in the Geniza one reads so little—if at all—about furs as an item of bedding.

Trunks and chests.—Along with the outfit, the future wife was expected to provide its storage. And just as the objects brought in should be as beautiful as possible, so also should their repositories.

This was true, in particular, of the *muqaddama*, the bridal trunk, which contained the wife's lingerie and main personal effects. The term appears in almost every complete trousseau list, usually, at the end, and is regularly accompanied by the euphemistic phrase "and that which is in it."[161] Muqaddama means put first, leading, probably because the donkey carrying it headed the procession that transported the outfit from the bride's domicile to that of her future husband.[162]

The muqaddama was inlaid with *d(h)abl*, tortoiseshell and ivory, as was the *kursī*, stool, or folding chair, on which it stood.[163] Additional ornamentations are noted, also a cover of *kaymukht*, leather with a granular surface, shagreen, which probably was a protection for the textiles.[164] Sometimes a mirror was included, a practical accessory since the trunk contained the wife's wardrobe.[165] Finally, there was a *mandīl muqaddama*, a piece of cloth, no doubt embroidered, serving as a decorative cover for the bridal trunk.[166] I have no doubt that the woman of the house wore the key to the trunk on her belt. Occasionally we find in a trousseau list precious objects such as silverware or "seven pieces of amber with golden covers" described as contained in the muqaddama. Such references are exceptional; at the evaluation of the dowry (see *Med. Soc.*, III, 124) costly items were exhibited, not concealed. In life, a wife's most cherished possessions were properly placed in the bridal trunk.[167]

Only one can be first. Consequently the muqaddama, "the one coming first," never appears in the dual or plural.[168] By contrast, the *ṣundūq*, the general term for crate, chest, or coffer, is regularly mentioned in the dual and listed with bedding. Just as one had two firāshes or mattresses, one needed two ṣundūqs for storing the bedding during the day.[169] Occasionally, such pairs were inlaid with mother-of-pearl and ivory, or covered with shagreen leather, like the muqaddama, or were described as *Ḥākimiyya* or *Mustanṣiriyya*, probably because those types were first seen at the weddings of the caliphs al-Ḥākim (996–1021) and al-Mustanṣir (1036–1096).[170] Instead of a matching pair one could have one ṣundūq made in Byzantium and another manufactured in Fustat.[171] When a bride brought in only one, the clerk would note "a single ṣundūq."[172] A Jewish couple marrying in Palermo 1479, still had "a pair of large sundūqs" (spelled with *s*).[173]

In addition to the muqaddama, the trunk for the wife's personal effects, and ṣundūqs, crates for the bedding and other large items, the trousseau lists often mention a case or box called *safaṭ*, mostly made of a strong variety of bamboo and usually placed upon one or two stools of the same material.[174] In overseas trade, the safaṭ was a middle-sized box for transporting textiles and products such as saffron, cloves, or coral. Two or more of them could be put with other voluminous packages into one container.[175] The household safaṭ, which was of moderate size and regularly put on a stool, thus easily accessible, seems to have contained the materials needed day in, day out; being made of bamboo it could be moved conveniently from one room to another.

The dakka bench, described above as part of the seating and bedding equipment, also had a place in the kitchen. In this role it is either listed as "a dakka for the copper" or mentioned with kitchen implements. As in the living room and bedroom, it could be used for both rest and storage.[176]

Another and far more frequently mentioned furnishing serving both as seat (*takht*, throne) and repository seems to be used in the Geniza almost exclusively in the latter sense, namely, as a container for textiles.[177] A bride would bring in two chests full of silk, another "with bandages, bags of siglaton and sachets of cloves," several others "with bandages and brassieres" or simply "clothes."[178] The takht is regularly listed with one or more other containers, and mostly was of low value. Even a Baghdadi takht was estimated to be worth only 1 dinar.[179]

Finally, there was the *khizāna*, cabinet or cupboard. The word designates a repository where one kept valuables and which could be locked. The word was also used for a small room in a house, where one could enjoy privacy.[180] As the Geniza shows, the khizāna was under the control of the husband, for either his work or personal possessions, or for both. On his deathbed he would declare to whom it should be left or entrusted.[181] A pharmacist, then as today, needed a cabinet that could be locked. His khizāna stood on a base, as did the bridal trunk and the safaṭ.[182] Glass vessels, even when encased in protective covers, were kept in a khizāna.[183] One of teak belonging to a Karaite government official was probably a wardrobe.[184]

Several khizānas are described as *dūlābiyya*, equipped with a wheel, *dūlāb*, which I take to designate a combination lock operated by dialing a sequence of letters or numbers arranged in a circle. Such a lock is described in a Muslim handbook of technical devices. There must have been decorative wheel locks that locked the cabinet but did not guarantee safety, for one inventory lists "a true," a real "wheel cabinet."[185]

Baskets of different materials, shapes, and sizes must have been conspicuous in the houses of the Geniza period. The most common type was the *qafaṣ*, cage, a basket with a cover made of palm fronds, in which were kept dishes, plates, cups, and other tableware made of brass or earthenware, glass of various descriptions, and food.[186] The "qafaṣ for copper" was a valuable item, listed separately in inventories, described briefly as either large or small. The open baskets which could be drawn closed and tied up were used for both storage and transport. A bamboo basket served as receptacle for vellum and other writing materials.[187]

The qafaṣ, like other repositories in the house, was covered with decorative laces, called *mandīl qafaṣ*, so often noted in the trousseau lists, once together with "two mandīls for the cooling jars."[188] It may well be, however, that in the course of time that expression came to mean any decorative cover with a basket pattern.[189]

In all these matters no uniformity should be expected. Some trousseau lists contain all or almost all the repositories discussed, others, none, not even the muqaddama, the bridal trunk. The most sumptuous outfit described in the Geniza lacked any item of storage, for what reason we cannot tell.[190] When a receptacle with a strange name, described as decorated with mother-of-pearl and covered with shagreen leather, appears at the end of trousseau lists, followed by the phrase "and that which is in it," we know that a muqaddama is intended.[191] Crates for bulkier articles, such as bedding, usually came in pairs, but a bride in modest circumstances could accommodate all she had in one cheap crate costing a mere dinar or a half a dinar, whereas another needed three, or a number of repositories of different types.[192]

Mediterranean people of the High Middle Ages did not need as many cupboards and armoires as did our grandparents. Like us they used recesses in the walls as repositories, although not as profusely and practically as we do since their khūristāns were limited in size and decorative in design. Scarcity of timber combined with the striving for spaciousness to keep the furnishings low and well distributed around the house.[193]

Lighting and heating.—"Enlivening the night" through the service of God was a concept pervading the religiosity of the Middle Ages. The rabbis had their nightly study, the monks their vigils, and the pious of Islam "fasted during the day and stood in prayer during the night." Jewish women, who, as a rule, did not study the holy law, donated oil for the synagogues to keep them illuminated until daybreak. Religion as practiced by the select few was an ideal embraced by the community at large.

The Geniza seems to show that inhabitants of the Egyptian capital of the year 1000 or so were in general inclined to spend more means and efforts on lighting than did their descendants at the beginning of the nineteenth century, when E. W. Lane so scrupulously described their primitive lamps made of glass and wood.[194]

Three different types of illumination are reflected clearly in our sources: lavish, in the synagogues—and, as we know, far more so in the mosques and churches; costly, in the reception hall of a private home, especially when it had to be lit for festive occasions; and by no means simple for regular household needs. None of the many lighting appliances for synagogues noted in *Med. Soc.*, II, 150, occur in the trousseau lists of brides, although there lamps and candlesticks are usually first in the Copper section (which includes bronze and brass); illumination of the majlis, or reception hall, was again a matter by itself. In the houses of worship lamps had to be suspended; hence the many *būqandalāt*, or chandeliers, triangles, and hoops—all bearing small glass vessels filled with water, oil, and wicks—or the grillwork lamps, which did not cast long shadows but permitted the light to be dispersed all over the building. In a majlis, chandeliers were hung as were the regular household lamps, but its pride was the wax candles and, in particular, the *ṣubḥī*, or bright ones (from *subḥ*, morning), that is, those of great height and diameter, which provided much light and could burn for hours. (Anyone visiting a museum with an Islamic collection must be impressed by the enormous candlestands from the Mamluk period, which are rarely absent; they are princely pieces and give an idea of the size of candles for great parties.) Beeswax, of which the candles were made, was very expensive, perhaps three times as much as the "good," that is, olive oil, let alone the linseed and other less valuable oils, which were commonly used. Only a very rich man could permit himself to light thirty ṣubḥī and over two hundred regular wax candles. In the synagogues, throughout the eleventh and twelfth centuries, no wax candles were used.[195]

We are comparatively well informed about household lighting because the wife was expected to provide the necessary appliances, at least for the more intimate rooms of a home. Whoever could afford it brought two "lamps" into the marriage, one described as "brides' lamp" and the other as "wax candles lamp," the former usually of a higher value than the latter. Only in one marriage contract (with realistic prices) was the wax candles lamp worth 10 dinars and the other only 6, and they were among the higher amounts noted for lighting implements brought in by a bride.[196] For all those lamps were of "copper," none of silver. The richest trousseau reported in the Geniza contained three lamps, one for candles and "two complete Andalusian lamps," but all three are lumped with other copper utensils. Even where a lamp is described as "artistically ornamented" its price is included in the total of the copper.[197] From all this I conclude that the illumination of the living room or rooms had to be provided by the master of the house. The wife's contribution probably was destined mainly for her personal domain—her sitting room, bedroom, and the kitchen. It is noteworthy, however, that even poor brides brought in at least one, and often more than one, lighting appliance made of copper.

Since the "brides' lamp" is listed with, but different from, "the one with wax candles," we shall not be amiss in assuming that it was lighted with oil. It was perhaps not much different from the wedding lamp drawn by E. W. Lane around 1835: a wooden device representing a six-pointed star (known today as Star of David, but previously named Solomon's Seal, not a Jewish emblem, but a magic sign, bringing good luck), from which were suspended one large and several small oil lamps.[198] Perhaps the "brides' lamp" of the Geniza had no fixed shape but was simply an oil lamp given and kindled at the wedding.

All examples given in note 196 of a brides' lamp noted together with a candles chandelier are from the twelfth century. In earlier documents it was called a "trousseau lamp," in one case called so even on the occasion of a divorce settlement, when some articles of the outfit had been sold by the husband and others had been lost.[199] In the thirteenth century the trousseau lists note a bride's "jug lamp," that is, a lamp in the form of a jug and made of decorative grillwork in bronze. Lamps of this type have been painstakingly described and profusedly illustrated by D. Storm Rice, the most ancient known one having the Solomon's Seal as its central decoration.[200] An exceptionally well-equipped thirteenth-century bride had two "Damascene lamps," two candle chandeliers, a small lamp, and a jug lamp, the latter, worth 3 dinars, being the most valuable of her six lighting appliances.[201] In other documents jug lamps cost 2, 8, and 10 dinars, respectively.[202] Unfortunately, no descriptions of the two Damascene and two Spanish lamps are given. The jug lamps were no doubt suspended from the ceiling. Other oil lamps in a private home were movable, and they were probably in the majority. Here is an order for one, sent from Aden to the west coast of India, which was renowned for its bronze industry:

> Make me a nice lamp from the rest of all the copper (*ṣufr*). Its column should be octagonal and stout, its base should be in the form of a lampstand with strong feet. On its head there should be a copper (*nuḥās*) lamp with two ends for two wicks, which should be set on the end of the column so that it can move up and down. The three parts, the column, the stand, and the

lamp, should be separate from one another. If they can make the feet in spirals, then let it be so; for this is more beautiful. The late Abu 'l-Faraj al-Jubaylī made a lamp of such a description. Perhaps this will be like that one.[203]

As this order shows, some people preferred a lamp that could be taken apart, so that it could be cleaned more easily from oil rests. We find one in a trousseau list, and in the estate of a scribe even a "joint" lamp made of wood. The "head," that is, the part containing two or more cavities for the oil and wicks, should be movable, up, to illuminate the room, down, for reading. Others preferred the head to be fixed to the body of the lamp.[204]

Some trousseau lists note lamps "with their appurtenances." Other lists specify what they are. Scissors were needed for trimming the wicks. A light was extinguished by a snuffer; blowing it out was unpleasant and regarded as ominous, for light is a symbol of the soul, and "Man's soul is a lamp lit by God" (Proverbs 20:27); as often today, the snuffer had the form of an inverted funnel; it is mentioned twice as being made of silver. Finally, a lamp had its tray on which it was put to avoid smudging its environment.[205]

In addition to oil lamps and chandeliers for wax candles many brides had one, two, or three candlesticks or prickets, *ḥasaka*, literally, thorn, all made of "copper." Despite the modest name, a bronze ḥasaka could be quite expensive. In an inventory from the year 1028 two were evaluated at 10 dinars. A rich bride had "a large candlestick"; but even "a small one," ordered in India, was supposed to weigh three pounds and to be constructed "in steps." This one is expressly described as "for a candle"; a letter accompanying a consignment of Lebanese copperware speaks of a ḥasaka for wax candles, in the plural.[206]

"Two candlesticks" were not more frequent in the copper section of the trousseau lists than, say, two buckets or two ewers. Nowhere do we read about "a pair of candlesticks," a sight so familiar to us. Candlesticks made of silver are noted as the property of men. The businesswoman Wuḥsha, in this matter, as in any others, was exceptional: she had two of them, costing a total of 20 dinars, a very high amount.[207]

Special attention must be paid to *sirāj*, a light, which, in addition to its general meaning, designates in the Geniza several specific utensils. Basically, sirāj is the ancient Near Eastern (Persian-Aramaic) term for a single small oil lamp; untold thousands of them have been found in excavations. In the Geniza this implement must have been intended when the sirāj is noted separately along with either a candlestick, or a chandelier of wax candles, or "a lamp" in general. We must keep in mind that it always signifies an object made of copper or bronze, not of clay. But the word could also designate the "head," or upper parts of an oil lamp, which comprised several cups containing oil and wicks, and even that of "a wax candle lamp."[208]

The silver lamp suspended on silver chains before the Holy Ark in the synagogue (and on the corresponding holy spots in churches and mosques) is always called *qindīl* (derived from Latin *candela* as is our *candle*), a word still common in Arabic but not used in the Geniza for a lighting appliance in the house.[209]

The standard of four lighting appliances brought by the bride—oil lamp, chandelier, candlestick, and portable small oil light—taken together with the assumption that the illumination of the living room or rooms was normally incumbent on the husband, induces us to imagine that, in Geniza times, a middle-class home was fairly well lit and did not look as "dull" as the interior of an Egyptian house when E. W. Lane saw it.[210] The long entrance corridor, dihlīz, however, seems not to have been regularly lit. In a report about an assassination attempt the writer mentions that he did not recognize the assailant because he went into the dark dihlīz without carrying a light. The same assumption underlies the humorous story from the *Arabian Nights* of the Jewish physician who ran down the staircase into the unlit corridor and fell over his patient, believing he had killed him.[211] When leaving the house at nighttime one certainly carried a lantern, probably called *miṣbāḥ*. For the time being, I have only one reference to this term from the Geniza. Whether it was made partly of glass, as occurs in the famous Verse of the Light in the Koran (24:35), I cannot yet say. It is worthwhile, however, to remember that in a house without windowpanes, where strong drafts were common, a "hermit's lantern" must have been quite practical even for use in the interior, especially in the kitchen.[212]

For igniting lamps one kept in the house a box containing flint stones, valuable enough to be noted in an inventory. Sulphur matches must have been common, for a householder would ask a neighbor in an adjacent apartment for one as we would ask for a safety match.[213]

Heating appliances were probably a regular feature in the outfit of a bride from Damascus and other more northerly places. She would have one or two *kānūns*, best translated perhaps as firepot brazier, or coal pan. But occasionally Cairo could be cold. When a physician, describing his excessive mourning over the death of a younger brother, writes, "I did not leave a single stove or brazier in the house from which I did not take ashes, putting them on my head," his home must have been well equipped with those utensils.[214]

Fumigating and freshening.—Unlike the kānūn, which was a heating appliance and appears in the Geniza as made of copper or bronze, other charcoal burners, made of various materials, served as fumigators. Aromatic woods were burned on them to deodorize a room after a meal. This custom, entirely unknown in our own society (if we disregard the homely aroma of cigars), had its roots in remote antiquity. Burning incense in the temple was the most precious and most holy of offerings; it concluded and topped the animal sacrifices in the houses of God, just as it followed a meal in the homes of men. The Church, in using its thurible, has preserved this ceremonial; the Synagogue had to forego it, because igniting fire was prohibited on a holy day. But as soon as the Sabbath was over, one lit the brazier, equipped it with odoriferous woods, and said the benediction over the *mugmār*, or burning aromatics. Later, one dispensed with the brazier and said the benediction over fresh or dried fragrant plants.

The *mijmara*, brazier or censer (derived, as the reader sees, from the same Semitic root), congruous with its noble function, was always made of silver. The silver classification in the trousseau lists did not include bronze inlaid with silver; the Geniza had a special term for that. Bronze incense burners from the Fatimid and Ayyubid periods, mostly in the form of animals, real or imaginary, may still be admired in our museums. Silver censers were rare. It is possible that those brought in by Jewish brides were especially destined for the rite at the termination of the Sabbath. Their aroma was intended not so much to be diffused in the room, as to be snuffed by the individual worshiper to enable him to pronounce the appropriate benediction.[215]

The fumigator, *mibkhara* (from *bukhār*, fume), appears in one document right after the mijmara and must therefore have been different from it in form and possibly function. The mibkhara was made of bronze, which seems to have been the rule, or of bronze inlaid with silver, or, in one case, of silver. It seems to have been the common utensil for deodorizing a room at the conclusion of a festive meal when the guests were still present and the party was going on.[216]

A third type of incense burner, called *midkhana* (from *dukhān*, smoke), presents problems. Some of those made of silver were evaluated as being worth 40 and 50 dinars, among the highest prices noted in the Geniza for a single object. "Smoke censers" made of, or encrusted with, silver are attested in documents from 995 through the beginning of the twelfth century. Inexpensive midkhanas were made of bronze. There was, however, one of ebony wood decorated with silver, and, even more puzzling, quite a number of others described as *midkhana khayāzir*, bamboo censer, one even as being "ornamented." They were made of the same sturdy variety of bamboo as the chests and stools with which they are mentioned in one line. It is difficult to visualize that contraption. Perhaps the incense burner itself was made of clay but was surrounded by a bamboo cylinder serving as a kind of smokestack. A midkhana khayāzir could be had for 1 dinar. Originally I took "bamboo censer" to mean "[bronze] censer with wickerwork decorations like plaited bamboo," as found in the India trade correspondence. But since this censer is listed with chests and stools, I am reluctant to retain this explanation.[217]

Fumigating was costly, and, as the Tunisian historian Ibn Khaldūn (wrote 1377) pointed out, remained a preserve of the affluent. Only a limited number of brides had in their outfit the braziers needed for that type of deodorizing.[218] Freshening appliances, that is, vessels with fragrant woods, whose pleasing scent was supposed to overcome bad odors wafting in the house or intruding from the street, were in general use, however, and appear regularly at the end of trousseau lists. Usually, two, three, or more of them were brought in, invariably called *barānī*, whether they were made of copper, silver, or wood inlaid with mother-of-pearl and ivory. I assume that many were earthenware vases, but, like other easily perishable materials, were not included in brides' outfits. Barānī are usually, but not always, defined as *muṭayyab*, scented with *ṭīb*, which in Arabic is the general word for perfume, but in the Middle Ages designated an Indian odoriferous wood of the aloe family. As explained in the note, an inexpensive variety of aloes must have been the main scenting material. The widespread use of these freshening devices seems to prove that they met a vital need. Fustat was blamed by one of its illustrious sons for its stench. The ginger vases of eighteenth-century England, seem to have served a similar purpose.[219]

Besides their deodorizing effects, the fumigating and freshening devices must have satisfied a human need, similar to that met today by smoking. The Talmud is quite outspoken in this matter: all earthly pleasures gratify the body; inhaling fragrant smells is the enjoyment of the soul.[220]

5. *Housewares*

Washing.—If not for reasons of cleanliness, a Jew was obliged by religious law to wash after arousing from sleep, before prayer (three times a day), before and after meals (forks had not yet been invented), and, of course, after a visit to the bathroom (even a short one). The Muslim laws of ritual purification were even more rigorous. In those days when houses were not equipped with running water, a basin with a ewer was an indispensable piece of equipment in every home, and two or more such pairs were desirable. Anyone present, a servant, a wife, a child, would pour water from a ewer on the hands of a person who wanted to wash, so as to waste as little of the precious liquid as possible. Moreover, the washed hand would not be defiled by seizing the handle of the ewer touched before by the hand that had not yet been abluted. A case in point is the story of beautiful Cassia, who rushed from her bed to serve her father at washing as soon as she perceived that he was readying himself for nightly prayer.[1]

Basin and ewer are often listed together in Geniza marriage contracts, and one may assume that in those cases they matched each other, particularly as in a thirteenth-century document that says "a Damascus basin *with its ewer*" (costing 5 dinars, whereas a Fustat pair, possessed by the same bride, was worth only 2 dinars). An Andalusian basin costing 8 (real) dinars was accompanied by "a large ewer" worth 3 dinars in 1156. A matching pair, and one of superb craftsmanship, created by a thirteenth-century metalworker from Mosul, Iraq, has actually been preserved.[2]

Well-off brides had two basins and two ewers.[3] People preferred to have one large and one smaller basin, the former especially needed when guests came to dinner. In the twelfth century it became fashionable to describe the larger one as caliphate-like, meaning huge and of top quality.[4] A thirteenth-century basin is labeled "pre-Islamic," that is, very old, "antique," and cost 12 dinars, an exorbitant price, seen by me only once more in a document from the year 1186. A basin with a pair of "ears," that is, handles, was among household goods received by a widow from the estate of her husband in 1128. Medieval basins preserved are rarely equipped with handles. When a list of copper vessels contains not a ewer but "a copper sparrow," one is inclined to believe that it refers to a small ewer decorated with or having the form of a bird.[5]

For washing the face and other parts of the body one had one, or preferably, two or more washbasins, named *maghsal*, made of copper, and also, I am sure, of earthenware, although our sources had no reason to make mention of the latter. One copper maghsal was given as a pawn for a loan of 2 dinars, but two used ones were evaluated as being worth only half a dinar.[6] Washbasins made of silver must not have been uncommon. We find them in inventories and, in a court record, as exported, together with other silver vessels, from Fustat to India. The latter was encrusted with gold and niello work and weighed fifty-two and a quarter dirhems, a little more than half an American pound. A basin of this type probably was reserved for washing the hands at a festive meal.[7]

The marble purification fixture, *maṭhara*, listed in inventories of estates, might have been something like the French bidet, or was the name of the (removable?) marble plate with a hole, which is still widely used in the Middle East instead of our toilet seat. In one document it is noted between two copper vessels and evaluated at 10 dirhems. Together with many other fixtures and utensils it was given to a widow in payment of the late installment of her marriage gift.[8]

Water for washing and cleaning was drawn from a well, apparently found in every house. A bucket and a dipper, both made of copper, formed as common a pair in trousseau lists as a basin and a ewer. A pair could be had for 1 dinar; but a well-off widow, who had two buckets and two dippers, evaluated them as being worth 15 dinars.[9] The bucket, *saṭl* (from Latin *situla*), appears in different shapes: round or quadrangular, small, middle, or large, and is repeatedly described as "with legs," which was a blessing for the housewife, inasmuch as she did not have to bend over every time she had to scoop water.[10] Copper and brass buckets were imported from Damascus and other places in Syria, from Baghdad, and even India, but, as far as our documents tell us, the imported ones were not more expensive than those locally produced. An India bucket cost 1-1/2 dinars, and a Damascene or Syrian one even less (same price together with a lamp). In one marriage contract (ca. 1125) a Damascene bucket is described as "ornamented with coins."[11]

The word translated as dipper, *karnīb* (from Greek *khernips*), basically means gourd, but, as in Europe, the dry shell of this fruit served as a vessel and gave its name to a utensil made of metal similar to it in shape. When we find in a list of used household goods "a small karnīb without a handle" we are led to assume that a handle was normally affixed to the karnīb mentioned with the bucket. This small improvement over nature was not only practical, but possibly had a ritual purpose, especially when one had to make a prescribed ablution without another person doing the pouring.[12]

Soap was an important article of import from Tunisia to Egypt, and sometimes the government confiscated all the consignments for its own needs. In the households represented in the Geniza, soap was used for washing clothes, not the body.[13] Instead, *ushnān*, pulverized ashes of alkaloid plants, served the purpose. Receptacles of different types containing this indispensable material are regularly included in the trousseau lists. An ushnān box had to have a lid to preserve its chemical properties and fragrance, if it was perfumed, as it often was, and, of course, had to be accompanied by a little scoop or spoon. Therefore the lists sometimes speak of a set, or a complete set, of ushnān. The receptacle, ushnāna, was normally made of brass. When, in addition to the regular utensil, a bride had two silver ushnānas, or a government official three, we understand that guests had to be honored not only by beautiful washbasins and ewers, but also by matching ushnān containers. An Arab literary source describing "the ushnān of the kings and great personages" emphasizes the care to be taken with this material. "It must not be touched by any hand except that of the person performing the ablution."[14]

For bathing one visited a bathhouse, normally once a week. The utensils used on that occasion are discussed in the subsection on health care and illness in *Med. Soc.* V (in preparation).

Storage and cooking.—The housewife of the Geniza period did not need the immense array of gadgets which makes modern kitchen work so efficient (and complicated). The intake of food was much more limited than ours and far less variegated. Moreover, bringing home cooked food from the bazaar was common practice. Although one document states that Jews did more cooking at home than others, we see that brides have in their trousseaus a meal carrier, a contrivance consisting of several compartments and a handle in which various warm dishes could be brought home at a time. The average cost of such a brass *porte-manger*, as the French call it, was 2 dinars. It was used throughout the Geniza times.[15] The Cairene museum of Islamic art possesses a complete porte-manger, of course, for princely use.[16] Pairs (not two) of these utensils appear both in marriage contracts and in inventories. It seems to prove that the pair was to be carried by a person, one in each hand, and not to serve the Jewish practice of dividing the kitchen into a meat and dairy section. In general I must observe that the details about kitchenware and tableware in the Geniza texts give no information whatsoever on how the Jewish dietary and Sabbath laws were then observed in those parts.[17]

Bread could be bought at the bazaar. But one did not leave the grain, that sustainer of life, to chance. Whenever possible, provisions were laid in for the year. One or several stone jars containing fixed measurements of wheat—for instance, seven and a half *wayba*s (approximately one hundred and twenty liters)—were put in a safe place in the interior of the house. A small vessel of fixed measurement and durable material, such as marble, was attached to the jar, which enabled the housewife to control the consumption. But it seems that grain could not be taken out of the jar without express permission of the master of the house. When he left town, it was stipulated how much she could take each month.[18]

The wheat was not ground at home. It was done in one of the many mills found all over the city. Only once have I come across a hand mill listed in a trousseau list, namely, in that of a very poor widow who perhaps could not afford to pay for the grinding; she remarried shortly after the death of her husband (probably forced to do so by dire need).[19] One or more hand mills are listed in inventories, but they were trade tools, not kitchenware.[20] By contrast, mortar and pestle were common items in a bride's outfit; their use was multifarious; two mortars, "one large, one small," were by no means a luxury. Even a pestle alone would be listed in an inventory as something valuable.[21]

The dough for the bread was prepared in the house. The ground wheat was separated from the bran with a "hair sieve."[22] As kneading troughs wooden *jafnas* are mentioned, which occur in letters as being ordered or sent from Alexandria to Cairo, but found by me in a bride's outfit only in a marriage contract from Tyre, Lebanon, a country that provided Egypt with good hardwood.[23] A kitchen was equipped with an oven for baking, frying, and cooking, but it seems to have been customary, to what extent we cannot know, to have the bread baked in a baker's oven.[24] "Bring your bread to the baker, even if he burns it," says a Near Eastern maxim. Good bread needs intense heat, which is costly to produce in a kitchen and, in a hot country, unpleasant.[25]

Drinking water was brought from the Nile by porters and kept in large earthenware jars, placed in or, preferably, near the kitchen. They themselves were not provided by the wife, but the copper cups attached to them and their copper covers were valuable objects and therefore could be parts of an outfit.[26] The "coolers," porous clay jugs, whose wind-cooled water tastes so much fresher than water from a refrigerator, are known to us from the Geniza solely through their bronze lids, the cups attached, and the lovely embroidered covers spread over them (a custom still alive).[27]

Next to bread and water a household had to have oil, equally needed for cooking and lighting. Every bride had an oil cruse. I purposely use this biblical word (I Kings 17:14), because that small vessel performed a special service and probably had some symbolic connotation as well. Most of the objects brought in by a bride appear in duplicate or triplicate, or in larger number, but always there is only one oil cruse. At first blush, it seems strange. From orders sent to grocers we know that different types of oil were used in a household. So why only one *kūz zayt*? This utensil was not a container in which the oil was kept, but a small jug, probably with a spout, constantly in the hand of the housewife when she moved around the house filling lamps, or when she stood in the kitchen cooking, frying, or preparing sweetmeats. It seemed to symbolize the wife's role as provider of food and light.[28]

I do not enumerate the usual kitchen implements that occasionally appear in the Geniza documents, but a few deserve special mention. The *zanjala* (or *zinjila*), tentatively translated by me as canister, or as spice box, is as ubiquitous in trousseau lists and inventories as it is absent from Arabic dictionaries. It must have been a common utensil, since a lane in Fustat, named after its manufacturers, is mentioned in at least two Geniza documents and in the writings of Muslim antiquarians.[29] Neither can its function be in doubt, when a court record lists "a small zanjala with its lid and another larger one, without lid," and the inventory of an estate notes "a small brass zanjala and another made of brass, at the pigeons," meaning, outside the house, containing food for the beloved pigeons kept by many.[30] A bride had "six lids and zanjalas" (in this sequence!) costing 6 dinars, another, one, from the small town of Malīj, had three, a third bride, two; but all the many others, as far as I can see, had only one. Since so many types of containers are mentioned in our documents, this indicates that the zanjala had a special form and function, but I do not know what they were. It was perhaps a small container for salt, pepper, cinnamon, and other spices, and in the majority of cases, when only one was brought in by a bride, it was destined to serve as a salt shaker. Bread and salt were inseparable. While breaking the bread and pronouncing the benediction, one sprinkled it with "the salt of the covenant with God" (Leviticus 2:13).[31]

It is worthy of note that pieces of regular kitchenware, such as pots, kettles, and caldrons, were rarely brought in by brides, and if they were, more often than not, they came in pairs, even frying pans.[32] The latter had both a Greek and an Arabic name, were made either of iron or of "stone," and were of two types, one for roasting nuts and seeds, and the other for regular kitchen use.[33] The kitchen was crammed with glass bottles, clay vessels, and metal containers. The countless orders to grocers preserved prove that although one carefully stocked the house with grain for a prolonged period, all the "accompaniments of bread" were bought in very small quantities—a few pounds, a pound, or less. The grocery store was around the corner. A child or servant would be sent there, carrying the appropriate receptacle, and the grocer would pour into it the quantity ordered. Hence we read in inventories and letters such items as "a small jug with some almonds and sugar, about three ounces," "a clay vessel with melted butter," and so on.[34]

To avoid congestion in the kitchen one suspended whatever one could from the walls and ceiling. There were "hooks for the kitchen," hangers, "thorns," that is, spikes for the cups, and a special contrivance, named *kab(a)ka*, a perforated copper board suspended from the ceiling on which one stacked the dishes. The documents in which this object is mentioned were written in the eleventh century. In one case it was given as a collateral; in a trousseau list it concluded the Copper section.[35]

Dining and amenities.—Meals were taken "at a table." In legal parlance (as early as pre-Islamic) "eating at *one* table" meant living together.[36] Yet the furniture called table, *mā'ida* (pronounced *mayda*), although mentioned sporadically in letters and inventories, seems not to have been in general use. We find it in the possession of a poor widow, a scribe, and of middle-class people; a physician had two; the amir, or governor, of Alexandria "took" one sent from Fustat, and one was ordered in Fustat "at any cost" by a merchant from Aden, South Arabia.[37]

The mā'ida seems to have been a large tray, which was placed on a stool; "a stool for a table" is listed as a separate piece of furniture.[38] As material a multicolored, veined hardwood named *khalanj* is mentioned, which to describe botanically would be futile, since that noted by Muslim geographers grew in Iran south of the Caspian Sea and in Russia, while that listed in Geniza inventories came from Sicily.[39] The *sufra*, or cover for the table, was not a tablecloth but a bag of leather or other strong material, in which the "table," like other precious furnishings, was stored when not in use. All in all it seems that the mā'ida was traditionally made of fine wood, the like of which was not found on the southern shores of the Mediterranean, and, was therefore not in widespread use.[40]

Normally a *ṣīniyya*, a round tray made of copper or brass, placed upon a stool, served as a table. It appears regularly in the Copper section of a bride's outfit, and, with one or two exceptions, always in the singular. Precious pieces of cloth serving as covers are also frequently listed.[41]

Silver sīniyyas were as common in the eleventh century as they were rare in the twelfth. When we read of their prices of 25, 30, or 50 dinars, or of one given as collateral for forty-four pieces of golden jewelry weighing fifty *mithqāls* (equivalent to slightly more than half an American pound), it is evident that a considerable number of persons could be accommodated around such a tray. Silver sīniyyas were ordered in Fustat for export to Tunisia as well as to Aden.[42]

Besides the tray around which one sat there were others on which food and drink were served. Throughout the centuries the *muʿtaṣimī*, called so after the Abbasid caliph al-Muʿtaṣim (ruled 833–842), was used. Fortunately we have a description of this object by Maimonides, written in, or shortly before, 1168: "This is a large board of wood into which many small compartments are carved, each containing a different dish." An affluent Karaite bride from the early eleventh century had one, but the only price I have found thus far for one was 1-1/4 dinars (ca. 1140). A man bought two for his father, and two were found in the estate of a scribe, a duplication hardly made for ritual reasons (meat and dairy dishes). An inventory from 1143 notes a "caliphate-like," that is, large, muʿtaṣimī, which was cracked, as often happened with wooden utensils. Except for the description by Maimonides I have not yet come upon this utensil anywhere outside the Geniza.[43]

Another service tray, the *ṣadr*, on which were put the bowls and cups to be used at a meal, was made of copper or brass, cost between 1 and 2 dinars, and was found in the homes of the poor and the rich. In trousseau lists and inventories of any kind only one is noted.[44] The *khūnjā* (Persian, little table), which served a similar purpose and cost about the same, must have been different from the ṣadr, since the two appear separately in one document. Safety pins decorated with khūnjās are listed among a bride's precious jewelry. Thus the khūnjā had the form of a plate, round or rectangular. All the references to it are from the thirteenth century.[45]

The most common vessel on the table was the *zabdiyya* (originally, container of melted butter), a deep bowl of different sizes, materials, and purposes. When a bride had one zabdiyya with cover and ladle, all made of silver, and costing 10 dinars, the word is perhaps best translated as tureen.[46] There were other trousseau lists with just one silver zabdiyya.[47] Frequently, however, this vessel appears in large quantities. Brides brought in five or six zabdiyyas made of china. A letter from Alexandria orders from Cairo fifty zabdiyyas "with decorations in color" (as against only ten platters of the same description). An inventory states "found in his domicile a basket with about ten zabdiyyas," and notes later an unspecified number of small ones. These must have been the regular eating bowls so frequently seen in museums. The word rendered here as china is *ṣīnī*, which should not be taken literally as porcelain, but as fine earthenware in general.[48] When it is described as translucent, or is included in a luxurious trousseau, it might have been porcelain. But when poor people have two "chinas," or when a camel load of ṣīnī weighing 450 pounds cost 24 dinars, and another camel load of the same, 63 dinars, clearly popular imitations (Maghrebi ware imported to Egypt) are meant.[49]

Fustat itself produced fine earthenware, *ghaḍār*. "A basket of good ghaḍār made in Āmid [today Diyarbakir, Turkey] or Fustat" was ordered in a memo sent from Aden to the capital of Egypt around 1140. "I happened to get here [Fustat or Alexandria] carnelian-red ghaḍār and everyone envied me for this."[50] A letter from Aden, sent slightly earlier, says this: "I asked him to buy [in Fustat] a basket of ghaḍār: bowls, platters, and cups," which gives the impression that one tried to match the various china vessels used at a table. But the tastes, or perhaps the purposes for which orders were made, differed, as we learn from another request for tableware sent from Aden to Fustat in 1135, at approximately the same time as the letter just quoted: "Please buy me six painted platters, made in Miṣr'; they should be of middle size, neither very large nor very small; and twenty [regular] bowls and forty small ones. All should be painted, and their figures and colors should be different."[51]

In Aden itself, genuine Chinese porcelain was not uncommon on the tables of the rich, and from there found its way to Egypt. A set of six tumblers of "Chinese transparent fine china" was sent in the 1130s as a gift to the head of the Jewish community in Cairo by an Adenese representative of merchants. These sporadic testimonies from the Geniza are confirmed by numerous references in Arabic literature and actual archaeological finds. But since earthenware was normally not included in a bride's outfit we do not learn much from the Geniza about its use at the table.[52]

The "small zabdiyyas," mentioned together with regular bowls (see above, n. 48), probably were used for nuts and other fruit, fresh or dried, which were served before and, especially, after the main meal. These "dessert bowls," when made of silver, were a special article of export from Fustat.[53] The fine silver zabdiyyas in the inventory of an estate were obviously of that type.[54] Dessert bowls were made of the same multicolored veined wood named khalanj used to manufacture tables.[55] As bowls they often had a special name, *ṭayfūr*, another term that is common in the Geniza but apparently absent from Arabic dictionaries. One inventory of an estate lists a set of six dessert ṭayfūrs, another a set of three from Baghdad, "and one from Baghdad, middle sized."[56] Once, a ṭayfūr is described as "of marble," which probably means alabaster.[57]

Unlike the zabdiyya, which is rare in trousseau lists, because it was mostly made either of earthenware or of silver, the *ṭāsa*, a shallow drinking vessel, made of either "red" copper or "yellow" brass, was a regular feature in a bride's outfit, especially in Ayyubid and Mamluk times. It is often described as "whitened," that is, tinned, a procedure necessary to prevent copper from deteriorating and endangering health.[58] A set of four brass ṭāsas could cost 5 dinars, another one consisting of three pairs of "covers and small ṭāsas," found in the same list, cost 4 dinars. But when we find four ṭāsas plus a lamp, evaluated at 20 dinars, or a single one, 5 dinars, they must have been pieces of refined workmanship.[59] It should be emphasized that sets appear only exceptionally and only from the thirteenth century, when I once found a *dast*, or set, consisting of sixteen ṭāsas. Usually one ṭāsa was brought in by a bride, and, we may assume, only one was used by all at the table. The drinking vessel was passed around, but since it is often described as large, the lips could be choosy.[60] Damascene ṭāsas appear in thirteenth-century documents and were assessed at comparatively high prices.[61] I found a silver ṭāsa only once: in a court record from the year 1028.[62]

The ṭāsa is repeatedly listed together with a vessel named *marfaᶜ* (or *mirfaᶜ*), a term with a checkered history in Arabic literature.[63] As far as the Geniza period is concerned, our documents leave no doubt about its character. Throughout the centuries, the marfaᶜ, whether of brass or of silver, came with a cover or a lid.[64] It was a container, and it was put to heavy use as we shall see. An Adenese merchant, ordering one from a brass factory on the west coast of India, writes:

> . . . A marfaᶜ, here in Aden we call it table jug. It should be decorated with wickerwork and fit into the center of the ten-cornered tray [described before], so that when water is poured into it from a waterskin, the drops should fall on the tray. The wickerwork should be like that of a bamboo basket; the table jug should weigh eight pounds, more or less, and the ten-cornered tray about four pounds.[65]

In the same letter a *small* marfaᶜ ornamented with fine bamboo wickerwork is ordered for another customer. "He wishes to place it on a platter on the table."[66]

It is evident from these descriptions that the lid-covered marfaᶜ table jug was a vessel containing drinking water and was kept either on a platter on the table or, when large, on a tray nearby. Even the richest bride in the Geniza had only one marfaᶜ, albeit of silver.[67] Inventories occasionally list two or more.[68] Another rich bride had one marfaᶜ of silver, but a second marfaᶜ of hers, of brass, is described as *sharābī*, for "potions," meaning wine and soft drinks.[69] This vessel was generally called *sharābiyya*.

The sharābiyya was as common at the table as the water jug, and, like it, formed part of a bride's outfit. Throughout, it is listed (and always as a single piece) in the copper section and, most frequently, as worth 3 dinars, a high price for a copper vessel.[70] In one marriage contract the sharābiyya, together with a meal carrier, cost 4 dinars. This combination was natural: one bought warm and other dishes in the bazaar, and then filled his jug at a sharābī, a seller of "potions" of all types.[71]

The common drinking cup, *kūz*, was made of fine earthenware, produced in Fustat or elsewhere, of regular earthenware (the Damascene—or Syro-Palestinian—one was recommended for medical reasons), of glass, which probably was the material mostly used, and even of crystal. An urgent order (sent from Alexandria to Fustat) for fifty kūz, "the finest available," but without specifying the price, probably was for cups in common use.[72] Silver cups were rare and, it seems, of massive structure, perhaps for ceremonial use. In a tenth-century marriage contract it cost 15 dinars.[73] A father, on his deathbed, left his silver cup to his son, while the jewelry was to be divided between his daughters.[74] Two silver cups sent from Egypt to the Maghreb around 1100 weighed 200 dirhems, that is, 625 grams, or 312.5 grams each. This detail is included in a statement under oath in which the merchant who had carried those cups together with many other pieces of merchandise confirmed having received them. Thus the weight noted must have been exact.[75]

The *qadaḥ* tumbler was made of china or glass.[76] Earthenware goblets, *sāghar*, with gold luster were ordered in Fustat.[77] The *qiḥf*, despite its name (skull), must have been a shallow drinking vessel of small dimensions, since it is mostly listed as being of silver, and the highest price for it noted thus far is 4 dinars. It was among the silverware exported from Fustat to India. An amber qiḥf with a golden rim or ornamental design probably was a toilet article.[78]

Spoons, forks, and knives were not used at the table. At least we do not read about them in connection with other tableware. In Arabic one "drinks" the soup. For eating, a piece of their soft bread was a perfect means for seizing a morsel of food and conveying it safely to the mouth. Meat was cut in the kitchen. Chicken and other fowl, when placed upon the table whole, could be dissected with the fingers. Our dishes of vegetables stuffed with small pieces of meat and other fillings are relics of the time when one did not use knives at the table. Knives occur in the Geniza documents, but always in the singular. The knife is described as being of silver, silvered, gilded, with a silver hilt, or kept in a sheath. This was not a ceremonial bread knife as in use today; bread was "broken," or, rather, torn, not cut.

Where the prices listed were minimal (1 dinar or less), it must have been a small utensil for general purposes.[79]

Fumigating the dining room after an elaborate meal was one of the amenities of life which anyone who could afford it would not forgo.[80] In addition to purifying the air and making one feel comfortable, it was customary to sprinkle those present, and, in particular, the guests, with rose water. We can hardly imagine today how widespread the use was of water distilled from rose petals in those times. One enjoyed their fragrance and believed in their comprehensive faculties of enhancing or restoring health. Rose water was traded in large containers, but for household use one had a long-necked brass bottle named *qumqum*. In a book on traditional life in Saʿudi Arabia this term is jokingly explained as a hint. In Arabic *qum* means "get up!" The sprinkling of the guests with rose water was a sign that the party was over and everyone was advised to go home. In Geniza times the qumqum was the bottle in which rose water was bought and kept in the house.[81] The actual sprinkling was done with the "sprinkler," invariably made of silver and one of the most common household utensils made of that precious metal.[82]

The ubiquitous flies caused great discomfort, especially during meals. Flyswatters with handles of wood, iron, or silver, and equipped with canvas, helped to dispel this nuisance. E. W. Lane in his drawing of a meal in a middle-class household in Cairo around 1830 depicts two attendants, one serving and the other operating the flyswatter. This picture does not fit the Geniza society. Even miniatures almost contemporary with the Geniza showing a slave swinging a flyswatter over the head of a governor during an audience should not be compared with life as it was in Geniza times. Jewish households did not keep male slaves; as far as slaves were kept at all, they were business agents and the like. Female attendants could not be employed at a meal where guests were present. The flyswatters were objects for personal use; the fact that silver handles (one costing 15 dinars) are mentioned points in the same direction.[83]

Similarly, fans were not large canvases constantly operated by slaves, as we know from Arabic literature, but small utensils. An order from Aden, accompanied by 3 dinars of local issue (worth about 1 Egyptian dinar), is carried out in Fustat thus: "He asked me to buy him fans and to frame them. I bought him twenty and had them framed." (The writer was a well-to-do merchant.)[84] When a rich Karaite girl in Fustat had four Baghdadi fans in her outfit, they were certainly of high quality (or did she wish to have some for her kitchen?).[85] When arguments grew acrimonious in an assembly of notables one VIP would hit another's knee with his fan, an occurrence worth reporting in a letter going overseas.[86] "Maker of fans" was a common Jewish family name.[87]

Did the Geniza people keep vases for flowers and pots for houseplants? The testimony of the documents is equivocal. A vessel called *narjis* or *narjisiyya*, narcissus or narcissus-like (both the Arabic and the English words are derived from the Greek), sometimes made of brass and sometimes of silver, occurs quite frequently.[88] In *The Arabian Nights* a narjisiyya of gold is described as a flowerpot; and the love of flowers is a well-attested characteristic of medieval Near Eastern society.[89] But when we read about "a pair of 'narcissuses' and their covers," or "a large tray and also 'narcissuses,' " a specific type of cup or bowl seems to be intended.[90] In another document, however, a pair of brass "narcissuses" is noted together with one of "violets," and another has four "violets" costing 2-1/2 dinars.[91] Could they be bowls for keeping flowers? Of Abū Saᶜd al-Tustarī, the Jewish "vizier," it was said that he had a roof garden of three hundred silver pots with trees; and a small garden within a house was nothing special.[92] When referring to a son in a letter to his father, one would usually call him "the lovely flower" (in Hebrew). The Jews of Sanᶜā, Yemen, had a lamp consisting of an upper, smaller container for the oil and a wider, hollow and open base. When not used as a lamp, the vessel was turned upside down and served as a vase for flowers. Whether one of the lamps discussed in the preceding subsection had a similar form and function cannot be said. As is well known, wide bases are a characteristic feature of medieval Islamic lampstands.

For the silver and crystal utensils adorning a woman's dressing table, see B, nn. 530–554, and Appendix D, below.

B. CLOTHING AND JEWELRY

1. Clothing

Attitudes toward clothing and general appearance.—"Waste on your back and save on your belly,"[1] that is, "spend on food and drink less than you are able to do, but on your clothing and outerwear as much as you can."[2] This ancient Near Eastern maxim, appearing in postbiblical Aramaic and Hebrew, is echoed in countless Arabic vernacular sayings—even of Bedouins.[3] I have not yet found it in a Geniza letter. The principle underlying it permeated the entire fabric of life to such a degree that there was no need, one might say no opportunity, to formulate it anew in words. Of all occupations connected with material things, those dealing with clothing were the most noble ones, more perhaps even than gold- and silversmithing; the clothier's profession was the most suitable one for a religious scholar.[4] In contrast, the processors of food belonged to the lowest ranks of society, or were women, whose status in society depended on that of their fathers or husbands, not on the work done by them.

The extreme concern with clothing and outward appearance found its expression in pre-Islamic Jewish and in Islamic religious literatures. How the Prophet dressed, perfumed himself, and dyed his hair is an extensive subject in the classical biographies of the Founder of Islam. Following this example, the vast biographical writings of the Muslims about their rulers, scholars, and holy men rarely fail to mention their types of clothing and other aspects of their personal appearance. Like the intellectuals of Late Antiquity those of early Islam dedicated considerable time of their nightly conversations to matters of the wardrobe.

The boundless riches that fell into the hands of the conquering Muslims enabled them to adorn themselves lavishly. Naturally, the question arose whether such luxury was compatible with a religion that preached otherworldliness, forsaking this world and seeking the face of God in the next. The prevailing answer was in the affirmative. "When Allah bestows favors on a man, he wishes them to be apparent on him." This saying, attributed to the Prophet in the ancient sources, means to say that the display of riches was an expression of gratitude toward God who had provided them.[5]

Characteristically, the pietist response to the manifestations of worldliness was directed against sumptuous clothing and, connected with them, furnishings. "Sinful luxury, *isrāf*, is not perpetrated in eating; it is in furnishings and clothing," says Ibrahīm Adham (pronounce *ad-ham*), one of the founders of the Muslim pietist movement known later as Sufism. The word Sufism is derived from *ṣūf*, wool, then the clothing of the poor.[6] In the most representative Islamic code of the Ḥanafī school, Abū Ḥanīfa, the founder of the school (d. 767), is credited with having worn a cloak worth 400 gold pieces; this is adduced in order to emphasize what the law and the general consensus of the community permitted.[7] By contrast, the entire apparel of a pious man living in Qayrawān, Tunisia, in the ninth century, robe, undershirt, pants, and shawl, was worth only one silver coin.[8] Both reports probably are legend, which would enhance, rather than diminish, their meaningfulness.

The prophets of ancient Israel thundered against luxury in clothing, jewelry, and furnishings, so much so that Isaiah 3:16–24 presents to us a full picture of the haughty "daughter of Zion" at her dressing table.[9] But that was in the times of independence, before the steamrollers of the Assyrian, Babylonian, Persian, Macedonian, and Roman empires crushed the peoples of the Near East and impoverished, among others, its Jewish population. Now the old belief in the importance of proper clothing received new emphasis: the degradation of poverty should not be made worse by the neglect of one's outward appearance. "My garments make me respectable," said Rabbi Yohanan, one of the great teachers of ethics in the third century.[10] Even stronger utterings to this effect may be quoted.[11]

It was particularly true with regard to women's clothing. "The daughters of Israel are beautiful, but poverty disfigures them."[12] Therefore the advice that one should spend on clothing as much as one can is followed by the admonition: "And on his wife and children even more than one can."[13] Jewish law provided that women have precedence over men in matters of clothing, when the community had to take care of its poor. As the lists of distribution of garments preserved in the Geniza show, this law was heeded.[14]

Clothing at home and outerwear.—Both Arabic and Hebrew possess special verbs and nouns for expressing the different ideas of clothing and outerwear.[15] Types of mantles and raincoats as protection against cold and bad weather are found everywhere in climates that require it, but that is not what the Semitic term for outerwear, or cover, was intended for. Covering oneself meant arraying oneself in a way that showed respect toward one's fellowmen when one appeared in public and especially in the most gregarious of all places, the house of worship. There, the eyes of God were also felt to rest on those assembled. The *ṭallīth,* or so-called prayer mantle or prayer shawl, now something to be worn during prayer and the synagogue service, was nothing of the kind in ancient times. The ṭallīth was one of several general words designating the upper garment. The Jews attached to it fringes or tassels of a certain type as prescribed in the Bible (Numbers 15:37–41). As in so many other matters, the Yemenites preserved this old custom well into the twentieth century. Until a few decades ago one could see their old men leaving the house wrapped in a large piece of black cloth to which were fastened the prescribed tassels, reaching almost to the ground. The *ʿarḍī* shawl, which could be used as a prayer mantle in Geniza times, might have looked the same.[16] The admonition to make every effort to dress oneself and one's beloved properly clearly distinguishes between clothing and cover, just as the bridegroom in the Karaite marriage contract from Jerusalem, 1028, promises to provide his future wife with clothing "for home and street."[17]

The relationship between the two is thus defined in a description of the apparel of a scholar or any other person in the public eye, such as honorary officers of the community: "A scholar's robe should be such that no part of his body should be seen beneath it; a scholar's ṭallīth should be such that his robe should be seen beneath it for not more than a handbreadth."[18] For the process of dressing, the verbal terms specific to each piece of clothing, somewhat difficult to express in English, are applied: "He puts on his underwear,[19] dons his robe, girds his belt, covers himself with his ṭallīth, and finally puts on his shoes." Shoes came at the end, because one used them only when leaving the house.[20]

The climate of the countries from which we have Geniza letters and documents permitted people during most of the year to leave the house without fear of being caught in the rain or suffering from excessive cold. Life was organized in such a way that one spent a large part of his time in the open air. It explains in part the role of the upper garment as a status symbol rather than as a means of protection for the body.[21]

Another matter was involved. Nakedness was an abomination, so much so that no case of a naked person, inside or outside a house, is ever reported in the Geniza. The very frequent complaint about one's "nakedness" means having no proper clothing.[22] A respectable person's robe should conceal his entire body, and the robe itself should be covered almost entirely by the outerwear. By such precautions the complete opposite of nakedness was obtained: the limbs of the body and its contours were hidden from the eye.[23] This attitude toward clothing seems to have been more or less common to the peoples of the Mediterranean region during the High Middle Ages, to which, at least down to approximately 1100, Northern France, Western Germany, and England must also be reckoned to a certain extent. Medieval illustrations from all those countries tell an unmistakable story.

Male and female costumes.—The practice of concealing the body by a number of modestly tailored wraps—the Talmud speaks of five to ten robes worn one over the other—had the consequence that male and female fashions did not differ very much in their make.[24] If needed or desired, husband and wife could use the same outerwear. Examples of such occurrences are found in Talmudic and Arabic literatures and are mentioned in Geniza letters. It is reported of Rabbi Yehuda (b. Ilʿay), the great teacher of the Mishna (second century), that his wife wove for herself a woolen cloak which she wore when going out and which he covered himself with when attending public prayer. When the head of the Jewish community ordered a fast to be held, he sent R. Yehuda a scholarly upper garment for appearance at so solemn an occasion, but he refused to accept it. A similar story is told of the pious Muslim from Qayrawān referred to above. Once he appeared in the cathedral mosque at the Friday noon prayer, the main weekly Muslim service, in the robe of his wife; he himself had washed his own, and he possessed only one. "Robe" renders here the Arabic *qamīṣ*, which is derived from the same Latin word as French *chemise*, and is used today, as in French, to mean shirt.[25]

It was not only poverty that could induce a man to wear an article of his wife's clothing. Here is a story from the pinnacle of early Islamic society. When the caliph Othmān (644–656) was seen wearing a silken *muṭraf* worth 800 dinars—an unseemly luxury for a Muslim male—he explained: "I 'covered' *Nā'ila* [the wife of his old age] with it, but seeing *me* wear it gives her greater pleasure."[26]

Instances of garments worn by both husband and wife occur in the Geniza more than once. I noted these two. A man with a beautiful Hebrew hand and good Arabic style, writing from Benhā, Lower Egypt, on his way to Alexandria, reports the following misdeed, among others perpetrated by a fellow traveler: "He stole my new cloak, worth three quarters of a dinar; by the Torah of the living God, I do not possess another one for traveling or for town, nor does my wife, for going out on the street."[27] When a pietist disciple of Abraham Maimonides married a destitute orphan girl "for the sake of God, for no other purpose whatsoever," he "pulled out one of his robes from his wardrobe and clothed her with it," since she herself had no proper dress of her own.[28]

The girl probably did not wear that robe as presented but fixed it to look like a garment proper for a woman; the Geniza differentiates throughout between clothing suitable for women and that for men. Even so simple and formless an object as the *maʿraqa*, perspiration skullcap, worn beneath one's more elaborate head cover, is described in the list of a dead man's possessions as being for women. Precisely because the main words for clothing, such as *thawb*, robe, *ḥulla*, gala costume, *malḥafa* and *mulā'a*, cloak, wrap, *jubba*, gown (with sleeves), jūkāniyya, short robe for daily use, or *ghilāla*, undershirt, slip, were used for both male and female apparel, it was necessary to qualify a piece by gender. The very fact, however, that the most frequently occurring terms of clothing were common to both sexes shows that their basic forms were identical.[29] By contrast, the purpose of, and, consequently, the means lavished on, the outerwear of men and women were entirely opposed to each other. While a woman should show her respect to her fellowmen by making herself inconspicuous, if not invisible, a man should demonstrate by his clothing what he was. As one may expect, and as the Geniza shows, this principle was not always adhered to, especially on the female side.

The clothing handed out by the Jewish community to Fustat to the indigent and to lower officials reveals most tangibly that the same type of garment could be worn by men and women. In order to preserve equality, only one type of clothing was usually handed out at each distribution, such as a jūkāniyya, a *fūṭa* (a sarilike cloth), or a cover made of felt. Men and women lined up pell-mell, or in groups, and each received a garment of the same type. To illustrate this situation, the first fifteen items of a detailed list of recipients are translated here.[30]

Sulayman, the astrologer, a jūkāniyya.—The boy [servant] of Hoshaʿnā, same.—The mother of the fat woman, same.—The wife [= widow] of ʿImrān of Tripoli, same.—The wife of the son of the jeweler, same.—The son of the man from Baghdad, same.—The mother-in-law of the Kohen, same.—Joseph b. Ḥasan [a community official], a robe—Abu 'l-Faraj, the parnās, a robe.—The maidservant [probably emancipated], a jūkāniyya.—The son of the [female] astrologer, same.—The son of Abū Ghālib, the goldsmith, same.—The wife [= widow] of Karīm of Tiberias, same.—Abū ʿAlī, the blind man, same.—The daughters of Abū Ghālib, the goldsmith, same.[31]

Changing, especially for the Sabbath and holidays.—The division of the week into working days and a festive and pleasurable weekend is so natural to us that we are prone to forget that this institution was unknown to the majority of mankind until quite recently. It became widely accepted in the world only under the impact of Western, originally Christian, civilization. It all began with a startling socio-religious revelation, embedded in the fourth of the Ten Commandments: "The seventh day is a sabbath to the Lord, your God; you shall not do any work, you, your son or daughter, your manservant or maidservant . . . so that your manservant and maidservant may rest as you do" (Deuteronomy 5:14). The Sabbath belongs to God (Isaiah 58:13–14); we all are his servants; our servants must be free for him on this day like ourselves. The holidays, too, are "God's" (Exodus 10:9; 12:14; 13:6, and elsewhere).

The profound reverence for the sanctity of the Sabbath and the holidays found its expression in the clothing for those days. One wished to be buried in one's Sabbath vestments.[32] A person's wardrobe (women included) was divided into the sections "for the sacred," and "for the profane, ordinary" (days).[33] When a widow, whose only remaining son was murdered by marauding soldiers, applied to the community for new clothing, she argued: "I must honor God's holiday."[34] Requests for new clothing at the time of the holidays were common.[35]

It was particularly true for the Day of Atonement. In 1028/9, a factotum of the merchant prince Joseph Ibn ʿAwkal (writing from Alexandria to Cairo) asks his master to honor him with one of his used cloaks "for the day of fasting."[36] Two hundred years later a woman in Aden, South Arabia, orders her son, who had traveled to Cairo, to send her a fine new dress "for the Day of Atonement."[37] This custom of donning new clothing on the Day of Atonement seems strange, since the New Year High Holiday precedes it by only ten days. The reason, no doubt, was originally the Talmudic saying: "Since you cannot honor the Day of Atonement by food and drink, honor it by spotless outerwear."[38] It is possible, however, that practices of the Muslim environment were also influential. E. W. Lane reports from the 1820s that it was customary in Cairo to put on new clothes on the holiday concluding Ramadan, the Muslim month of fasting.[39] The same practice is alluded to eight hundred years earlier for Alexandria in the letter of Ibn ʿAwkal's factotum mentioned above. There he explains and excuses his request for the cloak by complaining that because of the impending Muslim holiday (concluding Ramadan) no clothing was to be had in his town.[40] I have not read that a similar custom prevailed among the Jews of medieval Christian Europe.[41]

Clothing for the seasonal, originally agricultural holidays (Passover-spring, Pentecost-summer, Feast of the Tabernacles–autumn) had its own special character. These holidays were, as a Talmudic opinion had it, "one half for God and one half for yourselves"; they should be divided between study and enjoyment.[42] Geniza letters referring to clothing on those holidays emphasize their joyous look. A cantor whose bundle of clothing was lost when it fell into the Nile, complains to the Nagid Mevōrākh: "I have nothing beautiful with which to celebrate the feast."[43] A jobless scholarly person, writing to a well-off acquaintance, says: "I need beautifying things for the holiday," alluding discreetly also to a new dress for his wife.[44] As far as dress was concerned, these holidays were even more demanding than Sabbaths, which ranked higher in sanctity. "One of my troubles is that my 'prayer shawl' for Sabbath is torn; I patched it, but it did not hold. . . . I am embarrassed in view of the forthcoming blessed feast [Heb.]. I am ashamed standing among the people on Sabbath, let alone on this holiday."[45] The word translated here as prayer shawl, *ṣīṣīth*, the Hebrew term for tassels, should not be taken to mean a vestment assigned for prayer only; it was the outerwear of that poor man for Sabbaths, and was probably made of silk, whereas during the week he wrapped himself in a shawl of less expensive material, which was also equipped with the ritual tassels.[46]

The Sabbath with its strict prohibition of all mundane occupations was the Day of the Lord par excellence and the very symbol of sanctity. Whoever was able to do so changed everything: his headgear, his robe, and above all, of course, his upper garment, whatever it was, a simple shawl or an elaborate cloak.[47] He who had nothing to change to should at least change the way in which he wrapped his body during the week. An example was given above.[48]

Since everyone made an endeavor to provide himself with proper attire for the holy day, he was prone to forget to look after his clothing during the week. But a businessman could not permit himself to neglect his outer appearance. To conclude this subsection I translate a passage from a long letter sent by a Tunisian trader staying in Cairo to his cousin in Alexandria, where he orders for himself four suits for "secular" use:

> When the Sicilian boats arrive, please buy me two narrow *farkhas* of excellent quality, costing about 2 1/2 dinars, and two attractive *thawbs* worth about 1 1/2 dinars, and bring them with you. And if you, my lord, depart before the arrival of the Sicilian [boats], bring me two attractive robes, which have some elegance, and give 2 1/2 dinars to Joseph for the purchase and forwarding of two farkhas, for I do not have anything to wear on weekdays.[49]

It has been suggested elsewhere that changing one's clothes must have been a favorite pastime with the Geniza people, and not only with women.[50] In contrast, to abstain from changing was a severe form of self-abnegation, destined, like fasting, to enhance the efficacy of prayer for a beloved person. A woman in al-Mahdiyya, Tunisia, writes to her brother who was on a business trip to Egypt, when it was reported that he had fallen ill in the foreign country: "I vowed that neither I nor my daughter would eat during daytime, change clothes, or visit a bathhouse." Fortunately, passengers from another boat soon reported that the traveler had recovered and enjoyed good health.[51]

Changing for the night was common. Certain outer garments, such as the *ridā* coat, the *mulā'a* cloak, the *malḥafa* wrap, and the *izār* mantle, are often qualified in the Geniza as *lil-nawm*, for sleep, meaning that they were similar in appearance to garments worn during the day, but differed from them slightly when used as nightly covers. It has often been asserted that in Roman and medieval times people did not change for the night, because they are seen in illustrations asleep wearing garments donned in the daytime. But this interpretation of the pictorial material does not apply to the Geniza world. A "ridā for sleep" was listed thus in a trousseau list, because the purpose it served was somehow recognizable. A poor scholar from Jerusalem complained: "My cover for night, day, and Sabbath is all the same." The norm was that the three be different.[52]

In late medieval and modern Arabic, the very word for suit or costume is *badla*, a thing to be exchanged and replaced. Readers of *The Arabian Nights* are familiar with the lover who at every visit wears a more ravishing attire, and the merchant who, coming to make a new offer, does the same so that he looks like "one emerging fresh from the bathhouse."[53] Hebrew *ḥlf*, like Arabic *bdl*, means changing (clothes). When the Psalmist wishes to express the idea that our world is doomed to perish and to be replaced by successive other worlds, he says: "They will perish and you will remain; you will exchange them like clothing, and they will disappear" (Psalm 102:27).[54]

Types of clothing: the parts of the body and their covers.—Anyone who has looked at the pictures of French Impressionists, drawn less than a century ago, remembers that men, even while sitting in a coffeehouse, wore top hats, and their womenfolk were adorned with equally impressive headgear. Only recently, and under very special historical circumstances, have most of us (not I) discarded head covers altogether. This newfangled manner has been imitated, and, again, for very specific reasons, by most Muslim intellectuals. A generation ago, no one would have dreamed of entering a mosque without having one's head covered.[55] During the last few centuries the religious custom of covering one's head during prayer (and for the more observant—constantly) has become general even among the Jews of Europe.[56]

In Geniza times everyone "belonging," schoolboys included, wore elaborate head covers.[57] The bigger the turban, the more important its bearer. Often more money was spent on the adornment of one's head than on that of all the rest of the body. The value of the *miʿjar*, or wimple, of the lower middle-class bride from Jerusalem, 1028, whose trousseau list is translated below, was twice as much as her best holiday dress.[58] According to the estimates of their nuptial outfit the headgear of the well-to-do girls from the middle of the twelfth century was worth three to five times as much as their finest costumes.[59] The ubiquity, elaborateness, and high price of the wimple, the decorative outer head cover of women, impress any student of the Geniza marriage contracts.[60]

We possess no similar lists for men. By chance, a letter from a small town contains orders for both a turban and a robe; the writer is prepared to pay 5 dinars for the former, but only 3 for the latter.[61] From a shipment of threads (of fine linen) sent from Fustat to Alexandria, a turban was made measuring 25 cubits, whereas the piece of cloth for a robe to go with it contained only 20.[62] For fine Sicilian turbans—much in demand—one paid 4–6 dinars. Like most other Sicilian textiles, they were made of silk.[63] But even cotton turbans of good quality could cost up to 3 dinars, whereas a man's robe was to be had for 1–2 dinars. Much material and high quality workmanship went into these fabrics of utmost thinness wound around the head.[64]

This intense concern for the head cover, as far as I can see, had its roots in two entirely different human dispositions: the wish to impress our fellowmen on the one side, and the awe for the divine, before which we have to humiliate (and perhaps also to protect) ourselves, on the other. The head is that part of our body on which the eye of persons facing us rests the most; the message we desire to convey by our appearance is affected the most by it. In antiquity Jewish common men, like Greeks and Romans, usually went bareheaded. The famous passage in I Corinthians 11:1–13, which presupposes this fact, so often quoted today because of its antifeminist stance, could be illustrated by many Old Testament and Talmudic references. Nevertheless, persons of special rank: kings, priests, and bridegrooms (who played the role of kings), wore turbans of different shapes and names. One of them (a common one) was *p'ēr*, a word combining the meanings of ornament and pride. It so happens in the history of clothing, those who could afford it imitated "the great." The prophet Isaiah castigates "the daughters of Zion" for their luxurious p'ērs (3:20), and the noble Judeans, who were exiled to Babylonia, wore p'ērs like the priest and prophet Ezekiel addressing them (24:17–23). By the time of the development of a large middle class in early Islam every respectable person had to ornament himself with a turban. It had become a status symbol like the upper garment.

The meticulous covering of the head was motivated also by religious sentiment. In the Aramaic language, which was spoken everywhere from Babylonia to Palestine for fifteen hundred years until it was replaced by Arabic, *bareheaded* meant *bold-faced*, defiant.[65] But we should not be irreverent in the presence of God, who is constantly with and above us. "I never walk even four cubits bareheaded, for God's presence is above my head," says one of the sages of the Talmud. His example was recommended as worth imitating by

Moses Maimonides in both his Code of Law and his *Guide for the Perplexed*, and a similar religious attitude toward head cover was alive in Islam.[66]

Medieval Islamic illustrations, whether in books or on objects of art, made of metals, ivory, or wood, usually show us the human body concealed by several layers of garments, mostly wide and flowing, so that often the contours and limbs of the body are hardly recognizable. (Only persons of low manual occupations, such as peasants, butchers, or bakers, possess a body and are also occasionally permitted to go around bare-headed).[67] Considering the medieval attitudes toward nakedness, clothing, and outerwear, this endeavor to conceal the body was to be expected.[68] The Geniza documents betray the same spirit, naturally in an indirect way. A man on his deathbed wishes to have a simple burial: "No wailing women, please; and of garments in which I shall be buried I wish to have no more than these: two cloaks, three robes, a washed turban of fine linen—it is already wound up—[69] new underpants of mine, and a new waistband of mine." Clearly, five covers of the body were regarded by persons of the class to which our dying man belonged as something very austere.[70]

When a person died without having made such specifications, the burial clothing had to be held to the minimum. Besides the clothing there were, of course, other funeral dues (detailed in the same document). The account lists the expenses in three coins: dinārs, qīrāṭs (1/24 dinar), and dirhems (worth approximately 1/40 dinar).

Account for the 'Shroud'

A tunic	19 qīrāts
A robe of Dimyaṭī [linen, probably white] and another of green silk	2, 2/3, 1/4 dinars
[for two robes a total of	2 dinars and 22 qīrāṭs]
A scarf	10 1/2 qīrāṭs
Underpants	9 dirhems
A turban	30 dirhems
A cloak	1 dinār
The tailor[71]	3 dirhems

The total payments for the clothing amounted to a little more than 5 dinars. The dead man belonged to the lower middle class; besides a tunic, two robes, and a cloak, he got a scarf, which also covered a large part of the body.[72]

The concealment of the body was made complete by wide, puffy sleeves, which gave the impression that the arms and trunk were one. This sartorial trait is described by a Muslim historian as an innovation of the Abbasid caliph al-Mustaʿīn (862–866); but it was so in conformity with the general concepts about clothing that no princely inventiveness should be sought for its origin.[73] The wide sleeves served as receptacles (instead of pockets, absent from medieval Near Eastern and European clothing). Men and women kept there a *mandīl kumm,* a sleeve kerchief, in which money and a wide variety of other objects could be stored. Such a mandīl could cost up to a dinar; its color was white, it was sometimes embroidered.[74] A man complaining about government extortion and tortures reports (in a letter sent from Cairo to the Fayyūm): "I had on [*thus*!] my sleeve 5 *nuqra* [good silver] dirhems, which fell from my sleeve on that Wednesday; before, my keys fell out together with 5 black [poor silver content] silver dirhems."[75] A question addressed to Moses Maimonides reports that a man who was asked by a friend to show the precious stone of a ring to a jeweler wrapped the stone and other things in his sleeve kerchief, but the kerchief fell out of the sleeve and the stone was lost.[76] The merchants carried their accounts there, the singers their songbooks, and our playing cards are oblong, because they came to Europe from countries where they were kept in sleeves.[77] Many other uses of the sleeve kerchief could be adduced from Islamic literature.[78] I have never found that it served for blowing the nose. The custom of using a piece of cloth for this purpose seems to be a later, European, invention. The English carry their handkerchiefs in their sleeves. But I do not believe that Richard the Lion-Hearted brought this custom back from his Crusade.

On most of the Islamic miniatures of the thirteenth century one observes that everyone, male and female, low and high, has on the upper part of his sleeves a stripe of material different in color from the rest of the garment and decorated with embroidered script or otherwise.[79] A marriage contract from the year 1239/40 lists a silken robe whose sleeves were beautified (literally, crowned) with pearls.[80] A teacher addressing a person of high standing and his brother writes this: "You have showered me with your favors from the crown of my head to the soles of my feet; your precious garments are on my skin, and there are these sleeves with embroideries on both sides."[81] The sleeves are mentioned separately because they could be given as a present (or purchased) without being attached to a garment. The upper arm is a symbol of strength. In the ancient Middle East a metal ring around it was an emblem of authority. I wonder whether this concept was living on in the ubiquitous decorations of the upper sleeve. The practice of attaching allusive verses to their sleeves, adhered to by the sophisticated ladies of early Abbasid Baghdad, was probably the direct model for the custom described in this paragraph.[82]

After all that has gone before, there is no need to explain why trousers, in the sense we use the word, were absent from the medieval Islamic wardrobe. Underpants were generally worn, but, except in business letters and inventories, they are mentioned only on special occasions, such as burials, when they formed an indispensable part of a dead man's attire.[83] Pants are practically absent from trousseau lists.[84] But it was a matter of propriety, and, besides, the value of the textiles used for that purpose was too little to be included in a document detailing a husband's "debt" to his wife. Only in a marriage contract from the little town of Damsīs in the Nile Delta are the pants listed, but in Hebrew, as we would circumscribe "unmentionables" by writing the word in Latin. The price, half a dinar, was exceptionally high. As illustrations show, the underpants of working people were short and tight, those of the middle class and women longer and fluffy, but entirely different from the later Near Eastern breeches, *sirwāl*, which were excessively wide in their upper part, but corded up beneath the knee.[85]

The shoe, like the turban, was the object of conflicting feelings. It was basically an "unmentionable," looked upon as "the mire of the streets" (Psalm 18:43 and elsewhere), through which it had to wade. When entering a mosque or an Oriental synagogue one took one's shoes off. My Yemenite interlocutors, who spoke Arabic, of course, never used the word shoe, but always circumvented it with a curiously intricate Hebrew phrase: "that which is beneath your honor [to be mentioned in your presence]." To refer to a person as a shoe was an expression of utmost contempt.[86]

Similarly, when a twelfth-century woman complains to the Head of the Jewish community of Egypt about her drunkard of a husband, she writes: "He hit me with something that cannot be mentioned."[87] Beating a person with a shoe was common; it could easily be taken off the foot and also symbolized one's despise of the foe. Having your face slapped with your own boot was the most extreme humiliation.[88]

Precisely because shoes were exposed to dirt and contempt, persons who were fussy about their outward appearance took particular care that their shoes be in proper shape at all times. Among the bourgeoisie of Geniza times there was a real cult of footwear. Abraham Maimonides, in his "Complete Guide for the Pious" says that most people were as concerned with keeping their shoes polished as with the proper setting of their turbans.[89] One ordered shoes from other towns or countries not only in mercantile quantities but also and often for personal use. In a large account from Fustat sent to Tunisia in 1065, listing precious Oriental commodities, such as perforated pearls of different types, camphor, and clover, one addressee gets a green *ʿaqbiyya* robe and a pair of red shoes, three others each get one pair (color not specified), and one customer gets a pair of *tāsūma* slippers.[90] In another memo by the same writer, addressed to Fustat, we read: "Buy me a first-class pair of yellow shoes and have them impregnated." I understand the latter expression to mean that the shoes were to be oiled to make them weatherproof.[91] A shipment of goods arriving from Tunisia in Alexandria during the same period was supposed to contain shoes "oiled" or gilded.[92] Islamic miniatures indeed show men wearing shoes of a variety of colors. I have never found black shoes mentioned in the Geniza, but doubt that it was due to a humorous story told at considerable length in the Talmud, according to which black shoes, being a sign of mourning, were not worn by Jews.[93]

A Sicilian writing from Qayrawān, Tunisia, where he passed the winter, orders from Cairo for his boy "a small cloak, a short robe, and small shoes," which gives the impression that the shoes, by similar or contrasting colors, should somehow go with the clothing.[94] Their shape is rarely described. Twice in orders the writers specify shoes "wide around the ankles," one adding, "but solid," apparently referring to low boots reaching just above the ankles, as seen in illustrations.[95] A most comprehensive order for textiles concludes with one for "twenty corkwood shoes of which ten should be made plain, of the type you have previously imported."[96] The cork sandals were probably worn by persons working in the kitchen or doing other housework such as washing the tiles on the floor. This eleventh-century document depicts a well-to-do society. No comparison should be made with a note in a fifteenth-century Muslim handbook of market supervision, where we are told that the poor Jews of Morocco either wore cork shoes or went barefoot.[97] A trousseau list written around 1200 mentions a shoe buckle worth 5 dinars, which would mean that it was made of a precious metal. The word used for shoe is Turkish; at that time many new terms appear in the marriage contracts, and it is likely that these terms also designated new shapes.[98] Two types of slippers have outlandish names. In the Geniza I found the Arabic word for mules (slippers without counter) only in the term designating their makers. The Arabic synonyms for cobblers are indicative of the variety of their products.[99]

Prices for shoes are difficult to come by in the Geniza. The sums noted in business letters are not accompanied by the quantities sent, and the price of about 1/4 dinar repeatedly mentioned was for persons in a state of dependence, whether free or slaves.[100] When we read, however, that a man in a stormy sea lost "11 dinars, a pair of new shoes, and a box with camphor," we understand that the pair lost, mentioned between two costly items, must have been quite valuable to its possessor.[101]

With one dubious exception, shoes never appear in the lists detailing a bride's outfit. Originally, I was inclined to ascribe this absence to their "unmentionableness." In view of the lively concern for footwear shown by Geniza people, however, I began to doubt the correctness of this explanation. Now I have learned from Professor Sylvia Haim-Kedouri that among the Jews of Baghdad it was customary for the groom to present shoes as a gift not only to his bride but also to her female relatives. In antiquity, the giving and removing of shoes were symbols for the conveying and withdrawing, respectively, of authority (see Ruth 4:7–8, Deuteronomy 25:9–10). This strange custom of sending shoes to the bride, which remained alive among the Jews of Baghdad until the beginning of the twentieth century, most probably was practiced also by the Jews of Egypt a millennium before. I have not yet found it in the Geniza, but it is attested in an Arabic papyrus. There, a list of *ḥawā'ij al-ʿurs*, the gifts sent for perfuming, bathing, and dyeing of the bride with henna and saffron, concludes with the item "Indian shoes with Tinnīsī [white linen] laces, costing a quarter dinar." Special attention to the laces was already fashionable in Talmudic times.[102]

Since many garments were little tailored, a cover of one part of the body could occasionally be extended over another. The ubiquitous female head cover miʿjar is described in one trousseau list as "cloaklike," which means that it was large enough to be wrapped around the entire body.[103] While traveling, one wound the end of the long cloth forming the turban around the neck to protect the body from dust and sand. Buttonholes had not yet been invented; the lapel of the turban formed a collar helping to close the cloak or mantle tightly. In short, it was not so much the parts as the entirety of the human appearance which was emphasized by the taste of those times.[104]

Fabrics and colors.—Of the four main fabrics provided by nature—

flax and wool (indigenous to the Middle East and Europe), cotton (systematically cultivated in India), and silk (used for millennia in China)—linen made of flax was by far the most common textile appearing in the Geniza. It was closely followed by silk, while cotton, for which Egypt has become so preeminent in modern times, lingered far behind during the High Middle Ages. Wool (of sheep, camels, and other animals), once the main fiber used by Arabs, became entirely overshadowed by the other fabrics. The astounding popularity of the upstart silk, which became widespread in the Mediterranean area in the centuries preceding and following the coming of Islam, is one of the most distinctive expressions of a refined and extravagant urban civilization. Clothes made of linen had been the national costume of Egypt since Pharaonic times.

These and other textiles, the countries of their cultivation, and technical aspects of their manufacture in Geniza times have been discussed in the subsection "The Main Industries" in the first volume of this book.[105] Their prices and economic significance, especially those of the staple goods silk and flax, have been explained there in the subsection "Commodities, Trade Routes, and Prices."[106] Here, their use for clothing, their combination with one another for this purpose, and their colors, prominently emphasized in the Geniza documents, are surveyed briefly.

While admonishing his colleagues, the religious scholars, to pay meticulous attention to their outward appearance, Abraham Maimonides (1186–1237) has this to say: "The ancient sages did not make it obligatory that the clothes of a scholar be silk in the winter and thin fine linen[107] in the summer, but that his garments should be spotlessly clean,[108] even though they consist of coarse cotton in the winter and secondhand[109] linen in the summer."[110] Wool, as we see, is not mentioned at all. Cotton was undesirable. Everyone wished to go around in silk or linen, even if he could not afford to change as often as desirable.

That being so, one is surprised to find the word "linen" only rarely in the trousseau lists of the Geniza and the terms for the various types of silk not so often as one would expect.[111] The reason for this apparent deficiency is the fact, well known to us from our own urban world, that yarns of different origin were often woven together, and besides, the fabrics on the market had a trade name bearing the name of a country, a town, or any other appellation, the origin of which cannot always be ascertained.[112]

The most common and really ubiquitous type of Egyptian linen, used for clothing as extensively as for bedding, was called Dabīqī. Its name is derived from the town of Dabīq, which disappeared from the face of the earth so completely that today even its exact location is not known. Although two fragments of material from the Fatimid period bearing the name Dabīq as its place of manufacture have been found, the town of Dabīq itself is never mentioned in the Geniza.[113]

Dabīqī was used for each and every type of garment, from the *ghilāla*, the slip or undershirt worn next to the body, to the mulā'a, the cloak a person put on when leaving the house, although one preferred even finer fabrics for the underwear as well as for the turban. As the phrase "whiter than Dabīqī garments" indicates, its natural color was white.[114] In the about two hundred cases of Dabīqī I came across, somewhat less than half do not note a color, which I take to mean that the fabric was white. Of the colors mentioned, about half were "white," followed by only a dozen cases of blue, a similar number of grayish ("cloud-," "manna" [light]-, "lead-" colored), while a few other colors occur only once, or at most three times (green). The average price of a substantial piece of female clothing—those forming part of a dowry—made of Dabīqī, such as a robe, cloak, or mantilla, was 3–6 dinars, a considerable expenditure. In about ten instances a Dabīqī is described as *ḥarīrī*, silken, or, vice versa, a silken cloth is called Dabīqī, which can only mean that linen and silk were woven together.[115] Dabīqī interwoven with gold threads, *mudhahhab*, occurs rarely, but it is likely that many or most of the numerous mudhahhab garments whose basic fabric is not noted were also made of linen.[116]

From the Dabīqī, the Egyptian linen in general use, is to be differentiated the *sharb*, an extremely fine and expensive linen, similar perhaps to a loosely woven gauze. It was used not only for the slip, the female undergarment (which an Arabic literary source, not the Geniza, describes as transparent)[117] and for the twenty-five cubits-long turban (which, to be wound around the head, had to be extremely thin)[118] but also for a gala costume and even a cloak. A list of clothing ordered in Cairo by a merchant writing from Aden, South Arabia, concludes: "The remainder should be with sharb [or made of sharb], whether it is a cloak, a head cover, ʿarḍi, or a 'Sevener.'" In hot Aden the thinnest linen was the appropriate fabric for all clothing.[119] In a late trousseau list it is described as "with silk," which might perhaps mean "with a silk border" or the like, rather than interwoven with that fabric.[120]

Compared with Dabīqī, other varieties of Egyptian linen are only occasionally found in the Geniza, lead by Tinnīsī, originally manufactured in the famous industrial center Tinnīs, situated on the shores of the Mediterranean. Tinnīsī was used mostly for bedding and cushions, not for garments. Getting wimples in Tinnīs, as ordered by a business friend, was a herculean task. Noteworthy is "Tinnīsī Rūmī mantilla," a European piece of clothing imitated in that Egyptian linen center.[121]

Linen from Tūna, an island between Tinnīs and Damietta, was renowned for its beauty. It is noted in the Geniza, and pieces bearing its name have been preserved.[122] The references to other towns famous for their linen industry, such as Damietta or Abyār (Ibyār), are so rare that they are probably not trade names but items actually manufactured in those places.[123] Iskandar[ān]ī, a frequently mentioned Alexandrian textile, served mostly for making blankets (for use both as clothing and as nightly cover).[124]

A linen fabric called Ḥāfiẓī appears regularly in the trousseau lists of the second half of the twelfth century, mostly at a value of 2 dinars. I am inclined to derive this appellation from the regnal title of the caliph al-Ḥāfiẓ (Keeper of God's Religion, 1131–1146), or rather of his imperial guard, the Ḥāfiẓiyya, whose uniform the inhabitants of the capital certainly often had opportunity to admire. Ḥāfiẓī garments are never identified by color; the attire of the Ḥāfiẓiyya corps probably was characterized by a certain combination of colors, which made further identification superfluous.[125]

Linen was a fabric of many different types. Since flax growing was a local, age-old agricultural industry in Egypt, each locality had developed its own style. The Jewish merchants, who traded the flax threads after they had been expertly treated,[126] carefully discerned between the various types, each of which had a tradename, mostly, but not always, taken from the name of the place where the flax was grown. To the twenty-two varieties listed in *Med. Soc.*, I, 455–457, I have since noted four more in the Geniza, and more will probably be found there and in literary sources. There can be no doubt that the finished linen products differed from one another in durability, smoothness, luster, and fineness, facts certainly well known not only to the dealers but also to the discerning customers. A Muslim handbook of market supervision indeed warns in the strongest terms not to mingle a poor variety of Egyptian flax with another.[127]

A similar and perhaps even greater multitude of varieties could be observed with regard to silk, a yarn produced in many countries, treated with different techniques, and often blended with other materials. To conclude from their writings, the Geniza people must have devoted a considerable part of their lives to discussing which kind of silk to choose for which garment and for which occasion. Until quite recently it was my experience that a new type of silk or, at least, a new aspect of the silk industry popped up whenever I came upon a previously unidentified Geniza piece, such as an extended business letter or a trousseau list. Here is a passage from a letter in the New Series of the E. N. Adler Collection, New York, written by a Maghrebi merchant, who, coming from al-Mahdiyya, Tunisia, had arrived in Alexandria at a time of civil unrest. As the names mentioned show, the letter was sent to Fustat during the turbulent 1060s or early 1070s:

> During the last few days the merchants from Constantinople have already agreed upon prices; those from Venice and Crete still hold back. . . . As to the goods brought by the Sicilians, cross [transverse] silk [threads]: 10 pounds cost 19 dinars; twisted ones: 1 pound—20 qīrāṭs (= 5/6 dinar); Spanish "cutting" [meaning: superfine] *khazz* silk: 10 pounds—25 through 26 dinars; *khazāsh*: 10 pounds for 20 dinars or less; Gabes silk is not to be had.[128]

In *Med. Soc.*, I, 102, it was stated on the authority of a Muslim geographer that Gabes was the only place in Tunisia where mulberry trees were planted and silk produced but that no mention of this could be found in the Geniza at that time. Here the Tunisian silk of Gabes ranks alongside the products of Sicily and Spain, the great centers of the silk industry.[129]

In the letters of the merchants silk means yarn. Where fabrics or garments are concerned, it is expressly stated. I render here a passage from a letter that exemplifies it and also demonstrates how diversified silks were, even when traded in small quantities, and how, on the receiving end, silk had to appeal to many different tastes and serve a variety of uses. The young Nahray b. Nissīm, besides doing many errands for the senior members of the family, sends (from Tunisia to Egypt) also a modest shipment of his own:

> After asking God for guidance I sent you a bundle containing 100 pieces of Sūsa cloth, of pure color, 40 3/4 pounds of Syracuse [silk] and pepper-gray "transverse,"[130] 11 2/3 of Andalusian "pickups,"[131] 6 pounds and 1 ounce of Palermo lāsīn,[132] and 23 pounds of lāsīn waste silk;[133] furthermore, a crate containing 15 robes and 1 mantle of fine silk, 52 hides . . . and other goods, as specified in the note inside the bundle.[134]

The recipient is asked to sell these items and others, such as brocade, Tustarī,[135] and Qayrawān cloth, belonging to an uncle, and with the proceeds to buy two bales of flax. A shipment of flax sent by the addressee had been transported by Nahray to the industrial city of Sūsa, where he hoped to sell it "during the winter" with great profit.[136] The flax of Egypt and the silks of Sicily and Spain were worked in Tunisia into world-famous textiles.

As in the passage just translated, Spanish silk, richly represented in the Geniza, is usually referred to by the general term "Andalusian." But the merchants knew well that Spain was as blessed with local varieties of silk as Sicily, or as Egypt was with flax. This detail from a long business order is characteristic: "Five pounds Shawdharī and Qurṭubī [Cordova silk], half-and-half; and another five, two-thirds Qurṭubī."[137] Cordova was famous for its silk; Shawdhar, a place southeast of Cordova and nearer to Granada, produced another variety. The writer wished to have the two yarns mingled in different proportions.[138] The woman from Jerusalem who ordered in Fustat five pounds of Shadhūna crimson—if it was to be had in the Egyptian capital—was perhaps herself a native of Spain or some other country of the western Mediterranean. Clothes made in, or in the style of, Manāra, a place near Shadhūna, were repeatedly sent from Aden to India.[139]

When Tustarī cloth is exported from Qayrawān, Tunisia, to Egypt (see n. 135), it is safe to assume that, like other silks bearing Iranian tradenames, this Tustarī was manufactured somewhere in the Muslim West and not in the city after which it was named. A father of a bride writing from Aden, South Arabia, to Cairo, orders as the first item of her outfit "four Jurjānī tunics with their wimples, and if no Jurjānīs are available, buy instead finest silk robes fitting women; they should be tailored."[140] When I first read this, I was much impressed. For Jurjān is a country southeast of the Caspian Sea, today a part of Central Asian Soviet Russia. How did those materials become the first choice of that girl living in a seaport on the India route?[141] My astonishment abated when I read that Jurjānīs were also manufactured in Almeria, a port city on the eastern coast of Spain, which was regularly visited by merchants from Egypt, including those who traveled to India via Aden.[142]

In the preceding pages I wished to illustrate by a few examples the wide diffusion and diversity of silkwear encountered in the Geniza world. Much has been said about this topic in *Med. Soc.* I, and more is coming in the following pages. The prominence of silk, however, was perhaps not as widespread as might appear from our documents. Egypt was an importer rather than a producer of that fabric. It is natural that costly items brought from distant countries and then often worked into high-priced specialties should loom large in business correspondence and in trousseau lists. Yet, the popularity of silk in the Mediterranean area during the High Middle Ages remains remarkable. This strong, clean, and fine yarn probably answered at that time many needs which are now fulfilled by the marvelous synthetic fabrics created in our own time.[143]

The emphasis in the Geniza with regard to silk applies, in reverse to cotton. I mean, that in actual life cotton was probably far more important than can be substantiated from the Geniza. Cotton is absent from the trousseau lists.[144] It was the clothing of the poor, as explained in *Med. Soc.*, III, 304–305, in connection with the lot of the orphans. Here is another characteristic item. A business letter from Alexandria to Nahray b. Nissīm concludes with this request:

> My lord, here in the house in which I live there is a poor young woman who has nothing to wear in this hard winter. As you know, I am presently not able to provide her with an outer garment. Perhaps you will collect among your friends half a dinar, for which a piece of cotton cloth could be bought here to serve her as a cover. By doing so you will acquire great *religious merit.*

One sees the writer is anxious to emphasize that he is asking for nothing extravagant, he wishes to obtain only the barest minimum needed for providing a poor girl with clothing.[145]

The absence of cotton from trousseau lists might have had its reason also in the requirement that a bride's outfit should be made of durable materials, and cotton, of course, is less durable than linen.[146] In lists of belongings of deceased persons cotton cloth occurs rarely, and then it is mostly from the India route, or the western Mediterranean, where cotton was produced.[147] Business letters from the Syrian ports frequently mention shipments of cotton, but only in small quantities, and definitely as a sideline.[148] Among the hundreds of occupations of Jews mentioned in the Geniza I have never come upon a *qaṭṭān*, a maker of or trader in cotton, as common as this appellation is today as a family name among North African Jews. The only bearer of this name that I found in the Geniza was a Muslim.[149] Importing large quantities of a cheap commodity of great volume had to be left to the rich Muslim shipowners, who would carry them whenever they had space available.[150]

In Egypt, cotton seems to have been used mostly for working clothes, pants, and bedding, in addition to serving as lining or filling for cloaks and wraps made from other fibers. A cotton robe worn by a Tunisian merchant over his main garments and left by him in Alexandria when he proceeded to Fustat, probably had served him as a means of protection while on sea. A man from Alexandria, describing himself as "naked" (see n. 3, above), writes "I have nothing on my body except an Aleppo robe," no doubt meaning one made of cotton. The Muslim topographers of Fustat speak only of an "alley of the cotton dealers," clearly a side street of limited size. A fragmentary Geniza letter mentions the "cotton market," visited by a Jewish woman, where she met an acquaintance.[151]

A textile constantly mentioned as a main export from India to the West, and especially from the north-Indian province of Nahrawāra-Gujerāt, requires some attention. It was named *miḥbas* (more commonly occurring in the plural *maḥābis*), which might be translated as wrapper.[152] It was traded in scores, consisting of twenty complete or half thawbs, a word usually denoting the robe worn by everyone, male or female, but also the piece of material needed for a robe.[153] The maḥābis were also used for the manufacture of pillows; red and black are mentioned as their colors, and their average price, approximately 1 Adenese, or 1/3 Egyptian dinar, makes it more than likely that they were made of cotton, the most important of Indian textiles.[154] The term "maḥābis" was not used in Egypt; when a Jewish merchant on the India route sends "a fine cotton robe" to a Muslim business friend in Qūṣ, Upper Egypt, he uses the regular Arabic term *quṭn* (from which the English word is derived).[155]

The Geniza people, indigenous to Egypt, never complain about heat, but often about cold. Sheep and camels abounded in that country, but wool seems to have been used for clothing far less than expected.[156] Like garments of cotton, those made of wool were not included in the outfits of brides, and, as in the case of cotton, the reason for this might have been partly technical. In the hot climate of Egypt, wool was much exposed to vermin and other damage. The Geniza letters show that their writers were very much aware of this. Wool sent from the Maghreb to Alexandria should not be forwarded to Cairo "until the air will become cooler."[157] Wool should be aired by being stretched out or by being hung up, weighted with stones, in a place with fresh air, but with no dust falling on it.[158]

The only garment repeatedly mentioned in the Geniza as made of wool was the *jubba*, or gown, worth an average of 10 qīrāṭs, or slightly less than half a dinar, according to an account from the mid-eleventh century, where three shipments of this material are noted.[159] According to a court record from Bilbays in Lower Egypt, written in December 1218, a widow possessed a woolen jubba, regarded as property of her late husband.[160] Since the standard minimum for a thawb, or robe, was 1 dinar, one sees that wool was regarded as an inferior fabric for clothing; it was the wear of beggars.[161]

This animal fiber, however, whose superior qualities include the thorough retaining of dyes, served, when dyed purple, as the adornment of kings. The various hues of purple are so expensive because a countless number of shellfish have to be crushed to obtain from them the desired dye.[162] In antiquity, the wearing of purple was restricted to rulers and other persons of high rank. In Geniza times the upper echelons of the bourgeoisie must also have indulged in this luxury, since shellfish gathering, the production of purple, and the dyeing of wool with its different hues appear in the Geniza as entirely private enterprises. Our sources show us Jewish purple makers at work. But this profession was by no means confined to Jews. When the rabbinical court of Fustat wished to evaluate a purple workshop left to an orphan, it invited non-Jewish experts to join in the inspection.[163] Purple cloth was probably used for the various borders and badges so often mentioned in the description of garments—similar to the *toga praetexta* of the ancient Romans—not for a complete garment. It would have been too expensive, and too warm during most of the year.[164]

The story of colors in the Geniza is full of surprises. Because of the passion of medieval people—and not only those of the Mediterranean area[165]—for brilliant and variegated colors, hence a flourishing dyeing industry, there was plenty of opportunity to touch upon these topics on other occasions. In *Med. Soc.*, I, 106–108, 419–420, it was emphasized that the predilection for colorful clothing was by no means confined to the fair sex, and that the differences in local usage and individual taste gave rise to a wide spectrum of hues and shades cherished. With the means then at the disposal of the dyers, serious efforts had to be made to satisfy the multifarious demands. The cost of the dyeing stuffs, often imported from distant countries, far exceeded the wages of the craftsmen working with them. The dyers seem to have been a mobile profession, migrating from one place to another, thus contributing to the diffusion of tastes and techniques (*Med. Soc.*, I, 51, 86).

Supplying dyeing materials and mordants (the ingredients needed for fixing dyes in textiles permanently)[166] was one of the main branches of international and local trades, as described throughout *Med. Soc.*, I, with indigo leading the list. Woad, mentioned in a tenth-century Hebrew document from Qayrawān as exported in considerable quantities from Egypt to Tunisia, is called there "*isatis* [Hebrew derived from Greek], known as Syro-Palestinian indigo." The *Isatis tinctorum*, once one of the most prominent dyeing plants, did indeed grow in that region, but was in the process of being replaced by indigo, a root,"stronger and more reliable than woad."[167] Indigo—originally cultivated in India (and sometimes referred to in the Geniza as Indian)—was also grown in other places, such as Egypt and the Jordan valley. Called *nīl* in Arabic (a Sanskrit word), indigo appears in the Geniza as a widely traded dyeing stuff, exported also to Europe, but never as a color, as is done in English. The reason for this seeming discrepancy was the use of this dye for producing a wide range of colors, from blackish and deep blue to green, depending on the type and quality of indigo selected, the mixture, density, and temperature of the solution prepared, the mordant added, and how often and how long each time the textiles were immersed.[168] Similarly, and for the same reason, brazilwood, a red tropical wood yielding various shades of red and purple, was one of the main items of both the India and Mediterranean trades, but it never occurs as a color.[169]

Zaʿfarān, grown in Tunisia and exported from there to Egypt and further afield, like its English derivative saffron, denoted both the plant and the orange yellow color produced from it. The names of the kermes, an insect, and the crimson, the dyestuff prepared from its dried body, go back to Arabic *qirmiz* (itself derived from Sanskrit), which, in the Geniza, stands for both the trading commodity and the color. Yet, both zaʿfarān and qirmiz are rarely used as descriptions of the color of a garment. Precisely because saffron and kermes were in such wide use as dyestuffs, their names were not well suited to provide the exact shade of a desired or reported color. The same could be said of other dyeing materials. Language had to be inventive to create conventional terms for identifying a color precisely.[170]

Unfortunately, the writers of the trousseau lists, our main source for the knowledge of clothing, were not very meticulous in their descriptions. The clerks were in a hurry; they were satisfied with labeling an object somehow, but did not oblige themselves to describe it in detail.[171] The merchants, naturally, were more precise. When a clothier placed an order, and his business friend filled it, the colors desired were carefully differentiated. But we do not have much of this material.[172]

Since whatever statistics can be compiled can be culled only from the richly available trousseau lists, those data concern the colors of female garments and home furnishings. The degree of favor enjoyed by the basic colors in Geniza times may be gauged by the frequency with which each appears in bridal outfits and similar sources. The list that follows is qualified considerably, however, by the subsequent discussion of the various shades of colors noticed in the same documents.

The leading role of white becomes even more impressive when complemented by its many shades, from glittering "snow-colored" (rare) to the very common pearl-colored, or pale white (noted 17 times). Cloud-colored, also frequent (14 times), could mean several things, but Arabic has various words for cloud, and *saḥābī*, the term

The basic colors noted in trousseau lists and cognate sources

	Total	For use other than clothing
1. White	83	10
2. Blue	62	8
3. Green	30	10
4. Red	22	10
5. Black	16	--
6. Yellow	12	9

used, designates the white, fluffy cumulus. Consider also this quotation: "A cloud-colored turban of thin fine linen was wound on and above his head so that it looked like a cloud heaped upon his head."[173] Since the same Arabic term is used for mercury, there is little doubt that a hue of silvery white was intended.[174] Silver, lead, borax, and starch were used for describing other shining or off-white hues. Of particular interest is the asparagus color. In a tenth-century comprehensive treatise on agriculture and many other matters, the color of the asparagus is praised as particularly attractive because its white shades into red, yellow, and wine, a diversity that is pleasing to the eye.[175] In the Geniza the term occurs in documents from the thirteenth and fourteenth centuries. "Glass" and "crystal" referring to textiles, probably describe them as translucent and lustrous, respectively. As a rule, Islamic glass from the High Middle Ages was translucent, not transparent.

The predilection of Geniza women for subdued shades of white is best expressed in the color *mannī,* after white and blue the color most commonly occurring in trousseau lists (45 times). *Mann,* derived from the biblical and qur'ānic word for manna, translated as honeydew, dust color, designates *ghubra,* a term for grayish white that is avoided in the Geniza. It is understandable; manna is preferable to dust.[176]

Blue was right behind white as the favorite color of Geniza women. It seems strange, considering that in Egypt, Palestine, and many other places blue was regarded as inauspicious, so much so that one said green when one meant blue to avoid uttering so ill-omened a word.[177] The freakish caliph al-Ḥākim (996–1021) was dreaded all the more because of his blue eyes, which he had inherited from his Christian mother.[178] Blue as a synonym for dismal and depressed is not unknown to the readers of this book.

Taking our lead from the Arabic idea of *ḍidd,* a word with two diametrically opposed meanings, we must remember that blue, particularly light blue, is an extremely pleasing color; and what woman would not like to look attractive? But because it is so pleasant blue may attract an "evil eye," wherefore one protected his children and pregnant wives by adorning them with blue pearls and the like, a kind of homeopathic repellent. Blue is represented in the Geniza also by a variety of different shades such as sky-color (two types, 10 + 6), bluish irridescent (6), and turquoise (blue-green, 2).

Green, the basic color ranking third in the Geniza, is outnumbered by its shades, not all of which may be exactly identified with regard to origin, especially the most common one, *masannī*, a bright green (14).[179] Pistachio (7) and emerald green (4) occur regularly in Arabic literature.

From the list on p. 174, it may be concluded that yellow was practically taboo for female clothing in the Geniza world, a remarkable fact, for according to a study by the late Aḥmad Amīn, yellow was the favorite color for everything in the house in Abbasid Baghdad, and especially for the attire of beautiful women. It would be farfetched to assume that in the capital of Fatimid Egypt they did everything contrary to the modes of living accepted in Abbasid Iraq. In Andalusian Arabic poetry yellow was a symbol of treachery, of separation from the beloved, and of unrequited love, which causes the suitor to languish to death.[180] Poetry permeated the life even of comparatively simple people in those days and might well have influenced popular attitudes concerning such delicate matters as female dress, which, we remember, was mostly displayed in the intimacy of the house. Arabic poetry from Spain, like its Hebrew counterparts, had found its way to Egypt by the eleventh century. And the poetic symbolism itself probably had its origin in popular superstitions. As far as the Geniza goes, yellow seems to have been more popular among males.[181]

Varieties of yellow and orange, such as the colors of apricot, bitter orange, sandalwood, saffron, safflower, and others, are also rare. The yellowish-brown honey color is far less represented than one would expect in view of the richness of their palette in hues of brown. Only the yellowish-white of the wax was much favored (10).

Red fetched only 22 points in the list of basic colors. It was widely overtaken by the light reddish-brown of the pomegranate (36), the color of the beloved's cheek in the biblical Song of Songs. Red, pink, purple, and violet seems to have had the widest spectrum of diversity, from yellowish-bright red to crimson, to the deep red of the ruby, the purplish-brown of the basil flower, and the brownish-pink of the eye of the partridge.[182]

The common word for brown, *asmar*, described not only the color of the human skin but also that of textiles. In addition to asmar, the colors of Oriental perfumes, such as musk (reddish-brown), camphor (dark brown), and the odoriferous wood *ʿūd*, were used.

Unlike yellow, which beautified furnishings but was almost absent from the female wardrobe, black appears in the table solely as a color for clothing. Examination of the details reveals, however, that black was used for veils, shawls, belts, and borders, but only exceptionally for full robes, and then mostly in Palestine or by males. Arab treatises on color, mostly derived from the Greeks, explain that the lively colors of white, yellow, red, and green, being full of light, give joy to the human soul, which is itself a substance of light, and joy gives strength, whereas black, the absence of light, makes the soul feel miserable, as if locked within a dark prison.[183] Black was known as a color of mourning to Arabs and Jews as to many other peoples.[184] But it was also well known that the color black had a festive and dressy air; ceremonial attire at the Abbasid court was black, and the Talmud was well aware that a woman could believe that a black dress would best bring out her beauty.[185]

The deep, dark blackish-blue *kuḥlī* (cf. the eye cosmetic kohl) was commonly applied to textiles (11), but, like black, mostly for wraps and shawls.

To bring home how particular people were in choosing the right color for the various pieces of their toilet, a passage from a business letter aptly concludes the discussion of the subject. The letter was written in Tinnīs, the Mediterranean seaport on the northeastern corner of the Nile delta, famous for its linen industry. It was sent in the last third of the eleventh century to a Tunisian merchant sojourning in Fustat, who had definite orders from his customers, probably including some choosy ladies back home in al-Mahdiyya. Tinnīs was a difficult place because, as the letter mentions, it was thronged with merchants from the Maghreb, Syria, and Iraq, all eager to buy. The writer, also a Maghrebi, refers to an illness of his, as was often done in business letters.[186]

Searching for the desired colors

You asked me to buy you wimples. You know what a headache this is, especially buying textiles in Tinnīs, whether one comes [to the bazaar] early in the morning or late in the evening. I relapsed into my illness only twice[187] because of this trouble. Today, thank God, I am fine.

I purchased for you:[188]	*dinars*
A black wimple with a white [border?], as ordered by you	1 7/8
A six-cubits-long sky blue[189] one with gold threads	2 3/8

An oak green[190] one	1 2/3
A white one	1 13/24
A red one	1 3/8

You wished to have two others, a pearl-colored one and one honeydew light gray.[191] The pearl-colored wimples were few in number and of mediocre quality. I waited two months expecting to get one made by ʿAlī ibn al-Murābiṭ,[192] but only this week I succeeded in coming upon one of excellent make. Then I received a letter of yours asking for a soot-black one.[193] This cannot be had. A honeydew wimple, ten cubits long and decorated with gold thread, costs 3 1/2 dinars, but no profit can be made with it; it is not worth a thing.[194]

Garments of different colors are as common in medieval Islamic illustrations as they are difficult to find in Geniza documents. The clerks, interested only in identifying a piece by its main color, did not describe it in detail. In a business letter it is said of an extremely beautiful siglaton robe that it was white and blue. The siglatons donated to the synagogue of the Babylonians in Fustat (noted in 1080) were all of two colors each: black and white (twice), light green with blue-black and with yellow. These textiles probably had originally been parts of a bride's outfit.[195]

Tailoring and treatment.—Tailoring began at the weaver's. "In Egypt, where garments were often woven in a single piece, requiring minimal sewing, the finished look of the outfit was left to a great extent in the hands of the weaver."[196] The tidbits from the Geniza provided below confirm this statement. One delivered to the weaver the yarn, or yarns, for instance, linen and cotton,[197] carefully weighed, and described the piece of clothing desired—a robe, a cloak, a turban—specifying its length and width. Normally, the quantity of yarn delivered no doubt slightly exceeded that needed for the object ordered, in which case the remainder was returned to the customer; sometimes, however, the opposite happened: the yarn proved to be insufficient and it was not always easy to find material to match to complete the object. Before starting his work the weaver was supposed to clean the threads of their blackish crust with a pumice stone.[198] If not done, or if the finished piece was not uniform in color and showed brownish spots, a new agreement had to be made with the "craftsman," *ṣāniʿ* (as the weaver was politely called) to have the whitening done by a cleaner, *muṣaffī*, literally, a man who made the cloth *ṣāfī*, or pure, uniform, and homogeneous in appearance.[199]

The material that came from the loom is described as *khām*, raw, throughout the Geniza. For proper use the cloth had to be fulled, a process of treading it in a solution of fuller's earth, a soapy substance, by which it shrank, tightened, and became "full" and bulky. In Aramaic, Hebrew, and Arabic, this treatment is expressed by the root *qṣr*, to shorten (so named because of the shrinking of the woven fabric). The opposite of khām is *maqṣūr*, fulled; the fuller is called *qaṣṣār*, shortener.[200] Treatment of the completed garment by sprinkling and beating with a club is also mentioned. This operation seems not to have been a part of the fuller's work but a separate treatment, that of the *mumarrish*, for the two are mentioned together in a letter ("4 dirhems, wages for the sprinkler and the fuller"),[201] while another letter speaks of "two cloaks, one sprinkled and one raw," as if "sprinkled" had taken the place of "fulled."[202] The fuller's work was completed by using a teasel, referred to in Greek, Latin, and Hebrew simply as "thistle" and in Arabic as "currycomb," for roughening certain fabrics to give them a dense appearance.[203]

After completion, the garment was put into a press operated with a screw to make it smooth and shiny. The press was called *kamad* and the presser *kammād*.[204] I was surprised to find that the Geniza people had the pressing done by a professional, even by one who lived in another town or overseas. The smooth and shiny surface, the sheen, was probably more important to them than the stiffness produced by the pressing.[205]

Even more surprising is an order placed in Spain for a person in Morocco instructing that the robe desired be tailored, cut out, *tafṣīl*. The bridegroom for whom the robe was destined was personally known to the recipient so that he was able to figure out the approximate measurements; since garments did not fit tightly, the sartorial work could be done in absentia. But we also have a note where the tailor is requested to come to the customer's house, accompanied, it seems, by his partner or employee, for "cutting out" cloth for a maqṭaʿ robe.[206]

Embroidering, too, could be ordered from out of town. They, no doubt, had fixed patterns according to which the artisans worked, although I have not yet come across an express mention of one. Here is the account for a *shuqqa* Sūsī, a raw Sūsa (Tunisia) cloth, sent from Fustat to another town for treatment. Its cleaning, *ṣafy*, fulling, and embroidery cost—together with the gate toll at the entrance to the city—12 dirhems, plus 2 dirhems for the bearer, all paid in advance by the writer of the letter. He asked the recipient, his brother, not to deliver it to the proprietor before he had settled the bill. Often, when a garment was sent to another place, it was transported by a friend, but not always, as illustrated here and in other letters, and the cost of the work done with the Sūsī was very high. Perhaps some skilled artisans, like copyists of books, preferred to live outside the capital because life there was so expensive. Even the seaport Damietta, where a fuller personally known to the writer placing an order with him lived, was renowned for being cheaper than Fustat.[207]

As may be expected of a highly commercialized urban society, the practice of personally attending to the manufacture of a garment, beginning with the very provision of the yarns, although common, could not be shared by the majority of the population. The Geniza correspondence proved abundantly that ready-made clothing was the rule. A tailor, darner, or embroiderer, often probably the womenfolk in the house, made the necessary adjustments. Before turning to this topic I wish to translate some additional passages illustrating the procedures for custom-made clothing.

In previous letters I have informed you of what I have done with the [linen] yarn.[208] I had made for you a *baqyār* turban,[209] 25 cubits long and a *shuqqa* cloth, 20 cubits long.[210] I paid the artisan [= weaver][211] for the cloth, the turban, and the unraveling of the yarn 4 dirhems,[212] and after the completion of his work I arranged with him to pay 2 dirhems for you to the cleaner.[213]

Later ʿAṭiyya Ben Shammāʿ [Gift, son of Waxmaker] arrived and brought to me a blue kerchief containing cotton, [linen] yarn, and unraveled flax. I weighed the unraveled flax and found that its weight was eleven ounces. I shall have it spun on account of the half ounce.[214] From the yarn previously sent there are remains in the hands of the artisan, weighing one-and-a-quarter Miṣr [Fustat] pounds.[215] I shall put everything together and have another cloth made for you.

Concerning the malḥafa cloak, I have informed you that the linen is of varying color: its whitening came out unevenly and some brownishness is apparent in it. If you wish, I shall have it cleaned [literally, made completely uniform in coloring] and fulled here. Otherwise I shall send it to you as it is.[216]

The passage is taken from a letter by Mardūk b. Mūsā (Mordechai b. Moses), a native of Tripoli, Libya, who had settled in Alexandria, where he became an important overseas trader. As was common practice, Mardūk did personal services for business friends, such as supervising the making of a mat, a type of furnishing, for the production of which Alexandria was famous.[217] The letter was sent to Nahray b. Nissīm in his later years when he was already "Member of the Academy." The following passage is taken from another letter from Alexandria to Nahray, but written many years earlier, by a cousin of his, who expresses himself in a highly disrespectful way:

> I wish to report to you, my lord, the troubles I had with the malḥafa cloak—may God curse its hour.[218] The artisan and I almost went to court.[219] He ran out of cotton, but had only a little more to weave. I did not find the same variety, so I bought him half an ounce [of another one], which they put at the edge. The malḥafa is with the carrier of this letter. For yarn [of linen], cotton, and wages I paid 1 5/8 dinars.[220]

The ready-made standard robe was called thawb, a word that also designated a piece of cloth of the size needed to make it.[221] A specialty of Alexandria (and of Ascalon, southern Palestine, which depended on the Egyptian seaport) was the *maqṭaʿ*, literally, a piece cut off, which had the same double meaning.[222] In Tunisia they said *shuqqa*, ripped off. Qayrawān, then the capital of Tunisia, and Sūsa, of course, were as famous for their shuqqas as Alexandria was for its maqṭaʿs.[223] Sicily had its *farkha*, common in the Geniza, but seemingly absent from contemporary Arabic literature and dictionaries. The Sicilian farkha is often defined as broad or narrow, a detail not noted for the other varieties.[224] Since textiles were exported from one end of the Mediterranean to the other, these four terms for cloth or garment were found everywhere, but whereas thawb is common Arabic, the other three, as far as the Geniza is concerned, have retained their local connotation and seem also to have differed from one another in types of weave.

How ready-made garments sent overseas to a wholesaler looked may be gauged from a huge account for the year 1024, written in Tunisia. The opening section deals with a shipment of 674 shuqqas, costing 2,560 quarter dinars, coming raw from the loom. Before shipment an additional 202 quarters had to be spent on fulling, scraping, mending, and embroidering. This results in a total of 2,762 quarters, or 690 1/2 full dinars, almost exactly 1 dinar per piece, the average standard price for a regular robe. In Egypt, of course, such a Tunisian shuqqa would obtain a higher price, such as 1 1/4 dinars, found elsewhere.[225] The item *ṭirāz*, embroidering, seems strange in garments produced in such large numbers. I assume they had ready-made strips of simple embroidery which were sewn on each individual piece. But I must leave this to the experts.[226] In any case, a Tunisian shuqqa shipped to Egypt was supposed to be ready-to-wear. In a letter from Qayrawān the writer inquires about shuqqas sent to a business friend for his personal use; meanwhile the man had died and the recipient of the letter was requested to find out what they cost.[227]

Most of the numerous accounts for finished textiles sent from the Muslim West (mainly Tunisia and Sicily) to Egypt[228] do not contain the details noted in the large order from Tunisia in 1024. The shuqqas shipped in large quantities were ordinary, ranging in price between 1/2 and 1 3/4 dinars, and the recipient was, of course, able to estimate the approximate value of the materials received. In 1048/9, 103 Sūsīs cost in al-Mahdiyya 6,283 dirhems, exactly 61 dirhems per piece, or according to the rate of exchange of the dirhem in that year a bit less than 1 2/5 dinars.[229] With this tallies the sum of 173 2/3 dinars, the price of 98 (out of 100) shuqqas sold in Alexandria in 1046, that is, approximately 1 3/4 dinars per piece, a quarter dinar more than in the country where they were manufactured.[230] Some Tunisian robes were sold in Alexandria for slightly more than half a dinar, as when 80 shuqqas brought 45 dinars.[231] In all these transactions Nahray b. Nissīm was involved.

Unlike the orders and accounts for ordinary garments, costing approximately between 1 and 2 dinars, the correspondence about ready-made clothing destined for the well-to-do is more specific. In two letters from the eleventh century, one referring to shipments moving between southern Iran and Egypt, and another, dealing with specialties shipped from Cairo to Tunisia, a single piece of male clothing costs from "25 dinars or a little more" to 60 dinars, prices comparable with those of the prime items in the wardrobe of a wealthy bride. Moreover, the writers are very particular as to the exact colors and other features of the garments ordered or received.[232] Unfortunately, little of the correspondence of the really great merchants, such as the Tustarīs, addressees of the two letters referred to above, have found their way into the Geniza. The following passage from a large and detailed order sent, it seems, from Tunisia to Spain, will show the reader how a clothier catering to fastidious customers stocked his store. The first nineteen lines, which are only partly preserved, contain no fewer than twenty orders for specific hues of colors (several not found elsewhere), many other technical details, and orders from two, obviously renowned, manufacturers, one Muslim and one Christian. From the middle of l. 18, the text is complete with only one word missing at the beginning of l. 19:[233]

Six [men's] cloaks, faced,[234] fine, not coarse, with beautiful thin [. . .], made to order, some of them clean white, some bluish-iridescent, or otherwise; some should have sleeve stripes[235] without script, bars[236] without script, exquisite ones, running from end to end, both outside and inside.

Six fine sprayed cloaks with beautiful borders[237] and exquisite script, ten cubits long. Their colors: two silvery, two sandal-colored, two uniform, clean white, tending to yellow.

Twenty soft robes, of which twelve should be white, freshly fulled, and eight of varying colors, namely, silvery, bluish-iridescent, and olive green.[238]

Five large velvetlike ʿUbaydī robes,[239] sprayed, clean, of varying colors, fancy.[240]

Two cloaks of sea wool,[241] faced, without script, faced[242] with green and red silk, first class, no script; they should have sleeve stripes like those in the safsārī and the barrakān,[243] and outside and inside there should be two fine runners,[244] made to order, each twenty-four cubits long.

And have made five brown mantles, light as those of ʿUbaydī, light,[245] with a beautiful glitter, of varying colors. Mantles like those have come to our place.

Five cloaks, fine, velvetlike, should be made to order, cloaks with sleeve stripes like the *fasāsārī*,[246] without script, one gazelle-blood, one pure violet, one musk-brown, one silvery, and one intensive yellow.

Ten pairs of socks[247] without patterns, of varying colors, thin.

The customers of that clothier had a rich selection at their disposal. Nevertheless, the services of a tailor were often, albeit not always, required. When Nahray b. Nissīm made a list of his personal expenses during a calendar year, and noted, in addition to the garments concerned, the item "tailoring," we understand that such an additional expenditure was not needed in every case:

Half an Arjīshī robe, thawb, and the tailoring for it from the perfumed shuqqa 1 dinar, 1/2 qirāt.

Mending a gown, jubba, cotton, and tailoring 1/2 dinar.[248]

A shuqqa, as measurements occasionally provided and illustrations show, was a very roomy garment; a young and traveling man, as Nahray then was, could do well with one half its size. For this operation, of course, a tailor was needed. If "1/2 qirāṭ" referred to his wages, it represented about 2 percent of the value of the garment (1 dinar, a reasonable price for half an Arjīshī). For fixing the funeral outfit of a man, consisting of seven pieces and costing slightly over 5 dinars, the tailor received 3 dirhems, or about 1 1/2 percent.[249] The tailor, as the name of his profession indicates (*khayyāṭ*, from *khayṭ*, thread), was mainly a sewer, and when a man in Palermo, Sicily, is asked to deliver two "tailored" woolen *mayzar* covers, which had been deposited with him—the writer was ill "because of the winter"—and when a robe and a *niṣfiyya* half garment, cape, are described in an inventory as tailored, the meaning is sewn for the use of the wearer.[250] Cutting up, *tafṣīl* or *qaṭʿ*, had to be done, of course, especially for making and fitting the sleeves.[251] But despite the extensive division of labor characteristic of the period, I have never come upon a cutter. Tailors (male, and female, *khayyāṭa*) occur in the Geniza throughout the centuries as beneficiaries of, or contributors to, public charity and in nonprofessional, personal affairs. When we hear so little about their work compared with that of other wage earners, for instance, the weaver and fuller, we must conclude that it was indeed of far smaller scope than is customary in our society.[252]

Care and economic importance.—Clothes were kept in trunks or chests, not hung up, as we do. Racks for hanging up clothes were used for fumigating and perfuming them, but they are almost never mentioned; such luxury was for the great, not for the common people. They had to content themselves with sachets (filled with cloves or other easily available material) put between their clothes.[253] As the material and the circumstances required, garments kept in containers of any kind regularly had to be taken out and separated, shaken out, stretched, or hung up, even weighted with stones.[254]

The human body was cleansed with *ushnān*, pulverized ashes of alkaloid plants, but clothes were washed with soap, an important article of export from Tunisia to Egypt.[255] When a household ordered from a grocer half a pound of soap and another half of *nashā*, starch, one understands that a big wash was ahead, and that some, or most, linen was starched.[256] One misses, however, the washer woman, a popular figure in smaller towns of Central Europe not so long ago. A *ghāsila* is a female washer of the dead, not of garments.[257] Cleaning clothes was probably done mostly by professionals: the fuller, the "cleaner," and probably also the "starcher."[258] Pressing, too, was left to an expert, and probably also the re-dyeing, although housewives are reported in the Geniza as dyeing silk at home.[259]

Frequent washing impaired the color and general appearance of a garment and diminished its value. In lists of the possessions of living or dead persons, as well as in numerous marriage contracts, items are labeled as *ghasīl*, washed. One inventory counts no fewer than nine such cases.[260] It is noteworthy that each and every piece of clothing, from an undershirt to heavy outerwear could be classified as ghasīl.[261] "The History of the Patriarchs of the Coptic Church of Alexandria," known under the name of one of its authors, Severus Ibn al-Muqaffaʿ, reports that the caliph al-Āmir wore washed, that is, worn-out, clothes at the funeral of the viceroy al-Malik al-Afḍal (1121). I have not yet ascertained that custom of mourning from the Geniza, but it is implied by Jewish religious law, codified by Moses

Maimonides, which prescribes that a mourner should not wear white, or new, or newly pressed clothing.[262]

From washed-out garments must be differentiated those taken off, *khalīʿ*, secondhand.[263] Almost all types of secondhand clothes (and draperies) are represented in trousseau lists. It is remarkable that they also were a substantial element in overseas trading. In an important business letter from Palermo, Ḥayyīm b. ʿAmmār, a prominent merchant, notes that, together with silk and lead, secondhand (Sicilian) clothing was purchased for export to Egypt.[264]

Writing from Tinnīs, a man inquires, among other items, about the prices of secondhand Syrian silk clothing in Cairo (in order to buy from the Syrian merchants crowding the bazaar of that Mediterranean port).[265] A Maghrebi merchant, sojourning in Egypt, is asked to buy for the writer a secondhand Damascene or Iraqi ʿAttābī robe, *thawb mukhtalāʿ*, worth 7 or 8 dinars.[266] This, for an order of unusually high price, shows that secondhand did not at all imply inferior quality. People with a richly endowed wardrobe—so often revealed to us in trousseau lists—occasionally desired to get rid of some of their often hardly used belongings, exchanging them for something else in the store of a *qashshāsh*, or *qāshsh*, dealer in secondhand goods.[267]

Receiving the discarded garment of one's superior, and in particular of a ruler, was a high honor, customary in the Near East since remote antiquity (cf. Genesis 41:42, Esther 6:8). Such a gift was a sign of friendship and even intimacy (I Samuel 18:4, Jonathan and David). In Geniza times, the bourgeoisie, as in other matters, imitated the ways of the court.[268] The name of such a gift was *khilʿa*, a discarded piece, which then received the general meaning of robe of honor. In practice, the Muslim (and, before them, the Sasanian) rulers gave as presents not garments previously worn by them but those embroidered with their names.[269] Since members of the merchant class were themselves among "the receivers of khilaʿ, or robes of honor," it is natural that the custom of giving clothing embroidered with names and blessings spread among them.[270]

The intrinsic importance of secondhand garments is driven home by a study of the dowries brought in by brides. The dowry was her economic protection on which she could fall back in case of widowhood or divorce. Clothing formed a major, often the main, part of the trousseau. Selling a piece of her wardrobe could provide a woman with months, even many months, of sustenance. For clothing, compared with food, was expensive. Garments were cash, under certain circumstances even better than money, because their proprietorship could be more easily established than that of hard coin. A case brought before Moses Maimonides shows that for paying a remainder of his poll tax a man took a loan of three robes worth 39 dirhems—he might have handed them over to the tax collector in kind—but was able to deposit as collateral an object worth over 60 dirhems. It was not only poor people who lacked ready money.[271] When, at the time of the caliph al-Ḥākim a Jewish cortège was attacked by a Muslim mob, and twenty-three persons were beaten, imprisoned, and robbed of their clothing, the caliph subsequently intervened, the Jews were freed, and all their clothes "from a thread to a shoe latchet" (cf. Genesis 14:23) were returned. This spectacular event exemplifies that garments could be more easily retrieved than general goods, let alone money.[272]

In times of extreme personal misfortune, such as long illness entailing costly medical treatment and unemployment, or communal disasters, such as famine, or the breakdown of authority and general anarchy, one kept body and soul together by selling or pawning one's clothing (and, of course, if necessary, other belongings). The Geniza has numerous examples of these occurrences.[273] In normal times, too, clothes could serve as cash, for instance, easily marketable robes as a payment of customs dues on a large shipment of pepper,[274] or a cloak for buying wheat for the family back home.[275] For me the most impressive example of the cash value of clothing is this detail from the life of the Spanish Hebrew poet Judah ha-Levi, revealed in a Geniza letter: when the poet had already boarded the ship which was to take him to the Holy Land, a mailman from Spain arrived in Alexandria with a letter from a young relative announcing that he would soon travel to Egypt. An admirer of the poet brought the letter on board, whereupon ha-Levi handed him a turban with a note to his relative advising him to sell it and to finance his travel from Egypt to Palestine with what he got for it.[276] All in all, it is evident that besides serving as a cover, as protection against wind and weather, and as a status symbol showing a person's profession and place in society, clothing was capital that shielded its proprietor in time of need.

Nothing is more indicative of the economic role of clothing during the classical Geniza period than the fact that the dowry, this safeguard of the wife's economic security, never consisted of money, but comprised objects related to the wife: her jewelry, clothing, furnishings, and housewares. The teen-age bride knew little about money; it was handled by men. But the value of the things with which she had grown up in her mother's household (part of which would follow her into her husband's house), and, in particular of those especially acquired for her outfit, was well known to her.

Those objects had been discussed and their price estimated again and again, bit by bit. The estimates given of them in the trousseau lists must have been the outcome of long deliberations, within the family and of negotiations with the groom. The bride, of course, had not taken part in those negotiations, but she had heard or overheard her parents discussing these matters. If the time should come for her to take action based on the monetary value of her outfit—in consent or contest with her husband, during his absence, or after his death—she was well prepared. She had economic power (wherefore divorce was so widespread). As a rule, the dowry was worth a multiple of the value of the marriage gift presented at the wedding by the future husband; ten times as much was perhaps the most common ratio. And the foremost part of a wife's trousseau was her wardrobe.[277]

Because of the durability and cash value of jewelry and the proverbial infatuation of the authentic Near Eastern woman with this element of her general appearance ("Can a maiden forget her jewelry, a bride her adornments," Jeremiah 2:32), one might expect that this item of the outfit was the highest in value, as it was regularly the first to be listed in the Estimate section. This might well have been the case in Late Antiquity when the traditional sequence was established of the four sections of the dowry, the *nedunyā*—gold, clothing, bedding, copper. In Geniza times this was practically never the case. For reasons touched on below, clothing always took pride of place. In a marriage contract from Damascus, Syria, dated 24 March 956, jewelry was estimated as being worth 150 dinars and clothing 100. These sections are not itemized, as was general practice (also in Damascus), but lumped together in round sums, which is all the more suspicious, as the total was 395 dinars. The first installment, the marriage gift at the wedding, was 25 dinars (the minimum then required in Damascus), its second installment, to be paid at the husband's death or at a divorce—200 dinars, entirely exceptional and unrealistic.[278]

Be that as it may, we have to wait about two hundred years until we come across another, almost complete, ketubba in which jewelry outstrips clothing so markedly, our Doc. III in App. D., where jewelry is valued at 471 and clothing at 373 dinars. That ratio might have been habitual in the uppermost crust of Jewish society, whose dealings are almost never recorded in the Geniza. The total marriage gift here was 500 dinars, an amount recurring only once when the prominent Karaite notable David b. ʿAmram ha-Kohen married the daughter of another Karaite in 1033.[279] In actually preserved Muslim marriage contracts from this period (or, rather, about two hundred years later than Doc. III) I found this sum only once, when a noble amīr (prince) married an amīra in Aswān, Egypt, giving her 100 dinars at the wedding and promising another 400 dinars in ten yearly installments. To appreciate such sums it should be noted that in a Karaite betrothal document, written (in eloquent Hebrew, of course) around 1030, Japheth b. Abraham b. Sahl marries the daughter of a Karaite Nāsī (that is, member of a family tracing its origin back to King David), presenting her with 100 dinars at the wedding and promising a deferred installment of 200 dinars. This Japheth was none other than Ḥasan, who, after the assassination of his father Abraham, known as Abū Saʿd Tustari, the "vizier" of the Dowager and actual administrator of the Fatimid empire, embraced Islam and became full vizier himself, albeit for only a short time as was then the custom. Thus we are here in the company of Jews who reached the pinnacle of power and, as described in Muslim sources, of wealth.[280]

The Jewish upper middle class tried to emulate these leading families. In App. D, Doc. V, below, the ratio of jewelry to clothing is 124:196 dinars, and in the ketubba beginning on the same sheet on which Document V ends, 209:262 dinars.[281] Our Document II is even more indicative of this trend: both sections, although well itemized, amount to 171 dinars each, which could hardly be accidental. The value of the jewelry of brides from lower middle-class families amounted to about half that of their clothing, and that from families in modest circumstances to about one-quarter.[282]

Why, then, was clothing number one in the Geniza trousseau when the prestige and economic advantages of ornaments were so obvious? This question is the more pertinent, as the Jewish husband undertook in the marriage contract to clothe his wife, an obligation taken very seriously by Jewish law, as laid down in the strongest terms in Mishna and Talmud and codified by Moses Maimonides. The husband is obliged to provide his wife with winter and summer dresses in accordance with his means; if he is able to clothe her in silk, embroidery, or even in garments woven of gold threads, he is forced to do so, "forced" in that he may be sued in court for failure to do his duty. The same applies to everything else apt to make the wife attractive, such as colorful headgear, eye cosmetics, or makeup.[283]

The idea "that she should not be unattractive to her husband," which Maimonides, following the Talmud, gives as reason for his law on the wife's clothing, had deep roots in specific Jewish and general Near Eastern realities and notions. In the close-knit Jewish community with its abhorrence of any form of concubinage (very much unlike the Islamic environment) and where one was constantly watched by everyone, a husband normally could find sexual satisfaction solely in marriage. In the Near East the process of disrobing, with its delight in ever more gorgeous dresses emerging, was an intrinsic part of lovemaking. We remember the sad story of the captive beauty put on the slave market for sale; in order to make her even more attractive she was clad in seven robes. In love poetry, too, whether Arabic or Hebrew, yearning, not consummation, formed, in endless variations, the almost exclusive content.[284]

The wardrobe of Jewish brides as revealed by the Geniza must be evaluated in the light of these observations. As the prices show (only ketubbas in which "a dinar is a dinar" are considered), mostly choice pieces, higher in value than regular garments of the same type, were selected. The day-to-day needs were satisfied by the dresses given by the husbands, usually at the spring and autumn holidays. The costly cloaks, robes, wimples, and the like brought in at the marriage were spared for special occasions. This also explains why the number of garments even of a well-to-do bride was comparatively limited and why many of them could be passed on from mother to daughter. Sparing use contributed to durability.[285]

One special occasion requiring dignified attire was death, and men were no less fastidious in this matter than women.[286] One might meet the scrutinizing eye of God quite soon after interment. Who knows? As on the Day of Atonement, one wished to appear in new clothing. One should be a new person, not one soiled by the misdeeds of the past. Naturally, not everyone could afford it. But everyone, male and female, had earmarked pieces from his or her wardrobe as "shrouds," probably those that had been used little or were still new.[287] As in trousseau lists, the cost of the various items of the shroud are a multiple of that of regular garments of the same type. This is what Wuḥsha, a successful business woman, ordered for herself on her deathbed:

This should be expended on my funeral and on my shroud:	50 dinars
to be taken from the cash available.[288]	
Of this sum should be bought for me:	
a Dabīqī robe for	6 dinars
a mulā'a wrap for	6 dinars
a Talī[289] skullcap for	2 dinars
a wimple for	6 dinars
a Dabīqī kerchief for	2 dinars
a veil for	2 dinars
a Tustari *kisā* cloak[290] for	6–7 dinars
and a coffin.	

The balance was for the pallbearers, the tombstone, and "the cantors walking behind my coffin."[291]

Wuhsha willed the same sum of 50 dinars to various synagogues "for oil, so that they may study at night," and an additional 20 to the poor.[292]

The total for the burial dress was about 30 dinars.

A similar sum was earmarked for this purpose by a young woman with a baby, whose husband was abroad.

I am not pleased with the shrouds I have, and wish, therefore, that some should be bought for me. This I wish to be bought:

a Dabīqī robe,[293] a wimple, a wrap, a *mukhlaf* cloak, a half-and-half[294] as bedding, and a braid,[295] the total costing about 25 dinars; and a coffin for (9–10?) dinars.[296]

Jewelry never appears in a burial outfit. Respectable clothing—yes. Gold and silver—no. "Mine is the silver, and mine is the gold, says the Lord of hosts" (Haggai 2:6). Man must approach his Judge in humility, disrobed of all insignia of pride and vanity. As excavations all over the globe prove, this attitude was not shared by the peoples of antiquity, including the ancient Egyptians. But the Christian and Muslim contemporaries of the Geniza world, no doubt, were pervaded by the same spirit. I do not believe that the absence of jewelry was attributable to economic considerations. One could have a gold ring for less than 2 dinars, and a gold-and-amber necklace for 4 dinars, sums far smaller than those earmarked for garments by the two dying women in the wills just discussed.

In numerous marriage contracts the bride receives, as in App. D, Docs. II and V, shares in one or several houses in addition to her trousseau. One would like to know the monetary value of those shares to gauge the degree of economic security provided the bride by real estate as compared with her outfit, in particular, the clothing. Here our sources fail us; nowhere are the data about houses in the trousseaus accompanied by prices. We possess, however, some illuminating information about this subject in the dispositions made in contemplation of his death by one of the most prominent figures in the Geniza, Abū Zikrī Kohen, Judah b. Joseph, "Scion of the Gaons," a representative of merchants in the Egyptian capital and a great India trader.[297] In his will he instructed his son Sulaymān to provide each of his two minor stepsisters with a dowry worth 200 dinars and to buy for each of them real estate worth 50 dinars. Until their marriage the two together were to receive a monthly allowance of 2 dinars, to which Sulaymān added another half dinar as long as he had not yet acquired the shares in a house (which would earn rents). Clothing represented an average of two-fifths of a dowry, which in this case would be about 80 dinars, far more than the real estate. Considering that houses brought income, whereas the objects of the dowry did not, one wonders why the latter were given so much preference. A look at App. D, Doc. VI, provides the answer. The objects of the dowry, one at a time, could be easily turned into money, whereas the transfer of real estate or, indeed, any action with it, was a clumsy affair. The sentimental value of clothing was an additional and most cogent consideration.[298]

Finally, the economic importance of clothing is brought home by its prominent place in the family budget. The problem of the standards of living, including the price of clothing, is, of course, a very vast subject. The estimate that the cost of living for a family in modest circumstances was 2 dinars per month during most of the Fatimid period, however, seems well established.[299] There was a standard price for a robe, the basic garment, of 1 – 1 1/2 dinars, so that providing adequate clothing for husband, wife, and children devoured a high percentage of the family income. Many households were unable to carry this burden. The regular handing out of garments to the poor and to lower communal officials by the Jewish community of Fustat illustrates this situation.[300] Public aid was equaled, if not surpassed, by deeds of private charity, especially before the High Holidays, when everyone whose family could afford it got new clothing. With a boat sailing late in summer from al-Mahdiyya, Tunisia, to Egypt, a merchant sent his daughter's used garments to Cairo; they were to be sold and the proceeds sent to Jerusalem to buy clothes for the orphans there. When donning a new dress on a holiday one desired that everyone should share this joy of renewal.[301]

Cosmopolitan, local, and communal aspects.—Leafing through the pages of this book, through *Letters of Medieval Jewish Traders*, or other publications based on the documents of the Cairo Geniza, one is impressed by the number of textiles brought from faraway countries or places, or at least bearing their names. In many cases the circumstances in which a garment or fabric is mentioned enable us to decide whether the geographical definition is genuine or a mere trade name. When clothes named after remote regions of northern or southern Iran are imported to Egypt from Spain or North Africa, or produced in Ramle, Palestine, it is evident that a type of material, not its place of origin, is intended.[302] When, as often happens, both a Ṭabarī and a Ṭabaristān Ṭabarī are listed in a trousseau list, it must mean that both the genuine and the imitated product were on the market.[303] In other instances the matter cannot be decided. For example, when Ibn al-Qaṣbī, the eminent Rav of Fustat, sends (around 1135) "a Baghdādī cape" as a present to his brother in Lucena, Spain, a garment manufactured in Baghdad is probably meant.[304] The sender (who had to inconvenience a prominent merchant with the transport) certainly chose something special; Baghdad was geographically and politically (then as today) very remote from Egypt, let alone from Spain. On the other hand, as the Geniza proves, Baghdad robes, gowns, cloaks, turbans and other pieces of clothing were available in the bazaars of Cairo, as is evident from the Geniza trousseau lists and other documents.[305] Despite these considerations we cannot know for sure where that Baghdādī cape was made. Finally there are, of course, other cases in which there is no doubt where a garment bearing a foreign name was produced. When a merchant returning from Tunisia to Alexandria notices that he had not bought his wife the desired Qayrawānese costume (consisting of robe, veil, wimple, and cloak) and asks a business friend to send one "with the first caravan leaving," it is clear that a costume manufactured in Qayrawān is meant. It looked different from one made in Cairo, and was, therefore, particularly desirable.[306]

As the examples of the Baghdad cape and the Qayrawān costume demonstrate, it was not only the fabrics but also the very form and style of garments which became diffused through the Islamic world. There was another area of interterritorial penetration: the Mediterranean, of which we cannot yet say how far north it extended in Geniza times. One of the most common pieces of clothing Jewish brides, say, of Damascus or Fustat-Cairo received (from the middle of the tenth through the twelfth centuries) was a *mandīl* Rūmī, possibly best translated as "a European mantilla."[307] Because of its popularity it was imitated in Egypt, where we find "a European mantilla, made in Tinnīs."[308] The Rūmiyya, noted four times in App. D, Doc. III, must have been different from the Rūmī mantilla, since it is once mentioned together with a wimple as forming part of a "robe of honor," and both mantilla and wimple served as decorative head covers. The Rūmiyya might have been a kind of jacket, a type of dress not represented otherwise in the female wardrobe of the Geniza.[309] A thirteenth-century bride possessed three Rūmiyyas, one blue (like the rich bride of Doc. III), one "peacock," that is multicolored, and one white, "in the Yemenite fashion." Thus a dress of European style, after having undergone changes in Yemen, turned up as a specialty in Egypt.[310] The European bathrobe, already possessed by the poor Karaite girl of Jerusalem in 1028, appears again and again, for instance, in the ketubba of a lower middle-class bride written two hundred years later.[311]

The cosmopolitan character of clothing in Islamic times is well attested in Arabic literature. A look at the Index of Place-Names in Serjeant's *Islamic Textiles* and at the relevant texts translated there brings this fact home. The Geniza shows us how the attitude permeated the common people and even the lower classes. Nor was this attitude specific to or new in Islamic civilization. For thousands of years empires had "taken away the borders of nations" (Isaiah 10:13), dragged artisans and upper-class people from one corner of the earth to the other, but opened also new avenues for trade and exchange of goods. Samuel Krauss's meaty chapter on clothing in his *Talmudische Archäologie* (as he himself emphasizes in Vol. I, pp. 206–207) contains an amazing assortment of outlandish names and things. As the Mishna says, during the solemn hours of the Day of Atonement the High Priest in the Temple of Jerusalem wore precious fabrics of the finest Egyptian and Indian makes.[312] Elsewhere I tried to show that the Jewish seats of learning in Babylonia came into being when the silk route from China went through that region, when there was constant coming and going between Palestine and the Land of the Two Rivers, and when the leaders of the new learning, the first Amoras, had a hand in the silk trade.[313] Late Antiquity and the Early Middle Ages were periods of lively exchange of material goods throughout the Middle East and beyond. Islam, which united most of the regions once separated by the eternal enmity between the Roman and Persian empires, reinforced this trend. The obligatory pilgrimage to Mecca, which was taken very seriously, was another mighty incentive for international exchange. For, as the Geniza shows, most travelers were also carriers of goods.

Finally, as a consequence of the intensive population movements under Islam, especially from Iran and Iraq to the Mediterranean area, first as colonizers and later as emigrants and even refugees, the newcomers transmitted the customs and tastes they brought with them to both their own posterity and their new environment. When Almeria, Spain, became renowned for its manufacture of a certain type of female dress named after Jurjān, a country in the very heart of Asia, it must be that some families from that remote region (perhaps both customers and makers of that dress) had found a new home in that Andalusian port city. The frequent occurrence of Iranian and Iraqian terms for fabrics and garments in the documents of the Cairo Geniza is partly to be explained as the outcome of large-scale migrations.[314]

The very same Muslim geographers, including their greatest, al-Muqaddasī, "the man from Jerusalem" (wrote around 985), who tell us so much about the diffusion of textiles in the realm of Islam, never tire of registering the specialties manufactured in each region, the clothing worn by its inhabitants, and the fashion observed at the time of the visit. When we learn from Cairo Geniza that at least twenty-six different types of Egyptian flax were traded all over the Mediterranean, we understand that different places and manufacturers preferred different varieties.[315] Thus a merchant, writing from Mazara, a port on the southwestern shores of Sicily, orders a certain type of Egyptian flax, "because it is the fashion, the distinctive mark, of this place."[316] A postscript to a letter from Jerusalem reports that black and sky-blue silk might be sold there, but not crimson. This frivolous color obviously was not in conformity with the austere character of the Holy City. It was used in the more mundane cities of Palestine, such as Ramle, the administrative capital, and Ascalon, the Mediterranean port.[317] That postscript explains perhaps why a woman living in Jerusalem at approximately (or exactly) the same time had to order crimson silk from Fustat. Most characteristically, she did not simply order crimson silk, but silk from Shadhūna, a place near Sevilla, Spain, which specialized in this variety, as we know from a Muslim source.[318] Similarly, in Sicily, it was not only the great port cities Palermo and Syracuse which gave their names to varieties of silk, but also the small inland town Demona, famous for its silk and carpets (possibly made of silk like Chinese ones).[319]

Our trousseau lists do not lend themselves to a comparative study of local fashions, for the majority of them, probably more than ninety percent, originated in the Egyptian capital. But they vividly demonstrate the change of times. The outfit of the poor girl from Jerusalem, 1028, comprised many items similar to those possessed by the rich bride of TS 16.80, who was her contemporary and a Karaite like herself.[320] It differed markedly, however, from the dowries in App. D, Docs. II–V, all from around the middle of the twelfth century, and they, in turn, differed even more from those written sixty or eighty years later. The Damascene trousseau lists from the tenth century, still formulated partly in Aramaic, are a world unto themselves.[321] A study of these changes—and of a certain continuity preserved in spite of them—may produce an interesting contribution to the history of clothing.

The most surprising aspect of the Geniza data about clothing, as far as Fatimid Egypt is concerned, is the complete absence of details about the restrictions imposed by Islam on non-Muslims concerning their wearing apparel. This matter has been discussed in detail in

Med. Soc., II, 285–288, and a mere look at the Index of Norman Stillman's *The Jews of Arab Lands*, s.v. Clothing, brings home the spectacle of an obsession pestering the Muslims almost throughout their entire history.[322] This obsession is itself, of course, a sign of the excessive importance attributed to clothing and the status it confers by distinguishing the wearer from people lower in rank. Precisely because the Muslim was aware of how much his religion had in common with the older monotheistic religions (a mere reading of his holy scripture, the Qu'rān, with its biblical names, stories, and laws, reminded him of this connection), he needed this constant affirmation of Jewish and Christian inferiority to reassure himself of his own superiority.

Special historical circumstances might have contributed to the origin and constant renewal of these discriminatory laws. When the conquering Muslims overran the Near East, they at first amounted to a very limited percentage of the population. They had to disperse over wide tracts of land and were in constant danger of being attacked when in small groups. To protect themselves from unpleasant surprises, they imposed upon the inhabitants of the countries conquered the condition that no one should don the dress or otherwise have the appearance of an Arab (for instance, how he combed his hair). These ordinances were among the earliest made in Islam; they appear in the oldest law books, and thus became part and parcel of generally accepted Islamic law. The details changed from time to time, but the basic concepts remained and were renewed again and again in varying forms, for they were Islamic, that is, God's, law, and the religious scholars, the guardians of the law, felt themselves called upon to watch over their observance.[323]

Why, then, did these laws so often fall into desuetude? Primarily, because they were no longer needed. In the course of centuries the victory of Islam in countries over which it ruled became so complete that neither the physical, nor the psychological security of Muslims required protection. True, the qur'ānic precept that a Muslim should avoid social contact with unbelievers was very much in force, but Jewry and the various Christian denominations formed groups so distinct that their members did not need a badge to be recognized as such. There were also times of tolerance, not as a matter of principle but because secular pursuits weakened the barriers between religions. The ordinances were enforced in times of crisis, when scapegoats were needed, as by the infamous caliph al-Mutawakkil, who introduced the "yellow" badge in 850, a measure renewed in the Seljuk period two hundred and fifty years later. When the darkness of barbarian rule and bigotry encompassed the Arab world, molesting non-Muslims, especially with regard to their outward appearance, became a permanent feature.[324]

Yellow, as we remember, was an ambivalent color in Arab Islam, regarded as inauspicious by some and as attractive by others. Its choice as a distinctive sign for non-Muslims, Christians as well as Jews, probably had nothing to do with either concept but was made because of its conspicuousness. Al-Mutawakkil's decree, by the way, uses the term "honey-colored," whereas the later sources speak outright of yellow.[325]

Distinctive clothing was not only imposed by an oppressive majority but also preferred—to a certain extent, of course—by beleaguered minorities. From the time the prophet Zephaniah (1:8) thundered against "all those who don foreign vestments" the guardians of Jewish religion insisted that in his outward appearance a Jew should be distinct from his pagan neighbors. In a situation of guarded assimilation, as with our contemporaries, the Jews of Jerba, Tunisia, this semireligious attitude was seeking ways to satisfy the demands of both conformity and otherness. Udovitch and Valensi, in their study on the Jews of Jerba, have discussed this trend and illustrated it with interesting examples. One wears the same dress—whether indigenous or European—but puts it on in a slightly different way, marking the wearer as Jewish.[326] Naturally, the Geniza documents do not permit us such subtle observations. I am not sure, however, that the Geniza people tried very hard to make themselves recognizable as Jews. The Jerban Jews of 1980 live in a ghetto; they confine themselves to a certain habitat, to a small number of occupations, and to their Hebrew religious culture. The Jews of Fatimid Egypt knew neither geographical nor occupational ghettos; and the better-educated people among them were familiar with Arabic script and had some acquaintance with the literary and scientific accomplishments of their environment. A coppersmith possessing a book of poetry written in Arabic script, as in App. D, Doc. VIII, below, was hardly exceptional.[327] That being so, one probably dressed like the people of one's non-Jewish environment. The fact that a Jew, high or low, could be mistaken for a Muslim is indicative of this generally relaxed atmosphere, as is the remark, found more than once in a Geniza letter: "The bearer of this letter is a Muslim."[328]

In the Geniza, the most popular color mentioned, even for outerwear, was white. Can one imagine a Jew or Christian daring to appear in the streets of Cairo wearing a white garment before the middle of the nineteenth century?[329] But the Jewish physician whose estate is itemized in a Geniza document from the year 1172 possessed a white turban, a white "broad shawl," a white cloak, and a white scarf, all vestments one donned outside the home. Moses Maimonides, who ordered the writing of the inventory on Passover of that year, probably dressed in the same way.[330]

Consequently, when we find in reports by travelers, in nineteenth-century illustrations, and actually exhibited in museums specific Jewish attire worn in Muslim Mediterranean countries, we should not jump to the conclusion that the same apartness prevailed in eleventh-century Egypt or Tunisia. Some Jewish specifics probably did exist, especially with regard to women's garments, mostly worn at home. But the Geniza is not very helpful for finding them out.

The broad shawl, called *ʿarḍī*, and indeed any other quadrangular piece of cloth in which one wrapped oneself, could be equipped with the ritual fringes or tassels prescribed by the Bible so that their wearers, "while looking on them, should be remindful of God's commandments" (Numbers 15:39). The very purpose of this religious duty implied that the fringes should be fixed on outerwear, which, in biblical times, and, to a large extent, still in the Geniza period, consisted of a piece "with corners." When the India trader Abū Zikrī Kohen was away on one of his prolonged voyages, his son Sulaymān wrote to him at the end of a long letter: "Please have made for me an ʿarḍī, six and a half [cubits] broad and six, or less [cubits] long [thus!], which might serve me as a ṭallīth [prayer mantle]." A fine, stately, white *burda*, a Yemenite speciality, costing about 2 dinars, is ordered by Solomon, the son of Elijah, the judge, in Yemen with the request to fix on it the ritual fringes.[331] The izār, a large wrap or coat, is twice mentioned in inventories of synagogue furnishings—provided with fringes, of course—once "for prayer," and once "for the Kohanim," that is, to be donned by a Kohen pronouncing the priestly blessing.[332] When a young man from a scholarly family wrote to his father in Jerusalem, "buy me an Aleppo izār in which I can pray all the time," he was probably referring to an inexpensive piece of Syrian cotton.[333] The *shāshiya*, a long piece of fine material, to be used for a turban or as a shawl, also could serve as a prayer mantle. It was for this purpose, when, in a letter from Aden, South Arabia, to Cairo a shāshiya was ordered embroidered with the name of the wearer and also with biblical quotations. The writer refers to this order twice in his very long missive: "Please buy a Qurqūbī shāshiya with gold threads and write on it Abraham b. Joseph b. Abraham b. Bundār b. Ḥasan."[334] And twelve lines later: "The shāshiya should be in red gold. As to the Bible verses, for example: 'May the Lord bless you,'[335] or similar verses."[336]

Qurqūb was a place on the southern border between Iran and Iraq where the Sassanian kings had settled Greek and Armenian craftsmen and where the finest silk goods were produced.[337] "Write on it" means, of course, have it embroidered. Prayer shawls were decorated with Bible verses.

The upshot of all this seems to be that (*a*), in Geniza times the Jewish prayer mantle had no fixed form—any of at least four different types of square outer garments could serve the purpose, and (*b*), shawls with ritual fringes were worn mostly during prayer and religious study, and probably during banquets that had a religious character (as I observed it worn in Yemenite circles many years ago), but that on the street it was worn only on the way to and from the synagogue (which, as a rule, was a short distance). In Maimonides' time their use seems to have been far less diffused than in later Judaism and confined mostly to divines, religious scholars, and pietists. As far as the Geniza shows, the *tallīth meṣuyyeṣet*, the upper garment adorned with fringes, cannot be described as a costume setting the Jews apart from the rest of the population. It was, rather, a mark of rank and profession within the Jewish community itself.[338]

Another order for a garment embroidered with a name, presented by a father to his son, written, as usual, in Arabic language, but Hebrew script, raises problems. It is an incomplete draft of a memo to be sent from Aden to Egypt.[339] I translate in full, line by line, so that the reader may be the judge:

(1) Memo from the sheikh Mufliḥ [Successful]:
(2) A Dabīqī scarf, *radda*,
(3) five cubits long and
(4) five spans broad
(4*a*) of highest quality,[340]
(5) bordered by two embroidered inscriptions
(6) each running from one edge to the other,[341]
(6*a*) the first
(7) written in Hebrew script:
(8) Yaʿqūb [Jacob] b. R. Mufliḥ
(9) b. R. Benjamin
(10) [Given] to Ibn Ahwāzī[342]
(11) [A line in Arabic script erased. The remnants are illegible. The rest of the page is covered with scribblings in Arabic script.]

What was ordered to be written in the second band of inscriptions? Verses from the Bible or good wishes in Arabic script? I prefer the former, for the change of script would probably have required two different artisans, whereas embellishment of a quadrangular piece of outer wear with Bible verses was common practice. This conclusion may be drawn from the way in which the matter is introduced in the earlier order from Aden to Cairo ("As to the Bible verses . . ."), and is learned in detail from a lengthy and rather excited responsum of Maimonides on the subject. Maimonides, following the opinion of Spanish-Jewish scholars, while coming to Egypt, had forbidden the standard Hebrew script to be embroidered on a ṭallīth. That script was the one engraved by God on the tablets given to Moses; it was the holiest of the holy; how could it be affixed on the ṭallīth, a simple piece of clothing with no sanctity, which one was permitted to wear even while entering the toilet? The custom was too popular, however, and too much in conformity with the ṭirāz of the Muslim environment, to be eradicated at once. Maimonides was besought with this question: A person had chosen a ṭallīth[343] for "the fringes" and, since he wished to fulfill God's commandments with beauty, he had had the borders embroidered with silk in the finest craftsmanship and on the borders stitched verses from (Numeri 15:37–41),[344] writing the name of God with three *y*s.[345] Warned by the head of the local congregation that this was not permissible, he did not heed the warning but persisted in wearing that garment.

In his answer, Maimonides, although admonishing the complainant to handle the matter with moderation, goes so far as to opine that continuous refusal of that man to obey the law should be punished by excommunication. It is indicative of the deep-rootedness of the custom condemned by Maimonides that even after his death a scholar in Alexandria could ask the Jewish chief justice in Cairo whether the use of Hebrew standard script was indeed not permitted for secular purposes. The chief justice (who happened to be the father-in-law of Moses Maimonides' only son), quoting the master's letter just discussed, reiterated the answer given in it, adding that in Spain (and in other countries) a type of cursive script had been invented, so that Hebrew could be used for everything. Spanish-Hebrew cursive (as I know it from the Geniza), which imitated the thin and flowing Arabic script, lends itself to embroidery better than the massive and monumental standard Hebrew. I do not know, however, of any textiles embroidered with Hebrew inscriptions preserved from that period. Maimonides' authority was more influential than "the endeavor to beautify the fulfillment of God's commandments."[346]

Jewish women had fewer opportunities than their menfolk of meeting their Muslim and Christian counterparts. Consequently, some special tastes and styles of clothing very likely developed among them. For instance, the jūkāniyya, probably a variety of the regular robe, but shorter and therefore more practical for regular housework (and for use elsewhere), occurs innumerable times in the Geniza documents but is next to absent from Arabic literature. Thus one might be tempted to surmise that it was particularly popular with Jewish women.[347] The mukhlaf, which I have described as a patchwork cloth made up of different pieces, probably also of different colors, and which is listed over fifty times in the Geniza but not yet traced elsewhere, might have been a Jewish favorite. Perhaps a mark of poverty, originally, it became fashionable in the course of time.[348] The *makhtūma*, a cloth with an emblem, also not noted in Serjeant's painstaking *Islamic Textiles*, was perhaps adorned with a specifically Jewish symbol, such as the seven-armed candlestick, the Menorah, just as the breast of a Coptic tunic was sometimes ornamented with the Cross.[349] Concerning a tapestry Cross in a colorful pattern of jewels Dorothy Thompson says that it was a substitute for an actual pectoral ornament.[350] The Menorah, so visually described in the Bible and appearing on countless Jewish objects throughout the centuries, might well have decorated many a precious female dress in Geniza times.[351] On the island of Jerba and in other parts of Tunisia Jewish women used to wear a garment decorated with embroideries representing the Menorah, the tree of life, and the six-cornered star of David.[352] The star of David became a specifically Jewish emblem only a few hundred years ago, but the eleventh-century Tunisian merchant and scholar Nahray b. Nissīm used it as a mark on his bales of goods going overseas.[353]

In conclusion, the frequency of certain terms in the Geniza and their rarity or complete absence from other sources make it likely that Jewish clothing might have had some specific traits in Geniza times.[354] But we should not forget that nowhere in the Geniza is express mention of such deviations from the generally accepted modes of clothing made. If they existed, they were not conspicuous. When the Jews were suffered to appear in public dressed like the majority of the population, they did so with gusto—"They dress in the finest clothes while you wear the meanest"—writes a Muslim poet in Spain at a time when the Jews seemed to enjoy privileges not warranted by Islamic law.[355]

For Egypt itself, a Muslim writer on market supervision complains that the dhimmī (non-Muslim) "women, when they leave their houses and walk in the streets are hardly to be recognized. . . . They go into the bazaars and sit in the shops of the merchants, who pay them respect on account of their fine clothes, unaware that they belong to the dhimmīs."[356] In view of all this the data provided by the Geniza for Fatimid and early Ayyubid times should not be disregarded as a source for our knowledge of the apparel of the middle and lower classes in the capital of Egypt in general.

Jewelry

Definition.—

Oh those girls on the banks of the Nile
  [Light as] gazelles, but heavy,
For heavy are the bracelets on their arms
  And their steps are narrowed by anklets.
The heart is enchanted and forgets its age
  And fancies itself in the midst of boys and girls,
In that Paradise which is called Egypt,
  In the gardens and parks along the Pishon.[357]

These and similar lines were written by the Spanish Hebrew poet Judah ha-Levi while he enjoyed his stay in flourishing and tolerant Egypt in winter 1140/1, before setting out for the Holy Land, where he died soon after arrival. Looking at the luxuriant ornaments was his compensation for being deprived of viewing the beautiful faces by veils of many shapes worn by women of all religions.

Who were those girls on the banks of the Nile observed by the Jerusalem pilgrim (assuming that they were real and not merely creations of his imagination)? Hardly Jewish. For anklets were commonplace in the Geniza trousseau lists of the early eleventh century but almost absent from them around the middle of the twelfth.

We are able to form an idea of the weight of such artifacts from an ancient will by a Karaite mother of two girls, who was expecting another child. She wished to safeguard the rights of the newborn, "boy or girl,"[358] if she were to die in childbirth. To do so, she used the strongest terms ("like a drawn sword") and was very explicit with regard to the market value and weight of each piece of her jewelry. A single *siwār* bracelet of hers, described as "Scorpion's Venom,"[359] was worth 43 dinars—an exceptionally high price; its gold "without the fittings"[360] weighed 50 mithqāls, a total of around 230 grams, or about half an American pound. Since siwārs were regularly worn in pairs, the bracelets would weigh about a pound, indeed a heavy burden on the arms of "a gazelle." A pair of golden *dumluj* wristbands costing 100 dinars (if the price is not blown up in honor of the bride) would also have weighed approximately a pound.[361] The pregnant woman's anklets classified as "Breast of the Falcon"[362] contained, without fittings, 60 mithqāls of gold, or about 280 grams, also a substantial weight.[363] A weight of 20 mithqāls and a corresponding price of 20 dinars represent a fair average for a valuable pair of bracelets, which often headed a trousseau list. For this sum one could acquire indispensable household help.[364]

I started this part on jewelry with the aspect of weight because it indicates how one went about ordering a piece. One brought to or bought from the goldsmith a certain quantity of gold, weighing 10, 20, 30, 50, 60, or more mithqāls, and, naturally, for more modest items far smaller weights.[365] The value of the precious metal in an ornament largely, but by no means exclusively, determined its price. In the will of the expectant mother, a bracelet containing 50 mithqāls of gold was estimated as being worth only 43 dinars, but the price for an ornament weighing ("without fittings") only 30 mithqāls was set at 44 dinars. In addition to the renown of the artisan who created it much depended on the cost of labor which went into the making of a piece and its state of preservation at the time it was appraised. Yet the experts doing the estimates that appear in our trousseau lists were well acquainted with these circumstances, and since the gold coin dinar weighed only slightly less than the mithqāl (the weight unit for commodities), the price of an ornament, expressed in dinars, approximated its weight. In view of this, with almost no exceptions such as those just given, the weight of a piece of jewelry is practically never indicated in a trousseau list.[366]

Jewelry is simply introduced under the heading "The Gold" even when the ornaments were made of silver,[367] or it is separately listed under "Golden Objects" and "Silver Objects."[368] In daily life, naturally, other terms were in vogue for this part of a woman's possessions, such as *maṣāgh wa-ḥaly*, things artistically shaped and adornments,[369] or, generally, *aʿlāq*, objects to which the heart is attached, precious items.[370]

Before trying now to find out what the Geniza has to tell us about female ornaments, a warning must again be sounded. The trousseau lists, our main source, are legal documents specifying the financial obligations of a husband in respect to his wife's dowry. Only items of definable market value, such as objects of gold, silver, copper, pearls, or fine and durable textiles were noted. But do we not admire in our museums pieces of Egyptian jewelry, made three and a half millenniums before the Geniza period, which are graceful and of high technical perfection but still do not contain any precious metals? Is not the Geniza business correspondence replete with information about immense quantities of corals, cowry shells, Indian (or Chinese) beads, and so-called pearls, and other inexpensive but engaging mass articles for costume jewelry? Cloves, a major item of international trade, and sent to scholars as presents, went into attractive and sweet-smelling chains worn by peasant women, and today, and—who knows, also in Geniza times—even by discriminating women.[371]

In short, our trousseau lists provide some knowledge of the jewelry given to girls from families that had attained a certain degree of comfort, but let us only gauge the richness of invention that went into the adornment of women of the general population. As the lists from more modest homes show, everyone tried to obtain at least a small share of the real thing.

"Thy cheeks are comely with circlets, thy neck with beads. We shall make thee circlets of gold, with studs of silver." The poor shepherdess of the Song of Songs (1:10–11) was beautiful despite the plainness of her adornments. Love promised to replace them with gold and silver. The costly ornaments are what mostly occupy us here.

Materials.—One might expect that silver, which is so much less expensive than gold, was the more popular of the two precious metals. Were not almost all the delicate creations of the Yemenite Hebrew jewelers made of silver? The opposite was the case in Geniza times. With the exception of some silver pins and finger rings, and some rare examples of bracelets, especially of the *ḥadīda* type, all ornaments had gold as their basic material. R. A. Higgins, in his book on Greek and Roman jewelry, ascribes the paucity of silver ornaments preserved from antiquity to the perishable character of this metal and surmises that silver might have been as popular as gold.[372] In Geniza times, it should be emphasized, this was not the case. One may be induced to explain the paucity of silver ornaments by the general scarcity of silver during the Fatimid period, from which we have only limited amounts of silver coinage.[373] But silver *vessels* were common items in dowries and played an important role in international trade.[374] The preference for gold as the main material for jewelry as testified by the Geniza is explained perhaps by its absolute value, owing to its purity and the durability of its luster, unlike silver, which was of varying alloy and needed constant polishing. Of course, there is the magic of gold and the general human propensity for getting the best—"Gold is for the mistress, silver for the maid"—as Kipling has it—but we are concerned here with the special circumstances met with in our documents.[375]

The documents on clothing and jewelry translated in Appendix D show that even the poorest bride (Doc. I) possessed some ornaments made of gold worth at least 7 1/2 dinars. The richest bride (Doc. III), whose jewelry and precious vessels had a total value of 471 dinars, did not possess a single ornament made of silver. Only nine items, however, are expressly described as being entirely or part of gold, and they total 198 dinars. The writer of the document had no need to add this description to every item, for when a pair of bracelets cost 30 or 52 dinars, and a pair of pins 18 or 20 dinars, the very price indicated the material from which they were made. The middle-class brides represented in Docs. IV, V, X *b*, *d*, *e*, had no silver ornaments except one or two finger rings. But the *miʿḍada* armlet, worn on the upper arm, probably to keep the tucked-up sleeve in place, was always made of silver.[376]

Considering that bronze and brass were in daily use during the Middle Ages to a far higher degree than is so in our own times and that trousseau lists regularly contain a section headed "The Copper," one wonders that one never reads in the Geniza about pins, rings, or earrings, made of such materials. Whether gold pins, so often mentioned in our lists, were actually of bronze and only gilded or plated with gold should be decided in each case considering the price as well as ornaments other than gold, such as clusters of pearls, attached to the object concerned.[377]

After gold, pearls were the most desirable material for ornate jewelry. Already visible in the trousseau lists of the eleventh century, this trend becomes dominant in the twelfth and early thirteenth centuries, the period when the participation of Jews in the trade on the India route was at its peak. The technical term for "adorned with pearls" was *mukallal bi-lūlū*, or simply, *mukallal*, an Arabic word that has a history. It is derived from *iklīl*, crown, itself a loanword from Aramaic. Pearls were the adornment par excellence, the crowning finish of a piece of jewelry. Where they were missing, the piece would be described as *bi-ghayr taklīl*, without adornment.[378]

This list is the jewelry assigned by a middle-class India trader to his daughter as part of her dowry, when he returned to Egypt after a sojourn of twenty or more years in India and Yemen:[379]

A golden *ḥadīda* bracelet, without adornment	20 dinars
A pair of golden *ḥilaq* earrings, worth	6 1/4 dinars
Another pair of *hilaqs*, without adornment	4 dinars
A *miḥbas* collar necklace, without adornment	15 dinars
A pair of two peacock pins, without adornment	7 dinars
A *lāzam* necklace with pendants, without adornment	7 1/4 dinars
Pearls for "adorning" all the previously mentioned ornaments. Their weight 53 1/4 dirhems (ca. 165 grams), their price	40 dinars

The total (gold) value of these "unadorned" ornaments was 59 1/2 or approximately 60 dinars. Thus the pearls amounted to two-fifths of the price of this collection of jewelry.[380]

There follow some other items for which no "crowning" by pearls was foreseen:

A golden *ḥadīda* bracelet	8 dinars
A pair of bulging *aswira* bracelets	13 1/2 dinars
A pair of granulated *aswira*	16 1/3 dinars
Two pairs of silver pins with arrows, one pair gold-plated; a pair of spoon(-pins); a pair of open-worked sun disks; a kohl stick; an encased mirror, total	8 dinars and 2 qīrāts
A silver *dabla* finger ring	1 1/8 dinars
Total jewelry	150 dinars

The assumption that the predeliction for pearls had something to do with the flourishing India trade of the twelfth century seems to be strengthened by an examination of the engagement contract of Sitt al-Khāṣṣa (Mistress of the Elite), whose father and grandfather had been renowned India traders (see App. D, Doc. II, dated 1146]. Most of her jewelry was studded with pearls: her most costly a sumptuous diadem (costing 70 dinars), as well as her least expensive, a pair of pins, a *ḥanak* choker, and a *tannūr* cuff. Finally, she had a pearl bracelet held together by a rim of gold. A contemporary of hers (Doc. Xd, dated 1159), like her, had pearls on almost everything, including the necklace with the *maymūm* amulet. Earrings, pins, chokers, and bracelets were regularly adorned with pearls, but finger rings inlaid with pearls are rarely mentioned.

The choice of pearls as main or additional adornments was certainly also a matter of taste. Thus the Spanish women were known to Egyptian merchants as being particularly fussy in this respect. Thus "the rich bride," so often referred to (App. D, Doc. III), whose jewelry and precious utensils were worth about three times as much as those of her contemporary, the Mistress of the Elite, possessed only two objects decorated with pearls. At any rate, the fascination with pearls is already attested to in the Talmudic age, when they, like silk, were a comparatively new article of luxury (imported by Arabs). Perforators and stringers of pearls are repeatedly referred to in the Geniza documents.[381]

Arabic literature is replete with wondrous stories about precious stones of fabulous coloring, size, and weight, and costing tens of thousands of dinars. Islamic science, copying and following the

Greek model, devoted great efforts to the study of the provenance and properties of those marvels of nature.[382] "Precious stones and pearls" are a standard phrase in the Talmud for costly possessions.[383] Jewish merchants are known from both the Geniza and Arabic literature as dealers in highly prized gems.[384] In view of all this one is surprised by the complete absence of precious stones from the jewelry listed in marriage contracts during the Fatimid and Ayyubid periods. I do remember one small fragment of a very poorly written trousseau list from spring 1069, where Durra (Pearl!) b. Saʿīd has a gold ring with a ruby stone valued at 5 dinars; the sum is probably inflated in honor of the bride, and the real price of the ring was not more than half or less of that noted, approximately 2 dinars, the average of the value of finger rings belonging to well-to-do brides.[385] But that was an exception. Jewish brides of the classical Geniza period (950–1250), even the richest of them, possessed pearls, and some of them many pearls, but no precious stones.

In the Mamluk period, from the fourteenth century on, a change seems to have occurred. *Fuṣūṣ* (pl. of *faṣṣ*) best translated perhaps as cut semiprecious stones, now regularly make their appearance in trousseau lists. In a document from December 1310 the bride has a headband with blue fuṣūṣ, small "pearls," and amber beads having the shape of lupine seeds, altogether worth 4 dinars; among other modest items she possesses two chains, *silsila*, "with" fuṣūṣ and edges embroidered with gold, both together costing 6 dinars.[386] In a detailed but truncated marriage contract from the same century, the dowry contains three chains, each consisting of carnelians, gold, and "pearls," and each costing only 2 dinars; a finger ring with a turquoise inset fetches the same price; there are also items with balas-*balakhsh* rubies, but because of the defective state of the manuscript the exact details cannot be ascertained.[387] Finally, a fifteenth-century trousseau list mentions, inter alia, "five pairs of earrings of gold, pearls, fuṣūṣ, and yāqūt rubies" and "three rings of gold, one with a turquoise stone."[388]

As the numerous foreign (mostly Turkish) terms creeping into the descriptions of female attire from the end of the twelfth century prove, it is certainly true that fashions changed under the impact of Easterners who, beginning with Saladin, ruled Egypt.[389] But there must have been an additional reason for the presence of precious and semiprecious stones in Mamluk trousseau lists and their practically total absence during the preceding periods, for the business letters, accounts, and legal documents, especially of the eleventh century, reveal a very lively trade in these materials. For instance, carnelians, *ʿaqīq*, mentioned above [390] as the main stones of fourteenth-century chains but absent in earlier trousseau lists, were a staple article of export from Cairo. They are regularly noted in letters written by Nahray b. Nissīm (active 1044–1095) or addressed to him from Tunisia, Alexandria, or Jerusalem. How inexpensive these materials were may be learned from an account presented by Nahray for the year 1044/5, where two bags of carnelians sent from Egypt to Tunisia cost only 1 1/2 dinars, that is, 3/4 dinars each, and this in a report on transactions totaling more than two thousand dinars.[391] A business friend of Nahray's in Jerusalem wanted carnelians of a somewhat higher quality: "three bags priced 1–1 1/2 dinars, of deep color and without blemish."[392] Another one from the same city ordered "good 'tube,' that is, carnelians of longish shape, not excellent, but also not of poor quality."[393] An order from Alexandria placed in Cairo for red carnelians costing about 30 dinars is the highest I have seen thus far, and the sum of 63 1/6 dinars obtained for one-third of a casket with carnelians, returned to Fustat and sold there, is the highest payment actually encountered (1057/8).[394] These latter sums compared with the preceding ones show, however, that large quantities of carnelians must have been on the market. Since they are described as faṣṣ, they must have been used as ornaments for rings and not only for chains.[395]

Besides those already mentioned I noted, in an account written around 1100, 45 beryls, *faṣṣ bazādī*, worth 1 1/4 dinars and, in the draft of a marriage contract from autumn 1157, a neckband of lustrous jets, *khaṣr sabaj*, intersected with pearls, costing 7 dinars. In a lawsuit from June 1079 one partner claims from the other "one-third of a balas stone [spelled here *balaghsh*], weighing 5 1/3 dirhems, and one-third of an emerald 'tube,' weighing two mithqāls." Why balas should be weighed with dirhems, the weight for silver, and emeralds with that for gold escapes me.[396] In a letter to Aden, the leader of the Jewish community there is advised to send to the Rayyis, the Head of the Jews of Egypt, among other presents, a beautiful stone of exquisite quality. Precious stones, used for signet or regular rings, were the jewelry normally worn by men and appropriate as gifts for dignitaries.[397]

The Arabic term for gem or jewel, *jawhar*, never appears in trousseau lists and is rarely used in business correspondence. It was too general. Thus, a merchant in Alexandria acknowledges receipt of a bag with jawhar, containing, among other items, ten emeralds and eighteen pearls (*jumāna*, never mentioned as a female ornament).[398] Another complains that the year before a customer had sent him, against his wish, jawhar which had remained in his storeroom and was worn out and yellowed; such a description can refer only to something which certainly could not be described as gems.[399] As far as I can tell, jawhar, in the Geniza papers, refers to products of nature, not to artifacts. The *jawharī* is a dealer in "gems" of all descriptions; the creator of jewelry is a *ṣā'igh*.[400]

I have dealt with these matters at some length[401] because the all but complete absence of precious or semiprecious stones from the trousseau lists of the "classical" Geniza period has baffled me for years. Since trading in such stones was common among Jews, it is unthinkable that the ornaments of their women should have lacked those embellishments entirely. I explain this deficiency as a generally accepted practice of the court clerks who wrote those lists. It was not always easy to define the exact character of a precious or semiprecious stone, and in a legal document, such as a marriage contract, accuracy was the most stringent requirement. Hence, general terms such as *wāsiṭa*, middle piece, or *farīda*, solitaire, were used, in the extremely rare cases when gems were referred to at all; their function, not their identity, was stated.[402] Mainly, however, it was the comparatively low value of the semiprecious stones which dictated their exclusion; they were the "fittings" of a piece of jewelry, the intrinsic value of which was determined by the gold it contained.[403] The Geniza women did not have really precious stones. Their "precious stones" were their pearls.

Second to pearls in Geniza jewelry, but following close behind, was amber as a basic element, used in combination with gold. Its orange-yellow color, which is similar to gold, but, because of its translucency, contrasting so beautifully with it, made them ideal companions. Add to this the amber's magic qualities—its producing sparks when rubbed and its magnetism "catching straws," as the Persians say, and one understands why it was used for ornaments since early antiquity.[404] Yet, I have hardly come upon it in eleventh-century trousseau lists or in business letters.[405] Then, from approximately 1100, the lists are swamped with amber ornaments, a flood that becomes ever stronger down to Mamluk times. This change was probably a matter of supply. Amber came from the shores of the Baltic sea on the northwest edge of the world then known to Muslims, and probably arrived—or, we should say, arrived again—in mass quantity on the southern banks of the Mediterranean only by the late eleventh century.

Amber appears together with gold in various combinations, foremost as alternating beads in necklaces, shoulder bands, and frontlets, and especially in the *maymūn* amulet. This combination was so common that, in the thirteenth century, a new term was introduced: *ʿanbarīniyya*, amber neckband, defined as either *mufaṣṣala*, intersected with gold beads, or *sādhaja*, plain, consisting solely of amber. Siwār bracelets made of amber had rims (one or two, *fumm*, pl. *afmām*, literally, mouth) and "heads" of gold, the latter meaning either real heads, for instance, of lions, as was so common both before and during the Islamic period,[406] but unlikely in a Jewish ambiance, or simply decorative ends or clasps. But we read also about "amber apples with golden heads," that is, large beads crowned with gold ornaments. An amber solitaire costing 6 dinars makes its appearance as early as 1117, and another one, again "adorned with golden heads," is listed somewhat later.[407] Instead of gold, a ḥadīda armband of amber had rims made of enamel (and cost 5 dinars).[408] Finger rings made of amber are also mentioned, but rarely.[409] Finally, amber could be used for vessels on the dressing table. The "rich bride" possessed an amber *qiḥf* (shallow bowl) with a golden rim.[410]

The blueish and decorative lapis lazuli occurs in trousseau lists less than one would expect considering its relative frequency in business letters. It was used for bracelets and as a divider in pearl ornaments, but served also as an ingredient in medical prescriptions.[411]

Unlike pearls, amber, and lapis lazuli, *mīnā*,[412] an enamel-like type of pottery, is, of course, not a natural product but a man-made artifact. Nowhere in the Geniza, however, is it defined by composition, make, or color, which is the more surprising as a wide variety of processes was used in its manufacture.[413] I therefore conclude that the Jewish goldsmiths did not make that material but bought it ready-made in the bazaar. It was used mainly in bracelets and pins, but also as a decorative element, described as "sun disks," in a tiara consisting of seven pieces.[414]

Shapes and techniques.—As taciturn as the Geniza is with regard to the enamel-like mīnā, so loquacious is it with regard to the small decorative elements forming, or attached to, the main ornaments. Reading those trousseau lists I am reminded of Jewish silversmiths from Yemen, who, decades ago, while showing me their work, pointed out those tiny items, explaining the name, place, and function of each.[415] The Geniza terminology is easier to grasp than that of the Yemenite silversmiths because it mostly describes those small artifacts with the names of fruits, seeds, plants, geometrical figures, or objects of daily life, such as sticks, tubes, or spoons.

Pears seem to have been the most favored fruit imitated by the goldsmiths. Throughout, pears served as heads of decorative pairs of pins, that is, as their handles; they should not be compared with tearlike drops (as in pendants) since they stood with the broad end up. It should be noted that the Yemenite flat pieces named "pear" (twenty of which formed the fifth row in the gala pendant *labbah*), also hang with the round end up. Naturally, only the more costly pins possessed this decorative element.[416] Apples are less common than one would expect, perhaps because their almost round, smooth surface did not offer the artisan enough incentive for "fittings." As far as I can tell, they always used apple-shaped amber or gold beads either in chains, sometimes adorned with filigree (in one case alternating with myrobolans, or "cherry plums") or as a solitaire, "one big apple."[417] Garlic (forget the smell!), with its wrinkled and irregular appearance, which allowed their makers free play of the imagination, seems to have been more popular, always as *ḥilaq* earrings—so much so that garlic simply meant earrings.[418] Pomegranate never designated jewelry, but in the Geniza (and still in some Oriental communities, such as those from Iraq and Yemen) was the name for the openwork or filigree and niello ornaments placed on the upper ends of the two sticks on which the Torah scrolls are fastened. In North Africa pomegranates were called apples, although, of late, their form is rather like that of a tower embellished with bells, certainly an imitation of European models.[419]

Like pomegranates and garlic, some floral elements became the name rather than the description of ornaments. This is particularly true of the *khūṣa*, or palm leaf, made of silver (mostly), gold, and probably also of semiprecious stones. It was used by men and women alike and, therefore, probably served for keeping the headgear in place. A golden khūṣa was embellished with niello work.[420] When one reads lists like "a silver ring, two khūṣas, and two neckbands—1/2 dinar,"[421] or "three silver ḥadīda bracelets, a khūṣa, and three pins—1 1/2 dinars,"[422] and, in particular, "a silver ring, a silver ḥadīda for fastening the [sleeve] kerchief, a silver khūṣa, and two silver pins—3 [dinars]," it is evident that the word had become the name of an ornament.[423]

After having noticed "a pair of gold myrtle pins, worth 4 dinars" in a carefully written trousseau list from summer 1186,[424] I took *marāsīn*, occurring in at least three similar documents, to mean pins with handles imitating the flowers or leaves of myrtles. In a poorly styled thirteenth-century letter, when the writer asks a female relative to provide him with three rings, "either *marsīna*, or round, *mudawwara*," he probably means either decorated with floral designs, or plain.[425] Anemones, *shaqā'iq*, in silver, also formed adornments of pins and were therefore occasionally listed in this sense without mentioning pins expressly.[426] Houseleek, the Greek name of which, "ever-living," was translated into Latin *sempervivum* and

Arabic *ḥayy al-ʿālam*, decorated earrings.[427]

Birds in relief decorated the woodwork in the Geniza synagogue, and figurines of cocks formed knickknacks on the dressing table. The beautiful pendant from the Metropolitan Museum of Art, mentioned before, shows a pair of birds facing each other.[428] But no birds are mentioned in our trousseau lists—there was no need for it—except one, frequently noted: the peacock, that medieval symbol of glory and pride. When the rich bride had a pair of peacock pins costing 18 dinars, and other brides those of a value of 7 or 8 dinars, some expressly or implicitly described as not adorned with pearls, probably (half-)precious stones of bright and different colors were intended.[429] The term "peacock" could refer also to the shape of the spread-out tail of the bird and not to its coloring. A "silver peacock pipe" was probably a pendant.[430]

The crescent, found as an emblem on Arab-Sassanian coins as early as the first century of Islam,[431] was represented in the jewelry of the Jewish brides four hundred and more years later. A gold hilāl, adorned with small pearls, weighing 4 1/2 dinars and probably also worth that sum, most likely served as a pendant.[432] Another gold crescent, together with four pins, adorned the *shāshiya*, or turban cloth of a little boy; it was taken on loan, certainly for a special occasion, such as the first cutting of the boy's hair.[433] A miḥbas collar with five golden crescents adorned with pearls and with gold "pieces," *qiṭaʿ*, was the first of twenty-six items of jewelry owned by a lower middle-class bride.[434]

The decorative element named *shamsa*, sun disk (in Arabic the sun itself is called *shams*, not *shamsa*), appears in different combinations and has several functions. In App. D, Doc. X *d*, a bride lists first a tiara consisting of seven parts with enamel sun disks adorned with pearls and costing 50 dinars; her second item is a pair of golden hoop pins, again with enamel sun disks and clusters of pearls, worth 10 dinars; and later on in her outfit, a *ḥanak* choker with gold sun disks valued at only 2 dinars. This gives the impression that the mīnā (see n. 413) shamsas accounted for the high prices of the first two pieces.[435] The jewelry left by the India trader Ben Yijū to his daughter in 1156, described above, contained also a pair of openworked sun disks, probably to be used as pendants.[436] In a legal opinion written by this learned merchant (most likely in inland Yemen), a mother is reported as having given "her own sun disk" and *khannāqa* to her daughter on the girl's wedding day. This shamsa must refer to the large ornamental disk worn by women of the countryside of Yemen (and many other Oriental countries) on their foreheads (hanging down from their head covers). Those that

I could observe around 1950, when villagers formed the majority of emigrants from Yemen, had great charm.[437]

"Star" as a term for a decorative element has not yet been encountered by me in the Geniza. The ubiquitous five-pointed star (for instance, in earrings [Keene-Jenkins, *Djawhar*, fig. 19]) was called (King) Solomon's ring and served to decorate finger rings and, in particular, pins, as in "a pair of silver pins of the type *khawātīm Sulaymān* with enamel and adorned with pearls."[438]

Goldsmith terms derived from objects of daily life, especially as handles for or description of pins, are surprisingly numerous. Hoops, the most common ones, have already been mentioned. A pair of hoop pins could cost from 1 to 30 dinars.[439] Pins are defined by such terms as spoons, small trays, compartments, tambourines, pincers, arrows, clubs (or safety pins?), shepherd's staffs, and others.[440] Pendants are often described as having attachments such as boxes, pipes, tubes, cylinders, and the like, and some have been preserved.

Where gold tubes are mentioned independently and not as attachments to a pendant, hair ornaments might have been intended.[441] When we find small earrings described as cups, we are inclined to regard pairs of ornaments named "dervish cups," and even "stirrups," as earrings too.[442]

Among techniques of the jewelers, attention should be paid first to the general term *sādhaj*, plain, repeatedly referred to above. As in clothing, where it meant unpatterned, or of one color only, and the like, in jewelry it had a number of meanings. In the entry "four rings, two filigree and two plain,"[443] the meaning is evident. A sādhaj amber necklace had no alternating beads of gold or other materials.[444] Any ornament lacking easily removable attachments could also be described as sādhaj.

Bracelets of all types, as well as pins, are frequently described as *ṣāmit*, solid, as opposed to *manfūkh*, literally, puffed up, probably meaning hollow and protuberant.[445] With one exception, only siwār bracelets are listed as puffed up. But this might be fortuitous. No marked difference in price can be observed.[446]

Another important specification concerning the body of a piece of jewelry was whether it was solidly of a precious metal or only plated with it. If it was plated, the main material seems to be mentioned only when it is silver.[447] When the shank of an anklet or bracelet is braided or twisted, it is noted, although infrequently, or is described as "[like] the border of a basket."[448]

The most common way of beautifying a surface was filigree, named *mushabbak*, literally, latticework.[449] It is very often noted with regard to rings, but rarely with bracelets, necklaces, earrings, or tiaras; perhaps filigree was taken for granted on such objects. Silver vessels, especially those decorating the dressing table, are also occasionally noted as mushabbak.[450]

I noted "beaded," which I take to mean granulated, siwār bracelets (no other ornaments) only three times, all from brides marrying in summer 1156. (Did all buy their jewelry from one goldsmith?) The first of the three bracelets, which was also adorned by niello work, cost 18 dinars; the two others, which were not, were evaluated at 15 and 16 1/3 dinars. It looks as if the theory of the replacement of granulation by filigree, expressed decades ago by the author of a three-volume study of the history of goldsmithing, has found additional corroboration in the Cairo Geniza.[451]

The bride of 1156 with the filigree siwārs adorned with niello work had another pair with niello only, which cost 28 dinars. The same very high price was noted for a pair of niello bracelets in Doc. II, col. I, l. 8, dated 1146. And the "rich bride" (Doc. III, col. I, l. 8) had a pair valued at 52 dinars, an exceptionally high sum for any piece of jewelry. If filigree was common, niello was prestigious. R. A. Higgins defines the material and process of niello in his history of Greek and Roman jewlery: "a mat black substance, composed of one or more metallic sulphides, used for the decoration of gold, and, more commonly, silver. It is set in recesses cut in the surface of the metal". He concludes his description with the remark: "It was not until the eleventh century A.D. well beyond our period, that a niello suitable for fusion to metal was employed."[452]

As far as the Geniza is concerned, the twelfth century was the classical time for niello work. It was applied almost exclusively to objects made of gold, mostly to bracelets of all types. Only once have I found a silver *dabla*, a finger ring without a stone, with niello (but worth only 2 dinars), and once a silver box and a silver jug with the same decoration.[453] The term for niello is *mujrā*, treated, which seems to make no sense, and it took me years to identify it. Some documents mercifully added the word *(bi-)sawād*, (with) blackness, and the mystery was solved. But the very fact that in the great majority of cases in the Geniza, as well as in an Arabic text, mujrā is used without the addition of (bi-)sawād proves how widely this technique was applied. Among a tremendous array of costly gifts sent by a Byzantine emperor and his entourage to the caliph al-Rāḍī in the year 938, there was a battle-ax with a heavy hilt made of gilded silver, "treated [with black]," and inset with gems. Niello as a decoration for weapons was already known to the Egyptians in the second millennium B.C.[454]

The first dated Geniza document describing an ornament as treated with blackness is the oft-cited Karaite marriage contract of 1117. Two other, approximately contemporary sources have the same full expression (but without "with"). In these three cases, a ḥadīda bracelet is identified thus. In all the other documents the abbreviated term "treated" is used for niello applied to ornaments. I have not noted a case of niello later than say, 1180.[455]

The ornaments.—After this detailed discussion of the materials, shapes, and techniques of jewelry, there is no need for a lengthy description of the individual ornaments. Here, again, we are up against problems of terminology. When we encounter several terms for a common object, such as earrings or bracelets, we wonder if different types are intended, or if the variety of names is only a matter of linguistic usage. A few considerations help to overcome this difficulty, at least in part. When a bride brings in three or four pairs of bracelets with different names, they must represent different types well known to everyone. But when one trousseau list notes several pairs of earrings, always using the same word, and another list does the same, but with another term, a difference in time, ambiance, or linguistic usage must be assumed, not the shape and general appearance of the ornament.[456] The place in the list where a piece is mentioned and its price are also considerations, although they are indications of only relative value. Thus, in the Jewelry section, when the first item is an object named *ʿiṣāba*, (head)-band, costing 80 dinars, and, in the Clothing section also listed first is another object bearing the same name which together with a robe and a wimple costs 50 dinars, the place, even where no other details are provided (as often happens), defines the character of the pieces. The first was made of gold and other high-priced materials. The second was a textile set with precious ornaments. But matters are often not so simple as that.[457]

The head is the dominant part of the body and attracts attention first. From remote antiquity Near Easterners enhanced the dominance of the head with sumptuous headgear, such as gorgeous turbans of the finest linen, or, in the case of women and rulers, with extravagant jewelry.[458] In those circumstances, I translated the Geniza ʿiṣāba as tiara or diadem. Two different types seem to have existed. A golden ʿiṣāba of seven pieces with mīnā sun disks and adorned with pearls, costing 50 dinars, another consisting of seven pieces and described as (made) complete,[459] and a third having eleven parts convey the image of a kind of crown that has one prominent center piece with three or five other pieces on each side of diminishing heights.[460] But ʿiṣābas costing 80, 70, or 50 dinars, respectively, and described simply as golden, or made of gold and adorned with pearls, in the last case also with filigree work, leads one to visualize a hoop of gold inlaid with pearls.[461]

Tubes as hair ornaments, mentioned above, have actually been preserved.[462] Pairs of pipes made of silver or gold and known in Palestine to the present day as *barābekh*, are described by Yedida Stillman as attached to the coif near the temple and end in a hollow ball from which hang four braided chains.[463] A *barbakh* pipe is repeatedly mentioned in trousseau lists written around 1200, but always in the singular; I assume therefore that it must have had a form and function different from those of the modern barābekh.[464]

Special attention must be paid to the *khuyūṭ*, gilded strings for the head. In one case they cost only 1 dinar; in another, 20. In still another they are described as silk strings with gold-plated silver threads worth 3 dinars, and in the earliest instance noted by me, the clerk simply wrote "strings made of silk and other materials—6 dinars," a sum that points to the use of silver and gold. In all these cases "the materials for the khuyūṭ" were included in the trousseau lists.[465]

In the later part of the twelfth century the putting on by the bride of her head strings became a festive ceremony, comparable with the henna night when her body was dyed with that color of joy. The strings were a symbol of something else: A virgin wore her hair falling freely on her shoulders. With the entrance into the state of matrimony the hair was bound up forever. No wonder we read in a marriage contract of April 1243 that at the wedding the groom provided the expenses for the henna and the strings "as customary." Marriage brings with it both joy and restrictions.[466]

The palm leaf, khūṣa, a clasp for keeping the headgear in place, the Mamluk *kulband*, headcover, and the sun disk, shamsa, probably an ornament for the forehead, have been discussed.[467]

Earrings did not require detailed descriptions because of their obvious function, their small size, which clearly distinguishes them from other ornaments, and their constant appearance in pairs. They are mostly, if at all, defined as being of gold—otherwise they would not have been noted in the trousseau—and adorned ("with pearls," often omitted), their price varying between 3 and 6 dinars, 5 dinars being the most common price. Special elements of shape such as garlic, houseleek (sempervivum), cups, and stirrups, have been mentioned.[468] To them we may add "two small pepper earrings of gold," probably meaning that they were composed of tiny gold pellets,[469] and *mukhammas* earrings valued in one case at 8 dinars and in another at 7. The latter pair was listed in the marriage contract of the businesswoman Wuḥsha. Many years later, on her deathbed, she gave this pair to her brother (in addition to 100 dinars and other gifts); since she made gifts to a sister and left another pair of earrings to the daughter of her paternal uncle, one wonders whether Jewish men in those days, like some other Near Easterners, occasionally wore earrings.[470] *Mukhammas* might denote a five-pointed star; but this was commonly called (King) Solomon's ring. Tentatively I suggest, that, an ornament representing the *khamsa*, the five fingers of the magic hand, is meant; but we must wait for actual finds from the Fatimid period for comfirmation.[471]

The common word for earring then, as now, was *ḥalqa*, which simply means ring. In the Geniza documents, mostly from the tenth and eleventh centuries, however, another word, *turk*, pl. *atrāk*, or *turkiy*, pl. *tarākī* (also other forms), was in use. It is found in Syro-Palestinian documents from Jerusalem, Damascus, and Tyre, and, when it occurs in marriage contracts from the Egyptian towns Damsīs (in 1083) and al-Maḥalla, it may well be that the clerk (and possibly the families concerned) were immigrants from Palestine, as so often happened.[472] Descriptions refer only to Syro-Palestinian artifacts. Pairs from Damascus are repeatedly described as ribs, which might have had some similarity with the aforementioned hoops decorating pins. A Syro-Palestinian pair of golden atrāk weighed 8 1/2 mithqāls (about 40 grams), which corresponds approximately to the price of 8 dinars for a mukhammas, as already noted.[473]

A third term for earring, pronounced in the eleventh century as today either *khurṣ* or *khirṣ*, is not very common. As with regular rings, some are described as decorated with amber.[474] The *shunūf* "which are worn either on the ears, as is done today, or on the nose, as it was customary in ancient times" (as Maimonides writes) I have encountered in the Geniza only once. In his Commentary on the Mishnah, Maimonides provides an exact description (in this case accompanied by a sketch) of these objects and many others, which may be useful for students of the material civilization of the twelfth century.[475]

Like earrings, pins almost always appear in pairs, and as such have actually been recovered.[476] Unlike earrings, though, their function is by no means self-evident, and their decorative elements were of the widest imaginable variety. Consequently, they are more frequently defined and described than any other ornament. Much of what has been said on materials, shapes, and techniques also applies to pins. One gets the impression that a pair of pins was the jewelry a woman needed most. I assume they were used for keeping the headgear in place; there they would attract the attention of an onlooker first, and to that end the artisans had to come up with ever new ideas for making them different. Pairs of pins to fasten the ends of a necklace or a woman's clothing (as in Roman times) were hardly common in Islam. A single gold pin for keeping the ends of an outer garment together was absolutely exceptional.[477]

Ornaments for around the neck and down the chest are clearly divided into two groups: strings and the like to closely encircle the throat and loose chains, with or without pendants, to hang down, in some instances reaching almost to the girdle. The documents translated in Appendix D frequently note a choker made of pearls, sometimes combined with alternating gold or sun disks or golden spools, and named *ḥanak*, a word seemingly absent from our dictionaries.[478] The verb *ḥanaka* means bridling a horse; another term of horse trappings used for the description of a female ornament is discussed below.[479] The frequency of the term in our Appendix should not give the impression that it was used throughout the Geniza. All cases I have noted are found in documents dated between 1146 and 1159. Perhaps the connection with horse bridling drove the term out of use.

Unlike the pearl choker, ḥanak, listed only around the middle of the twelfth century, the *mikhnaqa* (from *khanaqa*, to smother, to strangle—also an unpleasant connotation) is known from a Damascus document dated 956, and throughout the tenth and eleventh centuries. It was made of gold; parts described as beads, drops, and a head are mentioned.[480] The *khannāqa*, derived from the same verb, occurs only in legal documents from the twelfth century with no descriptive details, but is known as a necklace from Arabic literature and is still in use in Morocco.[481] The pearl band, *khaṣr*, intersected by beads of gold (App. D, Doc. III, col. I, l. 12), or made of lustrous *sabaj* jets, divided by pearls (see p. 421, below) must also be a neckband; the regular meaning of khaṣr is waist, and I take the term, which I have not found elsewhere, as something laced up tight. In a fragmentary document khaṣr is found in the dual, perhaps worn, like the Yemenite subḥa, over the lower parts of a girl's sleeves, and then, of course, made of cheap costume jewelry.[482]

Another tight-fitting necklace, the *miḥbas* collar, the one decorated with five crescents, pearls, and gold pendants, we have already met.[483] The verbal root *ḥabasa* means to block, to confine, to jail. Thus the name of this ornament, like those of the other four necklaces discussed, denotes its close adherence to the throat. The long list of jewelry of a well-to-do bride, written in Fustat 1156, is headed by a gold miḥbas adorned with pearls and worth 75 dinars, far more than twice as much as any other ornament in her trousseau.[484] Another list, written a year earlier (1155), has this interesting description of a gold miḥbas: consisting of twenty-five pieces, nine large and sixteen small, that is, the large pieces formed the "head," or, as we would say, the center.[485] The miḥbas is again first in position and price in a trousseau list from al-Maḥalla, drafted at approximately the same time where it is valued at 12 dinars. But when we consider that the list from that provincial town concludes with an item worth 1 qīrāṭ (1/24 dinar), we understand how precious that necklace must have been to its wearer.[486]

The most common, one should say, classical, word for necklace in Arabic literature, *ʿiqd*, I came across in the Geniza only twice: in a marriage contract from Aleppo, dated 1107/8 ("pearl ʿiqd, divided by gold"), and one from the Egyptian town al-Maḥalla "the Great," where Jews from Aleppo were settled. It was complemented by M. A. Friedman, I believe correctly, in a small tattered fragment, probably also from Syria or Palestine. Words, like books, are exposed to the vagaries of fortune. To be sure, at that time Syria had preserved the traditions of classical Arabic more faithfully than Egypt.[487]

Of the ornaments decorating the upper chest, the gold *lāzam*, explained in detail in App. D, n. 142, is by far most frequently mentioned. It is repeatedly described as consisting of five rows, probably alternating strings of beads and small sheets of gold cut in different shapes. Since, in one case, it is noted as "a lāzam not adorned with pearls," one may assume that it usually was. In all other instances it is simply called lāzam, or *lāzam dhahab*. Its price varied from 7 to 13 dinars with one exception, when it was valued at 20 dinars.[488]

The shoulder band, *katifiyya* or *kitfiyya*, as its name and the parts of which it was composed indicate, was entirely different from the lāzam. In the trousseau of the "rich bride," where it takes second place after the tiara in both order and price (70 dinars), it is composed of eleven disks of gold and twenty of amber, which means that the center piece in front was a gold disk.[489] The katifiyya was essentially a long string of amber beads; its price depended on the number and size of the gold pieces put between them. A widow claiming the return of her dowry, which had a total value of 754 dinars, states that she had already received—among other items—"the amber of a katifiyya, worth 12 dinars," certainly only a fraction of the total value, as we see from the sums spent on other examples of this ornament.[490] "A shoulder band with twenty spools of gold, an apple and a myrobalan [cherry plum] of gold, and thirty apples of amber" had a total value of 30 dinars.[491] Even more characteristic is this entry in a marriage contract: "A gold katifiyya, the number of its gold beads: twelve, besides the amber—30 dinars." To the clerk the number of amber beads seemed of secondary importance; they probably were too numerous to be counted.[492]

The *qilāda*, still commonly used today, especially for a necklace composed of one or several longer strings, in the Geniza had three different shapes. Like the katifiyya, it was either an amber string intersected by gold "apples and myrobalans" (see App. D, n. 290), or a small necklace, such as "the gold qilāda, composed of eight grains and a middle piece, of a total weight of 5 5/8 dinars [thus, not mithqāls],"[493] or a fine piece of cloth trimmed with precious materials. "A light-gray qilāda trimmed solely with amber" is the first and most valuable item in the trousseau of a widow marrying a widower, both promising to bring up the children from their previous marriages.[494] A mother writing to her son complains that "only one piece of silver was on the qilāda."[495] The *silsila* chain, composed of precious stones and cloth embroidered with gold threads, similar to the third type of the qilāda, is discussed above; but we find also "three gold rings in a chain with gold grains."[496] An amber rosary, *subḥa*, is listed in a marriage contract of the early eleventh century. In an agreement written in Ascalon, Palestine, in January 1100, such a rosary, divided by filigree (or openwork) gold apples and a filigree gold center piece, was valued at 35 dinars.[497]

Finally, mention must be made of ornaments expressly described as amulets, especially the *maymūn*, auspicious, ubiquitous in the Geniza documents and, under other names, still popular all over the Islamic world.[498] Jewelry in general was partly intended to attract the looks and thus to divert a potentially evil eye from its bearer. But there were necklaces with pendants, either actually containing a *kitāb*, or script with a magic formula, or indicating by their shape—a lengthy box with spherical ends— that they might contain one. In a power of attorney written in Tunisia in 1074, a maymūn with gold spools and a silver kitāb was claimed from the family back in Egypt. That the main part of the maymūn was made of amber is not stated, since it was the rule, and is indeed indicated in all other instances I have noted.[499] In one case the maymūn consisted of thirteen amber beads, six gold spools, and four pearls; the most expensive maymūn noted thus far had thirteen amber beads, but I am not sure that this number did not have superstitious connotations.[500] In addition to their maymūn these two brides had a *mijarr* chain, in one case equipped with two boxes, *khizāna*, a type of ornament found in other jewelry serving as an amulet.[501] The mijarr, denoting also the rope of a draft animal,[502] became popular in Mamluk times, when it consisted of a large number of amber beads (sixty in two documents, seventy-two in another—multiples of twelve), but seemingly without the admixture of other, more costly materials.[503]

The four main types of bracelets: *siwār*, an ancient Semitic word; *dastaynaq*, from Persian *dast*, hand; *dumluj*, probably derived from the Ethiopian; and *ḥadīda*, about which later, occur side by side in App. D, Doc. X *d* (1159) and in an eleventh-century list;[504] the first three also in Doc. X *b* (1050) and in another document from the same century.[505] It shows that these terms denoted four different groups of bracelets, distinguishable by everyone, but, as additional descriptions indicate, comprising variations according to material, shape, and technique used. The first three types of bracelet were mostly of gold and were worn in pairs, one on each arm, as was customary in biblical times.[506]

The ḥadīda was different. It usually appears in the singular and was more often made of silver than of gold. Besides adornment it must have served a practical purpose. In some cases it is described as *laff al-mandīl*, keeping the kerchief in place, namely, the kerchief which was tucked into the sleeve, and which was used not for blowing the nose but for carrying money and anything else that one would keep in a pocket. Since it is repeatedly reported that people lost the sleeve kerchief and its contents, one understands why people preferred to fasten it with a buckle.[507] There might have been another and perhaps even more common use for the ḥadīda. Sleeves were wide, which was not always convenient while doing household chores such as cooking. The ḥadīda clasp, sometimes described as large or broad, might have helped to gather up and hold the ends of the right sleeve tightly together. This practice might explain the origin of the word; *ḥadīd*, as a noun, means iron, and ḥadīda might be understood as a piece of iron, which is unlikely; but ḥadīd, as an adjective, means adjacent, bordering on; thus the ḥadīda was essentially a piece for the border of a sleeve. In the course of time it became a general word for bracelet, and, in North Africa it seems to be the one most commonly used.[508]

The most prestigious bracelet was the "classical" *siwār*, still the term common in Egypt and Palestine.[509] When specified, it is always listed as being made of gold, and in the rare cases when its main materials were pearls or amber, it had at least one or two golden rims.[510] It is repeatedly described as puffed up, and niello work was its most costly adornment.[511] Filigree and granulation, it seems, were more common than noted.[512] The "Scorpion's tail" probably looked somewhat like the splendid piece in Keene-Jenkins, *Djawhar*, fig. 5*a*, while the "Basket's border" has some similarity to that in fig. 16*b*.[513]

Whereas the siwār was characterized by massive gold, the *dastaynaj* (a foreign word, pronounced in different ways) excelled in attachments. It is mostly described as adorned with, or intersected by, pearls, once as a single mīnā dastaynaj (App. D, Doc. IV, col. I, l. 9), and in a document from al-Maḥalla as made of, or decorated with, lapis lazulī and worth only 1/4 dinar. The highest price obtained for a single *tastaynaq* (spelled thus) was 10 dinars (App. D, Doc. V, l. 13), the average, 5 dinars.[514]

Like siwār, *dumluj* is an ancient word, and the bracelets bearing this name appear frequently in documents from the middle of the eleventh century. They were usually made of gold; a price of 15 dinars for a pair is repeatedly mentioned. A single gold dumluj with niello work cost 14 dinars.[515] A pair of silver dumlujs weighed 60 dirhems, about 200 grams, but the price of 14 dinars is given in Adenese currency, which had only about a third the value of that of Egypt.[516]

Other types of bracelet besides the main four occur in the trousseau lists, but too infrequently to warrant a meaningful discussion.[517] Mention must be made, however, of the *miʿḍada*, an ornament for the *ʿaḍud*, or upper arm; it is always noted in the singular and always as made of silver. A golden ring around the upper arm—the symbol of strength—was the insignia of nobility and royalty (King Saul wore one) in the ancient Near East, put, as the reliefs show, it was worn directly on the skin. Since a Jewish (and certainly a Muslim) woman should never uncover her upper arm, it was surmised above (at n. 376) that the silver miʿḍada, in addition to its decorative purpose, might have been used to hold a tucked-up sleeve in place.[518]

The adornment of sleeves with strings of pearls or colored stripes (sometimes bearing an inscription) is attested by Arabic literature and miniatures as well as by the Geniza.[519] The practice of adorning sleeves with a poetic inscription may help to identify as a bracelet a piece of jewelry named *shāhid*. The word denotes a verse by a classical poet adduced as a proof for correct linguistic usage. Found in Fustat in 1105 among the belongings of a dead foreigner were a golden shāhid and another made of small pearls. In a marriage contract written in the same town a year later, a pearl shāhid was valued at 1 dinar. If this explanation holds water, it would show that even a gold armlet could be worn above the sleeve.[520]

Finger rings seem not to have been objects suited for the display of affluence. Leafing through the trousseau lists of well-to-do brides in Appendix D, one finds that the number of rings brought in varied from one (Doc. X *d*, l. 21) to eight (four gold, four silver,

Doc. X *a*, l. 2) with four the average number, while their value varied between 1 1/2 and 2 1/2 dinars (Doc. II, l. 11; Doc. III, ll. 14–27; Doc. V, l. 14; Doc. X *c*, ll. 5–6). The reason for these low prices was the absence of precious stone settings, emphasized above.[521] While the hands of some of our contemporaries glitter with sparkling diamonds, even a modest carnelian is rarely mentioned in the Geniza, probably because the value of those half-precious stones was minimal in comparison with that of the gold or silver needed for a ring. *Khātam*, or *khātim* (as it was already pronounced in the eleventh century[522]), literally means seal ring. But a ring bearing the name of a Jewish woman is known to me only from Christian Spain, and when two golden filigree khātims plus two silver khātims were valued at 2 dinars, that is 1/2 dinar apiece, or when one could have a silver khātim for a quarter dinar, one doubts whether these rings had a stone at all.[523] Beside the occasional occurrence of stone settings, filigree, and pearls, amber is noted as an adornment or as the material; one bride had one ring of gold, two of silver, and one of amber.[524] The majority of khātims appear in pairs (two or four; eight [see above] is exceptional), but the term "pair" is rarely used. Thus, unlike bracelets, rings, as a rule, probably did not match.

The *dabla* (a term still common), a ring without a stone, seems to have been rather massive in Geniza times. One of gold was valued at 4 dinars in 1155; a pair of silver *dibal* was estimated as being worth the same in 1186; and of particular interest is the trousseau of a remarrying widow, where two gold khātims cost 2 dinars, three silver dablas, 9, and some silver khātims (their number is not preserved) together with a silver chain, 2 dinars. Most rings of this type were made of silver, one of which was adorned with niello work. The khātim occurs at least five times as often as the dabla.[525]

Anklets, like bracelets, could be easily displayed by furtively pulling the upper garment up or aside; therefore, both had to be heavy, which means expensive, betraying the bearer's means and social status. In the passage translated at the beginning of this section on jewelry it was the bracelets and anklets that attracted the attention of the poet. It seems that in the earlier part of the eleventh century anklets were particularly treasured; they repeatedly appear at the head of a trousseau list—like the tiara in the twelfth century—and the prices at which they were valued—25, 30, and even over 60 dinars—were among the highest noted in those documents.[526] Anklets were routinely wrought in gold. In the exceptional case when a poor woman in Tyre, Lebanon, marrying in November 1023, had silver anklets worth 8 dinars, their price shows these ornaments to have been very heavy.[527] The specific magical power of anklets is demonstrated by the fact that children, even boys, were equipped with them. In a postscript to a letter a teacher from a learned family writes to his brother: "Tell me, have you already made a 'Bible' for your boy—or only anklets?" Meaning: to study the holy scriptures is a better protection against any evil than to wear silver or gold.[528]

At the dressing table.—The list of ornaments in the marriage contract of a middle-class bride usually ends with some utensils made of precious materials such as silver, crystal, ebony, or ivory for her dressing table. Costly objects of lighting, heating, dining, fumigating, and freshening were occasionally brought in by the bride, but it seems to have been customarily the duty of the husband to provide them. They are treated in the subsections "Furnishings" and "Houseware" (A, 4 and 5), above. The trunks and chests, often ornamented with mother-of-pearl and ivory, in which the wife kept her wardrobe, regularly formed part of her dowry, and are also discussed under "Furnishings," because they contributed so much to the look of the interior of a house.

Needless to say, item number one on the dressing table was the mirror. The grooming and dressing of a woman is described in a family letter in this sequence: "She paints her face, combs her hair, puts on her pendants [or earrings], dresses, and goes out." Practically all the brides in our Appendix D had a *mir'āh muḥallāh*, an ornamented mirror, the "rich bride" (Doc. III, like that in Doc. X *e*) possessed two, one costing 10 dinars, the highest price noted, and another, a round one, valued at 6 dinars, which was the average price (5 being the most common).[529] Ornamented meant embellished with silver adornments, as is evident from those cases where the mirror is described as "ornamented with silver," or "with a silver decoration," or "inlaid with silver."[530] We read also about a round mirror with a silver cover and one "encased," costing 8 1/12 dinars.[531] In short, just as in jewelry adorned meant with pearls, in mirrors it meant with silver. A respectable bride could not do without a silver mirror. Silver, however, was scarce and expensive in the twelfth century. In two marriage contracts from the end of the century, iron mirrors, valued at 1/2 and 1 dinar, respectively, are noted, and others in a similar price range might have been set in the same material.[532] In a letter of the judge Elijah b. Zachariah (see Index) to his mother in Alexandria, she receives an Indian mirror (probably sent to him from Aden as a present). But Egypt was a great center for the manufacture of silver vessels; most of the objects mentioned probably were locally made.[533]

Next to the mirror in prestige on the dressing table was the jewel box. Its common name was *durj*, a general word for casket, but other designations were also used. A strange development is to be observed in respect to jewel boxes: whereas in the tenth and eleventh centuries much money was spent on them, in the twelfth comparatively little was expended because silver had then become scarce, and one preferred to use it for the adornment of the body and not for that of a utensil hidden away in a woman's dressing cabinet.

In the very first detailed trousseau list preserved (Damascus, 933) the "container of precious objects" was valued at 15 dinars. A silver jewel box from the early eleventh century cost from 10 to 20 dinars; at its end, a price of 14 dinars is quoted; and the Karaite bride of 1117 still had one worth 8 dinars. A business letter from the later half of the eleventh century with a big order for silver vessels from Egypt lists a beautiful durj as the first item.[534] In later lists I found only one instance of a silver durj worth 5 dinars (1156). Whereas in the dowries of the "rich bride" and her younger contemporary, the silver durj was lumped together with other objects and could hardly have cost more than 2 dinars, if not much less.[535]

The earlier listings occasionally include specifications concerning the make of a durj. A marriage contract from 995 describes it as *muḥraq*, burnished with gold, and another from 1050, as adorned with filigree and sandalwood. A document from 1063, written in Zawīlat al-Mahdiyya, Tunisia, but referring to objects left in Egypt and belonging to a woman, lists a box made of ebony adorned with copper; this combination of the dark-colored heartwood with the reddish shining metal must have been striking. An ebony durj for *sanūn*, tooth care materials (toothpicks and powder), costing 5 dinars, is noted in a marriage contract of a well-to-do woman written around 1028, a high price for a receptacle with so modest a purpose.[536]

Turning now to the utensils used for beauty care, one is impressed by the mass of material related to the application of kohl to the eyes. It was a ritual of almost religious significance. When Queen Jezebel knew that she was going to be killed, "she painted her eyes with kohl"—an indispensable adornment for dying in royal splendor (2 Kings 9:30). From the Geniza it is evident that neglecting this aspect of bodily care was an offense to the husband.[537]

The main equipment for eye paint was the *mukḥula*, or kohl jar, which, as I learned from Marilyn Jenkins, then, as in ancient Egypt and in Hellenistic times, as well as in nineteenth-century Egypt, had the shape of a tiny Greek amphora.[538] In the majority of cases it was made of *billawr*, which is usually translated as crystal, and was sometimes decorated with a golden rim or closed with a silver lid. In view of the low price, about 1 dinar, this crystal must have been of a very low grade, probably a kind of quartz. In one case we know from which part of the world the material came. After his return from India and Yemen (early 1150s), Ben Yijū notes, in one of his inventories, "3 crystal kohl jars." In 1156 his daughter had them in her trousseau—valued at 3 dinars. With one possible exception, all my references to crystal are from the twelfth century and later. A number of kohl jars were made of silver, or at least adorned with it, and worth at most 2 dinars.[539] The "rich bride" had an ivory kohl jar, costing 3 dinars. Naturally, she had to be different. But perhaps she was not so different from other girls of her status, for the word used here for ivory came to mean jar or flask in general, as happened with the word mukḥula itself.[540]

Kohl was appled with a small ornamented probe (*mīl*, derived from Greek), listed once as made of crystal, but mostly of silver, four of them in an eleventh-century document valued at 1 dinar. An admirably detailed description of this important part of female toilet may be read in Lane's *Modern Egyptians*.[541] Being ornamental, a mīl could be worn "on the cheek," probably hanging down from the headgear.[542] Together with its case, it is referred to as *mirwad*, a more elaborate piece of jewelry, repeatedly noted as being made of silver and worth 1 dinar.[543] A favorite place to store the kohl stick, a tiny, but essential utensil of makeup, was in a perforated figurine, such as a crystal cock, a lion, or an amber gazelle.[544] Numerous such figurines have been preserved, and I believe that the amber *tamāthīl*, or figurines, in the outfits of the Mistress of the Persians and the Mistress of Baghdad, and unspecified numbers of amber tamāthīl valued at 5 dinars found in twelfth- and thirteenth-century lists served the same purpose.[545]

Combs, if described at all, were made of silver, and one such could be had for 1 or 2 dinars. The "rich bride" had a silver comb for 4 dinars. But a Karaite widow possessed a golden comb worth 16 dinars, whereas her rosewater sprinkler was valued at only 8 1/2 dinars. Once an ivory comb is listed in an outfit.[546] When a mother in Fustat asks her son (who was staying in an inn in the Jewish quarter of Alexandria) to buy for her, among other wooden utensils, a very fine comb, she probably had in mind one made of European boxwood, according to a Muslim handbook of market supervision the only material to be used for combs for both men and women. The plea of the mother made in the same letter not to drink wine—strange, since the letter is addressed to "the scholar from Fustat, Abu 'l-Maḥāsin"—has also to do with a product imported from Europe: the Greek and Italian wines, relished by the Jewish *jeunesse dorée* of Alexandria.[547] Amshāṭī, Comb maker, was a very common Jewish family name throughout the centuries, borne by persons living in Fustat, Alexandria, and al-Maḥalla, but it is nowhere evident whether these "Comb makers" (or, rather, their forefathers) were engaged in making the toilet utensil or the wide-toothed brush used for carding textile fibers, designated in Arabic by the same term. Moreover, most of the Amshāṭis mentioned in the Geniza were well-off merchants, contributors to or organizers of public appeals, donors of costly gifts to synagogues, and the like.[548]

Anointing and perfuming oneself was an indispensable part of body care, particularly for women. When the Persian king Shahpur wished to enjoy pleasant scents—the Talmud relates—he sent for his daughter, whose well-groomed body provided the most effective fragrance. The Book of Esther 2:12 drastically reveals that only by intensive and protracted care could such perfection be obtained. Islam inherited this infatuation from Persia, and the Jews living under Islam (who had themselves an ancient tradition in this respect [Song of Songs 1:3; 4:10]) followed suit, although opinions about the propriety of male perfuming were divided. Concerning females there was no doubt. Supplying poor brides with aromatic ointments was a religious duty. As for the Land of the Nile, reliefs and countless little artifacts illustrate the variegated cosmetic activities of the women of ancient Egypt.[549]

Ointments and perfumes, like medications, were composed of various ingredients. The most needed utensil on the dressing table was therefore a mixing vessel in which the woman of the house could prepare mixtures to her heart's content to suit every occasion. In good Arabic this contraption was called *madāf*, vessel in which one mixed, a word as common in the Geniza, as it is absent from our dictionaries.[550] The "rich bride" possessed three madāfs (App. D, Doc. III, col. 1, ll. 18–20): one valued at 3 dinars, and probably of silver, like the silver one in Doc. X *d*, col. I, l. 22, which had the same value; one worth 5 dinars, made of crystal, like the one possessed by her contemporary Sitt al-Ḥasab (Doc. IV, col. I, ll. 14–15 "with *its* crystal probe [or kohlstick]"); and a very special one, "a compartment madāf with feet," that is, the vessel was sectioned off, or was composed of various jars each containing a different perfume or scented ointment, some probably also equipped with a small spoon or stick serving each, as described next. In addition to her crystal mixer, Sitt al-Ḥasab had another with four silver lids (Doc. IV, col. I, l. 12); naturally, the perfumes had to be preserved in tight compartments. Ancient Egyptian make-up jars show four cavities, or are composed of five cylinders, the one in the center probably serving as the mixing vessel. All have lids.[551] Madāfs were usually made of silver and were to be had for 1 to 5 dinars, 3, it seems, having been the standard price.[552] A particularly well-equipped bride of the early thirteenth century possessed a madāf made of sandalwood.[553]

Ointment jars are less represented in the trousseau lists, probably because they were made of inexpensive materials. The poor Karaite bride from Jerusalem 1028 had one (App. D, Doc. I, l. 24). A marriage contract written in 1105 lists "a small ointment jar, two very small silver ointment jars with one silver spoon for the labdanum, and another silver spoon for the *ghāliya*," and there are other such utensils from the eleventh and twelfth centuries.[554]

Returning now from the dressing table to the ornaments and their wearer, I wish to conclude with this remark in Graham Hughes, *Jewelry*: "The most popular, but the least public of all possessions, jewels intrigue one's close friends, not the crowd in the streets; they satisfy only in private, they reserve their charms for intimacy."[555] If such a statement could be made in the England of the twentieth century, how much more did it apply to a Jewish woman living in an Islamic environment a thousand or so years ago. In the Song of Songs (7:2) the body of the beloved is itself praised as a creation of the jeweler's art. Jewelry was intended not only to protect its wearer from need (and, possibly, the evil eye), but, above all, to enhance her charms in the intimacy of matrimonial life.

In this section it was necessary to dwell on the price of ornaments so as to assign each piece its proper place in the hierarchy of the artistic means of attraction. But one must never lose sight of the main purpose. On his deathbed a rich man willed his young wife from a second marriage (in addition to what was due her from her marriage contract, of course) "the items in gold," whereas the silver was left to the little ones. Silver, remember, was used mainly for minor ornaments, dressing-table utensils, and housewares. Gold adorned the wife herself. The dying man wanted her to have it for good.[556]

C. FOOD AND DRINK

1. *Food*

Talking about food.—We read much about hunger in the Geniza, but little about food. It is natural that hungry people make themselves heard, but it is not so easy to understand why the writers of the Geniza letters should be so utterly taciturn about the enjoyment of eating. According to a competent observer, even the Jewish scholars passed their time in taking delight in the vanities of This World: distinguished clothing and delicious food.[1] Muslim sayings singled out the Jews for being particularly dedicated to culinary relish. "Sleep in a Christian bed and enjoy Jewish food," says a widely known maxim.[2] Even more outspoken is this observation, made probably already in early Islamic times: "Of the good things of this world the Muslims enjoy most sex; the Christians, money, the Persians, status; and the Jews, food."[3]

The reputation of Jewish food in its Islamic environment was probably attributable to its specialities, necessitated by Jewish religious law. On the Sabbath all cooking is prohibited, but, naturally, one wanted warm food particularly on the day of rest, when there was time to enjoy it. Special preparations had to be made for this purpose, and it is a common human trait that dishes different from those to which we are accustomed arouse our curiosity and whet our appetite. A story about such a Sabbath dish for which Jews had already been renowned in pre-Islamic Arabia—and which Jews from Arabia, namely, those coming from Yemen, using the same term, still prepare—is too beautiful not to be told. The *harīs(a)* is a semolina dough which is stuffed with meat and fat, such as lamb's tail, and spices. During the long process of warming, the dough becomes saturated with the taste of meat, fat, and spices, unlike a regular harīsa that is consumed shortly after preparation.[4] The story centers on the jovial caliph Muʿāwiya (661–680) who loved poetry, fun—and wine.

At Muʿāwiya's request, a Jew at a party recited a poem by his father, in which the latter glorified himself. When the caliph remarked that such glory belonged only to the ruler, the Jew asserted that his father had more claim to high praise than anyone. Two boon companions of the caliph scolded the Jew for being so impudent, and the latter retorted angrily. To change the subject, Muʿāwiya asked the Jew: "Does your family still prepare the harīsa as well as it did in pre-Islamic times?" "Even better," replied the Jew, whereupon he was requested to prepare some, which the caliph consumed. The gist of the anecdote was probably that Jewish food was better than Jewish poetry.[5]

I should start by saying that I have not found in the Geniza a single description of a specifically Jewish dish or meal, or, for that matter, of any dish or meal. In view of the hospitality that prevailed in their society, with its invitations to weekends, holidays, weddings, and similar occasions, and the reverence shown to distinguished guests, this deficiency is hard to explain. Traveling from Cairo to Damascus, a physician was put up and entertained by the Jewish judge of Bilbays on the eastern fringes of the Nile Delta. In describing how he was honored by the judge with festive meals, he did not say a word about the food consumed, but pointed out that on each occasion the judge "refused to wash his hands and to say the benediction" (meaning, before breaking the bread and distributing the ceremonial morsels to those present at the meal, the religious privilege of the host); the guest, so to say, took over the role of the host, in accordance with the greetings extended to a newcomer, "My house is your house."[6] A passenger on the Nile, describes to his mother how his boat, because of the dread of pirates, was unable to cast anchor, and, while passing the night in fear of death, he missed his supper: "Believe me, I did not even make *ha-mōṣī*," meaning I did not even say the blessing over bread ("Blessed be He who brings forth bread from the soil"). On such an occasion, we probably would have mentioned some of the goodies we carried with us which we had been deprived of enjoying.[7] At traditional Yemenite receptions, a great variety of fruits and tidbits are served. The guest is invited to help himself not by reference to the individual dishes but by the simple word *bōrēkh*, bless God. The person thus addressed would choose the items appropriate to the blessing said for each dish[8] and slowly say the particular blessing aloud, pronouncing each word distinctly. The other participants, silent during the recitation of the benediction, would respond with a vigorous Amen, whereupon the food would be slowly carried to the mouth and silently eaten. One observer once said to me: "These people seem to relish the saying of the benedictions at least as much as the enjoyment of the food." One praised God instead of the host or his meal, just as in a Geniza letter, after receipt of a consignment or report of an action taken on the writer's behalf, he would say: "I thanked God for what you have done for me," or the like.

The hostess, if mentioned at all in a letter of thanks, would be referred to in general terms, or lauded for her piety and charity, never for her cooking. In general, a woman would be praised as efficient and tidy, not as a good cook.[9] This is somewhat surprising since cooking and baking were duties incumbent on a housewife by law.[10] But among the many virtues possessed by the biblical woman of valor excellence in the preparation of food is not mentioned.[11] Near Eastern traditional attitude to dishes consumed is dramatically described in this passage, expressing the feelings of an American anthropologist after she had toiled much to prepare a sumptuous meal for the local "Sheik Mohammed" according to all rules of Arab gastronomy:

> I felt let down and disappointed. I suppose I had expected Mohammed to comment enthusiastically on the excellence of each dish which we had

prepared for the sheik's pleasure. He didn't. No one did ever such a thing, I found out later. If the food was good, it was obvious; people ate it and there was little of it left. Why should one talk about it?[12]

The widely diversified civilization of the medieval Near East was not unified in its attitude toward food. The secularly minded, sophisticated courtiers and government officials, together with their company of litterateurs and philosophers, enjoyed talking about food, just as the intellectuals of Late Antiquity had done before them. An abundance of treatises on cookery was available as early as the fourth century of Islam.[13] In that century, the famous medical writer Isḥāq al-Isrā'īlī, known in medieval Europe as Isaac Judaeus, wrote a four-volume book on foodstuffs and their value for human health. Thus there was also much serious thinking and research on the subject.[14]

It is true, however, that the bulk of the population, which was in the bondage of religion, had scruples with regard to food: one might enjoy this sustainer of life, but should give praise to its provider, God. The disregard for the preparers of meals, male or female, was only one aspect of that general contempt for the *banausus*, the mechanic, the technician, which the Near East had inherited, at least partly, from the Greek. Finally, refraining from commenting on food was a part of good table manners, avoiding both the impression of gluttony and the pitfalls of half-hearted praise, which might be taken as blame for the quality of the dishes.[15]

"The Egyptians eat very moderately," writes E. W. Lane, a keen and competent observer, in the 1830s. The same impression is gained from the Geniza. To become obese by eating too much was regarded as a disgrace. A glutton, *mujalliḥ*, literally, a man who makes the tray "bald," empty, before others serve themselves, was an odious figure. One left his byname as family name to his son.[16] To be sure, for a refugee from Morocco, Egypt was the "Land of Life," and a Palestinian enjoyed Egyptian conviviality, food, drink, and music so much that he forgot to go home to his wife and children.[17] But the scarcity of references to the enjoyments of food in the Geniza letters seems to indicate that their writers were hardly Sybarites.

One normally ate two meals a day, a light morning meal, *ghadā'*, and a more substantial evening meal, *ʿashā'*.[18] This had been common custom in the Near East in antiquity (and is widely discussed in the Talmud), and was still habitual in Egypt in E. W. Lane's time. In other words, the "breakfast," the breaking of the nightly fast, was not yet divided into *déjeuner* and *petit déjeuner*; one ate only one morning meal. After prayer one went to work, and, approximately four hours after sunrise, some food was taken at work.[19] Therefore, as shown in countless Geniza texts, the morning meal of laborers was provided by their employers.[20] This was not done in kind, but in money, since food of all descriptions was prepared by specialists in the bazaar and could be bought from them.[21] A master mason, who received 1 1/4 dirhems for his lunch, could buy for himself a varied nourishing meal for this sum, whereas his helpers, who got no ghadā' at all, probably had to be content with bread and onions or the like, the usual fare of the poor.[22]

The evening meal, taken at home, consisted of a number of dishes.[23] How many? As far as the lower middle class, the bulk of the Geniza population, is concerned, we can get an inkling from the advice given by Abraham Maimonides to a disciple who, for reasons of piety, wished to confine himself to bread and salt.[24] Do not make the transition abruptly. If, for instance, you are accustomed to eating five types of food at a time, take four, and so on.[25] This contrasts sharply with the twelve and more delicious dishes at a time a proselyte from Europe claimed to have been served regularly when he still adhered to his old faith in his native country.[26] But there he was a high dignitary, whereas in Egypt he shared the lot of destitute refugees; no contrast between gluttonous Europe and a frugal East should be seen in this story, although cooler climates naturally required stronger nourishment.[27] To honor a special guest by serving him different main dishes and desserts every night is reported as something noteworthy in the *Arabian Nights*.[28]

Household accounts.—A quick introduction to the food world of the Geniza people may be obtained by reading some of the household accounts preserved, all of which are short.

a. Provisions for a holiday.

Expenditure for the Pentecost[29]—if I live so long with the help of the Almighty

Little chickens[30]—1 dirhem; meat—1 1/2 dirhems; a pound of fat tail (of sheep)—1/2 and 1/6 dirhem; a hen—1 1/2 dirhems; garden mallow—1/2 dirhem; cubeb and garlic—1/8 dirhem; sesame oil—1/4 dirhem; eggplants—1/2 dirhem; sesame oil—1/2 dirhem; this is for the first day, which is a Friday.

For the Sabbath: a lemon hen—2 dirhems; chard (leaf beets)—3/8 dirhem; onions—1/4 dirhem; safflower—1/4 dirhem; green lemons—1/2 dirhem.

The handwriting suggests that the writer of this list was a clerk. Bread and wheat were distributed to them by the community (*Med.*

Soc., II, 123) and are therefore not included here. The list is carefully written and probably the result of long deliberations between husband and wife, for an expenditure of approximately 10 dirhems was a serious matter for a lower official earning somewhere between 40 and 80 dirhems a month. "Garden mallow" is a tentative translation for the famous *mulūkhiya* (from Greek *molokhe*; botanical name, *Corchorus olitorius*), a herb still widely cultivated in Egypt, Palestine, and Syria, and made into a thick soup. It was also called *baqla yahūdiyya*, Jewish vegetable, perhaps because Jews liked it. But the mulūkhiya soup is a national dish of Egypt.

The repetition of the item "sesame oil" is not a mistake. One bought one measure of oil for the mallow soup and another for the eggplant vegetable.

Friends familiar with the Middle Eastern kitchen tell me that a hen cooked in lemon sauce and spices is still a delicacy. For this a fat hen, which already lays eggs, is needed. That's why the lemon hen cost more than the others. That dish was accompanied by a salad made of the thick leaves (not the root) of the chard, a beet plant.[31] Lemons are the only fruit, perhaps because other fruit was beyond the means of the clerk, or possibly such items as apples, nuts, and raisins had been bought before the prices went up on the eve of the holiday.[32]

b. Meat for the New Year: A butcher's bill.

On weekends the standard fare was chicken, but for the two days of New Year, when many guests were expected, more substantial meat was needed. Here, obviously, two additional pounds were fetched, when unexpected newcomers arrived.

Mutton was preferred to beef and was therefore more expensive. The most expensive meat was the fat tail of a sheep. A mutton's head, symbolizing a beginning, was a favored dish for the New Year's dinner. At the time of this bill the silver dirhem was worth 48 copper fals.

On the eve of the New Year: Five pounds and again two pounds of mutton. The price: 5 1/4 [dirhems]. Also beef, five [pounds. The price:] 2 dirhems and 4 fals. Total: 7 1/3. Received: 7 dirhems. Balance: 1/3. Price for one pound sheep's tail: 1 1/8 dirhems. Total balance: 1 1/2 dirhems less 2 fals.[33]

c. Expenditure for a Sabbath.

The court clerk, cantor, and schoolmaster Solomon, son of the judge Elijah,[34] jotted this note on the reverse side of a letter of his, which was returned to him:

Cucumber, *faqqūs* (cucumber),[35] parsley,
apples, bread, mul[ūkhiya?]
a chicken, asparagus.[36]
Cheering money for the wife.[37]
Expended on Friday.[38]

d. Midweek shopping for the kitchen.

This text has neither superscription nor postscript, but appears to be fairly complete. Besides kitchen items it contains payments to five persons mentioned by first name only (two receiving 2 1/2 and 2 1/4 dirhems, respectively, probably daily wages of workmen), a payment of 1 1/2 dirhems "to the *ʿarīf*,"[39] a dirhem for the public bath (visited by the wife), and 3 (copper coins) to a fuller (for washing or fulling[40] garments). Most of the sums in dirhems, if not otherwise indicated, are written in words; they are rendered here in numerals.

Colocasia[41]—1/2 and 1/8. Coriander—1 fals.[42] Garlic—1 fals. Spices for the soup[43]—1 fals. Sesame oil—1/4 and 1/8. Pepper—1 fals. Meat—2 dirhems. Total 3 dirhems.[44]

Bath—1 dirhem. Fuller—3 (fals).[45] Barakāt—2 1/2. Hiba—2 1/4. Dates—1/4 and 1/8. Chickpeas—1/4. Bitter oranges—1/8. Radishes—1 fals. Baking of bread[46]—1/8. Water carrier[47]—3 fals.

Here follow sundry smaller payments and the total 12 1/2 (dirhems, in Coptic numerals).[48]

e. Food and general care for a sick foreigner put up at the house of a (retired?) judge.

Various medical prescriptions conclude with the note: "Meal—cooked chickens." How this worked out in practice is seen in the daily accounts listing the sums expended for a sick foreigner and the sums showing how they were collected, as summarized here.

The list is in the unmistakable hand of the judge Nathan b. Solomon ha-Kohen, who was active in the Egyptian capital in the years 1125–1150, but who signed (as first signatory) a document in Tyre, Lebanon, as early as 1102. (Tyre was conquered by the Crusaders in 1124.) At the writing of this account he seems to have been an old man and was probably retired.[49] The account refers to the first twelve days of the month Shevat (Jan.–Feb.). The sums refer to the silver coin dirhem.

Expenditures
Daily
Bread—3/4; on Saturday a larger amount: 7/8 or 1
A chicken—2 1/8, or (mostly) 2 1/2
(Medical) potion—1

Weekly
Hot oil[50]—1

Listed only once
Rose water[51]—3/4
Creme[52]—1/2
Honey—1/2
Lentils—1/4
Saffron—1/4
Nile water[53]—1/4

Larger sums were spent on bandages, cotton, laundry, and a new cloak. The patient was probably treated gratuitously by a physician of the community.

The expenditure was covered by (*a*) income from a house belonging to the community; (*b*) six donations, in one case a husband and his wife—referred to as "his house"—contributed separately; (*c*) a collection made in the two rabbinical synagogues of Fustat (which brought only 7 dirhems); (*d*) 1 dinar less 1/24 (qīrāṭ), worth at that time 35 1/2 dirhems, donated by "our lord," meaning the Head of the Jewish community, probably the court physician Samuel b. Hananiah (1140–1159).[54]

Starting an evaluation of the accounts with the last one, the absolutely dominant role of bread is impressive. The patient daily consumed bread worth 3/4 dirhem, approximately one-third of the price of the chicken, whereas the daily allowances for an orphan, at that time, usually amounted to not more than 1/2 dirhem.[55] For Saturday, which was honored with three, instead of two daily meals, the ration was increased. Chicken was the preferred meat for weekends, holidays, and times of illness. This might have been partly a Jewish speciality, because the ritual slaughtering of a chicken was a far less risky matter than that of cattle; *dajājī*, dealer in chickens, was a quite common Jewish family name. Special historical circumstances might also have contributed to this phenomenon. But Egypt was renowned for its fowl, as the scenes in Pharaonic tombs depict. In the postscript to a communal letter sent from Palestine to Fustat the addressee is asked to urge a relative, who had a family in Jerusalem, to return to that city "to eat onions in Jerusalem instead of chickens in Egypt."[56]

Good food should be rich in fat. Therefore on holidays one permitted oneself the luxury of a costly sheep's tail, that embodiment of fattiness.[57] Honoring a holiday with fat food was already taken for granted in biblical times.[58] But the Talmud reports a popular saying from Palestine condemning the sheep's tail, not for medical reasons, but as a luxury. Vegetables were preferable.[59] The sheep's tail is still popular in Egypt.

Another remarkable trait of the lists presented is the writers' predilection for vegetables. This Jewish proclivity is attested to in the Bible and the Talmud; as we have seen, even the intrinsically Egyptian mulūkhiya had—and still has—the byname "Jewish vegetable." According to Rav Huna, the outstanding Babylonian sage, a scholar was not permitted to live in a place that had no vegetables.[60] Roger Le Tourneau's observation that the Jewish infatuation with vegetables was sufficient reason for the Muslims of Fez to shun eating them has been already noted.[61] As Cérès Wissa Wassef's book on presenting Coptic cooking shows, all the vegetables noted above are still richly used in the modern Egyptian kitchen.[62]

It is to be expected that lists originating with people in modest circumstances include only the more common fruits such as dates, apples, lemons, and bitter oranges.[63] But fruits were eagerly sought after. When the somewhat eccentric clerk Solomon b. Elijah excused himself for not expressing his sympathy to a friend in person, on account of illness, he adds this postscript so that everyone would understand how really sick he was: "Bananas, figs, grapes, watermelon, fish, and beans, by my soul, none of these were tasted by me this week." Indeed, none of these delicacies was offered to the sick foreigner mentioned above.[64]

Wheat and bread.—My assertion in the very first sentence of this section, that the Geniza contains little about food, seems to be belied by the countless reports and inquiries about the prices and availability of wheat and bread found in the Geniza letters throughout the centuries.[65] The data from the Geniza, which reflect actual experience, are generally more realistic and reliable than those provided by Islamic literary sources, which are often given in round sums and written down long after their occurrence.[66] But the Geniza data, too, betray bewildering fluctuations. Future research may establish the chronological sequence of the (as a rule, undated) Geniza letters to a higher degree than we are able to do now, and a closer scrutiny of their historical context may contribute to a better understanding of the data contained in them (see below). Be that as it may, one crucial fact of medieval life in the Near East—even in a country of proverbial fertility such as Egypt—emerges with frightening clarity from the mass of information about the prices and availability of wheat and bread. The mind of the average man, that of the middle class included, was constantly preoccupied with providing his household with the most urgently needed life-sustaining food. In times of a low Nile and other disasters befalling agriculture, famine, epidemics, breakdown of public order, or, who knows, shameless grain speculations, such apprehensions were natural.[67] But the Geniza letters seem to betray that state of mind even when the prices reported appear to have been normal, as far as such a thing existed. This is a story not of food but of its scarcity. All one can do here is explore how the insecurity surrounding the most basic food of the population influenced the organization of its daily life and affected its thinking.

Whoever had the means to buy wheat at harvest time laid in a sufficient supply for the year. Hence the strong admonitions in letters "I have no more urgent request from you than the [purchase of] wheat and grapes" (for making wine, see below), or "do not neglect the wheat, for it is one of the most basic of all things," or the assurance "Don't worry, I have taken care of the purchase of the wheat, put it into jars and put [the jars] into the sun."[68] The wheat was ground at a local mill, and the dough, prepared at home, was baked at a bakery. This procedure had the triple advantage of being cheaper than buying bread daily, of affording safety against the fluctuations of the market or the outright unavailability of the foodstuff, and, finally, of knowing what went into one's bread, although its quality perhaps did not differ as much as in Europe (perhaps slightly later than Geniza times).[69] Laying in provisions carried the risk that the wheat would deteriorate or spoil altogether, or that burglars or robbers would take them away. To avoid such disasters one stored the wheat in big jars of porous clay, put them on the uppermost floor of the house, and, if feasible, on its sunny side, probably to protect it from humidity.[70]

The standard measurement of wheat was the irdabb, measuring about 90 liters and weighing about 70 kilograms. It was divided into six waybas, also extremely common. At the distribution of wheat to the needy (on the eves of holidays or fasts) quarters or halves of a wayba were handed out to each.[71]

Twelve irdabbs per year, or one per month seem to have been the quantity of wheat needed for an average middle-class household. Twelve are ordered as yearly provisions in a letter written around 1210,[72] and ten in another missive sent from Alexandria to Cairo at approximately the same time. "In case the wheat cannot be had, please, bring with you instead three camel loads of flour." Since the recipient, Moses ha-Kohen, the Pride of the Merchants, commuted, as the letter shows, between Cairo andAlexandria, it would not have burdened him to have three camels added to his caravan.[73] In a letter to ʿArūs b. Joseph (dated documents 1088–1116), a traveling merchant with his seat in Alexandria orders one irdabb of sieved wheat every month; he clearly did not wish to receive the entire quantity of the yearly provision at once, because, as he mentions, the price was high (only four waybas for 1 dinar).[74]

When the size of the household was reduced by the absence of husband or wife, the average yearly provision was six irdabbs, and the monthly one was half, or three waybas. The convert and newcomer from Europe, referred to above, who stipulated his right to put six irdabbs on the upper floor occupied by his partner certainly had not yet founded a new family in Egypt (Al-Maḥalla, 1121).[75] When a well-to-do merchant went away on a long journey (probably to India or beyond), he earmarked the regular twelve irdabbs of wheat per year for his wife; her household comprised only a little boy and a servant with a daughter. But her old parents lived in the same house (Fustat, 1143).[76] In a similar case, where, however, no old parents were in the house, the wife of an India trader, a mother of two little girls, received five irdabbs per year, and the same quantity was foreseen by the court clerk Mevōrākh b. Nathan, when he traveled away from home. A merchant who had his business in a provincial town, left six irdabbs to his wife in Alexandria.[77] A merchant from Tyre, Lebanon (which then was menaced by the Crusaders), who sought greener pastures in Egypt, provided his wife with three waybas, half an irdabb, per month (plus the cost of the grinding).[78] Women ate less than men, or, rather, did not have to entertain business friends and other guests during the absence of their husbands; under those circumstances monthly provisions of two waybas were reasonable. We find such monthly provisions of wheat for a mother of one child (dated 1081)[79] and for a mother with several children, where, as in that of the woman from Tyre, the cost of grinding was also borne by the husband (1133).[80]

The weekly bread ration handed out by the Jewish community of Fustat to a destitute person was four loaves, each weighing approximately a pound, a total of about 1,750 grams.[81] This meager share was, at least ideally, supplemented by charity from other quarters. We find, however, the same ration of four pounds of bread (per week) allotted by a husband to his working wife, together with one pound of meat. With this nourishment she was supposed "to sit and to make Rūmī garments."[82] Ten communal lists written in or around

1107 presuppose that a hundred loaves of bread could be had for half a dinar. Since half a dinar corresponded approximately to 20 dirhems, five loaves of bread could be had for one dirhem, and, of course, more at wholesale. One baker provided the community with about 500 loaves. The individual buyer probably paid a little bit more. Yet, those painstaking lists (betraying a concern that no one should get more than he deserved) give the impression that they were compiled in times of stress. The average number of loaves to be had for a dirhem was probably more than five loaves.[83]

A number of passages reflecting the fluctuations in the prices of wheat and bread will enable the reader to judge for himself how far the Geniza is able to illustrate the social aspects of this intricate problem of economic history. The time of our first example is fixed by a postscript: "The sheykh Abī[84] Munajjā occupies today a very high rank and place." Abū Munajjā, a Jew in the service of the Egyptian viceroy al-Malik al-Afḍal, supervised the construction of a canal in the eastern Nile Delta named after the supervisor during the years 1113–1119.[85] The time of writing, therefore, was the beginning of the second decade of the twelfth century. The writer, a Maghrebi living in Cairo, implores his brother-in-law, a physician, to return his wife to him, who, as often happened, had fled from her husband to her brother. The letter concludes with this note which is written around the four margins of the second page and which is followed by the postscript:

> By God, do not disappoint me, my lord, but kindly send my wife back to Cairo in the company of her Maghrebi relatives. For leading the life of a bachelor in Cairo is very, very difficult; I can't bear it. Our prices in Cairo: nine pounds of pure bread—1 1/8 dirhems. Wheat (regular)—two irdabbs [for 1 dinar]. Good [wheat]: nine and a half waybas [for 1 dinar]. Bread does not sell, it is cheap. After the first third of the night some of mine still remained in the bazaar.[86]

These lines were written at a time of oversupply. As we shall learn, an irdabb of wheat costing half a dinar was indeed exceptional. A weak economy is unable to control glut, just as it is powerless against scarcity. The big difference between regular and good wheat is remarkable, and the quotation "nine pounds of good bread—1 1/8 dirhems" instead of "a pound of bread—1/8 dirhem," seems to indicate that larger quantities were lower in price. The writer, himself a baker, or proprietor of a bakery, certainly knew what he was talking about. The extensive letter shows him to be a man of some learning.

This cannot be said about the man who, about a hundred years later, dictated a letter which also reports very low prices of wheat in Cairo and a story of unsold bread. The scribe took his words down verbatim and they appear here as confused and slightly ridiculous as they had come out of the speaker's mouth:

When you were in the Fayyūm, eight [pounds of] bread could be had for 1 dirhem. When you came here to Maṣr [Cairo-Fustat], the world collapsed. On Friday, as you know: four for a dirhem! Then you traveled away from us on Monday. On Monday—by the holy religion—six [pounds of market bread] could be had for 1 1/8 dirhem and six of home bread[87] for 1 dirhem. Then the price remained steady: the market bread—six for 1 dirhem and the home bread—seven for 1 dirhem. By our religion, what I just told you is not a lie. Had you remained in Maṣr for another week, we would have been unable to buy bread.[88] But God had mercy upon us at the time you departed for the Fayyūm. Majdiyya[89] sold on Monday, the day of your departure—by the holy religion—she sold her tiara for 105 dirhems!

Good wheat of first quality—an irdabb costs 36 [dirhems], and one of lesser quality, 30 [dirhems]. Every night, ten hundred pounds of bread remain in every market [becoming stale].[90]

Again, a time of glut. Thousands of loaves remained unsold in the bazaars overnight, and an irdabb of first quality wheat cost 36 dirhems, corresponding to 1 dinar, a modest, or, perhaps, standard price. But the writer had to invoke his religion three times to make credible the unbelievable fluctuations during one week, from 1/8 to 1/4 to 1/6 dirhem per loaf. Did the bakers conspire to drive the prices up during the weekend of the three religions, when everyone was supposed to eat more than on weekdays? If so, they received swift punishment for their wickedness.

We read about a real bakers' strike in a large thirteenth-century family letter sent from Alexandria to Fustat written immediately after the autumn holidays (Sept.–Oct.):

On the second day of the Sukkot feast there were great disturbances in Alexandria because of the bread, which could not be found all over the city, until God brought relief by the end of the day; the governor and the superintendent of the markets rode out and threatened to burn down [the houses of] the bakers because of the bread, after they had inquired with the people at one oven in the east and one in the west. At the end there remained fifty hundred weights of bread in the ovens that night. So do not worry.[91]

A quite different situation is revealed in this letter from Alexandria written between September 26 and October 1, 1200.[92] The great famine of 1201/2 is, of course, a landmark in Egyptian history. But here we see that Alexandria, which in general was provisioned less well than the capital, was already in deep trouble in the autumn of 1200. The writer must have been a respectable person, since he gives personal greetings to Moses Maimonides and to the French rabbi, Anatoli (who temporarily sojourned in Fustat). He must have been a man of some means, as may be concluded from his order of ten irdabbs of wheat when it was so costly, a quantity sufficient for approximately a year.[93]

Alexandria is in great trouble: the price of wheat from Upper Egypt,[94] bought from the houses,[95] is 225 dinars per hundred [irdabbs];[96] every wayba costs 14 *waraq* dirhems.[97] The mediocre Rīfī (Delta) wheat costs 200 dinars a hundred, the bread—one and a half loaves—1 dirhem.[98] People eat up one another. This catastrophe came upon the population quite suddenly, may God grant relief in his mercy. Your slave was able to purchase only three irdabbs and most of it has already been consumed. May I ask you to get the wheat under all circumstances. Your servant is [like one] of your family. May I never miss you.[99]

Please instruct the Muslim who takes care of the wheat that he should enter the city relying on his high rank,[100] for this [Jewish] nation is closely watched[101] by the gentiles, who menace them with plunder every day.[102]

In another letter, from a provincial town it seems, we read indeed about seventy irdabbs of wheat taken from a house during a pillage.[103]

The price of 2 dinars or so for one irdabb seems to have been common in times of scarcity. In a report to a notable, who appears in numerous Geniza documents around 1200, he is informed that a man was paid 30 dinars for fifteen irdabbs, bought for the Fustat community, probably to provide bread for the indigent.[104] Sixty years earlier, in the 1140s, there were some bad years, reflected in the Geniza by the many lists of the poor preserved from that period. Abū Zikrī Kohen, from whose hand we have many dated documents from that decade, paid 6 1/4 dinars for three irdabbs.[105] The time of the great famine, 1063–1073, is represented in the correspondence of Nahray b. Nissīm by wild fluctuations of prices, sometimes referred to in one and the same letter (see below). One irdabb costing 2 dinars seems to have indicated that hunger and anarchy prevailed in the writer's place. "Everything edible is sold [or salable]. The *wheat*: three [waybas] for one *gold piece* [that is, one irdabb for 2 dinars; both words are written in Hebrew, a kind of secret code]. The city, as you know, is afflicted by hunger—may God make it easier for you," we read in a letter to Nahray from Alexandria.[106]

From the same city we hear again about the same price (and in Hebrew) in the remark: "It is difficult to get wheat, for the roads are not safe."[107]

Naturally, when confronted with prices even higher than 2 dinars for one irdabb, one preferred the latter. "Tell ʿIwāḍ that I have not bought anything for him, for hunger is in the countryside, wheat—one and three-quarter waybas [costing 1 dinar, and six waybas = one irdabb, over 3 dinars] and beans the same,[108] while I have heard that in your place an irdabb of wheat can be had for 2 dinars." The letter is addressed to the Square of Perfumers in Fustat.[109] This is not the only case where the capital is better provided with victuals than the countryside that produced them. A traveling silk merchant, who had passed weeks, including a holiday, in the Rīf, after visiting Alexandria, where for only 1 dinar four and a half waybas could be had, asked his partner in Fustat to send two irdabbs to him in Rosetta (on the Mediterranean coast). Despite the cost of transportation grain was cheaper and more easily available in the capital than in the countryside.[110] The recurrent price of 2 dinars, probably twice the "normal," for an irdabb was perhaps fixed by government order in the big cities at the time of scarcity.

The 1020s saw another period of famine, again reflected in the Geniza by extended and carefully executed lists of recipients of handouts.[111] Here some noteworthy data can be observed. A business letter sent from Cairo to Qūṣ, the terminus of the India trade in Upper Egypt, around 1030 or earlier, notes in the midst of a very long list of prices prevailing in the capital: "Wheat, one *tillīs* 3 [dinars]." The tillīs, weighing about 67.5 kilograms, was almost identical with the irdabb (about 70 kilograms).[112] Thus this price was extraordinary and is noted by the Fatimid historian al-Musabbiḥī for the hunger year 1024.[113] But the writer of the letter does not mention this horrid price with indignation. Quite the contrary. He introduces his list with the remark "The [prices in the] bazaar are as you love it." Here the supplier, not the consumer, is addressed. Cairene merchants went up to Qūṣ to purchase Indian and other Oriental specialities, but used the occasion to carry with them some of the wheat of Upper Egypt, which was renowned for its quality.[114]

A letter from Alexandria shows how those exorbitant prices were combated: one imported wheat from abroad. "Eight to nine waybas of the Rūmī wheat we have here cost 1 dinar; we do not miss a thing; life is cheap here, and people have it far better than before."[115] Another letter from Alexandria and the same period has this: "The price of new wheat: nine waybas per dinar, old wheat—eleven waybas."[116] Thus a price of 1 dinar for nine waybas of good wheat, or 1 1/2 irdabbs, was regarded as cheap. A similar picture emerges from a report fromTunisia sent to Nahray b. Nissīm, when he had already become a merchant of substance in Egypt, say, around 1060: "Prices in Ifrīqiya [Africa, approximately Tunisia today] are extremely low: 25 thumns of wheat cost 1 dinar in Qayrawān [the capital]." This corresponds approximately to 1 2/3 irdabbs, *very* cheap if compared with the "cheap" 1 1/2, listed in Alexandria.[117] But not long before, we read about a terrible rise of prices in Ifrīqiya: for 1 dinar only 4 thumns could be had![118]

The upshot of all this seems to be that to draw generalizations about the times and regions in terms of the prices mentioned in the Geniza is hazardous. In particular, one must avoid the pitfall of accepting as normal prices noted as a relief from former hardship. The correspondence of Nahray b. Nissīm is full of such cases. Examples from the early thirteenth century, some time after the great famine of 1201/2, illustrate the problem. In a letter to judge Elijah b. Zechariah, then still in Alexandria, the writer notes that he was unable to buy wheat because of its exorbitant price of 20 (dirhems a wayba, 120 dirhems, or over 3 dinars, an irdabb). An unhappy father in that Mediterranean port, whose son had disappeared, reportedly "to the army," sends several missives to Elijah's son, a physician in the capital, with the request to contact the fugitive, assuring him that the situation in the country had improved: "Alexandria is now quiet, no disturbances have occurred—may God make the end well—an irdabb of wheat costs 1 5/8 dinars." The writer does not mean to say that 1 1/2 dinars or so was an acceptable, normal price, but that, compared with times of anarchy and insecurity of the roads, the price was an improvement.[119] When a silk weaver escaped from the tax collector to Aswān in Upper Egypt, he was assured by his family in Fustat that he had nothing to fear and that times had become better. "An irdabb of wheat of middle quality costs 42 dirhems—may God make it cheaper." Low-grade wheat should be priced somewhat below, not above, 1 dinar (see above). But the somewhat high price is reported to convince the fugitive that he could make ends meet anyhow, if he returned.[120]

In extraordinary times, the price of wheat fluctuated so wildly that the change is reported in one and the same letter. "It was 4 dinars for one irdabb and stands today at 2 1/2 dinars," we read in a letter from Alexandria to Nahray b. Nissīm. Since in the same letter the writer reports that he had already purchased wheat for the higher price and put it aside for the recipient, some time may have elapsed between the two quotations.[121]

This cannot be said of a letter sent to the notable Judah b. Moses

Ibn Sighmār by his wife, when the capital was menaced by Arab tribes (1069). Many Jewish families had left the city, but were held up on their way; even the prominent Dōsā family was considering leaving. Numerous maidservants had run away to the Bedouins, and the writer was afraid that the slave agent whom her husband had left behind to look after the business might do the same. And worst of all: "The tillīs [of wheat, approximately = one irdabb] has already reached 30 [dinars]." In a long postscript she reports that the Dōsās had left on the very day she was writing, that the chief vizier had expelled all other viziers from the town, "and we are exposed to *anarchy and hunger* [both words in Hebrew], one tillīs [of wheat] costs 25 [dinars] and bread 4 1/2 [dirhems] a pound." The prices quoted by a Muslim historian for this period are four times as high.[122]

The writer speaks only of Jewish families leaving the city because she probably knew few Muslims, and because the latter had less to fear than the former. An exodus of Muslims from a city smitten by famine is reported by a Jew to emphasize the magnitude of the disaster. The Jewish judge of Barqa, eastern Libya, who sojourned in Alexandria on his pilgrimage to Jerusalem (which he failed to carry out), writes that he was forced to return home, for he had received bad news from his native town: "It is in ruins; most Muslims have gone into exile from there, the wheat costs one wayba a dinar, and business is at a standstill" (1060 or so).[123]

Moving to Tripoli, the capital of western Libya, during "a year, the like of which no one has witnessed and no one knows even from hearsay," we read that at Passover-Easter half a wayba cost 1 dinar (one irdabb = 12 dinars), but at the time of the writing of the letter, in August or slightly later of the same year, three waybas could be had for that price (one irdabb = 2 dinars). A new harvest had intervened and some import of wheat must have helped, but both were not enough to reduce the price to so-called normal completely. Yet, the letter concludes: "We are now all right, and the city is quiet."[124]

The transport of grain was supervised by the government, partly, perhaps, to insure that the relevant taxes had been paid, and partly for the purpose of confiscating it in times of emergency. Hence, in such times, we find the terms for wheat and coins written in Hebrew, serving as a kind of code, or reports about actual attempts to conceal consignments of wheat. "I tried to transport, together with the flax, 50 or, at least 30, irdabbs [of wheat], but was unable to do so, for the clerk came in," we read in a letter from the flax district of Bahnasā sent to Fustat.[125] A missive addressed to a business friend in Tunisia contains this instruction: "Buy me 3 qafīz[126] of wheat or whatever [quantity] you can get, grind it and put it inside the hazelnut bales." Flour, although generally regarded as less desirable than fresh wheat, possibly was believed to escape detection more easily than grain.[127]

Since wheat was laid in by everyone in a position to do so, we read little about flour in the Geniza. When the court clerk Mevōrākh b. Nathan on coming home discovered that a friend had failed to provide his family with wheat during his absence on a journey, he found it worth mentioning in a letter to an esteemed friend that it was extremely burdensome for him to buy five pounds of flour costing 1 1/8 dirhems every day.[128] A large section of the population bought flour because they did not possess the means to buy wheat at harvest time but still preferred to prepare their bread dough at home, or were simply too poor to buy any wheat at all, so they had to apply to the flour dealer when they had a penny available or a pawn to leave with him.[129] Moreover, many types of food, such as sweetmeats or the harīsa hamburger, were admixed with flour. Thus it seems likely that just as Jews, with few exceptions, did not deal in grain, they did not engage in the sale of flour. One ordered flour in large quantities only when wheat was not available, or for other special reasons.[130]

On the preceding pages I have used the word *loaf* for the sake of convenience, although Near Eastern bread is flat, round, and soft, to be easily broken by hand (no knife being needed) into pieces, which can be used, instead of forks or spoons, for picking up morsels from a tray. I must remark, however, that in a very detailed account of household expenses the writer constantly uses, in addition to the general word for bread, two other terms designating its form. It escapes me whether this was a mere play on words, or whether indeed two different shapes of bread were intended.[131]

Barley was completely absent from the table of the urban population, as far as the Geniza goes. This testimony of a respectable merchant, who had to flee from Alexandria before an oppressive government official and to hide in the western desert for years, underlines this fact: "Then I passed a year and a half in other people's houses, and most of the time begging for a *ṣāʿ* of barley, which I ground with my own hands. . . . I sent home two flat cakes of unleavened barley bread, each weighing only fifteen dirhems, to show them on what food I lived." In the very rare cases where the price of barley is noted, the reference is probably to fodder for animals.[132]

To sum up. The quality of life in a city was defined in Geniza letters by the prices of wheat available to the common people. The frightening instability of supply, caused by nature as well as by human factors, made the daily bread a constant concern for everyone. I have tried to bring this situation—so strange to us—home to the reader by ample citations from both times of scarcity and abundance. They reflect the extraordinary place occupied by wheat in the daily diet of Near Eastern–Mediterranean peoples.

Another remarkable aspect seems to emerge from the texts provided above: a certain standardization of consumption achieved by that age-old measurement of wheat, the irdabb, introduced during the Persian occupation of Egypt, about fifteen hundred years prior to the period of the Geniza documents. Twelve irdabbs a year, one a month, seem to have been the average need assumed for an urban household, and one gold piece seems to have been the ideal price for one. A pound was the average weight of a loaf of bread. Such standardization, imposed not from above, but derived from experience, would indicate that eating habits were common to a fairly large section of the urban population.[133]

"*All the things men eat with bread.*"—When the Byzantine emperor Alexius I Comnenus (1081–1118) founded a town for the poor and the crippled, he endowed it with good lands "so that they should have all the things that men eat with bread."[134] This note from the *Alexiad* of the emperor's gifted daughter Anna Comnena reminds us that the absolute prominence of bread as human nourishment was not confined to the Muslim society of the Mediterranean, nor did it originate there. On the contrary. Witness the cry of the Roman masses for "bread and games" and of the Roman soldier who conquered the world, while receiving as daily fare rations of bread and wine (which often had the taste of vinegar). The Bible expresses the idea of having one's meal by the sentence: "They sat down to eat bread" (Genesis 37:25). And it has already been noted that both Hebrew and Arabic possess special terms for "the things taken together with bread."[135]

I hasten to add that, even though we do not have the description of a full evening meal in the Geniza, the variety and quantities of spices, flavorings, and fruits, as well as the many details about meats, cheese, oils, honey, and sugar appearing in the documents point to the fact that the table of families that could afford them was as rich in appetizers, dishes, and desserts as could be observed in well-to-do traditional homes in the Near East not long ago. Spices of all descriptions were the most frequently mentioned items and, consequently, must have been equally well represented in the pantry. And one did not need so many spices except when one prepared a good many dishes which needed different flavoring.

Starting at the bottom, for the broad mass of laborers and employees with scanty earnings, greens, such as onions, garlic, thyme, or radishes, formed natural complements to bread, moistening its dryness and stimulating the appetite. Vegetables fulfilled also a more substantial task in the nutrition of the indigent. I do not know when and where it was said that eggplants are "poor man's meat."[136] But it certainly applies to Geniza times. A woman scolding her husband for his long absence writes: "The children had no one who would buy a pound of meat for them. Their holiday meal consisted of *burayq*[137] for half a dirhem and fried eggplants for a quarter."[138] Not that eggplants did not also find their way into a shopping list for the kitchen of those higher up, for example, a Nagid, or head of the Jewish community of Egypt.[139] In Geniza times, the thick mulūkhiya soup, the daily fare of the Egyptian fellāḥ, had been adopted, at least by the urban lower class, as shown by the household notes translated above and the sobriquet "Jewish vegetable," listed, it seems, by Maimonides.[140] The sturdy and substantial root of the colocasia must also have been a regular item on the table of the Geniza people, since we find it not only in a household account but also in a letter showing that it was grown on land belonging to the recipient.[141] Beans could substitute for bread when the wheat failed. Since we do not have in the Geniza any descriptions of prepared food, nowhere do we read about the delicious Egyptian dishes made of beans or chickpeas. But when we find in one shopping list a limited quantity of chickpeas taken home together with a number of other kitchen items and in another some *ṭaḥīna* (sesame-meal paste), we can be sure that it was made into something similar to the tasty *ḥummuṣ*.[142] The extremely long list of plants, used cooked or raw (as in salads or dressings) by the most indigenous of all Egyptians, the Copts (many of which are mentioned in the Geniza), proves that the local diet was predominantly vegetarian.[143]

Since vegetables are best eaten when fresh, they were picked up at the market or brought or sent in by relatives or friends from the countryside. Thus we read about them, if at all, in household accounts or in letters exchanged between the city and the Rīf. For places outside Egypt we have only stray notices: In a letter to Aleppo in northern Syria, written during the first third of the eleventh century, the writer honors the spiritual leader of the local Jewish community by sending him two and a half pounds of truffles and excuses himself for failing to send additional presents because unexpected guests had emptied his pantry during the holidays just ended.[144] In letters from Tunisians we read about a wild herb, *ḥurrayq*, which grew in a ruin of the then capital al-Mahdiyya or on a small island not far away; it was eaten in springtime, raw or cooked, when the Norman invaders had destroyed the crops in the country and when on that desolate island nothing else was to be had.[145] Maimonides' book on the names of medicinal (and culinary) plants listed the different names given to identical plants in the countries of the Mediterranean region. But his modern commentator often had opportunity to note that the different names were for different plants.[146]

The contrast between Egypt and the neighboring countries was particularly marked in the supply of fruits. The mass and variety of imported fruits recorded in the Geniza are indeed astounding. In *Med. Soc.*, I, 121, where the subject is treated, I surmised that the tastes and eating habits of the many immigrants from Palestine, Syria, and Iran had been influential in this matter. I should add here that I did not have in mind only the Jews. The Muslim merchants, officials, and scholars were as mobile as their Jewish counterparts, if not more so. At one time, the daily government revenue from the Cairene Market of Apples and Dates, which I take to mean Imported and Local Fruits, was higher even than that from the slaughterhouses and equaled only by that from the fish market.[147] Since many fruits imported from the eastern shores of the Mediterranean, such as apricots, peaches, and plums, are highly perishable, they must have been transported in a dried or half-dried state and were then sold in the street of the *naqliyyīn* or *nuqliyyīn*, the Street of the Sellers of Dried Fruit, partly to be consumed glazed with sugar or as preserves.[148] Fruits of this type were also grown locally.[149] A great variety of nuts, such as shelled almonds, walnuts, pistachios, and hazelnuts, were brought to Egypt from both the East and the West, and were often made into sweetmeats and candies. The processors of almonds, the *lawwāzīn*, had a lane for themselves in the bazaar, and persons bearing this family name, both Jewish and Muslim, appear in the Geniza from the eleventh century.[150] A sweetmeat named *qaṭā'if*, made of almonds, honey, fine meal, and sesame oil, spawned another family name; almonds also went into the making of chewing gum.[151] It is therefore not surprising to find in the Geniza a store for fruit and sugar, the ingredients for homemade candy for those who wished to enjoy the fruit in a state other than natural. An inventory lists a large amount of regular sugar and a small one of rock sugar, a hundred pounds of hazelnuts and smaller quantities of pomegranate seeds, sumac, pistachios and two types of raisins. Banana leaves were among the equipment of the store, probably used for wrapping.[152]

When Maimonides was asked by a fledgling student of philosophy what a scholar should eat "together with bread," he recommended almonds combined with a few seedless raisins, both praised by him also in his medical writings. This combination of almonds and raisins as ideal food remained alive in Jewish folklore.[153]

Vine-growing must have been extensive in medieval Egypt, since wine, as the Geniza shows, was made from local grapes. Numerous letters speak, however, of importing of raisins for both eating and making beverages. Black raisins were preferred for eating.[154]

Dates were the main indigenous fruit of Egypt. As far as urban consumption is concerned, there was no need for laying in provisions; pressed dates were available, but as the household accounts reveal, one fetched one's requirements of fresh dates from the grocer. The situation was different in times of famine, that is, scarcity of wheat. Then the Geniza letters become replete with orders for dates of all descriptions and with notifications how such orders were carried out. These letters are worth studying in the wider context of the replacement of one major element of nutrition by another.[155] As quick food for a scholar and as an alternative for almonds and raisins, Maimonides, in a holograph preserved in the Geniza, recommends honey made of good, fresh dates mixed with water, taken with bread. With a letter from the Fayyūm, chicken and dates were sent as a present for the Day of Atonement. Did Jews, like Muslims, break the fast with dates? They are a bit hard to digest, but replace the missing carbohydrates in minutes.[156]

The moving novel, *A Handful of Blackberries*, by the Italian writer Ignazio Silone, derives its title from the hero's experience that in his youth he often "had nothing to eat together with a piece of dry bread" except some blackberries picked on the mountains surrounding his native village. A few fresh dates or sycamore figs might have performed a similar service to a poor boy in medieval Cairo.

The second great provider of sweetness, sugar cane, was not indigenous to Egypt. It was transplanted there in early Islamic times from southern Iran and Iraq (to which countries it had come from India and farther east) and gave rise to a great industry, in which the Jews had a disproportionally high share.[157] This might have had its roots in a phenomenon found elsewhere, namely, that the sugar industry was a new field of economic activity, and an oppressed minority could get a foothold in it more easily than in long-established enterprises. The fact that many Jewish families in Egypt had come from southern Iran and Iraq might also have played a part. Finally, the Jewish propensity for sweetness, attested by Bible and Talmud, might have found the concentrated power of sugar particularly attractive.[158] Several sorts of sugar (depending on the number of cookings of the raw material and the fluids used for the process) appear in the Geniza, as well as a wide diversity of prices, not easy to explain. But no detailed descriptions of its use in the kitchen or the food industry has been found.[159]

Despite the diffusion of sugar, bee honey retained its prominent place in the diet of the urban population. Although Egypt possessed a highly developed apiculture, the quantities imported from the West, mainly Tunisia, and the East, Palestine and Greater Syria, were considerable. The extraordinary fluctuations of prices, reflecting the vicissitudes of an import trade, betray the eagerness of the demand for the sweet commodity "which brightens the eyes."[160] The combination of honey and vinegar, of sweet and sour, and the potion made of it, the Greek oxymel, was of such dietetic importance, that two Muslim medical writers, including the great Ibn Sīnā (Avicenna), dedicated special treatises to it. The oxymel is a regular household item in the Geniza, which shows that scientific theory and daily life were not as separated from each other as one might perhaps assume.[161] Honey, as we have seen, was used for the preparation of sweetmeats, and especially, together with fine, "white" flour and melted butter for making the *ʿaṣīda*, a thick paste or cake (presented also as a gift on special occasions such as childbirth). A man from the countryside writes to a relative in Fustat: "Please try to find bee honey and fine 'white' flour for the ʿaṣīda. *With the help of the Almighty* I shall come to town on Sunday; have the ʿaṣīda packed for me in a basket." He wished to bring this special dish home, for at his place neither bee honey nor fine meal was to be had.[162]

The variegated spices and flavorings bought in small quantities for the household have been surveyed in our section on the vocations of the druggist and perfumer, (*Med. Soc.*, II, 269–271). Orders from drugstores and inventories after the death of the proprietor are also of considerable interest since they show how diversified and demanding the tastes even of ordinary people seem to have been.[163] Chewing gum made from fruits such as almonds or pistachios were so popular that they were sent as gifts via Aden to Mediterranean merchants in India.[164]

If any partaking of food was a religious ceremony, opened and concluded by benedictions, the eating of meat was surrounded by an unending plethora of rituals reminding man that killing an animal was permitted only when conceived as a kind of offering to God.[165] In Islam, as in Judaism, the name of God has to be invoked at the slaughtering of the animal—a sacramental act—and blood, the essence of life given by God, cannot be consumed, but must be poured out, that is, to be returned to the earth from where it ultimately came (Deuteronomy 12:16).

The contentment of common people to consume meat on weekends, holidays, and festive occasions of religious character had its origin perhaps not only in its cost but also in its character of a treat to be reserved for "the days of the Lord."[166] For Jewish (and, maybe, also partly for non-Jewish) consumption, animals were slaughtered during "the nights of Fridays," that is Thursday evenings, to supply the community with fresh meat for the Sabbath.[167] During the week, the less privileged had to be content with leftovers. The orders for small quantities of pepper and other spices used for preservation prove that they knew how to keep meat edible for some time. This note from al-Maḥalla, a provincial capital with a considerable Jewish population, presupposes the same: "At present, there is no communal ritual slaughtering here, neither good nor bad. When they feel the desire for meat, they buy a sheep and slaughter it, each in his house."[168] In Fustat, people who could afford it had a lamb slaughtered for their private needs whenever they wished. In an account written at the time of the caliph al-Ẓāhir (1021–1036), or slightly later, such a lamb (sold for a household, not to a butcher) cost 1 1/4 dinars. Considering that at the same time the price for a pound of meat was about 1 1/4 dirhems, a household would have something between thirty to forty pounds of meat from such a purchase.[169]

Mutton was the fare of the privileged, as indicated by its considerably higher price than that of beef. "My stepbrother is beef," says a Yemenite bon mot, meaning, second best.[170] Yemen was nevertheless renowned for this type of meat, and a fifteenth-century Egyptian author praises the beef of his country.[171] How one wished beef to be is evident from this charming note, sent from the countryside to an elder brother in the city: "Your slave Barakāt kisses your hands and feet. Your brother is fine. Let him know when you will come. Please buy me two pounds of beef, which should be yellow, dry, and good. If you can't get it, don't buy any. Your welfare [may increase]."[172]

Since "red meat" in Arabic described it as lean and without fat, "yellow" probably meant the opposite. The brother was invited for the weekend, and for the Sabbath harīsa, I am informed, one preferred fat beef. In the absence of the latter, the guests would be feasted with fowl, plenty of which was available in the country and, as many Geniza letters tell us, was sent from there to relatives in the city.[173]

The proverbial popularity of chicken in Egypt had its roots in the poverty and unprotected state of the peasants. Chickens were easy to acquire, easy to feed, and easy to replace, when taken away by a rapacious government official or a marauder. For the urban consumer in a country with little wood they had the additional advantage that their preparation required far less fuel than the meat of cattle. Add to this their dietetic value, especially for infants and the sick, so much emphasized by the physicians—of course in cooked, not in fried state. (The Geniza people seem to have been constantly suffering from stomach troubles.)[174] The cold lemon hen, described above, was an ideal dish for the hot summer months, and, in particular, for Jews on the Sabbath, when no cooking was permitted.[175] Coops with chickens were sent to friends and relatives in town; the recipients probably had facilities in their houses for storing them. Pigeons were ordered for the kitchen from the countryside together with chickens. But the pigeons kept in one's house were carrier pigeons, trained for races, a sport much enjoyed by Jews (and not only in Fustat), who were preceded in this hobby by Greeks, Romans, Byzantines, and Muslims, high and low.[176]

As much as we read in the Geniza about chickens, as little we learn from it about the consumption of eggs. The reason might have been technical: one bought them in the market, or peasant women brought them over; so there was no occasion to mention them in letters. Or perhaps the transport of fresh eggs in quantities sufficient for the population of a town was then so difficult that this nutritious commodity was consumed far less than was done in our societies. A man writing to his mother in Cairo, who wished him to marry a woman in that city, says this: "If, coming to Cairo, I could earn there every day two to three dirhems of full silver, I would come. Then, buying two eggs, I would find someone who would make them for me." The words are meant, of course, sarcastically. For two full silver dirhems (equivalent to six regular ones), one could have three hens, not two eggs. Cairo, he wishes to say, was so expensive that even if he earned well, all his future wife would be able to prepare for him was an omelette, a dish obviously not highly regarded. Once, when Abū Zikrī Kohen (see the Index) went shopping for his household, he bought eggs for 1 1/2 dirhems. For this sum he must have got a huge amount. The household account from the ninth century discussed in C, 2, n. 33, twice notes the item eggs costing 1 dirhem each time.[177]

The infatuation of the Egyptians (and their guests, the ancient Israelites) with fish of all descriptions and states of preparation: fresh, smoked, salted, minced, is discussed in *Med. Soc.*, I, 126. Fish, along with fruits, were the delights of life, and the fish market in Fustat was equaled only by that of fruit in the amount of revenue collected by the government.[178] Because of the variety of fish available on the market, their sellers were named according to the specialty they sold.[179] How fish got from the wholesaler to the retailer is illustrated by this letter, probably from a Greek Jew, for he writes in Hebrew and not in Arabic, commonly used for business and technical matters: "As requested, I am sending you a basket with fifty fish, ten of which are torn open and forty uncut, ten of which are salted, with their spawn[180] not taken out. Everything has been done with cleanliness, according to the law, and reliably. I enjoyed very much your learned remarks; please never withhold them from me." The recipient of the letter, the judge Solomon b. Nathan, served as a convenient address, since he was found in the synagogue compound most of the day. The Jewish fish market probably was situated in the vicinity of the synagogue.[181]

Besides meat, fowl, and fish, a variety of cheeses, both local and imported, were substantial sources of protein. Since, for Jews, the production, transport, and sale of cheese had to be done under the supervision of a responsible religious person, the Geniza supplies much information about this subject.[182] Of particular interest is this certificate issued in Alexandria on 9 October 1214:

Mr. Farājī Kohen, son of the late R. Joseph Kohen, the Sicilian, one of those Sicilian merchants who commute to Alexandria, appeared before the undersigned and declared that he sold to Bu 'l-Faraj b. Barakāt, son of the late Sulaymān, 160 Jarwī[183] pounds of Sicilian cheese, 95 molds in number, and that this cheese was ritually unimpeachable ["kosher"] beyond any doubt. Since Bu 'l-Faraj wishes now to travel to various places in the Egyptian Rīf and to sell the cheese there, he asked us to issue him a certificate about the information supplied to us by Farājī, the seller. We acceded to his request and issued this certificate on the fourth of Marheshvan 4971 in No Amon [Alexandria], etc.[184]

The reference to the merchants commuting between Sicily and Alexandria meant that the rabbinical court of Alexandria knew Mr. Farājī well and trusted him. This certificate confirms what could have been deduced from previously cited Geniza documents, namely, that there was a steady import of cheese into Egypt and that it reached not only the big cities but also provincial towns. This is further corroborated by the letters of Abū ʿAlī Ezekiel to his brother, the prominent India trader and communal leader Ḥalfon b. Nethanel, about his trade in Sicilian cheese.[185] Abū ʿAlī had his seat in the provincial town of Qalyūb and was succeeded by one of his sons, who traded in cheese, each mold of which bore the name of the importer.[186]

There is no need to assume that the Jews were particularly keen on Sicilian and Greek cheeses, since we read so much about locally produced cheese and Jewish cheese makers in Egypt.[187] For Tunisia, too, we read about a Jew making cheese in a village near Qayrawān, then the capital of the country.[188] The European cheese was possibly more durable than the one locally produced, or was preferred, as we prefer foreign cheeses, for idiosyncrasies of taste. The average price of 2 1/2 dirhems for a pound of imported cheese, as compared with the same price for a chicken, was not exorbitant.[189] Cheese was urgently needed in situations where meat was not easily available, as when traveling, so often undertaken by Geniza people, or in small communities, or, in general, during the week, when one did not wish to cook a meal. A late Geniza source reports that eight imprisoned persons got cheese for both morning and evening meals, of course, with bread. They must have been pampered people. Other prisoners were happy if they got bread.[190]

About dairy products other than cheese, the Geniza is virtually silent. When a man was advised to undergo a milk cure, that is to consume only milk, he had to hire a cow.[191] The milkman, *labbān*, probably delivered mainly the sour milk, *laban*.[192] Thus we must assume that with regard to dairy products the situation in Geniza times was similar to that still prevailing in the Jewish community of Jerba, Tunisia; with the exception of cheese they played no significant role in the daily diet. The dichotomy of the kitchen into a meat and a milk section, so basic in an observant Jewish household, is unknown in Jerba and never mentioned in the Geniza.[193]

To the degree that the Geniza is lacking in information on milk products, it is abundant in details about olive oil. It is no exaggeration to say that the importing of olive oil from Tunisia and Sicily (or via Sicily) into Egypt, its prices and the vicissitudes caused by nature, wars, or overreaching governments, form a major part of the business correspondence of the eleventh century. Throughout the years I have taken great pains to collect this material, but I do not see that its publication here would contribute much to the understanding of the role of oil in the diet of the city population of Egypt. The question is: for whom were these massive imports destined, and why were the governments so eager to lay their hands on them? For more elaborate cooking, as the household accounts translated above show, the indigenous sesame oil, which, at least in certain periods, was more expensive than olive oil, was chosen even by people with limited means.[194] The olive oil, transported from Palestine into Egypt already in biblical times (Hosea 12:2), probably had become in the course of centuries an indispensable accompaniment of bread for the urban population, including the army, and its supply had to be safeguarded. On the other hand, "good olive oil" was also the regular fare of the well-to-do.[195] The fact that *zayt*, literally, olive oil, became the general word for oil in Arabic, betrays its all-comprising importance.[196]

Looking back on the foodstuffs consumed by the urban population, as revealed to us by the Geniza, we are impressed, as with clothing, by their cosmopolitan character. Most of the oil and nuts and much of the cheese and honey were imported. The major food industry, "the Egyptian sugar," had been transplanted there from Iran. And even such widely used vegetables as eggplants and colocasias or fruits like bananas had come from the remote East.[197] Spices and medical plants (the latter often used as constituents of the daily diet) came from all four corners of the then known world. This process, which began in remote antiquity, received new momentum in Islamic times, giving the urban kitchen its international character. On the other hand, "the fleshpots of Egypt" (Exodus 16:3) and "the grain which is in Egypt" (Genesis 42:1–2) singled out the country as the land of plenty in the Fatimid period as in Pharaonic times. As the biblical accounts show, the predilection for sweetness and fat was not confined to the land of the Nile, nor, I believe, to any age preceding the acceptance of modern medical views. But this tendency was counteracted by the frugality of the diet of the broad masses. The feasting of the rich has left only insignificant traces in the Geniza.

2. *Wine and Other Beverages*

Wine as daily diet and for festive occasions.—Alcoholic beverages were prohibited in Islam; and there can be no doubt that in the course of centuries, and, as far as the broad masses were concerned, this prohibition was honored more by compliance than by transgression. The reader of Arabic literature should not be misled by those endless stories that show caliphs and generals wasting half their lives in drinking bouts, or by Arabic (and other Muslim) poetry saturated with wine songs *ad* nauseam. With the rising and deepening of religiosity the prohibition was taken more and more seriously, and substitutes for wine as stimulus and nourishment had to be found. When religiosity turned into bigotry, widely felt as from the thirteenth century, but appearing in passing fits before, abstinence turned into rage against those who were permitted by their religion to enjoy intoxicating beverages, and who used wine in their most sacred rituals, Christians and Jews.[1]

As reflected in the Cairo Geniza, Fatimid Egypt exhibits a sound balance in this matter. The ancient and all-pervading tradition of the Mediterranean area, where wine was almost as basic a constituent of the regular diet as bread, was still much alive. Wine was openly sold. This tallies with the observation of a visitor to the country that fresh grapes were hard to come by because they were mostly made into wine.[2] A Street of the Wine Sellers was found in Cairo as early (or as late) as 1038, and in Fustat in 1156, although Muslim historians seem not to have noted them.[3] An early papyrus shows Aḥmad the wine seller doing business.[4] The word for wine used in all these cases is the innocent *nabīdh*, which could also designate beverages made of dates, bee honey, and the like, which were sometimes, but by no means always, not inebriating. (The spicy Egyptian honey wine whose recipe is translated below, definitely was.) The experts on Islamic law were of divided opinion as to which, if any, type of nabīdh was permissible, but this proclivity for fooling oneself (and others) had the advantage that one was able to talk openly about wine without causing offense. In the Geniza (and, I believe, also in Arabic literature) nabīdh is as commonly used for grape wine as the true word, the offensive *khamr*; and both, referring to the same stuff, appear in two consecutive lines of a letter containing the usual orders for laying in supplies of wheat and wine.[5]

Yet the proliferation of wine substitutes, and, in particular, of soft drinks made with fruits, flower petals, vegetables, or spices, or combinations of some of them, appearing in the Geniza as daily diet of the middle class proves that wine had been largely replaced by other beverages, not only in Islam but also in a minority group living in its midst.

Wine was consumed by middle-class Jews, and probably in considerable quantities on Sabbaths, holidays, and at family or community feasts, such as betrothals, weddings, or circumcisions. It was taken before the meal, when the relevant benedictions were pronounced (and when the wine, as Talmudic medicine has it, served as an "opener of the intestines"), after the meal (or even during it, if one wished), and again after grace was said, when a cup, held in the right hand during the long prayer after a meal, was emptied, preceded by a blessing and followed by a special grace over wine. This sequence of drinks and thanks for the gift of wine, elaborated in the Talmud and codified by Maimonides, is still observed in traditional households, with the qualification that the lovely custom of holding sweet-smelling herbs in the left hand during the grace has fallen into desuetude.[6] Formal dinners with wine served in the order described above were also held after bloodletting or a visit to a public bath (especially after an illness and restoration to good health), as again codified by Maimonides and reflected in this short note from the Geniza written in a spirit of revelry rather than devotion:

In [Your] Name, oh Mer[ciful].

Your excellency, my lord, our Master, Ḥiyyā, The Pride of the Godfearing,[7] promised me last Saturday a jug of excellent wine, so that we might renew with it our ancient *Kingdom*.[8] Now, today, after bloodletting, the doctor prescribed wine for me to drink. So, please let me have the most excellent sort to be had, as I know your spirit and noble aims, and as I have experienced on occasion of your previous kindnesses. [There follow seven good wishes in Hebrew rhymes for the recipient and his still unmarried sons.][9]

Since good wine was a delicacy, it was often given, or, as here, solicited as a gift. Numerous examples could be provided from the Geniza and Arabic and Hebrew poetry. A letter accompanying the gift of "a little juglet of wine" from the court clerk Solomon, son of the judge Elijah, whose family dabbled in the wine trade (see n. 37, below), illustrates the mores of the time. The recipient was the old physician Rashīd, who is described as the writer's "father" and benefactor. Rashīd is five times implored to receive the insignificant gift and not to embarrass the sender by refusing or paying for it or by reciprocating with a return gift. It was a light wine, to be taken with cooked (not roasted) meat.[10] Moreover, the time of the pressing of new grapes was upon them, and Solomon himself did not drink wine "in these very hot days," and so on. Reading the letter again, I feel it may be characteristic not so much of the environment in which it was written as of the idiosyncratic personality of its author. But he, too, belonged to the Mediterranean scene.[11]

It must be emphasized that during the entire period that concerns us here, wine was not a luxury but a daily need, best to be obtained when the grapes were picked in quantities sufficient for a year. In contracts of partnerships or other forms of commercial cooperation or when an heir undertakes to maintain his brother, the provision of wine, together with that of wheat, was singled out to be guaranteed by the common income or otherwise.[12]

The same impression is gained from the quantities of wine, stored or traded, noted in our documents. In this respect we encounter a serious difficulty. If our knowledge about medieval measurements in general is somewhat hazy, that for standard containers of wine is practically absent, since wine could not be legally traded in

Islam. The little the Geniza has to offer in these matters is therefore doubly welcome.

Containers and prices.—The container of wine most often mentioned was the *jarra,* a jar (the English is derived from the Arabic), probably with two handles like the Greek amphora.[13] A document from October 1099 about a complicated lawsuit mentions a payment of 9 dinars for ninety jars, corrected in a postscript to ninety-one, which makes it likely that 1 dinar was a standard price for ten jarras.[14] A detailed letter about the pressing of grapes and the making of wine, written at least a hundred years later, informs a relative that for his 3 dinars thirty jars of wine were produced; since the local supply of grapes was exhausted, his additional requirements would be satisfied elsewhere.[15] In summer 1150, or slightly later, a man inherited from his father, among other items, 1,937 jars of wine, which were auctioned, during at least four days, mostly in units of 10, 20, 30, 50, 90, 100, 150 or 200 jars, occasionally also in sums other than tens, such as 15, 65, or 19, 89. The list of the buyers is quite intersting (see the note).[16]

Instead of the general word jarra, another term, clearly derived from the Greek, *ṭamāwiya,* was frequently used as a standard term for a wine container. This vessel must have had a special form, for empty clay ṭamāwiyas, for instance, 350 costing 70 dirhems, which makes 0.2 dirhem apiece, were stored in a cellar, or a quantity worth 4 dirhems by a small dealer. Ten ṭamāwiyas of wine—like ten pounds of silk—were traded as a unit. The court clerk Mevōrākh b. Nathan (active ca. 1150–1180) had seven ṭamāwiyas filled with wine in the provincial town Minyat Ziftā; through a friend he asks his brother to let him have another three so that he may be able to sell his wine.[17] Of particular interest is a document referring to spring 1149, the beginning and the end of which are missing; it seems to represent the dissolution of a partnership between a large number of members. Of a wine cellar containing 2,565 ṭamāwiyas, 965 were sold as follows:

Ṭamāwiyas	Dinars
250	20
250	20 1/2
240	20
225	19

Thus, the average price for ten ṭamāwiyas was something between 0.8 and 0.88 dinars.[18] Another piece of information from approximately the same time (1165) may be compared in which a payment of 28 dinars for 250 jars of wine is reported, which makes a little bit above 1 dinar for ten ṭamāwiyas.[19] In both these cases and numerous others, wine is not called by the common term "nabīdh," but by *laṭaf*, literally, a precious gift, or sweets, which seems to be another euphemism for the forbidden fluid, since it never appears compared with another type of wine.[20] When a young man, before traveling to Aden, South Arabia, received a down payment of 2 1/4 dinars for fifty ṭamāwiyas of nabīdh, held by a third party, we can safely assume that this sum represented half the total price of 4 1/2 dinars, or 0.9 dinars for ten receptacles.[21]

Domestic and imported.—The idea of standardizing wine prices or, rather, vessels containing quantities averaging a certain price seems to be absurd. Is it not the variety of wines which makes them so attractive? The answer is that our texts speak about local wine mostly laid in for yearly consumption and awaiting the pressing of fresh grapes in the coming summer. The soil and climate of Egypt are not particularly well suited for viniculture. But when the wine-loving Greeks, in the wake of Alexander's victories, became the masters of Egypt for almost a thousand years, they made considerable efforts to expand wine-growing in the country. As our documents show, these efforts were crowned with success, and even today, as I learned from the late Professor Rudolf Mach, a connoisseur, Egyptian wine is not to be dismissed easily. There were, of course, good years and bad, and, as we shall see, even a small producer would be able to offer different qualities. The deviation of about 20 percent, from the average of 1 dinar for ten jarras or ṭamāwiyas observed above, would leave enough latitude for such differences. A glimpse from the consumer's side sheds additional light on this problem.[22]

In the month of Av (July 17–Aug. 15) 1140, two payments for grapes, totaling 6 7/12 dinars, and one of 2 dinars for raisins were made by Abū Zikri Kohen Sijilmāsī, the representative of merchants in Fustat so ubiquitous in these volumes.[23] In an account settled in June 1134 for the preceding year, Abū Zikrī had spent 5 1/24 dinars for one purchase of grapes.[24] About eighty years earlier, when Nahray b. Nissīm, the Tunisian merchant resident in Egypt, was still very active in Palestine and Lebanon, his agent in Jerusalem bought for him grapes for 5 Nizāriyya dinars (which were then regarded as having particularly good value).[25] According to the data on the preceding pages, one could get fifty to sixty jars of wine for 5 or 6 dinars spent on grapes, a reasonable quantity for the household of a respectable merchant: a jar per week, with extras for holidays and special occasions, less weeks of abstinence such as Lent for Christians and the mourning period of the months of Tammuz and Av for Jews, when festive meals with meat and wine were unthinkable.[26]

Naturally, the majority of the population was unable to spend on wine a sum of 6 dinars or so at a time (which was about one-half of what one needed for a yearly provision of wheat). Since Jews were supposed to drink only wine produced, transported, and stored under the supervision of reliable coreligionists, a ramified wine trade was a necessity of life. A Jew selling 221 1/2 small jars of wine appears in an Antinoopolis papyrus of the year 542, more than a hundred years before the conquest of Egypt by the Arabs.[27] Ancient Arabic literature is full of stories of Christian and Jewish taverns. Four types of traders in wine are discernible in the Geniza: merchants investing in wine as in any other business venture; professional *nabbādhīn*, who, as usual, carried that commodity as both retailers and wholesalers; religious dignitaries, who could dabble in this trade because they were naturally regarded as particularly reliable by the scrupulous; and, finally, physicians, because wine was not only delicious and nutritive but also much used in medical treatment. In a treatise still extant, Moses Maimonides recommended the drinking of wine to an Ayyubid ruler for the cure of melancholy, leaving it to him to follow medical advice or the commands of his religion.[28]

Wine cellars stocking two to three thousand jars seem to have been nothing exceptional, and quantities of two to two hundred and fifty jars changing hands are mentioned repeatedly.[29] A successful Egyptian doctor practicing in Seleucia (today Selefke), Asia Minor, boasted of possessing four hundred barrels, each containing ten *ṭamāyas* (thus), which would make four thousand jars. But measurements in Byzantium were probably different from those prevailing in Egypt.[30] A retailer, who at the opening of the store had 650 ṭamāwiyas in his makhzan, sold quantities ranging from a quarter jar (twice) to 110 jars.[31]

I said that wine was traded in units of ten jars, probably the minimum on which a wholesaler or any passer of a toll station at the entrance to a city had to pay a tax.[32] The average price for this unit, I surmised, was 1 dinar, and, for one jar 0.1 dinar, or about 4 dirhems. A bill of expenditure for a grand dinner, written on an Arabic papyrus of the ninth century, lists two items of wine, one costing 4 1/2 dirhems and another 6 dirhems, probably two jars of different quality.[33] In a contract between two physicians, 91 + 9 = 100 jars of "good" *laṭaf* wine cost 657 1/2 cut-up dirhems which were the legal tender in Egypt around 1220. The price of 6.575 dirhems for a jar was probably attributable less to the quality of the wine than to the weakness of the dirhem.[34] But when a man writes to his son, "If anyone would come and buy a hundred jars of wine, taste it, and carry it away for 250 or 240 [dirhems, of course], let him come and take it, for I have not made a dirhem's worth sale since you left," an extraordinary situation was involved or a smaller jar is meant.[35]

Wine was also stored and sold in smaller vessels, which we read about in the papers of minor dealers. The cellar of one such merchant was arranged in four rows, each containing 150–290 ṭamāwiyas, 17–29 *lājiyās* (see the note), and 5–40 "small ones." In the Tower, that is, a tower of the ruined Roman fortress, which was possessed by the Jewish community and converted into stores and apartments, smaller quantities of the same three categories were kept.[36] An inventory made on 5 Oct. 1230 by Solomon b. Elijah of the quantities of wine kept in the underground storeroom of the family house for his father, the judge, his brother, the physician, and himself, he notes, alongside ṭamāwiyas (31–37 for each) a measurement named "olive," certainly a very small one. Most of the wines are described as *muwallad*, crossbred, possibly meaning mixed with an inferior type of wine, and only a few (totaling ten) as khamr, real wine.[37] About a hundred years earlier, Toviah b. Eli, who was in charge of the Jewish community of Bilbays, sent to his cousin and brother-in-law, the judge Nathan b. Solomon in Fustat, ten samples of two qualities of wine, of which he had made a total of one hundred and fifty jarras, asking him to offer them "to the best Jewish wine sellers." He implores the judge in the most urgent terms to break the clay seal of a jar marked by a sign, and, if he liked "the smell," that is the bouquet, to use it.[38] When the superintendent of "the small synagogue in Alexandria" revoked the engagement of his daughter to a nephew, he had to return to the latter among other things sixty jarras of wine, supplied by the prospective son-in-law as a partnership planned. Dealings in comparatively small quantities of wine, we see, were a favorite sideline for persons holding religious office.[39]

Recipes for wine.—Samuel Krauss describes thirty kinds of wine found in Talmudic literature, which is, we remember, of an intrinsically religious and juristic character.[40] Nothing of the kind can be offered from the Geniza, although most of its content is concerned with daily life. I have not even come across "old wine," familiar from *The Arabian Nights*, the Talmud, and, of course, the Ancients. In *The Arabian Nights*, Rūmī, that is, Greek or Italian, wine, is called "matured."[41] In the Geniza we find Rūmī wine in Alexandria (never in Fustat), where the jeunesse dorée wasted their parents money in the taverns of foreign nabbādhin.[42] Even "a scholar from Fustat sojourning in the al-Qamra inn in Alexandria" had to be warned by his mother not to damage his health by succumbing to the temptations of that sinful port city.[43] The "crossbred" wine made or, at least, traded by the family of Judge Elijah was probably intended to meet the demands of thrift rather than of the palate. Thus far I have come upon only one grape wine created for the delight of the connoisseur, an imitation of the ancient Roman *conditum* (from which our condiment), a wine enriched by bee honey on the one hand and pepper and other spices and ferments on the other. This luxury wine was so popular in Talmudic times that the study of the Torah with its many contrasting facets was compared with it. The spicy recipe translated below, however, is not specifically Jewish. It is part and parcel of an ancient Mediterranean tradition.

A Recipe for Good Wine

Take two and a half dirhems' weight of each of the following: lichen,[44] ginger, pepper, and barley flour, and half a dirhem of saffron. Mix all these together, pound them and bind the mixture with the same quantity [weight] of Egyptian bee honey and put it aside. Put two and a half dirhems' weight of this, together with one dirhem of colophony,[45] into each jar and plaster it over.[46] Leave it in the sun for seven days, after which it can be used.

If you wish to have vinegar, put only one and a quarter of this stuff into each jar and leave it in the sun for eleven days.[47]

Exposure to the sun for fermenting wine, known to the Ancient, was not forgotten in the Middle Ages. From the Geniza it appears that it was a common way of making wine.[48] The Arabic expression "sun matured" is a translation from the Greek.[49]

The tiny quantity of honey listed in the recipe proves that it served as a condiment, not as the main substance of the beverage described. The mixture prepared was poured into a jarra of grape wine, the measurement of which was known to everyone, although it seems not yet to have been defined by modern research with certainty.[50] A real honey wine is described in the recipe translated below, which was written in Aden, South Arabia. The *dādhī*, an edible lichen, with which it was mixed, is frequently mentioned in the letters and accounts of the India trade, and one Muslim author asserts that wine could be made with that lichen alone.[51]

A Recipe for Dādhī Wine

Take fifteen pounds of honey and put on it one pound of dādhī. Stir it up every day until it loses the tạste of honey. Then take it, clarify it, put it into a gl[āss] vessel [and pour] over each pound of honey three pounds of water.[52]

This alcoholic honey wine is the honey sherbet, the *fuqqāʿ*, "which God has permitted [to drink]." It is mentioned in both Arabic papyri and the Geniza; Jewish vendors sold it in Egypt and Jews made it in al-Mahdiyya, Tunisia. It was so popular that the *fuqqāʿa*, the bottle in which it was kept, became a general term for that vessel. The prohibition to drink honey sherbet, one of the fitful edicts of the caliph al-Ḥākim, was made in connection with the chiliastic expectations of the Muslim year 400 (1009/10), and was certainly only temporary.[53]

Beer.—The white Egyptian beer, *mizr*, made from wheat, must once have been popular among Jews, since it was brewed at the holy shrine of Dammūh so that it should be easily available to the pilgrims' gathering there. We learn about it when this practice was prohibited along with many other things around 1010.[54] We hear again about mizr from Acre (Akko) in Crusader times when purple shellfish gatherers from Alexandria were reproved there for drinking it in a tavern of bad repute.[55] I have not found that beverage mentioned elsewhere; it was probably popular in circles not much represented in the Geniza.

Soft drinks.—Besides the invigorating and much demanded oxymel, the combination of honey and vinegar discussed above, the table of a middle-class family was well provided with refreshing beverages, made of the juices of fruits and vegetables, fetched customarily from the *sharābī*, the seller of potions. Particularly popular besides juices made of lemons, pomegranates, apples, plums, sorrels, and unripe grapes was rose water, highly recommended by physicians, and so was the *tamar hindī*, the tamarind drink, sought after in the western as in the eastern Mediterranean. Only a few decades ago, the cry of the tamar hindī vendor was a very familiar sound heard in the bazaars. A type of asparagus, different from the one providing the medical potion mentioned before, supplied the material for a regular drink. Household lists, business correspondence, and religious texts in the Geniza confirm that Muslim society had found substitutes for alcoholic beverages and that a minority group had adapted to the dietary habits of its environment.[56]

Aspects connected with the drinking of wine, such as conviviality and drunkenness, are treated in *Med. Soc.* V, A, 1 (in preparation).

D. MOUNTS

The riding animal as status symbol.—In the chapter "Travel and Seafaring" (*Med. Soc.*, I, 273 ff.), riding animals are mentioned only in passing, and their role in intraurban transport is not touched upon there at all. Something must therefore be said about them before concluding this chapter dealing with a person's physical environment and possessions and his attitudes toward them.

Islamic literature reveals that the quality of the riding beast and of its harness was almost as important for the outer appearance of its rider as his own looks and attire. This was not an innovation of Islam. The Prophets of ancient Israel proclaimed "we shall not ride on horses" and had the Messiah ride on an ass—protests against human vanity and haughtiness as demonstrated in the choice of mounts, always in the public eye like our cars. Naturally, only the higher echelons of society could permit themselves luxurious exposure, often fraught with danger. Christians and Jews, as is known from many stories, had to be particularly cautious not to arouse the envy and anger of the majority population. Yet the example of the leading classes was seductive. Even within the narrow circle of the Jewish community a person's status was marked by the value of his riding beast. The gift of a mule with its harness from a Tunisian princess's own stable was no less a distinction for a Jewish court purveyor than the bestowal of a robe of honor.[1] This passage from a letter to a brother carousing with an Arab chieftain, the brother of a general who held sway over most of Lower Egypt, is a telling example.

The least that the Jews and others say (under oath!) about you is that you earned on this journey a thousand dinars; not enough with this: one, by-named Abu 'l-Faḍl of the companions of the Rayyis [. . .] al-Dawla[2] said to me yesterday night in the reception hall of the Rayyis and in the presence of guests: "Your brother has got from Fakhr al- ʿArab[3] what is worth five hundred dinars, namely, a mule with its saddle worth two hundred dinars, and three hundred dinars in cash."[4] That man added that he was in al-Maḥalla and had seen all this with his own eyes.

God knows how I felt when I heard this. Not that I have any responsibility in this affair, but because of the spreading of gossip and exaggerated rumors, while the truth of the matter is often the opposite. . . . I say only this: May God protect you from *wicked people* and those who envy you, and turn away from you *the evil eye* in his mercy.[5]

The solicitous brother had good reason to be fearful of the evil eye, for a price of 200 dinars for a mount was out of reach of virtually everyone in the Jewish community. The price of 20 dinars for a mule sold to a person connected with the government, as reported in the letter summarized below, although by no means inconsiderable, was only a small fraction of that frightening sum. In a letter written in beautiful Arabic script and style, but crowned with biblical blessings in Hebrew, the writer mentions that he had sold his mule for 20 dinars, to be paid in monthly payments of 1 dinar; the first installment had been paid, and a government clerk, mentioned by name, had already "transferred" the sum; the addressee's mule was well; "One-Eyed," no doubt also a riding beast, was fine; the purchase of a mount by one acquaintance for another had run into a hitch, and the recipient was asked to do something in that calamity. The latter, addressed as "illustrious sheykh," "my lord," but also as "my boy," must have been a younger, but respected, partner or relative (or both), who shared a stable with the writer and probably with others. They did not deal in animals, for their common business is described as a shop, *ḥānūt*, but they cherished their mounts as our contemporaries do their cars. "One-Eyed" was probably a riding ass, destined to serve the writer after he had sold his mule, reason unknown.[6] Larger mansions would have one or even two stables, but we rarely hear of them, for most of our documents deal with the transfer of single houses or—even more frequently—parts of houses. In any case, our letter reflects an environment of persons at ease, not only because of the government connection but in view of the price: for 20 dinars one could have a good maidservant—or ten pounds of silk, with which one could start a business. The value of most of the mounts referred to was far lower.[7]

In the letter summarized, the same expressions are used for the well being of animals as for human beings. The acquisition of a mount by an acquaintance was an event worthy of being reported.[8] When the donkey of a scholar who bore the honorific title al-Ḥāfiẓ (one who knows the Bible by heart) brought forth a young, a friend was asked to convey to him the writer's congratulations. Later in the same letter, the addressee is given wishes that his own ass, which was with young, be granted a similarly sound delivery; the wish is accompanied by the appropriate Bible quotation: "Blessed shall be the fruit of your beast" (Deuteronomy 28:4 and 11).[9]

Prices.—On the prices of mounts, it has already been noted that 20 dinars for a mule was a very considerable sum. In a letter to a qadi, which had found its way into the Geniza, a horse cost 17 dinars.[10] Nowhere in the Geniza have I come upon a horse owned by a Jew. In a letter on vellum, probably from the tenth century, if not earlier, a pregnant young donkey was bought for 4 1/2 dinars, and a pair of oxen went for 15 "large" dinars.[11] Such agricultural husbandry is not found in later letters. The navy physician, whose acquiescence in a very generous settlement of a debt due him is described in a previous volume, bought, after arrival in the Mediterranean port of Damietta (probably on board ship), a saddled mount for 4 dinars.[12] The price range of donkeys is well illustrated in the letter of another physician, also met before: no one would choose to buy those offered for 2 dinars or less; those costing 5–6 dinars were not worth more than 4; therefore he refrained from buying any.[13] When the Keeper of the Sepulchers of the Patriarchs in Hebron, Palestine, complained that his son was robbed of his donkey worth 6 dinars, while traveling to Ascalon, he probably exaggerated; the gist of the letter was a cry for help (late eleventh century).[14] A donkey purchased for 3 1/12 dinars by a troubled businessman, from whom we have many letters, was offered for sale unsaddled for 2 dinars; its "outfit" was evaluated as worth 20 dirhems, or about half a dinar (May 1140).[15]

Thus, a lower middle-class physician or merchant could have a modest riding beast for about 4 dinars. If for any reason he did not keep one, he at least kept in the house saddles and harness for both mule and donkey to be used when one bought or hired a mount for travel. We find such equipment in the estate of a druggist (1143) and in that of a woman from Fustat (1083).[16] An order for one, inserted into a long business letter written by the prominent merchant Barhūn b. Isaac Tāhertī in al-Mahdiyya, Tunisia, on 9 August 1048, deserves attention. "Buy for me a Cairene saddle, a small one, for a donkey, of excellent material; if used, I do not care; price 1/2–2 dinars; also a rein of black leather with a heavy iron, for my donkey has a strong head." Obviously, Barhūn, who commuted between Egypt and Tunisia, kept a mount in Alexandria but ordered its harness from Miṣr, the capital, probably the central market for riding beasts (often imported from Nubia) and their equipment. Barhūn had to specify "donkey," because a merchant of his status was supposed to ride a mule.[17]

Riding animals then, as now with cars, were lent to friends, occasionally even for extended trips. Such favors could lead to mishaps. One in which prices were involved is briefly reported: a donkey whose proprietor claimed it cost him 5 dinars was lent to a friend for a trip to Malīj; on the way the donkey was lost and its rider died, but not before having asserted that it was worth only 2 dinars—a complicated case indeed.[18]

Renting mounts.—People who had neither money nor friends who possessed animals rented them. To do so meant hiring donkey drivers, or muleteers, who seem to have formed some loose corporations. Some were reliable, others not, and experts had to be consulted before choosing one. Although Jewish couriers were comparatively plentiful, Jewish muleteers and donkey drivers were not, or cannot be identified as Jews, because such persons are usually referred to with names that were common to Jews and Muslims.[19] The practice seems to have been that one traveled only a comparatively short distance with the mukārī(s) (probably until one stayed overnight), and then hired new ones. Thus a friend is warned: "When you arrive in Malīj, you must hire mounts, for our animals are on the spring pastures." The company obviously had expected to use their friends' donkeys.[20] A scholarly person from Alexandria who had tried in vain to find employment in the capital asks Abū Naṣr, possibly the famous one, the Tustarī, for 3 dirhems to hire a riding beast and try his luck in one of the congregations of the Rīf. Although 3 dirhems was hardly a negligible sum, our scholar would not get very far with such a fare. But he could be sure that any community that did not wish to make use of his talents would be glad to get rid of him by paying for the continuation of his journey.[21]

Traveling in stages had another purpose. As long as the aim was to cover a certain distance as quickly and conveniently as possible, the main requirement was a strong and steady animal, whatever its looks. When approaching his destination, however, one wished "to enter the city" on a fine mount in an equally ornate harness. In a strikingly calligraphic Hebrew letter with wide space between the lines (as in the caliphal chancelleries) a VIP informs Sahlān b. Abraham, the head of the Iraqian congregation in Fustat, that he had arrived safely in Minyat al-Qā'id via Ṣahrajt, and sends him respectful greetings. In a one-line marginal note, written in Arabic, he politely suggests that Sahlān's messenger bring back a saddled mount "so that entrance could be made while riding on it."[22]

A person of standing, such as a government official of rank, a renowned physician, or prosperous merchant, would normally leave his house mounted. Since Jews were not permitted to ride on Saturday, noble families tried to live near the synagogue. When Cairo was founded and a Jewish house of worship was erected in it, three court physicians of the Fatimid caliphs had their houses just around it.[23] This complaint from the pen of a Hebrew poet to his maecenas is particularly illustrative: "At midnight you came to me on foot asking me to compose a letter of condolence and to adorn it with verses. You found me and I wrote. And I composed booklets of dirges to be recited by the community each day of the period of mourning." The maecenas was in such a hurry that he did not take the time to have his mount saddled, which shows that the distance between his house and the dwelling of the poet was short. Under normal circumstances, though, he would always cover it while mounted.[24]

The preceding pages seem to show that a respectable middle-class person would be content with a riding animal worth 5–6 dinars, approximately equivalent to the yearly rent for an acceptable domicile.[25] A donkey worth 2 dinars or less betrayed his rider as being in somewhat strained financial circumstances. A mule worth 20 dinars symbolized high status. A mule with its harness costing ten times that much was regarded as ostentatious affluence and dangerous for a non-Muslim. Commoners, the majority of the population, did not possess riding animals; they had no need for them because of the comparatively short distances within a medieval town. To the contrary, a respectable middle-class person, when leaving his house, would ride wherever practicable to avoid not only the dust and dirt of the narrow streets but also the jostling crowd.

The material things. A retrospective.—This short note about riding animals tallies with the economic activities, possessions, and standards of living of the majority of the people represented in the Geniza documents. It was an industrious but by no means affluent community. The volume of business conducted between two merchants as reflected in the yearly closing of the accounts was usually in the hundreds, in any case only exceptionally above two thousand dinars.[26] Tens and hundreds of dinars were the sums regularly handled. Profits were modest and losses abundant.[27] Numerous letters and even legal documents are concerned with sums in dirhems, often worth less than 1 dinar. Estates, at least those registered by clerks of the rabbinical court of Fustat, rarely surpassed a thousand dinars in cash and promissory notes.[28]

The public chest was even more restricted in means than private coffers. The yearly revenue from twenty-five properties—pious foundations belonging, completely or partly, to the rabbinical community of Fustat—amounted in 1164 to 3,683 dirhems. At that time the community possessed about sixty such houses. From this and other data has been calculated an average yearly income from pious foundations of 12,000 dirhems, or about 300 dinars.[29] Some of those buildings were out of repair and had probably been donated by their proprietors when moving to (New) Cairo. But others were well kept, as their long life, testified by the Geniza, proves,[30] and a yearly income of 5 dinars from a modest house was normal for the people described in these pages.[31]

Another characteristic of the material well being of Geniza society was its relative uniformity. The differences between the lower and higher income brackets, although considerable, were gradual, not staggering. The really wealthy few belonged to another world outside the Geniza. At the same time distinct strata of prosperity were clearly discernible. Both phenomena can best be studied by a perusal of documents on real estate transactions and on the conclusion of marriages. One could buy a complete house for 20 dinars, but also build one costing 600 dinars. In between, naturally, values of properties varied widely, but seven clearly distinct groups stand out, and within each group a certain standardization of prices seems to have been achieved.[32] For instance, in App. A, Group III (houses worth 50–80 dinars), five out of eighteen properties were worth 50 dinars (including one of 52 dinars), and seven, 60 (one 58); in Group IV (90–140 dinars) five out of thirteen were around 100 dinars, three, 120, and another three, 140 dinars.

Less than one-half of the Jewish community of Fustat can have possessed houses.[33] But almost everyone married. Consequently, the gradation in value of marriage gifts and dowries from the poor to the well-to-do was far narrower than that of the prices of real estate. Yet, here too, seven distinct groups are discernible, and standardization was very pronounced.[34] The groups of values of houses do not coincide at all with those of the economics of marriage. But the interplay of a high degree of uniformity with marked stratification was operative in both fields.

Add to these a third element: the closeness of living quarters, caused perhaps in part by progressive impoverishment and the availability of inexpensive housing owing to the exodus to Cairo, a process probably more marked in the Muslim population than in the Jewish. Parts of, or shares in, houses changed hands more often than complete buildings. Taking the three middle groups of Appendix A, we find being sold in Group III three eighths, one sixth, five fourths, two halves, and only one complete house; three houses served as collateral or security, that is, remained in the hands of their proprietors. In Group IV, only two complete houses were sold, as against one sixth, five fourths, and two halves; in Group V there was not a single case of an entire property purchased (except one in Byzantium). In the rare instances when a relative bought part of a house from another, he probably intended to round up an estate that had become split in the process of inheritance. Otherwise, shares were acquired either because the buyer wished to live there himself or to derive income by leasing. Whether as tenants or as proprietors of shares, the inhabitants lived close together and had to take care of many common concerns: the well providing water for washing and cleaning, the drainpipes needing constant attention, repairs (a concern also for tenants since the landlords were not always eager to carry them out), payments for the night watchmen and garbage removal, agreements on where to hang linen or to store provisions. All these and various other aspects of life in a condominium are touched upon in the Geniza and we get a sense of how that way of life must have affected those who were exposed to it.

Yet, while weighing the Geniza evidence we must always consider the circumstances under which it came into being. Partners frequently had occasion to go to court, not only to settle a squabble but also simply to establish their individual rights. Siblings and relatives in general were often partners in a house, but the honor of the family required that it conceal its affairs from the public eye as much as possible. The family mansion was still a strong institution in Geniza times, and, in view of the durability of buildings, lasted for generations. We frequently read about it, especially in engagement and marriage contracts. But its importance reached far beyond what was confided to writing. The information gleaned from the Geniza is a starting point; we must gauge its implications. Only in exceptional cases have we the good luck to find a number of documents referring to the same case, thus permitting us to put together a full story. In App. D, Doc. II, we read about Sitt al-Khāṣṣa who received five out of twenty-four shares—approximately a quarter—of the house of her grandfather and one-half of that of her father, both long dead at the time of her engagement in 1146. The grandfather, Joseph Lebdi, a native of Tunisia, had purchased that "large" house in 1102 for the exceptionally high price of 500 dinars, when he, a seasoned India trader, preferred to settle in the capital of Egypt. He left the main part of that house (19/24 or approximately three-quarters) to his daughter, certainly because his son, as our document shows, had already acquired a domicile for himself. When this girl (Sitt al-Khāṣṣa's aunt), after a romantic interlude, finally married, she brought that big chunk of a large house to her husband, whom we therefore find in our document as partner of Sitt al-Khāṣṣa. We see that old Joseph Lebdi provided well for his progeny when he gained possession of that expensive mansion.[35]

The moving story of a brother who gave his sister at her marriage half a large house and half a small one confronting it and, four years later, on his deathbed, the other two halves, can be reconstructed only because three documents could be identified as belonging together. According to Jewish law the son was heir to the entire property of his father, but he was expected to enable his sister to found a family with the aid of the estate he had received.[36]

Besides those who had work (or had means enough not to need

to) and possessed shelter, food, clothing, and the other things required in daily life, there was the large mass of those who were unfit or unable to find a regular source of income and suffered endless privations. How the Jewish community of Fustat tried to alleviate the lot of those unhappy people is described in detail in the chapter on the social services.[37] How this stringent human obligation of the fight against poverty was conceived and fulfilled by the individual is treated in the next and final volume of this work. There I explore the inner world of the Geniza person, his response to the challenges of life, his dreads and hopes in this world and for the world to come, his concept of his role as a servant of God, and his acting out of that role. The striving of the select few for perfection, for an all-around education encompassing all aspects of knowledge available in those days, has also left its traces in the documentary Geniza. Its description completes the picture of the society which I have attempted to draw in these volumes.

A Note on Sachkultur

Since the term *Sachkultur* is not familiar in this country, I should like to draw the attention of the reader to some publications carrying this word in their titles.

Die Funktion der schriftlichen Quelle in der Sachkulturforschung (The Function of Written Sources in the Study of Material Civilization), a collection of studies edited by Heinrich Appelt (Vienna, 1976). Naturally, Geniza research is directly concerned with this problem. *Klösterliche Sachkultur des Spätmittelalters* (The Material Civilization of the Monastries of the Late Middle Ages), containing the proceedings of an international congress held in September 1978, and attended by contributors from most countries of Central Europe (Vienna, 1980).

Europäische Sachkultur des Mittelalters, a collection of articles by authors from all over Europe, including France and Italy (but not Great Britain), edited and introduced by Heinrich Appelt with a methodological essay on the subject (Vienna, 1980). A jubilee volume honoring the tenth anniversary of a branch of the Austrian Academy of Sciences, entitled, in English, Institute for the Research on Medieval Austrain Daily Life and Material Culture (p. 8).

Most of the studies in these publications pertain to the Late Middle Ages, when life in Europe had become totally different from that depicted in the Geniza documents, which originated on the southern shores of the Mediterranean during the High, or middle, Middle Ages. There is some common ground with regard to the methodological approach.

A forceful appeal to the Orientalists to bring *Sachkultur* within the orbit of their studies was made by Eugen Wirth (see A, 1, nn. 8 and 9, above), in his programmatic address "Orientalistik and Orientforschung," *ZDMG*, Supplement III, 1, 1977, lxxv–lxxx.

Appendixes

Appendix A

Prices of Houses in Geniza Documents

(antedating 1250)

The circumstances in which the prices listed below were obtained are indicated to enable the reader to evaluate their significance. For instance, when one-eighth of a house was sold for 30 dinars, the total price of 240 dinars represents only the approximate value of that property. A good illustration of this situation is found in Group V, the entry dated 1246, where out of 24 shares of a property two were sold for 27 d. on 16 April 1246, whereas one share was sold for 15 d. three months later, on 29 July 1246. The total value of that compound, which consisted of two houses, was thus approximately 324–360 d.

Similarly, the sum against which a house was given as collateral was very probably smaller than the price of that house. In exceptional cases, the opposite might have been the case, namely, when the debtor did not possess anything else except the mortgaged property (see Group I, the entry dated ca. 1220).

(R) indicates that the house was situated in a residential quarter. This is assumed where either a detailed description of the boundaries shows that a house was surrounded by private homes or where the neighborhood is known as residential from fairly contemporary documents. (B) stands for bazaar. Business and/or industrial areas are assumed when a house is adjacent to one or several bazaars. In most cases the relevant data are either absent, or lost, or not sufficiently evident.

Attention is drawn to the tables and discussion of the prices of houses in Fatimid and Ayyubid times presented by Ashtor, *Prix*, pp. 183–190. This Appendix contains a number of Geniza items not listed by Ashtor, and the reader will occasionally discover some discrepancies between the two tables. To discuss these minutiae would lead too far afield and would not change essentially the conclusions which each of us drew. As its arrangement and details show, this Appendix, which was compiled years before Ashtor's book appeared, sets out to illustrate the different standards of living apparent in the Geniza society.

It is noteworthy that the prices of Muslim houses in the Maghreb during the tenth through the twelfth centuries, as registered by Idris, "Vie économique en Occident musulman," pp. 81–82, are within the range of sums listed in this Appendix (3, 14, 50, 60, 100, 300, 500 d., respectively).

GROUP I.

Houses for less than 20 dinars

Source	Date	Circumstances	Price of house in dinars
Dropsie 335; cf. *Med. Soc.*, II, 533 and n. 59	1041	Gift to a sister (or two sisters) of a house in the Jaᶜfariyya quarter of Sahrajt, worth 10 d. See *Med. Soc.*, III 282–283.	10
TS 8 J 7, f. 7; cf; *Med. Soc.*, III, 281 and n. 24	Twelfth century	One-half of a house with a store in Malīj was bought by a mother from her son for 6 d. with the money received from her second husband at divorce. On her deathbed she divides that half between a grandson and a granddaughter in equal shares.	12
TS 8 J 11, f. 15; cf. *Med Soc.*, III, 113–114 and n. 74	1127–1139	Deposition in court claims that a house in Malīj was sold for 17 d.	17
Bodl. a 3 (2873), f. 8	1134	A house given as a collateral for a debt of 10 d. See A, 3, n. 18, above	10
TS Misc. Box 28, f. 234	April/May 1141	Farajiyya, the daughter of the late Ṣedāqā, sells her house in Minyat Ziftā for 9 d. of which she renounces 1 d. when making the settlement before a Jewish notary in Fustat (who happened to be Ẓāfira's husband [see *Med. Soc.*, III, 216–217]). The buyer had delivered 6 1/3 d. and promised to pay the balance of 1 2/3 d. during the month of the forthcoming High Holidays (Sept.–Oct.), while she would register the sale with the Muslim authorities "as was customary."	8
Bodl. d 66 (2878), fs. 110*v*–111*r*	1150	Joseph b. Saᶜīd must cede 3/4 of a house (probably all he possessed of it) and half of a ruin situated opposite it to the orphan Hibat Allah if he does not pay him 6 d. by Sivan (April–May) 1150.	ca. 10

Source	Date	Circumstances	Price of house in dinars
TS 8 J 35, f. 5	1153	Joseph, the cantor, sells "a small house" (of which half belonged to him and the other to his daughter, the wife of the beadle Hiba) to the water carrier Ibrahīm for 6 d.	12
TS 8 J 14, f. 3*v*	ca. 1180	Question addressed to Joseph Rōsh ha-Seder about half a house given as a collateral for a debt of 8 d., but worth less.	Less than 16
Abraham Maimuni, *Responsa*, p. 203	ca. 1220	A woman possesses half a house worth 6 d. Her husband used it as a collateral against a debt of 8 d.	12
Bodl. b 3 (Cat. 2806) fs. 7–8; see *Med. Soc.*, II, 400–401	1232	The widow Tujjār (Queen of the Merchants) claims that ten shares in a house in Bilbays belongs to her children as heirs of her husband Abu 'l- ʿAlā' b. Joseph Kohen. The husband of her sister-in-law produces Arabic deeds, not confirmed by a Jewish court, showing that the children's grandmother had sold him those shares. He asserts (before the court in Fustat) that in Bilbays such confirmations are not customary. Tujjār produces a Hebrew document, witnessed, but not validated by a court. At the advice of experts, Abu 'l- ʿAlā' agrees to pay his nephews 300 dirhem *fulūs*. Assuming an exchange rate of 1:40, the total value of the house would be 18 d. In reality the price was certainly considerably higher.	More than 18
Bodl. d 66 (2878), f. 21, *India Book* 177	ca. 1230	A woman in Aden, South Arabia, gives her house as a collateral against 30 (Maliki) d. due as poll tax of her two sons who were away on business voyages. A Maliki d. was worth about 1/3 Egyptian d.	10

GROUP II.

Houses for 20–45 dinars

Source	Date	Circumstances	Price of house in dinars
TS 16.132	998	A woman in al-Banā near Fāqūs, Nile Delta, sells a quarter of a third of a house to her son-in-law for 3 1/2 d.	42
TS 12.577	Tenth century	A woman purchases a house adjacent to the *saqīfa* (A, 1, n. 150) of Yazīd the perfumer. (B)	30
Bodl. b 12 (2875), f. 31	Early eleventh century	Part of the dowry of a Karaite bride: half a house in the Street of the Turners worth 20 d. (B) Her Copper: 15 d.	40
Bodl. d 66 (2878), f. 3	ca. 1100	A house in an industrial area belonging to orphans in Aleppo, worth "because of the slump" only 30+ d. (B)	More than 30
TS 24.5	1111	An amount of 14 d. forms part of dowry for buying half a house. The groom is a freedman.	28
Merx, *Paléographie*, p. 39	1124	Sale of a "small house." See A, 2, n. 38. (R)	20
TS 13 J 20, f. 27	ca. 1150	A noble woman, widow of a physician and distant relative of the Nagid Samuel b. Hananya, is forced to sell a quarter of her smaller house and to mortgage half of it (on the rent of which she lived) against a debt of 12 d.	ca. 24
Bodl. b 11 (Cat. 2874, no. 34), f. 35	Dec. 1156/ Jan. 1157	His wife agreeing, the dyer Makārim b. Salāma sells to his brother Abu 'l-Ḥasan one-eighth of a house in the Surayya quarter, formerly known as the residence of Joseph, father of the water carrier Abu 'l-Khayr. Price 5 d. (B)	40

Source	Date	Circumstances	Price of house in dinars
TS 8 J 9, f. 17*c*, item I	1160	Sale of two out of twenty-four shares in a house containing two interconnected apartments and a silk worker's qāʿa for 3 d.	36
Antonin 1064	1174	Sale of a quarter of a burnt house in the Mikā'īl Lane, Qaṣr al-Shamʿ, Fustat, for 6 d.	24
Maimonides, *Responsa* I, 103 n. 64	ca. 1190	House of a widow offered for sale by auction and acquired by the community.	36
TS 8 J 32, f. 4 and TS 10 J 21, f. 17 (two fragments of one document)	1229	One dyer sells to another half a house for 430 dirhems, total 860 (exchange rate probably 1:43). The seller remains in the house for a yearly rent of 66 dirhems; see A, 3, n. 24. (R)	ca. 20
TS 12.231*v*	ca. 1230	Half a house in the Qadi Badr alley of the al-Mamṣūṣa quarter sold for 1,000 *waraq* dirhems (exchange rate 1:40). The house had been converted into workshops, its arched portal was boarded, and as its parts solely two storerooms, two rose-water pools with two drain-pipes are listed. The seller possessed twenty out of twenty-four shares and sold twelve (see l. 7., in l. 3, the first *min* is erroneous).	25
TS Arabic Box 54, f. 92	1233/4	The house Ibn Sibāʿ sold through a real estate broker.	23
TS Arabic Box 54, f. 92	1233/4	House bought from a woman, Umm Abu 'l-Ḥasan, by the same broker, "repairs excluded" (incumbent on the seller). See also Group V, same year.	40
BM Or 10.126; see *Med. Soc.*, II, 400–401	1239	House in Bilbays, given as a collateral for a debt of 36 d. is returned to the proprietor with the right to buy it back within twelve years.	36

TS 8 J 6, f. 15	1243	The paternal cousin of a man's wife renounces his inheritance right on 1/4 of a house belonging to her against 10 d. promised to him by her husband in case she precedes him in death.	40

GROUP III.

Houses for 50–80 dinars

Source	Date	Circumstances	Price of house in dinars
TS 12.499	969	Two houses, each pledged for a debt of 50 d. (see A, 3, n. 17). (R)	50
Bodl. a 3 (2873), f. 32*v*	1064 or 1078	A mother in Ramle, Palestine gives her daughter as part of her dowry half a house, which half is valued 25 d.	50
ULC Or 1080 J 117	1088	A house in Alexandria bordering on Christian and Muslim properties, described in full in an Arabic deed, sold for 60 d. (R)	60
TS 12.502 frag., ed. G. Weiss, *Gratz Coll. Annual*, I, 72–73; 77–78	1123	A woman sells half her house for 25 d., receiving the right to buy it back within two years and two months. The rents paid by her tenants will be hers and she has to pay no rent. For similar arrangements see A, 3, n. 24	50

Source	Date	Circumstances	Price of house in dinars
Bodl. e 94, fs. 19 and 25; TS 12.482; TS NS 306, f. 1, l. 15; see *Med. Soc.*, III, 329, 333, and nn. 70–71, 90; Gil, *Foundations*, p. 298 n. 9; G. Weiss, *Gratz Annual*, I Philadelphia 1972, 66–72	In and around 1124	Jayyida, wife of a scholarly grape-presser (family name), gives two-thirds of a house in the Ḥudayjī Street, which was her share, as a collateral against a loan of 50 d. granted by a dyer. She remained in the house promising to pay 16 d. as rent for two years. The remaining third was or became communal property.	75
ENA 2558, f. 4	ca. 1130	A woman sells one-sixth of a house with two shops, one in the Mamṣūṣa, one in Saqīfat Shaʿīra. (B)	66
TS 12.694	Jan. 1139	Dalāl, daughter of Maḥbūb, sells to Munā, daughter of Isaac, a quarter of a house with two shops on the Great Bazaar for 14 1/2 d. (B)	58
TS 13 J 2, f. 25	1140	A property, *milk*, on the Jazīra (isle of Roḍa opposite Fustat) pledged against 50 d. deposited with the proprietor.	50
ENA 2558, f. 3	1141	The son of a water carrier sells to a woman one-eighth of a house in a blind alley in Cairo for 10 d.	80
Bodl. 65 (2877), f. 21	1156	The son of a money changer sells to another money changer one-quarter of a house in which the latter was a partner, for 15 d. (R)	60
TS Misc. Box 28, f. 33*v*, ll. 1–6, *India Book* 215	ca. 1176	A merchant traveling to Sicily gives his house in Alexandria as collateral against a loan of 50 d. (mentioned in letter).	50

TS 16.117	July 1179	A seller of potions sells to a perfumer one-eighth of a house "in the Great Bazaar, in the Surayya Lane, a blind alley," for 7 1/2 d. Half the house belonged "to Christians," and one-sixth to a seller of oil. (B)	60
TS 12.166; see *Med. Soc.*, II, 290	1202	A woman sells a quarter of a house (in the Jewish quarter of al-Maḥalla), of which half belongs to her and half to her husband, for 13 d., to a silk merchant. The house bordered on that of a Christian.	52
Bodl. b 3 (2806), f. 6	1213/4	The Nagid Abraham Maimonides is given the right to repurchase a tower in the ancient Byzantine fortress of Fustat, which he had sold for 60 d., for a period of five years and to live in it without paying rent. See A, 3, n. 24.	60
TS Arabic Box 51, f. 118	1232	A real estate agent notes sale of two-thirds of a house for 40 d.	60
ULC Add 2586	1233	A father sells to his son a quarter of the apartment belonging to him in a house in the al-Muʿtamid passage (*khawkha*) of the Tujīb quarter for 17 d. (R)	68?
TS 13 J 25, f. 19	ca. 1235	A woman sells to another (with the consent of her husband and her father) one-quarter of the house of her father, which had been given to her as part of her dowry, for 15 d. The house was situated in a lane near the al-Qubba (The Dome) mosque, bordered on the residence of the Nagid, a mill belonging to a qadi, and on the house of the purchaser. Its eastern border was formed by the wall of the al-Mamṣūṣa quarter. (R)	60

Source	Date	Circumstances	Price of house in dinars
TS 8 J 6, f. 14*v*	1241	A woman from the frequently mentioned Ibn Zabqala family sells to her brother one-eighth of a house belonging to her and held in partnership with a silk weaver, *qazzāz*. The property was situated in Alexandria, in the District of the Prisons (or Baths, *Khuṭṭ al-Dayāmis*, from Greek *demosion*). The sale was made in Fustat, with the consent of her husband, a dyer, after the brother had declared that he had inspected the house (see A, 3, n. 33, end) and delivered the price, 9 d.	72

GROUP IV.

Houses for 90–140 dinars

Source	Date	Circumstances	Price of house in dinars
TS 16.181; Assaf, *Texts*, p. 66	933	A bridegroom pledges one-quarter of a house, worth 35 d. as a security for the promised marriage gift. Damascus. (R)	140
TS 13 J 13, f. 27	ca. 1060	A man acquires "gardens and a house" in Sicily from a Christian for 100 d.	100
TS 20.126	1066	An unmarried woman (probably a widow) sells one-quarter of two stores with an apartment above them for 35 d. to Abraham, son of Nathan, the President of the Court. (B)	140

ENA 4020, f. 54	ca. 1090	Purchase of one-quarter of a house, described as adjacent to another one, for 24, 27, or 29 d.	96–116
TS 24.44	1102	A mother buys for her daughter half a house in the Harrānī Street for 51 d. See A, 2, n. 62. (R)	102
Dropsie 333 and TS 16.155 (fragments of one document)	ca. 1100	A woman sells one-quarter of a house in the Ṣaqāliba quarter of Cairo given to her by her father as part of her dowry for 30 d.	120
JNUL 3	1103	Half a house in Alexandria is sold to one of its partial proprietors for 60 d. See A, 3, n. 24.	120
TS 10 J 15, f. 26; cf. *Med Soc.*, III, 150 and n. 33	ca. 1136	Because of famine and debts a man on the island of Jerba sells his large house for 90 d. (For dating the letter cf. TS K 6, f. 47.)	ca. 100
Bodl. d 66 (2878), f. 109	1145	Cash received for the sale of a house in the Mamṣūṣa quarter. (B) (This document is translated at the end of this Appendix.)	123
TS Arabic Box 53, f. 70	1157	Sale of one-quarter of a new house for 27 1/2 d. (Arabic deed) (R)	110
TS 16.176	1182	A physician sells one-sixth of a house in the Zuwayla quarter, Cairo, known as his (former?) domicile to a dyer, who already possessed other parts, for 21 d. with the right to buy it back after seven months. During this period the rent from that sixth belonged to the physician.	126
ULC Or 1081 J 31	1226	Two brothers in Cairo sell to another two (by another father) a house for 120 d.	120
Bodl. d 66 (2878), f. 92	1229	Ibn al- ʿAjamī, a public leader, sells one-fourth of his house to the wife of a money assayer for 1,000 dirhems (exchange rate 1:40). (R)	ca. 100

GROUP V.

Houses for 150–250 dinars

Source	Date	Circumstances	Price of house in dinars
TS 28.3	1004	A representative of merchants, son of an immigrant, buys one-third of a house for 70 d. (R)	210
TS 16.115, ed. *Tarbiz* 9, 206–208	1006	A will makes mention of one-twelfth of a house sold for 14 d. (R)	168
TS Misc. Box 29, f. 23	ca. 1100	Ibrahīm b. Mūsa b. Ṣāliḥ al-Isra'īlī buys 1 1/2 out of 24 shares of a house from Da'ūd b. Azhar Ibrāhīm b. Azhar for 15 d. Deed in Arabic characters.	240
ṬS 12.156	ca. 1130	Brother sells to sister one-sixth of house inherited by him for 35 d. Two-thirds already belonged to sister, who had inherited the other sixth.	210
ENA 4020, f. 53	ca. 1130	One-sixth of a house adjacent to a physician's house is sold for 28 d.	168
ENA 4020, f. 52*v*	1132	A woman sells to another one-half of a house in the Ḥarrānī Street for 117 d. "free of charges." (R)	234
TS 13 J 21, f. 17; see *Med. Soc.*, I, 399 and n. 56	1137	A physician from Egypt who had emigrated to Seleucia (Silifke) in Asia Minor, built there a house worth 200 d.	200
PER H 89, ed. *Sefunot*, 8 (1964), 119 ff.	1137	Half a house sold for 100 d.	200
TS NS J 27, col. III, l. 4	1143/4	Sale of half a house in the Ḥudayjī Street for 75 d.	150

TS 16.126	1204	One-eighth of a house in Alexandria is sold on behalf of orphans for 30 d. after having been estimated by "famous experts."	240
TS Arabic Box 54, f. 92; see A, 2, nn. 38, 166	1233/4	A broker buys one-quarter of a small house and (with) a garden for 40 d. from the sons of Maḍmūn.	160
Bodl. d 66 (2878), f. 136	1246	Two out of 24 shares of a property consisting of two adjacent houses are sold for a total of 27 d., and, three months later, one for 15 d. The seller had the right to repurchase those shares under certain conditions. (B)	162–180
TS AS 148, f. 15	ca. 1250	A man in Fustat is prepared to pay 1,000 dirhems for 2 1/2 out of 24 shares of a "well-known" house in Alexandria. Total worth about 9,600 dirhems, corresponding to ca. 240 d. The fragment contains instructions to a scribe. The transaction summarized is preceded by another in which Abu 'l-Faraj b. Abū Mufaḍḍal al-Marāwiḥī buys a Nubian maidservant. This man lived in the early days of the Nagid David b. Abraham Maimonides. See *Med. Soc.*, II, 495, top, for further details.	240

GROUP VI.

Houses for 270–360 dinars

Source	Date	Circumstances	Price of house in dinars
TS 16.83, see A, 1, n. 95	976–1040	Sale of a compound, consisting of a larger and a small building on the Market of the Jews in Damascus for 280 d. (B)	280
TS Arabic Box 53, f. 61; see A, 1, n. 50; A, 2, nn. 11, 72	Early eleventh century	An apothecary buys from three Christian women one-quarter of a house, in the Rāya district, three-quarters of which already belonged to him, for 70 d. (R)	280
Dropsie 389*v*, l. 37	ca. 1063	A Tunisian merchant writes that he bought himself a house in Sicily for 300 d.	300
TS 16.146 and 12.176; see A, 3, n. 7	1143	Sitt al-Sāda, widow of the India trader Abu 'l-Barakat b. Joseph Lebdi, acquires one-sixth of two stores at the end of the Wax Makers Street from the physician Abu 'l-Faḍā'il Ibn al-Nāqid (see *Med. Soc.*, I, 250) for 53 3/4 d. One of these stores served as *sukn* (residence and/or office) of another physician. Abu 'l-Faḍā'il had acquired that sixth from the two sons of his late brother for the same price and granted them the right to repurchase it, which right is confirmed by the buyer Sitt al-Sāda. For the term of the repurchase reference is made to another document.	ca. 322 1/2
TS 12.544. See A, 3, n. 14	1147	A widow is adjudicated one-sixth of a house (situated at two bazaars) as an equivalent for 40 d. due her as marriage portion and other obligations of her late husband. The place is used as living quarters. (B)	ca. 300

ULC Or 1080 J 283. Munajjā b. Solomon, one of the parties, signed TS 13 J 3, f. 6 in 1145	Early twelfth century	Fragmentary deposition in court concerning a house estimated to be worth 300 d. and for which 270 d. were offered. Complicated case of inheritance and heirs who had become Muslims.	270–300
Firkovitch II, 1700, f. 8*b*	1156	A widow buys from her brother-in-law half of her late husband's house for 160 d.	320
TS NS J 190*v*	ca. 1240	Two and a quarter out of 24 shares of a sugar workshop in which its partial proprietor, a physician, lived, are sold for 25 d. (B)	270

GROUP VII.

Houses for 400 dinars and above

Source	Date	Circumstances	Price of house in dinars
ULC Or 1080 J 7; see A, 1, n. 93; A, 2, n. 35	1040	The uppermost story, worth 295 d., of a large house in Qayrawān, Tunisia, is ceded by a husband to his wife at divorce. He owed her 300 d. (R)	ca. 600
Mosseri A 82; see A, 1, n. 88	ca. 1060	Nahray b. Nissīm buys from his brother-in-law and the sons of the latter's late brother one-third of a house worth 150 d.	450
TS 8 J 9, fs. 2–3, esp. f. 2*v*, l. 14, *India Book* 284	1102	Complicated lawsuit between the buyer, the India trader Joseph Lebdi, and the seller, Nājiya, the wife of Japheth b. Abraham, The Pride of the Congregation, about a house bought for 500 d.	500

Source	Date	Circumstances	Price of house in dinars
AIU VII D 7; see A, 3, n. 8	1102	Joseph Lebdi acquires half a house for 300 d. and retains the former proprietor as tenant.	600
TS K 25, f. 284. See A, 1, n. 79	ca. 1120	Six and two-thirds of the twenty-four shares of a compound consisting of two houses and two stables with upper floors cost 220 d. (R)	ca. 800
Bodl. e 98, f. 63	1136	With the consent of his wife, a husband mortgages one-twelfth of a house on the Jazīra isle against a debt of 55 d. to be repaid during six years.	660
Bodl. d 66 (2878), f. 99; see A, 2, n. 55	1139	Two partners build a house in the Muṣāṣa quarter, and one sells to the other one half of it at a price of 300 d. to be paid in three installments, once every five months.	600
Firkovitch II, 1700, f. 18a; see A, 1, n. 86	1156	One-eighth of a house is bought in the Street of the Wine Dealers in the neighborhood of the Little Market of the Vizier for a minor sister by her brother at the price of 50 d. (B)	400
Maimonides, *Responsa*, I, 32	ca. 1202	One forty-eighth of a house is sold in times of famine for 12 d.	ca. 600
Bodl. d 65 (2877), f. 44	Dec. 1217	One government official sells to another one-quarter of a house for 150 d.	600
TS NS J 190	ca. 1240	Two and a quarter shares in a sugar factory, known as the *sukn* (residence and/or office) of the physician al-Rashid Samaw'al are sold (to a third person).	550

TRANSFER TAX AND COMMISSION

As a rule, neither the Muslim nor the Jewish contracts on the sale of houses mention the taxes or commissions involved. A rabbinical court record that does is translated here. See A, 3, nn. 36, 37.

A Court Record on the Sale of a House
in the al-Mamṣūṣa Quarter, Fustat

Bodl. MS Heb. d 66 (Cat. 2878), f. 109, Item II

Translation

Received by the Trustee as the price of the house in the al-Mamṣūṣa quarter: 123 dinars.

Paid from this: the taxes on it (*mu'an-hā*), kept by The Glory: 3 + 1/3 + 1/4 dinars, also 4 1/2 dinars commission (*dalāla*), and 8 dinars and 2 qīrāṭs [1/12 dinar], and also 1/3 dinar, kept by The Glory.

We have made the symbolic purchase [see *Med. Soc.*, II, 329] from The Glory, the elder Abū Saʿīd b. Thābit, on Friday, 29th Sivan 1456 [June 22, 1145]*, that he has received the sums recorded in this document in his name.

[Signatures]

Ḥiyyā, son of R. Isaac [active 1129–1159,
(may he) r(est in) E(den) see *Med. Soc.*, II, 513]
Nathan, son of R. Samuel [active 1128–1153, see
(of) b(lessed) m(emory) *ibid.*]

[Nathan also wrote the Court record.]

[Added on the left margin in the same hand, but in larger script:]

The total amount [of 123 dinars including the sums delivered to The Glory] went to Abū Saʿd b. Abu 'l-Ḥusayn [the seller].

COMMENTS

The two agents active in this transaction appear together in TS NS Box 246, f. 22, ll. 25–28, a list of notables compiled around 1142 (ed. N. Allony, see *Med. Soc.*, II, 480, sec. 26). They act together also in a court session recorded on the reverse side of our manuscript (d 66, f. 109), where a woman receives from The Glory 24 dinars kept for her by The Trustee. The latter, whose full title was Abu 'l-Faḍl, The Trustee, the Delight of the Congregations and Glory of the Yeshiva, no doubt, was a well-to-do merchant, whom the courts, as here, entrusted with sums belonging to an absent person, a widow,

*A. Neubauer and A. E. Cowley (*Catalogue of the Hebrew Manuscripts in the Bodleian Library* [Oxford, 1906], p. 394) read the two numerals *nw* (56) erroneously as one, namely, as an Alif (1), and dated the MS as written in 1090. The date 1145 is absolutely assured by the time of the signatories and other persons mentioned in the document. (Ashtor, *Prix*, p. 184, has to be changed accordingly.)

or an orphan. The Glory is an abbreviation of the title Glory of the Cantors. The cantor dabbled in financial matters, and it is likely that he himself was the sale's agent. The third sum (besides the tax advanced by him and the commission) probably represented expenditure for repairs in the house prior to its sale and a small bonus (1/3 d.) to a clerk.

As I understand this record, the sale's tax and commission (and repairs) had to be borne by the seller, but he indemnified himself by charging them to the purchaser.

Appendix B

The Cost of Rents

In Communal Buildings

The stated purpose of the donation of properties to the community was not to provide cheap housing. The gifts were made for maintenance of the synagogues, their lighting for study at night, for weekly distributions of bread to the needy, and for other religious or charitable objects. In practice, most of the premises belonging to the communal chest were inhabited by poor people. In normal times, the payments of rent were comparatively regular. Even beggars were advised: "Just as you beg for your food, beg for your rent." One account is particularly impressive where, in the course of twenty-one consecutive months, in nineteen, 3 dirhems were paid, in one, 2 1/2, and in another, 2; the tenant, as the sums show, must have been a needy person (ENA 1822 A, f. 68*v, Med. Soc.*, II, 432, sec. 161; Gil, *Foundations*, p. 476, does not have the *verso*). Consequently, the massive testimony of the Geniza accounts from the eleventh through the thirteenth century is an important source for the study of housing, especially of the poorer sections of the population. The conclusions drawn from the analysis of seven accounts undertaken in this appendix in comparison with other material on the subject are summarized in A, 3, above.

The accounts analyzed are described in *Med. Soc.*, II, App. A, and printed with a translation and important comments in Gil, *Foundations*. They are referred to here according to their numbers in *Med. Soc.*, II, and in Gil's book, for example, A 6 = *Med. Soc.*, II, 414, sec. 6; Gil 22 = Gil, *Foundations*, p. 193, no. 22.

Gil, *Foundations*, pp. 485–509, lists chronologically 105 houses with the monthly revenue from the individual rooms, apartments, and stores. An alphabetical list of the same houses is found in Gil's Index, s.v. "*dār*," pp. 540–543. His alphabetical list of tenants and their monthly rents (pp. 517–520), mentions only the persons noted in the chronological list of houses, that is, of whom it is not stated in which house they lived. Finally, Gil's table 2 (p. 72), also chronologically arranged, lists the stores and the rents paid for them.

In the analysis that follows, the lists are arranged according to the amount of rent paid. The lists also show how many tenants paid each amount. Other details are added when found in the sources. The amounts are in dirhems, of low silver content, about 40 of which represent the equivalent of 1 gold dinar. The term *bayt* may mean "for a room," or "by a family," and in many instances it is difficult to decide which is meant.

GROUP I (1042–1043)

A 6 and 7 (Gil 22 and 26) belong to a group of communal accounts, all written by the cantor and court clerk Japheth b. David Ben Shekhanya, complementing one another.

A 6 and 7

Amount of monthly rent	*Number of tenants paying this amount*
2 3/4	Four, two of whom women, all for a *khuṣṣ*, a room made of reeds or other light material.
3	Three, one for a *qaṣr*, a structure only partly connected with the main building, one for the shop of a flax worker, and one by a person mentioned by name only.
4	Four, one for the shop of a maker of spindles, one for a *qāʿa*, or room on a ground floor (occupied by a woman), one for a qaṣr, and one for a *bayt*, or room.
5–5 1/2 (two monthly payments of 2 1/2 and 2 3/4	Four, one for a *dār*, house.
6 1/2	One.
7 3/4–8	One, for two rooms, occupied by an apothecary.

9	One.
12	One, from a family.

Ten parties living in one house; four occupied a bayt, five a *khuṣṣ* (one of whom did not pay his rent), and one a *qaṣr*. Two *khuṣṣ*, one described as small, were unoccupied (A 7 [Gil 26], 11. 4–14).

A 8 (Gil 16)

In two cases the rent here is higher by half a dirhem than in A 7, and in one case by a full dirhem.

Amount of monthly rent	*Number of tenants paying this amount*
2 1/2	Two, one of whom occupied a *khuṣṣ*.
2 3/4	Four, three of whom were women; one is described as "the European," and another as "the wife [that is, widow] of the goldsmith."
3	Two, a porter and "the slavegirl of the wool merchant." The girl appears with the same rent in an account written in Arabic characters and dated 1041 (A 5). The wool merchant was probably unmarried and, according to Jewish law, not permitted to live with a maidservant under one roof. See *Med. Soc.*, I, 134.
4	Two, an astrologer and a maker of spindles.
4 1/2 and 5 1/2	Two, a porter and a man called Baghdādī, who, in A 6, paid 4 and 5, respectively.

A two-room apartment and a small room are listed as unoccupied.

GROUP II (1181–1184)

Twelve monthly and bimonthly accounts of revenue from public buildings have been preserved from the years 1181–1184 (see *Med. Soc.*, II 417–419, secs. 25–36; Gil, *Foundations*, pp. 327–361). Here are presented the data for one building. The House of the Glassmaker, because the rents paid by its tenants are listed in accounts A 32 and 33 (Gil 88 and 87) for three consecutive months (July 22–October 18, 1183), when they remained constant. One place, indicated here in parentheses, was unoccupied during the third month. In the first two months, the house was inhabited by fifteen parties, referred to by name without specification of the premises occupied. The groundfloor most probably served as a workshop or as a store. The rents paid were as follows:

Amount of monthly rent	*Number of tenants paying this amount*
1 1/2	One
2–2 1/2	Four, three of them women
4	One
5	Four
6	Two
(7)	One
9	One
15 1/2	One, ground floor

A later account A 43 (Gil 101) dated June 1201 (see Group III) records only ten parties in the same house, with one apartment unoccupied and a deferment granted for the payment of the rent for the ground floor. (I read now *musallakh*, from *salkh*, end of month, deferment granted until the end of the next month. In *Med. Soc.*, II, 420, sec. 43, I took *mslk* as *maslak*.) The rents in that house were then as follows:

Amount of monthly rent	*Number of tenants paying this amount*
2 1/2	Two, one a Muslim
3 1/2	One, "an inner upper apartment"
4	One
5–5 1/2	Four, two Muslims
6	Two

The rooms in the lowest category were perhaps rearranged so that three of them brought the same revenue of 8 1/2 dirhems as four in accounts A 32 and A 33.

GROUP III (THIRTEENTH CENTURY)

The catastrophic decline of Fustat in the wake of the great famine and plague starting in 1201 (see *Med. Soc.*, II, 141) is evidenced by the many unoccupied places noted in A 43 (Gil 101). It is all the more noteworthy that the prices of the premises, as a rule, remained steady.

The rents paid for all the properties listed in A 43 (Gil 101) were as follows:

Amount of monthly rent	*Number of tenants paying this amount*
1	One, for a *ṭārma*, or light structure.
1 3/4	Two, one for a *ṭabaqa*, or an apartment on an upper floor.
2	Four
2 1/4	One, for a storeroom
2 1/2	Two, one of them a Muslim.
3	Two, one for a room on the ground floor, *sufl*, of the tower of the Fortress.
3 1/2	One, for an inside *ṭabaqa (juwwāniyya)*.
4	Two [14 in Gil, 378, (a) 2 is a misprint].
5	Eleven, one for an apartment in the tower, another for a *qāʿa*, or ground floor, a third for a *mustaraqa*, or loggia, and a fourth for a *ṭabaqa*. At least one tenant was a Muslim.
5 1/2	One
6	Six, one for "a small shop." One was occupied by a Christian, Ben Qosṭā [Gil, p. 379, b, 3, read *w* for *q*].
8	One, for a *qāʿa*.
1/4 dinar (ca. 9 dirhems; *r* stands for *rubʿ*, a quarter)	
10	One, for "a house."
12	One. Occupied by Abū Zikrī who paid 10 and 12 in other accounts.
13	One. Occupied by Abū (not Akhū) Sahl who paid 10 and 13 in other lists.
18	One, for the house on the Jazīra (island in the Nile).
20	One. Occupied by a physician.
45	General revenue from a caravanserai.

Three ground floors, two upper floors, four apartments (*sukn*), and one house, ten places altogether, are listed as vacant.

Account A 95 (Gil 142) is from June 1247 and lists in an orderly way the income and expenses for one month. The rents are as follows:

Amount of monthly rent	*Number of tenants paying this amount*
1	One
2	Three, one a tax collector, another a Syro-Palestinian; one place was a storeroom.
2 1/2	One, a European or Byzantine Jew.
3	Four, a wailing woman, a water carrier, a coppersmith, and a Kohen.
3 1/4	One, "The [former] neighbor of Hānī from (Minyat) Ziftā.
3 1/2	One, a *bayyāʿ*, or seller of foodstuff.
4	Three, a dyer, a gravedigger, and "the son of the carpenter."
4 3/4	One, a maker of wax candles.
5	Three, one a *firnās*, or social service officer, another bore an honorific title (ʿImād, support [of the government]), the third party was from a well-known family named Ghuzūlī, Netmaker.
6	Three, a money assayer, a *mutasawwiq*, or purveyor, and a *mugharbil*, or "sifter" (worker in the building branch).
7	One, a Kohen.
8	One, a *bayyāʿ*.
10	One, a *dahhān*, or oil painter, a dyer, and "the son of a nākhudā, or ship-owner" probably an immigrant from Yemen.
11	One, not specified.

Appendix C

Furnishings

The Geniza documents have several terms for furnishings in the widest sense of the word, comprising everything movable in the house. In the trousseau lists the words used mostly referred to (travel) outfit or equipment (*jahāz, raḥl, shuwār, shūra*) (see *Med. Soc.*, III, 124). The most general term for furnishings was *qumāsh*, household effects (from *qamash*, to collect), as in TS NS J 228 (Malīj, 1134): "Estimate of the qumāsh of Lady Splendor"; or TS NS J 231 (Fustat, 1225): "We were present in the place where the qumāsh jihāz, the household effects forming the outfit of the virgin Noble, were assembled for evaluation." But when a newlywed asks her mother to send her her qumāsh (ENA NS 22, f. 20*v*, l. 6), the context shows that only the copper vessels were intended, and in the trousseau list TS K 25, f. 269 (early thirteenth century) qumāsh is the specific name of the Clothing section, coming, as usual, between Jewelry and Bedding. Such shifting and narrowing of terms is a common occurrence in human speech in general. See now N. A. Stillman, "*Ḳumāsh*," *EI*², V, 373–374.

When a household was dissolved, all that was found in it was comprised under the term *qashsha* (from *qashsh*, also meaning to collect, to gather). While settling the estate of his wife, which went to his son, Meir b. al-Hamadānī, the correspondent of Moses Maimonides (*Med. Soc.*, II, 248, 577 n. 37) writes to the judge Elijah b. Zechariah: "From the entire qashsha nothing should remain, except three pairs of round cushions, the most precious among them, two long leather cushions, also the finest ones, the woolen *martaba*, the silk robe, the chandelier, and the silver scales, please may your honor send all these to your servant, my son Mūsā [Moses]. All the rest should be sold." Immediately three other items were added, an implement for making fire (*zinād*), a knife for cutting meat (*sāṭūr*), and a mirror. There follows an incredible variety of articles, deposited with different persons, and instructions how to dispose of them (TS 10 J 12, f. 10, ll. 19–23, and passim). But qashsha was used also in a narrow sense, for instance, "articles of personal use" as in the will Bodl. MS Heb. b 13, (Cat. 2834, no. 27) f. 46, l. 25, or even one's old clothing as in TS 13 J 25, f. 9, ll. 18–19, *Nahray* 181 (in the plural: *qishāsh*). Hence the dealers in secondhand objects, who occupied a street in the bazaar of Fustat, were called *qāshsh*, or the like (see *Med. Soc.*, I, 437, bottom, n. 5).

Thus one sees that a comprehensive term for furnishings was in living use when it was needed for legal purposes, in particular, when the furnishings were part of either the bride's trousseau, before she moved to her husband's house, or the estate of a deceased person, when it had to be decided how to dispose of them.

In the following, wherever feasible, the class to which the proprietors of a piece of furnishing belonged is noted. These abbreviations are used:

LMC	Lower middle class
UMC	Upper middle class
VMod.	In very modest circumstances

With a few exceptions the classification adopted in *Med. Soc.*, III, 418–419, is followed.

If not otherwise stated, the prices are in dinars, the place is Fustat or unknown, and Rūmī means Byzantine.

1. Seating and bedding: terminology.—Sitting and sleeping facilities, together with draperies and carpets, usually formed the third part of a trousseau list, preceded by jewelry and clothing. Occasionally the group had a name (either in a superscription or in the summary of its total value): "What is spread out and what is hung up," *al-busuṭ wal-taʿālīq* (TS J 1, f. 29, col. III, l. 24 [ca. 1140]), or, in inverted order, "al-taʿlīq[!] wal-busuṭ" (TS 24.1 [1082]).

When summarized separately, sitting and sleeping facilities were described as *busuṭ* (TS K 15, f. 65, col. IV, ll. 4–11 [no date]), or *furush* (Firkovitch II, 1700, f. 24 b, l. 1 [1156]; both written by the same scribe, Mevōrākh b. Nathan). The two words are derived from similar but slightly different roots, the first meaning "spreading out," the latter, "laying out on the ground." When the two are used together, *furush* refers more to bedding and *busuṭ* to sitting facilities, as in the will Bodl. MS Heb. b 13, (Cat. 2834, no. 27), f. 46, l. 25. A person's individual sleeping equipment was designated by the rhymed expression *ghaṭā' wa-waṭā'*, cover and bedding (*ibid.*, l. 24), or waṭā' alone, as in TS 28.6, sec. C (1074), a power of attorney:

"The waṭā' of my daughter consists of a *muzarra* sleeping bag, or dressing gown, a Ṭabarī pad, a Ṭabarī mattress, and two pillows."

The Heb. equivalent of busuṭ and furush (*kelē maṣṣā'ōt*, textiles spread out, is based on pre-Islamic usage (TS 20.47*v*, l. 13 [Karaite]).

2. *The* martaba, *or divan, and its alternatives.*—The long divan or sofa, the main piece of furnishing in a house, usually consisted of several sections, *qiṭa'*. In many of the cases in which the number of sections is not indicated, we may infer from the high prices that the items registered did indeed have more than one section. The prices are in dinars.

MS Mark	*Material*	*Price*	*Class*
HIGH-PRICED MARTABAS, NUMBER OF SECTIONS NOT NOTED			
ENA 2738, f. 33*v*, l. 10	Rūmī brocade with two cushions and back	50	UMC
Bodl. a 3 (2873), f. 43, ll. 12–13 (1059)	Brocade	40	UMC
Firkovitch II, 1700, f. 25, ll. 2–3 (1156)	Silk with two cushions and back of Rūmī brocade	40	UMC
TS 12.12, l. 13 (ca. 1020)	Brocade with back	35	UMC
TS 20.7 (1050)	Rūmī brocade	30	UMC
TWO SECTIONS			
Bodl. d 75 (no Cat.) f. 20*v*, l. 5, *Nahray* 94 (ca. 1055)	Ṭabarī (silk), sent from Ascalon, Palestine, to Egypt	—	(LMC)
THREE SECTIONS			
Bodl. f 56 (2821), f. 47*v*, margin (ca. 1182)	Ḥāfiẓī (tradename) Dabīqī (linen)	25	LMC
Ibid., l. 5	Ṭabarī (silk)	2	LMC

MS Mark	*Material*	*Price*	*Class*
TS J 1, f. 29, col. III, l. 18 (ca. 1140)	Jazā'irī (Greek islands stuff; brocade)	15	Rich
Ibid., l. 19	Rūmī brocade	15	Rich
Bodl. f 56 (2821), f. 48, ll. 21–22 (1186)	Silk	12	LMC
Firkovitch II, 1700, f. 26 b (1156)	Brocade	12	UMC
ULC Or 1080, Box 5, f. 15	Brocade	9	UMC
TS Arabic Box 6, f. 2, col. II	Ṭabaristān (genuine Iranian)	8	UMC
TS 12.167*v*, l. 9 (ca. 1050)	Muṣabbagh (dyed)	—	LMC
TS 20.8 A, l. 11 (1155)	Dabīqī (linen)	5	LMC
ENA 1822 A, f. 10 (ca. 1165)	White Dabīqī	3	Modest
Ibid.	Ṭabarī	2	Modest
Bodl. d 66 (2878), f. 77 (1161)	Dabīqī	2	Poor
TS 16.86, l. 9 (ca. 1166/7)	Dabīqī	2	Poor
TS 12.526, l. 8 (ca. 1170)	—	2	Modest
TS 8 J 9, f. 17 a (1116)	—	1	VMod.
Ibid.	Ṭabarī	1	VMod.
FOUR SECTIONS			
TS J 1, f. 29, col. III, l. 17	Bahā'ī (tradename)	15	Rich
Bodl. f 56 (2821), f. 47*v*, margin (ca. 1182)	Brocade	15	LMC

MS Mark	*Material*	*Price*	*Class*
BM Or 5561 b, f. 3, l. 22 (1164)	Silk	5	Poor
ENA 1822 A, f. 10 (ca. 1165)	—	5	Modest
TS K 15, f. 100, col. II, l. 5 (1199)	Silk	5	LMC
TS 12.141, l. 8 (ca. 1200)	–	4	Modest

FIVE SECTIONS

TS Arabic Box 6, f. 2, col. II (ca. 1100)	Brocade	60	UMC
Ibid.	Ṭabarī	5	UMC
ENA 2743, f. 2, l. 16	–	60	UMC
Ibid., l. 17	–	20	UMC
ENA 2808, f. 13, l. 15	Dabīqī linen	50	UMC
Bodl. a 3 (2873), f. 42, l. 24 (1117)	Brocade	40	UMC
TS Misc. Box 8, f. 97 (ca. 1090)	Dabīqī	25	?
TS 8 J 29, f. 7 (eleventh century)	Brocade	20	LMC
TS 24.15, l. 3 (1125)	Dabīqī	20	LMC
Bodl. a 2 (2805), f.6 (1127)	Dabīqī	20	LMC
Ibid.	Ṭabaristān	15	LMC

MS Mark	*Material*	*Price*	*Class*
TS 10 J 21, f. 4 b, l. 15 (ca. 1100)	Maghrebī (brocade)	15	LMC
TS 28.23, 1.4 (1106)	White Dabīqī	11	Mod.
ULC Or 1080, Box 5, f.15, l.8	Brocade	9	UMC
TS 12.488, l.8 (1108-1119)	Ṭabaristān silk	8	VMod.
TS 16.86, l.9 (ca. 1160)	—	6	Mod.
TS NS J 410, col. II, l.1 (ca. 1100)	Ṭabarī	5	LMC
TS 24.5 (1111)	Ṭabarī	5	Destitute
TS K 15, f. 111, col. I, l.17	Ṭabarī with mattress	5	VMod.
Bodl. d 66 (2878), f. 47, m., col. II (1146)	Ṭabaristān	4	UMC
TS 20.8 A, l.11 (1155)	Ṭabarī	3	LMC
TS NS J 390	Rūmī brocade	—	LMC
TS K 25, f. 166, l.19	Ṭabarī with mattress	—	VMod.

SIX SECTIONS

Firkovitch II, 1700, f. 26 b (1156)	Brocade	42	UMC
TS J 1, f. 29, col. III, l.15 (Ca. 1140)	Rūmī brocade	40	Rich

MS Mark	*Material*	*Price*	*Class*
Bodl. d 66 (2878), f. 47, m., col. II (1146)	Brocade	25	UMC
TS Arabic Box 6, f. 2, col. II, ll. 3–4	Dabīqī, two of the six sections sūsānjird	20	UMC
TS J 1, f. 48, col. II, ll. 4–7	Two martabas, each of six sections, plus ṭarrāḥa	—	LMC
TS 20.8	Rūmī (brocade)	14	LMC

This list (which could be expanded) shows that neither the number of sections, nor the type of materials, nor the economic position of the proprietor was a safe indicator of the value of a martaba. A person could own one for 60 dinars and another one for 5, and a Dabīqī linen martaba consisting of three sections could be had for 25 dinars or for 2. The wide diversity is to be explained by the fact that many pieces were much used heirlooms or secondhand, and were destined for different purposes (reception hall, bedroom). This diversity would have been even more pronounced had the list not been confined to items consisting of several sections and a few high-priced martabas.

On the other hand the standardization of the fabrics used for martabas is remarkable. Brocade and Ṭabari(stān) silk are represented in approximately equal number, whereas Egyptian linen, number one for other purposes, falls somewhat behind as a martaba fabric.

Brocade.—Of twenty-five martaba covers of brocade, noted at random, ten are designated as of Byzantine provenance; hence their high price. It is likely that most of the unspecified ones came from the same source. I translate here Rūmī as Byzantine (and not Christian Europe), because in the trousseau lists Rūmī is often mentioned together, and opposed to, Ṣiqillī, Sicilian, the island from which Western textiles were imported. "The rich bride" (TS J 1, f. 29) had, in addition to martabas made of Rūmī brocade, two of Jazā'irī—which should not be translated as "Algerian" (the regular meaning in later centuries), but as "from Greek islands" (see *EI*[2], II, 521/2). A Jazā'irī back on a brocade martaba is noted in a marriage contract from the same period (TS K 15, f. 65, col. IV, l. 5), and a ṭarrāḥa daybed made from this material is noted half a century earlier (ENA 2747, f. 1, l. 6). Maghrebī, that is Tunisian, fabric, used exceptionally for a martaba of five sections (see TS 10 J 21, f. 4 b, l. 15) probably was also brocade; Maghrebī curtains, bedspreads, and pillows made of brocade are mentioned in several Geniza documents.

Ṭabari(stān) silk.—This renowned textile (see A, 4, n. 2, above) is always described as either genuine or imitation. Of twenty-five samples, eleven martabas were made of genuine Ṭabaristāns, and fourteen were imitated locally, five in Ramle: TS 12.12 (ca. 1020); TS 20.47*v* (long before 1080); Bodl. a 3 (2873), f. 43 (1059, two such martabas); TS NS J 390 (late eleventh or early twelfth century). In *Med. Soc.*, I, 50, n. 53, I left it open whether Ramle, Palestine, or a place of the same name in Egypt was meant. I have not found a single reference to the latter in the Geniza; during the eleventh century, however, the former appears in it as a great center of international trade. Many emigrants from Iran and Iraq settled, temporarily or permanently, in Ramle, Palestine, including Ibn Killis, later vizier of the first Fatimid caliph of Egypt. It is reasonable to assume that some of those Easterners developed an industry there with which they had been familiar in their countries of origin. When we find a two-section Ṭabarī martaba (see listing above) exported from Ascalon, the port of Ramle, it is reasonable to conclude that it was manufactured in the latter city. For the Hārūnī Ṭabarī made in Ramle see p. 306, below.

This heavy silk fabric was also used for the alternatives of the martaba, the *majlis*-seat and the *ṭarrāḥa* daybed (see above, A, 4, nn. 3–5, 8), and for parts of the bedding, namely, the *barda*ʿ*a*, the pad laid on top of the mattress, and the *maṭraḥ* (see *ibid.*, n. 7). If my memory does not fail me, I have never come across a *firāsh*, the basic equipment of bedding, which may be tentatively translated as mattress, made of Ṭabaristān or its imitations.

Ṭabarīs were so popular that in the earlier half of the Geniza period brides brought into the marriage a *bayt Ṭabarī*, literally, a Ṭabarī-house, meaning a trunk filled with that costly material (ENA NS 3, f. 24, l. 19; see Friedman, *Marriage*, no. 1, l. 26, where the sources about these occurrences are collected). I suspect this usage is pre-Islamic, for *bayt*, in the meaning of container, is Aramaic rather than Arabic. The semi-independent rulers of Ṭabaristān sent such material to the Sassanid kings as a yearly "gift" centuries before they were forced to do the same for the caliphs of Baghdad (see A, 4, n. 3).

The Geniza uses a similar expression for another textile called Buzyōn or Fizyōn. A Karaite bride in modest circumstances, who married in Jerusalem in Jan. 1028, had, besides a Ṭabarī martaba, a Buzyōn one, presumably named after Buzyān, a place near Herāt, Afghanistan (Persian long *ā* is pronounced *ō*) (ULC Add. 3430; see App. D, Doc. I, below). Buzyān brocade was highly valued in early Islamic times; its colors and patterns are described in al-Jāḥiẓ's treatise on international trade (see Serjeant, *Islamic Textiles*, 15–16, p. 66). In an ancient Geniza marriage contract (TS 24.30, ed. Friedman, *Marriage*, no. 5, l. 28) a bride has a bayt Fizyōn (= Buzyōn) together with a bayt Ṭabarī, a container for each of these precious fabrics. But in the marriage contract of Karīma b. ʿAmmār (= al-Wuḥsha; see *Med. Soc*, III, 346–352) written around 1090, a Buzyōn ṭarrāha with its two cushions cost only 2 dinars (ENA 2727, f. 8, l. 18). They had probably been in use for several generations. The poor bride in TS NS J 461, l.16, ENA 2747, f. 1, l. 6 (Med. Soc. III, 396, no. 36) had a Buzyōn. (Originally, I derived Fizyōn from Greek *fasian(os)*, pheasant, designating a textile with figures of brilliantly colored pheasants; but because of the ō pronunciation and the wide use of Buzyōn-Fizyōn in early Islamic times I prefer the derivation from an Iranian place. The fact that a Rūmī Buzyōn is mentioned once does not prove Byzantine origin. Just as one had Ṭabarī Ramlī, that is, Ṭabaristān imitated in Ramle, one had Buzyōn imitated by the Rūm. (See Serjeant, *Islamic Textiles*, 15–16, p. 77 [from Ibn al-Faqīh]).

Dabīqī linen and sundry fabrics.—The third major textile serving as cover for a martaba and similar furniture was Egyptian linen, although it was somewhat less used for this purpose than brocade and Ṭabari(stān). Wherever the Dabīqī is described as white, the divan it covers was probably intended predominantly for nightly rest.

Silk martabas are rarely noted. Silk (ḥarīr) was manufactured in those days almost everywhere, but good silk normally came to Egypt from Spain or Sicily (see *Med. Soc.*, I, 102–104). The *siglaton*, a heavy damask renowned during the Middle Ages in Europe under this name as in the Near East (see Goitein, *Letters*, p. 77), occurs as a martaba cover only in the trousseau of "the rich bride" (TS J1, f. 29, col. III, l. 21) and perhaps once or twice as a decoration of a martaba made of another material.

Wool is virtually absent. Thus far, I have found a woolen martaba only in the letter of Meir b. al-Hamadāni, mentioned above (TS 10 J 12, f. 10, l. 20). Armenian martabas were bought in Fustat and sold in Tinnīs on the Mediterranean coast by a merchant traveling to Ascalon and Jerusalem around 1060 (TS 10 J 16, f. 10, l. 17, *Nahray* 156).

As in our own times, textiles and other manufactured goods could have trade names. The Dabīqī linen of Ḥāfiẓī make was used not only for martabas but also for a variety of clothing. It is probably named after the Fatimid caliph al-Ḥāfiẓ (1131–1149) (see B, n. 125). To the best of my knowledge, none of the Geniza documents mentioning it precedes his reign. The Bahā'ī brocade martaba of "the rich bride" was produced in a workshop of a Mr. Bahā', Splendor. Several men with this name or title appear in our documents. In a report by Nahray b. Nissīm to Tyre, Lebanon, about prices in the capital of Egypt, the Hārūnī Ṭabarī martabas cost about 2 dinars per piece (JNUL 2, l. 11, ed. E. Strauss, *Zion*, 7 [1952], 152 [for *'l-'bry 'l-mk'tb* read *al-Ṭabarī al-marātib*]). Hārūnī, derived from Aaron, means Kohen, or Mr. Cohen, in Arabic. The recipient of this letter was on his way back from Tyre to Ramle, Palestine, and the price list was sent to him from Egypt to instruct him on how to buy. Thus Mr. Cohen in Ramle was the, or one of the manufacturers of the Ramle Ṭabarī. Since he is called in a letter exchanged between two Jews, Hārūnī and not Kohen, it is evident that his Ṭabarī was sold in the bazaar of Old Cairo under that Arabic trade name.

3. Cushions and pillows as comfort and decor.—The materials for these furnishings were to a certain extent the same as those used for divans and daybeds. But two fabrics were used exclusively or predominantly for cushions. The first and most precious one was an embroidered, originally Iranian material named *sūsanjird*. Opinion was divided whether the first part of this word was derived from *sūsan*, lily, that flower originally forming the main theme of decoration, or *sūzan*, needle, describing the textile as a piece of artistic tapestry. In all the Geniza documents I have seen the word is invariably spelled with *s*, not with *z*. Ernst Herzfeld (*Geschichte der Stadt Samarra*, pp. 223–224, with bibliographic notes on the subject) asserts that the material is named after a town (Shushankird), as are so many other Iranian textiles. Figures of birds are the only embroideries of sūsanjird noted in the Geniza (see A, 4, n. 32). Sūsanjird could be white and decorated with ornamental stripes (see *ibid.*, n. 28).

The other favorite precious textile used for cushions was *sharb*, a very fine linen manufactured in Tinnīs on the Mediterranean coast, mostly of pomegranate color. Both sūsanjird and Tinnīs sharb were popular throughout the "classical" Geniza period.

In the first half of the eleventh century it seems to have been customary not to indicate the color of the cushions, and frequently to list only their number: six (TS 12.167, poor, 1027/8), seven (Bodl. MS Heb. a 2 [Cat. 2805], f. 4, poor, 1029), eight (TS 12.690, l. 4, scribe Japheth b. David), eleven (TS 12.156, l. 12, Karaite, old), twelve (ENA NS 17, f. 12, l. 6, poor, ca. 1000; ULC Or 1080 J 140, col. II, l. 9, modest, 1045), fourteen (TS 8.97, LMC, Karaite, old), twenty (TS 20.6, 1. 20, LMC, 1037). Later, the clerks became more specific, probably in order to keep the dowry separate from materials acquired by the husband.

An average of four or five pairs of living-room cushions seems to have been standard for a middle-class bridal outfit. The number of over forty cushions noted in ENA NS 3, f. 24, l. 17, is a special case. That girl brought in also a bridal canopy worth 150 dinars and a bridegroom's ceremonial seat (*takht*) worth 50 dinars (ll. 17 and 20), two items, as the editor rightly observes, not found elsewhere. Clearly, that bride's late father had been a caterer who provided, for a compensation, the furnishings required at a wedding: a canopy for the bride, a ceremonial seat for the groom, and partly precious (fifteen for 100 d.), partly regular (eighteen for 20 d.) cushions. Now that the father was dead, that business equipment was part of her trousseau. The commercial or gratuitous provision of jewelry and attire for weddings is recorded for pre-Islamic Mecca and is still habitual in Arabia. The lending of furnishing requirements for that purpose is to be understood in the same way. Cf. p. 122, above, where a woman is requested to lend precious hangings for a festive occasion.

4. *Representative listings of seating and bedding facilities.*—Now that the various constituents of the seating and bedding facilities have been discussed individually, here a few complete listings are translated; d. stands for dinar.

(*a*) TS 24.80, ll. 18–22 (Oct. 1039. Total worth of outfit: 140 d. Modest).

[Seating]	[Price]
Two Ṭabaristān martabas and six cushions with borders	20

[Bedding]	40
A bedstead with ebony decorations, two Sicilian firāshes, a Ṭabarī pad, [four] pillows for sleep, six pillows of different colors, two cloaks [for sleep], a Maghrebi brocade blanket, and a sky blue canopy	

A sum of 60 dinars for seating and bedding out of a total outfit of 140 d. was exceptional. The bedding of this bride in modest circumstances is representative of one of the middle class. Most of the objects, no doubt, were heirlooms.

(*b*) TS Box J 1, f. 48, col. II, l. 4– col. III, l. 16 (ca. 1100. Total value of marriage gift and dowry 238 d. LMC).

[Seating]	
Two martabas, each of six sections One ṭarrāḥa Two blue Dabīqī cushions	Prices not preserved
Two pomegranate-colored Tinnīsī, two Sūsanjird, and two white cushions of fine linen	12
[Bedding]	
A white Sicilian firāsh, a Ṭabarī pad, four pillows "for the cheek," a cloak for sleep, a red blanket	15

(*c*) TS 12.12, ll. 13-17 (ca. 1020. Dowry 865. UMC. For her jewelry see App. D, X *a*, below).

[Seating]	
A brocade martaba with a support	35
A Ṭabarī majlis (seat) with two sections of genuine Ṭabaristān and two made in Ramle	50
Eight cushions of fine Tinnīsī linen	20
Two Dabīqī cushions with borders	15
[Bedding]	
Two Dabīqī firashes, two others, Sicilian, and a Ṭabarī pad	15
Nine sušanjird pillows	25
Three wraps for sleep and a kerchief	5
A Qurqūbī (heavy silk) blanket	15
[An item mostly destroyed]	2

A white canopy without patterns and with ornamental stripes	50
Total	232

A sum of 232 for seating and bedding as compared with the total outfit worth 865 (1:3.7) was normal.

Complete lists of seating and bedding facilities are included in App. D, Docs. I–V.

Appendix D

Selected Documents

DOCUMENTS I–V. FIVE TROUSSEAU LISTS

Introduction

Five trousseau lists with their usual division into jewelry, clothing, furnishings, and housewares, are presented here in full, because all these belongings serve to portray the outward appearance and, indeed, world of the medieval Mediterranean woman, who was largely confined to her home. Jewelry is part of any woman's attire, but the colorful and richly patterned sofas, couches, pillows, spreads, and hangings, which often were made of the same materials as a Geniza woman's dresses, could be regarded as an extension of herself; or, vice versa, she in her attractive clothing formed, so to speak, the most impressive item of the interior decoration of the home.

The first three trousseaus were chosen because of their diversity. The families of the first document, dated Jerusalem 1028, lived in modest circumstances, as did a very large section of the population represented in the Geniza.[1] They were by no means destitute, however, nor do they seem to have suffered from the Bedouin attacks that afflicted Palestine in the 1020s, for the composition of the dowry appears to be perfectly regular. The marriage gift of the groom (5 dinars given, 35 promised) and the dowry brought in by the bride (61 1/2 dinars) totaled 101 1/2 dinars, less than one-sixth of the amounts listed in the second document (40 + 100 marriage gift, 500 dowry), an engagement contract drawn up in Fustat in November 1146 between two well-to-do parties, representing the upper crust of Geniza society.

The third document is neither a marriage nor an engagement contract, but merely a trousseau list, originally attached to a ketubba, and therefore bearing no date or names of place and persons. It is written in the hand of the judge Nathan b. Samuel he-ḥāvēr of Fustat, of whom dated documents have been preserved from the years 1128–1153 and who lived for at least ten years after he ceased to appear as a signatory.[2] Thus Documents II and III are fairly contemporary. This bride's marriage gift (500 dinars) and dowry (1,600) amounted to 2,100 dinars, more than three times as much as that noted in the engagement contract of 1146.

There were also differences in kind. The well-to-do girl brought in with her, as usual, one maidservant, a confidante from her mother's home, who would help her to overcome the difficulties awaiting her in a strange household dominated by her mother- and sisters-in-law. The wealthy bride possessed a staff of two maids and two personal attendants. Her dowry included a library worth 250 dinars—a sum on which a modest family could live for ten years. She was probably the daughter of a rich physician who had recently died (for who would part with his library during his lifetime?), and about to marry another physician who was avid to have the books. Collections of books left by physicians were the most valuable ones recorded in the Geniza. The average price of a book in a physician's library sold publicly on two consecutive Tuesdays in November 1190 was approximately 1/4 dinar. Thus, this bride's library might have contained about a thousand manuscripts.[3]

The really wealthy Jews are scarcely represented in the Geniza. Most of them lived in (New) Cairo, and the Geniza synagogue was in Fustat. Moreover, the higher the status of a family, the more it tried to conceal evidence of its riches—too many rapacious government men watched out for easy prey. Under these circumstances the list of the "rich bride's" trousseau (probably discarded in the Geniza by chance because it had been replaced by a revised copy) is particularly welcome.

Document I differs from Documents II and III by its place and time, being written in Jerusalem 1028, whereas the other two were produced in the capital of Egypt around the middle of the twelfth century. Document I is distinguished also by the fact that it is a Karaite document, whereas all the other ketubbas translated here originated in the Rabbanite community, the main bulk of the Jewish population.

The Karaite ketubba differs widely from the Rabbanite. It was created during the "bourgeois revolution" of the early centuries of Islam and was, therefore, far more refined, expressive, and outspoken about the relations between husband and wife than the rigid Rabbanite ketubba, a remnant from antiquity. It was written in Hebrew, a language that could easily be handled, whereas Aramaic, obligatory in the Rabbanite ketubba, soon became a dead language. Finally, it spelled out the specific injunctions that a Karaite couple had to observe. I translate the document in full because I believe that it reflects the attitude toward marriage in Geniza times in general and not solely with respect to the Karaite denomination.

Documents IV and V, dated 1146 and 1156, were selected because they list the trousseaus of two sisters, leading to the assumption that they were more or less identical. They were, but not to the extent one would expect. This diversity reflects the general truth that each ketubba in the Geniza was unique and depended on the special circumstances in which the two families and the couple itself found themselves at the time of the engagement and marriage. Yet, these same documents, and, indeed, the trousseau lists from Fatimid and early Ayyubid times in general, prove that there were certain standards of clothing and other items for each layer of society. When the outfit of a bride fell considerably short in one respect, but exceeded her status in another, special reasons (often, but not always, easy to guess) must have prevailed.

To give just one, but very telling, example: In the often-discussed ketubba of Sahlān b. Abraham, the *payṭān* (writer of synagogal poetry) and leader of the Babylonian congregation of Fustat, the bride brings in clothing worth only 70 dinars, but furnishings and housewares worth 120 dinars (80 + 40 [see *Med. Soc.*, III, 378, sec. 36]). This utterly exceptional imbalance of the dowry may be explained as follows.[4] The bridegroom already bore all the titles a spiritual and communal leader could obtain in those days: *ḥavēr* of the Palestinian, the *allūf* of Hay Gaon's Babylonian yeshiva, *segan* Leader—probably of the other Babylonian yeshiva, *ḥemdat*, Delight, of the Nesī'ut, the family of the Exilarch. Thus he must have been well advanced in age, and this marriage was not his first.[5] The repudiated wife had taken with her the furnishings noted in her ketubba. Consequently, while discussing with his future in-laws the items of the dowry, Sahlān probably emphasized Bedding and Copper; for clothing, he himself would provide in due course, as promised in the ketubba. Naturally this is nothing but an educated guess. But those figures in the marriage contracts were of vital significance for the parties concerned, and we must try to understand them.

To repeat, the selection of trousseau lists and cognate documents translated and discussed is confined to the Fatimid and early Ayyubid periods. By the beginning of the thirteenth century a complete change in the nomenclature, and presumably also the look of clothing, occurred, no doubt under the influence of the Turkish

Easterners who now ruled Egypt. Another change was the reduction or complete disappearance of furnishings and housewares from the outfit of a bride.[6] Upper-class trousseau lists are almost absent from the Geniza after 1200.[7] This probably was a result of the catastrophic plague and famine of 1201–1202 which decimated the size of the population and depleted its resources, as well as of the accelerated exodus from Fustat to Cairo, a migration movement initiated long before by the upper class. Finally, Muslim bigotry, which reached its culmination in Mamluk times (1250–1517), had in the later Ayyubid period already begun to affect all aspects of life, including the attitude toward clothing of non-Muslims.

Documents II–V were all written during the middle of the twelfth century when the Jewish community was led by two high-standing court physicians, Abū Manṣūr Samuel b. Hananya (1140–1159) and his successor Hibat Allah Nethanel b. Moses ha-Levi, both known also from Arabic sources.[8] Although this period has been described (because of its incredible court intrigues and the heinous murders connected with them) as "one of the darkest chapters of Egyptian history,"[9] it is documented in the Geniza by many items that seem to show the Jewish community in an orderly and comparatively prosperous state.[10] The massive documentation in four detailed trousseau lists from this period provides us with a realistic notion of the wardrobe of a Jewish woman in twelfth-century Egypt and the interior of her house.

I had an additional reason for selecting documents II–V. Any evaluation of a bride's trousseau must start with a consideration of whether the prices listed are real or inflated in honor of the young couple and their families. The remark in Doc. II, fol. 47*v*, ll. 11–12, "a dinar is worth a dinar, real value, not doubled," and a similar statement in Doc. V, fol. 25 a, l. 18 assure us that we are dealing here with the real value of the outfit. Doc. II was written by judge Nathan b. Samuel he-ḥāvēr, Doc. V by his son Mevōrākh. Both seem to have adhered to the rule of giving the real estimates—unless expressly stated otherwise.[11] Doc. III was also written by Nathan b. Samuel; the proviso "a dinar is a dinar," if made at all, was included in the marriage contract, which we do not possess. Doc. IV, in which the elder of two sisters receives her trousseau back after she was widowed, is signed by Nathan b. Samuel and, I believe, also written by him, albeit in a more cursive script than the estimates. Since the purpose of the court record was to show that the trousseau had been returned in full, no prices are noted. According to all we know from contemporary documents the prices in the Karaite ketubba from the year 1028 (Doc. I) were real.

Words deleted in the original are put between two sets of square brackets [[ ]].

Document I

A Karaite Marriage Contract from Jerusalem
January 26, 1028

Translation

University Library Cambridge, ULC Add. 3430.[12]

In the Name of the Living God.
"And they built and were succesful."[13]
"In God they will triumph and glory."[14]
"And the Judean elders build and are successful."[15]

On Friday, the twenty-sixth of the month of Shevat of the year 1339 according to the era of the Greeks,[16] in Jerusalem, the Holy City, may it be rebuilt soon, Amen. On this very day appeared Hezekiah, the fine young man, son of Benjamin, before the elders signing this document and said to them:

Give witness against me, and make the symbolic purchase from me, write down and sign as a legal obligation on me, conveying rights, that I make the following declaration without being compelled, mistaken, erring, or forced, but acting in full capacity and out of my free will.[17]

That I take, gain possession of, and marry Sarwa,[18] the virgin maid, the daughter of Ṣadaqa b. Jarīr,[19] by means of the nuptial gift, this contract, and consummation, as ordered by Moses, the man of God, of blessed memory, and in accordance with the law of Israel, the pure and holy.

I shall provide her with clothing for home and street, as well as food, supply all her needs and appropriate wishes according to my ability and to the extent I can afford. I shall conduct myself toward her with truthfulness and sincerity, with love and affection. I will not grieve or oppress her but let her have food, clothing, and marital relations to the extent habitual among Jewish men, who. . . .[20]

As nuptial gift I have assigned her *fifty pieces of silver*, as due a virgin,[21] with an additional gift of *forty* good and complete gold pieces of full weight. Of these, I have already given her *five* gold pieces. The fifty silver pieces I am giving her today at the wedding ceremony, and thirty-five good gold pieces remain as a fully certified and established debt incumbent on me and on my possessions during my lifetime and after my death.[22]

The above-mentioned Sarwa listened to the words of Hezekiah and agreed to marry him and to be his wife and companion[23] in purity, holiness, and fear of God, to listen to his words, to honor and to hold him dear, to be his helper,[24] and to do in his house what a virtuous Jewish woman is expected to do, to conduct herself toward him with love and consideration, to be under his rule, and her desire will be toward him.[25]

Sarwa, out of her free will, appointed as her representative Joseph b. Abraham ha-Kohen[26] to take care of the affairs of her marriage. Two trustworthy persons, Mevōrākh b. David and Jacob b. Faḍlān, were the witnesses of this appointment.[27]

This Joseph, the representative, appeared before the elders and testified that he had received from Hezekiah the preliminary payment of five gold pieces and that he agreed to marry off the above-mentioned Sarwa to Hezekiah with this nuptial gift on the conditions specified above in this document.

These are the valuables brought in by Sarwa to the house of her husband Hezekiah:

The Gold [meaning jewelry in general]

A pair of wristbands[28]	5	dinars
A pair of earrings, *atrāk*	2	
One finger ring of gold and three of silver	2	
Jewelry total	9	dinars

[*The Clothing*][29]

A greenish gala costume, *ḥulla musannī*	3	dinars
A translucent veil[30]	1	
A mantlelike wimple[31]	6	
A kohl-colored *ʿaq(a)biyya*[32]	2	
A Sicilian robe	2 1/2	
A snow-white slip and wimple	2	
A wrap[33]	2	
Two white robes and a veil[34]	2	
Two red robes, a cloak[35] and two wimples	2	
A Rūmī bathrobe[36] and a piece of red *lādh* silk[37]	1	
A kerchief for the face	1	
A gown, *jubba*, of *khazz* silk[38] and a pink slip	2	
A linen mantle[39]	1 1/2	
A Sicilian robe	1	
Four kerchiefs and a bathrobe	1	
Clothing total	30	dinars

The Copper [household and toilet utensils and containers]

A Baghdadi bucket and its dipper	3 [?]	dinars
A basin and a ewer	2	
A chandelier and an [oil] lamp	2	
A Damascene bowl[40]	2	
A large *qashwa*[41]	1 1/2	
A bucket	1 1/2	
A complete set for soda ash,[42] a *marfaʿ* water container, a wash basin, a small bucket, a dipper	3	

A vase with perfumes and musk[43]	5	
A box for ointments, a chest [for jewelry] and a purse	2	
18 pieces		
Copper total	22	dinars

[Bedding][44]

A Ṭabarī[45] sofa and pad	3	dinars
A brocade bed cover	3	
A Buzyōn sofa[46]	2	
A quilt coverlet[47] and six pillows	1 1/2	
Bedding total	9 1/2	dinars
Total value	61 1/2	dinars.[48]

The above-mentioned Hezekiah declared in the presence of the elders that all these valuables had come into his house and were now in his possession and under his hand; and that he had undertaken to keep them as if they were his own;[49] and that he would not make any change with them without the knowledge and consent of his wife Sarwa.[50] He took upon himself and upon his estate after his death responsibility that nothing should be lost or spoiled.

The two agreed between themselves that should Sarwa, God beware, leave this world without a child from him, all that she brought in with her would go back to her heirs from her kin.[51] Contrariwise, her heirs would have no claim on the final installment of the nuptial gift incumbent on Hezekiah.

They also agreed to keep the holidays by the observation of the new moon and of the ripening of the ears in Eretz Israel; that they would not eat beef and mutton in Jerusalem until the altar of God was erected; and that they would not apply to a gentile court in exchange for the laws of the Torah.[52]

We made the symbolic purchase from Hezekiah, son of Benjamin, with regard to all that is written and stated above. We have written down all that happened in our presence, signed the document and put it into the hand of Sarwa, the daughter of Ṣadaqa, so that it should be in her hand as a proof, an instrument of claims, and a testimony in accordance with the law of Moses and Israel.

And they built and were successful.

Ṣ.[53]

Solomon b. David ha-Kohen ha-melammed, witness. Joshua b. Eli ha-Kohen Ben Ziṭā,[54] witness. Nathan ha-Kohen b. Yḥy, [may his] s[oul] r[est in peace].[55] Joshua b. Adayah ha-Kohen, witness.

Bushr[56] b. Abraham ha-Levi, witness. Nathan b. Nisan ha-Levi ha-melammed, witness.

Eli b. Maʿmar, maker of potions, witness.

ʿOmar[57] b. Joshua, witness. Joseph b. Samuel [witness. Sim]ḥa b. Zechariah, witness."

Note that the document is signed by ten witnesses, of whom four were Kohens, two Levis, and only four, ordinary Jews. The bride's representative (n. 26, above) was also a Kohen.

Sarwa's Outfit

It is somewhat puzzling that a girl in very modest circumstances should have so many duplicates in her small trousseau: two Sicilian[58] robes, one costing 2 1/2 dinars and another 1 dinar, two white, and two red robes with two wimples, two veils of the rare type *qināʿ*, two bathrobes, two buckets with dippers (and a third bucket)—and most of them mentioned not together as pairs but in different places of the list. Perhaps outfits had been readied for two sisters; one had died, and the survivor received all the family could afford.

Of particular interest is a comparison of Sarwa's ketubba with that of her contemporary, the rich Rayyisa, also a Karaite, whose assets totaled 1,170 dinars. Rayyisa, like Sarwa, had "a greenish gala costume" (but worth five times as much as Sarwa's, and, of course, she had others), linen *izārs* (n. 39, above), one *minshafa* bathrobe, Buzyōn bedding (n. 46, above), a Baghdadi bucket, and a Damascene bowl. Such details seem to reveal that the common people, when outfitting their daughters, tried to emulate the more favored classes despite the natural limitations to which they were subjected.[59]

Document II

A Rabbanite Engagement Contract from Fustat (Old Cairo)
November 11, 1146

The original of this contract (Hebrew script, Arabic language) is printed in *AJSreview*, 2 (1977), 104–106.

This document is translated in full because it shows the reader the arrangements and conditions common at a Rabbanite marriage in Geniza times. The basic stipulations specified in this engagement contract were also included in the marriage contract, ketubba, and were fairly common. Both the engagement agreement and the ketubba were real contracts, reflecting in each case the social and economic positions of the contracting parties.[60]

The bride, Sitt al-Khāṣṣa (Mistress of the Elite), was the granddaughter of Joseph Lebdī, an India trader.[61] Her late father Barakāt (Blessings) also was engaged in the India trade. Both possessed houses in Fustat. Of her grandfather's house Sitt al-Khāṣṣa had inherited or had been willed or given five out of twenty-four shares; of her father's house, half the property. Her mother Sitt al-Sāda (Mistress over the Lords) daughter of a physician, acted on her behalf, for the girl, despite her exalted epithet, no doubt was a teenager who knew little about men and money. In general, only women previously married dealt directly with their future husbands.

Translation

Bodl. MS Heb. d 66 (Cat. 2878), fs. 48 and 47 [in this order].

[Fol. 48*r*]

(1) This is a copy of the engagement contract of Abū Manṣūr Ṣemaḥ,[62] son of Rabbānā Japheth [known as] the elder
(2) Abū ʿAlī, the perfumer, to Sitt al-Khāṣṣa, the daughter of the elder Abu 'l-Barakāt Ibn al-Lebdī.
(3) On Monday, the fifth day of the month of Kislev of the year 1458
(4) of the era of the documents [November 11, 1146], in Fustat, Egypt, which is situated on the Nile River and which is under the jurisdiction
(5) of our lord Samuel, the great Nagid—may his name be forever, M. Ṣemaḥ, the young man, son of M.
(6) and R.[63] Japheth the elder, son of M. and R. Tiqvā, the elder, the Friend of the yeshiva—may he rest in Eden—concluded a match with Sitt al-Khāṣṣa, his fiancée,
(7) a virgin, the daughter of M. and R. Berakhōt, the elder—may he rest in Eden.
His obligation is a first installment of 40
(8) certified dinars, to be given as a gift at the time of the wedding, and a final installment of 100 certified
(9) dinars. Abū Manṣūr Ṣemaḥ, the fiancé, presented the 40 dinars of the first installment,
(10) and the elder Abu 'l-ʿAlā' Musallam, the perfumer, son of Sahl, received them from him.[64] The wedding is set for the month of
(11) Kislev of the coming year—may we be destined for life in it—which is the [coming] year 1459 [1147].
Ṣemaḥ assumed these obligations toward Sitt al-Khāṣṣa: She
(12) will be regarded as trustworthy in all that concerns food and drink
(13) in the house, no suspicion may be cast upon her, nor can he demand from her an oath concerning any of these
(14) things, not even a supplementary oath.[65] He may not marry another woman, nor retain
(15) a maidservant whom she dislikes. Should he do any of these things, the final installment is hers, and he must
(16) release her [from the marriage bond by divorce]. In the case that there are no children, half of what remains of the dowry returns to her family.[66] She may choose the place
(17) and the domicile where she wishes to live. The rent of her proper-

ties is hers, she may spend it for whatever purpose she prefers;
(18) he has no say in the matter.
Should he nullify this engagement contract and not
(19) marry her during the said Kislev, she will receive 20 dinars. This is a debt
(20) and an obligation, binding [as from now]. We made the symbolic purchase[67] from M. Ṣemaḥ, the young man, for Sitt al-Khāṣṣa, the fiancée,
(21) according to all that is recorded above, a purchase which is definite and strict, made with the proper object for such a transaction.
(22) We also made the symbolic purchase from Sitt al-Sāda, the daughter of the elder Abū Naṣr, the physician, the mother of Sitt
(23) al-Khāṣṣa, the fiancée, in the most rigorous terms, binding as from now: Should her
(24) daughter Sitt al-Khāṣṣa nullify the engagement contract and refuse to marry
(25) the fiancée during the said month of Kislev, she would owe the fiancée
(26) 20 [dinars . . .] This has taken place after the verification of her identity.[68]
(27) Signatures: Mevōrākh b. Solomon [of] b[lessed] m[emory]. Ṣadaqa b[torn away].

[Fol. 47*r*]

(1) The Estimate

[Jewelry and utensils of precious metals]

(2)	A pair of *ḥilaq* earrings adorned [with pearls]	5 dinars
(3)	A gold tiara adorned with pearls	70
(4)	A pair of pins with clusters of pearlike ornaments [in gold], with *mīnā*	20
(5)	and adorned with pearls	
(6)	A pair of pins adorned [with pearls]	3
(7)	A wristband[69]	6
(8)	A pair of niello-work[70] bracelets	28
(9)	A *tannūr*[71] inlaid with pearls	6
(10)	A *siwār* bracelet of pearls with a gold rim	4
(11)	Four gold rings	6
(12)	A *ḥanak* choker of pearls	3
(13)	An amber maymūn[72] necklace	6
(14)	An ornamented mirror	8
(15)	Two crystal kohl containers	3
(16)	A silver (jewel) box and two silver kohl containers[73]	3
(17)	and a kohl stick	
(18–19)	[Jewelry]	total 171 dinars

[Clothing]

(20)	A white brocaded "robe of honor," and its wimple[74]	20 dinars
(21)	A pomegranate-colored "robe of honor," and its wimple	15
(22)	A *jūkāniyya*[75] of fine *Dabīqī* linen and a scarf, *radda*, of Dabīqī linen	5
(23)	A kerchief of blue Dabīqī and a blue scarf	8
(24)	A *jūkāniyya* of cloud-colored Dabīqī and a cloud-colored hood[76]	8
(25)	A gown with *ḥamā'ilī*[77] ornaments and a Maghrebi veil, *khimār*	5
(26)	A kerchief of white Dabīqī and a grayish *mannī*, headband	10
(27)	A broad belt, *wasaṭ*, and a scarf	3
(28)	A basket cover and two covers for cooling jars	8
(29)	A silk skullcap with *ḥamā'ilī* ornaments	2

[Marginal Column I]

(30)	A Dabīqī wrap in two pieces and a pearl-colored face cover[78] with gold threads	
(31)	A fastened cloak, *malḥafa muqran*,[79] and a pearl-colored *niqāb*	5
(32)	A cloud-colored chest cover with gold threads and a bureau[80] cover	
(33)	and a serving-tray cover	8
(34)	Thirteen pieces of worn clothing and two chests for silk	16
(35)	Eight *bukhnuq* (pl. bakhāniq) cloths	16
(36)	One brocade center and two side curtains[81]	30
(37)	Two new dabīqī *maqṭaʿ*s[82]	6
(38)	A brocade dressing gown[83]	15
	[Clothing total	171]

[Marginal Column II]

[Bedding]

(39)	A brocade sofa, six pieces	25
(40)	A brocade couch, five pieces	7
(41)	A Ṭabarī sofa from Ṭabaristān,[84] five pieces [[2 dinars]]	4
(42)	A Ṭabaristān couch, three pieces	2
(43)	A pair of tapestry, *sūsanjird*,[85] pillows	8
(44)	A pair of pomegranate-colored pillows of fine	5

(45) linen and a gray-colored pair and a green pair
(46) A pair of pillows of Dabīqī linen 3
(47) A pad of white Dabīqī linen and one of blue Dabīqī
(48) and four sleeping pillows[86] 5
(49) A brocade bedcover and a saffron-yellow wrap 10
[Bedding total 69]

[Fol. 47*v*]

[Copper and other utensils and containers]

(1) A wax candle wedding lamp and a small wedding lamp, 40
(2) a pitcher, a large and a small basin, a bucket, a candlestick, a
(3) box, a soda-ash container,[87] a ewer, a bucket, and a dipper, and a jug for olive oil,
(4) a [portable oil] lamp and a bathrobe
(5) A chest and its stand decorated with mother-of-pearl 15 and ivory and a bureau and all that is in it [women's lingerie]
(6) and its stand of mother-of-pearl and ivory
(7) Two receptacles[88] of mother-of-pearl and ivory 3
(8) Two painted receptacles 4
(9) A maidservant named Zuhr (Flower) 20
[Total varia 82]
[Grand total, dowry 496 dinars, estimated 500 dinars]
(10) The entire ketubba, namely, the nupital gift, the additions, and the dowry amounts to:
(11) 640 dinars, a dinar being worth a dinar,
(12) real value, not doubled,
(13) plus five shares in the house which is in Miṣr [Fustat] in the Fortress of the Candles[89]
(14) which is known as that of Ibn al-Lebdī Abu 'l-Surūr, the perfumer, the Levi,
(15) b. Binyām [= Benjamin] shares it,
(16) and half of the house which is in the Mamṣūṣa quarter and which is known as that of the elder Abu 'l-Barakāt
(17) b. al-Lebdī,
(18) may God have mercy upon him.[90]

Document III

The Dowry and Nuptial Gift of a Rich Bride
In the hand of Nathan b. Samuel he-Ḥāvēr
ca. 1140

The original of this list (Hebrew script, Arabic language) is printed in *AJSreview*, 2 (1977), 107–110.

TS J 1, f. 29

[Column I]

(1) With good luck and success	
[Jewelry (and vessels, made of costly materials)]	
(2) A gold tiara	80 dinars
(3) A shoulder band, *katifiyya*, with eleven disks of gold and twenty of amber[91]	70
(4) A pair of pins with clusters of pearls	20
(5) A pair of peacock pins	18
(6) A pair of earrings	5
(7) A pair of pins	5
(8) A pair of niello-work bracelets, *aswira*	52
(9) A pair of filigree bracelets	30
(10) A single enameled [bracelet]	25
(11) A *maymūn* necklace of amber divided by golden spools	8
(12) A pearl band divided by [beads of] gold	8
(13) Gold tubes[92]	6
(14) Two rings	4
(15) An ornamented mirror	10
(16) A water container[93] [for the table], and a cover, a silver goblet, and a ladle	15
(17) A shallow bowl, *qiḥf*	4
(18) A bowl[94] and a compartmented[95] mixing vessel[96] with feet	5
(19) A crystal mixing vessel	5
(20) Another mixing vessel	3
(21) A gold [. . .]	2
(22) An ivory kohl container	3
(23) A crystal cock[97]	4
(24) A pen box made in China, with two knives, a sand sprinkler [for blotting], and an ivory plate [on which the pen is nibbed]	13
(25) A silver comb	4
(26) A pair of gold bracelets	15
(27) Three gold rings	4
(28) A locally made qimaṭra [jewel box] of "porcelain" ṣīnī, with silver luster, *muḥallāh bifiḍḍa*	20

(29)	A round ornamented mirror	6
(30)	A lion[98] and a probe [literally, needle] for perfuming	5
(31)	Two silver caskets and a [jewel] box	5
(32)	An amber *qiḥf* [shallow bowl] with a gold rim	5
(33)	A bureau and its stand	10
(34)	Equipment for bloodletting	2
	Total [value of jewelry]	471 dinars

[Column II]

(1)	The Clothing	
(2)	A cloud-colored "robe of honor," consisting of a robe,	50
(3)	a wimple, and a grayish headband	
(4)	A white wimple with gold threads	15
(5)	A hood with stripes, "as the pen runs"[99] and a robe, both with gold threads	10
(6)	A kerchief of Dabīqī linen	8
(7)	A skullcap of Dabīqī linen,	22
(8)	a wrap with two edges in gold threads	
(9)	and a face cover with gold threads	
(10)	A wrap of Dabīqī linen and silk	4
(11)	A blue Rūmiyya[100]	6
(12)	A silk wimple in double layers	6
(13)	A silken "robe of honor" consisting of a robe	
(14)	[damaged	?]
(15)	A grayish robe of silk and Dabīqī linen and a grayish Rūmiyya	15
(16)	A grayish patched garment	5
(17)	A pomegranate-colored "robe of honor" and its wimple	15
(18)	A blue wimple with gold threads	5
(19)	A *jūkāniyya* with bird patterns	4
(20)	A poultice-colored wimple	5
(21)	An apricot-colored jūkāniyya with gold threads, a silken patched garment,	10
(22)	and an apricot-colored silk Rūmiyya	
(23)	A green robe with gold threads, and a wax-colored wimple	5
(24)	A homemade *makhtūma*[101]	6
(25)	A jūkāniyya of siglaton[102]	3
(26)	A jūkāniyya of red siglaton	4
(27)	A makhtūma of siglaton	7
(28)	A homemade (?) tabby makhtūma	6
(29)	A starch-colored tabby makhtūma	5
(30)	A jūkāniyya of brocade with borders of [two or more] different colors	10

[Column III]

(1)	A jūkāniyya of red brocade	10
(2)	A makhtūma of pistachio brocade	15
(3)	A greenish "robe of honor," consisting of a robe, a wimple,	30
(4)	A headband, and a Rūmiyya	
(5)	Paneled robes and pieces of cloth	30
(6–7)	[Total deleted, because there was an addition:]	
(8)	A dressing gown of siglaton	12
(9)	A dressing gown of blue brocade	20
(10–11)	Total of the clothing	373 dinars

[Bedding]

(12)	A bed cover of Rūmī brocade	10
(13)	Another bed cover	10
(14)	Two chameleon-colored canopies	60
(15)	A sofa of Rūmī brocade, six pieces	40
(16)	A sofa of Islets[103] brocade	15
(17)	A sofa of brilliant color,[104] four pieces	15
(18)	An Islets sofa, three pieces	15
(19)	A sofa of Rūmī brocade, three pieces	15
(20)	A siglaton couch	5
(21)	A siglaton sofa	5
(22)	A couch made of reeds[105]	3
(23)	A brocade pad	5
(24–25)	Total of bedding and hangings	198 dinars

(26)	The Copper	
(27)	A candle lamp, an oil lamp, two complete Spanish	
(28)	lamps, a large box and another box inside it,	
(29)	a pitcher, a spacious[106] washbasin, a large ewer	
(30)	and another washbasin, a ewer, a soda-ash container, a box,	
(31)	a part of a box, an oven, a round bucket, three candlesticks,	
(32)	a copper bowl, and a bathrobe with hems[107]	
(33)	Total	200 dinars
(34)	Vases with their perfume	8 dinars

[Column IV]

(1)	The Maids	
(2–3)	ʿIzz [Glory] and Dalāl [Coquetry] and two	100

	personal attendants, Nusā [Rainbow, Lantern] and Wafā [Fidelity]		
(4–5)		Total [of outfit]	1,350
(6)	The books		250
(7)		Total	1,600
(8)	The first and the final installments		500
		Grand total	2,100 dinars

Document IV

Return of Her Outfit to Sitt Al-Ḥasab after the Termination of Her Marriage
September 1146

ULC Or 1080 J 49

Sitt al-Ḥasab (Lady Noble) was the elder daughter of Abu 'l-Faḍl (Generous) Shēlā[108] ha-Levi of the Ben al-Baṣrī (from Basra, Iraq) family, who bore the Hebrew titles Prince of the Levites, Glory of the munificent, and Delight of the yeshiva, which shows that he was well-to-do and of a philanthropic bent. At the time of our document he was already dead, and since Sitt al-Ḥasab's (as far as we know, first) marriage seemingly was of short duration, he had probably not witnessed her wedding. In a document from Aug./Sept. 1121 he was involved in a business partnership.[109]

In his will, written on or shortly after Jan. 30, 1160, Shēlā's son Abu 'l-Ḥasan, describes his elder sister Sitt al-Ḥasab as the widow of al-rayyis (Doctor) Bu 'l- ʿAlā'.[110] I do not believe that he would have referred to her on his deathbed thus if he had in mind the marriage terminated fourteen years earlier. Consequently, we must concede that we do not yet know for sure whether our document of 1146 concerns a widow or a divorcée. The duration of the marriage reflected in our document must have been short, for the numerous items of clothing were returned without exception; of the jewelry Sitt al-Ḥasab had only exchanged a ring for a pair of pins and given a pair of bracelets as a collateral; and of furnishings some items had been removed "to them," that is, to her paternal family, to which she probably had moved. This seems to make it likely that the marriage had been terminated by divorce.[111]

In November 1157, Sitt al-Ḥasab gave liberty to a maidservant of hers named Ṣalaf (Pride and Prudishness).[112] About twenty or more years earlier, an Indian slave girl with the same name, worth 20 dinars, formed part of a dowry in a huge marriage contract, which is so damaged, however, that even the names of the couple are not preserved. The bride was not our Sitt al-Ḥasab.[113]

In a court record dated Oct. 31, 1161, Sitt al-Ḥasab drops many claims against one of her agents who happened to be a tenant in one of her houses.[114] Besides purely commercial matters, such as the sale of a hundred pounds of rose oil, she was concerned in the claim about a gala costume which he allegedly had sold her for a higher price than "she had accepted in the bazaar during the auction."[115] The costume, a blue *ḥulla*, consisted of three pieces, a skullcap, a wimple, and a *mukhlaf*, probably "a patchwork piece," "one of which was embroidered with three border ornaments and two 'rows' [stripes paralleling the lower edge]."[116]

A short discussion of the term *mukhlaf* is apt to shed light on the problems of the terminology of clothing in general. Although the word occurs in the Geniza more than fifty times throughout four centuries I was unable to locate it in any Arab dictionary.[117] The Hebrew letter *k* corresponds to Arabic *k* and *kh*. For a long time I preferred the first choice, reading *mukallaf*, ornamented, precious.[118] But when the term began to occur in the outfits of both the poor and the rich, I had second thoughts and read it as *mukhlaf*, a patchwork cloth, changed through replacing some parts by others.[119] We should not be surprised that the rich bride of Doc. III had in her outfit two such pieces. Just as one did not shun old, secondhand, and laundered clothes, one was not ashamed of patched ones. "He who mends does not go unclothed,"; says a proverb found in many Arabic venaculars, and "replacing" essentially means "improving."[120]

Just to mention in passing: the fact that we find here three siblings connected with five documents: two trousseau lists, written under very different circumstances, a will, a bill of manumission of a slave, and a lawsuit, proves, like many similar occurrences, that families kept their papers together until a member of a later generation disposed of them in the Geniza, where they became dispersed until modern research reunited them.[121]

Translation

ULC Or 1080 J 49[122]

(1) This is what the sheikh Abu 'l-Surūr, *Rav Peraḥya* (2) *ha-Levi, the elder, son of Rav Benjamin, the elder m(ay their) R(ock keep them)*, received[123] (3) on order of his excellency, the *Nagid*,[124] *(may) G(od) exalt (his rank)* (4) and on order of the *Courts*,[125] of the *nedunya* belonging to (5) Sitt al-Ḥasab, the daughter of our *prince, The Prince of the Levites*, may God have mercy upon him:

(6) A complete golden tiara consisting of seven pieces with . . . ; (7) a pair of large earrings, inlaid with pearls, and a pair of small ones, cups;[126] (8) a pair of golden pins ornamented with clusters of pearls; (9) a pair of sticklike pins; a pearl-choker; a single enamel wristband; (10) a *maymūn* necklace of amber and gold, namely, consisting of eight beads of amber and six of gold; (11) a lapis lazuli bracelet (*ḥadīda*); an ornamented mirror; five stools decorated with d(h)abl tortoiseshell; (12) a mixing vessel, four silver covers;[127] a silver box; two gold rings; (13) a silver ring. A ring listed in the ketubba was exchanged for a pair of golden pins. (14) Two crystal kohl containers with golden rims; a mixing vessel made of (15) crystal; . . . of crystal; a wristband; a kohl stick.

(16) Clothing.[128]

(17) A white Dabīqī (linen) robe with gold threads and a white silken wimple; (18) a . . . gala costume—robe, wimple, and headband—grayish; (19) a pomegranate-colored "robe of honor"—robe and wimple; (20) a sky blue "robe of honor"—robe and wimple; (21) a headband with gold threads; a Dabīqī cloak; a . . . robe; (22) a blue silk wimple; a pearl-colored face cover with gold threads; (23) a homemade *makhtūma*; a skullcap of *lālas* silk; (24) a skullcap of lālas;[129] a . . . with gold threads; a Maghrebi veil; (25) a . . . kerchief; a blue Dabīqī belt; (26) a white . . . a green kerchief [serving as] basket(cover);[130] (27) a paneled skullcap; a laundered half cloak; two blue scarves (28) in double layers; a black face cover; a new *malḥafa* cloak and a face cover; (29) a laundered malḥafa; four polo robes (*jūkāniyya*); two kerchiefs (serving as) covers for trays; (30) two kerchiefs (serving as) covers for the cooling jug; a brocade carpet; seven kerchiefs; (31) a . . . kerchief; two brocade sofas (martaba); four brocade pillows; (32) a brocade mattress (*ṭarrāḥa*) with its pillow; two *sūsanjird* tapestry pillows; (33) . . . blue pillows; and a pair of green pillows made of fine linen.

Verso

(1) A pair of Dabīqī pillows; a Dabīqī trunk and a pad; (2) a large blanket (*liḥāf khilāfī*) and a siglaton cloak.

(3) The Copper

(4) A wedding (oil) lamp; wax candle lamps; two washbasins and a ewer; (5) . . . a large tray (*ṣadr*); [[a pitcher]]; a candlestick; a complete soda-ash container; (6) a washbasin; a jug for olive oil; an oil lamp; a complete box; (7) a bureau decorated with mother-of-pearl and ivory with its stool; a chest with its stool; (8) a bathrobe; a perfuming vase.

(9) Everything in the ketubba has been accounted for and received by the aforementioned sheikh (10) Abu 'l-Surūr; nothing is missing except (11) a pair of beaded bracelets, of which it is recorded that it is in the hands of the sheikh Abu 'l-(12) Faraj.[131] A Ṭabaristān mattress is in the house of (13) . . . Rabbēnū Ḥiyyā, *may Heaven keep him*. Of a siglaton . . . (14) it is recorded that it is with them;[132] the pit[cher] is with them, [also?] (15) a maidservant named Shuᶜ[a]b.[133]

This happened in the middle ten days of (16) *the month of Tishri 1458* (Sept.

1146). *The document was written in order to serve as a title of right* (17) [*and as a proof*]. *I joined*[134] *the judges and signed.* (18) David, the Refugee, *pālīṭ* (Heb.), son of R. Joseph (may he) r(est in an) h(onored place and. . . .[135]
Ḥiyyā b. Isaac (may he) r(est in) E(den)[136]
Nathan b. Samuel, he-Ḥāvēr (of) b(lessed) m(emory).[137].

Document V

The Dowry of Sitt al-Riyāsa
August 1156

Firkovitch II, 1700, fs. 24 a-b, 25 a.

Two leaves from the record book of Mevōrākh b. Nathan, written during spring and summer 1156. Our document is not dated, but the entry immediately preceding it bears the date "Last third of the month of Av." The last day of that month coincided with Aug. 18, 1156.

In several respects our document is the model of a marriage contract for a bride from a well-to-do family in Fustat during the High Middle Ages. True, Sitt al-Riyāsa (Lady Leadership) did not have a golden tiara, like her elder sister Sitt al-Ḥasab of Doc. IV and the two brides known to us from Docs. II and III; she had no crystal, of which her sister possessed several pieces, no gala costume (*ḥulla*; she had a robe of honor, *khilʿa*), not even a perfuming vessel for freshening the house. But the distribution of the expenses for the various sections of the outfit (jewelry and utensils made of costly materials, 124 dinars; clothing, 196; furnishing, 96; housewares, 80; total, including a maidservant, 520) represents the ideal average; the marriage gift (50 + 100 dinars) shows the two parties as belonging to the same social level; and the individual items, especially of clothing, are variegated and convey a good idea of how the wardrobe of a woman of her station might have looked.

Translation

(1) Estimate of the sheikh Bu 'l-Makārim (Man of Noble Deeds), the Goldsmith[138]

(2) Joseph b. Samuel. The bride: the virgin Sitt al-Riyāsa, daughter of Shēlā

(3) ha-Levi, (may he) r(est) in E(den).
Immediate (installment of the marriage gift of the husband:) fifty [dinars], *a gift.*[139]

(4) Deferred (installment:) a hundred [dinars], certified [by a money assayer]

(5)	And the well-known conditions imposed by the girls.[140]	
(6)	The Dowry	
(7)	A pair of granulated golden bracelets with niello work[141]	18 (dinars)
(8)	A pair of golden bracelets with niello work	28
(9)	A pair of golden pins adorned with pearls	7
(10)	A pair of adorned earrings	8
(11)	A golden *lāzam*[142]	10
(12)	A golden *khūṣa* with black niello work[143]	6
(13)	A wristband, *tastaynaj*, adorned with pearls	10
(14)	Two golden inlaid rings	5
(15)	An amber *maymūn* necklace with gold spools	4
(16)	A pearl choker with gold spools	8
(17)	[Circle with dot in center ⊙][144]	
(18)	A silver kohl container	2
(19)	A silver mixing vessel	2
(20)	A silver presser[145]	1

[Column II]

(1)	A tray for . . .	. . .
(2)	and a spoon, a kohl stick, another[146]	
(3)	pair of pins, and two silver rings	
(4)		3
(5)	A pair of golden pins	. . .
(6)	A silver jewel box	6
(7)	An embellished[147] mirror	5
(8)	Total	124
(9)	124 [repeated]	

Firkovitch II, 1700, f. 24 b

[Column I]

(1)	The Clothing	
(2)	A [[kerchief]] sky blue Dabīqī (linen) wimple with gold threads	12
(3)	A blue Dabīqī robe with gold threads [[15]][148]	20
(4)	A Dabīqī kerchief with gold threads	8
(5)	A white Dabīqī "robe of honor"	15
(6)	Its wimple	15
(7)	[[a green "robe of honor"; its robe]][149]	
(8)	A green *jūkāniyya* (polo robe)	6
(9)	A green wimple	3
(10)	A green kerchief	6
(11)	A white Dabīqī *jūkāniyya*	5

(12)	A white hood, *kṣy*[150]	7
(13)	A blue jūkāniyya	3
(14)	A blue wimple	4
(15)	A red, wimplelike hood, kṣy	5
(16)	A red skullcap	2
(17)	A blue half kerchief	5
(18)	A black kerchief	4
(19)	A piece of red *lādh* silk[151]	1
(20)	A Dabīqī jūkāniyya in double layers	3
(21)	A half cloak	5

[Column II]

(1)	A sleeve kerchief[152]	1
(2)	A grayish Dabīqī kerchief	4
(3)	A Dabīqī wrap with two (ornamented) ends [[12]]	15
(4)	A pearl-colored face cover	1
(5)	A cloak	3
(6)	A blue Dabīqī scarf	2
(7)	A Dabīqī headband of two layers	1
(8)	A grayish headband	1
(9)	A white Dabīqī scarf	2
(10)	A kerchief of two layers	1
(11)	A basket cover	8
(12)	Four paneled jūkāniyyas	8
(13)	Two skullcaps	4
(14)	A white Dabīqī scarf	1
(15)	A cloak in double layers	1
(16)	Two jūkāniyyas [[2]][153]	1
(17)	A bathrobe and a *fūṭa*[154]	1
(18)	[[A fūṭa]]	
(19)	A silken waistband	2
(20)	Sixteen *bukhnuq* cloths of diversified colors[155]	
(21)	[[deleted and changed into]]	8
(22)	A siglaton kerchief	2
(23)	Total	196

Firkovitch II, 1700, f. 25 a

[Column I]

(1)	The Furnishings[156]	
(2)	A silk *martaba* [[five pieces]]	
(3)	Two pillows, and a support of Rūmī brocade	40
(4)	A *ṭarrāḥa* mattress with two brocade pillows	15
(5)	A ṭarrāḥa mattress with two brocade pillows[157]	15
(6)	A white Dabīqī martaba	3

(7)	[[A pair of green pillows]][158]	
(8)	A Ṭabaristān ṭarrāḥa with a pair of pillows	2
(9)	A Ṭabarī pad	3
(10)	A pair of green pillows	2
(11)	A pair of pomegranate-colored pillows	2
(12)	A pair of "feathered"[159] (pillows) [[2]]	4
(13)	A pair of red (pillows) [[2]]	4
(14)	A white single one	1
(15)	A brocade *nūna* bedcover[160]	5
(16)	A cloak Total	96
(17)	The Copper	
(18)	A lamp for wax candles	5
(19)	A wedding (oil-)lamp	5
(20)	A complete large copper box[161]	18
(21)	A bowl	5
(22)	A pitcher	3
(23)	An Andalusian washbasin[162]	8
(24)	A large ewer	3
(25)	A small washbasin	1
(26)	[[A large box]][163]	
(27)	[[A small box]]	

[Column II]

(1)	A bucket, a dipper, a jug for olive oil	2
(2)	A bureau *and that which is in it*[164]	4
(3)	A bathrobe	2
(4)	A box for jewelry	1
(5)	A chest, its stool, and a small bureau	
(6)		5
(7)	A pair of *jūkāniyya*s, a Dabīqī scarf	
(8)	and a cloak	4
(9)	A Dabīqī "goblet" kerchief[165]	5
(10)	A white kerchief of *lālas* silk	2
(11)	A maidservant called Beechtree[166]	20
(12)	(rounded up) Total	100
(13)	A dyeing trough[167]	4
(14)	Total [[with immediate]]	
(15)	[[and deferred installment]] 500	[[100]]
(16)	Total with immediate and deferred installment	
(17)	Six hundred and seventy [dinars],	
(18)	each dinar being worth a dinar.	
(19)	Also the entire half of the well-known house in	
(20)	Cairo in the Zuwayla quarter that her	
(21)	brother gave her, which is in the lanes of the Christians.	
(22)	Also the entire half of the small house which is	

(23) close to it and which the sheikh
(24) Amīn al-Dawla gave her.[168]

Document VI

Pawning of Garments and Other Items of a Trousseau
ca. 1049–1052

ULC Or 1080 J 48*v*

How a woman managed to keep body and soul together in an emergency by using her clothing and other items of her bridal outfit is illustrated by the notes of a pawnbroker referring to the Muslim years 441–444 (corresponding approximately to 1049–1052). The beginning of the notes was written on another piece of paper and, as far as we know, is lost. At the end the writer broke off in the middle of a sentence, clearly because he had become confused and intended to make a new draft. Despite these deficiencies this paper contains some valuable documentary evidence.

The situation in which that woman found herself was only too common in Geniza times. Her husband had been away for a far longer period than anticipated.[169] He probably was away in some countries of the Indian Ocean, had suffered shipwreck or other misfortunes and remained away from home for years; legal documents mention absences "in the lands of India" of nine and ten years.[170] The travelers sent home "gifts" for the upkeep of the family; but such shipments often were lost, or were not delivered in time by the merchants who had to take care of them, or—did not arrive because they had not been sent.[171] When the provisions left or sent by the sustainer of the family were exhausted, the wife approached the rabbinical court and received permission to sell or to pawn items of her trousseau. This permission was required, since the husband was obliged to restore the value of the dowry in full. After his return, accounts were made between him, his wife, and third parties concerned. The pawner's draft translated here reflects such an occurrence.

Translation

ULC Or 1080 J 48*v*

(1) A bangle[172] and two . . . robes against . . . dinars less 1/3 dinar and (2) 1 grain.[173]

New moon day (first) of Muḥarram (I) of 441: (3) a dressing gown[174] against 1 dinar (deposited during) the first ten days of that month. A brocade mattress[175] (4) deposited on New moon day of Shawwāl (X) of the same year against 1 dinar.

New moon day of Muḥarram (I) (5) of the year 442: two siglaton robes against (6) 6 dinars of full weight. And during the first ten days of that month: a carpet[176] (7) and a golden ring against 3 dinars of full weight. New moon day of Shawwāl (X) (8): a *jubba*[177] against 4 dinars, and three wimples[178] against 6 (9) dinars, another *jubba* against 1 dinar, a . . . of siglaton against 1 dinar, an unpatterned[179] (10) robe and a slip against 1 dinar, and a washbasin[180] for 2 dinars.

New moon day of Shaʿbān (VIII)[181] (11): a mortar and a wickerwork basket against 3 (dinars) and 9 qīrāṭs;[182] two pairs of wool curtains against (12) 2 dinars, New moon day of (13) Dhu 'l-Qaʿda (XI) (14); and[183] a couch made of fine reeds against 1 dinar,[184] and (15) New moon day of Dhu 'l-Qaʿda,[185] a wrap[186] and a pitcher against 1 dinar, a wimple (16) against 1 dinar.

New moon day of Ṣafar (II):[187]

Comments

This draft is written on the reverse side of a note sent by Elhanan b. Shemarya, the famous spiritual leader of Egyptian Jewry, flourishing around 1020, to a communal official asking him to take care of the affairs of a blind man.[188] Thus the note lingered in the Geniza as waste paper for about a quarter of a century before being reused by the pawnbroker.

Since no names of pawners are mentioned, all pawnings must have been effected by one woman. During a period of four years she pawned

15 or 16 pieces of clothing
5 or 6 pieces of bedding, hangings and carpets[189]
2 pieces of jewelry
4 utensils

These were the sums received by her in the course of the years 1049–1052:

Muslim date	Corresponding to	Sums in dinars
1[190] Muḥarram (I) 441[191]	5 June 1049	1
1 Shawwāl (X) 441	26 Feb. 1050	1
1 Muḥarram (I) 442	26 May 1050	6 + 3
1 Shawwāl (X) 442	16 Feb. 1051	4 + 6 + 1 + 1 + 1 + 2
1 Shaʿbān (VIII) 443	8 Dec. 1051	3 3/8 + 2
1 Dhu 'l-Qaʿda (XI) 443	5 March 1052	1 + 1 + 1
1 Ṣafar (II) 444	2 June 1052	Draft discontinued

The very small allowances granted to the pawner in 1049 and 1052 prove that the means provided by the husband in those years were regarded by the court as sufficient; the sums adjudicated were for extra expenses, such as for medical treatment. The 9 dinars received for nine (Muslim) months as from 1, I, 442, show that her regular alimony was 1 dinar per month, a modest, but common appropriation to a woman of the middle class, to which our pawner, as the objects deposited by her prove, belonged.[192] The 15 dinars approved for the following ten months (1, X, 442) certainly included some special items.

We see that clothing, both in the number of pieces pawned and the sums received for them, outstripped by far the other sections of the bridal outfit, although they were by no means negligible. For pawning of clothing in general see B, n. 273, above.

DOCUMENTS VII–IX. FROM THE INVENTORIES OF THE ESTATES OF MEN

Nothing found in the Geniza with regard to the wardrobes of men compares with trousseau lists. Business and private letters contain much information concerning the fabrics, materials, and market value of garments, but they do not tell us what constituted the sartorial equipment of a male individual. We are better off with wills or official statements about burial attire. The *kafan*, or shrouds, as this attire was called, was of very deep concern; it was to be as perfect as possible, as sumptuous or modest as feasible, depending on the religious mood and the means of the person concerned. Examples for modest male "shrouds" were provided in B, pp. 188–189 above. There even the will of a pious man of limited means foresaw five covers of the entire body as the limit to which restraint could go.

Inventories of the estates of men should yield more information about the subject. Unfortunately only a few of them deal with clothing, except in the cases of travelers overtaken by death, which are, of course, not representative. Houses, or parts of them, given by parents to children had to be registered, like all transfers of real estate.[193] But the receipt by gift or inheritance of movables such as clothing was normally done by the mutual understanding of the relatives concerned. Whatever could be achieved without attracting the attention of the watchful eyes of the authorities was done without the writing of documents, which had to be witnessed by at least two persons. On one's deathbed one sometimes left selected pieces to relatives or friends, or poor people would divide the little they had in jewelry and clothing among the heirs,[194] but from such occasional instances little can be learned about the clothing worn by an average individual.

The documents translated below remedy somewhat this deficiency. The inventory of the physician's possessions (Doc. VII), recorded, with Moses Maimonides' express permission, during a Passover week (when usually no documents were written), must have been made only a few days after his death, if not the day thereafter. The same may be said of the action of a court that visited the premises of a coppersmith to seal it for safeguarding his estate (Doc. VIII). The Geniza has preserved a detailed record of such an action in the case of the demise of a foreigner, undertaken when the dead man's body was still in the house.[195] Thus Docs. VII and VIII should give us some idea of the types of clothes worn by a physician of limited means and by a successful artisan.

Doc. IX does not indicate who owned the pieces listed and under which circumstances they were offered for sale, but it is valuable because of its inner completeness.

Document VII

Inventory of the Estate of the Physician Abu 'l-Riḍā Ha-Levi Taken on Order of Moses Maimonides April 13, 1172

ULC Or 1080 J 142 and TS Misc. Box 25, f. 53

The physician Abu 'l-Riḍā ha-Levi and his brother Abu 'l-Ḥ(asan) are known from a document written in the provincial town of Minyat Ziftā, where both undertook a trusteeship (probably for an orphan) "solely for seeking favor before God." Thus Abu 'l-Riḍā was probably a "country doctor," settled in the capital and not very well off.[196]

The absence of bankers' and promissory notes (the most conspicuous part of a man's pecuniary possessions), cash, and jewelry does not necessarily mean that the doctor had not possessed any. These matters were taken care of by another court action.[197]

Abu 'l-Riḍā's wife was dead. Otherwise, her presence at the time of the taking of the inventory would have been imperative,[198] and the clothing, carpets, hangings, and houseware would not have been transferred to the house of her dead husband's brother.

The data indicates that "our lord Moses," who ordered the taking of the inventory, was none other than Moses Maimonides.[199] "The Great Rav" is not merely a laudatory epithet but the exact title of his office; he was recognized as the highest religious authority in the country, whom the judges had to consult whenever doubt of the legality of an action arose. This office can be rightly described as corresponding to that of the Muslim Grand Mufti.[200]

In our case there was indeed some reason for doubt. The seventeenth of the month of Nisan, on which our document was written, is one of the *waṣṭāniyyāt*, or middle days, between the first and the concluding days of the Passover holidays. The Geniza contains much material illustrating the question whether business should be conducted and documents written on these days. The answer was generally in the affirmative, although some misgivings about this permissiveness were expressed.[201] In order to be on the safe side, the judges asked Maimonides, who ordered the action because of the urgency of the matter. The brother of the deceased had already transferred a part of the latter's housewares to his place. If this went on, they could easily be mixed up with and disappear in the brother's own belongings.[202]

As often happened, our document is preserved in two different collections: the University Collection of Geniza manuscripts, acquired by the Cambridge University Library by purchase or gift, and the Taylor-Schechter Collection, brought to England by Solomon Schechter in 1898. The two sheets are continuous, but the lower part of the first sheet is torn away, causing a loss of about three to four lines on each page.[203]

Two actions, supervised by the rabbinical court of Fustat,[204] are reported in this document: the taking of the inventory and the transport of the objects noted to the brother's house, which happened on the same day. Therefore, the record is dated both at the beginning and the end, a very rare occurrence. The objects were moved in five different receptacles, the copper in a saddlebag and the rest in four "sleeping carpets."[205]

Translation

ULC Or 1080 J 142

(1) List of what the sheikh Abu 'l-Riḍā, the physician, the Levi, has left, which has been taken into (2) trusteeship for his orphan ʿImrān on order of *his excellency, our lord Moses, the Great* (3) *Rav, may his name endure forever*, on Thursday the 17th of Nisan 1483 (13 April 1172):

(4) Three used curtains of Maghrebi brocade, the length of each of which is approximately five (5) and a half cubits, and its breadth three cubits; its valances[206] are blue, lined with white.

(6) A gala costume fastened by two "pieces"[207] from one side and pointed ribbons[208] from the other; (7) its "plaited palm leaves"[209] are blue.

A white center carpet[210] with blue borders, twenty-two cubits long.

(8) A blue scarf with red decorative bands.[211]

All this is in a new sleeping carpet.

A white sleeping carpet containing (9) a white turban with a camphor-colored "eye"[212] and with three "pieces" on each side. A red *kahramāna*[213] (10) of silk, twenty-seven cubits long. A white *talthīma* scarf[214] with three yellow "pieces." (11) A red *kahramāna*, eighteen cubits long. A plain white "broad" shawl[215] with blue (12) borders. A new white Dabīqī *mulā'a* wrap with two ornamental edges.[216] A white robe, fastened (13) by one "piece" on [each side]. A new blue male *burd*[217] robe. A robe (14) . . . . a paneled . . . ten cubits (long) (15) . . . . a yellow . . . ten (or twenty) cubits long (and here three or four lines are missing.)

verso

(1) a yellow. . . . Five remainders of cloth, one of them of silk. A new Iraqi *burd muqaddar*.[218] (2) A female washed belt. A Mosul[219] remainder of cloth, fulled, (3) five cubits long. A new, . . . mandrake and patterned kerchief.[220]

Total of the items contained in this (4) bundle: thirty, in addition to the five fulled remainders.[221]

A fourth sleeping carpet, (5) a new one, contains a small burd muqaddar with borders of [two or more] different colors.[222] A large laundered *maqṭaʿ* robe. A (6) laundered paneled robe. A *jūkāniyya* of princely fabric.[223] A laundered black jūkāniyya. A laundered (7) maqṭaʿ robe. A laundered paneled jūkāniyya and a veil.[224] A white Dabīqī scarf with a "piece." (8) A laundered paneled jūkāniyya. A laundered plain scarf of two layers. A laundered cotton (9) cloak. A Dabīqī robe. A laundered black belt.

A pair of new green Dabīqī (10) pillows, each pillow [decorated] with two "pieces." A pair of Tinnīsī *bukhnuq* cloths[225] in two layers on a string. (11) A sachet[226] with gold threads for cloves. [. . .] A pair of white embroidered (12) Dabīqī pillows. [A carpet] (13) with decorative bands, . . .[227] cubits long [This lost section starts listing the contents—mainly housewares—of the saddlebag.]

TS Misc. Box 25, f. 53

(1) Small [. . .]. Three broken canisters.[228] A mirror. The pestle of a mortar. Two buckets [one large,] (2) and one small. A slipcase[229] made of bamboo canes containing four black silk borders. An iron (3) dip[per]. A bandage container[230] // for bandages; a *dāwardān*[231] // for kohl containers. Two wash basins and two tables [. . . .] (4) A broken wash basin and a pillow. All the above-mentioned items of copper (5) and the dāwardān are in the saddlebag.

In addition, sheikh Abu 'l-Ḥ[asan], (6) the brother of the deceased, declared that, of the above-mentioned estate he had received before the following items, which are presently in his possession: (7) two stands[232] for cups, two covers, a mortar pestle, a narc[issus]-like vessel,[233] (8) two trays, a set[234] of copper vessels, a lamp for wax candles. Four small remainders (9) of cloth, a remainder of pieces with gold brocade. A knife in a sheath.[235]

A sleeping carpet of two lay[ers] containing (10) the belongings of Musk, the maidservant of the deceased, namely a . . . belt in two layers; (11) a locally made *maqṭaᶜ* in two layers; a white laundered cloak with black borders, [a . . .] (12) blue; half garments; a new paneled *jūkāniyya* in two layers; a face cover; [. . .]; (13) and a laundered maqṭaᶜ; a pair of socks of different colors.

The sheikh Abu 'l-Ḥ[asan], (14) the "perfumer," received all the belongings listed above in our presence and had them transferred [. . .] (15) to a separate place in his domicile as a deposit in trust for ᶜImrān, the orphan of the sh[eikh Abu 'l-] (16) Riḍā, the above-mentioned physician.

Thursday, the seventeenth of N[isan of the year 1483 of] the Era of the Documents.[236]

Document VIII

A Coppersmith's Personal Belongings

Jewish Theological Seminary of America, ENA 1822, f. 46

This coppersmith functioned not only as craftsman, but, as was often done, also as a dealer in copperware. The list contains about one hundred and forty brass, bronze, and copper vessels of all descriptions, kept on the middle floor of the house where he lived, while, as usual, his workshop was on the ground floor. There, no doubt, he exhibited other products of his art for his customers. The middle floor harbored also his personal belongings, and the third floor was probably occupied by a tenant or by the proprietor of the house.

The time of our document can be gauged from its script, which is identical with that of the scribe who wrote the communal lists of distributions of bread to the poor, discussed in *Med. Soc.*, II, 442, secs. 17 and 18. These lists were drawn up at the end of the eleventh or the beginning of the twelfth century and show that there was always an influx of foreigners to Egypt from all directions, including the Muslim West.

It is likely that this coppersmith came from Spain, the country famed for its export of copper and copperware at that time. Most of his geographically defined clothes were manufacured in the Muslim West, two even in Nūl, a place in southern Morocco, to the best of my knowledge not mentioned elsewhere in the Geniza. In addition to the generally accepted prayer book of R. Saadya Gaon, he possessed a Maghrebi prayer book as well as a volume of poetry in Arabic script—the infatuation of Spanish Jews with Arabic poetry is well-known.

A comparison of the physician's wardrobe (Doc. VII) with that of the coppersmith should not induce us to assume that the latter was poorer than the former. The opposite might have been the case. But the artisan stayed in his workshop and store most of his day, whereas the doctor—unless he was a very prominent one—left his house early in the morning, to visit patients, or work part time in a hospital, or participate in communal activities. He was constantly in the limelight. Not in vain do Muslim historians of medicine praise the spotless outward appearance of some physicians described by them.[237]

Translation of the sections pertaining to personal belongings

ENA 1822, f. 46

(1) List of what is on the middle floor. . . . (10) Three old[238] carpets; a *mulḥam* (11) robe;[239] an "overall";[240] a threadbare[241] blue robe; pants; another (12) mulḥam robe; another "overall"; another pair of pants; a worn[242] (13) linen robe; an Iraqi *burd* gown;[243] A Nūlī *biqyār* (big turban);[244] (14) a scarf; a new Spanish robe; a "raw" [unfulled] Spanish robe; (15) a Sūsī[245] scarf; a small Nūlī biqyār with its "Compartment";[246] still another (16) pair of pants; a threadbare robe. . . .

(17) A small chest containing the prayer book of Rabbēnū Saadya (of) b[lessed] m[emory], and a section of the (18) Book of Psalms, a Maghrebi prayer book,[247] and a book of poetry in Arabic characters.

(26) A lined chest (27) containing ten Spanish "raw" [unfulled] robes,[248] a Sicilian piece of cloth (28) and two gowns [[shrouds]] in which some china is packed.[249]

(31) A single ʿAbbadānī mat,[250] a small copper (32) dipper, a small copper canister, a woolen curtain; (33) another copper canister at the pigeons;[251] a copper (34) bucket with a base, two water jars made of stone[252] and two large copper (35) jar cups for the jars.

Document IX

A Male Wardrobe Offered for Sale

TS Arabic Box 51, f. 80

A long narrow strip of paper, containing notes concerning a deal in secondhand clothes.

The first section, written in Arabic script with Coptic numerals, does not belong to the main part, which is in Hebrew script with Hebrew numerals. As the amounts indicate, the deal recorded in the first section was made in dirhems, the second in dinars. In the Arabic part the prices are written beneath the items to which they belong—a definite sale; in the Hebrew part they are inserted between the lines above the items—an estimate, not yet completed.

Translation
(In Arabic script)

A tailored piece; a robe; an untailored piece

40	23	16 1/2

a "waistband"[253]

1

(In Hebrew script)

1	2

(1) A sesame-colored tailored piece,[254] a new, faded[255] robe
3
(2) A new piece of cloth, twelve cubits long
1/2
(3) A waistband, also new; a "cleaned"[256] broad shawl
(4) A new broad *lānas* shawl;[257] a piece of the same material, two cubits
(5) A new gown
8 1/2[258]

[about two lines blank]

(6) A faded linen robe
(7) A faded multicolored[259] robe
(8) A faded sesame-colored robe
(9) A turban with ornamental borders[260]
(10) A white turban
(11) Two "waistbands"; a worn broad shawl
(12) A faded and worn linen robe

Comments

The list of clothing gives the impression that their owner, preparing for a voyage, had bought a number of new pieces, but death overcame him; his estate, as so often happened, was contested, and the belongings left by him could not be touched. By the time the matter was settled, it was found that many garments, including a new one, had lost their colors (which probably had not been very strong to begin with). The dealer to whom the wardrobe was offered divided it into two heaps, one consisting mostly of the new pieces, each of which he tried to evaluate separately, and another of items seemingly of little account to him. We find that the former proprietor, probably a small merchant, owned all in all two turbans, five robes, three "broad shawls" (for going out), one gown (with sleeves, for special occasions), three underwear, and a *tafṣīla*, a piece of clothing appearing only in the early thirteenth century, probably a kind of jacket.[261] Add to that what the man took with himself into his tomb.

The document is in the hand of the court clerk Solomon b. Elijah b. Zechariah (ca. 1230).[262] Since the proceeds from this sale were probably to be paid to a widow or orphan, the action had to be supervised by a communal official. What we have is the draft, which the clerk made for himself. The final record would contain all the details we tried to surmise, as well as the names and date.

Document X a–e

Documents on Jewelry and Silver Utensils

Documents I–V translated above contain complete lists of trousseaus, including the ornaments brought in by the bride and the precious objects adorning her dressing table. Three other lists of jewelry are added here because they refer to well-to-do people of the eleventh century not represented in the preceding selections, and they have items not found in the texts treated before.

A fourth list, from the year 1159, is included because it is a telling counterpart to its contemporaries, Docs. II–V. Taken together these five lists illustrate the standards and tastes prevalent in the middle and upper echelons of a minority group near the end of the Fatimid period.

The fifth one is a somewhat elusive trousseau list: in content it is similar to Doc. X *a* (TS 12.12), which is from the earlier part of the eleventh century; in script it appears to belong rather to its end. In any case, it complements Docs. I and X *a–c* substantially, and rounds off the picture of an earlier stage of female ornamentation as represented in the Geniza.

(*a*) TS 12.12

This is the list of a trousseau from the 1020s, estimated to be worth 865 dinars. The total value of the jewelry and precious toilet articles was 181 dinars. The marriage gift of the husband amounted to 40 dinars paid, plus 60 dinars promised (see *Med. Soc.*, III, 375, sec. 19).

Translation

(2)	Four gold and four silver rings	10 (dinars)
	Two golden anklets	30
	Two golden *siwār* bracelets	30
	Two *dumluj* bracelets	30

(3)	A solitaire[263]	10
	A pair of "ambered" earrings adorned (with pearls)[264] and another pair of gold	10
	A silver tray	25
(4)	A silver box	20
	A sleeve ornament[265]	10
	A *khurdādī*[266]	6

(*b*) TS 20.7, dated Jan. 1050

The marriage contract of Abraham, son of Isaac the scholar, often mentioned in this book (see *Med. Soc.*, II, 512, sec. 10). The marriage gift consisted of 30 + 50 dinars; the jewelry and dressing-table objects were evaluated as worth 150 + 10 = 160 dinars.

Translation

(6) *This is the dowry she brought in to him from her father's house:* (7) Two *siwār* and two *dumluj* bracelets, a tiara, a *jān*,[267] a solitaire, two *dastaynaj* bracelets, adorned [with pearls], and three rings, all made of gold, and two silver rings,[268] total value 150 dinars; a filigree box ornamented with (8) sandalwood and a silver flask;[269] total value 10 dinars.

(*c*) ENA 2743, f. 2a

The bridegroom Peraḥyā b. Nathan *al-Ḥayfī* (of Haifa, Israel) appears in a document dated 1107 as a *zāqēn* (Heb.), or "elder." Thus, his marriage probably took place a few decades earlier. The script of the document, too, points to the late eleventh century. Peraḥyā's marriage gift amounted to 40 + 50 dinars,[270] and the total of jewelry brought in by the bride came to 121 dinars.

Translation

(3) A gold tiara (4) adorned (with pearls)	50 dinars
Two pairs of plain gold [bracelets],[271]	15 dinars
(5) A filigree solitaire	5 dinars
A pair of adorned earrings	4 dinars
Four (6) rings, two filigree, and two plain	7 dinars
A pair of *siwār* (7) amber bracelets with two gold rims,	10 dinars
A shoulder band,[272] consisting of twenty (8) gold beads, a gold apple, a gold myrobalan ["cherry plum"], and thirty amber apples.	30 dinars

(*d*) TS 13 J 3, f. 10, item III, 1159[273]

The marriage gift amounted to 30 + 80 dinars. The ornaments and dressing-table objects brought in by the bride were evaluated as worth 155 dinars. The stipulations for the "daughters of Israel" were the usual ones, except that the condition that the bride was entitled to choose the place where the couple would live was crossed out. Both spouses were Kohens and possibly cousins.

The document is in the clear and beautiful hand of Mevōrākh b. Nathan, who also wrote Docs. V (1156) and VII (1172).

Translation

(8)	A gold tiara, of seven pieces,[274] with mīnā sun disks and adorned with pearls	50 dinars
(9)	A pair of pins with gold hoops, *ṭārāt*, mīnā sun disks, and clusters of pearls	10 dinars
(10)	A pair of gold earrings adorned with pearls	6 dinars
(11)	A gold *lāzam*[275]	7 dinars
(12)	A pearl choker[276] with gold "sun" disks	2 dinars
(13)	A pair of gold *siwār* bracelets with niello work[277]	16 dinars
(14)	A single gold *dumluj* bracelet with niello work	14 dinars
(15)	A gold *tastaynaj* bracelet adorned with pearls	5 dinars
(16)	A gold *ḥadīda* bracelet with niello work	5 dinars
(17)	A gold [[*ḥadīda*]] palm leaf[278] with enamel rims	5 dinars
(18)	A single amber ḥadīda with gold rims	4 dinars
(19)	An amber *maymūn* necklace with gold beads, a tassel,[279] and pearls	5 dinars
(20)	A pair of pins of yellowish(?, or, rather: ẓāfirī)[280] gold	3 dinars
(21)	A ring of jujube-colored [dark-red] gold	2 dinars
(22)	A silver mixing vessel[281]	3 dinars
(23)	A silver spoon	1 dinar

[New page]

(1)	A silver presser[282]	2 dinars
(2)	A silver kohl jar, a *barniyya* container, and a pear-shaped shovel[283]	4 dinars
(3)	A silver comb and a bowl	3 dinars
(4)	A round mirror with a silver cover	5 dinars
(5)	Nine silver pins and a spoon	1 dinar
(6)	Five pieces of crystal[284]	2 dinars
	Total	155[285] dinars

(*e*) TS 13 J 17, f. 8 and TS NS J 390[286]

Yeshūʿā (Salvation) b. Abraham gives to Mubāraka (The Blessed) b. Ṭoviyā (Tobias) a marriage gift of 20 + 30 dinars. Her jewelry, as usual listed first, is estimated as worth 125 dinars and her total dowry, 480 dinars.[287] At the end, ll. 21–22, are noted one bureau with her lingerie containing a mirror with silver ornaments and another with a smaller mirror of the same type. It was normal for a mirror to be kept in a bureau, and it also occurs in other trousseau documents.

Translation

(2) . . . The Outfit:[288] (3) Two anklets and two golden *siwār* bracelets		50[289] dinars
Two *dastaynaq* [thus!] bracelets, adorned with pearls, four gold rings, (4) two earrings adorned with pearls, and two silver rings		20 dinars
An amber chain[290] (5) divided by nine gold beads, their number [namely, of the amber beads] being twenty-three, partly apples, partly "cherry plums," and two gold (6) earrings with amber		40 dinars
A silver *khurdādī*[291] and a small silver jewel box[292]	worth	15 dinars
[Total 125 dinars]		

Trousseau lists were customarily itemized. Occasionally, only the totals of the main sections (jewelry, clothing, and so on) were noted. The system followed here—rounding off the estimate of groups within the main sections—is rare, but reasonable. The evaluation of the objects was a matter of give and take rather than of exact computation, so it was often easier to lump a number of them together than to fix the price of each individual item.

Here, as in TS 12.12 (Doc. X *a*), the list notes first a particularly valuable ornament—the anklets of massive gold—just as Docs. II, III, IV, and X *c* open with the golden tiara. It concludes with the enigmatic *khurdādī*, as the context shows, a dressing-table object.

Notes

Notes

CHAPTER IX: *Daily Life*
Housing, Clothing, Food, and Mounts

A. THE HOME

1. The City

[1]About agriculture in the Geniza papers see *Med. Soc.*, I, 116–127.

[2]In the eleventh century the European merchants were already visiting the markets on the Islamic side of the Mediterranean regularly, but no Jews from there traded in the Christian cities (see *Med. Soc.*, I, 44–47). But southern Italy (Amalfi, Salerno, Bari) and Greece (Thebes, Salonika) belonged to the Geniza world.

[3]A single Geniza document (BM Or 5544) induced Norman Golb to write his massive book *History and Culture of the Jews of Rouen in the Middle Ages* (Tel Aviv, 1976; in Heb. An English version is in preparation). The document from Kiev (TS 12.122) is treated by him in Norman Golb and Omeljan Pritsak, *Khazarian Hebrew Documents of the Tenth Century* (Ithaca and London, 1982).

[4]See E. Ashtor, "Migrations de l'Iraq vers les pays méditerranéens dans le haut Moyen Age," *Annales*, 27 (1972), 185–214, esp. pp. 201–208; Claude Cahen, "L'Emigration persane des origines de l'Islam aux Mongols," in *La Persia nel Medioevo* (Rome, 1971), pp. 181–193.

To the places in Iran, mentioned in *Med. Soc.*, I, 400 n. 2, others could be added, e.g., Qumm (TS 18 J 2, f. 12, l. 21, a man from Qumm died in Aleppo, 1050). In Iraq-Mesopotamia, besides larger cities, such as Baghdad, Basra, Mosul, and Wāsiṭ, many smaller places, such as ʿĀqūl (near Baghdad), Hīt, Irbil, Nahrawān, Raqqa, Sarūj, and ʿUkbara, appear in family names.

[5]The towns of the India route will be considered in the *India Book* (see *Med. Soc.*, I, xxii, bottom; the documents thus far collected number 384).

[6]"Von der muhammedamischen Stadt im vierten Jahrhundert," *Zeitschrift für Assyriologie*, I. Goldziher Jubilee Volume 27 (1912), 65–74. The paper was later incorporated as chap. 22 in Mez's posthumously published classic *Die Renaissance des Islams* (Heidelberg, 1922; Engl. trans., 1937).

[7]On this point see A, 2 nn. 23–25, 52–54, below.

[8]"Die orientalische Stadt. Ein Überblick aufgrund jüngerer Forschungen zur materiellen Kultur," *Saeculum*, 26 (1975), 43–94, comprising a valuable bibliography of more than 160 items and many instructive plans of Islamic cities. See also n. 15, below.

[9]"Zum Problem des Bazars (sūq, çarsı). Versuch einer Begriffsbestimmung und Theorie des traditionellen Wirtschaftszentrums der Orientalisch-islamischen Stadt" (On the Problem of the Bazaar: An Attempt to Formulate a Definition and a Theory of the Traditional Economic Center of the Oriental-Islamic City), *Der Islam*, 51 (1974), 203–260; 52 (1975) 6–46. It is significant that simultaneously with Wirth's study on the bazaar (and not yet included in his bibliography on the Islamic city) appeared the voluminous and solid *El "señor del zoco" en España: edades media y moderna, contribucion al estudio de la historia del mercado* (The "Inspector of the Bazaar"

in Spain in Medieval and Modern Times: A Contribution to the Study of the Market), by Pedro Chalmeta Gendron (Madrid, 1973). Heinz Gaube and Eugen Wirth, *Der Bazar von Isfahan* (Wiesbaden, 1978), is a superb model for the application to an individual case of the principles evolved in the article mentioned above. See n. 69, below. A. Raymond and G. Wiet, *Les marchés du Caire: Traduction annotée du texte de Maqrīzī* (Paris 1979) reached me after the completion of this volume.

[10]Oleg Grabar, "Cities and Citizens," *The World of Islam*, ed. Bernard Lewis (London, 1976), pp. 89–116.

[11]Jean Sauvaget, *Alep. Essai sur le développement d'une grande ville syrienne des origines au milieu du XIX siècle* (Paris, 1941); Roger Le Tourneau, *Fès avant le protectorat: Étude économique et sociale d'une ville de l'occident musulman* (Casablanca, 1949); idem, *Les villes musulmanes de l'Afrique du Nord* (Algiers, 1957); André Raymond, *Artisans et commerçants au Caire au XVIIIe siècle* (Damascus, 1973, 1974). It is an indication of the great French tradition on Near Eastern urbanism that the comparatively small town of Qūṣ in Upper Egypt is treated in an excellent monograph of 657 pages: J.-C. Garcin, *Un centre musulman de la Haute-Égypte médiévale: Qūṣ* (Cairo, 1976). See *Speculum*, 53 (1978), 362–363 (review by S. D. Goitein).

[12]École Pratique des Hautes Études, Sorbonne, Sixième Section, Division des Aires Culturelles, *Les Villes. Entretiens interdisciplinaires sur les sociétés musulmanes* (Paris, 1958).

The state of research in the mid-fifties on the general character of the medieval Near Eastern cities is best represented in Gustave E. von Grunebaum's beautiful paper "The Structure of the Muslim Town," in his *Islam: Essays in the Nature and Growth of a Cultural Tradition* (Chicago, 1955), pp. 141–158.

[13]It cannot be argued, as has been done, that Jewish commerce and industry might have been organized differently from the Muslim. The Jews formed an integral, but only small, sector of the economy of their environment and could not have existed without adapting themselves to it. In addition, there was constant contact, and even cooperation between Jews and Muslims of the same socioeconomic level (see *Med. Soc.*, I, 82–99, 164–192; II, 294–297).

[14]*The Islamic City: A Colloquium*, ed. A. H. Hourani and S. M. Stern (Oxford, 1970); *Middle Eastern Cities: A Symposium on Ancient, Islamic, and Contemporary Middle Eastern Urbanism*, ed. Ira M. Lapidus (Berkeley and Los Angeles, 1969) (Lapidus has written copiously on the Islamic city, and more, I understand, is in preparation); *From Madina to Metropolis: Heritage and Change in the Near Eastern City*, ed. L. Carl Brown (Princeton, 1973). The introductory essays by A. H. Hourani and L. Carl Brown provide good introductions to recent research on the Islamic city. The Princeton book is richly illustrated with plans, photos, and artistic views of traditional cities, and so is Bernard Lewis's *World of Islam* (see n. 10, above). Special mention must be made of the profuse and superb picture material in Dominique Sourdel and Janine Sourdel, *La civilisation de l'Islam classique* (Paris, 1968), the value of which is enhanced by the detailed commentaries accompanying each picture.

[15]Michael E. Bonine, "Urban Studies in the Middle East," *Middle East Studies Association Bulletin*, 10, 3 (Oct. 1976), 1–37; idem, *The Islamic City: Factors of Change, Social and Moral Aspects. Colloquium on the Islamic City, Middle East Center, Cambridge University, July 1976*, A UNESCO publication, ed. Yusuf Ibish (1977); idem, "From Uruk to Casablanca: Perspectives on the Urban Experience of the Middle East," *Journal of Urban History*, 3 (1977), 141–180; Dale F. Eickelman, "Is There an Islamic City? The Making of a Quarter in a Moroccan Town," *IJMES*, 5 (1974), 274–294.

[16]*The Cambridge History of Islam*, ed. P. M. Holt, Ann K. S. Lambton, and Bernard Lewis (Cambridge, 1970), II, 456–457.

[17]*Ibid.*, pp. 520–521.

[18]TS 16.200, l. 12 (Oct. 1225), even has *Miṣr wal-Qāhira*! The proof for *Miṣr* having been pronounced *Maṣr* as today is its spelling as *mṣr* throughout. Had the word been pronounced *miṣr*, writers of Hebrew letters certainly would sometimes have spelled it *myṣr*.

[19]Thus, paper manufactured in Damascus could be called *kāghidh shāmī*: TS 13

J 20, f. 26, l. 14, *Nahray* 34, or *waraq dimashqī*, DK VI, ll. 14–15, *Nahray* 146, two letters addressed to the same person (ca. 1070). The latter form is found also in TS 12.383*v*, l. 5, a letter to Ibn ʿAwkal, early eleventh century, ed. S. D. Goitein, *Tarbiz*, 37 (1968), 171.

[20]TS NS J 6 (Feb. 1092).

[21]Hence, Madīnī (not: Madanī) in the Geniza letters means a citizen of Palermo.

[22]See A. L. Udovitch, "A Tale of Two Cities: Commercial Relations between Cairo and Alexandria during the Second Half of the Eleventh Century," Miskimin et al., *The Medieval City*, pp. 143–162. The Geniza contains sufficient material for a comprehensive study of that port city. ENA 1822, f. 47, l. 23: "Nothing is worthwhile buying here." Ink: Ibrahīm b. Farāḥ, representative of merchants in Alexandria (see *Med. Soc.*, I, 304 and n. 20) orders two ounces of ink to be bought in Fustat "from the Persian at the gate of the mosque" (TS 13 J 17, f. 15*v*, ll. 8–9). The recipient knew, of course, which mosque was intended.

[23]See the Index for the towns mentioned in this paragraph.

[24]JNUL 10, ll. 14–16: *fa-fariḥat alladhī lam taqaʿ maʿ ahl miṣr.*

[25]TS 8 J 5, f. 2 a–c (1132).

[26]N. Golb, "The Topography of the Jews of Medieval Egypt," *Journal of Near Eastern Studies*, 24 (1965), 251–270, and esp., 33 (1972), 116–149. My card index of Geniza material on places in Egypt was at Golb's disposal and he could also use E. Ashtor's important article, "The Number of Jews in Medieval Egypt," *Journal of Jewish Studies*, 18 (1967), 9–42, and 19 (1968), 1–22. Thus, for the time being, Golb's study is the final work on the subject. As far as my card index is concerned, I must remark, however, that I entered only matters that for any reason appeared to be significant for the characterization of the locality concerned. At a later stage of Geniza research, when all the relevant texts will have been properly transcribed, more mechanical methods may be applied. In the 1972 continuation of Golb's article, p. 117, s.v. "Akhmīm," I must correct a mistake of mine. In TS 13 J 22, f. 24*v*, l. 9 (see n. 161, below), I read *ʿwlm* for *ṭlm* (which stands for *ẓulm*). The letter does not say "that many Jews lived in Akhmīm," but that travelers were molested there. Golb (*ibid.*, p. 145): the locality Faraskūr is attested in the Geniza, TS 24.76, l. 31 (see *Med. Soc.*, II, 438), where *bēt faraskūr* receive eight loaves of bread at a communal handout in Fustat (ca. 1025). See also n. 220, below.

[27]For Damietta–al-Maḥalla see *Med. Soc.*, III, 178 and n. 89. See also S. D. Goitein, "Townsman and Fellah: A Geniza Text from the Seventeenth Century," *Asian and African Studies*, 8 (1972), 257–261.

[28]The use of the term *Rīf* for the towns of Palestine as opposed to Jerusalem (see *Med. Soc.*, I, 426 n. 19) is exceptional.

[29]ULC Or 1080 J 276. See on this city-Rīf complex in marital relations *Med. Soc.*, III, 150 ff. and 177 ff.

[30]TS 13 J 18, f. 25, see *Med. Soc.*, II, 528 n. 57

[31]TS 13 J 16, f. 6, l. 7: *ḥāmās* (Heb.) *al-Rīf*; TS 10 J 8, f. 2, l. 23 (Solomon b. Elijah to the judge Hananel): he cannot find in the *balda*, small town, anyone *fīhi faḍīla*, perhaps to be translated "a civilized person."

[32]TS 24.78, passim, ed. S. D. Goitein, *H. A. R. Gibb Jubilee Volume*, ed. G. Makdisi (Leiden, 1965), pp. 270–284.

[33]JNUL 4°577, f. 10, l. 6: *wa-aḥwajanī al-zaman* (no *ā*) *ʿayyadt al-ʿunṣura barrā*: "I was forced by circumstances to pass the Pentecost outside [the city]."

[34]See A, 3, below.

[35]See *Med. Soc.*, I, 54 and 404 n. 72; Ennen, *Europäische Stadt*, p. 202. Although 90–95 percent of medieval towns had fewer than 2,000 inhabitants they still were economically important.

[36]E.g., Eli, son of Hillel b. Eli, clerk of the rabbinical court of Fustat, was *nā'ib al-nāẓir bil-Bahnasā*, "deputy overseer of the B. district," and lived there, as is evident from his correspondence with his sister and her husband, the court clerk Ḥalfōn b. Manasse (TS 13 J 21, f. 18). A Jewish *ʿāmil al-Buḥayra*, "director of finances in the B. district," is mentioned in TS 24.78.

[37]Physicians, e.g., in Ashmūm (also called Ashmūn) Ṭannāh: TS 16.335 (1228); in al-Maḥalla and Ibyār (also called Abyār): TS 10 J 12, f. 1; in Qūṣ: TS 8 J 6, f. 12 (1216); two physicians and one apothecary in Minyat Ziftā: TS 12.543 (1265).

[38]Wealthy bride: Firkovitch II, 1700, f. 25 b. In TS 12.695, l. 5, the bride is obliged to live in Fustat (to exclusion of which other place is not preserved [ca. 1140]). Divorce: TS 12.588.

[39]Maqrīzī, *Khiṭaṭ*, I, 342, ll. 20 ff. See also G. Wiet, *Cairo*, p. 49: Ibn Saᶜīd describes Fustat also as cheaper because it was situated nearer the Nile than Cairo. He visited Egypt in the 1240s (see *EI*², III, 926).

[40]Maqrīzī, *Khiṭaṭ*, p. 363, l. 5. As the examples from the Geniza prove, these restrictions were not in force to the very end of the Fatimid period, as assumed by K. A. C. Creswell, *Colloque 1969*, p. 127.

[41]See *Med. Soc.*, II, 243–244, 345–355; TS 16.188 (Jan. 1105); TS 16.286, l. 25 (Oct. 1219).

[42]TS Arabic Box 40, f. 113, *India Book* 319; JNUL 5 (1133), ed. S. D. Goitein, *Kirjath Sepher*, 41 (1966), 267–271; TS Arabic Box 48, f. 270, *India Book* 86, ed. S. D. Goitein, *Sinai*, 33 [1953], 234–237: Ḥalfōn b. Nethanel asks his brother, a judge in Maṣlī'aḥ's court, to put up two distinguished India traders in the family house in Cairo, not in Fustat.

[43]In 1141 the son of a water carrier sold an eighth of a house in Cairo for 10 dinars (ENA 2558, f. 3). The three couples betrothed in Cairo in the years 1107–1110 (see *Med. Soc.*, III, 90–91) were very poor.

[44]See *Med. Soc.*, I, 18–19, II, 141–142. Abraham Maimonides: Bodl. MS Heb. b 3 (Cat. 2806), f. 6 (1213/4, his house). TS NS J 59: visit to Cairo.

[45]*Colloque 1969*. Contains also summaries in European languages of papers printed in a three-volume Arabic publication, *Nadwa 1969*. The book of the sociologist Janet L. Abu-Lughod, *Cairo: 1001 Years of the City Victorious* (Princeton, 1971) is concerned mainly with the modern era. Susan Jane Staffa, *Conquest and Fusion: The Social Evolution of Cairo*, A.D. *642–1850* (Leiden, 1977).

[46]See A, 2, nn. 15–25, below.

[47]Spelled *khwṭ*, TS K 25, f. 251, l. 3, ed. S. D. Goitein, in Miskimin et al., *The Medieval City*, pp. 163–178; Gottheil-Worrell, VIII, p. 40, l. 10.

[48]The sources for this and partly also for the following paragraphs in A 2, 3, below. See also E. J. Worman, "Notes on the Jews in Fustat etc.," *JQR*, 18 (1905/6), 1–39. An outline map of Fustat in *EI*¹, s.v. "Cairo," shows all the names cited.

[49]TS K 25, f. 251*v*, ll. 3–4. See George T. Scanlon, *Colloque 1969*, p. 415.

[50]TS Arabic Box 53, f. 60: *al-shāriᶜ al-maslūk minhu ila 'l-ḥāra 'l-maᶜrūfa bi-Saqīfat Shaᶜīra wa-ila 'l-ḥāra 'l-maᶜrūfa bil-Mamṣūṣa*. In TS Arabic Box 53, f. 61, Mahra is called *ḥāra*, while Maqrīzī, *Khiṭaṭ*, I, 297, speaks of *khuṭṭ Mahra*. TS Arabic Box 30, f. 263: *bi-Khawlān fi 'l-ḥāra 'l-maᶜrūfa bi-masjid Mālik bin Shuraḥīl*. TS Arabic Box 53, f. 66, l. 8: *bil-rāya fi 'l-ḥara 'l-maᶜrūfa bi-maḥbas Banāna*, "in the Rāya, in the ḥāra known as Banāna prison." Here ḥāra designates a subdivision of the Rāya quarter.

For the use of the terms *ḥāra*, *darb*, in Mamluk and Ottoman times, see Nawal al-Messiri Nadim, "The Concept of the Hara," *Annales Islamologiques*, 15 (1979), 313–348. The reference to Lapidus 1969: 80, on p. 313, sends the reader to my paper, "Cairo: An Islamic City in the Light of the Geniza Documents," a first attempt to summarize the subject treated here in A, 1.

[51]The Great Bazaar: TS 12.694 (1139). Mamṣūṣa: TS K 25, f. 251, l. 9. Fortress of the Candles: TS 16.72 (ca. 1070).

[52]For *taṣqīᶜ* (also spelled with *s*) cf. Ibn Muyassar, p. 65, second line from bottom, and Dozy, *Supplément*, I, 839; for *taṣqīᶜ al-rubᶜ*, or *taṣqīᶜ jibāyat al-shaykh Abu 'l-Bayān* see the sources listed *Med. Soc.*, II, 417–418, secs. 25, 27, 28, 30, and elsewhere. See Gil, *Foundations*, p. 592, s.v.

[53]TS Arabic Box 30, f. 30*v*, l. 3: *nāḥiyat banī Ḥasan* (November 1132); TS 12.586; *nāḥiyat al-Qashmīrī* (thirteenth century). Also *khuṭṭ al-Dāyamis*: TS 8 J 6, f. 14*v* (1241). The Maṣāṣa (Mamṣūṣa) is called *nāḥiya* in TS 12.694 (1139).

[54]The Alexandrian quarter most frequently mentioned in the Geniza is al-Qamra,

e.g., TS 10 J 12, f. 16*v*, a letter addressed to the *funduq* in that quarter; TS 10 J 18, f. 3 (silk weavers, dyers, market criers); TS 13 J 18, f. 29; 13 J 36, f. 11 (a Jewish neighborhood). Hence the family name al-Qamrī (TS NS J 36). One letter is addressed to Bīr Jabr, the synagogue of the Iraqians in Alexandria (ENA 154 [2558]). A rather spacious house was in al-Qarāfa quarter (Maimonides, *Responsa*, p. 2).

[55]For the pronunciation *rubᶜ* cf. the spelling of *rwbᶜ*, Bodl. MS Heb. b 11 (Cat. 2874), f. 5, ll. 7, 28 (see *Med. Soc.*, II, 413, sec. 5). For the compounds of the poor and of the Jerusalemites see *ibid.*, p. 437, and Gil, *Foundations, passim.* Muqaddasi, p. 31, l. 4, identifies *ṣāḥib al-rabᶜ* with *maslaḥa*, police (station) and *ṣāḥib al-ṭarīq*, guard. In Cl. Cahen, "Histoires Coptes d'un cadi médiéval," *BIFAO*, 59 (1960), 12–13, *ribāᶜ* are pious foundations as in the Geniza. The editor of Muqaddasi vowels *rabᶜ*, plot, site, but the Geniza spells *rubᶜ*. The pronunciation accepted today is *rabᶜ* (see Spiro, *Dictionary of Modern Arabic*, p. 187; Mona Zakariya, "The Rabᶜ de Tabbāna," *Annales Islamologiques*, 16 [1980], 275).

[56]See *Med. Soc.*, II, 608 n. 37.

[57]This was the Arabic name of a notable otherwise known as Samuel, the Pride of the Congregations, son of Nethanel, the Head of the Congregations (Bodl. MS Heb. e 98 [no Cat.], f. 63*v*, item I [ca. 1138]; see *Med. Soc.*, III, 310 and n. 169). His Hebrew titles show that he was a prominent man.

[58]The term " ᶜĀnānī," named after ᶜĀnān, the "founder" of the Karaite sect, designated in the Arabic speech of this period simply a Karaite, it seems, with a slightly pejorative touch. See *EI*², s. v. " ᶜĀnāniyya."

[59]Partly effaced, perhaps to be read *al-kattān*, the flax merchant.

[60]ENA NS 2, I, f. 20, ll. 1–9 (middle of the twelfth century).

[61]ENA 4011, f. 29*v*, l. 11 (1181/2), see *Med Soc.*, II, 423, sec. 112, and Gil, *Foundations*, p. 367: a darrāb receives a payment of 6 dirhems from the Jewish community. For Spain see Dozy *Supplément*, I, 429*b* (with the interesting detail that the darrāb was accompanied by a watchdog).

[62]A. H. Freimann, "Responsa of R. Maimon, the Father of Maimonides," *Tarbiz*, 6, 3 (1935), 174, ll. 16–18. Epiphany: Mez, *Renaissance*, chap. 23, p. 398, citing al-Masᶜūdī, *Murūj*, ed. C. Barbier de Maynard and Pavet de Courteille (Paris, 1861–1877), II, 364 ff. Also: Al-Ḥākim: *EI*², III, 79, based on Maqrīzī, *Khiṭaṭ* (suggested by Paula Sanders).

[63]In *Med. Soc.*, I, 411 n. 8, a money changer is mentioned as having his office in the Street of the Coppersmiths. From ENA 4020, f. 43, an important business letter sent from Būṣīr to Fustat, it is evident that the Dār al-Baraka, The House of the Blessing, the great bourse, where the money changers had their offices, was situated in that street. This House hardly was identical with one bearing the same name, which was given by Abdallah the son of Omar I to the caliph Muᶜāwiya (or Marwān I), as Ibn Duqmāq, IV, 6, reports, for then the building would have been in existence about four hundred years. But the site was perhaps the same, in which case the House would have preceded in time the street. "[The Mamluks] did not leave a mill, a press, or a house without plundering it": TS 8 J 23, f. 17, ll. 5–8.

[64]For references see nn. 77–82, below.

[65]TS 16.146, ll. 5–6, *India Book* 286: *al-dakākīn allatī bi-Fusṭāṭ fī ṭaraf al-shāmmāᶜīn alladhī al-wāḥida*(!) *minhum sukn al-shaykh Abu 'l-Barakāt al-ṭabīb*, "two stores in Fustat at the end of the street of the wax makers, one of which is the domicile of the physician A.B."); ENA 1822 A, f. 64: *musammirīn*, "horseshoers"; Judge: ULC Or 1080 J 23, see *Med. Soc.*, III, 220 and n. 244.

[66]TS NS J 190*v*: *al-maṭbakh al-maᶜrūf bi-sukn al-Rashīd Samwāl*, Ibn Duqmāq, IV, 41, ll. 1–3, speaks of a (sugar-)workshop in a Jewish residential neighborhood, in which a prominent Muslim lived (*yaskunuhu*).

[67]TS 13 J 20, f. 5, ll. 20–21: *lā fī mulk sukn wa-lā fī maṭbakh* (actually two drafts).

[68]TS 8 J 27, f. 15 (ca. 1200).

[69]See, in particular, *Der Islam*, 52 (1975), 287 ff. Since the writing of these lines the monumental work of Heinz Gaube and Eugen Wirth, *Der Bazar von Isfahan* (Wiesbaden, 1978), has appeared, matched by André Raymond's creations in this field:

A. Raymond and G. Wiet, *Les marchés du Caire: Traduction annotée du texte de Maqrīzī* (Cairo, 1979); André Raymond, *Artisans et commerçants au Caire au XVIIIe siècle* (2 vols; Damascus, 1973, 1974). Clifford Geertz, "Suq: The Bazaar Economy in Sefrou," in *Meaning and Order in Moroccan Society* (Cambridge University Press, 1979), although dealing with a small town, is an eye-opener for the understanding of the nature of dealings in the bazaar and is of special interest for the student of the Geniza, since the once considerable Jewish population of Sefrou was very much involved in this intricate socioeconomic process.

[70]Bodl. MS Heb. b 12 (Cat. 2875), fs. 6 and 29, ed. S. Assaf, *Tarbiz*, 9 (1938), 202–204, Engl. trans., S. D. Goitein, *Mélanges Le Tourneau* (Aix-en-Provence, 1973), pp. 401–403.

[71]TS 20.85, a large and very beautiful fragment; the last digit of the date is missing. It was written in 948–958.

[72]TS 12.499, ed. S. Assaf, *Tarbiz*, 9 (1938), 205–206.

[73]TS 28.3, the house of the goldsmith appears here again, but in the form of "the house known as that of *the son* of the goldsmith." The Fatimid caliph Muᶜizz ruled 972–975. About the role of a representative of the merchants see *Med. Soc.*, I, 186–192. In TS 13 J 1, f. 5, ed. Braslavsky, *Our Country*, p. 101, the daughter and heir of that representative of the merchants appoints an attorney to claim the estate on which some women (probably the heirs of the other two-thirds of the house) had laid their hands (1024/5).

[74]This Wool Hall is of course not identical with the famous one, called so, or after its founder, *qayṣāriyyat al-Maḥallī*, the Hall of the Man from al-Maḥalla, which was in the new, Muslim section of the city (see Casanova, *Reconstitution*, p. 307).

[75]See A, 2, nn. 118–124, below.

[76]TS 16.116. Three out of the five properties surrounding the house in question belonged to the wives of the persons mentioned.

[77]TS 20.96, ll. 9 and 17, ed. S. D. Goitein, *Eretz-Israel*, L.A. Mayer Memorial Volume, 7 (1964), 85, l. 16; see Gil, *Foundations*, p. 137.

[78]See TS K 21, f. 98*v*, ll. 5–19 (ca. 1037), TS NS J 264 (ca. 1040), Gil, *Foundations*, pp. 155 ff., 182 ff., which clearly refer to the same property. On p. 156, translation to *b*, l. 5, read "the two storerooms (*makhzanayn*) and two shops," referring to ll. 14–18. "The large and the small rooms" and "the two shops" repeatedly mentioned identify the building.

[79]TS K 25, f. 284, ed., as transcribed into Arabic characters, and trans. Goitein, *Mélanges Le Tourneau* (see n. 70, above). The compound was in the part of the Fortress of the Rūm, which was included in the Rāya quarter, originally the seat of the Muslim High Command.

[80]TS 12.694. Interesting, but not completed. In the hand of Nathan b. Samuel.

[81]ENA 2558, f. 4. Detailed, but fragmentary. In the hand of Ḥalfon b. Manasse.

[82]TS 20.126 (1066). Left half of a Hebrew deed signed by many important personalities. Abraham, the son of Nathan, the former (temporary) Head of the yeshiva, buys from a woman a quarter of two stores with an upper apartment (l. 5: *we-ha-dīr]ā she-ᶜalēhem*) for 35 dinars (total value, 140). The location of the property is not preserved.

ULC Or 1080 J 239 (1220). Two-thirds of a property on the Mamṣūṣa street consisting of two stores with an upper apartment are given by their Jewish owner as security against a loan of 480 dirhems (later increased to 500 d., approximately 12 dinars). The other third was owned by a Christian. Total value, ca. 20 dinars.

[83]About the Tujīb of Fustat see *Ibn ᶜAbd al-Ḥakam, Futūḥ Miṣr*, ed. Charles C. Torrey (New Haven, 1922), p. 352, (index); about their leader, Muᶜāwiya b. Ḥudayj, *ibid.*, p. 347; about the Tujīb of Spain, *EI*[1], s.v. "Tujīb." "The man in the yellow silk robe": *Al-Balādhurī, Ansāb*, ed. S. D. Goitein (Jerusalem, 1936), V, 89, l. 19. "Ḥudayjī" designates a client of the clan of Ḥudayj, a non-Arab acquiring membership in the clan while embracing Islam. Thus the street was indirectly named after Muᶜāwiya's father.

[84]Bodl. MS Heb. d 66 (Cat. 2878), f. 99, l. 7. Cf. Gil, *Foundations*, p. 242 n. 9. To the readings noted there add *al-Maṣṣāṣa*.

[85]P. Heid 1451.

[86]Firkovitch II, 1700, f. 18*a*. For The Little Market of the Vizier, see Casanova, *Reconstitution*, pp. 114–115.

[87]TS K 25, f. 251.

[88]TS 16.72, l. 7, *Nahray* 216. The document refers to the end of Nahray's life, but the house might be identical with the one that was originally the property of his father-in-law, TS 8 J 11, f. 18 (1066) and Mosseri A 82, see *Med. Soc.*, III, 37 and n. 13, and A, 3, nn. 43 and 76, below.

[89]Bodl. MS Heb. d 66 (Cat. 2878), fs. 47–48.

[90]Ibn Duqmāq, IV, 108. The Geniza papers speak of the *majlis*, or Meeting House, of the Karaites, but do not refer to its location (see *Med. Soc.*, II, 266).

[91]S. Runciman, *Byzantine Civilization* (New York, 1959), p. 159.

[92]Houses on the Jazīra: Bodl. MS Heb. e 98 (no Cat.), f. 63: one-twelfth of a house mortgaged against a debt of 55 dinars (April 1136, hand of Nathan b. Samuel). TS 8 J 34, f. 4: in a prestigious neighborhood a house with two shops belonging to the son of the proprietress which bordered on an open space; TS 13 J 2, f. 25, l. 14 (1140), ed. M. A. Friedman, *Tarbiz*, 40 (1971), 337–340, see *Med. Soc.*, I, 68 and n. 40, III, 148 and n. 21 and *passim*; see also A, 2, n. 47, below.

[93]Qayrawān: ULC Or 1080 J 7 (1040) and Bodl. MS Heb. c 28 (Cat. 2876), f. 41, ed. S. Assaf, *Tarbiz*, 9 (1938), 214–215, refer to the same property. Both documents were written in Fustat (see *Med. Soc.*, III, 203 and nn. 195, 196; Bodl. MS Heb. a 2 (Cat. 2805), f. 23, ed. S. Assaf, *Tarbiz*, 9 (1938), 215–216, see *Med. Soc.*, III, 150 and n. 32).

[94]TS 8 J 4, f. 13 + TS 20.92, ed. S. D. Goitein, *Eretz-Israel*, 8 (1967), 288–293. The brothers fled in the 1060s in order to escape seizure by an oppressive governor, their property formed the object of a lawsuit in 1094 and 1095. The potter: TS K 6, f. 106, l. 4, see *Med. Soc.*, II, 416, sec. 16, and Gil, *Foundations*, p. 229. The *dār Quzmān* is designated here as *darb*, street.

[95]TS 16.83, damaged and not completed. Damascus in l. 5: *d[msh]q*. Like the documents concerning properties in Qayrawān, this, too, was written in Fustat (see n. 93, above, and next note). The parties might have been Persians, for the deed states that it cannot be invalidated by any document produced in court, whether written in Hebrew, Persian, or Arabic (in this sequence, ll. 17–18). The tens and singles of the date are lost. ʿAzīzī dinars were first coined in 976 (see Lane-Poole, *History of Egypt*, p. 118 n. 3). The century mentioned ended in 1040.

The Market of the Jews might be identical with The Little Market of the Synagogue, mentioned in TS K 6, f. 106, l. 8 (see preceding note, and, for relevant literature, Gil, *Foundations*, pp. 217, 230, 232). Heb. *pōʿēl* corresponds to Ar. *fāʿil* (see al-Qasimy, *Dictionnaire des métiers Damascains* [Paris and The Hague, 1960], II, 333). Porters: see *Med. Soc.*, I, 84 and n. 16.

[96]BM Or 5566 B, f. 7; see *Med. Soc.*, II, 415, sec. 12, and Gil, *Foundations*, pp. 214–217. This document, too, was written in Fustat.

[97]TS Misc. Box 8, f. 22 *a*, ll. 1–5, ed. Gil, *Foundations*, pp. 230–232. The leaf preserved is not the beginning of the document and had no reason to specify "the great synagogue."

[98]TS 13 J 8, f. 25, see *Med. Soc.*, II, 423, sec. 107, and Gil, *Foundations*, pp. 482–484.

[99]Abraham Maimuni, *Responsa*, pp. 158–160; Schacht, *Islamic Law*, p. 141.

[100]TS MS, temporarily in TS K 27, f. 45.

[101]1156: Firkovitch II, 1700, f. 22a. The sister probably was the proprietor of the other half. 1143/4: TS NS J 27, p. 3, item 4, notes in the hand of the judge Nathan b. Samuel. For Ḥudayjī Street see nn. 83, 87, 88, above.

[102]TS 13 J 22, f. 2, ed. S. D. Goitein, *Sefunot*, 8 (1964), 111–113 (see *Med. Soc.*, II, 416, sec. 18, and Gil, *Foundations*, pp. 270–274). The document is a personal memo made by one of the witnesses present and does not describe the site of the house concerned.

[103]E.g., TS Arabic Box 53, f. 70 (Muslim document): a Jew selling a quarter of a new small house in a Muslim environment, 1157); TS 12.694, see n. 80, above; TS 20.92 (Damascus 1092), see n. 94, above; P. Heid 1451, see n. 85, above; TS 16.356, l. 33 (1120); TS K 25, f. 251, see n. 87 above; TS Arabic Box 38, f. 116 (Bilbays, 1519).

[104]TS Arabic Box 53, f. 60. Ḥassān b. Ibrahīm b. Azhar al-ṣayrafī is the Ar. equivalent of Heb. Japheth b. Abraham b. Yā'īr (see *Med. Soc.*, I, 362, sec. 2).

[105]TS 12.300*v*, ll. 1–5. Another case of rebuilding in n. 99, above.

[106]DK XXVI; see *Med. Soc.*, II, 397.

[107]Storerooms: see n. 87, above. Charitable foundations: TS K 3, f. 11 a, l. 14 (1183); see Gil, *Foundations*, p. 340; Bodl. MS Heb. f 56 (Cat. 2821, no. 16), f. 59*v*, l. 6; see Gil, *Foundations*, p. 351.

[108]Rubbish disposal: ENA 4011, f. 32.

[109]TS Arabic Box 53, f. 19 (Muslim document from Minyat Ziftā): *ʿāmir al-binā'*.

[110]See A, 3, nn. 109–116, below. The house in the Maḥras quarter (see n. 166, below): TS 13 J 18, f. 21, ll. 17–23. "Neighborhood," *ṣuqʿ*. "Its structure is solid": *marfaq-hā makīn al-binā*. The plural *marāfiq* designates appurtenances; but the singular *marfaq*, as opposed to *uṣūl*, foundations, must refer to the entire structure above them. "A place where I can put my head down," meaning safely: *wa-yaḥṣul fīhā masqaṭ ra's*, which may also be translated simply as a home.

[111]Dropsie 386, ed. Mann, *Texts*, I, 461. For another part of this letter see *Med. Soc.*, III, 48 and n. 3. Ghuzz: Bodl. MS Heb. d 76 (no Cat.), f. 60, ll. 14–20.

[112]TS 8 J 41, f. 13, l. 12. TS Arabic Box 54, f. 20 (1124–1126).

[113]TS 20.168; see *Med. Soc.*, II, 414, sec. 6, and Gil, *Foundations*, p. 194. But, TS Misc. Box 8, f. 86 (*Med. Soc.*, II, 414, sec. 10 (1059), and Gil, *Foundations*, pp. 222–224) does not exactly belong here. The relevant passages say: ll. 2–3: M., a Jewess, for one month, 6 (dirhems), and she vacated (in the preceding line a Muslim was listed); ll. 13–14: the storeroom of the goldsmith, 25, and he vacated; *verso*, ll. 15–16: the baker, for two months, 12, and he vacated. It does not necessarily mean that the places concerned remained unoccupied after their former tenants left. Church: see Grohmann, *World of Arabic Papyri*, pp. 160–161.

[114]TS Arabic Box 18 (1), f. 155, l. 13; see *Med. Soc.*, II, 417, sec. 24, and Gil, *Foundations*, p. 300.

[115]TS K 15, f. 13d, col. II, ll. 18–19; see *Med. Soc.*, II, 419, sec. 36, and Gil, *Foundations*, p. 360. The payment was for three months, thus approximately the same as in the preceding case.

[116]TS 8 J 11, f. 4, l. 11; see Gil, *Foundations*, p. 338.

[117]See *Med. Soc.*, II, 141, and the lists edited by Gil, *Foundations*, pp. 378–392.

[118]Ibn Muyassar, pp. 65–66. See Bernard Lewis, *The Assassins: A Radical Sect in Islam* (New York, 1968), pp. 60–61.

[119]Gil, *Foundations*, p. 87; also p. 383, s.v. "*sadd bāb*."

[120]E. Ashtor, *A Social and Economic History of the Near East in the Middle Ages* (Berkeley, Los Angeles, London, 1976), p. 207. For a detailed description of the years 1062–1072 see Lane-Poole, *History of Egypt*, pp. 145–150.

[121]The Geniza contains dated documents for practically every year during the period 1060–1090—sixteen for the historical year 1066 alone—but not one, as far as I know, issued by an administration of communal real estate. The document from March 1085, discussed in *Med. Soc.*, II, 415, sec. 13, is a receipt for a payment to the poor of Jerusalem.

[122]See *Med. Soc.*, I, 186–192.

[123]*Ibid.*, pp. 194–195.

[124]TS 12.367, address, ed. S. D. Goitein, *Tarbiz*, 37 (1968), 71, top.

[125]Bodl. MS Heb. b 3 (Cat. 2806), f. 20, l. 20, *Nahray* 7. We say: "Such a quantity for approximately such a price." They mentioned a fixed price and asked that the quantity be adapted to it.

[126]ULC Or 1080 J 36, ll. 20–21, *Nahray* 178: *tajʿal quʿūdak fī dār al-jawhar fī kull sūq an waqaʿ*.

[127]TS 8 J 19, f. 24, ll. 21–22. See *Med. Soc.*, II, 296.

[128]DK 14, l. 12: *zurumbāq muṭabbaq min ʿamal [al-An]dalusī fī dār al-jawhar*. An order from al-Mahdiyya, addressed to ʿArūs b. Joseph, a native of the Tunisian seaport, who had settled in Fustat.

[129]See Casanova, *Reconstitution*, pp. 25–26. The sketch on p. 26, naturally, is a mere suggestion. For *saqīfa*, roofed passage, see n. 150, below.

[130]See Claude Cahen, "Un texte peu connu [ralatif=] relatif au commerce oriental d'Amalfi au Xe siècle," *Archivio Storico per le Province Napoletane*, 34 (1954), estratto 4.

[131]E.g., Bodl. MS Heb. d 65 (Cat. 2877), f. 18, l. 4 (Account for Ibn ʿAwkal), ed. S. D. Goitein, *Tarbiz*, 37 (1968), 180; TS J 1, f. 1, col. III, l. 9 (Nahray b. Nissīm, 1058).

[132]For Market of the Greeks see n. 70, above.

[133]See *Med. Soc.*, II, 366, and, *ibid.*, p. 281.

[134]*Dār mānak* is mentioned in a Muslim handbook on the revenues of Egypt in Fatimid times, written by the judge al-Makhzūmī in the early years of Saladin's rule (see Cl. Cahen, "Douanes et commerce dans les ports méditerranéens de l'Égypte médiévale d'après le *Minhādj* d'al-Makhzūmī," *JESHO*, 7 [1964], 256–257). The reading *mān·k* (and not *Mālik*, as Cahen doubted) is established by the Geniza documents, since the letters *n* and *l* in Hebrew, unlike Arabic, are totally different.

In *JESHO*, 5 (1962), 141–142, Cl. Cahen explains that the *Minhādj* pictures the Fatimid world. This tallies with the fact that the term *dār mānak* is not found in the Geniza later than the eleventh century. Anyhow, Ibn Duqmāq's note refers to an entirely different building, a house inhabited by Ibn Muljam, who was installed by the caliph Omar as Koran teacher for the Arabs of Fustat, but later became famous as the murderer of Ali, the fourth caliph. Ibn Duqmāq, IV, 6, l. 6, has *dār mān·k*, but I suspect it is a misprint, for it is referred to in the index of that volume as *dār Mālik*.

[135]TS 8 J 21, f. 29, l. 9, a letter of Mūsā b. Abi 'l-Ḥayy, Alexandria.

[136]Address: ENA 4020, f. 43, letter of Faraḥ b. Ismaʿīl to Judah b. Mūsā (Moses) b. Sighmār, addressed to the *dukkān*, or office, of Joseph, Purses: TS Arabic Box 54, f. 15*v*, trans. *JESHO*, 9 (1966), 40, l. 17 (a purse of 20 dinars), l. 21 (9 d.).

[137]DK 18 and TS 12.374, ed. Goitein, *Palestinian Jewry*, pp. 206–213.

[138]TS 8 J 33, f. 8*v*. The sister of Sālim writes to Abū ʿImrān al-Bāḥīr (The Chosen, Heb.) b. al-Muwaffaq at the *murabbaʿat al-ṣarf*.

[139]See Lane-Poole, *History of Egypt*, p. 103 n. 1, and my Index s.v. "Mint." For the operations of the Cairene Mint see A. S. Ehrenkreutz, "Extracts from the Technical Manual on the Ayyubid Mint in Cairo," *BSOAS*, 15 (1953), 432–447.

[140]TS Arabic Box 38, f. 86, l. 13, in the description of the boundaries of a newly erected oil press, given by a father to his daughter: *ilā darb al-ḥadīd wal-ṣaffayn wa-ilā kanīsat Bū Sarga* (spelled, of course, *srjh*). Fragment of a beautiful Arabic document.

[141]See *Med. Soc.*, I, 193, 195, 224, 227. ULC Or 1080 J 130 margin: "The prices of *pepper* and flax in the Qālūṣ" (spelled here with *ṣ*, as often). The small house: TS NS Box 306, f. 1*v*, l. 5; see *Med. Soc.*, II, 419, sec. 39, and Gil, *Foundations*, p. 298 n. 16, p. 305, text col. I, l. 9. For the meaning of the word (cheering, welcoming) see Fraenkel, *Aramäische Fremdwörter*, p. 284. Misṭāḥ: TS 12.174. When the twelfth of the site was purchased by an outsider, a partner acquired it for the same price by right of preemption, *shufʿa*. For *misṭāḥ* see also *Med. Soc.*, II, 114 and 545 n. 4.

[142]See *Med. Soc.*, I, 194. "The Colonnade and the Qaysāriyya": TS 8 J 16, f. 31*v*, margin. "Carpet house": TS 10 J 7, f. 6 *b*, sec. 3, see *Med. Soc.*, I, 365, sec. 13.

[143]See n. 74, above, and Bodl. MS Heb. a 3 (Cat. 2873), f. 35, l. 4: "the qaysāriyya known by ʿAbd al- ʿAzīz, in which cloths are sold." This market hall, which was situated at *mawridat al-ṣiqāra*, "the wharf [on the Nile river] of the falconers (or: bandits)," is not noted by Casanova, nor is the wharf.

[144]See *Med. Soc.*, II, 113–114, 135, 420, 434, 465, 545, 548, and Gil, *Foundations*, pp. 112–115, and Index, p. 549. Structural details: *qāʿa, sufl, ʿulūw, ṭabaqa*, see A, 2, *passim*, below.

[145]*Med. Soc.*, II, 154.

[146]*Ibid.*, I, 349–350.

[147]TS 20.104, ll. 8–10, see *Med. Soc.*, II, 227. Meanwhile the document has been edited by me in *Shalem*, 1 (1974), 21–25.

[148]The Muslim mail couriers had their seat in the market at the Bath of the Mice (see *Med. Soc.*, I, 293).

[149]Ibn Duqmāq, IV, 25, bottom, through 26, l. 2: *ḥānūt majzarat al-yahūd.*

[150]*Saqīfat Shaᶜīra*, ENA 2558, f. 4, l. 14, see n. 81, above; TS Arabic Box 53, f. 60, l. 3, leading to, or adjoining the Mamṣūṣa. Both Shaᶜīra and Mamṣūṣa are nicknames. Shaᶜīra, Grain of Barley, a little woman, Mamṣūṣa, Emaciated, lean (f.). Since women were often proprietors of houses, it is natural that a house named after one should become also the name of a neighborhood. TS Arabic Box 53, f. 60, a Muslim document, designates a *saqīfa* as *ḥāra* (see n. 50, above). Bodl. MS Heb. f 56 (Cat. 2821, no. 16), f. 56, l. 15 (1186), places half a house in *Maḥaṭṭ al-saqā'if*, the Depot of the Passages, not mentioned elsewhere.

[151]Ṣabaṭ Ibn Ayyūb: Mosseri L-197, ll. 13, and margin, l. 2, ed. S. D. Goitein, "A Maghrebi Living in Cairo Implores His Karaite Wife to Return to him," *JQR* (in press for 1983); TS 12.628, l. 2; Fraenkel, *Aramäische Fremdwörter*, p. 13, regards *sābāṭ* as Persian. Prisoner: TS Arabic Box 42, f. 130, ed. Cl. Cahen, "Une lettre d'un prisonnier musulman des Francs de Syrie," *Mélanges E.-R. Labande* (Poitiers, 1974), pp. 83–87.

[152]See Casanova, *Reconstitution*, p. 140. Ibn Duqmāq, *passim.*

[153]TS NS J 3, l. 16 (see *Med. Soc.*, II, 384).

[154]See nn. 9 and 69, above.

[155]Ennen, *Europäische Stadt*, p. 133.

[156]Johannes Pedersen's book-length article on the mosque "Masdjid" in *EI* is still a classic and cites the sources on which my remarks on the role of the mosque are based. See also George Makdisi, *The Rise of Colleges: Institutions of Learning in Islam and the West* (Edinburgh, 1981).

[157]Mosques are mentioned in the Geniza documents as boundaries, as endowed with premises occupied by Jewish tenants, or for other practical purposes, but there was no occasion to enlarge on their social or religious functions.

[158]See Norman A. Stillman, "Charity and Social Service in Medieval Islam," *Societas*, 5 (1975), 105–115.

[159]See E. Rauschenberger's map in M. Sobernheim and E. Mittwoch, "Hebräische Inschriften in der Synagoge von Aleppo," *Jacob Guttman Jubilee Volume* (Leipzig, 1915), and Alexander Dothan, "On the History of the Ancient Synagogues in Aleppo," *Sefunot*, 1 (1956), [7]–[8] (Engl. summary of the original Heb. pp. 25–61). The map *ibid.*, p. 37.

[160]See *Med. Soc.*, II, 143–145, 152–153.

[161]Ibn Duqmāq, IV, 10, ll. 17–25. The *dār al-imāra* was essentially the residence of the governors. How far it once served also as the center of administration is not evident from the description. The *dār al-sulṭān* in Jerusalem (1196) designated the residence of the members of the Ayyubid royal house who happened to be there (TS 13 J 22, f. 24, margin, ed. Goitein, *Palestinian Jewry*, p. 324). (Al-Malik al- ᶜAzīz, Saladin's son, and his nephew, al-Malik al-Muᶜaẓẓam, are mentioned as being absent from the town at the time of the writing of that letter).

[162]See Lane-Poole, *History of Egypt*, pp. 195 ff. A man whom the government wished to squeeze for money was tortured first in the *dīwān*, or general administration building, and then in the Citadel; the procedure was repeated in the same order: TS 10 J 7, f. 4, l. 13, *verso*, l. 4 (qalᶜa); ll. 6, 10, 20, 21, *verso*, ll. 1, 3 (dīwān). Ca. 1240. A Genoese "Frank" emissary entering the Citadel: TS Misc. Box 20, f. 153, etc.

[163]E.g., ENA NS 22, f. 2, l. 2: "I went to the dīwān" (nonpayment of poll tax). See also the preceding note.

[164]*Med. Soc.*, I, 340–341, 345, and *passim.*

[165]*Ibid.*, II, 380–392, III, 277 ff. For instance, there was a special office dealing with Christians and Jews from Syria-Palestine and not yet registered as permanent residents in Egypt (*ibid.*, II, 385).

[166]Arabic *bn'n(h)* may be pronounced in different ways. I take it as *bunāna*, pl. *bunān*, beautiful garden, an ancient Arabic name (see Werner Caskel, *Ǧamharat al-Nasab* [Leiden, 1966], II, 229). For Gardens, in the plural, as a female name, compare TS Arabic Box 18(1), f. 130*v*, l. 15, and Bodl. MS Heb. f 22 (Cat. 2728), f. 43, *riyāḍ*, which means the same (see *Med. Soc.*, II, 433, sec. 164). It also explains why Bunāna and Bunān were used indiscriminately. Casanova, *Reconstitution*, writes Banānat throughout, but no such name is known to me.

[167]TS 8 J 16, f. 6: address *ḥbs bnyn*, Bunēn = Bunān (Imāla). TS 13 J 3, f. 3, l. 8, ed. S. D. Goitein, *Sefunot*, 8 (1964), 122: "the large house in the neighborhood of *ḥabs Bunān*" (1143); TS Arabic Box 40, f. 53, col. II: *ḥabs Bunāna*; TS Arabic Box 53, f. 66, l. 8: "in the Rāya quarter in the district known by the *maḥbas Bunāna*" (in Arabic characters); Casanova, *Reconstitution*, p. 19 n. 2, has these three versions (which reflect real usage and not carelessness of copyists), as well as *maḥras* Bunāna. The maḥras ʿAmmār gave its name to a neighborhood mentioned in an eleventh-century document (ULC Or 1080 J 66, l. 2, see also Ibn Duqmāq, IV, 25, l. 3). ENA 2558, f. 4, l. 16: maḥras al-Sāriya (not mentioned elsewhere, it seems) and Abī [qurba] (see Ibn Duqmāq, IV, 23, l. 4), both near the Mamṣūṣa quarter. The word for police, *shurṭa*, could designate also a police station (see *Med. Soc.*, II, 607 n. 26).

[168]The Sicilian twelfth-century geographer Idrīsī has *maḥras* in the sense both of barracks and of a hospice for students, travelers, and paupers (see Dozy, *Supplément*, I, 270 *a*–*b*). Since the word was used in Egypt interchangeably with *maḥbas*, jail, the former meaning should be assumed as being commonly intended.

[169]TS 16.65, ll. 4, 8, 9: *al-sūq al-maʿrūf bi-ḥubs yūnus wa-yajrī fī dīwān al-jawāmiʿ wal-masājid*. This place seems not to be noted by the Muslim topographers.

[170]*Med. Soc.*, II, 368–372. Mounted police also *ibid.*, I, 243.

[171]See nn. 55–61, above.

[172]For the *ḥirāsa* see Gil, *Foundations*, pp. 88–90, and p. 241 n. 3. Table 6 (*ibid.*, pp. 89–90) is very useful, but includes matters other than ḥirāsa (which should not be translated as night watch). On the ṭawwāf see *Med. Soc.*, II, 86, and 540 n. 96. In the documents analyzed in *ibid.*, pp. 442–443, secs. 18–22, a night watchman receives regularly five loaves of bread; *ibid.*, p. 440, sec. 6: a payment of 3/8 dirhems; *ibid.*, p. 451, sec. 43: for three weeks 1 dirhem per week. The *bayyāt*, lit., night man (Bodl. MS Heb. f 56 [Cat. 2821, no. 16], f. 61, and Gil, *Foundations*, p. 352), is probably identical with the ṭawwāf. He is not mentioned by name, and therefore almost certainly was not Jewish.

[173]A payment of an average of 9 1/2 dirhems per month appears *seven* times in the accounts of the communal official Abu 'l-Bayān in the course of the years 1181–1184 (see the list, Gil, *Foundations*, p. 90). Gil (p. 89) assumes that this sum represented 4 percent of the gross revenue from the rent of the houses of which he was in charge.

[174]TS Arabic Box 52, f. 247*d*, esp. ll. 2–3, 10–11 (*Med. Soc.*, II, 427, sec. 137, and Gil, *Foundations*, pp. 324–325). The name of the watchman, Abū Kallabūṣ, seems to contain the Maghrebi *kallabūsh*, the man with the cap, with slight change of the sibilant (sh-s-ṣ) (see Dozy, *Supplément*, II, 482 *a*). *Khifāra* is the same as *ghifāra* (*Med. Soc.*, I, 469 n. 26).

[175]Gil, *Foundations*, p. 336, l. 12 (1182): 1/2 dirhem; p. 354, l. 16: 16 dirhems.

[176]*Ibid.*, pp. 353–354, ll. *a*4, *c*4, *c*14; see also *e*10 (1183/4): 1 1/2 dirhems for *ramy turāb*, or garbage removal. *Ibid.*, p. 302, ll. 6 and 11: 3 1/2 dirhems for "the funduq between the two synagogues" and the same for the synagogue of the Iraqians (1164). *Ibid.*, p. 97, referring to p. 474, ll. 11/12, where it is stated that for the Synagogue of the Babylonians 20 dirhems were paid, is a mistake. The payment was 5 3/4 d., including a fine or tip.

[177]Al-Kindī, Muḥammad, *Kitāb al-Wulāh* . . . , ed. R. Guest (Leiden, 1912), pp. 383, 395, quoted by Gil, *Foundations*, p. 83. The word for disposal, *kans*, sweeping, used here, is rare in the Geniza. But in Jerusalem in the 1930s we paid (to the Municipality) "for security and sweeping," *ḥerāse kenāse*, see p. 35, above. For "consideration," *juʿl*, see *Med. Soc.*, I, 185, II, 607 n. 7, and Gil, *Foundations*, p. 91, and 472*b* l. 11.

[178]TS 10 J 20, f. 5*v*, ed. S. D. Goitein, *Tarbiz*, 32 (1962/3), 184–188. See Gil,

Foundations, pp. 321–322.

[179]*Ibid.*, p. 396, ll. 18–21.

[180]*Ibid.*, p. 355*e*, ll. 5–8.

[181]George T. Scanlon, "Housing and Sanitation: Some Aspects of Medieval Islamic Public Service," in *The Islamic City*, ed. Hourani and Stern, pp. 179–194; Gil, *Foundations*, pp. 159–160. See A, 2, n. 21, below.

[182]The list of manual occupations described in *Med. Soc.*, I, 101–127, could now be considerably enlarged.

[183]TS 16.115, l. 9, see *Med. Soc.*, II, 413, sec. 1 and Gil, *Foundations*, p. 121.

[184]TS NS J 215, "For the entrance half ḥikr has to be paid to the Ministry of the Charitable Foundations": *dihlīz-hu muḥtakar li-dīwān al-aḥbās.* "The rest of the plot of that factory is free and not subject to ḥikr": *bāqī arḍ hādha 'l-maṭbakh ṭaliq lā ḥikr ʿalayh.* The property was in the Basātīn, or Garden, district (which should not be confused with the famous place bearing that name in our time) near the *maʿārij*, the stairs leading down to the Nile, a prominent landmark equally distant from the Fortress and the ʿAmr mosque (see Casanova, *Reconstitution*, p. 312).

[185]Maqrīzī, *Khiṭaṭ*, I, 196; see Gil, *Foundations*, p. 242 n. 5.

[186]See *ibid.*, pp. 87–88.

[187]Merx, *Paléographie hébraïque*, pp. 23–35.

[188]The accounts are listed in *Med. Soc.*, II, 418–419, secs. 31, 32, 35, and Gil, *Foundations*, pp. 342–346, 350–357.

[189]TS K 25, f. 240, entry 1.

[190]TS 20.3 (1117); see *Med. Soc.*, II, 435, sec. 176, and Gil, *Foundations*, pp. 232–240.

[191]TS 13 J 2, f. 3 (1093); see *Med. Soc.*, III, 92 and n. 79).

[192]TS 8 J 15, f. 17, ll. 10–11, ed. S. D. Goitein, *Tarbiz*, 34 (1965), 233–236; see Gil, *Foundations*, p. 365. In this letter the writer complains about the expenses he had made for the house.

[193]TS K 6, f. 44*v*, l. 23 (1247): *lil-ḥikrī*, for "payment to the man collecting the ḥikr." Had this man been an "official" (Gil, *Foundations*, p. 87), the text would have noted, as in so many other cases, simply ḥikr. The meaning of the passage: this time the tax farmer had collected the ḥikr in person.

[194]Government as coproprietor: TS 13 J 22, f. 2*v*, l. 2 (*sharikat al-sulṭān*); TS K 25, f. 251, l. 11 (*dīwān al-aḥbās*). In arrears to the dīwān for five months of rent: ULC Or 1080 J 27, l. 10. A building of the dīwān serving as synagogue: Westminster College, Frag. Cairens. 51*v*, ll. 1–9, see *Med. Soc.*, II, 284 and n. 42. See also A, 3, *passim*. A Jew contemplating donating his house to the government: TS 24.78*v*, l. 24.

[195]TS 8 J 5, f. 12, trans. Goitein, *Mélanges Le Tourneau*, pp. 405–406.

[196] See Gil, *Foundations*, p. 355, l. 12; 440 *c*, ll. 9–10; 464 *b*, II, ll. 1–3. *Ibid.*, ll. 14–16: a muhandis, his colleagues, and his employee receive 5 *nuqra* dirhems, the approximate equivalent of 15 regular dirhems. Since *muhandis* is derived from Persian *andāz*, measurement, the spelling with *z* is the original and older one.

[197]See n. 118, above.

[198]INA D 55, f. 14, l. 12: *qad nazzalt ismī fi 'l-qānūn wa-anā ʿalā shirā dār.*

[199]TS 8 J 5, f. 9, ll. 3–4 (July, 1130): *warrāq kabīr bil-wirāqa.* For the term see *Med. Soc.*, II, 597 n. 41.

[200]TS 10 J 11, f. 26, l. 6 (1038), TS 8 J 13, f. 18, l. 14 (1044), TS K 25, f. 240, ll. 3–5 (1218): *iṣlāḥ al-darb.* See *Med. Soc.*, II, 424, sec. 113, 414, sec. 9, 420, sec. 48–92, and Gil, *Foundations*, pp. 164, 208, 420–421.

[201]Firkovitch II, 1367. The merchant's name: al-Ṣafī Abu 'l-Maḥāsin b. al-Asʿad Abu 'l-Ḥasan Kātib al- ʿArab, four honorific names, but no proper name—in accordance with the custom of that late period. Kātib al- ʿArab, or Clerk of the Bedouin Levies, was a distinguished Karaite family (see *Med. Soc.*, II, 379 n. 28). For the persecution of 1301 see Lane-Poole, *History of Egypt*, pp. 300–301; Strauss, *Mamluks*, I, 84 ff.

[202] See *Med. Soc.*, II, 354–371. About the state of the city population in the times of anarchy see D, 2, below.

[203]See *Med. Soc.*, I, 59–70.

[204]DK 18 (ca. 1051), ed. S. D. Goitein, *Palestinian Jewry*, pp. 206–217. The reference there is to 2 Samuel 20:37.

[205]Bodl. MS Heb. b 11 (Cat. 2874), f. 7, ed. *ibid.*, pp. 251–253.

[206]TS 12.347, l. 32, ed. Mann, *Texts*, I, 385.

[207]AIU VII A 17.

[208]Gottheil-Worrell XXXIV, p. 157, l. 14.

[209]TS 10 J 15, f. 2, l. 9, *India Book* 110.

[210]TS 8 J 5, f. 13 (Jan. 1138), *India Book* 115.

[211]TS 10 J 15, f. 26*v*, *yāgēn ʿal malkāh we-ʿalēhā.*

[212]TS 16.106; Psalm 87:5.

[213]Ibn Jubayr, p. 302, l. 15. This usage was common.

[214]Jeremiah 29:7. In that chapter Jeremiah refers to letters he had received from the captives in Babylonia. They may have contained curses on the writers' city and blessings on Jerusalem—just as was done by their descendants two and a half millennia later in Yemen. Jeremiah taught them better.

[215]See n. 208, above.

[216]See Maqrīzī, *Khiṭaṭ*, I, 366, l. 9. Ibn Saʿīd quotes al-Bayhaqī, the older, I assume, see *EI*², I, 1130–1132.

[217]Quoted by Ch. Pellat, "Basra, patrie du réalisme et du rationalisme," *Colloque sur la sociologie musulmane, Actes, 11–14 Septembre 1961* (Brussels, n.d.), p. 337.

[218]Ennen, *Europäische Stadt*, p. 74. The meritorious author is, of course, aware of the fact that "each city had its individuality," each was a case by itself (p. 96).

[219]TS 18 J 1, f. 27, l. 6. An Abu 'l-Riḍā known as al-Subkī left all his property to his wife (Alexandria, 1185). TS 13 J 21, f. 29: a note from Cairo listing several persons, among them two called Qarqashandī, one, a schoolteacher, and another a Levi. The form with *r* seems to be the original, for Yāqūt, IV, 64, has only this one. But cf. *EI*², IV, 509 *b*. One or several persons named al-Shaʿrānī appear in the lists of beneficiaries of the community chest (*Med. Soc.*, II, 439, sec. 2 b, p. 440, secs. 4–5 [eleventh century]); one is a money changer (*ibid.*, II, 508, sec. 137); another in TS Misc. Box 25, f. 39).

Following S. Abramson, *Tarbiz*, 31 (1961), 200 n. 104, I listed al-Qifṭī as a Jewish family name. But an examination of the MS TS 13 J 22, f. 16, showed that the correct reading is al-Qafṣī (from Qafṣa in Tunisia). Golb, *Topography*, p. 136, is to be corrected accordingly. But Qifṭ in Upper Egypt had a Jewish community (see *ibid.*).

[220]E.g., Bahbītī (a father of two married daughters), TS Arabic Box 6, f. 28, ll. 9–10, *Med. Soc.*, III, 4–6 and nn. 10, 18. Balaqsī (a contributor to charity), TS K 15, f. 58, *Med. Soc.*, II, 495, sec. 67. Bathanūnī (Samuel ha-Levi b. Japheth al-Bathanūnī sells his maidservant, Cairo, 1207; the genealogy of his family in TS K 15, f. 47). Dakarnasiyya (a woman receiving clothes and wheat from the community), see *Med. Soc.*, II, 463, top. Faraskūr family, see n. 26, above. Ghayfī (his wife receives bread, TS 24.76, l. 38, *Med. Soc.*, II, 438. For further examples see Golb, *Topography, passim.*

[221]Damīrīs with differing personal names appear as contributors in lists of charitable fund raising in Fustat, *Med. Soc.*, II, 492, sec. 55, 494–495, secs. 62, 63, 64. Meshullām b. Mevassēr "known as Ben Pinhas al-Damīrī" gives a loan of 120 1/2 dinars, an exceptionally high sum, in spring 1100: TS 8 J 9, f. 6.

In the 1050s the deliberations about the formation of the leadership of the Jewish community were held "in the house of the Damsīsī": TS K 25, f. 244, ll. 17 and 33, ed. S.D. Goitein, *Shalem*, 2 (1976), 56–63.

[222]1087: TS 12.479, l. 9. Letter: ULC 1080 J 264.

[223]See *Med. Soc.*, III, 260–272.

[224]See D, 2, below.

[225]Al-Jāḥiẓ's essay "Yearning after the Home" is treated in a Ph.D. dissertation by Ṣāliḥ Habal, prepared under the supervision of Franz Rosenthal at the University of Pennsylvania.

[226]See esp. G. E. von Grunebaum, *Kritik und Dichtkunst* (Wiesbaden, 1955), p. 39 n. 56, where the literature on the subject is reviewed.

[227]TS 8 K 22, f. 12*v*.

[228]Yāqūt, II, 934, l. 19. Geniza letters from Zoar: Goitein, *Palestinian Jewry*, p. 204. The document edited there is not from Zoar.

[229]Ibn Jubayr, p. 307, l. 2. See n. 213, above.

[230]TS 16.102, l. 7: *faᶜādahū ᶜayd min tidhkār al-waṭan wal-ḥanīn ila 'l-waṭan*. The petition is written in clear Arabic script and proper language.

[231]TS Arabic Box 51, f. 107, l. 14, ed. S. M. Stern, *Oriens*, 15 (1962), 182: *al-muqām bi-waṭanih.*

[232]TS 24.14, l. 3: *bi-ḥukm al-ahliyya allatī baynanā wal-baladiyya*, ed. Gershon Weiss, *Haifa Studies*, vol. 4 (Haifa, 1978), 165, Heb.

[233]TS 16.262, l. 30, *India Book* 307: *wa-hū aydan baladīnā wa-yakhuṣṣnā kathīr*.

[234]See *Med. Soc.*, II, 274, 295–298. Other examples could be added. The learned father-in-law of Solomon, the son of judge Elijah, writes from Alexandria: "If the faqīh [Muslim divine] Jamāl al-Dīn travels [to Fustat], I shall accompany him": Bodl. MS Heb. c 28 (Cat. 2876), f. 64, l. 12.

[235]See *Med. Soc.*, I, 20–21; II, 67, 167. On p. 167 correct: the people from Ghaza sojourned in Ascalon, not in Hebron. I assume that those from both Ghaza and Hebron fled to the fortified port city of Ascalon at the advent of the Crusaders (see Goitein, *Palestinian Jewry*, p. 222). Tripoli-Alexandria: ENA NS 22, f. 1*v*.

[236]See nn. 45–62, above.

[237]E.g., Friedrich Heer, *The Medieval World*, trans. Janet Sondheimer (Cleveland and New York, 1961), p. 255.

[238]TS AS 150, f. 1 (early thirteenth century). The letter ENA 154 (2558), see *Med. Soc.*, I, 157 and n. 32, is addressed to Bīr Jabr, Synagogue of the Iraqians.

[239]BT Ketubbot 110 *b*. Small or middle-sized town: *ᶜīr* (biblical Heb.); big city: *kerākh* (postbiblical). Geniza: Mann, II, 190, l. 28 (from a private MS, owned by A. Harkavy). The reason given here is the dire economic situation, caused by the anarchic state of the country.

[240]About all this see *Med. Soc.*, V (in preparation), X, A, 2 nn. 241–254.

[241]See *Med. Soc.*, III, 178 and n. 89; D. Herlihy, "The Florentine Merchant Family in the Middle Ages," nn. 83–85.

[242]*Med. Soc.*, III, 53 and n. 21. The relevant document Mosseri L 197 is ed. and transl. in *JQR* 1983 (in progress), cf n. 150 above.

[243]"Jerusalem, a city of many curses," is absolutely exceptional and was written at a time of extreme hardship (in the letter cited in n. 239, above, ll. 28–29).

[244]Derekh Erets Zuta 10, BT Eruvin 55 *b*, bottom.

[245]Al-Shaᶜrānī, *Laṭā'if al-Minan* (Cairo, 1938/9), I, 33, cited by Michael Winter, "Shaᶜrānī and Egyptian Society in the Sixteenth Century," *Asian and African Studies*, 9 (1973), 327. 'Exodus" translates *hijra*, which has religious merit like Muhammad's exchange of the then pagan town of Mecca for Medina, where he was recognized as prophet. Winter refers to G. E. von Grunebaum, *Medieval Islam* (Chicago, 1953), pp. 173–174.

[246] Cited in BT Taᶜanit 23 *a* (Aramaic).

2. *Domestic Architecture*

[1]BT Berakhot 57*b*. Home first: BT Soṭa 44*a*, based on Deuteronomy 20:5–7.

[2]Midrash Esther Rabba 3:10 (commenting on the Book of Esther 1:9): the men enjoyed drinking, while the women were pleased to be seated in the beautiful rooms of the royal harem; *battīm meṣuyyārīm* probably means rooms with figurative paintings. A *Midrash* is in form an exposition of the Scriptures, but in substance a freewheeling sermon quoting many authorities as well as popular sayings.

[3]BT Pesaḥim 114*a* (in Aramaic). Cf. B, nn. 1, 2, below.

[4]See A. Arthur Schiller, "The Budge Papyrus of Columbia University," *JARCE*, 7 (1968), 81. The Greek terms used: *symposion* and *koiton*.

[5]See Krauss, *Griechische und lateinische Lehnwörter*, II, 274, *triklinion* (dining room); 528, *koiton*, both with numerous references to sources, some late. The Latin-Greek

terms for cellar, storeroom, *kellarion*, appears also in both the Coptic papyrus and Talmudic-Midrashic literature, see *ibid.*, 531. Mansions of the late Mamluk period had a "sleeping closet," see Richards, *Arabic Doc.*, p. 152, l. 11 (dated 1438), p. 138 (1513). But this development was new, cf. n. 103, below.

[6]Gershon Weiss, "Formularies (Sheṭarōt) Reconstructed from the Cairo Geniza," *Gratz College Annual of Jewish Studies* (Philadelphia), 2 (1973), 38–42.

[7]Jeanette A. Wakin, *The Function of Documents in Islamic Law: The Chapters on Sale from Ṭaḥāwī's Kitāb al-Shurūṭ al-Kabīr* (Albany, N.Y., 1972).

[8]"No description necessary," e.g., TS Arabic Box 5, f. 1, sec. B (Muslim, 1032); TS 13 J 4, f. 4*v* (Jewish, 1229).

[9]Beginning with south, e.g., PSR 1451 (Muslim); TS 16.116 (dated 1010); TS 16.356 (1120); TS 13 J 25, f. 9 (around 1250). East-west-south-north, e.g., TS 28.3 (July 1004) and TS 12.773 (same period). E-W-N-S: Dropsie 335 (Ṣahrajt in Lower Egypt, 1041). E-S-W-N: TS 16.132 (Egyptian countryside, 998). Cf. W. Hoenerbach, "Some Notes on the Legal Language of Christian and Islamic Deeds," *JAOS*, 81 (1961), 35: The sequence S-N-E-W was already common in the Demotic, Greek, and Coptic papyri of Egypt, but was recommended by the Muslim scholars as being religiously "the most noble direction." Hoenerbach states that in Spain the Muslims followed the Christian custom of starting with the East (p. 36). The reason for this difference between Egypt and Spain presumably was that in Spain the *qibla*, or direction of Mecca, was to the east rather than to the south.

[10]More about this in, A, 3, nn. 2–4, below.

[11]No commission for the broker: e.g., TS Arabic Box 53, f. 61. About broker's commissions see *Med. Soc.*, I, 160 and 184. "Bonus for the handclasp": TS NS J 27, case no. 4 (2 out of 75 dinars, 1143/4). TS 12.694: (1 dinar paid to the agent in addition to 14 1/2 dinars, the price of one quarter of a house, Jan. 1139).

[12]See *Med. Soc.*, II, 112–121, 413–437, "Appendix A: Documents Regarding Charitable Foundations." Moshe Gil, *Documents of the Jewish Pious Foundations from the Cairo Geniza* (Leiden, 1976).

[13]See, in particular, Grohmann, *APEL*, I, 159–273.

[14]See Richards, *Karaite Doc.*, and Richards, *Arabic Doc.*

[15]Aly Bahgat and Albert Gabriel, *Fouilles d' al Fousṭāṭ* (sic) (Paris, 1921).

[16]Albert Gabriel, *Les fouilles d'al-Foustat et les origines de la maison arabe en Égypte* (Paris, 1921).

[17]"The Dwellings of Fustat as Revealed by the Excavations" (in Arabic), *Nadwa 1969*, Vol. I (Cairo, 1970), pp. 223–251. Based on the excavation of the remains of one building, laid bare in 1964, which the author believed to have been erected in the Fatimid period. According to him it was only this discovery which made it possible to form an idea of how an Egyptian house looked at that time. See also the summary, entitled "Les habitations d'al-Fusṭāṭ," *Colloque 1969*, pp. 321–322.

[18]Beginning with "Preliminary Report: Excavations at Fustat, 1964," *JARCE*, 4 (1965), 7–30. See also "Fustat Expedition: Preliminary Report 1968, Part I," *JARCE*, 11 (1974), 81–91.

[19]George T. Scanlon, "Fusṭāṭ: Archaeological Reconsiderations," *Colloque 1969*, pp. 415–428; W. Kubiak and G. T. Scanlon, *Re-dating Bahgat's Houses*, Art and Archaeology Research Papers 4 (1973).

[20]*JARCE*, 10 (1973), 12.

[21]TS Box K 21, f. 98*v*, ll. 14–16 (see A, 1, n. 78, above): *ᶜamal qanāt dār Quṭayṭ wa-tajriyat-hā ila 'l-baḥr thamāniya ᶜashar dirhem*, "work on [or: construction of] the drainpipe of the house of the Little Tomcat and conducting it to the Nile—18 dirhems." The house itself was new, see Gil, *Foundations*, p. 141, l. 33, and p. 488, sec. (10).

[22]Ibn Riḍwān (see *EI*², III, 906–907), *Risāla fī dafᶜ maḍarr al-abdān bi-arḍ Miṣr* (Treatise on the Avoidance of Damage to Health in Egypt), trans. Max Meyerhof, *Comptes rendus du Congrès International de Médecine Tropical et d'Hygiene*, Vol. II (Cairo, 1929), pp. 211–235. The passage is quoted in Wiet, *Cairo*, p. 37.

[23]For the sources see Mez, *Renaissance*, chap. 22, pp. 390 nn. 1, 2, and the article of

Lézine cited in the next note. The passage from Nāṣir-i-Khosraw is translated in Wiet, *Cairo*, p. 39.

[24]A. Lézine, "Persistance de traditions pré-islamiques dans l'architecture domestique de l'Egypte musulmane," *Annales Islamologiques*, 11 (1973), 1–22, quoting A. Gabriel. A. Mez, in his paper on the Islamic city written in 1912 (cited in A, 1, n. 6, above), made the same observation.

[25]See, e.g., Wendell Phillips, *Qataban and Sheba* (London, 1955), p. 60, a look of Shibām in the early 1950s, where the houses dwarf the trucks of the American expedition. The German traveler Hans Helfritz called his first picture book on South Arabia *Chicago der Wüste* (Berlin, 1932), meaning Desert Cities of Skyscrapers. See the magnificent photos of Shibām on pp. 92, 97, 98, 110–111. The impression of Shibām "looking like a mountain" is well conveyed in illus. 63 in D. van der Meulen, *Aden to the Hadhramaut* (London, 1947). See *ibid.*, illus. 65–71.

[26]Lane, *Modern Egyptians*, pp. 4–22. His linguistic remarks sometimes need qualification. *Sidillā* (see n. 113, below), is Latin, not Persian.

[27]Description: see nn. 72, 97, 137, 142, and *passim*.

[28]Edmund Pauty, *Les palais et les maisons d'époque musulmane au Caire* (Cairo, 1932).

[29]Briggs, "The Saracenic House," and Martin S. Briggs, *Muhammedan Architecture in Egypt and Palestine* (Oxford, 1924), pp. 145–165.

[30]A. Lézine and Abdel Tawwab, "Introduction a l'étude des maisons de Rosette," *Annales Islamologiques*, 10 (1972), 149–205.

[31]Brandenburg, *Islamische Baukunst*, esp. pp. 57–96.

[32]Reuther, *Wohnhaus in Baghdad*, esp. pp. 19–24, 72 (for Jewish houses); *idem*, "Qaᶜah." Samuel Tamari's *Qāᶜah; A Lexico-Architectural Study* (Tel Aviv, 1981) (in Heb.) reached my desk when this volume had gone to the publisher.

[33]Hassan Fathi, *Colloque 1969*, "The Qaᶜa," esp. pp. 135–150. See also the same author's "Constancy, Transposition and Change in the Arab City," in Brown, *Madina*, pp. 319–333. I was particularly pleased to find that my characterization of the house in Geniza times, the result of laborious years of study and thought, resembles Hassan Fathi's concepts about traditional Egyptian domestic architecture. For a comprehensive bibliography on the subject, see K. A. C. Creswell, *A Bibliography of the Architecture, Arts and Crafts of Islam* (Cairo, 1961).

[34]See also J. Revault, "Espace comparé des habitations citadines du Caire et de Tunis," *Annales Islamologiques*, 15 (1979), 293–311, with its most instructive illustrations.

When this volume was about to go to the printer I received the gorgeous opus of J.-C. Garcin, B. Maury, J. Revault, M. Zakariya, *Palais et maisons du Caire*, Vol. I, *Époque mamelouke (XIII–XVI siècles)*, (Paris, 1982). While the 1975 volume by J. Revault and B. Maury with a similar title was of a more archaeological character, this new publication, also lavishly illustrated, undertakes a vast historical inquiry into the development of the habitations of the Cairene elite during the centuries concerned. Jean-Claude Garcin, an authority on the Mamluk period, examines archaeological data in the light of literary and documentary sources.

[35]In documents emanating from the rabbinical courts *ḥāṣēr* is the common term for house. In a Karaite marriage contract, Bodl. MS Heb. b 12 (Cat. 2875), f. 31, Arabic *dār* is rendered by Hebrew *dīrā*, which is derived from the same Semitic root. The same usage occurs in the ancient documents TS 16.181 (Damascus, 933), ed. Assaf, *Texts*, pp. 66, 68, S. D. Goitein, *Lešonenu*, 30 (1966), 202 (*dārā*, Aram.); TS 16.132 (from al-Bana near Fāqūs in the Nile Delta, 998); ULC Or 1080 J 7, l. 10, and Bodl. MS Heb. c 28 (Cat. 2876), f. 41, l. 7, the latter ed. S. Assaf, *Tarbiz*, 9 (1938), 214, both referring to "a large house" in Qayrawān (dated 1040); also in the late fragment TS 8.162 (around 1260). In TS 16.116, l. 17 where "house" is differentiated from "court," the former notion is expressed by *bayit*, although in ll. 9–12 *ḥāṣēr* corresponds to dār.

[36]TS 16.185: *al-binā' al-qā'im fi 'l-dār* (around 1120). Fustat: TS 10 J 14, f. 27, l. 11: *bāᶜ al-dār alladhī fī dār al-Khalīj*. Damascus: see n. 41, below. Church: Grohmann, *World of Arabic Papyri*, pp. 160–161.

[37]Bodl. MS Heb. a 3 (Cat. 2873), f. 35, ll. 1 and 3: *al-kabīra al-jāmiʿa* (tenth or eleventh century). Other instances, e.g., TS 12.172*v*, l. 5 (same period); TS 16.83, l. 7; TS 20.3 (Feb–March 1117); TS Arabic Box 38, f. 116 (Bilbays, 1519). For Qayrawān see n. 35.

[38]Merx, *Paléographie hébraïque*, p. 30 (1124); Bodl. MS Heb. d 66 (Cat. 2878), f. 3, ed. S. Assaf, *Tarbiz*, 19 (1948), 107 (around 1100); TS Arabic Box 38, f. 119 (1137); TS Arabic Box, 54, f. 92, col. I. Also: TS 13 J 20, f. 27, where half a *duwayra* was mortgaged against a loan of 12 dinars (around 1150), TS NS Box 306, f. 1, l. 10, etc. See Gil, *Foundations*, p. 547.

[39]E.g., TS 12.792, margin, l. 3, *Nahray* 9.

[40]TS 13 J 18, f. 26: a letter addressed to "the dār of the *muʿallim* (teacher, or: master craftsman), to the *dār al-ghazl* (the spinnery), the old one." The two spinneries are referred to by the Muslim historians, cf. Ibn Duqmāq, IV, 24 and 34. One was a pious foundation given to the Jewish community, cf. TS Arabic Box 18 (1), f. 155, *Med. Soc.*, II, 417, sec. 24, and 545 n. 3.

[41]TS 20.92, B, l. 7; TS 8 J 4, f. 13, l. 5 (Damascus, 1094). Similarly in Old Cairo: "He sold the dār which is in the house at the Nile canal," TS 10 J 14, f. 27, l. 11, see n. 36, above.

[42]See A, 1, nn. 122–139, above.

[43]"The residence (*sukn*) of Hāni, the room (*bayt*) of Samḥūn": TS Box J 1, f. 47, col. II (Old Cairo, 1234), see Gil, *Foundations*, p. 437; TS Arabic Box 53, f. 19 (Minyat Ziftā); TS 13 J 19, f.3, l. 10 (*buyūt maʿrūfa fī dār* (Jerusalem); TS 16.181 (Damascus).

The "classical" term for room, *ḥujra*, is rare and denotes a separate building consisting, it seems, of one room, e.g., *al-ḥujra al-maʿṣara al-mustajadda li-ʿaṣr al-zayt*, the newly erected oil press, TS Arabic Box 38, f. 86; *ḥujra tuʿraf bi-bayt Ben Quzmān*, the building known as the room of B.Q., mentioned as a boundary in TS 20.92, B, l. 6 (see n. 41, above). When a bride in Alexandria receives as part of her marriage portion "half a *ḥujra in the neighborhood of the al-Qashmīrī* mosque" (TS 12.586), and when "a *ḥujayra* (little *ḥ*.) near the Jewish quarter" is rented in Jerusalem (Gottheil-Worrell, no. XXVII, ll. 29–30), one has the impression that in both cases a separate building rather than a single room is meant. A Spanish merchant, writing from Morocco, refers by this term to a storeroom: *wal-lāk jamīʿuh ḥaṣal ʿindī fi 'l-ḥujra*, I keep all the lac in my storeroom: TS 13 J 21, f. 12, l. 21. In Tyre, a man is given at his marriage a ḥujra adjacent to the living room: (TS NS J 382, l. 5, end of twelfth century, ed. *Eretz-Israel*, 8 [1966], 293–297). A chamber erected above a tomb was also called ḥujra, see *Med. Soc.*, III, 479, nn. 145–146.

[44]ULC Or 1080 J 80, l. 9: *lil-bayt*. For the expression "the lady of the house" see *Med. Soc.*, III, 164 and nn. 25, 26. TS 20.6, l. 12, ed. S. Assaf, *Tarbiz*, 9 (1938), 30: *dār bēt al-ghallāq*, the house of the al-Ghallāq family.

[45]The general word for residence or dwelling place in the Geniza is *sukn*, used also for an apartment occupied by a tenant. For *manzil* see n. 38, first source. Also TS NS J 185, fragment 8, ll. 3 ff.: "I hereby give my daughter an eighth of this house (dār), two slave girls of mine and all that the manzil belonging to me in which she lives comprises, and there are no claims against her brother with regard to the manzil belonging to me in which *he* lives."

A place to live in: *mawḍiʿ*, e.g., TS 8 J 20, f. 18, l. 8, *Nahray* 82; P. Heid 913 (both referring to Fustat), and TS 8 J 4, f. 13, ll. 5 and 9 (Damascus, 1094); or makān, TS 13 J 2, f. 16 (Fustat, 1112).

Other words for apartment: *maskan*, habitation, e.g., TS 20.1, l. 20; pl. *masākin*, e.g., TS 8 J 5, f. 9; *ghalq*, a place that can be locked, *ʿaqadt jumlat al-ghalq ʿalā nafsī*, TS 13 J 6, f. 22, l. 6 (Jerusalem). See n. 136, below.

[46]These two prices in App. A, group II, no. 5 and group VII, n. 3, below.

[47]See A, 1, nn. 70 and 92, above. Also Mosseri A-108: Deathbed declaration of a man who had sold to his daughter and her son two-thirds of two shops inclusive of the upper apartment: *wal-ṭabaqa allatī aʿlāhum*.

[48]See A, 1, n. 77, above.

[49]A. O. Citarella, "Patterns in Medieval Trade: The Commerce of Amalfi before

the Crusades," *Journal of Economic History*, 28 (1968), 533 n. 6, bottom. The value of a solidus was approximately that of a dinar.

[50]A, 1, n. 80, above; Lane, *Modern Egyptians*, p. 21; he refers to "shops" in the plural. See n. 64, below.

[51]Bodl. MS Heb. a 3 (Cat. 2873), f. 35, see n. 37, above. The section of the Rāya quarter in which this house was situated was called Aṣḥāb al-ḥaḍar, Townspeople, meaning the original Arab townsmen coming from Arabia, as opposed to the tribesmen who formed the bulk of the new Islamic city. "Wharf of the Falcons": *mawridat al-ṣiqāra*, Wiet, *Cairo*, p. 40. For *qaysariyya* (with *s* also in the Muslim document) see *Med. Soc.*, I, 194, and A, 1, nn. 142, 143, above.

[52]Muqaddasi, p. 198; TS K 25, f. 251, see A, 1, nn. 47, 87, above.

[53]See n. 125, below.

[54]Ibn Ḥawqal: Wiet, *Cairo*, p. 36. It has not escaped me that A. R. Guest in his well-known article, "The Foundation of Fustat and the Khittas of That Town," *Journal of the Royal Asiatic Society*, n.v. (Jan. 1907), 82, describes this and other newly founded Arab towns as "a long straggling colony of mean houses and hovels." It can be true only for the very beginning. We have testimony for very substantial structures also from Basra and Kufa. See Ibn Zūlāq, *Akhbār Sībawayh al-Miṣrī* (Cairo, 1933), pp. 21–22.

[55]Bodl. MS Heb. d 66 (Cat. 2878), f. 99, dated 1139, see A, 1, n. 84, above.

[56]TS 16.140. See n. 30, above.

[57]TS Arabic Box 53, f. 19.

[58]ULC Or 1080 J 117 (1088), l. 17: A Christian neighbor has the right to push a wall forward in order to include a *sāḥa*, or open space, belonging to him. TS 13 J 4, f. 14 (Jan. 1214): The proprietor of a *mamraq*, or passage, allows two neighbors to build on it. TS 12.172*v*, l. 6: The sāḥa of an adjacent house mentioned as a boundary.

[59]E.g., Bodl. MS Heb. b 12 (Cat. 2875), f. 4 (1102); Firkovitch II 1700, f. 22*b*–23*a* (1156).

[60]Tilting house: TS 8 J 5, f. 12, trans. *Mélanges Le Tourneau* (Aix-en-Provence, 1973), I, 405–406. Portico: ENA 2558, f. 2, l. 25, cf. A, 1, n. 150, above.

[61]TS 20.96 (1040), ll. 31–33, ʿAbd al-Laṭīf, p. 179, see Wiet, *Cairo*, p. 46.

[62]Arched doorway, *al-bāb al-maʿqūd ḥaniyyuh*: e.g., TS 16.356, l. 23 (1120); TS 24.44, l. 10 (1102); this house was worth 102 dinars. Two door leaves, *darfān*: TS K 25, f. 251*v*, l. 6 (ca. 1190); Richards, *Karaite Doc.* 17, l. 10 (1285). Rectangular gateway, *murabbaʿ* (Hebrew *merubbaʿ*): e.g., TS 12.773, l. 9; Merx, *Paléographie hébraïque*, p. 25 (1124; this house cost 20 dinars); TS Arabic Box 53, f. 19 (in Minyat Ghamr); TS Arabic Box 38, f. 116 (in Bilbays, dated 1519). One arched and one rectangular: TS Arabic Box 53, f. 73 (1317; the arched doorway was on the main street).

[63]TS 12.660 (around 1120), fragment.

[64]TS 12.694 (dated 1139): house on the Sūq al-kabīr, the large bazaar.

[65]TS 12.172*v*; Maimonides, *Responsa*, I, 162. The alley is called *khawkha*.

[66]PSR 1451, ll. 5, 6, 17, 18.

[67]TS 16.185, l. 15; TS K 25, f. 284*v*, ll. 48–49; Maimonides, *Responsa*, I, 3, l. 2 see n. 135, below. This responsum contains a document, dated 1194, referring to a house in Alexandria. For the quotation see Briggs, "The Saracenic House," p. 238.

[68]TS 13 J 30, f. 6: The house behind the synagogue of the Iraqians, which is adjacent to the secret door, through which the womenfolk of the Jews ascend. TS 13 J 8, f. 11*v*: repairs of the "secret door" of the Palestinian synagogue, see Gil, *Foundations*, p. 403, bottom. Women's entrance, *bāb al-nisā*, e.g., TS 20.96, l. 14.

[69]TS 13 J 15, f. 24, l. 14: *aduqq al-ḥalq* (plural, not: *ḥalqa*).

[70]Bodl. MS Heb. d 66 (Cat. 2878), f. 6, l. 12.

[71]See *Med. Soc.*, I, 109 and 421 n. 61. *Ibid.*, last line: for *ḍabbāb* should be read *ṣabbāb*, enamored.

[72]Sinnārī mansion: Revault-Maury, *Palais et maisons*, p. 88, fig. 23 (after *Description de l'Égypte*), Plate LVI (two photos of the present state). See also *ibid.*, Plates I and XVIII. TS Arabic Box 53, f. 60, l. 5 (using *ʿaskar*). TS Arabic Box 53, f. 61, l. 8: "Its doorway and its ʿaskar which belong to the rights of this house are on this street. This ʿaskar

overlooks the ground in front of the doorway and the lane mentioned before and occupies the whole eastern boundary of the house opposite the house of So and So." ENA 2558, f. 4, l. 22: *ʿasākir hādhih al-dār*. Hebrew *gesosṭrā*: TS 12.773, ll. 8, 16 17 (around 1000); or gezoẓtrā: TS 28.3, l. 23 (July 1004). In modern Arabic: *mashrabiyya*.

[73]TS 18 J 2, f. 6, ll. 11–19: a letter by Simḥa Kohen to Abu 'l-Manṣūr, (it seems, from Alexandria, ca. 1205). Three court records: TS Misc. Box 24, f. 5 (1108).

[74]TS 16.140, l. 9 (1121).

[75]TS Arabic Box 38, f. 117, l. 22 (second half of the twelfth century); TS 8 J 4, f. 13 (Damascus, 1094); TS 12.773, l. 16: *pethāḥīm pethūḥōth(!) mushqāfōth ʿal ha-derekh* (Heb.), openings looking on the street in the upper floors.

[76]Bodl. MS Heb. f 56, f. 43, col. II, l. 12: *ṭāqat zujāj*, see Gil, *Foundations*, p. 328. Glass windows were already known in ninth-century Islam, cf. Carl J. Lamm, *Das Glas von Samarra* (Berlin, 1928), pp. 101–102 (communication of Richard Ettinghausen).

[77]Bodl. MS Heb. b 12 (Cat. 2875), f. 4, see n. 59, above: *bāb al-rīḥ*.

[78]Bodl. MS Heb. c 13, (Cat. 2807, no. 17d), f. 22, *verso*, l. 7, dated April 1028: *nāfidha*, in modern literary Arabic the general word for window, but never used in this sense in the Geniza.

[79]Windows and "wind opening": Richards, *Karaite Doc.* 17. View held: see Wiet, *Cairo*, pp. 88–89. Agreement: TS 16.35 (1118).

[80]A large doorway with corridors: Maimonides, *Responsa*, I, 162. A second corridor: TS K 25, f. 251. The term "dihlīz" is of Persian origin. For the turn in the entrance passages see Revault-Maury, *Palais et maisons*, p. 4, fig. 2, detail no. 4, and p. 91, fig. 24, no. 1.

[81]The second source cited in the preceding note.

[82]ULC Or 1080 J 117, l. 8 (1088); PSR 1451.

[83]Small house: Merx, *Paléographie hébraïque*, p. 30. Large building: Richards, *Karaite Doc.* 17, l. 17. See n. 154, below.

[84]Richards, *Karaite Doc.* 5, l. 8: *zawj abwāb*.

[85]TS 8 J 9, fs. 2*v*, l. 9, and 3, l. 7, *India Book* 284 (1102).

[86]See n. 151 and, for the *majlis*, n. 100, below.

[87]TS Arabic Box 30, f. 53.

[88]TS Arabic Box 53, f. 70 the house is described as a duwayra; and with a (decorative) ceiling: *musaqqaf*.

[89]TS 16.140, l. 4: the *qāʿa* of the ground floor; l. 6: the qāʿa *muʿallaqa* in the *wasṭānī*, or middle floor.

[90]See *Colloque 1969*, p. 137.

[91]TS 8 J 9, fs. 2 and 3, see n. 85, above; TS Arabic Box 5, f. 1, sec. B (1032); TS K 25, f. 251, l. 7 (ca. 1190). The photo of the Razzāz mansion in Cairo (fifteenth century) in Revault-Maury, *Palais et maisons*, Pl. xx, gives a good idea of the look of a house with two inner courts.

[92]TS 16.356, l. 24: *al-qāʿa al-suflā dhāt al-majlis* (1120); PSR 1451, l. 12. Maimonides, *Responsa*, I, 2: [*al-qāʿa*] *al-kabīra wal-ḥurmiyya* (1194). TS Arabic Box 30, f. 30*v*: The large *qāʿa* and the women's *qāʿa* (1132). TS 16.116: *ū-vayit ze yesh bō shālōsh ḥaṣērōt qeṭannōt (Heb.)*.

[93]PSR 1451, l. 12, see n. 109, below.

[94]Small: e.g., n. 88, above. Large: TS K 25, f. 251.

[95]Pair of columns in front of a room: Bodl. MS Heb. d 68 (Cat. 2836, no. 22), f. 100, l. 18 (spring 1156); before a *majlis*: TS Arabic Box 53, f. 70, l. 6 (1157). Marble columns (plural, not dual) in a qāʿa: TS 16.356, l. 24.

[96]Wall hangings: see A, 4, nn. 78–96. Plain (*sādhij*) doors: Richards, *Karaite Doc.* 5, l. 13 (in an upper apartment).

[97]TS K 25, f. 251. Wind catcher, *bād-hanj*, abbreviated from *bādāhanj*, a Persian word. See Revault-Maury, *Palais et maisons*, p. 98, fig. 28 (cross section from *Description de l'Égypte* showing the position of the wind catcher within the house); Pl. LXVI (photos showing it protruding above the roof). See n. 172, below, and Franz Rosenthal, "Poetry and Architecture: The *bādhanj*," *Journal of Arabic Literature*, 8 (1977), 1–19, a

collection and discussion of Arabic poems in praise of the wind catcher. The mass of verses dedicated to the topic proves how much relief was provided by that structure. While resting in it after the day's heat one could catch a nasty cold, however, as one poet had it (p. 19):

Don't sleep in the bādhanj.
There is no cure for those made sick by it.

One detail in TS K 25, f. 251, has not yet been identified: *al-'nbd'ryh al-mudhahhaba al-dā'ira bihi* (l. 12). The same in TS 16.356, l. 26: *'nbd'ryh dā'ira muqābila li-hādha 'l-majlis*, translated tentatively: The living room is encircled by a gilded cornice. See the photos of gilded cornices in Revault-Maury, Pls. x and xv.

[98]TS Arabic Box 38, f. 119 (dated 1137): *al-majlis alladhī fī wasṭihi fisqiyya*. Richards, *Karaite Doc.* 17, l. 13: *bi-wasṭihi fisqiyya murakhkhama*. The word fisqiyya is the Latin *piscina* and came to the Arabs via Aramaic.

[99]TS K 25, f. 284, l. 7 (ca. 1130). Cf G. Marçais, "Salsabīl et šādirwān," *Lévi-Provençal Memorial Volume*, II (Paris, 1962), 639–648.

[100]ENA 4020, f. 6, ll. 15–19, ed. Mann, II, 172. The letter refers to Ramle, Palestine, not to Damascus, as assumed by Mann, I, 150.

[101]Majlis in upper apartment: TS 16.356, l. 28 (1120); Mosseri A 6.2 (written by the same scribe); Richards, *Karaite Doc.* 17, ll. 18, 20, 21.

[102]TS K 25, f. 251, l. 10: *wa-fīhi maqṭaᶜān khashabiyya manqūsha kullun minhumā bi-bāb yudkhal minhu ilā fard kumm mujāwir lahu*. PSR 1451: *majlis bi-farday kumm*. TS Arabic Box 38, f. 102, l. 11: *majlis bi-kummayn*. Same in Richards, *Karaite Doc.* 5, l. 8, where also *kummayhi*, its vestibules. Without doors: TS Arabic Box 53, f. 73, l. 7. TS Arabic Box 38, f. 117, l. 3: *bi-akmām (!) bi-ghayr abwāb*. Cf. Dozy, *Supplément*, II, 487*a*: sortie étroite. Dardīr: Revault-Maury, *Palais et maisons*, p. 7, fig. 5, details no. 7. For Yemen see Rathjens, *Sanᶜa*, p. 51. Classical antiquity: see n. 174, below.

[103]Synagogue: TS 18 J 4, f. 12, l. 36 (ca. 1100). Sultan's palace: DK 245, ed. S. Kandel, *Genizai Keziratok* (Budapest, 1909), Table I, l. 22. Divorce: TS 18 J 2, f. 13, ll. 18–21 (1117). Nahray: ULC Or 1080 J 170, l. 13, *Nahray* 10. Mosul: TS 20.128 (May 1237). Rent: ULC Or 1080 J 117, *verso*, second entry.

[104]Mosseri L-95. The complaint is addressed to the Nagid Abraham Maimonides (d. 1237).

[105]See n. 38, above, first item. Dozy, *Supplément*, I, 362*a*. Barthélemy, *Dictionnaire*, s.v.; Reuther, "Qāᶜa," p. 205. In Bodl. MS Heb. f 56 (Cat. 2821), f. 50*v*, ll. 16–17, ed. R. Gottheil, *Israel Abrahams Jubilee Volume* (New York, 1927), pp. 149–169, the word designates the shelves of the library of the synagogue, which were situated in the recess of a wall. TS 13 J 7, f. 22, ll. 6–7: He gave him the rest of the white quires which were *fī 'l-khuristān*.

The Persian word *khuristān* is derived from *khor*, food, and designates a pantry, in that language: Steingass, *Persian-English Dictionary*, 484*a*, where the word is spelled *kh-w-r-s-t-'n*. Arabic texts leave the *w* out, and so do the texts in Hebrew characters. The shelves in the wall recesses of private homes had decorative purposes, displaying beautiful vessels, knicknacks, and the like. The visitor to the Metropolitan Museum of Art in New York should not miss the Syrian room with its wall recesses and its decorative ceiling, see n. 88, above.

[106]Richards, *Karaite Docs.* 5, ll. 9, 10, and 17, l. 14.

[107]Ahmed Fikri, "The Characteristics of Cairene Architecture in the Ayyubid Period," *Nadwa 1969*, I, 163–192, esp. pp. 168–172. The term *īwān* is older, at least in a letter of a man from Mosul, Iraq. He terms thus the sitting room of Maimonides: TS 8 J 14, f. 18, ll. 9, 12, 16.

[108]Richards, *Karaite Doc.* 5, ll. 20–22.

[109]See nn. 96–98, above.

[110]See Lane, *Modern Egyptians*, pp. 10–13, with two illustrations, one opposite p. 1, and one on p. 12. Hassan Fathi (*Colloque 1969*, p. 138) says that the covered *dūrqāᶜa* replaced the open court, *ṣaḥn*, wherefore it is one step deeper than the īwāns, "as if it were still open to the sky, so as to stop rainwater from seeping into the īwāns." In Richards, *Karaite Doc.* 17, ll. 19 and 21, a house sold in 1285 had a dūrqāᶜa on both the

second and third floors; it was paved with *kadhdhān* (or *kaddān*), tuff gravel, see Dozy, *Supplément*, II, 450*a*–451*a*.

[111]PSR 1451, a document written by a Muslim notary; the hundreds have not been preserved, but the names clearly point to the fourteenth century. The name of the son, Faraj Allāh (God Has Helped, namely, at the birth) appears first at that time, e.g., twice in a list from October 1335, analyzed in *Med. Soc.*, II, 496, sec. 69; the first contributor in the slightly earlier list (*ibid.*, p. 495, sec. 67) also bears this name. In two documents the cantor Faraj Allāh receives orders from the Nagid Joshua (d. 1355): TS NS Box 31, f. 7, and TS 6 J 6, f. 21. The name continued to be in use later, see Strauss-Ashtor, *Mamluks*, III, 127. In Hebrew, the son was called Yeshūᶜā b. Elᶜazar ha-Levi. It is likely that he was related to a man with the name Elᶜazar b. Yeshūᶜā ha-Levi, of whom we have a document dated Dec. 10, 1310, see *ibid.*, p. 68.

[112]Lane, *Modern Egyptians*, pp. 11–12. Illustration: opposite p. 1. Two *ṣuffas*, one opposite the other: TS 16.356; TS K 25, f. 251; PSR 1451. Four: TS 16.140, l. 6. Opposite the *majlis*: TS Arabic Box 53, f. 73, l. 6 (1317). Beneath a wind catcher: Bodl. MS Heb. d 68, f. 100, ll. 1–2. For a bench under a bower placed at a fountain see the sketch in Reuther, "Qaᶜa", p. 208. Looking on the lane: Richards, *Karaite Doc.* 17, l. 19.

[113]Lane, *Modern Egyptians*, p. 12; Briggs, "The Saracenic House," p. 237; Mosseri A-6.2, l. 5; TS 16.356, l. 26; PSR 1451, ll. 10–11; Richards, *Karaite Doc.* 5, l. 10; Wiet, *Cairo*, p. 89.

[114]The word *fisqiyya* (see n. 98, above), seems to comprise both the basin and the fountain. In a letter from Alexandria, written in 1141, however, reference is made to both *zarrāqāt*, fountains (in the plural), and a *fisqiyya*, pictured in his poems by the Spanish Hebrew poet Judah ha-Levi during his stay in that city: TS 13 J 24, f. 8*v*, l. 1, ed. *Tarbiz*, 28 (1959), 353. Well: TS 10 J 7, f. 13; PSR 1451.

[115]Alexandria: TS Arabic Box 30, f. 30*v*, l. 5. Maimonides, *Responsa*, I, 151 and 155. Repair of a cistern for 1 1/2 dinars: TS 10 J 17, f. 21*v*, ll. 7–11, *Nahray* 115. Brackish or no water: ENA NS 19, f. 10*v*, ll. 1–4 (Sept./Oct. 1200).

[116]Kitchen on upper floors: Mosseri A-6.2; uppermost: TS 16.140, l. 7; Maimonides, *Responsa*, I, 3. Three washrooms upstairs: TS K 25, f. 251. *Mirḥāḍ* (washroom): TS Arabic Box 53, f. 19 (Minyat Ghamr); Mosseri A-6.2 and often. *Bayt al-mā'* (room with water): TS 8.257, margin, *Nahray* 153. *Mustaḥamm* (bathroom): TS NS J 4, l. 11: in a prison (the context proves that a toilet is intended). *Mustarāḥ* (restroom), *murtafaq* (convenience): ULC Or 1080 J 117, l. 8. *Bēth kissē* (Hebrew), room with a chair: TS NS J 338, l. 8. A *kūkh murakhkham*, a cabin paved with marble, mentioned in a Geniza fragment, seems to be another term for the same room: TS 8.150, l. 5. Hamadhānī's twenty-second *maqāma*, or story in rhymed prose, and al-Ḥarīzī's thirty-fourth.

[117]Qāᶜa as living quarters, *sukn*, *maskan*, or *manzil*: e.g., TS 13 J 8, f. 11*v*; TS 13 J 18, f. 8, l. 18; Bodl. MS Heb. f 56, f. 61; TS K 15, f. 54, l. 5. Rent of a house with a *qāᶜa dhāt al-manāzil*: TS Arabic Box 38, f. 119; TS Arabic Box 5, f. 1, sec. B. *Majlis ḥayrī* (on both lower and upper floors): TS Arabic Box 38, f. 102, l. 11; TS 16.356, l. 28; Richards *Karaite Doc.* 5, l. 8; Doc. 17, l. 12. See *EI*², s. v. "Ḳaṣr al-ḥayr," and the bibliography provided there.

[118]TS Arabic Box 18 (1), f. 101, l. 11: *ᶜan al-qāᶜa* (eleventh century).

[119]*Med. Soc.*, I, 157 and n. 29.

[120]TS 10 J 5, f. 16, l. 4.

[121]Maimonides, *Responsa*, I, 177–178. Cf. TS 8 J 9, f. 17*c*, item I (1160): *qāᶜat qazzāz*, workshop of a silk weaver, topped by two adjacent upper apartments.

[122]TS 10 J 28, f. 13, see *Med. Soc.*, I, 382, sec. 59; II, 428, sec. 143, and Gil, *Foundations*, pp. 372–375. Litharge: *martak*, Gil's reading is to be corrected.

[123]Go to the qāᶜa where so-and-so teaches: TS 10 J 13, f. 23.

[124]Maqrīzī, *Khiṭaṭ*, II, 406, ll. 14 and 23: *fa-'abqā al-qāᶜa ᶜalā ḥālihā wa-ᶜamilahā māristānan*. See Wiet, *Cairo*, pp. 128–129.

[125]Nine floors: TS K 25, f. 251, l. 9. Instead of *ᶜalw*, one occasionally used *jamīᶜa ᶜālīhā*, all its upper structures: TS 8 J 29, f. 9.

[126]ULC Or 1080 J 66 (no date preserved; written by Hillel b. Eli, 1066–1108). The second document is printed in full in Worman, *JQR*, 18 (1905), 37, at a time when it had not yet been "classed." Its original has not yet been identified. It is a hasty note on a strip of vellum. Worman's misreadings can easily be corrected: *wal-mustaraqāt* for *w'lmstwq't*, *wal-sullam* for *w'lsly*, *wal-darābazīn al-khashab* for *w'l-dr'kzyn 'l-bshr*. The Ḥujja mosque seems not to be known by this name, but its location (in the Maḥras ʿAmmār district [see A, 1, n. 166, above] on the Abī Dalāma lane identifies it as the one known from Ibn Duqmāq, IV, 24 and 29. Samuel's stepson, after the death of both his father and mother, gives a quarter of the house (which he had been given by his stepfather or inherited from his mother) to his sister (gives, not sells, because in the latter case the note would have contained a price).

[127]Richards, *Karaite Doc.* 17. See n. 178, below.

[128]Mosseri A-6.2. Uppermost: *fawqānī* (usually opposed to *wasṭānī*, middle floor). Unfortunately, rodents destroyed the middle part of ll. 6–10, so that a consecutive translation is impossible. The stalactite vault, *al-muqarnaṣ al-muttaṣil bil-ʿumud*, is remarkable, because the muqarnaṣ makes its appearance in this part of the Muslim world only about this time, see Ernst Herzfeld, "Damascus: Studies in Architecture," *Ars Islamica*, 11 (1946), 17. As I learned from Richard Ettinghausen, the earliest example of the muqarnaṣ in Egypt is found in the Juyūshī (Giyūshī) mosque of Cairo (1085). Pantry as translation for *mustakhdam* suggested by Paula Sanders.

[129]Lane, *Modern Egyptians*, p. 21.

[130]Rathjens, *Sanʿa*, pp. 7 and 14. According to the author "in the Muslim house, all the rooms on its many floors are always to be found on the same level." To be sure, in Fustat there was no basic difference in the structure of Jewish and Muslim houses, because in Egypt, unlike Yemen, the urban Jew and urban Muslim of the High Middle Ages were of the same social type, using the same domestic architecture.

[131]Wiet, *Cairo*, pp. 45–56, see n. 61, above.

[132]Assaf, *Texts*, p. 66, ll. 4–9; Goitein, *Lešonenu*, 30 (1966), 202, l. 15. I take the Aramaic *mwsnwy* as derived from Greek *meson*, middle, cf. Krauss, *Griechische und lateinische Lehnwörter*, p. 337. See n. 35, above. Friedman, *Marriage*, no. 53d, reads *mys[y]ny*, explaining it as "textiles from Maysān", a province of Iraq.

[133]TS 10 J 7, f. 13, superscribed *maʿrifa*, memo, specifying the outfit of Malīḥa b. Ezekiel al-Kohen (father alive), to which Eli ha-Kohen b. Yaḥyā (1057–1107, see *Med. Soc.*, II, 79), in his characteristic hand, added the name of the groom and the details about his marriage gift.

[134]ULC Or 1080 J 117, l. 9. Hay storeroom: *bayt al-tibn*. Vault: *qabw*.

[135]Maimonides, *Responsa*, I, 3. Read *bāb al-sirr*, see *Responsa*, III, 119.

[136]TS 13 J 4, f. 4*v*, ll. 19–20. Unit that can be locked, *mughlaq*, or *mughallaq*, called *ghalq* in Jerusalem: TS 13 J 6, f. 22, l. 6. See n. 45, above, and *Med. Soc.*, V, A, 1, n. 104 (in preparation). The rather confused draft does not mention a qāʿa prior to the passage translated. The house, as often, had two qāʿas.

[137]Compare with this the sketches from *Description de l'Égypte*, in Brown, *Madina*, fig. 34, where three stories are the rule, but no additional structures are visible.

[138]Cf. *EI*², II 114, s.v. "Dār (G. Marçais); Reuther, *Wohnhaus in Baghdad*, pp. 2, 8, and 18.

[139]Maqrīzī, Khiṭaṭ, I, 444: *bayt min khashab*. For Maimonides' explanation see *Med. Soc.*, I, 295 and n. 1.

[140]TS 8 J 5, f. 10, item II; MS Sassoon, *verso*, l. 16, see H. Z. Hirschberg, *I. Baer Jubilee Volume* (Jerusalem, 1961), p. 143, *India Book* 263; TS 6 J 1, f. 1, and Gil, *Foundations*, pp. 269, 270, 379, ll. 19 and 35, 389*d*, l. 12.

[141]Five *akhṣāṣ* in one house: TS 20.168, ll. 27–32 (1042/3). Seven: TS K 15, f. 45. Mats: ULC Or 1080 J 117, l. 16. Donated: TS Arabic Box 18 (1), f. 35, l. 3. In private houses: TS Arabic Box 5, f. 1, sec. B. al-Afḍal: Ibn Muyassar, p. 42, l. 11. The word translated in Gil, *Foundations*, p. 178, l. 39, and p. 181, l. 15, as apartment is *khuṣṣ*.

[142]Lane, *Modern Egyptians*, p. 17. Loggia with entrance door: Revault-Maury, *Palais et maisons*, p. 93, fig. 25 (after *Description de l'Égypte*), Pl. VII. Screened: *ibid.*, Pls. XIII, XIV.

[143]See Brian Doe and R. B. Serjeant, "A Fortified Tower-house in Wādī Jirdān (Wāḥidī Sultanate)," Part II, *BSOAS*, 38 (1975), 293: "*masrūqa* [the stolen one, designates in Tarīm, Hadhramaut], a small room between two larger rooms, or a cupboard, storeroom, made from the area of one of the larger rooms."

Until recently, I translated *mustaraqa* as mezzanine, but since the documents describe it as a place from which one looks down, its identification with the more modern *maqᶜad*, loggia, is assured.

[144]PSR 1451, ll. 11–13.

[145]TS K 25, f. 251*v*, l. 19: *mustaraqatayn muṭillatayn ᶜalā ṣāḥn qāᶜat-hā.*

[146]TS Arabic Box 53, f. 73, l. 8 (dated 1317): *mustaraqatayn mutajāwiratayn iḥdāhumā muṭilla ᶜala wajh bāb-hā wal-thāniya muṭilla ᶜalā qāᶜat-hā.*

[147]TS NS Box 225, f. 25 (1133), and Gil, *Foundations*, p. 224 n. 5. Maḥfūẓa, daughter of Joseph, who bore the title *zayn al-tujjār* (the ornament of the merchants) sells part of her property, inclusive of *al-mustaraqa al-jawwāniyya*. In another deed she and her husband Salāma b. Joseph and three other coproprietors lease a mansion to Abū Zikrī b. Joseph ha-Kohen, the renowned India trader: TS Arabic Box 38, f. 115 (a magnificent document of which only part of the beginning is preserved).

[148]TS 16.356, l. 28 (1120); TS Arabic Box 38, f. 102, l. 5.

[149]TS 13 J 1, f. 21 (1150), ll. 3 and 9; TS 8 J 4, f. 14*a* (1098); TS K 25, f. 284, ll. 51–56; Richards, *Karaite Doc.* 17. For the rent of a *mustaraqa* as a separate entity see Gil, *Foundations*, p. 574.

[150]Damascus: TS 20.92, l. 2. Tyre: TS NS J 338, l. 8. In Hebrew: *akhsadrā* (which is Greek *exedra*): TS 16.181*v*, Item III, l. 9.

[151]Courtyard: ULC Or 1080 J 25*v*, l. 25. Street: TS Arabic Box 38, f. 86, l. 11. In *majlis*: Richards, *Karaite Doc.* 17, l. 12. Creswell: *Colloque 1969*, p. 130.

[152]*Mashraqa*: ULC Or 1080 J 71, l. 9, cf. Dozy, *Supplément*, I, 751*b*. Damascus: see Gil, *Foundations*, pp. 231–232.

[153]*Mafrash*: TS Arabic Box 53, f. 70, l. 6, cf. Dozy, *Supplément*, II, 254*a*; TS 16.140.

[154]Stone and wood: TS 20.3 (Feb.–March 1117), *salālimhā al-ḥajar minhā wal-khashab*. Stone arches: the sources in nn. 144 and 145, for instance, TS Arabic Box 38, f. 117, l. 3. Baked brick: *sullam ṭūb ājurr*, Richards, *Karaite Doc.* 25, margin, l. 4. Landing, *basṭa*: Bodl. MS Heb. b 11 (Cat. 2874), f. 14*v*, l. 3. TS 16.140, l. 7: *basṭa kabīra*, a large landing. First corridor: TS 8 J 29, f. 9, ll. 5–6. Apartment house: TS K 25, f. 284, section C. Mansion: see n. 145. Connecting two houses: TS 8 J 20, f. 16. For repairs, see Gil, "Maintenance." Staircases dangerous for children: TS 8 J 22, f. 24, ll. 7, 15.

[155]TS 16.137, l. 12; Richards, *Karaite Doc.* 17, ll. 21–22, see n. 178, below.

[156]Wall around the roof: TS 18 J 2, f. 8. Rail, *darābizīn* (from Greek *trapezion*): TS K 25, f. 251*v*, l. 26. Gable roof, *jamalūn*: TS 20.96, l. 32 (Fustat), and Gil, *Foundations*, pp. 175–177. TS 12.581, l. 15 (Minyat Ziftā). In private house (not permitted to add): TS 16.137; jamalūn is derived from Syriac, see Fraenkel, *Aramäische Fremdwörter*, p. 29.

[157]TS Arabic Box 18 (1), f. 127, l. 3 (1230); Dropsie 340, ll. 7 and 14 (1093). TS 12.773, l. 22: *bēth ginzēhōn*, their treasure room (Aramaic).

[158]Deed of gift: TS 16.137, ll. 9–10, in the hand of Nathan b. Samuel he-Ḥāvēr, see *Med. Soc.*, II, 513, sec. 18. 1260: Richards, *Karaite Doc.* 5, ll. 9, 15, 16, 18, 19. Steingass, *Persian-English Dictionary*, p. 1054*b*, defines *kandūj* as an arabicized form of Persian *kandū*, with the meaning "a clay vessel in which grain is kept." The kandūj of our documents clearly had a different purpose and structure.

[159]TS NS J 382, l. 5 (Tyre); TS Misc. Box 28, f. 137*v*, margin (Damietta); TS 12.231*v*, ll. 20–21 (al-Mamṣūṣa). *Makhzan sukn*: TS K 15, f. 3, ll. 6–9, see *Med. Soc.*, II, 420, sec. 42, and Gil, *Foundations*, pp. 375–376. *Ibid.*, ll. 6–9, like l. 13. Translate: "The storeroom which is inhabited by" instead of "the storeroom of the apartment of." Separate building: cf. *makhzan Ḥammūd* (not: Ḥāmūd); Gil, *Foundations*, p. 157, identical with *qaṣr Ḥ.*, *ibid.*, p. 518. For funduq-makhzan see *ibid.*, pp. 549 and 568. A storeroom with grille windows and an elaborate portal in Revault-Maury, *Palais et maisons*, Pls. VII and XII.

[160]In a house with two doorways, one, which led through an alley to a stable, was

converted into a main entrance: Maimonides, *Responsa*, I, 162. Separate stable: TS 12.50, l. 4. Living quarters above stable: TS 12.172*v*. Building with two stables: TS K 25, f. 284, section C. Room for hay: ULC 1080 J 117, l. 9, see n. 134, above.

[161]TS Arabic Box 18 (1) f. 181: The "castle" of the donkey driver brings 36 dirhems a year (1037–8); TS 20.169, ll. 19 and 23 (1043); TS K 15, f. 45*a* l. 14 (about the same time), and Gil, *Foundations*, p. 579.

[162]Merx, *Paléographie hébraïque*, p. 25; ENA 2558, f. 4, l. 17, TS 12.172*v*.

[163]Two "castles": TS Arabic Box 38, f. 102. E. W. Lane's definition is quoted in Dozy, *Supplément*, II, 356*a*. Grohmann, *APEL*, I, 268 and 270, no. 72, also refers to an isolated *qaṣr*. For ḥujra, see n. 43, above. For later developments of the qaṣr, see Samuel Tamari, *Qā ʿah* (n. 32, above), pp. 51–62.

[164]Aden: Mosseri L-12, trans. Goitein, *Letters*, p. 213 n. 6. The term is still used in Yemen, see Rathjens, *Sanʿa*, pp. 7, 73. Mosul: TS 20.128, l. 15, and *verso*, l. 26. Fatimid caliphs: suggested by Paula Sanders. The *manẓara* in the traditional houses of Cairo corresponds roughly to the majlis of the Geniza period, see Lane, *Modern Egyptians*, p. 10, and Revault-Maury, *Palais et masions, passim*. Alexandria: TS Arabic Box 30, f. 30*v*. Qalyūb (the guests in the *ghurfa*, or upper room, stole the wheat stored there): TS 13 J 20, f. 12, l. 16. Tamīm (b. Joseph) writes to his brothers, see Gottheil-Worrell, Pl. XII, dated 1231. In Grohmann, *APEL*, I, 181, no. 59, l. 4, *ghurfa* should be read instead of *ʿizba*, for a farm cannot be on an upper floor. See also Oleg Grabar, *Ars Orientalis*, 5 (1963), fig. 30. Lodging for travelers in synagogue: TS 8 J 37, f. 5, l. 13.

[165]See nn. 38 (dated 1137), 87 (ca. 1100), 136 (1229), above.

[166]ULC Or 1080 J 117, l. 17; TS Arabic Box 54, f. 92, superscribed 1545 (= 1233/4). Same note about "the little house and the garden" in TS Arabic Box 51, f. 118, where the sale is registered in the month of Tishri, Sept./Oct. 1233.

[167]Maimonides, *Responsa*, I, 195; Richards, *Karaite Doc.* 17, p. 112 (read *al-nakhla*); TS Arabic Box 53, f. 19, l. 8; TS Arabic Box 38, f. 116. The word used for tree is *aṣl*, pl. *uṣūl*, lit., stem, trunk. The same in TS Arabic Box 30, f. 53, see n. 87, above. Orchards: see *Med. Soc.*, I, 116–126, and Gil, *Foundations*, pp. 79–81.

[168]E.g., TS 18 J 2, f. 1, analyzed in *Eretz-Israel*, 7 (1964), 87: four palm trunks for a *miẓalla*; TS K 25, f. 190. The feast of Tabernacles is called in the Geniza Sukkā (in the singular), not Sukkōth, cf. TS 18 J 4, f. 12, l. 32. For pleasure pavilions along the Khalīj of Fustat see Brown, *Madina*, fig. 35.

[169]Speros Vryonis, ed., *Individuality and Conformity in Classical Islam* (Berkeley and Los Angeles, 1977).

[170]See A, 1, n. 4, above.

[171]See n. 72, above, and Robertson, *Greek and Roman Architecture*, pp. 297–298.

[172]See n. 97, above, and Alexander Badawy, "Architectural Provision against Heat," *JNES*, 17 (1958), 122–128, and Hassan Fathi, *Colloque 1969*, p. 144, with an illustration of the ancient Egyptian house of Neb Amun; the two triangles protruding from the roof of the house are understood to be the upper ends of wind shafts. In modern Arabic the contraption has an Arabic name: *malqaf*.

[173]Coptic quarter: see Abu-Lughod, *City Victorious*, p. 59 (from Georg Ebers, *Aegypten in Wort and Bild*). Baghdad: Reuther, *Wohnhaus in Baghdad*, p. 37; Brown, *Madina*, ill. 17 and 18 (from David Roberts).

[174]Pauly et al., *Real-encyclopädie der Classischen Altertumswissenschaft*, Supplementband VII (1940), pp. 258, 266, 273–274, "predominance of one large and broad frontal room, opening frequently into two smaller rooms behind it."

[175]The same applies to the Jewish house in Sanʿa, Yemen, which was transplanted there from the Mediterranean area. "A house without a large hall is not called a house"—thus begins the description of housing in a book in which an emigrant from Sanʿa describes life in his native city. Likewise, each house had its inner court open to the sky (not on the ground floor, which comprised stables and storerooms, but on the second floor), see Yehuda Levi Nahum, *Miṣṣefūnōt Yehūdē Tēmān* (Tel Aviv, 1962), pp. 32–33.

[176]See A, l, nn. 49 and 50, above.

[177]TS K 25, f. 251, see A, 1, n. 47, above. The document is incomplete. It was written around 1190.

[178]Richards, *Karaite Doc.* 17; Richards, *Arabic Doc.* IV. The name of the emir: Shams al-Dīn Ṭuquz, son of the emir Sayf al-Dīn Qilij al-Nāṣiri, of the al-Baḥriyya al-Manṣūriyya regiment. The very uneven distribution of shares (the eldest sister receives more than a brother and the youngest only 1/12 of the price) finds its explanation in the simple and natural assumption that the five had inherited other properties and belongings (such as costly jewelry, taken by the youngest sister), and those who here received less had already been indemnified by other items of the estate.

[179]The document, TS 16.140, has been referred to above, n. 56, and *passim*. The Jew bore the same name as his father, which was uncommon among European Jews in later times, but rather frequent during the Geniza period. At conversion, the proselyte received the name Abraham, meaning member of the community regarding itself as the "seed of Abraham"; this usage was common. The family name Son of Moses was a special honor. The convert probably was a learned man, see *Med. Soc.*, II, 308–309.

[180]A quarter in al-Maḥalla outside the Jewish quarter (in which also Christians lived), see *Med. Soc.*, II, 290. The word might be Greek, cf. the name Qālī Qōrī (Beautiful Girl), in a list of recipients of wheat, *ibid.* p. 444, sec. 26; TS K 15, f. 113.

[181]Text: *kandūman*, occurring only here. I take it as another Arabic derivative from Persian *kandū*, see n. 158, above.

[182]This structure, not known to me from elsewhere, might well have been called after the vizier al-Ma'mūn al-Baṭā'iḥī. Despite the shortness of his incumbency (1121–1125) several important innovations are ascribed to him, which he probably initiated in part before assuming office. (We are here in February–March 1121: al-Ma'mūn's predecessor, al-Afḍal, was murdered late in 1121.)

[183]One irdabb of wheat measured about 90 liter and weighed about 70 kilograms, see Hinze, *Masse*, p. 39. "What belongs to them" refers to the receptacles of wheat.

[184]Here follow the statements that the parties had acted out of their free will and in the prescribed manner and that each of them had received an identical copy of the contract.

[185]The underlined words are a quotation (in Heb.) from the Mishna Bava Meṣiʿa 6:2.

3. Socioeconomic Aspects of Housing

[1]See *Med. Soc.*, III, 36–39, 143–144, 150–152, 171–179, and *passim*. Compare Diane O. Hughes, "Kinsmen and Neighbors in Medieval Genoa," in Miskimin et al., *The Medieval City*, pp. 95–111.

[2]In Arabic: *mushāʿ*, or *shāʿī ghayr maqsūm*.

[3]For the division of a house ownership into 24 shares cf. A. Grohmann, *APEL*, I, 172, no. 57, l. 5. A share of 1/48: TS Arabic Box 53, f. 66, l. 5. The beginning of the line is to be read: *al-ḥiṣṣa 'l-latī m(ablagh-hā)*. 1/18: TS 16.72; Maimonides, *Responsa*, I, 32. 1/16: TS 16.41. 1/9: TS 12.668. 1/8: TS 13 J 22, f. 2; TS 16.117; ENA 2558, f .3 (Cairo 1141). A share is called *sahm*, but also *qīrāṭ*, e.g., in TS 16.79, ed. Israel Abrahams, *JQR*, 17 (1904/5), 428. (Concerning the date of this document see *Med. Soc.*, II, 534 n. 80); qīrāt: TS 8.150, l. 4.

[4]See *Med. Soc.*, I, 169–183, and Index, I, 544, s.v. "Partnership(s)."

[5]TS 8.150, middle, fragmentary, part of a document. One partner was a Muslim, another a Christian.

[6]TS 13 J 22, f. 2.

[7]Bodl. MS Heb. c 28 (Cat. 2876), f. 37, top, ll. 9–14, *verso*, ll. 1–2.

[8]TS 16.146 and TS 12.176, *India Book* 286*a* and *b*, dated 1143, cf. A, 1, n. 65, above. AIU VII D 7, ed. B. Chapira, *REJ*, 56 (1908), 233–237, *India Book* 283, and TS 8 J 9, fs. 2–3, *India Book* 284, both dated 1102.

[9]TS 16.140, see A, 2, n. 176, and *passim*, above. Inspection of drainage pipe: TS 12.601 (early twelfth century).

[10]TS 8 J 5, f. 10, item B: a man was assigned a *ṭārma* (see A, 2, nn. 138–140, above) to live in, also part of the rent for the ground floor, and would share the costs of repairs with the other occupants.

[11]Maimonides, *Responsa*, I, 155. The term for occupying a part of a house is here and in TS 16.140 (see n. 9): *ḥāz*.

[12]*Ibid.*, p. 151. The contract from Tyre has been put together from three fragments: TS NS J 338 and 382, and TS 12.177, ed. S. D. Goitein, *Eretz-Israel*, 8 (1966), 293–297 (with facsimile), cf. A, 2, n. 43, above. Shemarya (1000): TS 12.115. Here the main hall is called *qīṭōn*, which is Greek *koiton*, bedroom, but was already used also as a general word for room in Late Antiquity.

[13]TS NS J 185 (8) and (12), fragments of one deed.

[14]TS 12.544, dated 1147.

[15]See n. 43, below.

[16]See *Med. Soc.*, III, 243–244, 326–328, and *passim*. Husband: *ibid.*, p. 252, and TS 12.538. (Two stepsons contending the widow's rights to the house twenty years after the death of her husband.) New house of old aunt: *Med. Soc.*, III, 285 and 490 n. 45.

[17]TS 12.499, cf. A, 1, n. 72, above.

[18]Bodl. MS Heb. a 3 (Cat. 2873), f. 8, l. 9.

[19]Goitein, *Jemenica*, p. 173, no. 1348.

[20]Grohmann, *APEL*, I, 194, no. 61 (June/July 1032: 5/8 dinar); 188 ff., no. 60 (Jan. 1016: 5 dinars); 224 ff., no. 65 (Feb. 1050: 5 1/4 dinars); 248, no. 68 (Aug. 1067: 4 2/3 dinars). Murabbaᶜāt: A. Grohmann, "Les grottes de Murabbaᶜāt," Benoit *et al.*, *Discoveries in the Judean Desert*, II, Oxford, 1961, 285. House and ruin: Bodl. MS Heb. d 66 (Cat. 2878), fs. 110*v*–111. Frag. of a copy (not the original) of a court record.

[21]For the actual (not nominal) value of *nuqra* silver in Mamluk times see *Med. Soc.*, I, 386, sec. 79, and Ashtor, *Prix*, p. 275.

[22]Seven months: TS 16.176, a special case, see App. A, group IV, entry dated 1182. For the more extended periods see n. 24, below.

[23]BT Bava Meṣiᶜa 65*b*. The sale of real estate with the right of redemption, granted as a favor by the buyer, *bayᶜ al-wafāʾ* (see Schacht, *Islamic Law*, p. 78), and the special case that the seller pays rent for the occupation of the property sold, *bayᶜ bil-istighlāl*, are well-known topics of Islamic law and incorporated in the Ottoman *Mejelle*, §§ 118 and 119, discussed by A. Ben-Shemesh in *Hapraklit*, 23 (1967), 283–284 (Heb.).

[24]Alexandria 1103: JNUL 3, ed. S. D. Goitein, *Kirjath Sepher*, 41 (1966), 264–265. Abraham Maimonides: Bodl. MS Heb. b 3 (Cat. 2806), f. 6. The buyer Abū Isḥāq b. Sayyid al-Ahl al-Abzārī (Trader in Seeds) renounced the rent. 1246: Bodl. MS Heb. d 66 (Cat. 2878), f. 136, see App. A, group V, entry dated 1246. The dyers: TS 8 J 32, f. 4, and TS 10 J 21, f. 17, which together form a complete document. Bilbays: BM 10.126. The mill in Ḥudayjī Street: TS 12.485. In addition to the three documents referred to in *Med. Soc.*, III, 329, a fourth refers to the case of veiled interest discussed there: TS 12.482, ed. G. Weiss, *Gratz College Annual*, 1 (1972), 70–72.

[25]For details see *Med. Soc.*, III, 326–329, and *passim*.

[26]TS 13 J 22, f. 2, see *Med. Soc.*, I, 135.

[27]Bodl. MS Heb. d 65 (Cat. 2877), f. 13 (Alexandria, 1196).

[28]TS 20.3. Dated 1117. Ar. *takhdumnī*, "that she serves me."

[29]Provisions for old age in general are treated in *Med. Soc.*, V, A, 2 (in preparation).

[30]See *Med. Soc.*, II, 112–121, 413–437; Gil, *Foundations*, pp. 5–24.

[31]Bodl. MS Heb. d 66 (Cat. 2878), f. 88, *Med. Soc.*, II, 415, sec. 14; Gil, *Foundations*, pp. 217–219.

[32]Fustat, 1006: TS 16. 115, see A, 1, n. 183, above. Ca. 1161: TS 8 J 5, f. 22, *verso*, written on the reverse side of a court record dated 1161, see *Med. Soc.*, II, 427, sec. 134. Bodl. MS Heb. f 56 (Cat. 2821), f. 48, see *ibid.*, p. 419, sec. 38. In both cases, the woman is called Naẓar, but the other details differ.

[33]Good examples: TS 24.81, a *ṣulḥa*, or settlement, in which the guardians of two minor orphans hand over the deeds of a house to the latter's elder sister to whom the

house had been left by her father, and promise to register it in her name *bil-yahūd wal-muslīmīn* (May 1207), see *Med. Soc.*, III, 291–292, and 492 n. 72. TS 10 J 21, f. 17, l. 6: *wa-sallamt ilayh kutubha 'l-ʿarabiyya wal-ʿibrāniyya.* "I delivered to him the Arabic and Hebrew deeds of the house," see n. 24, above. The "deed of transfer" preceding the registration was called *kitāb al-intiqāl*, TS 8 J 9, f. 3, l. 6 (*India Book* 284*b*), the "original deed"—*kitāb al-aṣl.* Inspection: *qallab al-mulk*, TS 8 J 6, f. 14*v*, l. 9 (1241).

[34]Cf. *Med. Soc.*, III, 123 and n. 27. Sugar factory: TS 8 J 9, f. 11, Makīn, son of Moses, the judge, agreed to sell to Ibrahīm b. Abū Saʿd.

[35]TS Arabic Box 53, f. 73. ULC Or 1080 J 117 has three entries on the reverse side. Richards, *Arabic Doc.*, pp. 110 ff.

[36]TS 18 J 2, f. 6*v*, ll. 1–16. See A, 2, n. 73, above.

[37]ENA 4020, f. 52*v* (charges: *mu'an*). Sale of the house in the al-Mamṣūṣa quarter: Bodl. MS Heb. d 66 (Cat. 2878), f. 109, item II. See App. A, end.

[38]Abraham Maimuni, *Responsa*, p. 196, cf. *Med. Soc.*, I, 160.

[39]Jan. 1139: see A, 2, n. 11, above. Real estate agent: TS Arabic Box 54, f. 92.

[40]BT Ḥullin 95*b*. TS Arabic Box 54, f. 66: *Allāh yajʿal fī dukhūlih al-khayr.* In the letter, the writer apologizes for not having presented his congratulations earlier and in person.

[41]For Nāṣir-i-Khosraw cf. Lane-Poole, *History of Egypt*, p. 139; for Judah ha-Levi, TS 13 J 19, f. 17, ll. 19–20, ed. *Tarbiz*, 28 (1959), 351–359.

[42]TS 8 J 20, f. 18, *Nahray* 82, ll. 8–11. Joseph b. Faraḥ Qābisī writing to Nahray b. Nissīm.

[43]TS 8 J 19, f. 21, ll. 2–4, 6–12. For Ibn Rajā see *Med. Soc.*, II, 295 and 590 n. 18.

[44]TS Misc. Box 28, f. 72, Abu 'l-Faḍl b. al-Dhahabī had a house in Alexandria and a *ṭabaqa* (an upper floor or an apartment on an upper floor) in Fustat and asks ʿArūs b. Joseph to (sub)let it and to send him the rent.

[45]TS 8 J 11, f. 18; TS Arabic Box 30, f. 215, see Goitein, *Letters*, pp. 290–291.

[46]TS 13 J 18, f. 8*v*, ll. 18–20, postscript to a letter from Fustat by Barhūn b. Ṣāliḥ Tāhertī to his cousin Barhūn b. Mūsā.

[47]Fustat: TS 16.72, l. 7, see A, 1, n. 88, above. Alexandria: TS 10 J 17, f. 21*v*, ll. 7–11, see A, 2, n. 115, above. Jerusalem: TS 8.257, see A, 2, n. 116, above.

[48]P. Heid. 913.

[49]See *Med. Soc.*, III, 152 and nn. 46–53.

[50]See n. 31, above.

[51]Muslim renting an apartment house: TS Arabic Box 5, f. 1, sec. B. See A, 2, n. 141, above. Orphans: see *Med. Soc.*, III, 299 and n. 99.

[52]Six months: ULC Or 1080 J 10 (1180). ULC Or 1080 J 117 (after 1088). A year: TS Arabic Box 5, f. 1, sec. B (1032); TS 16.5 (1076); TS 8.260 (1132).

[53]Muḥarram: Gottheil-Worrell, XXVIII, 131 (referring to Jerusalem). TS 16.356 (1120). TS Arabic Box 39, f. 17 (both Fustat). TS Arabic Box 30, f. 30*v* (for twenty-six months, beginning two months before the end of the Muslim year, November 1132, Alexandria). TS AS 147, f. 38 (June 1178), a house belonging to the Jewish community of Minyat Ziftā. Lease continued in Ramaḍān: TS 12.777 (1143).

[54]Two years: Bodl. MS Heb. d 66 (Cat. 2878), f. 137*v*, l. 12, *India Book* 132; TS 13 J 4, f. 4 (1229). Maimonides, *Responsa*, I, 117, and TS AS 147, f. 38.

[55]Four years: TS Arabic Box 38, f. 119 (1137). Five years: TS 12.477 (1180); Maimonides, *Responsa*, I, 123.

[56]Arrears: see Gil, *Foundations*, p. 58, sec. 79, and p. 74, sec. 105. Son-in-law warned to pay rent "without delay or argument": see *Med. Soc.*, III, 151 and n. 44. Deferment of four months granted: TS AS 151, f. 4 (dated A.H. [4]38 = 1046/7), similar in content to TS 20.168, *Med. Soc*, II, 414, sec. 6 (1043), Gil, *Foundations*, pp. 193–195. See also *Med. Soc.*, II, 116, with reference to App. A, secs. 28, 33, 35.

[57]Bodl. MS Heb. f 56 (Cat. 2821), f. 43 d, sec. 2 (1186), see *Med. Soc.*, II, 419, sec. 37. Advance payment (*taqdima*): TS 12.487 (1180–1182). *Med. Soc.*, II, 422, sec. 102, and 545 n. 8. Possibly also *ibid.*, sec. 29 (1191–1193), see Gil, *Foundations*, Introduction, p. 74, sec. 104.

[58]See *Med. Soc.*, II, 112–121, 413–437.

[59]*Ibid.*, p. 422, sec. 101, ENA 2743, f. 4.

[60]Maimonides, *Responsa*, I, 123.

[61]A. Grohmann, *APEL*, II, 76, no. 89.

[62]*Med. Soc.*, II, 423, sec. 111 (Gil, *Foundations*, no. 38, l. 5), dated 1096. The same sum was paid for a building serving as a synagogue in the province: Westminster College, Frag. Cairens. 51.

[63]Mosseri L-95. See A, 2, n. 104, above. Ascalon: TS 16.122, see *Med. Soc.*, II, 416, sec. 17, and Gil, *Foundations*, no. 57.

[64]Alexandria: A, 3, n. 24; advance payment: n. 56, above.

[65]India trader: TS Arabic Box 30, f. 258, *India Book* 323, ll. 11–16. The tenant claimed that the price was less. Fragmentary contract: TS Arabic Box 39, f. 17.

[66]*Khizāna*: see A, 2, n. 103, above. Store: TS 12.777. See A, 3, n. 53, above.

[67]TS NS J 378.

[68]Alexandria 1132: TS Arabic Box 30, f. 30*v*. 1165: TS 13 J 3, f. 12. Jerusalem: Gottheil-Worrell, XXVII, 121, ll. 27–28. Garden house in Fustat, 1137: TS Arabic Box 38, f. 119. 1229: TS 13 J 4, f. 4, see *Med. Soc.*, I, 122 and n. 46. In 1230/1, again a rent of 300 dirhems per year for the duration of seven years is stipulated for a property on the Nile river: TS 6 J 2, f. 22.

[69]Maimonides, *Responsa*, I, 8–9. The case is complicated. Two-thirds of the house was rented for 14 dinars for a period of six months. This means that the total rent for the entire house for a year was 42 dinars. One-third of that house, however, was large enough to harbor two families. Thus the rent required for one family would be 42/6 = 7 dinars.

[70]See the last source cited in n. 8, above, and those in n. 54.

[71]See n. 45, above.

[72]Maimonides, *Responsa*, I, 2.

[73]See n. 41, above.

[74]TS K 3, f. 21, bottom, see *Med. Soc.*, II, 428, sec. 142, and Gil, *Foundations*, no. 139.

[75]The contract of 1076: TS 16.5; that of 1120: TS 16.356. The Geniza has preserved a third document related to this house: University Museum Philadelphia E 16 510, cf. *JQR*, 49 (1958), 38.

[76]TS 8 J 9, fs. 2–3, cf. n. 8, above. Alexandria: JNUL 3, cf. n. 24, above.

[77]TS 13 J 2, f. 3, Dec. 1093.

[78]TS Arabic Box 54, f. 20, ll. 3, 6–7 (1124–5). Only the left side of the document is preserved. Maghrebi people, as indicated by the names Lebdī and Makhlūf.

[79]TS 12.624, see *Med. Soc.*, III, 460 n. 66: Alexandria, ca. 1090. As is proved by ENA 4010, f. 19 (1089), TS 20.121, TS 20.129, Merāyōt ha-Kohen b. Joseph Av ha-yeshiva, the presiding signatory of TS 12.624, had as colleagues Shēlā b. Mevassēr and Mawhūb b. Aaron, known as members of the rabbinical court of Alexandria.

[80]TS Arabic Box 7, f. 5. The addressee is requested to deliver the rent to Nahray (b. Nissim). The writer would use the amount for paying his own rent. Son ordered to vacate apartment let to his father: TS 8 J 23, f. 10.

[81]TS 10 J 28, f. 13, see *Med. Soc.*, II, 428, sec. 143, Gil, *Foundations*, no. 98, and A, 2, n. 122, above.

[82]TS 8 J 41, f. 13, l. 10. The reverse side of this letter was used for a communal list, see *Med. Soc.*, II, 460, sec. 75.

[83]See App. B, Groups II and I, respectively.

[84]See n. 51, above.

[85]Maimonides, *Responsa*, I, 19.

[86]TS 28.3; TS 13 J 1, f. 5, ed. Braslavsky, *Our Country*, pp. 101–102.

[87]See n. 75, above.

[88]Bodl. MS Heb. b 12 (Cat. 2875), fs. 6 and 29, ll. 12–13, see A, 1, n. 70, above; TS 12.462, 1.3, ed. S. Assaf, *Tarbiz*, 9 (1938), 204; TS 20.6, ll. 11–12, see A, 2, n. 44, above.

[89]See *Med. Soc.*, II, 119–120, and Gil, "Maintenance," pp. 145–146, and *Foundations*, pp. 86–87, where some details need further study. The early disappearance of houses mentioned before from subsequent communal accounts must also be considered.

[90]One expects Sarwa, but the manuscript has clearly a *t* at the end of the name.

[91]TS 16.207: *al-rayyis al-jalīl al-ʿajamī*, son of Simḥa ha-Levi, probably a brother of Isaac (b. Simḥā ha-Levi) Nīsābūrī, see *Med. Soc.*, I, 538, Index, a prominent Persian merchant, living in Alexandria. The date of TS 16.207 is lost, but the scribe Ḥalfōn b. Manasse, who wrote it, made an entry on the reverse side dated Nov./Dec. 1119. The strange name Mistress over her Enemies is also found elsewhere, see *Med. Soc.*, III, 316 and n. 14.

[92]TS 16.51. Abu 'l-Karam Nādīv ha-Levi b. Saʿadya. When his mother-in-law had so formidable a name, it is not surprising that a daughter of his was called Sitt al-Sāda, Mistress over the Lords, TS 12.771.

[93]TS 8.224. The beginning and end of this document have been cut away and with them its date. The final transaction recorded in it may have been made around 1130. The first one, the sale by the amir to the clergyman, could have occurred at the beginning of the century or even earlier.

[94]Richards, *Arabic Doc.* no. II, pp. 107–108 (dated by him tentatively May, 1209). The price was 50 *nuqra* dirhems (corresponding at that time to about 150 *waraq*, or ordinary, dirhems, worth approximately 4 dinars, see *Med. Soc.*, I, 382).

[95]See *Med. Soc.*, II, 148.

[96]See A, 2, n. 108, above and the passage translated on p. 80. We are here exactly in the period when īwāns became fashionable in the Egyptian capital.

[97]Mann, *Texts*, II, 270, ll. 237–244. The Hebrew names Yeshūʿā b. Saʿadyāhū have the same meaning as the Arabic ones noted in the deed. That a banker should lead a congregation in prayer was, of course, nothing exceptional, see e.g., Goitein, *Letters*, p. 224 n. 15, but it seems that the Karaite congregations, in general, were of a presbyterian character. Throughout the Karaite Geniza documents "the elders," not "spiritual leaders," are acting.

[98]Mann, *Texts*, II, 260–261. Kirmān is a town in Iran. But the family name al-Kirmānī is already well attested in the Geniza in the twelfth century, e.g., TS K 15, f. 91, col. I, l. 5: "an order of payment of 50 dinàrs by Ibn al-Kirmānī" (ca. 1130). Firkovitch II, 1700, f. 21 *a* and *b* (1156): a woman owes Abu 'l-Makārim b. Bu 'l-Ḥasan Ibn al-Kirmānī 8 dinars.

[99]Richards, *Arabic Doc.*, p. 110, B, i-iii. About the exchange rate of nuqra dirhems at that time see *Med. Soc.*, I, 386, sec. 79, and Ashtor, *Prix*, p. 275.

[100]Richards, *Arabic Doc.*, p. 110, B, iv.

[101]Plurals of abstract notions, such as Virtues, Maḥāsin, or noble Character Traits, Makārim, often formed names. The word Abū, Possessor of, has to be complemented.

[102]Richards, *Arabic Doc.*, p. 111. There are some slight oversights on this page. Maḥāsin b. Abi 'l-Fakhr in B, v is, of course, not identical with Maḥāsin b. Abi 'l-Ḥasan mentioned in B, ii. For 1/6 in B, v or vii, probably 1/4 is to be read as in vii and viii.

[103]Mann, *Texts*, II, 261, l. 67.

[104]The reader is reminded that the deeds described by Richards were not found in the Geniza, but are kept in the collection of documents in the possession of the Karaite community in Cairo.

[105]Richards, *Arabic Doc.*, pp. 115–117, 152–162 (the Arabic text). Numerous Muslim deeds of houses have been preserved from this late period, still awaiting publication.

[106]See A, 1, nn. 100–110, above.

[107]See A, 3, n. 40, above; Briggs, "The Saracenic House," p. 233; TS 13 J 18, f. 27, see *Med. Soc.*, III, 34.

[108]Bodl. MS Heb. d 66 (Cat. 2878), f. 88, see *Med. Soc.*, II, 415, sec. 14.

[109]Maimonides, *Responsa*, I, 117.

[110]Renovation of ground floor: TS 13 J 1, f. 21, see *Med. Soc.*, III, 347 and n. 165. Restoration of upper floor: TS 12.417, ll. 12–14, *verso*, ll. 1–5 (ca. 1200).

[111]Bodl. MS Heb. d 68 (Cat. 2836, no. 22), f. 100, *Med. Soc.*, II, 416, sec. 21, Gil, *Foundations*, p. 287.

[112]TS 8 J 9, f. 3*v* (1102). Props: *arkān*.

[113]TS 16.115, ll. 14–15. For the repair of a wall "bearing the beams" of two

contiguous houses "up to 100 dinars" were promised and 25 dinars actually paid (in monthly installments of half a dinar). Summer 1156. Firkovitch II, 1700, fs. 22*v*–23.

[114]Bodl. MS Heb. a 2 (Cat. 2805), f. 7.

[115]TS 8 J 11, f. 9, see *Med. Soc.*, II, 416, secs. 19–20, and Gil, *Foundations*, pp. 264–265.

[116]TS Arabic Box 18(1), f. 155, *Med. Soc.*, II, 417, sec. 24, where expenditure on administration is included.

[117]See Gil, "Maintenance," *passim*.

[118]Shihāb al-Dīn Ibn Faḍl Allāh al-ʿUmarī (d. 1349) writes (Masālik al-Abṣār, MS Bibl. Nat., Paris 2325, f. 163 a): "Few of the buildings in Egypt are made of stone." Quoted by Richards, *Arabic Doc.* p. 118 n. 1.

[119]TS 20.96, ll. 20–21. The synagogue had been renovated only a few years before it was demolished at al-Ḥākim's command. For the history and description of the building see *Med. Soc.*, II, 145.

[120]TS 18 J 2, f. 1, ll. 7–25, see A, 2, n. 168. A breakdown of that account is instructive in various respects. All prices are in dinars.

Two donkeys (for the transport of earth, etc.)	6 5/6
Payments made by R. Samuel [sometimes head of the congregation]	21 5/8
Seventeen columns, a large base and a large capital [both for the large column listed below]	58 3/4
Transport of these items	6
Broken stones	1 5/12
Stone of ʿAyn Shams [Heliopolis, that is taken from ancient Egyptian ruins as explained to me by the late Ahmed Fakhri]	6
[Illegible]	6 14/24
Hewn stones, *majādīl* [used as lintels and thresholds]	1 3/8
Eighteen fir trunks, *shūkha*, and their transport	23
Fifteen elm trunks, *dardāra*	7 1/2
Four half palm trunks	3 7/12
Eleven small old hewn stones, *murabbaʿ* [see Dozy, *Supplément*, I, 505*a*]	2 1/12
Various deliveries of bricks [about 21,000, according to the prices of that time]	3 1/2
Four *maltiyya* [not identified] palm trunks for the *miẓalla*, or tabernacle	4 2/3
To the veterinary for the treatment of the donkey with the sprained ankle	1/4
Old iron locks, *derwend*	5/8
The large white column	11 3/4
Two payments for fir and elm trees (Here the manuscript breaks off)	16 11/12
Total [as far as preserved]	182 3/4

[121]In the account analyzed in the preceding note timber is second in quantity only to columns. For the import of wood from Europe see *Med. Soc.*, I, 301. In TS 13 J 14, f. 20, Judah b. Israel of Fustat orders in Alexandria (or Damietta) twenty long and twenty short logs of fir, sixty of elm, and ten of pine, *ṣanawbar*.

[122]See Gil, "Maintenance," pp. 168–170. The bushes: *nashūsh*; flock or oakum: *sās*.

[123]See A, 2, n. 97, above.

[124]Firkovitch II, 1700, f. 8*b*.

[125]TS Arabic Box 53, f. 37*v*, l. 11, ed. S. D. Goitein, *Sefunot*, 11 (1973), 19 and 22.

[126]Antonin f. 1064. Read: [*al-maḥ*]*rūqa al-dāthira*.

[127]See Lane-Poole, *History of Egypt*, p. 184. I doubt, however, that this surmise can be sustained. The house was situated in the Mikā'īl Lane, in the innermost part of the

Fortress of the Candles, and the Geniza seems to prove that the 1168 conflagration did not extend that far, see *Med. Soc.*, II, 141.

[128]See nn. 80–81, above, and *Med. Soc.*, I, 114–115.

[129]See also the list of wages in Gil, *Foundations*, pp. 512–516.

[130]Bodl. MS Heb. c 50 (no Cat.), f. 14, see *Med. Soc.*, II, 429, sec. 147; Gil, *Foundations*, pp. 408–409. On *verso*, ll. 6–7, a mishap occurred in the translation: *wa-fī ʿāshir ithnayn* cannot mean "twelve," of course. After *ʿāshir* the word Kislev (the month) was omitted (On the tenth of Kislev). Consequently, the dates on p. 409 nn. 6–8, have to be changed; *ithnayn* refers to the following word: "two pillars." For the scarcity of skilled labor see also N. A. Stillman, "A Case of Labor Problems in Medieval Egypt," *IJMES*, 5 (1974), 194–201.

[131]Popular wisdom was divided as to the effect of sumptuous buildings on viewers from the rank and file. "He who sees the Sultan's palace demolishes his own house," says an all-Arab maxim. But another has it: "I slept in the Sultan's palace—it cannot compare with my home." See Goitein, *Jemenica*, p. 153, no. 1156. The second runs like this: *nimt bi-bayt as-sulṭān—wa-mithl baytī mā kān.*

[132]Cf. the story of Wuḥsha, who lived on the third floor, and her relations with the people downstairs, *Med. Soc.*, III, 346–352.

[133]See Goitein, *Jemenica*, p. 164, no. 1269. To the examples given there one from classical Arabic literature should be added. In the *Ḥilyat al-Awliyā'* of Abū Nuʿaym al-Iṣfahānī (948–1038, a contemporary of the Geniza), vol. III, p. 72, l. 5, the warning is sounded: "Moving from one habitation—*manzil*—to another makes life miserable."

4. *Furnishings of the Home*

[1]On seating and bedding in Arabic literature, see Sadan, *Mobilier*, pp. 25–56, 99–133. The Geniza sources on the *martaba* are discussed in App. C, 2, below.

[2]*Mikhadda lil-khadd* (four—two pairs—brought in by a bride): Bodl. MS Heb. d 66 (Cat. 2878), f. 47 margin, col. II, l. 10 (as against five pairs for the living room); TS 20.8 A, l. 12; TS 24.15, l. 4; TS 10 J 21, f. 4 b, l. 21; TS Arabic Box 6, f. 2, col. II, l. 7; TS J 1, f. 48, col. II, ll. 12–16.

[3]See A, 2, nn. 95–101, above. In several documents a *majlis* is listed alongside a *martaba*. The *majlisiyya* given on trust to the synagogue of the Iraqians of Fustat (Bodl. MS Heb. f 56 [Cat. 2821, no. 16], f. 50*v*, l. 6, 1181) probably was a furnishing of the same type as the majlis.

[4]See Serjeant, "Islamic Textiles," pp. 74–80; Goitein, *Studies*, pp. 239–240. Ṭabarī sent from Nahrawāra, Gujerāt, India, to Aden: TS 28.22, l. 14, *India Book* 14 (ca. 1090). Kings of Persia: see Ibn Isfandiyār, *History of Ṭabaristan*, trans. E. G. Browne (Leiden and London, 1905), p. 118.

[5]ENA 2738, f. 33 b, l. 9 (1028): 80 dinars. For the circumstances of this contract see *Med. Soc.*, III, 214 and n. 234. TS 12.12, ll. 13–14: *majlis Ṭabarī thintayn Ṭabarī Ṭabaristān wa'ākharayn Ramlī.* Support: Bodl. MS Heb. a 3 (Cat. 2873), f. 39, l. 12: *majlis Ṭabarī bi-misnad.*

[6]See Dozy, *Supplément*, II, 32*b*; *al-maṭāriḥ wal-masānid*, maṭraḥs with supports.

[7]Bodl. MS Heb. a 3 (Cat. 2873), f. 40, ll. 16–17: maṭraḥ and firāsh (dated 1128). TS K 15, f. 79, col. II, ll. 1 and 5 (ca. 1100), and TS 13 J 3, f. 10, col. III, ll. 17–18: two maṭraḥs (1149).

[8]A brocade *ṭarrāḥa* of five pieces cost 7 dinars, and a Ṭabaristān one of three pieces, 2 dinars: Bodl. MS Heb. d 66 (2878), f. 47, m, col. II, ll. 2 and 4 (daughter of a well-to-do India trader, 1146). A Ṭabarī ṭarrāḥa of three pieces cost 1 dinar; PER H 20, l. 10 (a woman in modest circumstances, 1171).

[9]TS 20.7, ll. 13–14. On Abraham, the Son of the Scholar, see *Med. Soc.*, I, 238–239, and *passim*. The total value of the dowry was about 640 dinars. For translation of Rūmī here as "Byzantine" see p. 303. Milāḥ: Bodl. MS Heb. a 3 (Cat. 2873), f. 43, l. 12.

[10]TS 20.8, l. 11. The total value of the dowry was about 310 dinars. Only the grand

total (marriage gift plus dowry) of 360 dinars is preserved. The early installment of the marriage gift was 15 dinars, which was followed by an average of 35 dinars for the late installment: 360 − (15 + 35 =) 50 = 310.

[11]TS NS J 390, ll. 10–11. First installment of the marriage gift: 20 dinars. Part of the right side unevenly torn away.

[12]ENA 1822, f. 10 (ca. 1165).

[13]See App. C, I, 2. When ʿAli Ibn al-ʿAddās was appointed treasurer "a special room was assigned to him in the caliphal palace and his martaba was covered with brocade": Ibn Dawādārī, *Kanz al-Durar, Fatimid Period*, ed. S. Munaggid (Cairo 1961), p. 229, bottom.

[14]See A, 2, n. 97, above.

[15]1117: Bodl. MS Heb. a 3 (Cat. 2873), f. 42, ed. Mann, *Texts*, II, 177–180, but without the trousseau list. 1125: TS 8 J 29, f. 7. 1156: Firkovitch II, 1700, f. 25.

[16]In the large contract from early Mamluk times, TS Misc. Box 29, f. 29, ed. Strauss (Ashtor), *Mamluks*, III, 32–37, the bride receives a marriage gift of 30 + 70 dinars and possesses an outfit, nominally 460 dinars and actually worth 230. She has only two pieces of bedding valued at 12 dinars (but = 6), and her jewelry was estimated at 122 dinars (but = 61). The slightly later contract Misc. (not: Arabic) Box 28, f. 217, ed. *ibid.*, pp. 72–73, lists a dowry of over 500 dinars (in *Med. Soc.*, III, 408, no. 234, delete: [1 = 1/2]), but had no bedding at all. Her Damascene cushion worth 8 dinars, and the Alexandrian worth 2 dinars, were showpieces.

[17]Bodl. MS Heb. f 56 (Cat. 2821), f. 48, ll. 21–22 (1186).

[18]ULC Or 1080 J 126, l. 19 (ca. 1150).

[19]TS K 25, f. 269, col. II, l. 2 (early thirteenth century).

[20]ENA 2808, f. 13, l. 14 (ca. 1100). Borax-colored: *dinkār*.

[21]Karaite contract: TS 13 J 37, f. 11: . . . with a support, but without cushions—30 dinars. Two Ṭabaristān martabas, but without [(probably:) cushions]. Husband's receipt: PER H 20 (1171), *martaba dībāj wa-mikhādd-hā mustaʿmala.*

[22]*Abulkasim, ein Baghdader Sittenbild*, ed. A. Mez (Heidelberg, 1902), p. 36. For the lust for color in Islamic art see R. Ettinghausen, "The Man-made Setting," in *World of Islam*, ed. Bernard Lewis, (London, 1976), pp. 68–70. "Garden pillows": TS 8 J 29, f. 7*v*, l. 13.

[23]ENA NS 3, f. 24, l. 17, ed. Friedman, *Marriage*, no. 1. Crate: *ṣundūq;* chest: *takht*. Such chests were used for sending high-quality textiles overseas. See Goitein, *Letters*, pp. 36–37.

[24]*Abulkasim* (see n. 22), pp. 36 and 52.

[25]On colors see pp. 172–177.

[26]Dabīqī with border, *muʿlam*: TS 12.12, l. 15 (ca. 1020). Tinnīsī: Bodl. MS Heb. a 3 (2873), f. 43, l. 14 (1059).

[27]*Muṭarraz*: TS K 25, f. 269, col. II, l. 2; TS K 25, f. 42, l. 12 (seven pillows with badges of embroidered script costing 10 dinars), both early thirteenth century.

[28]Ornamental stripes, *muwashshah*, from *wishāḥ*, a belt decorated with precious or semiprecious stones: TS 10 J 21, f. 4*b*, l. 18 (ca. 1110); TS K 15, f. 65, col. IV, l. 7 (ca. 1150).

[29]Fringes, *murayyash* or *murāyash*, literally, with feathers: TS 20.8 A, l. 12 (1155), explained to me thus by the late Egyptian archaeologist Aḥmed Fakhri. Serjeant, *Islamic Textiles*, Index, p. 299: striped stuff. It cannot mean "filled with feathers," for garments are often described thus.

[30]See *Med. Soc.*, I, 419 n. 41. *Mulawwan* literally means colored, but this translation makes no sense. Since the term is also used for clothing and ceramics, I took it as designating a plain surface decorated with patterns or figures in different colors. As explained in B, 1, nn. 171, 238, the correct translation is a fabric of different colors. On pillows: TS 20.7, l. 14 (1050); TS Arabic Box 6, f. 2, col. II, l. 6 (ca. 1100); TS NS J 390, l. 16 (12th century).

[31]"Gilded," *mudhahhab*. TS 12.488, l. 9 (1108–1119).

[32]Figures of birds: *muṭāyar*, TS K 15, f. 65, col. IV, l. 9 (ca. 1150; on white); TS NS J 390, l. 14 (on *sūsanjird*, see p. 306); TS NS J 392, l. 12 (same), TS K 15, f. 79, col. II, l. 2 (same). On animal decorations in general see Serjeant, *Islamic Textiles*, p. 160,

p. 113 n. 186, and p. 212, p. 76, n. 5. Lions: see n. 87, below.

[33]TS 10 J 12, f. 10, a letter, see App. C, Introduction; TS 20.175*v*, ll. 12 and 14 (also a letter); TS K 25, f. 42*v*, l. 1 (a postscript to a large outfit, no price; *mudawwara*, without *mikhadda*).

[34]ENA 2747, f. 1, l. 5 (ca. 1100): *mikhaddatayn, wa-miswaratayn wa-misna[d]*. TS 8 J 4, f. 3 b, *v*, l. 7 (1028): *miswaratayn Ṭabarī*. Same: TS K 15, f. 99, col. II, l. 3 (of brocade). TS 12.530*v*, col. II, ll. 8–10 (1105): also with Ṭabarī. As these examples show, the definition "leather cushion" given by classical dictionaries does not fit the Geniza period. But since leather cushions were round, any round cushion was called miswara. See Dozy, *Supplément*, I, 701*a*. The root of the word is *swr*, wall of a city.

[35]For further details see App. C, sec. 3.

[36]Bedstead: *sarīr*; ebony wood: *sa'sam*. Westminster College Frag. Cairens. 5, l. 5 (first item of the dowry); Bodl. MS Heb. b 3 (Cat. 2806, no. 11), f. 12, l. 11; ENA NS 17, f. 12, l. 16.

[37]Karaite ketubbas: TS 20.156 (10 dinars), TS 8.97 (same, with two ṣundūqs). Yemen: ENA NS 2, f. 25, l. 13: "a mattress (firāsh), six pillows, a bedstead, and a mat—9 dinars." The dinars referred to in the marriage gift were Malikiyya, Aden dinars, whose rate of exchange with the Egyptian dinar, the dollar of the period, fluctuated between 2.2:1 and 4.5:1, as proved by the documents on the India trade. The evaluation of the dowry might have been made in Fustat. The document is continued in ENA NS 1, f. 13 (formerly Laminated 49). See Friedman, *Marriage*, p. 355 n. 10.

[38]1059: Bodl. MS Heb. a 3 (Cat. 2873), f. 43, l. 15, see n. 9, above. 1039: TS 24.80, l. 20. See *EI*², *I*, 200–203.

[39]Hebrew Union College, Geniza MS 15, col. III, l. 8.

[40]TS 13 J 7, f. 8, l. 19: *dakka lil-nawm thalāth qiṭa*ᶜ. The present-day Egyptian pronunciation of the word is *dikka*, see Spiro, *Dictionary of Modern Arabic*, p. 176.

[41]TS 24.2, l. 15. This bride had a "seat" for the living room, *ibid.*, l. 14, cf. nn. 2–5, above.

[42]Bodl. MS Heb. a 3 (Cat. 2873), f. 39, l. 11. This bride, too, had a *majlis*, see n. 5, above.

[43]Persian *takht*, throne, and hence ceremonial seat of bridegroom (see p. 307). As far as I can see throughout the Geniza it designates a chest and not a seating or sleeping facility. See nn. 177–179 below.

[44]"Sicilian" and "Spanish" firāshes are always listed without a definition of the type of material of which they were made. But silk was the principal textile imported from those countries.

Sicilian firāsh, e.g., TS 24.2, l. 15 (with *muthallath*, "triple-thread") and TS 13 J 17, f. 14, ll. 13–14 (with Dabīqī), both from the first half of the eleventh century; TS J 1, f. 48, col. II, ll. 12–16 (ca. 1100); Bodl. MS Heb. a 3 (Cat. 2873), f. 40, ll. 16–17 (1128); and those noted in nn. 45, 56.

Muthallath is best translated twill, a stuff produced when the first weft is passed over one warp, then beneath three warps, again over one, "while with every throwing of the shuttle the one covered warp is moved in echelon to the left or the right," which gives the finished material the look of diagonal parallel ribs. This technique was well known to Greeks and Romans (who also called it "three-thread") and in the Talmud (where it is named "furrowed"), see Krauss, *Talmudische Archäologie*, I, 153; Donald Strong and David Brown, *Roman Crafts* (New York, 1976), p. 175; and Weibel, *Two Thousand Years of Textiles*, p. 18.

Muthallath exported from Egypt: ULC Add. 3418, l. 12, *India Book* 1.

[45]Two Sicilian firāshes: TS 20.7, l. 15 (1050). Two firāshes, one Dabīqī and one Sicilian, priced as worth 20 dinars (ENA 2738, f. 33 b, l. 12), probably were worth only half that amount.

[46]TS 12.12, l. 15.

[47]TS 12.763, l. 9. Yemenite bedspreads (and pillows): ENA 2727, f. 5, col. II, l. 2; TS K 25, f. 42, l. 13; TS K 25, f. 269, col. II, l. 3. Westminster College, Frag. Cairens. 119.

[48]Of ten Ṭabarī maṭraḥs I have noted four Dabīqī and one made of brocade. A

wajh al-maṭraḥ, together with a choker, served as collateral against a debt of 6 dinars: TS 8 J 4, f. 16, l. 9 (1100).

[49]A maṭraḥ with two pillows costing 4 dinars: TS K 15, f. 79, col. II, l. 5; TS 10 J 21, f. 4 b, l. 17; 5 dinars: ENA 2808, f. 13; ULC Or 1080 J 126, ll. 17–18 (two examples); Bodl. MS Heb. a 3 (Cat. 2873), f. 40 (10 dinars representing 5); 1 dinar: TS 12.653; TS 13 J 3, f. 10, col. III, l. 17.

[50]TS K 15, f. 79, col. II, l. 1.

[51]Bodl. MS Heb. a 3 (Cat. 2873), f. 40: a white Dabīqī maṭraḥ with two pillows of the same material and color, plus a white Sicilian firāsh, equipped with two pillows and a sleeping cloak: TS 10 J 21, f. 4 b, ll. 17, 22.

[52]*Ṭarrāḥa* listed together with sleeping equipment (*bardaʿa, liḥāf, ridā'*): see nn. 53–57, below; TS 20.116*v*, col. II, ll. 3–5 (ca. 1090); and often.

Several sections: see n. 8, above.

Fine reeds: TS J 1, f. 29, col. III, l. 22, Ar. *sāmān*, growing near Baysān in Palestine, see Dozy, *Supplément*, I, 622*a*, and Claude Cahen, "Quelques chroniques anciennes relatives aux derniers Fatimides," *BIFAO*, 37 (1937), 5, where a collection of three hundred sāmān ṭarrāḥas is cited as the most luxurious item in the treasures of the rapacious "Monk" (d. 1129, see *Med. Soc.*, II, 28). Also in ULC Or 1080 J 48*v*, l. 14.

Ṭarrāḥa with gilded pillows made of leather, *adam*; TS NS J 208, ll. 6–7 (12 c.).

[53]Ṭabarī *bardaʿa*: too many to be listed. Brocade: TS J 1, f. 29, col. III, l. 23. One of white and one of blue Dabīqī linen: Bodl. MS Heb. d 66 (Cat. 2878), f. 47, margin, col. II, ll. 9–10. Greeks: Richter, *Furniture*, fig. 316 (Achilles with Priam and the dead Hector) and p. 60; Ransom, *Couches*, p. 67.

[54]Two beds (firāshes): TS 8.97, TS 12.12, l. 15; TS 12.167, l. 8; TS 16.32, l. 14; TS 20.156, l. 12; TS 24.2; TS NS Box 320, f. 34; ULC Or 1080 J 100; ULC Or 1080 J 140*v*, ll. 8–9.

[55]TS 16.70.

[56]A Byzantine brocade liḥāf with a Tustarī band of geometrical ornaments (*mafrūz*, derived from *ifrīz*, a word having the same meaning, but perhaps not the same origin, as English frieze) cost 10 dinars in 1033/4; TS 24.12, l. 9; another brocade bed-spread, together with eight Dabīqī pillows, 20 dinars in 1050: TS 20.7, l. 14; and again 10 dinars together with a saffron-colored wrap in 1146: Bodl. MS Heb. d 66 (Cat. 2878), f. 47, margin, col. II, l. 11. At approximately the same time, "the rich bride" had "one and another one," each for this price: TS J 1, f. 29, col. III, ll. 12, 13. That girl had multiples of everything; but how the liḥāfs were listed shows that they did not form a pair.

I listed ten saqlābī (sometimes spelled with *ṣ*) liḥāfs, the earliest dated one in a ketubba of 1156: Firkovitch II, 1700, f. 26 b, l. 13. For the role of Slav slaves, mostly eunuchs, at the Fatimid court, see Marius Canard, *Vie de l'Ustadh Jaudhar* (Algiers, 1958), pp. 15–16. For Yemenite liḥāfs see n. 47, above. See also Friedman, *Marriage*, Index s.v. "Saʿīdī."

In some ancient marriage contracts from Lebanon-Palestine and the Egyptian countryside, a quilted blanket, *mudarraba*, takes the place of the liḥāf: JNUL Heb. 4 577/4, no. 98, l. 27, ed. Friedman, *Marriage*, no. 2 (Tyre, 1023, worth 1 dinar); ULC Add 3430, l. 25, App. D, Doc. I (Jerusalem, 1028, costing, together with six pillows. 1 1/2 dinars); TS 12.154, l. 14 (Qujandim 945, evaluated 2 dinars with firāsh), see Friedman, *Marriage*, no. 14, who rightly corrects the reading in my edition of the document.

[57]"Cloak for sleep," *ridā' lil-nawm*, noted a dozen times in Geniza trousseaus; blanket, *malḥafa*, e.g., TS 13 J 3, f. 10 c, col. III, l. 16; PER H 20, l. 9 and often; wrap, *mulā'a*, TS 12.12, l. 16 (three), TS 20.6, l. 15 (three); TS 16.184, l. 9 (two), TS 20.7, l. 11 (two): *mulā'atayn nawmiyya*; TS 16.58, l. 9, etc.; mantle, *īzār*: ENA 4020, f. 3; ENA NS 17, f. 31*v* (1084).

Roman and Greek: see Richter, *Furniture*, and Ransom, *Couches*, *passim*. Medieval: Grabar-Nordenfalk, *Early Medieval Painting*, *passim*. The poor scholar: TS 10 J 10, f. 5, l. 13, Ṣādōq ha-Levi b. Levi (first half of eleventh century).

[58]*Muzarra* stands for *muzarrara*, from *zirr*, button, see Dozy, *Supplément*, I, 584*a*. For buttonholes see B, n. 104, below.

[59]Details in App. C, 1, end.

[60]Grabar-Nordenfalk, *Early Medieval Painting*, pp. 213–214, picture illustrating the dream of Joseph, Mary's husband, and showing in its lower part his servant asleep, and p. 171, garments with hoods (Spain, 975).

[61]A brocade muzarra is listed as costing 20 dinars in a trousseau list from 1028, ENA 2738, f. 33 b, l. 9, see *Med. Soc.*, III, 471 n. 234 (Byzantine), and again around 1150 as part of the outfit of "the rich bride," TS J 1, f. 29, col. III, a ("blue"), who had another one of siglaton worth 12 dinars, *ibid.*, l. 8. The Iranian heavy silks, Qurqūbī (TS 24.16, l. 11; TS K 15, f. 99, col. II, l. 23; ULC Or 1080, Box 5, f. 15, l. 11, misspelled) and Tustarī (TS 24.12, l. 9, spelled Dustarī) were also very expensive. "The muzarra of the boy," taken by a woman from her husband's house, is one of the few cases where we learn in the Geniza about children's clothing, Dropsie 402, l. 13.

[62]The *killa* in both meanings is repeatedly referred to in Talmudic literature, see Krauss, *Talmudische Archäologie*, I, 65, 394.

[63]TS NS J 27, l. 10 (an inventory from 1143): a woolen *ḥajala*, canopy, and two woolen curtains; TS J 1, f. 29, col. III, 14: two surādiqs (spelled with *ṣ*)of chameleon color (*qalamūnī* for *būqalamūnī*) costing 60 dinars. Both expressions seem to designate a drapery hung over a quadrangular structure.

[64]Canopies in outfits or inventories: Bodl. MS Heb. a 3 (2873), f. 39, l. 12; ENA 4100, f. 8 B, l. 6; TS 12.12, l. 17; ENA 2738, f. 33 b, l. 10; TS 24.12, l. 7; TS 13 J 17, f. 14, l. 12; TS 12.180; TS 20.6, f. 19; TS 13 J 7, f. 8, l. 12; TS 20.7, l. 12.

[65]Three canopies, one *qābisiyya*, sent to Nahray (when in Egypt) from Sicily: TS 10 J 5, f. 24, l. 4 (*Nahray* 186). A brocade canopy sent from al-Mahdiyya: Bodl. MS Heb. b 3 (Cat. 2806), f. 19, l. 21 (*Nahray* 7).

[66]Bresc-Goitein, *Inventaire dotal*, pp. 908, 910.

[67]Richards, *Karaite Doc.* 17, l. 20.

[68]Richter, *Furnishings*, p. 119.

[69]See A, 2, nn. 102–104, above.

[70]Ettinghausen, *Arab Painting*, illustrations on pp. 87 and 113, the first from a manuscript of the *Materia Medica* of Dioscorides in the Metropolitan Museum, New York, the second (frontispiece) from the Maqāmāt, or Assemblies, of al-Ḥarīrī in Leningrad.

[71]See A, 2, nn. 105–106, above.

[72]See Richter, *Furnishings*, fig. 555, and the comments of the author, pp. 115 and 120.

[73]Iraqians: TS 20.47, ll. 15–16; Palestinians: ENA 4010, f. 1, ll. 20–21, see Goitein, *The Synagogue and Its Furnishings*, p. 92. See n. 112, below.

[74]See Samuel Krauss, *Synagogale Altertümer* (Berlin and Vienna, 1922), pp. 376–381, and *Studies in Textile History in Memory of Harold B. Burnham*, ed. Veronika Gervers (Toronto,1977), pp. 68–81.

[75]Picture of library in Paris manuscript: Lewis, *World of Islam*, p. 112 (O. Grabar). Curtains suspended behind decorative spandrels: Ettinghausen, Arab Painting, p. 87; Grabar, *A Manuscript of the Maqāmāt of Ḥarīrī*, pl. 13, fig. 25.

[76]See Y. Eche, *Bibliothèques arabes* (Damascus, 1967), pp. 333–337, esp. p. 337.

[77]Governor: Ettinghausen, *Arab Painting*, p. 106. Judge: *ibid.*, p. 107. Meal: *ibid.*, p. 113 (with central curtain knotted). Other curtains pulled up: *ibid.*, p. 150, Grabar, *A Manuscript of the Maqāmāt of Ḥarīrī*, pl. 7, fig. 14. Drawn: *ibid.*, pl. 13, fig. 25. "Keeper of the curtain", *parda-dār* (Persian): TS 8 J 14, f. 18 *v*, l. 12.

[78]For descriptions see Ibn Zubayr, *Dhakā'ir*, p. 329, s.v. "*sitr*" and the story, *ibid.*, p. 134, and its sources.

[79]ENA 2738, f. 33*v*, ll. 10–12.

[80]ENA 2591, f. 12, ll. 6–8, a large fragment in Nahray's hand. The length of the cubit differed in each town and for each item of merchandise, see Hinz, *Masse*, pp. 55–62. The Cairene cloth cubit measured 58.187 cm, about two-thirds of a yard. Good: *jayyid*; high quality: *rafī'*. For Bahnasī see nn. 84–87, below.

[81]Bodl. MS Heb. a 3 (Cat. 2873), f. 42, ll. 25–26.

[82]Bodl. MS Heb. d 66 (Cat. 2878), f. 47, margin, col. I, l. 7. Sidepiece, *mijnab* from *janb*, side, see App. D, Doc. II.

[83]1156: Firkovitch II, 1700, f. 26*v*, l. 1. Unfortunately, while in Leningrad, I could not make out the two words preceding *wa-mijnabayn*. The total of that line is 120 dinars. The brocade ṣadr wa-mijnabayn: TS 12.465, a small fragment in the hand of Mevōrākh b. Nathan.

[84]TS 20.142, l. 10 (Bahnasā, not Bahnasī, as usual); TS 12.619, l. 7. Two pairs and one single: TS 24.2, l. 18.

[85]Two pairs of Bahnasī woolen curtains, *zawjayn sutūr, ṣūf Bahnasī:* TS NS J 390, l. 13. A pair of woolen curtains costing only 3 dinars around 1090 is not described as Bahnasī: ENA 2727, f. 8 A*v*, l. 20.

[86]See *EI*², I, 926 (Gaston Wiet).

[87]TS Misc. Box 25, f. 14: *zawjayn sutūr sudāsī Bahnasī musabbaᶜ*. For *musabbaᶜ*, derived from *sibāᶜ*, lions, as meaning "with figures of lions," see n. 32, above, and Ibn Zubayr, *Dhakhā'ir*, p. 134, ll. 2–3. The measurement was provided here probably because this pair was cut from a longer piece.

[88]Bodl. MS Heb. d 65 (Cat. 2877), f. 30; Friedman, *Marriage* no. 18, ll. 18–19. She also had a pair made of *qazz*, silk; together both pairs were worth 20 dinars.

[89]1028: ENA 2738, f. 33*v*, ll. 10–11, see n. 79, above. 1030/1: TS 13 J 17, f. 14*v*, ll. 18–19.

[90]1172: ULC Or 1080 J 142, ll. 4–5. Ornamented bands: *farāwiz*, see n. 56, above. Two red Maghrebi silk curtains cost 10 dinars in 1033/4, TS 24.12, l. 10.

[91]BM Or 5566 B, f. 32: Shlmw (Solomon in Arabic transcription) b. Mūsā al-Mahdawī writing to Frḥy' (Peraḥyā) b. Joseph. Span, *shibr*, the length of the extended hand from the tip of the thumb to the tip of the little finger.

[92]Siglaton: ENA 2747, f. 29, l. 11; ENA 4020, f. 3, ll. 3–4. With Dabīqī: TS 12.12, l. 18. Two pairs of Dabīqīs costing 30 dinars: TS 12.635, l. 2. Bahnasī: TS 13 J 17, f. 14*v*, l. 19; TS 12.619, l. 7. Pair of woolen curtains: 12.781, l. 6 (late eleventh century). See also nn. 85, 86, above.

[93]A single Wāsiṭī curtain: Bodl. MS Heb. a 3 (Cat. 2873), f. 42, l. 26, see n. 81, above. A single Qurqūbī, costing 15 dinars: TS NS J 86, l. 9. Caliphal palaces: see Ibn Zubayr, *Dhakā'ir*, p. 134, a Wāsiṭī described as large; *ibid.*, p. 250: Qurqūbī pillaged from the (Fatimid) caliphal palace and bought by merchants.

Kingly hangings: TS 20.7, l. 12 (1050), *maqṭaᶜān Khuṣrawānī* (*ṣ* for *s*) costing 40 dinars, while two Bahnasī pairs cost 20 dinars. See Ibn Zubayr, *Dhakhā'ir*, p. 86, l. 6: *sutūr Khusrawānī. Maqṭaᶜ* means piece, namely, one large enough for being made into a curtain or carpet. See *ibid.*, p. 196, para. 258, and p. 250, l. 3 from bottom, and bottom. Khusrawānī taken as merely meaning sumptuous: Wiet, "Tapis," p. 5. For the ominous carpet of the patricidal caliph see Herzfeld, *Geschichte der Stadt Samarra*, pp. 221–222.

[94]Maimonides, *Responsa*, II, 379–380. See *ibid.*, n. 5, for literature on the subject.

[95]For wall paintings in Romanesque churches see the impressive Introduction to the magnificent volume by Otto Demus and Max Hirmer, *Romanische Wandmalerei* (Munich, 1968).

[96]TS 6 J 5, f. 10.

[97]TS 16.80, l. 7; TS 8.97, l. 6; ENA 2747, f. 2, l. 11; ENA 2727, f. 8 A, l. 7.

[98]TS NS J 228, l. 13: *sitrayn li(l)-ṭāqa*, which I take as arch, like *ṭāq*, see Dozy, *Supplément*, II, 71*a*, namely the one with the decorative spandrels behind which curtains were fastened, see n. 75, above.

[99]PER H 2, containing Jeremiah 17:7 and Psalms 34:9–10, 112:1 in nine monumental lines. TS 12.459*v*: only the last word is preserved, but only Psalm 106:4 could be intended. TS 8 J 19, f. 19: ca. forty Bible verses in a scribal hand fit for wall decorations.

[100]ULC Or 1080 J 50. Richard Ettinghausen examined the print, and ascribed it to the late Mamluk period. *EJ* 7, 912, contains a reduction of it. But this is a placard, not "a fragment from a Bible".

[101]For *anmāṭī* see Wiet, "Tapis," p. 9.

[102]ULC Or 1080 J 77, ll. 26–27, in a huge order for textiles of most variegated description, see n. 120, below.

[103]Partnership in *dār al-māṭ* = *al-anmāṭ*: *Med. Soc.*, I, 365, sec. 13; see Wiet, "Tapis,"

p. 10. Kātib: Gottheil-Worrell, XIII, p. 66; *Med. Soc.*, II, 474. He donated half a dinar.

[104]Antonin 635, l. 18, ed. Friedman, *Marriage*, no. 29. I prefer the pronunciation *ṭunfusa* (for the more common *ṭinfisa*), because it is spelled with *w* in several Geniza texts, e.g., those noted in n. 106, below.

[105]TS 20.116*v*, item II, l. 5.

[106]One person sitting on a ṭunfusa: Wiet, "Tapis," p. 6 n. 2. Pilfering: Dropsie 402, l. 8. Pawning: ULC Or 1080 J 48*v*, ll. 6–7 (May-June, 1050).

[107]Coppersmith: ENA 1822, f. 46, l. 10. Foreigner: TS 12.530*v*, col. II, l. 20 (1105). For prayer carpets see nn. 118–119, below.

[108]Ibn Muyassar, p. 58, l. 3 from bottom: *suṭūr ʿamal ṭanāfis.*

[109]TS 24.66*v*, ll. 7–8, *India Book* 26: *ṭunfusa burūjī*, price 5 (Malikī, Yemenite) dinars, worth at most 2 Egyptian dinars; cf. n. 37, above. Basin: Wiet, *Objets en cuivre*, pp. 103–104, no. 4022, pl. 47.

[110]Rotation: *lil-dawr*; whereas each of the other items was earmarked for one of the two synagogues, this one had been donated "for the two synagogues," and therefore rotated between them.

[111]TS NS J 296, ed. Goitein, *The Synagogue and Its Furnishings*, p. 95. The right side containing the beginnings of the lines is torn away in this manuscript but is found in TS Misc. Box 28, f. 51. They read as follows: l. 13, *al-kanīsatayn*; l. 14, *mamzūja*; l. 15, *wa-namaṭayn*; l. 16, *ithnayn*; l. 17, *mā qad.*

[112]See n. 73, above.

[113]Lane-Poole, *History of Egypt*, pp. 171–173.

[114]*Ibid.*, pp. 215–216.

[115]Mosseri IX–163. "Orange," *nāranjī*, the fruit of the bitter orange. ". . . wine-colored": in Homer the sea has the color of wine.

[116]ULC Or 1080 J 142, ll. 7, 9, 11, see n. 90, above. A cubit measures about 60 cm or two-thirds of a yard, see n. 80, above. The two red pieces are called *kahramāna*, not known to me from anywhere. I take it as *qahrmāna*, the woman in charge of a great household (like the qahrmāna of the caliph al-Ma'mūn, who sometimes presided over an administrative court of justice), the word being originally Persian, where *q* was pronounced *k*. One could also think of a derivation from *kahramān*, amber, on the assumption that those doctors' carpets originally were that color. But then the ending *a* would be uncommon.

[117]Seating: nn. 9–15, above; hangings: nn. 79–84, above.

[118]Herzfeld, *Geschichte der Stadt Samarra*, p. 222.

[119]Pair of prayer carpets, *muṣallāyatayn*, ordered (mostly from Tunisia): TS 12.229, l. 12 (ca. 1050); ENA 4100, f. 9 A*v*, l. 11; ENA NS 22, f. 25*v*, margin; in inventory: TS 12.530*v*, col. II, l. 20. See next note.

[120]Runner: *nakhkh*, pl. *ankhākh*. ULC Or 1080 J 77, ll. 26–27, dark blue, *kuḥl.*

[121]TS NS J 27, ll. 6–7 (1143).

[122]See nn. 79–84, above, and Herzfeld, *Geschichte der Stadt Samarra.*

[123]The Egyptian archaeologist Ahmed Fakhri explained to me the function of the *ʿataba* and told me that the word was still used so in his country. An ʿataba made of Yemenite material is noted in an inventory of the library of the synagogue of the Iraqians written in 1181, see Goitein, *The Synagogue and Its Furnishings*, p. 96, col. II. This was a textile, not a mat, as I originally assumed (n. 90).

[124]See *Med. Soc.*, II, 52 and n. 79.

[125]Bodl. MS Heb. b 11 (Cat. 2874), f. 5, ll. 24–25, see Goitein, *The Synagogue and Its Furnishings*, p. 88, Gil, *Foundations*, pp. 176–177.

[126]See *Med. Soc.*, II, 318, and n. 33.

[127]TS 13 J 16, f. 2, l. 13, a letter from Alexandria to ʿAllūn b. Yaʿīsh in Fustat (1057–1107, see *Med. Soc.*, II, 78).

[128]TS NS J 128, l. 4. Demona rugs: *busutDimanshī.* For Demona see Goitein, *Sicily*, pp. 31–32.

[129]TS 16.80, ll. 7–8. Amber: *karmī*, see Dozy, *Supplément*, II, 460*a*.

[130]Single: e.g., TS 13 J 7, f. 2, margin, *Nahray* 76 (sale); TS NS 320, f. 52 (legal document).

[131]TS 20.69*v*, l. 21, a huge business letter, sent on Aug. 9, 1048, by Barhūn b. Isaac

Tāhertī, Tunisia, to his younger partner Nahray b. Nissim in Egypt, see *Med. Soc.*, I, 372, sec. 14. The *zarbiyya* cost together with two covers, *kisā'*, and the freight for some other merchandise listed before, 105 dirhems, worth at that date 2 1/3 dinars.

[132]Wuḥsha: ENA 2727, f. 8 A*v*. Husband: ULC Or 1080 J 23. Merchant: Bodl. MS Heb. d 75 (no Cat.), f. 20, margin, l. 4, *Nahray* 94. Norman Stillman drew my attention to W. Marçais, *Textes arabes de Tanger*, (Paris, 1911), p. 269, which contains a rich bibliography about the *ḥanbal*.

[133]Bodl. MS Heb. b 3 (Cat. 2806), f. 20*v*, ll. 17–20, *Nahray* 7. Two pairs of mats ordered: TS 12.404, bottom.

[134]Probably called so after the Fatimid caliph al-ʿAzīz (reigned 975–996). The beginning of this passage is lost. The words in brackets are conjectural.

[135]"And a half" is written above the line. While jotting down the letter, the writer checked his measurements.

[136]Entrance piece: *ʿataba*, see n. 123, above; sidepiece, *mijnab*, see n. 122, above. "Of the same model": *qiṭʿa wāḥid(!)min al-nuskha*." The Heb. equivalent of ʿataba was probably *reṣūʿā* (belonging to a synagogue, TS 8 J 31, f. 4, l. 1).

[137]Houses, *bayt*, indicating the density of the plaiting, see Dozy, *Supplément*, I, 131*b*, "a quadratic figure in the texture of a stuff."

[138]TS 8 J 20, f. 8*v*, ll. 1–11, *India Book* 192. The letter was written in midwinter when the Khalīj, or canal connecting Alexandria with the Nile, was still full of water and navigable. In *The Synagogue and Its Furnishings*, p. 96, I assumed that the letter was written in Aden, South Arabia, because it contained important news from that city. A closer study revealed that it was sent from Fustat to Alexandria. It is in the hand of the India trader and representative of merchants in Fustat, Abū Zikrī Kohen, see Index.

[139]Bodl. MS Heb. d 66 (Cat. 2878), f. 93, ll. 6–12. Writer: Abraham II b. Nathan I, when his father was still alive (see *Med. Soc.*, II, 597, top). The letter was written before 1066, when his father was dead (TS 20.126, see *Med. Soc.*, III, 327). Recipient: Yeshūʿā b. Ismaʿīl, a prominent Tunisian merchant living in Alexandria, see Goitein, *Letters*, Index, p. 359.

[140]ENA 4010, f. 1, ll. 18–19. Round pieces: *al-qawwarāt*, cf. Marzouk, *Textile Industry in Alexandria*, p. 96; TS 12.12, l. 22: *qawwāratayn siglāṭūn*. The MS has *'l.wr't*. See A, 6, n. 40, below.

[141]Maqrīzī, *Khiṭaṭ*, II, 274. See Mez, *Renaissance*, chap. 19, p. 323; Maimonides, *Code*, book "Love of God", sec. "Prayer," ch. 11:5. In Palestine special collections were made for replenishing a synagogue with mats: TS 8 J 41, f. 11 (in Ascalon), ed. Goitein, *Palestinian Jewry*, p. 222.

[142]See EI^2, I, 5.

[143]Muqaddasi, p. 203, l. 12.

[144]See Grohmann, *APEL*, VI, 127–128.

[145]TS 10 J 12, f. 10*v*, l. 3: mats were transported wrapped in a piece of ʿAbbādānī. Nice ones with designs, *malīḥ manqūsh*: TS 8 J 25, f. 4, l. 8.

[146]Young woman: TS 20.187, l. 11. Tyre: PER H 1, l. 23. Late: TS Arabic Box 4, f. 4*v*, l. 8.

[147]Dropsie 402, l. 6. See n. 106, above.

[148]ENA 1822, f. 46, l. 31. See n. 107, above.

[149]TS AS 151, f. 4, ll. 17–18, where plaited mats (in the plural, not dual), to be used for the *sukka*, or hut of the Feast of Tabernacles, were expected to cost 16 dirhems, less than half a dinar. In an account published by Grohmann a small mat cost 2 dirhems, *APEL*, VI, 128. In another Geniza text worn-out mats were used for the sukka, see Goitein, *The Synagogue and Its Furnishings*, p. 92 n. 56.

[150]*Ṭarrāha*: see n. 52, above. Sāmān mats: TS 12.658 (small fragment in exquisite script).

[151]TS 13 J 6, f. 22, l. 10: concluding leaf of a letter by Moses b. Jacob to Nahray b. Nissim. See Dozy, *Supplément*, I, 682*b*, Wehr, *Modern Written Arabic*, p. 429*a*. Mat with a lining: Ibn Saʿīd, *Kitāb al- Mughrib*, ed. K.L. Tallquist (Leiden, 1899), p. 34, l. 25.

[152]TS 13 J 25, f. 8, margin (*Nahray* 183): *zawjayn ḥuṣr wāḥida farsh wal-ukhra thāniya lahā*, a clumsy vernacularism.

[153]Mat as wall hanging: *dirra*, Dozy, *Supplément*, I, 428*b*, (Spain, fifteenth century).

[154]TS 13 J 26, f. 8, margin, a letter sent shortly after 1067 (mentioned) from Alexandria to Fustat. The recipient of the mats was Mevōrākh b. Saᶜadya, later Head of the Jewish community, at the time when his elder brother Judah already bore the title of Nagid.

[155]Goitein, *Letters*, p. 191 and n. 19. A hide sent by a father in Qūṣ, Upper Egypt, to his son in Fustat was probably of Sudanese origin: TS 13 J 26, f. 6, l. 28.

[156]TS 24.66*v*, ll. 5–8, and n. 109, above.

[157]For *faylam* see Johnson, *Persian and Arabic Dictionary*, p. 942*c*. Actually two faylams were ordered: TS 28.22, l. 13 (*India Book* 14). The word is probably Hindu. The genuine Arabic faylam has different meanings. Thanks: TS 16.298, ll. 11 and 27, *India Book* 190.

[158]ENA NS 2, f. 25, l. 13, see n. 37, above. The first letter of the word following *naṭᶜ*, hide, is indistinct. If *n*, the word would be *nuzl*, "for putting up guests", if *gh*, it could be *ghazāl*, gazelle, although there is no *aliph*. Buckskins, *jild ayyil*, were traded in large quantities (seventy-six were once sent from Sicily to Egypt, see Goitein, *Sicily*, p. 31); but I have not yet read about gazelles' hides. TS 8 J 26, f. 5, l. 16: a husband sends from Alexandria to his family in Fustat victuals and many pieces of clothing, and also "a white hide," hardly the skin of a "white gazelle," see *EI*², II, 1037, bottom. Since we also have "red" hides, e.g., ENA 2591, f. 13, l. 13, different types of dressing the skin must be intended.

[159]PER H 24, l. 13; revised edition in Friedman, *Marriage*, no. 16.

[160]TS NS J 359.

[161]See *Med. Soc.*, III, 128 and n. 57, where details about prices are also provided. The phrase "and that which is in it" is mostly in Aramaic, which might indicate that the custom of noting this might be pre-Islamic. The phrase can refer solely to the bride's underwear; her outer garmets were exhibited during the evaluation of the outfit and itemized in the marriage contract. At the bridal procession they were put, of course, into the muqaddama.

[162]The term *muqaddama* is ubiquitous in the Geniza, but absent from Arabic dictionaries, and I have not yet come across it in Arabic literature. My spelling of the word is based on that of the most prolific scribes of the Geniza, Halfon b. Manasse, TS J 1, f. 48, col. III, l. 1, and Mevōrākh b. Nathan, TS 12.552, l. 3 (which is l. 14 of the document, most of which is preserved in TS 20.8).

[163]Tortoiseshell, *dhabl*, see Albert Dietrich, "Aus dem Drogenbuch des Suwaidī," *Armand Abel Memorial Volume* (Leiden, 1974), p. 97. Ivory, *ᶜāj*, see n. 38, above: TS 24.15, l. 5; TS J 1, f. 48, col. III, l. 1; ULC 1080 J 49, col. II, l. 6; ULC Or 1081 J 56*v*, l. 16; TS Arabic Box 6, f. 2, col. II, ll. 12–14; Bodl. MS Heb. d 66 (Cat. 2878), f. 47*v*, l. 5 (all from the twelfth century, mostly its first half).

[164]TS 12.12, ll. 20–21: *muqaddamat dhabl* (no *ᶜāj*) *muḥalla'a*, probably encrusted with silver. Shagreen, *kaymukht*, see Steingass, s.v.: ENA NS 17, f. 12 a, l. 8 (early eleventh century); ULC Or 1080 J 140, col. II, l. 11 (1045); TS 13 J 7, f. 8. ll. 21–22 (eleventh century).

[165]Mirror: TS 20.7, ll. 16–17, TS 24.15, l. 5; TS K 15, f. 65, col. II, margin.

[166]Bodl. MS Heb. d 66 (Cat. 2878), f. 47, margin, col. I, l. 3. See n. 188, below.

[167]Silver: TS NS Box 320, f. 34, l. 11 (ancient Karaite). Amber: Bodl. MS Heb. a 3 (Cat. 2873), f. 43, l. 10 (1059). An amber gazelle found in a muqaddama: ENA 2700, f. 33 b.

[168]In two cases I have found alongside the muqaddama "with its content" another one, one described as *biyāḍ*, "with white (linen)," TS 13 J 17, f. 14, ll. 10 and 16, and the other "(covered with) shagreen," TS 13 J 7, f. 8, ll. 21, 22. As the line numbers show, the two muqaddamas are not mentioned together.

[169]Two *ṣundūqs*: e.g., TS 8.97, l. 4; TS 16.30; TS 24.2, ll. 14–16; TS 24.80, l. 18; TS AS 147, f. 20; ULC Or 1080 J 140, col. II, l. 10 (all from the first half of the eleventh century).

[170]Inlaid: TS 12.586, l. 5 (costing 5 dinars). Shagreen: TS 16.184, l. 13; TS 20.7, l. 15. Mustanṣiriyya: TS 12.160, l. 5.

[171]TS Arabic Box 4, f. 4*v*, ll. 6 and 8 (thirteenth century).

[172]TS 16.178 (the clerk Japheth b. David, ca. 1040).

[173]Bresc-Goitein, *Inventaire dotal*, pp. 909, 912.

[174]"A *safaṭ* with *its* stool": ULC Or 1080 J 49, col. II, l. 6. One with two kursīs: TS 20.7, l. 12 (cost 12 dinars). A bamboo, *khayāzir*, safaṭ: ENA 3652, f. 8; TS 12.621; TS 12.635; TS NS J 390, l. 18. A kursī of this material: ENA 4100, f. 8 B, ll. 15–16. Both safaṭ and kursī made of khayāzir: TS 12.12, l. 21 (cost 5 dinars); TS NS Box 320, f. 34, l. 17 (6 dinars). See n. 182, below.

[175]TS 8.73*v*, postscript: TS 20.76*v*, l. 1 (in both cases corals and saffron, see Goitein, *Letters*, p. 118). ULC Add. 3418, l. 8, *India Book* 1; TS AS 149, f. 3, l. 19, spelled *ṣafad* (in both cases textiles, *matāʿ*).

[176]TS NS J 409, col. II, l. 6: *dakka lil-naḥās*, 3 dinars. Together with "copper": TS 10 J 21, f. 4 c, l. 12; ENA 1822 A, f. 10, l. 9 (less than half a dinar). See nn. 40–43, above.

[177]See nn. 23 and 43, above.

[178]Silk: App. D, Doc. II, fol. 47*v*, l. 34. Siglaton: ENA 2738, f. 33 b, ll. 7–8. *ʿAṣā'ib wa-rafā'id*: TS 12.12, l. 22; TS 20.7, l. 16; Bodl. MS Heb. a 3 (Cat. 2873), f. 43, l. 16. For the translation brassiere see Stillman, *Female Attire*, p. 189 n. 5. Clothes: TS 28.6, l. 16 (1074). *Rifādatayn*, 2 dinars: TS NS J 86, l. 7 (an old Karaite ketubba) must have a different meaning; mentioned in clothing section and not as contained in a chest.

[179]*Takht Baghdādī*: TS 24.15, l. 5.

[180]See A, 2, nn. 103–104, above.

[181]Left: TS Misc. Box 24, f. 137, p. 4*v*, ll. 8–9. Entrusted: PER H 22, l. 16 (1137), ed. Goitein, *Wills*, p. 116. TS 13 J 3, f. 1, l. 25 (1141), ed. M. A. Friedman, *Tarbiz*, 40 (1971), 324: deposited with the court as a security for wife. TS 13 J 3, f. 10 e, l. 7 (1159): estate of a husband.

[182]DK XX (1229), see *Med. Soc.*, II, 267. Base: *kursī*. The explanation of the term as a chair on which one put one's turban during the night (Ashtor, *Prix*, p. 178) does not apply here, since this is the inventory of a drugstore.

[183]ENA 1822, f. 46, l. 36. See n. 186, below.

[184]TS 20.187, l. 11 (1063).

[185]Cf. n. 178, above. Also TS J 1, f. 15d (taken from Ashtor, *Prix*, p. 178; the explanation provided there, "a cupboard built into the recess of a wall," is doubtful, since everywhere a piece of movable furniture is intended). Real, *khizāna dūlābiyya ṣaḥīḥa*: TS NS J 208, l. 5.

The translation of Dozy, *Supplément*, I, 478*a*, top, "armoire ronde tournant sur un pivot," is taken from a nineteenth-century dictionary and cannot be taken as a source for the usage of the term in the eleventh century. Today *dūlāb* simply means cupboard, especially in a wall, see J. Revault, *Annales Islamologiques*, 15 (1979), Pl. IX, B. See A, 3, n. 34, above.

For combination lock see Ibn al-Razzāz al-Jazarī, *The Book of Knowledge of Ingenious Mechanical Devices*, trans. Donald R. Hill (Dortrecht and Boston, 1974), pp. 199–201, 274–275, and E. Wiedemann and F. Hauser, "Über eine Palasttüre und Schlösser nach al-Gazari," *Der Islam*, 11 (1921), 213–251. Ibn al-Razzāz, who wrote his book in 1204 or 1206, notes that combination locks were made before him. He uses the word *dūlāb* for his "wheel lock."

[186]ENA 1822, f. 46 a, l. 19: *qafaṣ nuḥās lil-kīzān*, a qafaṣ for the copper, namely the cups. For glass see *Med. Soc.*, I, 486 n. 9. For food, *lil-ṭaʿām*: TS NS J 184, l. 24 (inventory).

[187]A large qafaṣ for the copper: TS 20.187, l. 8. The same document, l. 10, lists a basket, *salla*, containing twenty deep dishes, *zubdiya*, five plates, *ṣuḥūn*, and twenty drinking bowls, *ṭāsa*, given into storage. Dropsie 402, l. 10: a salla with ṣuḥūn taken by wife from her husband's house. TS NS J 27, l. 7; *qafaṣ naḥās laṭīf* (small). Bamboo basket, *khayzurāna*: HUC Geniza MS no. 15, col. II, l. 6.

[188]Bodl. MS Heb. d 66 (Cat. 2878), f. 47, l. 28: *mandīl qafaṣ wa-mandīlayn barrāda*, 8 dinars. See also n. 166, above.

[189]See Stillman, *Female Attire*, p. 124 n. 3. Cf. the expression *mandīl muqaffaṣ*, a

kerchief with a basket pattern: ULC Or 1080 Box 5, f. 15, l. 3.

[190]TS J 1, f. 29, App. D, Doc. III. Compare with this Bodl. MS Heb. a 3 (Cat. 2873), f. 43 (1059), which has muqaddama, ṣanādiq, safaṭ, takht, plus *zanfalīja*, see next note.

[191]ENA NS 18, f. 34, l. 7: *zanfalīja kaymukht*; ENA 3652, f. 8, l. 14: . . . *wa-zanfalīja dhabl wa-mā fīhim*; TS 16.32, l. 16; TS 12.619, l. 4. The word means slipcase for a book, see App. D, n. 229, and obviously describes a flat trunk.

[192]See nn. 169–173. A *ṣundūq* for 1 dinar: TS 10 J 21, f. 5, l. 21; TS K 15, f. 65, col. II, l. 12, col. IV, l. 20. For 1/2 dinar: TS 12.526, l. 9; TS 16.198, l. 15 (Tyre); ENA 2727, f. 5, col. II, ll. 5–6.

[193]For *khuristān* see A, 2, nn. 105–106, above. The bamboo *kummiyya* probably was called so because its place was in the *kumm*, the vestibule adjacent to the living room, see A, 2, n. 102, above. Bodl. MS Heb. a 2 (Cat. 2805), f. 4 (1029; together with muqaddama); ULC Or 1080 J 140, col. II, l. 11 (1045; with martaba); TS 8.97, l. 5 (Karaite, ancient; with safaṭ).

[194]Lane, *Modern Egyptians*, pp. 156 and 167 (with illustrations).

[195]See A, 2, n. 100, above. For oil and wax as burning materials see M. Gil, "Supplies of Oil in Medieval Egypt: A Geniza Study," *Journal of Near Eastern Studies*, 34 (1975), 63–73, and O'Dea, *Social History of Lighting*, p. 19. In *Med. Soc.*, II, 492, sec. 55, and 463, sec. 88–89, a single wax candle distributed to each of twenty persons and some possibly needed for a synagogue (not expressly stated) is a sign of the impoverishment of the community in the 1230s. The absence of wax candles from synagogues possibly had its reason in the apprehension that their guttering (so much complained of by literary men in more modern times, see O'Dea, pp. 4–5) may lead to a desecration of the Sabbath. About the illumination of mosques see *EI*, III, s.v. "Masdjid," section D, 2, h.

[196]"Brides' lamp," *manāra ʿarā'isī*; "one with wax candles," *shamʿī*, prices mostly between 2 and 4 dinars. Listed together: TS 12.552, l. 13; TS 16.86, l. 10; TS 10 J 21, f. 4 c, col. III, ll. 6–7; Bodl. MS Heb. d 66 (Cat. 2878), f. 47*v*, l. 1 (here, the manāra shamʿī is also called ʿarā'isī); Bodl. MS Heb. f 56 (Cat. 2821, no. 16), f. 47*v*, margin, col. II, l. 3; PER H 20, l.11; ULC Or 1080 J 49, col. II, l. 3; TS K 15, f. 65, col. II, ll. 15–16, col. IV, ll. 12–14.

[197]TS J 1, f. 29, col. III, l. 27. If that bride's Spanish lamps looked like one from the year 1305, now in Madrid, see Migeon, *Art Musulman*, I, 384, it differed much from those manufactured in Egypt and Syria in that period. "Artistically ornamented" translates *manāra muqaddara*, ENA NS 2, f. 45, l. 6, cf. Dozy, *Supplément*, II, 312b, "travailler artistement." This qualifies my remarks on *muqaddar* in *Med. Soc.*, II, 130, and 547 n. 28.

[198]Lane, *Modern Egyptians*, p. 167.

[199]"Trousseau lamp": *manāra mushawwara*, from *shuwār*, trousseau, see *Med. Soc.*, III, 124 and n. 34. Different from chandelier of candles, *manāratayn al-wāḥida sham[ʿī wal-ukhrā] mushawwara*: ULC Or 1081 J 56*v*, ll. 12–13. *Manāratayn mushawwaratayn*, two: TS Misc. Box 25, f. 14; TS 16.184, l. 12. One: TS AS 145, f. 10. In divorce settlement: ENA 2700, f. 32 a, worth 4 1/2 dinars.

[200]D. S. Rice, "Studies in Islamic Metal Work, Part V," *BSOAS*, 17 (1955), 206–231, esp. pl. X, showing the lamp with Solomon's Seal (1090).

[201]TS K 25, f. 42, l. 8, continued in TS Arabic Box 4, f. 4*v*, l. 1.

[202]*Manāra sharābiyya*: ULC Or 1080 J 185, l. 9 (8 dinars); TS NS J 231, col. IV, l. 2 (2 dinars; dated 1225); TS NS J 409, col. II, ll. 1–3: *manāra ʿarāʾisiyya wa-sharābiyya* (10 dinars), *shamʿī wa-sirāj* (3 dinars). I assume that before the word *sharābiyya*, *wa* was added erroneously.

[203]Goitein, *Letters*, p. 195 n. 10. For "yellow" copper, *asfar*, or *ṣufr*, see p. 194 n. 8.

[204]Lamp which could be taken apart, *manāra mufakkaka*: TS 20.48, ll. 31–32. "Joint," *mu'allafa*: HUC Geniza MS no. 15, col. I, l. 6. Head fixed to the lamp, *manārā*(!) *bahnas* (not: *Bahnasī*) *wa-ra'shā ʿalayhā marbūṭ*, among copper utensils sent from Lebanon to Fustat: TS 10 J 10, f. 29, ll.12–13 (*Nahray* 193). The writer might have meant that the head was taken off and fastened to the body of the lamp for

transport. I do not know what *bahnas* is.

[205]"Their appurtenances," *wa-hawā'ij-hā*: TS NS Box 320, f. 34; TS 20.7, l. 16; TS NS J 390, l. 19. Wick trimmer, *miqaṯṯ lil-shamʿ*: ENA 2808, f. 13 a, l. 21 (ca. 1100); TS 12.530*v*, col. II, l. 4 (1105). Candle snuffer made of silver, *qimʿ*; TS 12.530*v*, col. I, l. 24; TS K 15, f. 91, col. II, ll. 21–22 (both inventories of estates). See Dozy, *Supplément*, II, 406*b* for *qimʿ* as inverted funnel. "A large lamp with its tray," *wa-ṣīniyyat-hā* (costing 10 dinars): ENA 2738, f. 33*v*, l. 14; another lamp and tray in the same line: ENA 4100, f. 8B, l. 14. "Two candle basins," *ṭastay shamʿ*: TS 24.64, l. 18, *India Book* 56.

[206]Three candlesticks: TS J 1, f. 29, col. III, ll. 31, 32. Two bronze *ḥasakas* costing 10 dinars: ENA 2738, f. 33 b, l. 15 (1028). Ordered in India: TS 8 J 7, f. 23, l. 12, *India Book* 219.

[207]Silver candlesticks: TS 8 J 21, f. 14, l. 14 (continued in TS 8 J 8, f. 12), a deathbed declaration made by a husband in presence of his wife (but she did not get the candlestick; June 1085); TS 8 J 5, f. 1, l. 19, inventory of a rich man's estate (Aug., 1114). Wuḥsha: ENA 2727, f. 8 *a*.

[208]Fraenkel, *Aramäische Fremdwörter*, p. 95, Sirāj as different from candlestick: TS 10 J 21, f. 4 e, l. 11; from *manāra shamʿī*: TS J 1, f. 29, col. III, l. 27; Bodl. MS Heb. d 66 (Cat. 2878), f. 47*v*, ll. 1 and 4; TS NS J 409, col. II, l. 3; TS K 15, f. 65, col. IV, l. 11 (chandelier, sirāj, and oil jug together cost 2 dinars); from a lamp in general: ULC Add. 3430, l. 23. Sirāj as "head" of a lamp of any type: TS K 25, f. 269, col. II, l. 7; *manārat sirāj*; Bodl. MS Heb. f 56 (Cat. 2821), f. 49, l. 5; *lil-sirāj*; Firkovitch II, 1700, f. 26*v*, ll. 18–19; *shamʿī wa-sirāj-hā* (two, one costing 5, and the other 4 dinars).

[209]The statement in *Med. Soc.*, II, 150, that the Babylonian synagogue in Fustat had two such lamps must be corrected. The missing part of TS NS J 296 is preserved in TS Misc. Box 28, f. 51, where, l. 13, it is stated that the two silver lamps belonged to the two synagogues. L. Bauer, *Wörterbuch des palästinischen Arabisch* (Jerusalem, 1933), p. 200*b*, notes that qindīl denotes predominantly the church lamp. The estate inventory TS NS J 27, l. 3 (1143) lists one qindīl.

[210]See n. 194, above.

[211]"I did not carry a light," *wa-lam yakun maʿī ḍaw'*: TS 10 J 16, f. 6, l. 20, see *Med. Soc.*, II, 111–112. Amusing story: *ibid.*, p. 257 and n. 85.

[212]TS 12.619, l. 5: *miṣbāḥ*. Fragment of a marriage contract. Richard Ettinghausen drew my attention to a suspendable and portable totally enclosed Muslim lamp with a square base, Metropolitan Museum, 91.1.133.

[213]Box with flint stone, *ḥuqq fīh zinād*: TS NS J 184, l. 22 (early twelfth century). Sulphur match, *kibrīt*: TS 16.35 (1118), see *Med. Soc.*, III, 174 and nn. 70–71. The extensive article "Kibrīt" in *EI*, III, 1064, does not explain its daily use in a household.

[214]*Kānūn*: TS 16.181*v*, item II, l. 11 (933); Bodl. MS Heb. d 65 (Cat. 2877), f. 30, l. 21 (956), both Damascus; TS 24.30, l. 23, ed. Friedman, *Marriage*, no. 5 (probably Byzantium: two coal pans); TS 12.12, l. 20 (ca. 1020); TS J 1, f. 29, col. III, l. 31 (ca. 1140), both rich brides. Ashes from stove, *mawqida*: TS 24.72, ll. 5–6.

[215]*Mijmara*: TS 24.2, l. 9 (1020s); TS 8 J 4, f. 3 b*v*, ll. 5–6 (1028); TS 13 J 17, f. 14*v*, l. 2 (1030/1), all of silver; TS NS Box 264, f. 13, ed. Friedman, *Marriage*, no. 23, l. 20, mentioned between perfuming vessels, costing 5 dinars. Incense burners in the form of animals: Rice, *Islamic Art*, p. 75, fig. 72, p. 95, fig. 93; Dimand, *Muhammadan Art*, p. 138, fig. 80; *Metropolitan 1975*, p. 2 (with Solomon's Seal). Silver incense burner: *L. A. Mayer Memorial*, fig. 11. *Mugmār* (from *gumrā*, charcoal): BT Berakhot 42*b*–43*a*.

[216]A copper *mibkhara*: TS 12.465, l. 3; TS 13 J 6, f. 9*v*, l. 24. Inlaid with silver: ENA NS 3, f. 24, l. 16, *muḥallā kesef* (Heb.). Silver: TS 13 J 17, f. 14*v*, l. 2, see preceding note.

[217]995: TS 16.70, l. 12. Silver, 40 dinars: TS NS J 86, l. 5, Karaite; 50 dinars: ENA 2727, f. 8 A, l. 13 (Wuḥsha). Copper *madkhan* (without final *a*): TS NS J 410, col. II, l. 7 (ten copper utensils cost 25 dinars). Ebony wood: ENA 2738, f. 33 b, l. 2 (1028). From the same year one of silver: TS 8 J 4, f. 3 b*v*, l. 5. *Midkhana khayāzir muḥallā'a*: Bodl. MS Heb. a 3 (Cat. 2873), f. 39, l. 15; together with stool: ENA 4100, f. 8 B;

1 dinar: TS J 1, f. 50, l. 27. Bamboo wickerwork, *tashbīk khūzurān*: TS 8 J 7, f. 23, ll. 7 and 10, *India Book* 219.

[218]See Mehmet Aga-Oglu, "About a Type of Islamic Incense Burner," *The Art Bulletin*, 27 (1945), 28–45, esp. p. 28 n. 3. The article contains a short general introduction on incense burners in medieval Islam, including the Coptic and Byzantine antecedents, but knows of only one term: *mijmara*. (I owe the reference to Richard Ettinghausen.)

[219]The freshening vessel *barniyya* is mostly described as *muṭayyab*, that is, filled with *ṭīb*, perfume, meaning a cheap variety of aloes, or *ʿūd*. Instead of *muṭayyab*, the Geniza texts often have *muṣabbagh*: e.g., ENA 2808, f. 13 a, l. 22; TS AS 145, f. 10; TS NS J 410, col. II, l. 9; Firkovitch II, 1700, f. 25 a, col. II, l. 13; or *ṣabāgh*: TS 10 J 21, f. 4 c, l. 14, which designates a special type of ʿūd; cf. TS Arabic Box 54, f. 93, l. 23, *India Book* 375: *al-ʿūd al-ṣibgh al-lawn*, the dark brown aloes. About ṭīb and ʿūd see Maimonides-Meyerhof, pp. 144–145, and n. 221, below.

The number of freshening vases brought in by a bride is often not specified, which means that there were three or more. In the outfit of a bride which totaled 30 dinars, the *barānī* cost 2 dinars: Bodl. MS Heb. d 66 (Cat. 2878), f. 77 (1161); in another, 6 dinars: TS Arabic Box 6, f. 2, col. II, l. 15. But two cost 13 dinars in TS 16.184, l. 14, and three, 15 dinars in TS 16.80, l. 13 (Karaite), both from the first half of the eleventh century. The "rich bride" had barānī muṭayyab for 8 dinars and two silver barānī worth, together, with a small casket, 5 dinars: TS J 1, f. 29, col. III, ll. 31 and 34. Another well-to-do girl from the same time (1146) had two barniyyas decorated with mother-of-pearl and ivory worth 3 dinars and two muṣabbagh, 4 dinars: Bodl. MS Heb. d 66 (Cat. 2878), f. 47*v*, ll. 8–9.

The poor Karaite bride from Jerusalem, 1028, had one barniyya muṭayyab and one *mumassak*, that is, one with aloes and another with musk, both together worth 5 dinars (out of a dowry totaling 61 1/2 dinars): ULC Add. 3430, l. 24.

Stench: Ibn Riḍwān's complaint, see Wiet, *Cairo*, pp. 37–38.

[220]BT Berakhot 43*b*; cf. Maimonides, *Code*, book "Holidays," sec. "Sabbath," ch. 29:29.

5. *Housewares*

[1]Servant: cf. Lane, *Modern Egyptians*, illustration on p. 147. Cassia: see *Med. Soc.*, III, 32–33.

[2]"Copper" basin and ewer, *ṭast wa-ibrīq*, mentioned together, costing between 1 (PER H 20, l. 11, 1171) or 2 (TS K 25, f. 269, col. II, l. 5) and 5 dinars (TS NS J 409, col. II, l. 4). Numerous other examples.

Damascus: TS K 25, f. 42, l. 15. The Fustat equivalent of Damascene *wa-ibrīq-hū* is *wa-msykt-hū*. Dozy, *Supplément*, II, 592*b* notes *māsika* as belonging to a trousseau, but does not know what it is. As our Geniza text shows, it must have been a vessel like a ewer.

Andalusian basin: Firkovitch II, 1700, f. 25, col. I, ll. 23–24. In view of the paucity of references to Spanish copperwork in literary sources, the Geniza items are worth collecting, cf. A, 4, n. 197, above; see L. Golvin, "Note sur l'industrie du cuivre en Occident musulman au Moyen Age," *Cahiers de linguistique, d'orientalisme et de slavistique*, 1–2 (1973), 117–126.

Mosul: See E. Kühnel, "Zwei Mosulbronzen und ihr Meister," *Jahrbuch der preussischen Kunstsammlungen*, 60 (1939), 1–20, with numerous illustrations. Kühnel identifies twenty metal-workers from Mosul active between 1220 and 1320 (pp. 9–11). A master from Mosul made a chandelier in Fustat in 1269/70, see Wiet, *Objets en cuivre*, no. 1657, pl. 27.

[3]Two pairs: TS 16.80 (early, Karaite); ENA 2738, f. 33*v*, l. 15 (1028); TS 13 J 17, f. 14, l. 16 (1030/1).

[4]One large and one small basin: Bodl. MS Heb. d 66 (Cat. 2878), f. 47*v*, l. 2; TS J 1, f. 29, col. III, ll. 29–30; TS Arabic Box 30, f. 201*v*, ll. 2–3. "Caliphate-like," khilāfī: the two sources noted at the beginning of this note; TS K 15, f. 65, col. IV, l. 15; TS

NS J 27, l. 11. At first I derived the word from *khilāf*, the Egyptian poplar tree, but the derivation from *khilāfa*, caliphate, makes more sense.

[5]"Pre-Islamic," *ṭast jāhilī*: TS 24.9, l. 43 (thirteenth century); 12 dinars: Bodl. MS Heb. f 56 (Cat. 2821, no. 16), f. 48*v*, l. 3 (1186). *Ṭast nuḥās bi-zawj udhnān*: TS NS J 392, l. 15 (1128). A basin (caldron?) with handles: L. A. Mayer, *Islamic Metalworkers and Their Work* (Geneva, 1959), pl. II. "Sparrow," *ʿuṣfūr nuḥās*: Bodl. MS Heb. d 66 (Cat. 2878), f. 111*v* (poor orphans' belongings, 1150), cf. Dimand, *Muhammadan Art*, p. 134.

[6]One *maghsal*: ULC Add 3430 (Jerusalem, 1028); TS 16.80, l. 10. Two: TS 13 J 3, f. 10 e, l. 9 (1159, costing 1/2 dinar); Mosseri L-233, l. 15, *Nahray* 250. "Several": TS Arabic Box 4, f. 4*v*, l. 3. Pawn: ULC Or 1080 J 48*v*, l. 10, App. D, Doc. VI.

[7]*Maghsal fiḍḍa*: TS 8 J 5, f. 1, l. 19 (inventory, 1114); ULC Or 1080 J 55*v*, l. 4 (letter; sent with other silver vessels). Export: ULC Add 3418, ll. 16–17, *maghsal mujrā sawād mudhahhab* (in a list of silver vessels). Cf. Ibn Zubayr, *Dhakhā'ir*, p. 149, l. 14: golden *maghāsil*.

[8]TS NS J 27, l. 2 (1143; between a copper vessel and a glass cup). Widow: TS 13 J 3, f. 10 e, l. 11 (1159).

[9]Bucket and dipper, 1 dinar: TS 20.8 A, l. 13 (1155); PER H 20, l. 11 (1171). Two pairs worth 15 dinars: ENA 2738, f. 33*v*, l. 14. "A Baghdad bucket with its dipper": ULC Add 3430 (1028), l. 23.

[10]"Round" bucket, *mudawwar*: TS J 1, f. 29, col. III, l. 31; Bodl. MS Heb. a 3 (Cat. 2873), f. 40, ll. 17–18 (Damascene). Quadrangular, *murabbaʿ*: TS NS J 27, l. 8 (small). Small, large: common. "Middle": TS NS J 392, l. 16; (and with feet): TS 12.530*v*, col. I, l. 3. With feet (and cover), *ṣaṭl* (*ṣ = s*) *bi-arjul wa-ghaṭā*: TS K 15, f. 99, col. II, l. 16; *murjal*: ENA 1822, f. 46, l. 34.

[11]Damascene bucket: see preceding note; *shāmī*, costing 1 1/2 dinars together with a lamp: TS K 25, f. 269, col. II, l. 7. A large *riḥānī* bucket of *isfādirā'ī* tinned copper (see below), costing 2 dinars, was probably made in Rīḥā, a small town in northern Syria, see *EI*, III, 1250*b*. Baghdad: see n. 9 above; TS 16.80, l. 9. India: TS K 25, f. 42, l. 8. "Ornamented with coins," *muqaddar bi-fulūs*: ENA NS 2, f. 45, l. 6, written by Ḥalfon b. Manasse. For *muqaddar* see IX, A, 4, n. 197, above. Only the *l* of *saṭl* (or *sufl*) is visible.

[12]Handle, *widn* (see n. 5, above): Mosseri L-233, ll. 16–17, *Nahray* 250 (ca. 1075). The handle was ritually defiled by being touched by an unwashed hand; the other hand over which water was poured and thus had been purified could then touch any other part of the vessel for concluding the ablution.

[13]See *Med. Soc.*, I, 547, s.v. Soap. Half a pound of soap ordered from a grocer together with half a pound of starch: Mosseri L-159, frag. 3, *India Book*, 344*b*.

[14]For *ushnān* see Maimonides-Meyerhof, p. 15, no. 24, Grohmann, *APEL*, VI, 207–208, and Rice, "Islamic Metal Work" (see IX A, 4, n. 200, above), p. 230 n. 2, quoting Ghuzūlī, *Maṭāliʿ al-budūr* (Cairo, A.H. 1299, A.D. 1881/2), II, 66.

The regular word for ushnān container in the Geniza is *tawr*: TS 20.7, l. 16, and extremely common. "Set," *dast*: e.g., Bodl. MS Heb. a 3 (Cat. 2873), f. 39, l. 14. "Complete set," *dast kāmil*: ULC Add. 3430, l. 24; or *tawr mukmal*: TS Arabic Box 30, f. 201*v*. Two silver containers, *ushnānatayn*: TS 13 J 17, f. 14*v*, l. 3 (1030/1); in same list, l. 17, a regular brass container. Three: TS 20.187, l. 12 (1063).

[15]Meal carrier, *ḥāmil*: TS 24.16, l. 12; TS 13 J 6, f. 9*v*, col. I, l. 23, costing 2 dinars; TS 12.519, l. 10; Dropsie 402, l. 7. Jewish cooking: see A, 3, n. 80, above.

[16]Wiet, *Objets en cuivre*, no. 3953, pls. 66–69.

[17]*Zawj ḥawāmil*: TS 16.155, l. 12 (before 1088); TS K 15, f. 99, col. II, l. 26; ENA 1822, f. 46, l. 24. Professor A. L. Udovitch informs me that the very observant Jews of Jerba, Tunisia, do not practice the division of the kitchen into a meat and a dairy section.

[18]The grain jar, *zīr ḥajarī wa-kaylaja*, 1 1/2 dinars: TS 13 J 3, f. 10 e, l. 12 (1159). Kaylaja is a measurement containing about two liters, see Hinz, *Masse*, pp. 40–41, but seems to have been used in Egypt especially for the vessel attached to the grain jar; *al-zīr al-ḥajarī alladhī kaylajatuhu 'l-rukhām ʿind al-mawlā*: TS 10 J 12, f. 10, l. 27. Seven

and a half waybas: TS 10 J 11, f. 3. Two stone jars in a house: ENA 1822, f. 46, ll. 34–35; TS NS J 27, l. 13.

[19]TS 20.166*v*, item II, l. 5 (ca. 1088). In Dropsie 402, l. 12, a wife pilfers a *ṭāḥūna* from her husband's house.

[20]Two hand mills in inventories: ENA 1822, f. 46, ll. 10, and 35–36; "another, small one": TS NS J 184, l. 24; "iron implements, a mill for the grinding of gallnuts [for the preparation of ink]": HUC 15*v* l. 3.

[21]Mortar and pestle, *hāwun wa-yaduh*: TS NS J 392, l. 16 (1128). Large and small: TS Arabic Box 4, f. 4*v*, l. 9. Pestle alone: Bodl. MS Heb. d 66 (Cat. 2878), f. 111, l. 1 (1150). As wife's property: Dropsie 333, l. 12; TS 12.98; TS 20.116*v*, items II, l. 6 (the poor widow, see n. 19, above), and elsewhere.

[22]TS NS J 184, l. 21: *ghirbāl shaʿr lil-daqīq*.

[23]Kneading troughs, *jifān lil-ʿajīn*: ENA 1822, f. 46, l. 9. Tyre: 16.198, l. 13 (mentioned after ṣundūq). Taken from the house by the wife: Dropsie 402, l. 13. A *jafna* made of almond wood ordered in Alexandria: TS 12.434, l. 3. Three jafnas sent from Alexandria: TS 13 J 26, f. 8, margin.

[24]As utensils for operating the oven *safāfīd lil-tannūr*, rods (made of copper), are listed in the inventory ENA 1822, f. 46, l. 29, and in the trousseau list of Palermo, 1479, Bresc-Goitein, *Inventaire dotal*, p. 908, l. 24.

[25]Goitein, *Jemenica*, p. 148, no. 1109.

[26]TS NS J 208: *ghaṭā zīr wa-kūz zīr . . . kullhum nuḥās*. ENA 1822, f. 46, ll. 34–35: *kūzayn zīr nuḥās kibār lil-azyār*. Dropsie 402, ll. 11–13: *ghaṭā lil-zīr wa-zīrayn lil-mā*.

[27]ENA 1822, f. 46, l. 21: *zawjayn aghṭiyā lil-barrādāt*. TS 12.452, l. 3: *kūz lil-barrāda*. Bodl. MS Heb. d 66 (Cat. 2878), f. 47, l. 28: *mandīlayn barrāda*. TS 20.8 A, l. 10: *bukhnuqayn lil-barārīd*, 6 dinars.

A series of Iraqian copper vessels brought in by a bride in Damascus in 956 contained also a barrāda: Bodl. MS Heb. d 65 (Cat. 2877), f. 30, l. 22. This must have been different from the vessel bearing that name in the Egyptian documents.

[28]About thirty examples noted. Lowest price, 1/2 dinar: TS 13 J 3, f. 10 c, col. III, l. 14. Highest: 4 dinars (realistic; martabas in the same trousseau cost as little as 1 1/2 or 3 dinars): Bodl. MS Heb. f 56 (Cat. 2821, no. 16), f. 48*v*, l. 4. Wife and lighting the house: see A, 4, nn. 196–199, above, and C, 1, n. 196, below.

[29]See *Med. Soc.*, I, 109 and n. 63; II, 264 and n. 19; and App. D, n. 228, below.

[30]Bodl. MS Heb. d 66 (Cat. 2878), f. 111*v*. Pigeons: ENA 1822, f. 46, ll. 32–33.

[31]Six *zanājil*: Bodl. MS Heb. f 56 (Cat. 2821, no. 16), f. 48*v*, l. 3 (1186; see n. 28, above). Three: TS NS J 228 (1134). Two: TS K 15, f. 111, item I, l. 23 (ca. 1100). Six zanājil in a drugstore, which were worth only 4 1/2 dirhems, probably were made of earthenware: DK XX.

[32]Pair of cooking pots, *zawj qaṣārī*: Dropsie 333, l. 13; TS 16.155, l. 12; TS NS J 208, l. 12 (spelled here with *s*); ENA 1822, f. 46, l. 23; TS 20.187, ll. 8–9, "one large and two small copper pots." The three last sources are inventories. *Zawj birām* (earthenware): TS 20.116*v*, item II, l. 5. The large copper caldron *qidr*, and the vat, *ṭanjara*, seem to have been destined for industrial purposes rather than the kitchen: TS 18 J 1, f. 10, ll. 9–10 (1072): "Iraqian copper caldrons, *qidar*, full of copper vessels." ENA 1822, f. 46, l. 1: "Two caldrons with large pots for the boiling of paint (*li-ṭabkh al-duhn*) and two others for cooking." For the kitchen the diminutives *qidra* and *qudayra* were used, but rarely.

A common word for cooking pot was *sifl*, see Dozy, *Supplément*, I, 659*b* (connected with biblical *sēfel*), no longer known in this meaning. The Karaite girl from Jerusalem, 1028, had one from Damascus: ULC Add. 3430, l. 23; and so did her contemporary and coreligionist: TS 16.80, l. 10. In the first instance and two other twelfth century trousseaus the price was 2 dinars: TS 12.519, l. 10; PER H 20, l. 11 (1171); 4 dinars, a high sum for a cooking pot: TS K 15, f. 65, col. IV, l. 18 (ca. 1170), and TS NS J 409, col. II, l. 3 (ca. 1230).

[33]"Two frying pans of iron, one large and one small": TS K 25, f. 42*v*, l. 1 (trousseau). One of iron: HUC Geniza 15, col. I, l. 6; TS 12.56*v*; Goitein, *Letters*, p. 189 n. 11. One of "stone": *ibid.*, Greek *ṭājin* and Arabic *miqlā* were used indiscriminately.

For roasting seeds: *maqālī ḥadīd lil-qaly.*

[34]TS NS J 184, ll. 18–19, and TS 8 J 9, f. 19, l. 3: in both the vessel is named *barniyya.*

[35]"Hooks," *khaṭaṭīf . . . al-maṭbakh*: ENA 1822, f. 46, ll. 28–29. "Hanger," *ʿalāqa wa-khuṭṭāf*, and "spike for the cups," *shawkat kīzān*: HUC Geniza, no. 15, col. I, l. 3. Drying board, *kabaka*: see Dozy, *Supplément*, II, 440*b* (based on Mohīt, Beirut, 1870); or *kabke*: Barthélemy, *Dictionnaire arabe-français*, p. 702; TS 10 J 11, f. 15 (collateral); TS 13 J 17, f. 14*v*, l. 17 (trousseau).

[36]TS 20.1, l. 20, see *Med. Soc.*, III, 311; TS 13 J 2, f. 16, l. 4 ("he will eat with his son at one table, and she will not separate them").

[37]Widow: TS 20.116*v*, item II, l. 5 (ca. 1090). Scribe: TS K 3, f. 28, l. 5. Taken from house by wife: Dropsie 402. Physician: TS Arabic Box 25, f. 53, l. 3 (1172). Amir: TS 13 J 20, f. 19, ll. 21–22, *Nahray* 174 (ca. 1060). Aden: Westminster College, Frag. Cairens. 9, l. 31, *India Book* 50. On tables in Arabic literature see Sadan, *Mobilier*, pp. 64–85, and figs. 4 and 10.

[38]*Kursī (lil-)mā'ida*: TS 20.187, l. 8 (1063); TS 16.198, l. 12 (Tyre, Lebanon; ca. 1100).

[39]*Mayda kabīra khalandj Siqillī*: TS NS J 392, l. 15 (1128); TS K 15, f. 99, col. III, l. 13; see Dozy, *Supplément*, I, 400*a*–*b*; Mez, *Renaissance*, chap. 24, p. 423, nn. 1–2; V. Minorsky, *Ḥudūd al-ʿĀlam* (Leiden, 1937), p. 465. The description of a table as broken, or split, *mashqūqa*, in an inventory also indicates that it was made of wood: TS NS J 27, l. 11.

[40]"A *sufra* for the table, a middle-sized table, and a sufra for a lamp": TS 12.530*v*, col. II, ll. 20–21 (1105). "A large leathern *ṣufra* (*ṣ* = *s*) and a *qwbrh* [see below] for the table": TS 20.187, l. 12 (1063). "A blue *qw'rh* (*qawwāra*, see A, 4, n. 140, above) for the table": ENA 1822, f. 57, l. 21. In the latter document a tablecloth might have been intended, and *qwbrh* in TS 20.187 was perhaps a slip of the clerk for *qw'rh.*

[41]Two trays: Dropsie 333. A shawl and a *mandīl ṣīniyya* for 6 dinars: TS 10 J 21, f. 4b, l. 10 (Cairo, ca. 1110). *Bukhnuq lil-ṣawānī*: ULC Or 1080, Box 5, f. 17, and often. A ṣīniyya with its stool in Lane, *Modern Egyptians*, p. 147, fig. 45 (with Solomon's Seal).

[42]Silver *ṣīniyya*: e.g. TS 8 J 4, f. 3*v*, l. 5 (1028); TS 13 J 17, f. 14*v*, l. 2 (1030/1); TS 24.12, l. 6 ("burnt silver" *muḥraqa*, said also of another object in that document; 1034); TS AS 148, f. 7; TS 12.12, l. 3 (25 dinars); ENA 2727, f. 8 A, l. 9 (30 dinars); ENA NS 3, f. 26, l. 15 (50 dinars). As collateral: ULC Add. 3420 c (1097), *India Book* 15. Another case of a silver ṣīniyya given as collateral: Mosseri A-69, ll. 4 and 14. Exported to al-Mahdiyya: TS 13 J 28, f. 2, l. 30. To Aden: Westminster College, Frag. Cairens. 9, l. 8 (first item in list of silver vessels).

[43]Muʿtaṣimī: see I. Friedlaender, *Arabisch-deutsches Lexikon zum Sprachgebrauch des Maimonides* (Frankfurt a. M., 1902), p. 78 (from Maimonides' Commentary of the Mishna). Karaite bride: TS 16.80, l. 11. Price: TS 20.80*v*, l. 37, *India Book* 273 (1140). Two: Maimonides, *Responsa*, I, 135–136; HUC Geniza 15, col. IV (spelled here with ṭ). Cracked, *mashʿūb*: TS NS J 27, ll. 12–13. For khilāfī, large, see n. 43, above. For meat and dairy dishes see n. 17, above.

[44]A large copper *ṣadr* for 40 dirhems (ca. 1 dinar): TS NS J 359, l. 14; 50 dirhems: TS 13 J 3, f. 10 e, l. 11 (1159). Of brass, costing 2 dinars: TS K 25, f. 42, l. 7; Bodl. MS Heb. f 56 (Cat. 2821, no. 16), f. 53 a (1184). Inventories: TS NS J 163, l. 11 (see *Med. Soc.*, III, 493 n. 95); TS NS J 208, l. 8.

[45]TS K 25, f. 42, l. 7: a brass khūnjā, 2 dinars (see preceding note). TS Arabic Box 4, f. 4*v*, l. 4: one of copper, *nuḥās aḥmar*, 1 1/2 dinars. (These two manuscripts form part of one document.) TS 24.9, l. 13: *ibar khūnjāt*; see Dozy, *Supplément*, I, 414*b*.

[46]Bodl. MS Heb. a 3 (Cat. 2873), f. 42, l. 20 (1117).

[47]TS 24.9 (one silver *zabdiyya*, 5 dinars); TS J 1, f. 29, col. I, l. 18; TS NS J 453, l. 2, fragment of court record.

[48]Five chinas: TS 16.80, l. 11. Six zabdiyyas: TS 16.198, l. 14. Fifty ordered: TS 8 J 25, f. 20, ll. 4–6. Inventory: TS NS J 184, ll. 20 and 26 (small bowls: *zubaydiyyāt*).

[49]Translucent, *ṣīnī shifāf*: TS Arabic Box 4, f. 4, l. 9. Poor woman and inventories with "two chinas": TS 20.116*v*, item II, l. 5; TS 12.530*v*, col. I, l. 26; TS K 15, f. 99, col. I, l. 23. Maghrebi ware: TS 8 J 19, f. 21*v*, an unheaded list of consignments, mostly of wax and saffron, the most common articles of export from Tunisia to Egypt. Cf. Marilyn Jenkins, "Western Islamic Influences on Fatimid Egyptian Iconography," *Kunst des Orients*, 10 (1975), 91–107 (dealing with popular ceramics).

[50]Westminster College, Frag. Cairens. 9, l. 17: *qafaṣ ghaḍār Āmidī aw Miṣrī milāḥ*. Carnelian-red, *ʿaqīq*: TS 8 J 41, f. 12*v*, l. 1.

[51]Bodl. MS Heb. a 3 (Cat. 2873), f. 19, ll. 49–50, *India Book* 32: *qafaṣ ghaḍār zabādī wa-ṣuḥūn wa-kīzān*; TS 18 J 5, f. 5, ll. 42–46, *India Book* 149. Small bowl; *suk(ku)ruja*: cf. n. 48, above. For the date, see S. D. Goitein, "Two Eyewitness Reports on an Expedition of the King of Kish (Qais) against Aden," *BSOAS*, 16 (1954), 250.

[52]Chinese porcelain in Aden, *al-awʿiya al-ṣīnī al-ghaḍār al-shifāf al-ṣīnī*: TS 8 J 37, f. 1, col. VII, ll. 5–11, *India Book* 33. Sent to Cairo *dast aqdāḥ ṣīnī al-ʿadad sitta aqdāḥ*: TS Arabic Box 5, f. 2, col. III, l. 6, *India Book* 34. A set of Egyptian aqdāḥ is sent from Aden to India: ULC Or 1081 J 3, l. 8, *India Book* 61.

[53]TS 13 J 28, f. 2, l. 29: *zabādī naqliyyāt*.

[54]TS 8 J 5, f. 1*v*, l. 1.

[55]TS 16.80; TS NS J 163, l. 12: *ṭayfūr(at)ayn khalanj*. Steingass, *Persian-English Dictionary*, p. 824, has "*ṭayfary*, a small tray," but seems to regard this as a misspelling for *ṭayqarī*, or even *ṭabaqrī*. In Arabic ṭayfūr is the "name of a little bird," *ibid*.

[56]TS 12.530*v*, col. II, ll. 1–2 (1105): *sitta ṭayāfīr naqliyyāt wa-thalātha Baghdādī wa-ṭayfūr Baghdādī wasaṭ*. A *mayda wa-ṭayfūr* together cost 1 1/2 dinars in ENA 3030, f. 6*v*, l. 5. An inventory notes three intact and four broken ṭayfūrs, as often with wood: ENA 1822, f. 46, ll. 26 and 40. A scribe had two: TS K 3, f. 28, l. 5.

[57]TS NS J 27, l. 14 (1143): *ṭayfūr rukhām*.

[58]TS 20.48, ll. 29–30: *ṭāsa mubayyaḍa*, 2 dinars. Also *ṭāsatayn bīḍ*: ENA 2727, f. 5, col. II, l. 1. *Ṭāsa 'sf'dryh* (from Persian *isfīd*, white), means the same: TS 24.3, l. 9.

[59]Sets: TS Arabic Box 4, f. 4*v*, ll. 2–3 (thirteenth century); TS 24.8, l. 22 (ca. 1337); 5 dinars: ENA 2727, f. 5, col. II, l. 1 (of brass; see also preceding note).

[60]A large ṭāsa: TS NS J 226, col. II, l. 6 (1224); TS Arabic Box 4, f. 4*v*, l. 1; TS K 25, f. 269, col. II, l. 5 (one costing 2 dinars). Set of sixteen ṭāsas: TS Misc. (not: Arabic) Box 28, f. 217, l. 14, ed. Strauss-Ashtor, *Mamluks*, III, 73.

[61]Damascene ṭāsa: TS NS J 231, col. IV, l. 3 (2 1/4 dinars [1225]); TS NS J 409, col. II, l. 3 (4 dinars); TS K 25, f. 269, col. II, l. 8.

[62]Silver ṭāsa: TS 8 J 4, f. 3 b, *verso* l. 6. I do not know what a *ṭāsa qallāba* (convertible) is, perhaps one that, when turned upside down, served some other purpose, especially when its bottom had a brim: Westminster College, Frag. Cairens. 120, l. 9.

[63]See Sadan, *Mobilier*, pp. 90–94, which needs qualification in light of the Geniza texts discussed here. With ṭāsa: Bodl. MS Heb. f 56 (Cat. 2821, no. 16), f. 48, margin, col. II, l. 3 (1186); TS 12.134, l. 1.

[64]*Marāfiʿ wa-aghṭiyat-hum*: TS NS J 208, l. 13; TS NS J 359, l. 15; HUC Geniza, no. 15, col. I, l. 7. *Marfaʿ wa-ghaṭā*: TS 20.33, l. 12; ENA 1822, f. 46, margin (all in brass or copper). Same in silver: ULC Or 1080 J 55*v*, l. 4 (eleventh century); TS J 1, f. 29, col. I, l. 16 (ca. 1140).

[65]TS 8 J 7, f. 23, ll. 7 ff., *India Book* 219. Table jug: *zīr khuwān*. Ten-cornered tray: *muʿashshara*.

[66]*Ibid.*, ll. 19–20.

[67]Last source in n. 64, above.

[68]The first three sources in n. 64, above. TS Arabic Box 4, f. 4*v*, l. 3 ("five marfaʿs costing 2 dinars") is part of a long list of objects usually included in a trousseau, perhaps from a store of bridal outfits. See next note.

[69]TS 16.80, ll. 3 and 9 (early eleventh century). The three marfaʿs in Antonin 635, l. 17, Friedman, *Marriage*, no. 29 (Tyre, 1054), might find a similar explanation: one for water, one, *sharābī*, for wine, and one for soft drinks.

[70]*Sharābiyya* worth 3 dinars: ENA 1822, f. 10; TS 12.586, l. 6; TS 20.8 B; Bodl. MS

Heb. f 56 (Cat. 2821, no. 16), f. 47*v*, margin, col. II, l. 4; TS 13 J 6, f. 9*v*, col. I, l. 23. The price of 12 dinars in Bodl. MS Heb. f 56 (Cat. 2821, no. 16), f. 48*v*, l. 3, is exceptional. The same bride had a basin, as well as a lamp, each for the same price. The sharābiyyas in the Damascus document TS 16.181*v*, item II, l. 12, from the year 933 probably were cups rather than jugs.

[71]TS 12.519, l. 10: *sharābiyya wa-ḥāmil*, see nn. 15–17, above. Seller of "potions": *Med. Soc.*, II, 271.

[72]Fine china: n. 51, above. Damascene earthenware: a medication prepared in a tumbler or bowl, *qadaḥ*, should be taken by the patient in a *kūz fukhkhār shāmī*: TS 8 J 14, f. 3, ll. 4–11. Glass: compare *qafaṣ kīzān milāḥ*, "a basket with good cups," ordered in Fustat without definition of the material they were made of (Westminster College, Frag. Cairens. 9, l. 19), with *qafaṣ zujāj*, a basket with glass vessels, bought there (TS 18 J 1, f. 10, l. 14) and *qafaṣ lil-kīzān*, taken from a house (Dropsie 402, l. 10). Crystal: *kūz billawr*, bought in Egypt for 3 3/4 dinars (TS 18 J 1, f. 10, l. 20). Fifty kūz: 12.373, top.

[73]TS 12.118, l. 6, Friedman, *Marriage*, no. 41. Probably from Damascus. In the marriage contract Antonin 635, l. 17 (Tyre, 1054), Friedman, *Marriage*, no. 29, the kūz is listed among the copper vessels and with a price less than 1 dinar.

[74]PER H 22, l. 14.

[75]TS J 1, f. 42, l. 6.

[76]See n. 52, above. Glass: TS NS J 27, l. 2 (1143); see also n. 72, above.

[77]TS 13 J 17, f. 1, l. 23, *Nahray* 107: *sāghara fukhkhār maṭliyya* or *muṭlaya*. For the Persian loanword sāghar, see Fraenkel, *Aramäische Fremdwörter*, p. 63 n. 1; for *ṭalā* (I and IV), Dozy, *Supplément*, II, 58*a*.

[78]Silver: TS 8 J 5, f. 1, l. 19 (1114); TS AS 146, f. 13, l. 10 (together with marfaʿ; ca. 1140); TS J 1, f. 29, col. I, l. 17 (also with marfaʿ, costing 4 dinars; ca. 1140). A small qiḥf costing 1 1/2 dinars: TS Arabic Box 30, f. 201, col. I, l. 7. Export: ULC Add. 3418, l. 17. Amber: TS J 1, f. 29, col. I, l. 32. Ornamental design: *zīj*, its common meaning: astronomical table. The translation as "ornamental design" (from the Persian) I owe to J. Clinton.

[79]Knife of silver worth 1 dinar: ULC Or 1080 J 126, l. 14 (ca. 1150). Silvered, *mufaḍḍada*: TS K 15, f. 91, col. III, ll. 12–13 (ca. 1130). Gilded and large, *mudhahhaba*: HUC Geniza, no. 15, col. I, l. 7 (scribe). Silver hilt(?), *jalba*: ENA 1822, f. 57, l. 27 (eleventh century). Sheath, *ghilāf*: TS Misc. Box 25, f. 53, l. 9 (1172). Listed together with toilet articles and worth less than 1 dinar: TS Arabic Box 30, f. 201, col. I, ll. 5–6; Bodl. MS Heb. f 56 (Cat. 2821, no. 16), f. 53*v*, l. 17 (1185). The kitchen knife for cutting meat, *sāṭūr*: TS 10 J 12, f. 10, l. 23.

[80]See A, 4, nn. 215–218, above.

[81]Container, *qarrāba* (cf. French *carafe*, German *Karaffe*): PER H 22, l. 20; ENA 1822, f. 46, l. 36 (seventeen in one cupboard). Two *qumqums*: PER H 22, l. 20; TS 16.215, l. 4, *India Book* 187. "An Iraqi rose water qumqum" ordered in Fustat (in letter from Aden): Westminster College, Frag. Cairens. 9, ll. 20–21. "Iraqi" refers to the brass vessel, not to its contents.

[82]Sprinkler, *mirashsh*, worth 8 dinars: ENA 2727, f. 8 A, l. 14; TS NS J 86, l. 4, here called *mirashsha* (Karaite). Also Karaite: TS AS 147, f. 20, l. 4. Exported from Egypt to the Muslim West: ULC Or 1080 J 55*v*, l. 4; TS 13 J 28, f. 2, l. 30; to India: ULC Add. 3418, l. 13. Inventory: TS 8 J 5, f. 1*v*, l. 1; Dozy, *Supplément*, I, 529*b*.

[83]Flyswatter, *midhabba*, with iron or wood handle and with canvas, *khaysh*: TS NS J 392, l. 13. Silver handle: TS 13 J 3, f. 1 (1141). Costing 15 dinars: TS 16.181, item IV, l. 9, according to the correct reading of Friedman, *Marriage*, no. 53*d*. See Lane, *Modern Egyptians*, p. 149, H. Buchthal, " 'Hellenistic' Miniatures in Early Islamic Manuscripts," *Ars Islamica*, 7, Part 2 (1940), figs. 6 (after p. 126), and 32 (after p. 130), both from Bibliothèque Nationale, Paris, Arabe 6094.

[84]Sassoon 713, ll. 34–35, *India Book* 263: *ishtari li . . . marāwiḥ wa-barwiz-hum wa-qad ishtarayt loh ʿishrīn marwaḥa wa-barwazt-hā*. Dozy, *Supplément*, I, 79*b*; and Qasīmī, *Métiers damascains*, p. 428.

[85]TS 16.80, l. 11.

[86]TS 20.37, l. 17, *India Book* 87, ed. S. D. Goitein, *Sinai*, 16 (1953), 231.

[87]Marāwiḥī, see *Med. Soc.*, I, 416; II, 495, top. Add, e.g., TS AS 148, f. 15; TS Misc. Box 8, f. 99 d, col. II, l. 2 = e, col. I, l. 8.

[88]Silver: TS 13 J 37, f. 11. Brass: TS NS J 208, l. 9, and probably also TS 13 J 3, f. 10 e, l. 9 (two *narjīsiyya*s costing 1 dinar); TS NS J 163, l. 7 (poor). Material not defined: TS K 3, f. 26, l. 18.

[89]See Dozy, *Supplément*, II, 655*b*, and Lane, *Arabian Society*, pp. 161–167.

[90]"A pair and its covers, 2 dinars:" TS 20.48, l. 33. "A large *ṣadr* worth 40 (dirhems) and also the *narājis*, 35 (dirhems)": TS NS J 359, l. 13.

[91]*Banafsajāt*: TS NS J 208; TS Arabic Box 4, f. 4*v*, l. 5.

[92]See Mez, *Renaissance*, chap. 21, p. 364 (from Nāṣir-i-Khusraw) and A, 2, nn. 165–167, above.

B. CLOTHING AND JEWELRY

1. Clothing

[1]BT Bava Meṣiʿa 52*a*.

[2]BT Ḥullin 84*b*. See nn. 13 and 17, below.

[3]"Eat what you like, but dress as other people do": Goitein, *Jemenica*, p. 9, no. 34; "A hungry man may appear in public, one not properly dressed [Ar. *ʿārī*, literally, naked] cannot": *ibid.*, p. 68, no. 423, both with parallels from other Arabic vernaculars. Bedouins: A. Musil, *The Manners and Customs of the Rwala Beduins* (New York, NY, 1928), p. 86.

[4]According to a Muslim (not Jewish) legend Abraham, the father of the faith, was a textile merchant. What else could he have been?

[5]The sources are cited in Goitein, *Studies*, p. 224 nn. 5 and 6.

[6]Abū Ṭālib al-Makkī, *Qūt al-Qulūb* (Cairo, 1932), IV, 61; see Zakī Mubārak, *Al-taṣawwuf al-islāmī* (Cairo, 1938), II, 196.

[7]Burhān al-Dīn al-Ḥalabī, *Multaqa 'l-abḥur* (Istanbul, 1853/4), cited in Ashtor, *Prix*, p. 54 n. 5, quoting H. Sauvaire, *Journal asiatique*, 1887, pt. 2, 218.

[8]M. Talbi, *Biographies aghlabides extraites des Madārik du Cadi ʿIyāḍ* (Tunis, 1968), p. 280, bottom.

[9]For furnishings see Amos 6:4: "They lie on sofas adorned with ivory, loll on their couches."

[10]BT Shabbat 113*b*.

[11]Such as "a scholar on whose garment a greasy spot is found deserves the death penalty," *ibid.*, 114*a*.

[12]BT Nedarim 66*a*; said by R. Ishmael when a rejected poor girl was "beautified" in his house, whereupon her suitor agreed to marry her.

[13]See n. 2, above.

[14]Mishna Horayot 3:7; *Med. Soc.*, II, 132.

[15]The roots *lbs* for "clothing" and *ksy* for "cover" are common to Arabic and Hebrew. The verbs and nouns derived from them, used in these respective senses, are found throughout the Geniza texts. The two languages have other specific roots for the outerwear or wrap, Ar. *lḥf*, and Heb. *ʿṭf*.

[16]This black cloth was called *shamlāh*, see E. Brauer, *Ethnologie der Jemenitischen Juden* (Heidelberg, 1934), p. 83. This Arabic word is identical with (and only phonetically different from) the biblical *simlā*. See n. 331, below.

[17]See nn. 2 and 13, above. Jerusalem 1028: App. D, Doc. I.

[18]BT Bava Bathra 57*b*. The translation of *ḥālūq* as shirt is misleading, and its derivation from *ḥālāq*, smooth, more than doubtful; ḥālūq means parted; this garment may have been called thus because it was open in the front and fastened by a belt; see "girds his belt" in next quotation.

[19]The word *prqs* used here in an inversion and abbreviation of *'pqrsyn*, Greek *epikarsion*, which is common in Talmudic literature, see Krauss, *Griechische und lateinische Lehnwörter*, II, 113.

[20]Derekh Ereṣ Rabbā, chap. 10, ed. with English trans. Michael Higger, *Massekhtot Derekh Ereṣ* (New York, N.Y., 1935). See *EJ*, 5, 1551/2.

[21]On the application in Geniza times of the Islamic laws on the wearing apparel of non-Muslims see *Med. Soc.*, II, 286–288, and here, pp. 193–195.

[22]See n. 3, above. "There is nothing more detestable and loathsome before God than a person walking naked in the street like those men from Barbaria and Mauretania [Roman North Africa]" (BT Yevamot 63*b*).

[23]When a scholar, while walking on a Sabbath, tucked up his cloak into his belt so that a leg of his became visible, his companion immediately loosened it so that it reached down to the ground (Genesis Rabba, sec. 11). Concerning sleeves see nn. 73–82, below.

[24]For the number of robes worn one above the other see Krauss, *Talmudische Archäologie*, I, 593 n. 467. While visiting Hungary in spring 1921, I had the opportunity to see peasant women painting their low houses in honor of the forthcoming Easter holiday. I could not help observing that as they moved their brushes from the roof to the ground, the girls exposed, beneath their beautifully embroidered frocks, five or more (I did not count) seemingly starched, white petticoats. This was interesting for me, since I had always doubted those numbers of overlapping robes given in the Talmud, and here I saw persons engaged in hard work wearing them. It is a general law in the history of human costume that the simple people continue to preserve the ways of clothing of the upper classes long after they have abandoned them. BT Gittin 58*a* reports about a noblewoman of extreme beauty who was captured by a bandit and put on the slave market for sale. For this purpose she was clad in seven robes. Nothing could illustrate the ancient concepts about an impressive appearance more poignantly than this sad story. For Geniza times see nn. 69–72, below.

[25]BT Nedarim 49*b*–50*a*. The story bears clearly hagiographic and antiestablishment traits. For the pious Muslim from Qayrawān see M. Talbi, *Biographies aghlabides* (see n. 8, above), p. 282, l. 9. About *qamīṣ* see Fraenkel, *Aramäische Fremdwörter*, pp. 44–45. When the caliph Othman was asked to abdicate, he declared: "I shall never take off a 'robe' with which God has clothed me," *qamīṣ qammaṣanīhi*, al-Balādhurī, *Ansāb* (see next note), V, 66, l. 10, and parallels.

[26]*The Ansāb al-Ashrāf of al-Balādhurī* ed. S. D. Goitein Jerusalem, 1936, V, 3, ll. 18–20 (with parallel sources). The wearing by men of clothes made entirely of silk is theoretically prohibited by Islam, see *EI*², III, 209, s.v. *Ḥarīr*. The muṭraf (or miṭraf) so common in ancient Arabic sources, never appears in the Geniza, nor, if I am not mistaken, in modern Arabic. But the adjective *muṭraf*, adorned with borders of a color different from the main piece of clothing, is frequently found in the Geniza.

[27]TS 8 J 20, f. 5, ll. 5–7. Relatives invited the writer to stay with them in a Christian land, but he seemed to decline (MS incomplete) (twelfth century). The word translated here as cloak is *malḥafa*.

[28]TS 12.289, ed. S. D. Goitein, *Tarbiz*, 33 (1964), 189–190; see *idem*, "Abraham Maimonides and His Pietist Circle," *Jewish Medieval and Renaissance Studies*, ed. A. Altmann (Harvard University Press, 1966), pp. 153–154. The pious young scholar, himself a pauper, also had to take care of the girl's father and stepmother.

[29]TS 13 J 22, f. 2, ll. 10–11: *qumāsh yaṣluḥ lil-nisā* "fitting women." TS NS J 184, ll. 8–10: *maʿraqa nisāwiyya zarqā wa-khūṣatayn nisāwiyya fiḍḍa liṭāf*, "a blue feminine skullcap and two small silver 'leaves' for women"; *khūṣa*, palm leaf, is a common Arabic word (derived from the Aramaic; see Fraenkel, *Aramäische Fremdwörter*, pp. 75, 146), but I have not yet found it as the name of an ornament.

Bodl. MS Heb. e 98 (no Cat.), f. 74, l. 10, *Nahray* 133: a man writes from Tinnīs, the great center of the linen industry, to Fustat: "I sent you two robes, one for women, *nisā'ī*, one for men, *rijālī*." TS K 15, f. 99, col. II, ll. 17–18 (list of a pawnbroker): "A Dabīqī robe for women." The *ghilāla*, an undershirt or slip worn directly on the body, had also to be defined by sex: *ghilāla rijālī ghasīla*, "a washed men's tunic": TS NS J 392, l. 11; cf. Dropsie 402, l. 5: "A ghilāla belonging to the husband's son."

[30]TS K 15, f. 48. See *Med. Soc.*, II, 444, sec. 25.

[31]While their brother got a jūkāniyya for himself, the two girls, probably still small, received only one between them. Because of their simple cut—or, rather, lack of cut—various pieces of clothing could easily be divided into two halves. The term *niṣf ridā*, "half a mantle," is more common in the Geniza than "mantle."

[32]ENA 4010, f. 39, l. 3: [*thawbī*] *al-sabt wa-ridā'ī al-sabt*, my sabbath [robe] and my sabbath mantle." The dying man meant to say that these were good enough, and there was no need to buy new "shrouds" (dated 1050).

[33]TS 20.99, l. 12: *al-malbūs lahā* (Ar.) *lil-qōdesh wa-lil-ḥōl* (Heb.). In his deathbed declaration the notable referred to in *Med. Soc.*, I, 117 and n. 3, states that all clothing of his second wife was her property (although bought by him).

[34]TS NS Box 31, f. 8, l. 9: *inna alladhī ʿalayy ʿīduh*. The word preceding *alladhī*: *'ldd* is a mistake and deleted, as indicated by the stroke above it. See *Med. Soc.*, II, 501, sec. 95.

[35]See *ibid.*, p. 37 and n. 65, and what follows here.

[36]TS 8 J 18, f. 14, ll. 15–17, ed. S. D. Goitein, *Tarbiz*, 37 (1968), 48–49. A used mantle of a merchant prince was as precious and "new" as a secondhand fur coat worn and then sold by a famous actress today.

[37]Bodl. MS Heb. d 66 (Cat. 2878), f. 21, l. 9 (*India Book* 177). The word used here is *tafṣīla*, "a tailored dress."

[38]BT Shabbat 119*a*.

[39]Lane, *Modern Egyptians*, p. 493. "The minor *ʿeed* [holiday]" is the one celebrated at the end of Ramadan.

[40]See n. 36, above (purifying oneself by fasting means becoming a new being, symbolized by one's wearing new clothes). The text of the letter speaks only of "the holiday of the Ishmaelites." But in 1028/9 the Jewish month of the High Holidays coincided with Ramadan.

[41]In general, it seems to me that in Jewish communities rooted in an Islamic ambiance the joyous confidence in God's forgiveness was felt more than the overwhelming awareness of man's sinfulness characterizing the Ashkenazi service.

[42]BT Pesaḥim 68*b*. The sages were of divided opinion about this point, but the view cited prevailed.

[43]Bodl. MS Heb. e 98 (no Cat.), f. 69: *mā lī mā uʿayyid bih ʿalā ḥaly*. The Arabic word for "beautiful," *ḥaly*, refers mostly to female ornaments. The Hebrew vowel Segol (three dots), put beneath the *ḥ* of *ḥaly*, was pronounced (and is still pronounced so by Yemenites) as a short *a* in Arabic.

[44]TS 24.27*v*, ll. 26 ff.: *'aḥtāj ilā tajammul fil-mōʿēd* (the last word is Heb.) . . . *an takūn mā'idatī wa-baytī mujammal*. The term for beautifying, *tajammul*, is also found in al-Balādhurī, *Ansāb*, V, 3, l. 19, in the story of the caliph Othman, see n. 26, above. The person addressed in this letter was Yehuda ha-Kohen Abu 'l-Barakāt al-kātib, a prominent government official, often mentioned in the Geniza.

[45]TS 8 J 15, f. 14, ll. 7–13. The holiday was Passover, which, as the writer states, is particularly "exacting" as far as expenses are concerned.

[46]See n. 16, above.

[47]TS G 1, f. 1, l. 20: *al-biqyār al-jadīd matāʿ al-sabt*, "the big turban for the Sabbath," reported as having been lost during a pillage. TS 12.312, ll. 10–15: an extensive passage concerning a Sabbath *thawb*. ENA 4010, f. 39, l. 3: . . . *al-sabt wa-ridāyī al-sabt*, "my Sabbath . . . and Sabbath cloak" (given on deathbed as *ṣadaqa* (Ar.), a religiously meritorious gift—not specifically to the poor).

[48]PT, Pea 21*b*, ll. 1–6. The Hebrew word for wrapping used here repeatedly is *ʿṭf*. For the example see n. 23, above.

[49]TS 13 J 18, f. 8. The Sicilian *farkha*, like the *thawb*, was a piece of cloth large enough for manufacturing a person's robe, see n. 222, below. "Attractive," *ḥafīy*; "elegance," *ḥalāwa*.

[50]*Med. Soc.*, III, 342.

[51]Woman from al-Mahdiyya: TS 10 J 14, f. 20, see *Med. Soc.*, I, 347 and n. 4.

[52]The poor scholar: TS 10 J 10, f. 5, l. 13. Zadok ha-Levi b. Levi (first half of the eleventh century).

[53]See Dozy, *Supplément*, I, 58*a*–*b*. *Alf layla wa-layla* (Būlāq, A.H. 1252/A.D. 1836/7) (and reprints), I, 76, l. 10; 78, l. 4.

[54]By an interesting coincidence biblical *ḥalīfā*, which has the same meaning as Ar. *badla*, has become in modern Hebrew the term for a man's suit.

[55]On uncovering one's head in Islam see the deep-searching study of I. Goldziher, "Die Entblössung des Hauptes," *Islam*, 6 (1915), 173–177. The exceptionally long and detailed article "Turban" (with its 66 names!) in the first edition of *EI*, IV, demonstrates the social and religious importance once attributed to the head cover in the Muslim world.

[56]For a useful bibliography on this subject see *EJ*, VIII, 6.

[57]For schoolboys see *Med. Soc.*, II, 182 and 557 n. 35.

[58]ULC Add. 3430, translated in App. D, Doc. I, item 3 of Clothing section, as compared with item 1. The *miʿjar*, like some types of wimples worn in medieval western Europe, was occasionally *musaftaj*, made of stiff material (from Persian *safta*): TS 10 J 5, f. 9, l. 14 (dated 1102).

[59]Bodl. MS Heb. d 66 (Cat. 2878), f. 47, l. 3; TS J 1, f. 29, l. 2, App. D, Docs. II, III, above.

[60]See n. 58, above, and n. 103, below.

[61]TS 13 J 15, f. 18, sent from Qalʿat Jaʿbar on the Euphrates river, a fortress taken by the Crusaders in 1104, see G. Le Strange, *The Lands of the Eastern Caliphate* (Cambridge, 1905), p. 102, bottom, and Yāqūt, IV, 164. Addressed to Aleppo, Syria, as is evident from the reference to "his excellency," R. Bārūkh (b. Isaac) *yārūm hōdō*, who was active there around 1100, see *Med. Soc.*, III, 288.

[62]TS 13 J 15, f. 19, l. 7, *Nahray* 108, addressed to Nahray b. Nissīm.

[63]TS 12.275, ll. 13–19: 4 1/3–6 dinars (actual price). TS 13 J 19, f. 9, l. 32: 4 dinars (ordered). (In Stillman, "Female Attire," p. 127, the passage on the *ʿimāma* for women, from which it would appear that TS 16.32, l. 12, refers to two Sicilian turbans worth only 2 dinars, is to be deleted. The MS has only *yn*, meaning two; the word for turban [*ʿimāmat*] was added in the copy by conjecture.)

[64]BM Or 5542, f. 19: seven *ʿamā'im quṭn jiyād* cost 80 quarters, or 20 dinars. Sent from the Muslim West, Sicily or Tunisia.

[65]Aramaic bareheaded: *rēsh gelī*, translates Heb. "with a high hand," Exodus 14:8 and *passim*.

[66]See nn. 55 and 56, above. The late Bahhāj Effendi, who more than anyone else initiated me into the world of the Middle East (Haifa, mid-1920s), opened my understanding of the significance of the turban. When I read Persian poetry or Arabic prose with him, he always kept his voluminous turban on, even on the hottest days of July. But before he entered the toilet he took it off and deposited it on a stool nearby clearly in view of its sacral connotation. One is reminded of a curious custom reported in BT Berakhot 60*b*, top: before entering the toilet one politely asks his guardian angels to remain outside.

[67]For illustrations see Ettinghausen, *Arab Painting*, pp. 84–85; Lewis, *World of Islam*, p. 104, illus. 2.

[68]See nn. 15–24, above.

[69]The wrapping of a piece of cloth many cubits long around a fezlike cap was a complicated affair; the dying man had seen to it that this task was done well in advance.

[70]TS NS J 284, ll. 2–4, "Waistband" translates *zunnār*, a word normally not used for Jewish clothing. The belt called zunnār was the "badge" of the Christians. When an angry letter writer in the Geniza wished to say "I might as well become a Christian," he writes "I might as well gird myself with a zunnār."

[71]The garments were bought ready-made—as far as one can use this term in Geniza times—and the tailor had to adjust them to the dead man's body.

[72]TS J 1, f. 31. About burial garments see also nn. 286–296, below.

[73]Al-Masʿūdī, *Murūj* (Paris, 1861–1877), VII, 402, quoted by Mez, *Renaissance*, chap. XXI, p. 367.

[74]A sleeve kerchief costing 1 dinar: TS 16.86, l. 8; TS 20.48, l. 25 (both late twelfth

century). White: TS K 15, f. 65; TS 12.526, l. 7. Embroidered: ULC Or 1080 J 64 (dated 1225), sold for 16 dirhems in the bazaar of the clothiers.

[75]TS 10 J 14, f. 27, ll. 6–7 (early thirteenth century, it seems), *kān ʿalā kummī khamsa darāhim, waqaʿat min ʿalā kummī*. It is noteworthy that the writer uses twice "*on* my sleeve," not "*in*."

[76]Maimonides, *Responsa*, I, 81–82.

[77]Account books: see *Med. Soc.*, I, 205–206. Book of Songs: Goitein, *Jews and Arabs*, p. 202. Playing cards: R. Ettinghausen, "Further Comments on Mamluk Playing Cards," *Gatherings in Honor of Dorothy E. Miner* (Baltimore, Md., 1974), p. 64.

[78]See Mez, *Renaissance*, as quoted n. 73, above. In Europe this usage seems to have been less common, see Holmes, *Daily Living*, p. 161.

[79]Ettinghausen, *Arab Painting*, e.g., pp. 106, 114, 116. On p. 121, the midwife and the maidservants have such decorative stripes embroidered with script on their upper arms. See also Golombek-Gervers, "Tiraz Fabrics," p. 89 n. 73.

[80]TS 20.77, l. 7. About ornamenting the upper arm with silver, gold, or pearls see nn. 518–520, below.

[81]TS 20.148*v*, l. 9: *battē amat yādām be-riqmātayim* (Heb.). The teacher Joel (a name not found by me elsewhere in the Geniza) addresses "Abraham the Pious" and his brother Joseph, "the Head of the Pious" as if they were government servants. Abraham the Pious was a physician and, in this capacity, probably was connected with the court.

[82]See *Med. Soc.*, III, 225 and 473 n. 8. The example of the ladies of Baghdad was followed by Wallāda, the eleventh-century poetess of Cordova, Spain, see A. R. Nykl, *Hispano-Arabic Poetry* (Baltimore, Md., 1946), p. 107.

[83]Besides the documents noted above in nn. 70–72, especially TS NS J 184 should be considered an only partial list of the belongings of a poor grocer; only a few of his clothes were selected for the burial, but the *ṣarāwīl* (*ṣ* = *s*), the pants, were among them.

[84]ENA NS 18, f. 34, l. 4: ". . . and two pairs of pants worth 3 dinars." Unfortunately, the word before *ṣarāwīlayn* is lost. Among the signatories of this much torn marriage contract (see *Med. Soc.*, III, 414, no. 322) was A[braham b. Jaco]b Derʿi, active in Alexandria around 1100.

[85]Damsīs: PER H 24, l. 14, revised ed. Friedman, *Marriage*, no. 16. Working people: see n. 67, above. Others: Ettinghausen, *Arab Painting*, pp. 82, 87, 106, 111, 114.

[86]Heb. *ḥūṣ mikkevōdokh*, often abbreviated to *ḥūṣ*, cf. Y. Ratzaby, *Dictionary of the Hebrew Language Used by Yemenite Jews* (Heb.) (Tel Aviv 1978), p. 86. Contempt: Goitein, *Jemenica*, p. 40, no. 206. A similar expression in Palestinian (non-Jewish) Arabic: S. ʿAbbūd, *5000 arabische Sprichwörter aus Palästina* (Berlin 1933), p. 18, no. 379.

[87]ENA NS 31, f. 21, l. 8. In *Med. Soc.*, III, 175, I was in doubt whether the young wife was hit by her husband's sister with a shoe or her foot. In view of *Highways*, II, 76, l. 8 (see n. 89, below) it is evident that the shoe was meant.

[88]Dropsie 363: record of a lawsuit, in which, of course, the shoe, *madās* (lit., the thing on, or with which, one treads), is expressly mentioned. Slapping with a boot, *khuff*: TS NS Box 298, f. 6, ll. 7–8, ed. M. Gil, *Tarbiz*, 48 (1979), 66. A Hellenistic relief shows a mother castigating her little daughter with a slipper.

[89]Abraham Maimonides, *The Highways to Perfection*, II, 244, l. 4: *ṣiqālat naʿl al-rijl*.

[90]Mercantile quantities: "30 pairs of Adenese shoes," *madāsāt*: Mosseri A-55, l. 22, *India Book* 166 (inventory of India trader). Order for personal use: TS Arabic Box 7, f. 3 (2), col. I, ll. 3–4, col. II, ll. 3–5. The account is in the hand of Nahray b. Nissīm. He is one of the participants in the large shipment, but, as usual in such accounts, mentions himself by name. For *tāsūma* see Dozy, *Supplément*, I, 138/139, and *Vêtements*, p. 104.

[91]ENA 2591, f. 12, ll. 9–10.

[92]TS 8 J 22, f. 8, ll. 7–13, trans. *Med. Soc.*, I, 153 and n. 17. (In the reference to that passage, *ibid.*, p. 422 n. 84, by error TS 8 J 22, f. 18 [for f. 8] is printed).

[93]BT Bava Qamma 59*b*, top (see *ibid.*, Tosafot). Krauss, *Talmudische Archäologie*, I, 628 n. 711, end.

[94]TS 12.251, l. 19, written on vellum (early eleventh century). In this letter "shoes" is rendered by classical *niʿāl*. The addressee: Khallūf b. Faraḥ Ibn al-Zarbī (originating from the isle of Jerba, Tunisia). The order for shoes in Goitein, *Letters*, p. 116, together with a blue ("green" is a mistake) costume with gold threads and two white wimples, was intended as part of a bridal outfit.

[95]TS 16.279, l. 21, *Nahray* 169: *wāsiʿ al-khalkhāl mutqan*. TS NS J 432: an order for a boy. Here the request for easy shoes is repeated twice.

[96]ULC Or 1080 J 77*v*, ll. 31–32: *20 zawj 'aqrāq wa-yuḍrab 10 azwāj sawādhij min al-qalb* [see Dozy, *Supplément*, II, 390*a*, middle: *qulūb* = *qawālib*] *alladhī jalabahu*. Cork shoes seem sometimes to have been painted.

[97]"Un traité de ḥisba de Muḥammad al-ʿUqbānī al-Tilimsānī (d. 1467)," ed. Ali Chenoufi *BEOIF Damas*, 19 (1967), 151.

[98]TS 20.48, l. 19: *maqmaʿat al-jizma* (to be pronounced thus, for the manuscript spells *gyzmh*); *maqmaʿa* is a hooked metallic instrument. I have not yet seen it in the sense of "buckle" or the like.

[99]TS 13 J 19, f. 9, l. 19 (second half of eleventh century), a large business letter, in which Faraḥ b. Ismaʿīl b. Faraḥ writes from Alexandria to his father in Fustat that he had not ordered *tāsūma* (see n. 90 above) and *shamshak* (see Dozy, *Vêtements*, p. 231) and had no need for them. "Maker of mules," *baṭūṭī*: Bodl. MS Heb. a 3 (Cat. 2873), f. 19, *India Book 32;* also *India Book* 136 and 377: name of a Tunisian family active in the India trade; Dozy, *Supplément*, I, 93*a*. Synonyms: see *Med. Soc.*, I, 422 n. 81.

[100]TS K 15, f. 53, col. III, l. 3: Nahray b. Nissīm, who in 1046 was a kind of trainee of an elder relative, notes in the account submitted to him: a pair of shoes, 7 1/2 dirhems. Dropsie 472*v*, l. 25, *India Book* 333: Abraham b. Yijū, the India trader, on his return to Cairo, bought for his Indian agent (legally, slave) Bama a pair costing 10 dirhems in 1152 or so. In his homeland Bama, although a respected elderly man, probably went barefoot. Grohmann, *APEL*, VI, 115, l. 5: two pairs of (low) boots, *khifāf* (see n. 88, above) cost 1 1/24 dinar, which would make about 20 dirhems per pair. I believe this papyrus is later than the ninth century.

[101]ENA 3616, f. 9. A letter from Ramle.

[102]Grohmann, *World of Arabic Papyri*, p. 156, referred to in *Med. Soc.*, III, 442 n. 29, where it is shown that giving the bride those wedding gifts was also Jewish custom. Laces: Krauss, *Talmudische Archäologie*, I, 628 n. 711. A quarter dinar corresponds to the price of 10 dirhems noted in n. 100, above. The possible exception is in the lovely marriage contract from Damsīs (see n. 85, above), where I take the last item "necessities" (Heb. *ṣerākhīm*), costing a quarter dinar, as shoes. While putting his shoes on, one said a benediction thanking God "who gave me all I need" (the same Heb. word is used). The price is repeatedly found elsewhere for shoes.

[103]ULC Add. 3430, l. 20 (1028), see nn. 58 and 60, above.

[104]Ettinghausen, *Arab Painting*, pp. 82, 152. For buttonholes see Lynn White, Jr., *Medieval Religion and Technology* (Berkeley and Los Angeles, Calif., 1978), p. 273 n. 36: "The first functional buttons appeared in central Germany in the 1230s."

[105]*Med. Soc.*, I, 99–116, 415–425, and, specifically, 101–108. See also the Index, s.v. "Flax," "Silk," and other materials.

[106]*Ibid.*, pp. 209–229, 452–456, and particularly pp. 222–228.

[107]Ar. *sharb rafīʿ*.

[108]Ar. *abyaḍ* (lit., white) and *naqī*. White is intended here not as a color but as a symbol of cleanliness.

[109]*Khalīʿ*, secondhand. For this translation see n. 263, below.

[110]Abraham Maimonides, *The Highways to Perfection*, II, 76–77.

[111]Conversely, *kattān* in the meaning of flax (in all its stages of treatment) is one of the most frequently mentioned commodities in the Geniza letters. For the various types of silk see *Med. Soc.*, I, 454–455 n. 53, and below.

[112]A provisional list of fabrics (used for women's clothing) occurring in the Geniza is provided in Stillman, "Female Attire," pp. 20–25.

[113]See the article Dabīq in *EI*², II, 72–73. The article in the first edition might also be consulted with profit.

[114]A piece of valuable *ʿanbar*, ambergris, is described in a letter written in or around 1085 as "whiter than Dabīqī garments (*thiyāb*)": Bodl. MS Heb. d 66 (Cat. 2878), f. 5, ll. 13–14. As the English (originally French) name of the substance indicates, its natural color was grayish. About this affair see *Med. Soc.*, I, 178 and n. 43.

[115]The *ḥarīrī* is mostly found in the *thawb*, e.g., "a violet silken Dabīqī robe, 10 dinars": TS 12.12, l. 6 (*Med. Soc.*, III, no. 344); but also in the *mandīl* mantilla: TS K 15, f. 79, col. I, l. 18; and in the *mulā'a* cloak: TS J 1, f. 29, II, ll. 9–10 (4 dinars, App. D, Doc. III, below). In the same list and column, l. 15, a light-gray silk robe is described as Dabīqī.

[116]Dabīqī *thawb mudhahhab*: TS 20.7 (1050); ULC Or 1080 J 49, col. I, l. 17 (1146).

[117]Slip, "a pearl-colored *ghilāla sharb*, costing 5 dinars": TS NS J 390, l. 9; another one, costing 4 dinars: TS 20.47*v*, l. 11. Transparent: *Med. Soc.*, III, 167 and n. 41.

[118]"A Damietta [*ʿimā*]*mat sharb* costing 12 dinars"(!): TS 20.2; a sharb headband, *ʿiṣāba*, worth 8 dinars: *ibid.* (an ancient Karaite list). "A laundered sharb turban," for burial outfit: TS NS J 284, l. 3. See n. 62, above.

[119]Gala costume: TS 20.76, l. 41, *ḥulla wa-miʿjarhā sharb*. Cloak: TS NS J 488, l. 2, *mulā'a*. Aden: TS 18 J 5, f. 5, ll. 40–42. "Sevener," *subāʿi*, originally perhaps "seven [spans] long": see Serjeant, *Islamic Textiles*, p. 130 n. 65.

[120]"With silk": ENA 2727, f. 5, col. I, l. 4, *qajījat sharb bi-ḥarīr*, "a robe of fine linen decorated with silk." See n. 143, below.

[121]Wimples in Tinnīs: n. 186, below. Mantilla: TS Misc. Box 8, f. 97, l. 15, *mandīl rūmī tinnīsī*. For Tinnīsī *bukhnuq* kerchiefs see App. D, Doc. VII, n. 225, below.

[122]Tūnī garments, noted in the Geniza: TS 20.2, l. 19; ENA 3030, f. 7*v*, l. l; Westminster College, Frag. Cairens. 9*v*, l. 14. For Tūna see *EI, Supplement* (1938), p. 267, s.v. "Ṭirāz." Two pieces of linen, dated A.H. 388 (A.D. 998, 3d Jan.–23d Dec.) and 390 (999/1000), respectively, bear the name of this town. The inscriptions say that the materials were made for the caliph al-Ḥākim, but in the *ṭirāz al-ʿāmma*, the factory serving the public, not that reserved for the needs of the court. This explains why Jewish brides could have Tūnī linen. Renowned for its beauty: Yāqūt, I, 901, where an ʿIraqī poet, son of a ṭirāz worker, praises it.

[123]"A very thin, snow-white or pearl-colored Dimyāṭī *miʿjar* costing from 10 dinars upward" is ordered in a letter sent from Fustat to Alexandria: ENA 2591, f. 12, ll. 5–6 (Nahray b. Nissīm writing to Mardūk b. Mūsā). See also n. 118, above.

Abyār (Ibyār) on the Rosetta arm of the Nile is described by Ibn Duqmāq, V, 99, as a flourishing town "in which merchants live, where the Abyārī cloth, *qumāsh*, is manufactured, as well as the *muḥarrar* (see n. 143, below), which is superior to Alexandrian cloth. There they also make the Bedouin mantles, *al-abrād al-ʿarabiyya* [which elsewhere were made of wool]. Such a linen *burd* costs over 100 dirhems [app. 2 1/2 dinars]." Jews lived there: Bodl. MS Heb. d 66 (Cat. 2878), f. 22, a marriage contract dated 1070; TS 10 J 12, f. 1, l. 30, a physician; ULC Or 1080 J 24, see *Tarbiz*, 24 (1955), 147–148 (a respected Jewish merchant living in Abyār and one from Alexandria visiting there. The Spanish Hebrew poet, Yehuda Halevi, traveling from Alexandria to Cairo, spent the Sabbath there). Serjeant, *Islamic Textiles*, p. 154, where another source is quoted.

[124]Alexandrian blankets: Bodl. MS Heb. a 2 (Cat. 2805), f. 6 (1127); TS NS J 392 (1128); ENA NS 7, f. 20 (same period), Firkovitch II, 1700, f. 27*v*, l. 9 (1156). Four or more from the year 1186: Bodl. MS Heb. f 56 (Cat. 2821), f. 48, l. 15; f. 55, l. 8; f. 55*v*, l. 11; f. 56*v*, l. 8 (all are different brides); TS 20.48, l. 26 (ca. 1200, or later): the *malḥafa* is valued 5 dinars, otherwise the price is 1–2 dinars, or cannot be stated, because the blanket is noted with another item.

[125]For the Ḥāfiẓiyya guards see *EI*², III, 54*b*, bottom. Ḥāfiẓī garments are either described as Dabīqī, e.g., Bodl. MS Heb. f 56 (cat. 2821), f. 47*v*, margin, l. 2; f. 53, l. 11; f. 56, l. 6 (all from the 1180s); or as "with silk," which means that the basic fabric was linen: TS K 25, f. 269, col. I, l. 19; or are not further defined at all: TS K 15, f. 65*v*, col. III, l. 19, see *Med. Soc.*, III, 368, no. 29.

[126]For the treatment of flax—from plant to yarn—as far as reflected in the Geniza, see *Med. Soc.*, I, 105. Cf. also Weibel, *Two Thousand Years of Textiles*, p. 4.

[127]Additional varieties of flax threads: *Ahnās*, a place in the flax-growing district of Bahnasā, south of Cairo, Goitein, *Letters*, p. 297 n. 13. *Sarqanāwī, ibid.*, p. 131, derived from Sarqanā in the Ashmūnayn district in the northwestern region of the Nile delta, Ibn Duqmāq, V, 20. *Zanjabīlī*, ginger-colored, ENA 2875, f. 35, l. 3, and *verso*, l. 9. *Nīlī*, TS 13 J 29, f. 9, ll. 14–17, ed. *Tarbiz*, 38 (1969), 30, term derived not from the name of the Nile river but from that of the indigo plant. The dark blue of the indigo is not the natural color of flax, but a certain variety of flax yarn might have come on the market after having been dyed.

It is noteworthy that practically all these varieties of flax appear in the Geniza documents of the eleventh century, that is, almost simultaneously.

Muslim handbook of market supervision: *Maᶜālim al-Qurba*, p. 46 of the English summary, p. 178 of the Bodleian MS. See also nn. 315 and 316.

[128]ENA NS 2, f. 13, ll. 3–4, 6–8. In no other letter of the eleventh century have I seen merchants of Constantinople, Venice, and Crete mentioned together as doing business in Alexandria. The Christian merchants from Europe are usually lumped together under the general term "Rūm." "Constantinople silk" (but not Venetian) is mentioned in the Geniza around 1000, *Med. Soc.*, I, 417 n. 21.

For "transverse," diagonally arranged, *muṣallab*, see Dozy, *Supplément*, I, 117*b* and 841*a*. Four or five of the 400–1000-yard-long threads originally forming the cocoon of the silkworm are reeled off simultaneously into one strong yarn, see Weibel, *Two Thousand Years of Textiles*, p. 6. Since "transversely" or "crosswise" is mentioned here and elsewhere, e.g., TS 13 J 19, f. 27, ll. 27–28, *Nahray* 14, together with and differentiated from "twisted," *maftūl*, contrasting methods of combining the threads of the cocoon must be intended. Because of the high price I do not believe that the terms refer to the spinning of waste or floss silk (about these see *Med. Soc.*, I, 104).

The epithet *qāṭiᶜ*, "cutting," "categoric," "strong," for *khazz*, the first quality of silk (see *Med. Soc.*, I, 454 n. 53) has not been seen by me before, but is explained in Pedro de Alcala's Arabic-Castilian Dictionary, printed in Granada 1505, as "fine," said of a thread; see Dozy, *Supplément*, II, 374*a*. To be sure, our letter precedes Pedro by more than four centuries.

[129]In a much-torn letter by Barhūn b. Mūsā to Nahray b. Nissīm, ENA NS 18, f. 24*v*, l. 1, Gabes silk cost 23 quarter dinars. For prices of silk, see *Med. Soc.*, I, 222–224.

[130]Sūsa, a town on the northeastern shore of Tunisia, was renowned for its textile industry, which worked the silk of the West and the flax of Egypt (see n. 136, below) into fabrics bearing its name.

The port city Syracuse, Sicily, provided the name for one of the varieties of silk produced on that island, e.g., TS 20.180, l. 20, *Nahray* 172 (dated Jan. 1048). For "transverse" see n. 128, above.

[131]"Pickups," an attempt to translate *iltiqāt*, found also in Goitein, *Letters*, p. 127 n. 4, and explained by Dorothy G. Shepherd as silk yarn produced by combing and spinning the waste silk, see *Med. Soc.*, I, 454, bottom.

[132]During the eleventh century, Palermo is referred to in the Geniza as (Madīnat) Ṣiqilliyya, (the capital of) Sicily. Here, where another Sicilian town is mentioned, Ṣiqillī can only mean Palermo. For *lāsīn*, a red silk, see S. D. Goitein, "Two Arabic Textiles," *JESHO*, 19 (1976), 221–224.

[133]Waste silk, *muqashshar*, literally, peeled off, see *Med. Soc.*, I, 418 n. 26.

[134]Bodl. MS Heb. b 3 (Cat. 2806), f. 19, ll. 16–20, *Nahray* 7.

[135]*Tustarī* (spelled here *Dustarī*), cloth originally manufactured in Tustar in southwest Iran, then imitated in other silk-producing countries.

[136]In the letter cited in n. 134, above, ll. 14–16.

[137]ULC Or 1080 J 77, l. 31.

[138] Cordova: Serjeant, *Islamic Textiles*, p. 169 and *passim*. Shawdhar: "A town between Jayyān [today Jaén, north of Granada] and Granada," Yāqūt, III, 333, l. 19.

[139]TS 13 J 6, f. 22*v*, l. 16. (The MS has *shadhūnī*, which is correct, not with a long *ā*, as

printed in *Med. Soc.*, I, 417 n. 21.) Shadhūna near Sevilla was renowned for its crimson, Serjeant, *Islamic Textiles*, p. 171*a*. Moses b. Jacob, who made the order for "the lady, my sister," is different from his namesake in *Med. Soc.*, I, Index, 542, and Goitein, *Letters*, pp. 89–95, see *ibid.*, p. 91 n. 15. In TS 13 J 17, f. 18, l. 15, *Nahray* 164, he speaks about his yearning for the Maghreb. Manāra: see "From Aden to India," *JESHO*, 23 (1979/80), 65.

140 Westminster College, Frag. Cairens. 9, ll. 10, 12–15, *India Book* 50.

141 Muqaddasi, p. 367, ll. 5–6 says: The people of Jurjān have head covers made of *qazz* silk (black and red, see *Med. Soc.*, I, 454 n. 53), which are exported to Yemen. But this was written around 985, when the land routes between Iran, Iraq, and Arabia were open. (The Zaydis, the sect still prominent in Yemen, who came mainly from northern Iran, arrived in Yemen by land.) Our letter was written around 1135 and directed to Egypt, by sea, of course.

142 Serjeant, *Islamic Textiles*, pp. 169–170. For Almeria see Goitein, *Letters*, p. 345 (Index), *Med. Soc.*, I, 530 (Index).

143 A note on terminology seems to be appropriate. When the name of a garment is followed by the word *ḥarīr* "(of) silk," it means that it was made of that yarn; e.g., a wrap of silk, *mayzar ḥarīr*; 6 dinars, two robes of silk, *qamīṣayn ḥarīr*, 20 dinars, ENA NS 2, f. 25, ll. 9 and 11 (ca. 1178). This is rare, since a garment was often defined by its tradename or by the frequently found term *ḥarīrī*, which either meant the same, or, when combined with another yarn, such as Dabīqī linen (see n. 115, above), only partly made of silk.

The term *bi-ḥarīr*, "with silk," probably means that the piece concerned was adorned with silk embroidery, tapestry, borders, or bands, see n. 120 above. "An ash gray waistband with new silk," TS NS J 414, l. 1 (see n. 144 below), would then mean that the old silk cord had been replaced by a new one. When the father of the Adenese bride orders two fūṭas (sarilike wraps) "either silk with silk, or silk with linen" (the source in n. 140, above, *verso*, ll. 23–24), he wishes to say that the ornament should be made either with silk, probably of another color, or with linen.

Finally, *muḥarrar* is defined in Pedro de Alcala's Vocabulary as silklike, that is, an imitation of silk, see Dozy, *Supplément*, I, 264*a*. Its production was mentioned in n. 123, above, as a specialty of Abyār, Egypt, but it was found also in Almeria, Spain: TS 13 J 21, f. 12, l. 6 (Goitein, *Letters*, p. 265, top, where I translated "silken"), and in the estate of an India trader, who died in Aden: Mosseri A-55, l. 7, *India Book* 166, *jubbatayn muḥarrar*.

144 The example in Stillman, "*Female Attire*," p. 211 n. 9, TS NS J 414, l. 1 *wasaṭ quṭnī*, stems from an erroneous entry in my card index. The MS has *qaṭawī*, the color of the sandgrouse, see EI^2, IV, 143–145. In view of the mass of material contained in the Geniza one or more exceptions may always turn up confirming a rule.

145 TS 10 J 15, f. 19*v*, ll. 3–7, *Nahray* 56.

146 Kiener, *Kleidung*, p. 95.

147 "A second-hand Rūmī [European] cotton turban," forming part of a *raḥl*, things left behind and sent from the Maghreb to Alexandria: ENA 1822, f. 57, ll. 12–14. "Two vests, *ṣadratayn*, of cotton," found among the belongings of a Maghrebi merchant who died in Suwākin on the Red Sea coast in 1110: TS K 15, f. 98*v*, ll. 5–6, *India Book* 165. "A cotton pillow," listed under similar circumstances, probably in Aden around 1133, Mosseri A-55, l. 23, *India Book* 166. "A bundle, *rizma*, with cotton," among the assets of a sick Maghrebi merchant in Alexandria: TS 18 J 1, f. 10, l. 8 (1072).

148 To the examples provided in *Med. Soc.*, I, 418, no. 35 (where, however, *rizmatayn*, should have been translated as "[small] bundles," not as "bales"), a number of others could be added. E.g., TS Misc. Box 28, f. 228, ll. 15 and 22, *Nahray* 99: a bundle weighing 2 1/3 pounds, sent from Tripoli, Lebanon, to Alexandria, cost 1 dinar. DK I*v*, ll. 2 and 7–8, *Nahray* 167: 4 pounds less 2 ounces (3 10/12 pounds) of mediocre cotton could be had in Ascalon, Palestine, for 1 1/24 dinars. TS K 15, f. 114*v*, p. 3, l. 11, *Nahray* 42: A huge account sent from Alexandria to Fustat about the forwarding of a shipment of flax worth 220 3/4 dinars includes an item of two-thirds of a pound

of cotton costing a quarter dinar. This tiny quantity was certainly needed for such purposes as lining a cloak. TS J 1, f. 53, l. 16, *India Book* 81: The assets in Aden of the India trader Ḥalfon b. Nethanel, which consisted of Indian textiles worth hundreds of dinars (see below) and other Oriental goods, comprised also an item of "cotton worth 2 1/2 dinars." If these were local, Adenese, dinars, the value of that cotton would have been again less than 1 Egyptian dinar. All the cases listed in this note refer to cotton yarn, not to fabrics.

[149]Qaṭṭān: see *Maᶜālim al-Qurba*, p. 177 (of the Bodl. MS) and Qasīmī, *Métiers damascains*, II, 360, no. 284. North African Jews: M. Eisenbeth, *Les Juifs de l'Afrique du Nord* (Algiers, 1936), p. 110. A Muslim India trader named Qaṭṭān: Goitein, *Letters*, p. 64; also: Westminster College, Frag. Cairens. 13, margin, *India Book* 96.

[150]The few references to wholesale of cotton do not indicate that the dealers were Jews. TS 13 J 19, f. 27, l. 20, *Nahray* 14: "[In the Maghreb] the Syrians sold cotton for [only] 10 dinars per qinṭār [100 pounds], for large quantities arrived there from the land of the Rūm [Europe]." Dropsie 385, ll. 14–15, *Nahray* 252: "The price of cotton went up by 5 dinars per camel load [500 pounds or so], but we did not sell for a dirhem." The writer, Mardūk b. Mūsā of Tripoli, Libya, who settled later in Alexandria, has left many letters in the Geniza, but nowhere appears as a wholesaler of cotton. Here, he and his brother, for reasons not stated, were unable to sell the little they had. The short letter shows that Mardūk at that time was still a novice in overseas trade.

[151]Tunisian merchant: Goitein, *Letters*, p. 242, sec. G; Aleppo robe: TS 8 J 22, f. 6, l. 11; a Sicilian turban made of cotton: *Letters*, 334; see also nn. 64 and 147, above. Cotton market: Casanova, *Reconstitution*, pp. 122–124, *khawkhat al-qaṭṭānīn*; TS 10 J 5, f. 4, l. 12, *sūq al-quṭn*.

[152]TS 28.22, ll. 14 and 20, *India Book* 14. One of the meanings of Ar. *ḥabasa* is "to wrap." See also Serjeant, *Islamic Textiles*, p. 130 n. 64.

[153]TS 13 J 25, f. 13, ll. 12, 14, 16, *India Book* 31; TS J 1, f. 53, ll. 3–5 and 19, *India Book* 81.

[154]Pillows: ULC Or 1080 J 95, sec. I, l. 6, *India Book* 67. Colors: TS 28.22, l. 14. Price: TS J 1, f. 53, ll. 3–5, TS AS 148, f. 9*v*, l. 15, *India Book* 363.

[155]TS Arabic Box 30, f. 145, *India Book* 156, trans. Goitein, *Letters*, p. 69, sec. 10, n. 13.

[156]Details about wool in *Med. Soc.*, I, 105, and 419 nn. 37–39.

[157]*Ibid.*, p. 153.

[158]Wool spread out: TS 13 J 14, f. 2, l. 21, *Nahray* 17; hung up: TS Misc. Box 28, f. 225, ll. 15–16, *Nahray* 161.

[159]TS NS J 28, col. I, ll. 10, 15; *verso*, col. II, l. 13:

5 jubbas of wool cost	2 dinars, 2 qīrāṭs
5 jubbas of wool cost	2 dinars, 4 qīrāṭs
8 jubbas of wool cost after dues	3 dinars, 6 qīrāṭs, 1/72 dinars

The account seems to be written by Nahray b. Nissīm in his early years.

[160]ULC Add. 3339 b, l. 19.

[161]See nn. 6 and 110, above.

[162]See Weibel, *Two Thousand Years of Textiles*, p. 11.

[163]Inspection of purple workshop: TS NS J 150 (June, 1099), cf. *Med. Soc.*, II, 297 and n. 25.

[164]On purple "dyeing and making" in the Geniza see the Index *Med. Soc.*, I, 544, s.v. Purple cloth. Unfortunately, the reference to pp. 126–127 about the Alexandrian gatherers of the purple shellfish, who drink beer in the taverns (of the Crusaders) in Acre, was omitted there. The "oyster gatherers," *ibid.*, p. 92, l. 1, are identical with these; "oyster" should be replaced by "shellfish." I followed there Wahrmund, *Handwörterbuch*, I, 725, s.v. "*mahāra*." Special attention is drawn to the story of the bale of purple sent from Fustat via Alexandria to Sfax in Tunisia, *Med. Soc.*, I, 339–343.

[165]Holmes, *Daily Living*, p. 162.

[166]Mordants, "the liquids with which fabrics were saturated to hold the dyestuff" were indispensable in the highly developed dyeing industry of the Middle Ages. Since they have not been treated coherently in this book, some data about those occurring in the Geniza may be in order. It is not surprising that they are identical with those used in Europe at the same time, see Weibel, *Two Thousand Years of Textiles*, p. 8.

Alum (potassium), *shabb*, the most common mordant, was priced in Alexandria at one hundred pounds for 15 dirhems (the reading is perfectly clear but perhaps a scribal error: TS 10 J 15, f. 14*v*, l. 3, *Nahray* 8. Hope to sell it to Europeans in Alexandria: Gottheil-Worrell XXXIII, p. 152, l. 22. (The printed text is faulty; the manuscript has this: *wa-hōn qawm rūm wa-naḥn naʿridhū ʿalayhim*). Brilliant alum (*shabb mudarham*, cf. Dozy, *Supplément*, II, 438*b*) ordered: TS 16.274*v*, l. 17. These three letters are from the later part of the eleventh century.

Large quantities of widely different qualities of alum were sent from Fez, Morocco, to Almeria, Spain, in Dec. 1141, Goitein: *Letters*, p. 267. For the importance of the quality of alum see R. S. Lopez, "Market Expansion: The Case of Genova," *Journal of Economic History*, 24 (1964), 458. Alum was the main product of the Chad in inner Africa, from where it was exported to Egypt and Morocco (and from both to Europe), see Mez, *Renaissance*, chap. 24, p. 412. Alum was also found in Egypt itself, as well as in Yemen, see *Med. Soc.*, I, 45.

The gallnut, *ʿafṣ*, an excrescence of oak trees in northern Syria, served as a medication against fever and intestinal troubles, but mainly as a mordant for fixing black dye. (It was also used to produce the excellent ink that we still admire in the Geniza documents), see Maimonides-Meyerhof, p. 144, sec. 295. It was a main article of import from northern Syria to Egypt, mentioned first among products arriving on five boats in Alexandria from Suwaydiyya, the port of Antioch, *Med. Soc.*, I, 213. The writer announcing that arrival notes that because of the high price (4 1/2 dinars per *qinṭār* [100 pounds], see below) he did not dare to buy those gallnuts, TS Arabic Box 18(1), f. 164, ll. 11–12 (eleventh century). A bale (ca. 500 pounds) of ʿafṣ was sent from Syria to the warehouse of a qadi in Fustat for two Jewish brothers forming a partnership (TS 16.87, l. 9, a court record written in spring 1097). Nahray b. Nissīm dealt in this commodity, once paying 5 1/4 dinars for "a qinṭār and something" (TS K 15, f. 114*v*, l. 13, *Nahray* 42, and DK I, l. 20, *Nahray* 167, which refers to the same shipment. See also TS 10 J 19, f. 8, l. 8, *Nahray* 212, for profits made with gallnuts). The family name *ʿafṣī*, processor and/or seller of gallnuts, occurs quite frequently in the Geniza around 1100, but they might all have belonged to the same stock (Abū Naṣr, a contributor to public appeals: TS K 15, f. 106, l. 5, cf. *Med. Soc.*, II, 477, sec. 16, and TS Misc. Box 28, f. 29, *Med. Soc.*, II, 477 sec. 17. Abū Sa ʿīd, recipient of letters: TS 8 J 15, f. 25, an order for spices and dyes, and Bodl. MS Heb. d 66 (Cat. 2878), f. 52, trans. Goitein, *Letters*, pp. 49–51; contributor: *Med. Soc.*, II, 476, sec. 15, and repeatedly mentioned in letters of others).

Tartar (Ar. *ṭarṭār*, derived from the same medieval Greek word as the English) was another mordant, also coming to the capital of Egypt via Alexandria. A quantity of 200 *jarwī* (somewhat heavier than regular pounds), sent to the purplemaker ʿArūs b. Joseph in Fustat, cost 10 13/48 dinars, that is, approximately the same as gallnuts (see above): ULC Or 1080 J 178, ll. 6–10, 23–27, *verso*, ll. 13–14. From another letter from Alexandria, in which the material is described as tartar powder (cf. English salt of tartar, *daqq al-ṭarṭār*) it appears that the best quality was to be had from the Maghreb: TS NS J 344*v*, ll. 4–7. A letter from Tlemçen, Algeria, complains, however, that ṭarṭār sold poorly, giving the impression that there it was an article of import: TS 12.274*v*, l. 10.

[167]TS 12.468, l. 4 (written in Qayrawān 977/8), ed. Mann, *Texts*, II, 362: isatis *demithqrē* (Aram.) *nīl shāmī*. In TS 8.12, l. 13, ed. Goitein, *Tarbiz*, 37 (1968), 164–166 (ca. fifty years later), Heb. *isatis* is used as a code for indigo, not for woad. In TS 12.468, too, "Syro-Palestinian isatis" may perhaps refer to the indigo grown in the Jordan valley. See Weibel, *Two Thousand Years of Textiles*, p. 9.

[168]See *Med. Soc.*, I, 538 (fifteen references to indigo) and 185, 210, 219 (varying

prices of indigo, in one report between 100 and 300 quarter dinars according to type and quality).

[169]*Brazilwood: ibid.*, p. 532 (Ar. *baqqam*).

[170]Saffron: *ibid.*, p. 545. Crimson: *ibid.*, p. 107, 420 n. 26. Madder, *rubia tinctorum*, Ar. *fuwwa*, Heb. *pū'a*, a plant for dyeing red, was grown in Egypt, where it gave its name to an important town (Fuwwa, *Med. Soc.*, I, 536), and was also imported, especially from the countries of the Eastern Mediterranean. Fuwwa was a great article of commerce (e.g., TS NS Box 308, f. 119, trans. N. Stillman, *IJMES*, 5 [1974], 200–201, ULC Or 1081 J 25, TS 8 J 19, f. 26, l. 18 [all eleventh century]; TS 12.434, l. 15, and *verso*, l. 25 [early twelfth century]; JNUL 8, l. 12 [thirteenth century]), but never served as the name of a color. See also Serjeant, *Islamic Textiles*, p. 207, quoting *Maᶜālim al-Qurba*, which states that most dyers fraudulently use henna instead of madder. In our century, henna was used in Palestine only as makeup, not as dyeing stuff for textiles, see Dalman, *Arbeit und Sitte*, V, 73.

[171]As a rule, only the main color of a garment is indicated. If no one color prevailed, it would be described as *mulawwan*, see n. 238, below.

[172]An order placed: ULC Or 1080 J 77, see nn. 233–247, below. One filled (and partly not carried out): nn. 186–194, below.

[173]Dozy, *Supplément*, I, 635*a*, quoting Ibn Jubayr, p. 148, l. 9.

[174]Wahrmund, *Handwörterbuch*, I, 880*a*. The common word for mercury or quicksilver in the Geniza is *zaybaq*, not *sahāb*.

[175]Fahd, *Couleurs*, p. 92, bottom. This observation may go back to a Greek source.

[176]Fahd, *Couleurs*, p. 86, bottom. Instead of *aghbar* (the adjective of ghubra, cf. Wehr, *Modern Written Arabic*, p. 664*b*). I have seen also *ghabrī*.

[177]Morabia, *Noms de couleur*, pp. 92–94; Dalman, *Arbeit und Sitte*, V, 340 and *passim*.

[178]Lane-Poole, *History of Egypt*, p. 125.

[179]Dozy, *Supplément*, I, 695*b*. Bodl. MS Heb. f 56 (Cat. 2821), f. 48, l. 14 (dated 1186), vocalizes musannī (with *u*).

[180]Aḥmad Amīn, *Fayḍ al-Khāṭir* (Cairo, 1942), pp. 322–326, cited by Morabia, *Noms de couleur*, p. 96 n. 2, and Henri Pérès, *La poésie andalouse en arabe classique au XIe siècle* (Paris, 1953), p. 321, cited Morabia, p. 95 n. 4. The wearing of yellow badges imposed on the Jews of Baghdad in 1121 is discussed n. 325.

[181]Yellow more popular with males: Goitein, *Letters*, p. 77 (robe); ULC Or 1080 J 77, l. 30 (cloak); also shoes, n. 91, above.

[182]The late eminent orientalist Rudolf Mach advised me that *ḥajalī*, partridge colored, refers not to the plumage of the bird but to its eye, like French *oeil-de-perdrix*, used for designating the color of a specific type of wine. Naturally, this interesting identification needs to be confirmed by an Arabic source.

[183]J. C. Bürgel, "Der *Mufarriḥ an-nafs* des Ibn Qāḍī Baᶜalbakk, ein Lehrbuch der Psychohygiene aus dem 7. Jahrhundert der Hiǧra," in *Proceedings of the VIth Congress of Arabic and Islamic Studies* (Stockholm, 1972), p. 206; Fahd, *Couleurs*, p. 93. For beautiful colors in bathhouse murals as a therapy for melancholy see the passage translated in T. W. Arnold, *Painting in Islam* (Oxford, 1928), p. 83, and Franz Rosenthal, *Das Fortleben der Antike im Islam* (Zürich and Stuttgart, 1965), p. 358.

[184]Morabia, *Noms de couleur*, pp. 91–92. Pre-Islamic women mourning in black: James A. Bellamy, "The Impact of Islam on Early Arabic Poetry," in *Islam: Past Influence and Present Challenge* (Edinburgh, 1979), p. 156, quoting Ṭirimmāḥ. For black in Judaism see Krauss, *Talmudische Archäologie*, I, 144–145, 550 n. 211.

[185]*Ibid.*, p. 550 n. 208*a*.

[186]TS 8 J 18, f. 33, ll. 3–9, 12–17: Nissīm b. Ḥalfōn b. Benāyā writes to Barhūn b. Mūsā al-Tāhertī al-Maghrebī, both prominent in the Geniza correspondence of the later part of the eleventh century.

[187]Meant facetiously: Considering the exertion required I might have relapsed ten times.

[188]I arranged the text in the form of a table and converted the clumsy numerical circumlocutions into simple fractions.

[189]Sky blue: *samā'ī* instead of the regular form *samāwī*.

[190]Oak green: MS *'b'by (ubābī)*, probably referring to the dark green leaves of the *Quercus coccifera*; cf. Dozy, *Supplément*, I, 1*b*, quoting an ancient Muslim source, which explains that *abb* was the indigenous Arabic word for oak, whereas *ballūṭ*, the commonly used term, was a loanword (it is indeed Aramaic, see Fraenkel, *Aramäische Fremdwörter*, p. 139).

The term *'b'by* might also be derived from *ubāb* or *abāb*, mirage, glistening by reflection. Since the word has not yet been found elsewhere, both my reading and explanations must be regarded as tentative.

[191]Honeydew: *mannī*, see n. 176, above.

[192]At the time of the writing of the letter this Muslim artisan happened to be in Fustat. Nissīm addressed to him a letter (in Arabic, of course, but in Hebrew characters), asking Barhūn to read it out to him.

[193]Soot black: MS *shhr'y*, cf. *shuḥḥār*, soot. The word may be read *shuḥrā'ī*, or *shuḥḥārī* (' preceding *r*). True, enduring deep black is the most difficult color to produce, and the best dye to be used for this, according to Weibel, *Two Thousand Years of Textiles*, p. 11, is lamp soot.

[194]How much profit was expected from the sale of a wimple may be seen from a contemporary account written by Nahray b. Nissīm, in which this detail occurs: "A wimple, 2 1/2 [dinars]; another one, 2 1/4; profit from this, 5 qirāṭs," about 4 1/2 percent. TS J 1, f. 1*v*, col. IV, first col. on the margin, l. 1. (dated 1059), see *Med. Soc.*, I, 374, sec. 17, and 521.

[195]Siglaton, Ar. *Siqlāṭūn*, was a heavy fabric of damask silk widely used in Geniza times for distinguished clothing, bedding, and hangings. It was popular also in western Europe during the Middle Ages. W. Heyd, *Histoire du commerce du Levant au Moyen-Age* (Leipzig, 1885/6), p. 700, says that "the Orientals" dyed it almost always in dark blue, while in Europe one preferred a lively red. Heyd probably referred to a period later than that represented in our documents.

For the siglaton garment see Goitein, *Letters*, p. 77; for the siglaton donated, *Eretz Israel*, L. A. Mayer volume, 7 (1964), 92 (Heb.), ll. 8–14, 171 (Engl.).

The bride in App. D, Doc. III, below, had three siglaton robes (col. II, ll. 25–27) as well as a dressing gown, a couch, and a sofa made of the same material (col. III, 8, 20–21).

[196]Golombek-Gervers, *Tiraz Fabrics*, p. 89*a*, bottom.

[197]See "Weaving a maqṭaʿ cloth in Alexandria" in Goitein, *Letters*, pp. 134–135, and below, n. 222.

[198]See *Maʿālim al-Qurba*, p. 136, trans. p. 43; cf. n. 205, below.

[199]See the passages translated below, nn. 206–217, for the terms mentioned here.

[200]A detailed discussion of the fuller's work in Greek, Roman, and Talmudic sources is found in Krauss, *Talmudische Archäologie*, I, 153–154, 570–574. This voluminous book is important for medieval studies because it shows how completely Greek and Roman techniques were assimilated in the Near East during Late Antiquity and the early Middle Ages. For a relief depicting a fuller treading cloth in a vat see Donald Strong and David Brown, *Roman Crafts* (New York, 1976), p. 176. The fuller was also employed for washing clothes. Female fullers occur in the Talmud (probably as laundresses), but not in the Geniza.

Because of the use of fuller's earth, *ṭafl*, the fuller was also called *ṭaffāl* (which could also mean "dealer in *ṭafl*"); TS 13 J 20, f. 18, l. 18, ed. Mann, II, 300, where the *ṭaffāl*'s son is described in Heb., ll. 16, 23 as *qaṣṣār* (spelled *qṣr*). Fuller's earth was also used in households: TS 8 J 25, f. 2, where Ḥalfon b. Manasse, Fustat, the court clerk, receives some from his brother Japheth of Alexandria. Dozy, *Supplément*, II, 48*b*–49*a*, has detailed information about the different varieties of this soapy cleaning stuff. "Fuller's earths," *ṭafūl*, in the plural, are indeed mentioned in a price list from Almeria, Spain; TS 12.285, l. 19, *India Book* 202, but only with the remark that none of them was in demand.

It must not have been easy to find a competent fuller. A scholar in a provincial town writes to his cousin, a judge in Fustat, as follows: "My Sabbath robe went down in the Nile together with So-and-so. I am sending you now another one; please give it to

So-and-so for forwarding it quickly to Damietta, to sheykh Abu 'l-Faḍl [the fuller], paying him 4 dirhems for fulling it as perfectly as possible": TS 12.312, ll. 10–15. Ṭōviyahū ha-Kohen b. Eli writing to Nathan, "the eminent member of the yeshiva" b. Solomon. Washing the clothes of a sick visitor for twelve days cost 1 + 1/4 dirhems: TS J 1, f. 26, col III, ll. 7, 19.

[201]TS 13 J 20, f. 8*v*, l. 11, an Arabic letter of Joseph b. Āraḥ to Nethanel b. Amram, whereas TS 13 J 20, f. 18, is a Hebrew missive by Moses b. Elijah, sent to a Gaon.

[202]TS NS J 3, l. 8, *ridā'ayn al-wāḥid mumarrash wa 'l-ākhar khām*. The word *marrash* is a denominative derived from *mirashsh(a)*, sprayer (the tool).

A third letter differentiates between spraying and beating: "In a previous letter I had asked to inquire whether his Excellency wished to have the *mulā'a* wrap to be sprayed or to be beaten. When no answer was received, I had it both sprayed and beaten and forwarded it; please let me know whether it has arrived": TS 10 J 14, f. 13, ll. 6–12 (abridged).

[203]ULC Or 1080 J 291 (dated 1024), trans. Goitein, *Letters*, p. 275, Dozy, *Supplément*, I, 309*a*. Dozy's *miḥakka* is the instrument. My voweling, *maḥakka*, designates the action.

[204]Previously I translated this as "mangler" (*Med. Soc.*, II, 474, where "manger" is a misprint) and the process as ironing (*Letters*, p. 265, sec. A and passim). But the mangle and the hot iron had not yet been invented; the Arabs used a press as the Greeks, Romans, and the Near Eastern peoples had done before them.

[205]In Goitein, *Letters*, p. 265, a man from Fez, Morocco, orders a silk robe from Almeria, Spain "to be pressed in the very best way" and to be sent to him as quickly as possible. A *malḥafa* cloak, woven and "whitened" in Alexandria, was pressed there before being transported to Fustat; TS 8 J 25, f. 13, l. 23. The wages for the weaving of 25 cubits of material amounted to 5 qirāṭs, and the whitening and pressing of the same quantity to 3 1/2 qirāṭs. Since "whitening," *bayāḍ*, was done both with yarns and fabrics (see *Letters*, p. 134 n. 4, and p. 135 n. 4), the term probably describes the cleaning of linen materials from their blackish crust, see n. 198 above. (The *mubayyiḍ*, common in the Geniza, is the man who makes copper vessels "white" by tinning them.)

[206]See preceding note and nn. 23, 24, above and App. D, n. 82.

[207]ENA NS 22, f. 17 *margin* and *verso*, ll. 1–10: Jacob b. Nissīm, writing to his brother Abu 'l-Khayr. Actually, the maternal uncle of the recipient had been given the Sūsī for forwarding it! For copyists see *Med. Soc.*, II, 238–239; for Damietta, *ibid.*, III, 178. For the fuller in Damietta see n. 200, above, end.

[208]Since linen was the main fabric used, the term *ghazl*, thread, without additional definition, designated linen yarn. Cotton and silk, occurring also in the letter, are mentioned as such.

[209]A large-sized turban, see Dozy, *Supplément*, I, 105*b*. In TS K 15, f. 95, l. 5 (dated May 1150), the word is spelled *byqy'r*, which indicates that around the middle of the twelfth century the word was pronounced *biqyār*.

[210]The seemingly strange fact that the turban consumed more material than a piece serving as a garment is discussed in nn. 55–66, above.

[211]The common word for weaver, *ḥā'ik*, is by no means avoided in the Geniza; even contributors to an important public appeal are referred to thus: Bodl. MS Heb. d 79 (no Cat.), f. 35, col. II*v*, see *Med. Soc.*, II, 479, sec. 21. Since the weaver was held in the Near East with a certain disrespect (from Talmudic times, Krauss, *Talmudische Archäologie*, I, 149), probably because weaving was originally a female occupation, the term *ṣāniᶜ*, artisan, was preferred for this occupation. The Jews of Ṣanᶜā, Yemen, called the weaver *ṣannāᶜ*, and derived from this the verb *yiṣniᶜ*, weaving. A similar usage might have been common in the Maghreb from which the writer of our letter hailed.

[212]This is, of course, only a partial and final payment. The real wages must have been a multiple of it. The wages for the *malḥafa*, mentioned in the last paragraph translated, amounted, after some haggling and discounts granted, to 36 dirhems. The reader is reminded that this letter was preceded by others dealing with the same matters.

[213]Purifying the yarn was incumbent on the weaver. Since it had not been done, or at least, not to the satisfaction of our writer, the weaver agreed that the work should be left to a "cleaner," *muṣaffī*.

[214]Here, as before (see n. 212, above), the writer refers to a detail mentioned in a previous letter. He had taken half-an-ounce from the recipient's yarn and now paid back the debt.

[215]Ar. *nufāt al-ṣāniᶜ*. It is common knowledge that weights differed even within the same country, but in the hundreds of Geniza letters sent from Alexandria to Fustat "Miṣr pounds" are rarely mentioned.

[216]TS 13 J 15, f. 19, ll. 6–17, *Nahray* 108.

[217]The mats, like garments, were made to order. They had to fit the rooms for which they were made.

[218]The inauspicious hour in which the idea of ordering that cloak was conceived, cf. Job 3:1. Such impolite outbursts are rare. The recipient of the letter was a young man at that time.

[219]Lit., "the government came between me and the artisan," meaning, we almost turned to a non-Jewish court.

[220]Bodl. MS Heb. d 66 (Cat. 2878), f. 91, ll. 16–21, *Nahray* 30. "They" refers to the men working for the weaver, in *Med. Soc.*, II, 479, sec. 21, see n. 211, above.

[221]Like *beged* in biblical Hebrew (cf. Numbers 4:6–9, 11–13; I Samuel 19:13; I Kings 1:1) and in a Karaite marriage contract, TS 16.80, l. 3, *bigdē malbūsh*, Clothes section, literally, cloths used as clothing.

[222]From the passage translated in Goitein, *Letters*, pp. 134–135, it appears that the *maqṭaᶜ* was normally woven from linen yarn with an admixture of cotton, but could also be made only of linen. In TS 10 J 13, f. 5*v*, ll. 3–4, the writer orders "a half-and-half *maqṭaᶜ*, two 'throws' [of the shuttle], *ramyatayn*, cotton, two 'throws' coarse linen." ("Half-and-half" is spelled munaśśafa, with a Heb. *sīn*, which stands for *ṣ*.) The twelfth-century Sicilian geographer Idrīsī describes the *maqṭaᶜ* as being made mainly of linen, see Dozy, *Supplément*, II, 374*b*.

The maqṭaᶜ, like the thawb, was worn by men and women alike. An old woman was asked whether she wished to get a maqṭaᶜ *muqaffal* (lit., locked, i.e., to be closed by loops), 13 cubits long and costing 10 dirhems, ENA 1822 f. 53. In the thirteenth century it became fashionable to wear a *tafṣīla*, a tailored piece, above the straight maqṭaᶜ; both were embroidered: "The embroidery on the white maqṭaᶜ and the *tafṣīla* is not yet completed," ULC Add. 3415 (dated 1237). In a fragmentary trousseau list from the same period the maqṭaᶜ has the color of rose marmalade, *ward murrabbā*, and the tafṣīla that of sesame, TS NS Box 325, f. 13. When we read in *Alf Layla* (Night 25), I, 77, l. 20, that a woman wore a tafṣīla made exclusively of gold threads, we are sure that this was an upper garment. In trousseau lists the item *jūkāniyyatayn maqāṭiᶜ*, two jukāniyya (short) robes in maqṭaᶜ fashion or cut, are common, e.g., PER H 20, l. 7, and Stillman, "Female Attire," pp. 84–85.

It must be noted that maqṭaᶜ was used also in its original meaning of "a piece," even when not referring to clothing. In the marriage contract TS 20.7 (dated 1050), when two *khusrawānī*, kingly, maqṭaᶜs are listed between an emerald-colored canopy and curtains, no doubt wall hangings or carpets were intended. When a maqṭaᶜ made of the precious *ṭalī* material, a full four spans broad and costing 3 dinars and 2 qirāṭs, was sent from Cairo *to* Alexandria in 1141 with the remark that no other piece like this could be found in the capital, its use was certainly different from that of the Alexandrian maqṭaᶜ: TS 20.80, l. 10, and TS 13 J 23, f. 21, margin and top, *India Book* 273 and 130, respectively.

It is interesting that in M. A. Marzouk, *History of Textile Industry in Alexandria 331* B.C.–*1517* A.D. (Alexandria 1955), pp. 58–61, where, based on literary sources, "The Kinds of Alexandrian Textiles" (in Islamic times) are listed, no mention of the maqṭaᶜ is made. This is not a reflection on the author, who seems to be more interested in pre-Islamic times, but another indication of the usefulness of the Geniza for the knowledge of socioeconomic conditions in medieval Egypt.

On the textiles of Ascalon, Palestine, see Goitein, *Letters*, p. 288 n. 7.

[223]The original use of *shuqqa* for textiles manufactured in Tunisia is well exempli-

fied by a huge letter sent by the then young Nahray b. Nissīm from there to Egypt. Garments of silk, most probably made in Spain or Sicily, the silk countries, are called *thawb*, but one hundred Sūsīs or fifteen Qarawīs (made in Qayrawān) are called shuqqas, Bodl. MS Heb. b 3 (Cat. 2806), f. 19, *Nahray* 7. Later in the letter (f. 20, l. 8) he promises: "I shall buy you profitable goods, and I have already started to buy raw Qarawīs." When he sends, this time from Fustat, two Sūsī shuqqas, each worth over 3 dinars, as well as a perfumed one, *muṭayyaba*, costing approximately the same, it is most likely that this and other shuqqas handled by Nahray at that time were of Tunisian make: TS 10 J 12, f. 26, ll. 13–15, *Nahray* 5. But when one Maghrebi writes to another in Egypt, he uses the term "shuqqa" also for a garment woven in Alexandria, cf. n. 210, above. Although, as in the case just referred to, measurements are provided for a custom-made shuqqa, the shuqqa in general must have had a standard size, as may be concluded from an order like this, sent by a Maghrebi in Buṣīr, south of Cairo, to another in Fustat; he wishes to have a *shuqqa and a half* of twill, to cut from it a thawb and pants: TS 12.227*v*, ll. 13–15. (For twill, *muthallath*, see A, 4, n. 44, above.)

[224]Dozy, *Supplément*, II, 249*b*, notes *farkha* in the meaning of "a sheet of paper" from Mamluk times, and it is still used in this sense in Egypt, see Wehr, *Modern Written Arabic*, p. 703*a*. "A piece of cloth" conveys a similar idea, but the origin of the word is not quite clear, and whether it has anything to do with the *farakh* (perhaps to be read *farkh*) cloth of Fars in southern Iran (Serjeant, *Islamic Textiles*, pp. 55–56) is also doubtful.

The farkha was traded in large quantities of 100 through 125 pieces, e.g., Bodl. MS Heb. a 3 (Cat. 2873), f. 13, l. 40; TS 12.229, l. 9; TS 12.389, l. 6 (all broad); Bodl. MS Heb. a 2 (Cat. 2805), f. 20, l. 34 (small); or 40 pieces, Bodl. MS Heb. d 66 (Cat. 2878), f. 42, l. 8 (narrow), *Nahray* 221; TS NS J 300, Goitein, *Letters*, p. 334. When a father orders "a Sicilian farkha and a shawl for my boy, the light of my eyes," TS 10 J 16, f. 18, l. 14, *Nahray* 35, or when two farkhas and two shawls are sent from Mazara, Sicily, via al-Mahdiyya, Tunisia, to Egypt, Dropsie 389*v*, l. 71, it is evident that garments were intended. When a merchant writes that he will offer for sale the Sūsīs (clothes made in Sūsa, Tunisia) and the *firākh* (pl. of farkha), it is clear that Sicilian materials are referred to, TS 13 J 14, f. 2, ll. 21–22, *Nahray* 17. When the boats from Sicily did not arrive in Alexandria, and two Sicilian farkhas ordered were not to be had, one had to content oneself with Egyptian *thawbs*, TS 13 J 18, f. 8, see n. 49, above. The two farkhas ordered in that letter are described as "narrow," and so were two others, sent to Egypt by Ḥayyīm b. ʿAmmār of Palermo, Sicily, TS NS Box 323, f. 1. The difference in price between the narrow and broad farkha was not much, TS Arabic Box 54, f. 88, trans. S. D. Goitein, "Sicily and Southern Italy in the Cairo Geniza Documents." *Archivio Storico per la Sicilia Orientale*, 67 (1971), 32:

Three narrow farkhas	23 (quarter dinars)
One broad farkha	8 1/2 (quarter dinars)

They were costly farkhas, worth about 2 dinars each. The average price for a regular one was 1 1/4 dinars, TS NS J 127, col. I, l. 9, col. IV, l. 7, and above, n. 49. TS NS J 127 is an account in the hand of Nahray b. Nissīm, but is not included in Murad Michael's corpus.

[225]See end of preceding note.

[226]ULC Or 1080 J 291, trans. Goitein, *Letters*, pp. 273–278.

[227]TS 12.92, top: "So that he may wear them," *shiqāq liyalbasahā*. Israel b. Joseph (b. Bānūqa) writes to Abū Sahl Manasse b. David, no doubt before the sack of Qayrawān in 1057.

[228]Egypt exported to the Muslim West either raw materials, like flax and indigo, or specialties of its industrial production, but not large quantities of finished textiles. Those were imported. At least, that is what we learn from the correspondence of the Jewish merchants.

[229]TS 20.69*v*, l. 16, an account by Barhūn Tāhertī to his junior partner Nahray (not

in Michael's corpus). For the exchange rate of dinar: dirhem, 1:45, see *Med. Soc.*, I, 372–373, sec. 14.

[230]Bodl. MS Heb. e 98 (no Cat.), f. 64 b, l. 4, trans. Goitein, *Letters*, p. 283. Nahray writing to Barhūn Tāhertī (not in Michael's corpus). The garments are described as *shiqāq ṣawāfī*, homogenized in appearance, being of completely uniform, not varying, colors, see n. 199, above.

[231]TS 12.369, l. 10, *Nahray* 165. The sender of the letter, Elijah b. Judah b. Yaḥyā, mentions that he wrote it while passing the night in a *qārib* (small boat), destined for al-Lādhiqiyya (in northern Syria), cf. *Med. Soc.*, I, 314. But various references show that the accounts provided concerned transactions made in Alexandria.

[232]Trans. Goitein, *Letters*, pp. 34–39, 73–79.

[233]ULC Or 1080 J 77. Types of silk specific to certain districts of Spain, see nn. 137–138, above, and cork shoes, also produced in Spain and Portugal, see nn. 96 and 97, above, are ordered. The script is very similar to (but not identical with) TS 12.133, Goitein, *Letters*, pp. 73–79.

Muslim manufacturer: l. 12, ten robes, *ʿamal al-Sayf*, made by one named Sayf al-Dīn (The Sword of the Faith). Again referred to in l. 17: order for five fine felt mantles, *ghafāʾir ṭaylaqān*, to be ornamented with Sayfī remainders, *wa-tuṭraf bil-fuḍūl al-Sayfiyya*. Christian: l. 16, *ʿamal al-Qiddīs*, manufactured by "the [Christian] Saint." Seems to refer to ten mantles ordered in l. 14. See also n. 239, below.

[234]Ibid., l. 18: *aksiya muwajjaha* (spelled *mwjh'*). The very common *kisā*, pl. *aksiya*, cloak, cover, must have been a man's garment since it is absent from trousseau lists. "To face" (not seen elsewhere) must mean to provide the edges of the garment with finishing, see n. 242, below. Made-to-order: *mustaʿmala.*

[235]Sleeve stripes (see n. 79, above), *shawāhid*, literally, quotations, because the sleeve stripes usually contained poetic quotations embroidered on them, here, l. 20, and l. 25, below (not yet found in this connection elsewhere). Therefore it is always emphasized here whether or not the clothier wished to have script embroidered on them.

[236]Bars, *quḍbān*, literally, sticks. A bar, *qaḍīb*, probably was thinner and longer than regular stripes or bands. "Outside and inside," Ar. *min al-wajhayn*, literally, on the two surfaces; also below *passim.*

[237]Sprayed, marshūsha (cf. nn. 200, 202, above). Borders, *muʿlamāt biʿalāma*(!) *milāḥ*, see Serjeant, *Islamic Textiles*, p. 255*a* (Index). Cf. Westminster College, Frag. Cairens. 9*v*, ll. 25–27, *India Book* 50: *fī kull ṭaraf ʿalamayn, yakūn al-mandīl bi-'arbaʿa aʿlām milāḥ*, "two borders on each end, so that the kerchief has four beautiful borders."

[238]Ar. *mulawwana, fiḍḍī wa-fākhiṭī wa-zaytī*. One piece of cloth had three different colors, probably produced by leaving it in the same solution different spans of time, cf. n. 171, above.

[239]ʿUbayd: another manufacturer, see n. 245, below. The name ʿUbayd was found among Jews, but not commonly, see *Med. Soc.*, III, 499, sec. 86. Velvetlike: *khāmil* (l. 20. In the plural, *khawāmil*, l. 29, said of robes. The regular form is *mukhmal*).

[240]Ar. *mustaṭrafa.*

[241]About the rare and costly sea wool see *Med. Soc.*, I, 106 and n. 40, with reference to our order.

[242]See n. 234, above. The writer notes twice "faced" and "no script." Such repetitions are common, see n. 245, below.

[243]North African garments, see the detailed descriptions in Dozy, *Supplément*, I, 658*a-b*, Stillman, "Female Attire," pp. 62–63, Dozy, *Supplément*, I, 76*b*, and Stillman, "Female Attire," pp. 42–43, respectively.

[244]Ar. *nakhkhayn*, normally used, like runner in English, for a long narrow carpet. This is followed, l. 27, by an order for ten *musallayāt* (s = ṣ), prayer carpets, four white, two dark blue (*kuḥl*), two green, and two red.

[245]"Light" is repeated, because felt, a compressed fabric, tends to be heavy, see nn. 233 and 242, above. The ʿUbayd felt (see n. 239, above), although preferred, probably was too expensive. Mantles, *ghafāʾir*, pl. of *ghifāra*, literally, cover, a male garment, almost never mentioned in the Geniza. TS Arabic Box 7, f. 3(1), contains an

urgent order for a red one (thirteenth century).

[246]A slip for *safsārī*, see n. 243, above.

[247]Ar. *jawārib sawādhij*. The man in the al-Ḥarīrī manuscript MS arabe 3929, f. 69, Bibliothèque Nationale, Paris, Ettinghausen, *Arab Painting*, p. 82, wears socks. Because of the description "without patterns" one might be inclined to translate "stockings." Holmes, *Daily Living*, p. 162, speaks indeed of stockings, but as is evident from the explanations of the author, these were intended to form part of a man's ornate appearance. No such use of stockings had its place in Mediterranean clothing as revealed by the Cairo Geniza.

[248]Bodl. MS Heb. e 98 (no Cat.), f. 64 a, ll. 10 and 14, trans. Goitein, *Letters*, p. 282. The translation here differs in some points because of the insights won during a closer study of clothing. For Arjīsh, a town in Armenia, and its textiles see *Letters*, p. 152 n. 18. Mending, *iṣlāḥ*, clearly was not done by the tailor, but by a weaver, who used the additional cotton for strengthening the fabric.

[249]See n. 72, above.

[250]For *tafṣīl* see *Letters*, p. 265 n. 6, for *qaṭʿ* TS 13 J 3, f. 2, ed. S. D. Goitein, *Sefunot*, 8 (1964), 113 (dated 1142), where a man on his deathbed asks that a Baghdadi *niṣfiyya* and an ʿAttabi gown be cut for his funeral clothing.

[251]TS 8 J 16, f. 25, l. 11: *mayzarayn ṣūf mukhāṭa* (Palermo: *al-madīna*); TS NS J 359, ll. 5–8: *niṣfiyya mukhayyaṭa, thawb sumsumī bi-ḥarīr mukhayyaṭ*, each valued in the inventory at 20 (dirhems).

[252]No tailor is mentioned in *Med. Soc.*, I, 89–99, where the earnings of craftsmen are discussed, nor do I see a *tailleur* for the Geniza period in Ashtor, *Prix*. To be sure, one must remember that agreements with tailors naturally were made locally and orally, while weavers and fullers could work for persons in other places, as reported above.

[253]TS 16.181, sec. IV, l. 14 (Damascus, 933), ed. Goitein, *Lešonenu*, 30 (1966), 202; *minṣabayn*, "two racks, costing 4 dinars," according to M. A. Friedman's suggestion, *Lešonenu*, 31 (1967), 160. Another name for such a rack is *mishjab*, Wahrmund, *Handwörterbuch*, II, 806*b*. The mighty viceroy al-Afḍal had hundreds of musk-perfumed garments on racks, but he possessed also 800 concubines. For sachet see App. D, n. 226, below.

[254]Taking asunder, *fattat*: TS 12.435*v*, l. 1. (In *Letters*, p. 54, I translated it "spread out." Shaking out, *nafaḍ al-aksiya*: ENA 3788, f. 6, l. 11. Stretching and hanging up: see nn. 157 and 158, above.

[255]See *Med. Soc.*, I, 184, 302, 344.

[256]Mosseri L-159, frag. 3, *India Book* 344b. See also n. 258, below.

[257]*Med. Soc.*, I, 129 and n. 18.

[258]Fuller, *qaṣṣār* and *ṭaffāl*: see n. 200, above; cleaner, *muṣaffī*; see n. 213. Starcher, *nashshā*, family name of the merchant ʿAbdūn: TS Arabic Box 53, f. 51*v*, l. 3 (dated 1038), ed. S. D. Goitein, *Tarbiz*, 37 (1968), 185. Another person is called Ibn al-Nashshā, TS NS J 111, col. II, 1.2 (dated 1059, in an account in the hand of Nahray b. Nissīm), according to dates and circumstances possibly a son of the former. More common is the form *nashāwī*, which might be translated "maker of starch," but usually the makers of such materials also worked with them. Maḥāsin al-Nashāwī lived in a house belonging to the community, Gil, *Foundations*, pp. 407 n. 9, and p. 444, a Ben al-Nashāwī was a beneficiary of public charity, TS NS J 179*v*, l. 18, *Med. Soc.*, II, 441, sec. 11. (The list is edited by E. Ashtor in *Shazar Jubilee Volume* (Jerusalem, 1973), pp. 805–809.)

[259]Pressing: see n. 205, above. Redyeing, *maṣbūgh*, Aramaic *ṣevīʿ*: TS 16.181, ll. 5, 7. Housewives dyeing: *Med. Soc.*, II, 360.

[260]ULC Or 1080 J 142, col. II, ll. 2–9 (an inventory of a dead physician's possessions, drawn up at the instructions of Moses Maimonides, dated 1172). Translated in App. D, Doc. VII, below.

[261]E.g., undershirt: *ghilāla rijāliyya ghasīla*, TS NS J 392, l. 11. Outerwear: *malḥafa iskandarānī rafīʿa ghasīla*, a fine Alexandria cloak, *ibid.*

[262]*The History of the Patriarchs of the Egyptian Church*, III, part 1, ed. A. Khatir and

O.H.E. Burmester, Ar. text p. 23, l. 15, communicated to me by Mark R. Cohen. Maimonides, *Code*, Book XIV, sec. "Mourning," ch. 5:3.

[263]E.g., TS NS J 443, ll. 3–4: *ma ͨraqa ghasīla*, 1 (dinar), a *mandīl khalīͨ* 1/2 (dinar), a washed skullcap, a secondhand kerchief.

[264]TS 20.122, l. 29 (middle of eleventh century).

[265]BM Or 5566 B 20, l. 11, *Nahray* 141.

[266]Bodl. MS Heb. d 75 (no Cat.), f. 14, last line and margin. Damaged. Salāma b. [. . .] writes to Abū Saͨīd Makhlūf, the Trustee. The recipient is referred to as al-Nafūsī (from Libya) in TS 8 J 13, f. 3, a letter of Isaac Nīsābūrī, see *Med. Soc.*, I, 538*b* (Index).

[267]These terms, repeatedly found in the Geniza, refer also to dealers in secondhand clothing, as in TS 13 J 25, f. 9, ll. 18–19, *Nahray* 181, where Joseph b. Mūsā Tahertī sends the discarded clothing of his daughter, *qashāsh* (or *qushāsh*) *mimmā kān*(!) *talbas-hū bintī*, to Fustat, for selling it there and sending the proceeds to Jerusalem for the support of orphaned children. Cf. *Med. Soc.*, III, 235.

[268]See n. 36, above.

[269]For the Sassanid period cf. *sarbalē ḥatīmē*, the robes of scholars bearing the name of the Jewish exilarch, no doubt an imitation of the Persian court, BT Sabbath 58*a*. Modern commentators have explained this custom of wearing clothing with the name of a ruler as designating its wearer as his slave. But can there be an honor greater than being "a servant of the king"?

[270]See *Med. Soc.*, II, 351 and 604 n. 28.

[271]Maimonides, *Responsa*, I, 116. Ready money: *Med. Soc.*, I, 200.

[272]Mann, *The Jews in Egypt*, II, 435 (= *Hebrew Union College Annual*, 3 [1926], 261, l. 2).

[273]The court clerk Ḥalfon b. Manasse sold everything, including his Sabbath suits, during a protracted illness: TS 13 J 25, f. 6, *India Book* 48. "We sold all we had, even our garments" (to pay for the treatment of a child): TS 20.149, l. 29, a late letter sent from Gaza, Palestine, to Samuel al-Amshāṭī in Cairo. "Last year we sold those few garments together with what you know, but this year nothing has remained to be sold": TS 13 J 36, f. 5, ll. 21–22, the Gaon Solomon b. Judah writing to his son in a time of famine and complete anarchy in Palestine, ed. Goitein, *Palestinian Jewry*, p. 99.

Pawning garments (to cover expenses for High Holidays): TS 12.34*v*, ll. 7–9. Giving eight pieces of clothing as collateral for 4 dinars: TS 16.341 (Aug. 1213). A traveler pawns his clothing for 40 dirhems (it seems, in connection with the payment of the poll tax): TS 13 J 28, f. 29, ll. 2–4. Clothing (probably given to the tax collector in kind) taken as a loan received against collateral: ULC Or 1080 J 264. A complete picture of the activities of a pawnbroker emerges from TS K 15, f. 99, where a man of that profession transfers his business to another. The pawners range from a slave girl to a sharīf (a Muslim noble), the loans granted from 1/8 dinar to 14 dinars, and the largest number of articles of clothing pawned by one person was five (against a loan of 3 1/2 dinars). See also App. D, Doc. VI.

[274]Goitein, *Letters*, p. 184 n. 18.

[275]*Ibid.*, p. 250 n. 8.

[276]TS 10 J 24, f. 4, margin, ed. S. D. Goitein, *Tarbiz*, 24 (1955), 44.

[277]The dowry and its relationship to the husband's marriage gift is discussed in *Med. Soc.*, III, 123–131.

[278]Bodl. MS Heb. d 65 (Cat. 2877), f. 30, reedited, with an important commentary in Friedman, *Marriage*, no. 18. The relationship between the (first installment of the) marriage gift and the dowry was here 1:16 approximately, which was not frequent, but also not exceptional.

[279]TS 13 J 32, ed. S. Assaf, *Joseph Klausner Jubilee Volume* (Jerusalem, 1937), p. 230. The document now bears the manuscript mark TS J 3, f. 47. Corrections in *Med. Soc.*, III, 456 n. 96.

In *ibid.*, p. 137, I mentioned as another example a marriage proposed in Aden, South Arabia, around 1150. I regret this. No doubt, Adenese dinars, worth approximately one-third of the Egyptian dinar, were intended.

[280]Museum of Islamic Art, Cairo, no. 4224, ed. Suʿād Māhir, *ʿUqūd al-Zawāj* (n.d.), pp. 17–18. The document was written on cloth in 1334. In Jewish law and custom such installment payments of the deferred marriage gift are unknown.

Ḥasan b. Abū Saʿd Tustarī: TS 16.50, see *Med. Soc.*, III, 455 n. 92. A Persian traveler visiting Cairo reported that Abū Saʿd Tustarī had three hundred trees on his roof garden, all planted in silver pots, see A, 5, n. 92, above.

[281]*Med. Soc.*, III, 365, nos. 8 and 10.

[282]Trousseau lists of (*a*) lower middle-class brides show jewelry valued about one-half, and those from (*b*) families with modest income about one-quarter of the price of clothing, e.g.,

(*a*) *Med. Soc.*, III, 370, no. 2 (42:83 dinars); no. 18 (23:55 d.); 378, no. 36 (30:70 d.).

(*b*) *Ibid.*, 368, sec. 28 (6:25 1/2 d.); sec. 29 (10:40 d.); Doc. I, below (9:30 d.).

[283]Maimonides, *Code*, Book IV, sec. "Marriage," ch. 13:1–5; Mishna Ketubbot 5:8; BT Ketubbot 64*b* ff. Maimonides does not mention jewelry here. For *takhshīṭīm* in 13:4 refers to such things as eye cosmetics and makeup, with which even the poorest of the poor was obliged to provide his wife. But, as the Geniza shows and as is natural, husbands who could afford it gave ornaments to their wives as presents, *Med. Soc.*, III, 167, bottom, and *passim*.

[284]Captive: n. 24, above. See S. D. Goitein, "The Sexual Mores of the Common People," in *Society and the Sexes in Medieval Islam*, ed. Afaf Lutfi al-Sayyid-Marsot (Malibu, Calif., 1979), pp. 43–61.

[285]If we disregard the smaller or less valuable pieces whose total numbers are listed, but which are not itemized, the well-to-do girls of Doc. II–VI possessed 23, 42, 31, 42 pieces, respectively. These numbers are illustrative, not completely accurate, because the manuscripts have lacunae and other little defects.

[286]A man on his deathbed wishes to have "a consummate shroud, *mujmal*, the last enjoyment I have from my possessions," TS 13 J 3, f. 2, ll. 14–17, ed. *Sefunot*, 8 (1964), 113. See also the deathbed declaration discussed in nn. 69–70, above. The ideas about death discernible in the Geniza are treated in *Med. Soc.*, V, A, 3 (in preparation).

[287]In almost every longer inventory of the estate of deceased persons pieces of clothing described as new are found, e.g., in App. D., Doc. VII, below, ll. 12, 13; *verso*, ll. 1, 3. In the deathbed declarations referred to in the preceding note the dying man wished to have at least some of the garments ordered by him to be new.

[288]She assures the rabbinical court supervising the funeral that there is enough cash available in her estate, and no excuses should be made for being remiss in carrying out her last wishes. Wuḥsha, Désirée, had a brother, sisters, and other relatives, and was a divorcée with a young boy born out of wedlock. See *Med. Soc.*, III, 346–352.

[289]"Ṭalā linen is finer than Dabīqī and more lasting in wear," Serjeant, *Islamic Textiles*, p. 72, quoting the geographer al-Masʿūdī. I spell *Ṭalī*, because the word is always written so in the Geniza (probably an abbreviation of Ṭalā'ī). Ṭalā, or rather Talā, since the Iranians do not know how to pronounce *ṭ*—as Yāqūt, III, 541, judiciously remarks—was a town in northwestern Iran near the Black Sea, but the textile named for it was produced also in Egypt. Thus a man writing from Aden to Cairo orders "four Ṭalī robes made in Ashmūn," a renowned Egyptian linen center, Westminster College, Frag. Cairens. 9, ll. 15–16 *India Book* 50. The Egyptian product was obviously of lower quality. Ten Ṭalī robes, sent from Alexandria to Nahray b. Nissīm in Fustat, cost 13 dinars, the regular price for an ordinary robe made of linen: ENA 2805, f. 5b*v*, l. 3. Ṭalī skullcaps costing 1 or 2 dinars are found in Geniza trousseau lists.

[290]A piece of male clothing, see n. 234, above. Common in business letters, where they occur with a wide variety of prices, but with the standard price of 1–2 dinars, or even less; prevailing colors: black or white, as appropriate for males: TS 13 J 28, f. 4, ll. 8 ff.

[291]Wuḥsha, who had spent most of her eventful life in the company of men, preferred the recitation of religious texts to the howls of wailing women. To the contrary, the dying woman described next (see nn. 293–296, below) wished to be

lamented by Muslim wailing women, who probably made more noise than Jewish ones.

[292]TS Arabic Box 4, f. 5, text and trans. in "A Jewish Business Woman of the Eleventh Century," *The Seventy-Fifth Anniversary Volume of the JQR* (1979), 225–242.

[293]Using the Tunisian term *shuqqa*, see n. 223, above. Whether she cherished the weave of Tunisia or was a native of that country is not evident: TS 13 J 3, f. 3, ed. S. D. Goitein, *Sefunot*, 8 (1964), 122.

[294]Ar. *niṣāfiyya*, "an Egyptian stuff, half silk and half cotton" (Steingass, *Persian-English Dictionary*, p. 1406), not to be confounded with the very common *nisfiyya*, which denotes the cut, not the fabric, of the garment concerned, probably one covering only the upper part of the body; a kind of cape. The *naṣāfī*, noted in Serjeant, *Islamic Textiles*, p. 202, is the plural of *nisfiyya*.

[295]Ar. *ḥuzza*, used also for a man's underwear, as when a physician, overcome by the tidings of his brother's death, threw off his clothing "and nothing remained on me except the *ḥuzza*": TS 24.72, l. 2, ed. Goitein, *Palestinian Jewry*, p. 268. Here it is probably the band that held the clothing together and the corpse in the proper position: cf. Lane, *Modern Egyptians*, p. 578.

[296]The absolutely exceptional price of the coffin (if the tentative reading suggested is correct) may be explained by the woman's wish to be buried in her house until one of her family (parents or brother) would die, when her body should be brought out to the cemetery together with that of her kin. Thus the coffin had to be more durable than usual.

[297]About him see Goitein, *Letters*, pp. 62–65, 181–185, 199, 299–300.

[298]The story of Sulaymān and his stepsisters, contained in four court records written during six weeks of summer 1156, is told in *Med. Soc.*, III, 282. His stepmother was the daughter of a government official and herself an influential person. She herself no doubt possessed real estate and a rich outfit. Her daughter's dowry would probably be a multiple of what their father had earmarked for them out of his estate.

[299]See Ashtor, *Prix, passim*.

[300]*Med. Soc.*, II, 130–132.

[301]TS 13 J 25, f. 9, ll. 18–19, *Nahray* 181. The term *yunfiqū* refers specifically to clothing. See n. 267, above.

[302]See *Med. Soc.*, I, 50.

[303]Cf. App. D, n. 84.

[304]TS 8 J 18, f. 2 and TS 10 J 15, f. 3, *India Book* 102 and 103, where Ḥalfōn b. Nethanel, who carried the cape, asks two business friends in Almeria, Spain, to forward it to Lucena, since he himself did not travel there.

[305]I, however, have not found in the Geniza a single business letter going from Baghdad to Cairo or vice versa or any reference to one. It can hardly be argued that such letters might have been deposited in Genizas found in the Iraqian or Karaite synagogues of Fustat, since much other material written by or to members of those synagogues has been preserved in "our" Geniza. In a period of constant warfare (tenth through fourteenth centuries) the long overland route from Baghdad to Cairo was impracticable for heavy transport by Jews, who did not travel on Saturdays. Thus the textile trade between the two cities was probably in non-Jewish hands. In Ottoman times the observance of the Sabbath by Jewish merchants was a big nuisance to the movement of caravans, see Norman Stillman, *The Jews of Arab Lands* (Philadelphia, Pa., 1979), p. 321, and, for the topic in general, *Med. Soc.*, I, 280–281.

[306]ULC Or 1080 J 35, ll. 30–31, and 20–21.

[307]See *Med. Soc.*, I, 46. A Jewish woman in Egypt made Rūmī garments, see C, 1, n. 82, below.

[308]TS Misc. Box 8, f. 97, l. 15. See n. 121, above, and *Med. Soc.*, III, 397, sec. 55.

[309]App. D, Doc. III, n. 100, below. Together with wimple: *ibid.*, col. III, ll. 3–4.

[310]TS 13 J 6, f. 9*v*, ll. 11–15 (ca. 1230; see *Med. Soc.*, III, 422, sec. 379): *Rūmiyya ṭarīq al-Yaman*.

[311]App. D, n. 36. TS 13 J 6, f. 9*v*, col. I, l. 20 (see preceding note), where it is

described as made of silk and costing 2 dinars. In ENA 3652, f. 8, l. 13 (ca. 1100): *minshafa mukhmal Rūmī*, "made of velvet." The very fact that the Rūmī minshafa could be made of two different fabrics proves that it was a type of a dress (worn at the visit to the public bathhouse).

[312]See Mishna Yoma 3:7, and the discussion in Krauss, *Talmudische Archäologie*, I, 521 n. 35.

[313]"Some Basic Problems in Jewish History," *Proceedings of the Fifth World Congress of Jewish Studies* (August 1969) (Jerusalem, 1972), pp. 102–103.

[314]See n. 140, above; and *Med. Soc.*, I, 42–70.

[315]See n. 127, above.

[316]TS 12.366, ll. 13–14, Ar. *shiʿār al-mawḍiʿ*. He wishes to have Barrānī, and, if it was not to be had, Sāwī. The terms are explained in *Med. Soc.*, I, 456.

[317]Goitein, *Letters*, p. 107.

[318]See n. 139, above.

[319]Palermo and Syracuse: see nn. 130 and 132, above. Demona (spelled in the Geniza *dmnsh*) silk: TS Arabic Box 53, f. 32, ll. 10 (mentioned together with, and, therefore different from, Sicilian *lāsīn* silk) and l. 15. Demona carpets (*busuṭ*): TS NS J 128. Visited by Jewish merchants from abroad: TS 20.9, ll. 4, 5, 7 (dated 1046), ed. Assaf, *Texts and Studies*, p. 138; TS Arabic Box 54, f. 88 (around 1050), ed. in S. D. Goitein, "Sicily and Southern Italy in the Cairo Geniza Documents," *Archivio Storico per la Sicilia Orientale*, 67 (1971), 31–33.

[320]See App. D, n. 59.

[321]*Med. Soc.*, III, 372.

[322]Including the year 1400 of the Islamic era, when, in the summer of 1980, a discriminatory badge was imposed on Jews (and probably also on Zoroastrians) in Iran. (Oral information from an Iranian who had received it from a relative living in the country and affected by that ancient and ever new tribulation. It is not excluded that this was a local affair brought about by an overzealous cleric.)

[323]"The Pact of Umar," trans. in Stillman, *The Jews of Arab Lands*, pp. 157–158, is a later compilation, but contains "security ordinances," already present in early Islamic writings. The point that the laws concerning the clothing of non-Muslims owe their origin largely to the need for physical and psychological protection of the Muslims and were so durable because they were incorporated into the most ancient law texts was made by me in some detail in *The Jewish World*, ed. Elie Kedourie (London, 1979), pp. 180–181.

[324]See Stillman, *The Jews in Arab Lands*, pp. 167–168 (al-Mutawakkil), and p. 251 (Seljuk period, described by Obadyah, the proselyte). Obadyah mentions two renewals of the yellow badge, one that he himself observed in 1121, well known from other sources, see *Med. Soc.*, II, 287, and one that happened a generation earlier.

[325]See nn. 180 and 181, above, and the references to Stillman in the preceding note.

[326]A. L. Udovitch and L. Valensi, "Communautés juives en pays d'Islam: Les Juifs de Djerba," *Annales*, 35 (1980), 766–767.

[327]The two "prayer books" possessed by him, that of Saadya Gaon of Baghdad (d. 942) and that from North Africa, were also written in Arabic (but probably in Hebrew script); only the texts of the prayers were, of course, in Hebrew. A *Siddūr* was not what is now understood: a simple prayer book, but a bulky compendium of all the religious rites to be observed throughout the year.

[328]See *Med. Soc.*, II, 286.

[329]See Lane, *The Modern Egyptians*, p. 537, describing the situation after Muhammad Ali's reforms.

[330]App. D, Doc. VII, ll. 9, 11, 12, *verso*, l. 7.

[331]For *ʿardī*, see David Solomon Sassoon Collection, no. 713 (dated Dec. 1147/Jan. 1148), ed. M. Toledano, *HUCA*, 4 (1927), 449–458; H. Z. Hirschberg, *I. F. Baer Jubilee Volume* (Jerusalem, 1961), pp. 134–153. To be reedited in *India Book* 263. About Abū Zikrī Kohen and his son Sulaymān see nn. 297, 298, above. The reading *ʿarḍā*, suggested in Ashtor, *Prix*, p. 168, is impossible since the word is spelled throughout the Geniza *ʿrḍy*. Unlike the *shāshiya*, see n. 336, below, it could not be

used for the turban because of its almost square form. For *burda*: TS 8 J 23, f. 30, ll. 13–14, and 19, *India Book* 267.

[332]Dozy, *Supplément*, I, 19; ENA 4010, f. 1, l. 20, ed. S. D. Goitein, "The Synagogue and Its Furnishings," p. 91; TS 20.47, l. 15, ed. *ibid.*, p. 92 (dated 1075 and 1080, respectively).

[333]Bodl. MS Heb. d 75 (no Cat.), f. 13 (dated March, 1112).

[334]The son of the writer of the order.

[335]The opening of the priestly blessing, still heard in the Synagogue and the Church (Numbers 6:24).

[336]Westminster College, Frag. Cairens. 9*v*, ll. 17–19, 31, *India Book* 50. The Mishna, Yoma 4:4, distinguishes between high-quality "red," and low-quality "green" gold. The latter expression probably corresponds to Ar. *wāḍiḥ*, bright, see Christopher Toll, *Al-Hamdānī, Kitāb Al-Ǧauharatain, Die beiden Edelmetalle* (Uppsala, 1968), p. 329.

Jacob Milgrom's lecture, "The Tassel and the Tallith," University of Cincinnati, 1981, is a popular and instructive exposition on the possible origin and meaning of this religious practice.

[337]The throne of the Fatimid caliphs was covered with a Qurqūbī. The costliest textile known to me from the Geniza is a red Qurqūbī canopy worth 100 dinars. See Serjeant, *Islamic Textiles*, pp. 45, 63, 79, and *passim*, and TS 24.12, l. 7. Another *shāshiya Qurqūbī* is mentioned in ENA 1822, f. 57, l. 23, where it is brought from the Maghreb to Alexandria as part of an estate. ENA 2805, f. 6 A, l. 14, shows that Qurqūbīs were embroidered with (gold) threads, *khayṭ* in Fustat.

[338]Maimonides, *Code*, Book II, sec. "Fringes," ch. 3:11. All the persons writing in Geniza letters about garments equipped with fringes belonged to families of religious scholarship or were themselves communal functionaries. When a poor schoolmaster and cantor writes to his brother that he had to pawn "the *ʿarḍī*" on the eve of Sukkot (for buying provisions for the holidays), TS 12.34*v*, l. 8, he certainly referred to the "broad shawl" which served as his prayer mantle.

[339]TS Arabic Box 43, f. 71, *India Book* 342. *Verso* contains a reference to the Furḍa port of Aden.

[340]Ar. *rafīʿa*. The words in ll. 4*a* and 6*a* are written between the lines.

[341]Ar. *maḥshiyya bi-ṭirāzayn ḥiwālayn kull ṭirāz*. Inscriptions embroidered on a textile running from edge to edge, e.g., Golombek-Gervers, "Tiraz Fabrics," pp. 109–112. The same aesthetic effect on a plate, *ibid.*, p. 91. For *maḥshiyya* see also App. D, n. 260, below.

[342]The writer noted for himself to whom he had given this order. Ahwāz is a province in southwest Iran, once famous for its textiles and now for its oil (and now the war between Iraq and Iran).

[343]Here used in the original sense: a piece of outer wear.

[344]The section dealing with the "fringes."

[345]Forming a triangle, of one letter, but not written out, so that the Name should not be desecrated. In the first letter from Aden quoted above, last line, the Name was written in the same way.

[346]Maimonides, *Responsa*, III, 510–515. As the introductory note on p. 510 shows, this letter was widely discussed in medieval rabbinical literature (and not always with approval). TS 16.292, ed. in Goitein, "Chief Justice Hananel b. Samuel, In-law of Moses Maimonides" (Heb.) in *Tarbiz Jubilee Volume* (1980–1981, actually 1982), 386–388, nn. 67–75.

[347]App. D, n. 75.

[348]*Ibid.*, nn. 117–120, esp. n. 119, below. The *muqaddar*, a predominantly male garment, see *ibid.*, n. 218, is also extremely common in the Geniza, but has not yet been identified elsewhere.

[349]*Ibid.*, n. 101. Deborah Thompson, *Coptic Textiles in the Brooklyn Museum* (Brooklyn, N.Y., 1971), nos. 7, 21, and 36.

[350]Thompson, *Coptic Textiles*, no. 24.

[351]See *EJ*, XI, 1355–1366.

[352]Communication of Professor Lucette Valensi, who possesses such a garment bought in Zarzīs, Tunisia.

[353]*Med. Soc.*, I, 337, see *EJ*, XI, 688 (where Nahray b. Nissīm's use of the star is not noted).

[354]Even where a garment or a piece of jewelry has the same name in Muslim and Jewish sources they might have differed in make and look, as was the case in Yemen, where the Jews themselves had been the artisans working for both communities. Cf. Aviva Müller-Lancet, "Jewish Ethnography at the Israel Museum," *The Israel Museum News* (1979), p. 57, illus. 13 and 14, where the *lebbe*, a chest ornament, is constructed of entirely different units when made for Muslim and Jewish women. In Fustat, however, the Jewish woman was not confined to a ghetto as was the case in the capital of Yemen. She could go to the bazaar and buy whatever she liked.

[355]See Bernard Lewis, *Islam in History* (New York, N.Y. 1973), pp. 158–165, esp. p. 160, who provides a new English version of this repeatedly translated and quoted poem and puts it into its proper historical context. The poet: Abū Isḥāq al-Ilbīrī (from Elvira) writing against Joseph (Yehōsēf) b. Samuel ha-Nagid of Granada. Lewis's translation is reproduced in Stillman, *The Jews of Arab Lands*, p. 215.

[356]*Maᶜālim al-Qurba*, p. 15, Ar. text, p. 43. The author, who writes "from an Egyptian point of view," died as late as 1329, but his work is based on that of an earlier, Syrian writer, see *EI*², III, 960, s.v. "Ibn al-Ukhuwwa" (Cl. Cahen).

2. *Jewelry*

[357]H. J. Schirmann, *Hebrew Poetry in Spain and Provence* (Jerusalem and Tel Aviv, 1954), p. 511. Cf. Joseph Yahalom, "Poetry and Society in Egypt . . .," *Zion*, 45 (1980), 294. The Eden river Pishon (Genesis 2:11) is identified by rabbinical commentators with the Nile.

[358]Since Heb. *yeled* means both child and son, she wished to make it clear that the rights conveyed by the will were irrespective of the sex of the newborn. For wills of expectant mothers see *Med. Soc.*, III, 232 and n. 54, where our document is not listed.

[359]Ar. *ḥumat al-ᶜaqrab.*The venom is ejected from the scorpion's bent tail. The same description in the contemporary Karaite ketubba TS 20.47*v*, where the ornament was valued as being worth only 7 dinars. Those were people in modest circumstances, *Med. Soc.*, III, 421, sec. 371.

[360]Ar. *ḥashw*, materials other than gold used for the making of the bracelet.

[361]An Egyptian *mithqāl* weighed 4.68 grams, see Hinz, *Islamische Masse*, p. 4. Worth 100 dinars: ENA 2727, f. 8 A, l. 6, the trousseau of Wuḥsha (about her see *Med. Soc.*, III, 346–352). Since a single other bracelet was valued at only 5 dinars (l. 8), the prices might have been realistic.

[362]Ar. *ṣadr al-bāz.* This should not remind us of the Roman god Mercury, who had wings on his heels. The plumage of a falcon's breast is not smooth, but stands up in flakes and scales. The goldsmith might have provided the anklets with a rough surface, which, besides the attractive look, would make the click of the anklets audible (as "the Daughters of Zion" of old loved, Isaiah 3:16, who emphasizes also the narrowness of their steps). "Breast of the falcon" is also an Arabic name for buckwheat, Dozy, *Supplément*, I 822–823. Ornaments are frequently given the form of flowers and plants, see below. The small buckwheat seeds might have been the model for a rough surface.

[363]TS 12.646*v*, ll. 7–10, fragment of a leaf from a book of court records (first half of eleventh century). The Karaite character of the document is evident from the Hebrew style and script, but even more so from the reverse side, which contains (in the same hand) a report about the state of the fields in Palestine in springtime. According to Karaite law, the intercalation of a thirteenth month to the current year is required, when the fields are not sufficiently progressed. A similar Karaite report from March 15, 1051, in TS 12.147.

[364]TS 12.163, l. 3, from bottom (1120; remarriage of divorcée to former husband). Price of household help: *Med. Soc.*, I, 137–139.

[365]All these weights (with the exception of 20 mithqāls, for which see n. 361) in TS 12.646*v*, see n. 363, above, where we have also 4 1/2 mithqāls for a pair of . . . (earrings, probably).

[366]The "classical" gold dinar weighed 4.233 grams; the Egyptian mithqāl, as we have seen, 4.68 grams, see Hinz, *Islamische Masse*, pp. 2–4. In commercial transactions in which ornaments were given as collateral their weights are occasionally noted, e.g., TS 18 J 1, f. 26, ll. 15–18 (in al-Maḥalla, May 1160). Against a loan of 13 dinars these ornaments were given by a cantor, probably a man of limited means: "A gold crescent adorned with small pearls, weight 4 1/2 dinars; a gold *qilāda* necklace consisting of eight beads, *ḥubūb*, and a middle piece, *wāsiṭa*, total weight 5 5/8 dinars; six silver bracelets, *ḥadā'id*, and a silver bowl, total weight 43 dirhems." It is notable that the weight here is indicated by the term "dinar," not "mithqāl."

Dirhem is the name of both the weight and the silver coin. Cf. ENA NS 2, f. 25, which notes the weight of two silver *dumluj* bracelets as being of 60 dirhems (or 187.5 grams). Their price was 14 Malikī, that is, Adenese dinars, a coin of far less value than the Egyptian dinar, a half of it or less. The data about the relationship between the two coins vary greatly from time to time.

[367]TS 16.142, l. 6 (dated 982), ed. Mann, *Texts*, I, 364, see *Med. Soc.*, III, 454 n. 65, and frequently. App. D, Doc. I, l. 1 (dated 1028), superscribed "The Gold," includes also silver rings.

[368]TS 24.1 (dated 1082), see Shaked, *Bibliography of Geniza Documents*, p. 76; Westminster College, Frag. Cairens. 47.

[369]TS 8.166, l. 5 (ca. 1128), when special care had to be taken with them in a time of an oppressive government. In a question addressed to Moses Maimonides (late twelfth century), Bodl. MS Heb. e 98, f. 28, l. 3, jewelry is referred to as *maṣāgh*, and, two lines later, as *ḥaly* (case of a mother giving her elder daughter textiles, *qumāsh*, and jewelry to be used for her minor sister when she marries; ed. M. A. Friedman in *Studies in [the] Geniza and Sepharadi Heritage, 1981*, p. 111.

[370]TS 16.198, l. 8, *Med. Soc.*, III, 407, sec. 210, where jewelry is opposed to cash; TS NS J 306, l. 4, where *ʿlq* (probably pronounced *ʿilaq*) opens the Jewelry section.

[371]Cloves sent as present: TS 8 J 18, f. 2*v*, l. 1, *India Book* 102, and often, Goitein, *Letters*, p. 68. Clove chains: Stillman, *Palestinian Costume*, p. 95.

[372]Higgins, *Greek and Roman Jewellery*, p. xlii.

[373]See *Med. Soc.*, I, 368 ff. and the literature noted there on p. 491. Also Ashtor, *Social and Economic History*, pp. 216, 292, and *passim*. But see M. L. Bates, "The Function of Fāṭimid and Ayyūbid Glass Weights." *JESHO*, 24 (1980/1), 88–90.

[374]See nn. 529–554, below. The Jewish "trade" in gold was, of course, far more important than that in silver, inasmuch as countless bags of gold coins constantly found their way from the Muslim West to Egypt and from there to the India route. The question whether the Jews participated in the Saharan trade in gold bars was discussed by E. Ashtor and L. Lewicki at the Spoleto High Middle Ages Conference of March-April 1978 (see *Gli Ebrei nell' Alto Medioevo* [Spoleto, 1980], pp. 465–466). The flourishing state of the Jewish community in Sijilmāsa, Morocco, the North African terminal of that trade, around the year 1000, makes it likely that the Jews had some share in that great international economic activity.

[375]The gold content of the Fatimid dinars shows the high degree of workmanship attained by the artisans who minted them.

[376]There might have been other armlets made of base materials and therefore not mentioned in our documents. See n. 518, below. Dr. Marilyn Jenkins informs me that there are gold Fatimid pins in the L. A. Mayer Museum, Jerusalem.

[377]Cf. Higgins, *Greek and Roman Jewellery*, p. 45, about the use of bronze for ornaments.

[378]Fraenkel, *Aramäische Fremdwörter*, p. 62. The Hebrew word for bride, *kallā*, probably has something to do with the tiara or diadem worn by her, see Krauss, *Talmudische Archäologie*, I, 185 nn. 752 and 754.

The beautiful gold and enamel pendant in the Metropolitan Museum, Theodore M. Davis Collection 30.95.37 (see Keene-Jenkins, *Djawhar*, fig. 20) would have been described as *bi-ghayr taklīl*, because the gold hoops around the edge through which strands of pearls were destined to be laced are there, but not the pearls themselves.

The term *mukallal bi-mīnā*, adorned with enamel-like earthenware, said of a pair of pins worth 2 dinars, has been seen by me only once, TS K 15, f. 65, col. I, l. 7. According to Marilyn Jenkins only a few mīnā pieces have been preserved from this period.

[379]Abraham b. Yijū; see about him Goitein, *Letters*, pp. 186–197, 201–206. Firkovitch II, 1700, f. 27 (1156), *India Book* 334. My addition is somewhat different but their arithmetic was better. Or perhaps the sum was rounded out. The date is effaced, but since all the preceding documents, as well as the next—the last one preserved (when I copied them in Leningrad in 1965),—were written in spring and summer 1156, there can be little doubt that this *taqwīm*, or estimate of the dowry, was made in that year.

[380]Pearls were, of course, of the greatest imaginable difference in type and value. Take this example from an account written around 1100 by ʿArūs b. Joseph (see Index). The two items are separated only by a stroke:

24 pearls weighing 1 1/4 dirhems (the silver weight, total ca. 4 grams)	Price 1 5/8 dinars
One pearl, weighing a quarter dinar (ca. 1 gram)	Price 1 1/4 dinars

Other items from this account in n. 396, below. A long business letter from Alexandria to Fustat contains this detail: "My brother has left with you 60 1/2 dinars belonging to me. Please buy with them pearls of first quality of those that are salable in Spain. If they are not to be had, leave the money until my arrival": TS 12.373, l. 13.

[381]For the Spanish women see the end of the preceding note, Krauss, *Talmudische Archäologie*, I, 200 and 659–660; *Med. Soc.*, I, 416 n. 2, and II, 440, secs. 4–5, where perforaters are listed (in the manuscript) as making partial payments of the poll tax.

[382]Literature about this topic in Keene-Jenkins, *Djawhar*, sec. 1, and Bibliography.

[383]Heb. *avānīm ṭōvōt u-margāliyōt.*

[384]In the Geniza we read that a merchant prince like Ibn ʿAwkal (see Index) had his seat in the *dār al-jawhar* and we learn much about his far-flung commercial undertakings, but never about his dealings in high-priced gems. I understand that today, too, dealers in such costly items prefer to handle their transactions orally and in person and do not entrust them to written documents.

[385]Bodl. MS Heb. d 65 (Cat. 2877), f. 1, l. 8: *khātim* (spelled: *k'tym*) *dhahab bi-faṣṣ yāqūt*. See *Med. Soc.*, III, 401, sec. 106. The price of a silver ring with a ruby, Bodl. MS Heb. a 3 (Cat. 2873), f. 39, l. 7 (ca. 1020), has not been preserved.

[386]TS 20.10, l. 12, ed. Strauss-Ashtor, *Mamluks*, III, 67–70: *klbnd bi-fuṣūṣ zurq wa-lūlū raqīq wa-turaymisāt ʿanbar*. For *klbnd*, the editor, *ibid.*, p. 35 n. 5, refers to Maqrīzī, *Sulūk* (Cairo, 1936), I, 494. From the context there it appears that this was a kind of turban wound around a helmetlike cap. Is this word composed of Persian *gul*, rose, and *band*, band?

[387]TS Misc. Box 28, f. 217, ed. Strauss-Ashtor, *Mamluks*, III, 72–74. (By oversight, the manuscript is listed there as *Arabic* Box.) L. 5: *khātam dhahab bi-faṣṣ fayrūzaj*. L. 6: *silsila ʿaqīq bi-dhahab wa-lūlū*. The *balakhsh* was a type of ruby found in the Badhakhshan (pronounced Balakhshān, with *l* for *dh*) region near the Oxus River in Central Asia, see Yāqūt, I, 528–529; Le Strange, *Lands of the Eastern Caliphate*, p. 436; Ibn al-Zubayr, *Dhakhā'ir*, p. 261, sec. 407.

English balas is derived from balakhsh.

[388]TS 20.101, ed. Strauss-Ashtor, *Mamluks*, III, 110–112.

[389]"Mamluk" influence made itself felt long before the so-called Mamluk period. Saladin himself was described as a mamluk.

[390]See n. 387, above.

[391]Goitein, *Letters*, p. 283, l. [15]. There I spelled it cornelians in the British (and French) way.

[392]TS 10 J 10, f. 24, ll. 10–11, *Nahray* 48. These bags must have had a fixed weight or number of pieces, or some other standard description.

[393]TS 12. 279, ll. 13–14, *Nahray* 154: *ʿaqīq qaṣab ḥasan lā jalīl wa-lā dūn*. See n. 395, below.

[394]Order from Alexandria: Bodl. MS Heb. d 66 (Cat. 2878), f. 91, ll. 5–6, *Nahray* 30. Returned: TS Misc. Box 8, f. 65, sec. IV, l. 2. The major part of this account is translated in Goitein, *Letters*, pp. 286–289. This casket, *safaṭ*, must also have been a standard container.

[395]TS 12.530*v*, col. I, ll. 22–23: a piece of cloth containing fifteen *faṣṣ ʿaqīq*, found among the belongings of a dead foreigner (1105).

[396]Beryls: TS K 15, f. 77, l. 15. The account is in the atrocious hand of ʿArūs b. Joseph (see Index), who notes goods sent with his partner Ibn Sibāʿ and others. The jet, *sabaj*, neckband: TS 8 J 5, f. 18d, l. 22. Arabic *sabaj* is derived from Persian *shaba*, which designates jets and other smallish black adornments, made of a variety of materials, see Steingass, *Persian-English Dictionary*, pp. 647, 732; Dozy, *Supplément*, I, 624*a*.

Emerald: TS 28.6 A, l. 10. The emerald was described as *qaṣaba*, tube, in view of its length and because it was perforated, see Keene-Jenkins, *Djawhar*, and n. 393, above. Attention is drawn, however, to Ibn al-Zubayr, *Dhakhā'ir*, p. 20, sec. 28, who has *qaḍīb zumurrud* instead. The account TS K 15, f. 77, ll. 12–14, notes two hyacinth gemstones, four hyacinths, *yāqūt*, and a *qaṣaba zumurrud* as having a total worth of 4 dinars.

[397]TS Arabic Box 54, f. 39, ll. 51 and 56–57, *India Book* 88: *faṣṣ malīḥ wa-yakūn ghāya* (written in or around 1134).

[398]Bodl. MS Heb. c 28 (Cat. 2876), f. 34, ll. 26–28. Since *jumāna* is immediately followed by *farā'id*, singularly large pearls, the term designated perhaps a smaller species. Another passage from this letter is translated in Goitein, *Letters*, pp. 134–135.

[399]Bodl. MS Heb. b 3 (Cat. 2806), f. 20, l. 32 *verso*, l. 2, *Nahray* 7. Ar. *khalaq wa-asfar*.

[400]It was, of course, correct to use "Djawhar" as entry title for the article on jewelry in the *EI*. Since jawhar is the general term for jewel, the reader would look for this word when seeking information about the subject.

[401]Here I have not considered "costume jewelry," which is again a world by itself and needs to be studied diachronistically as a phenomenon of an international subculture.

[402]Thus the list of gems, *jawhar*, cited in n. 398 above, contains, besides emeralds and pearls, items like "two blue *wāsiṭas*." The description by color shows that precious stones are meant, but which, is not said. When, however, in May 1160, a golden *qilāda*, or necklace, consisting of eight beads and a wāsiṭa of a total "weight" of 5 5/8 dinars, is given as a collateral (see n. 366, above), this "middle piece" was probably of gold, or it would hardly have been included in the total "dinar" weight of the necklace. For *farīda* see n. 398, above, and App. D, n. 263, below.

[403]For "fittings," see n. 360, above.

[404]Cf. Higgins, *Greek and Roman Jewellery*, p. 37. Our word electricity is derived from Greek *electron*, amber. Following European usage, one expresses the idea of electricity in modern Arabic and Persian with *kah-rubā*, the Persian word for amber, literally, attractor of straws.

[405]In TS 12.12 (ca. 1020), the term *muʿanbar* is used, which is translated in App. D, Doc. X *a*, as "ambered", because I did not find any meaning in the dictionaries which makes sense, see Dozy, *Supplément*, II, 180*a*. I take it as gold with amberlike coloring.

TS 8 J 21, f. 28, is a twelfth-century business letter (without names or dates) devoted entirely to the sale of one-and-a-half units, *bayʿa*, of amber. The writer assumed that a unit was worth 1 dinar, again a case of the standardization of prices, see *Med. Soc.*, I, 222–223, 229. The recipient replied in good Arabic script: "Price obtained 52 dirhems [which corresponds indeed to about 1 1/2 dinars], less the compensation for the auctioneer, *nidā'*. With the translation of the note on the weight I am in trouble: *al-wazn aqall, 'aʿsar mithqāl wa-nisf wa-rubʿ*, "the weight is less; hardly 1 3/4 mithqāls." I do not know whether *'aʿsar* literally, with difficulty, could mean hardly, on the other hand, it is impossible to assume that the clearly written *'aʿsar* could represent the number *ʿashara*, ten, which in those days (twelfth century) would be followed by *mathāqīl*, as in classical Arabic. If my translation is correct, the standard unit of amber would have weighed approximately 1.25 mithqāls or 5.25 grams; that means, amber would have cost only slightly less than gold, which seems to be rather unlikely.

[406]See Keene-Jenkins, *Djawhar*, figs. 11*a-b*.

[407]See App. D, n. 263, below.

[408]TS 13 J 3, f. 10c, col. I, l. 18 (second half of twelfth century). Other references are given below under the ornaments mentioned.

[409]"Two rings, amber and gold, 1 dinar," TS 10 J 21, f. 5, l. 8. "Rings, one of gold, two of silver, one of amber," TS K 25, f. 269, col. I, l. 8 (early thirteenth century).

[410]App. D, Doc. III, col. I, l. 32; valued as being worth 5 dinars.

[411]Lapis lazuli, *lāzuward* (also āzuward) bracelets: ULC Or 1080 J 49, l. 11 (1146), App. D, Doc. IV; TS 12.615, l. 3 (old). Between pearls: TS 16.73, l. 9 (fragment, dated 1030/1). Alexandria, to which lapis lazuli was imported from the East, served as distribution center, from where it was sent to Cairo and to the Muslim West: ENA NS 16, f. 32, margin; TS 13 J 26, f. 8; TS 20.180, l. 10, *Nahray* 172, and elsewhere (all eleventh century). In an account in the hand of Nahray, TS J 1, f. 1, col. I, ll. 5–6, for the years 1057–1059 a consignment consisting of 715 smaller and 105 larger pieces (referred to as *ḥabba* and *ṭabarz*) and weighing 3 1/2 *mann* (approximately 7 pounds) cost 14 1/24 dinars, and, together with freight and perforation, *naqb*, 17 1/3 dinars. For another package, weighing 4 1/4 *mann*, 14 7/8 dinars were charged. In the detailed medical prescription TS 12.307*v*, a quarter mithqāl of "Armenian stone and lapis lazuli stone" was added to many other ingredients. Since "cooked chickens" were prescribed as food, the patient's stomach probably was not particularly sturdy.

[412]I provide this pronunciation for the often discussed word because its spelling throughout the Geniza is *myn'*. Long ā, however, was often pronounced with *imāla*, that is, ä or ē. In a marriage contract from September 1225, TS NS J 231, col. II, l. 2, the clerk tried indeed to indicate this pronunciation by putting the Hebrew vowel sign for ē beneath the *n*, and ending the word with a *h*. Oleg Grabar spells *mina'i*, "Les arts mineurs de l'Orient musulman à partir du milieu du XIe siècle," *Cahiers de civilization médiévale*, 11 (1968), 184; M. Rosen-Ayalon, "The Problem of the 'Baghdad School' of Miniatures and Its Connection with Persia," *Israel Oriental Studies*, 3 (1973), 165 and *passim: minayy*.

[413]See Higgins, *Greek and Roman Jewellery*, pp. 23–24, and Keene-Jenkins, *Djawhar*, *passim*.

[414]Details in "Ornaments," below. See also n. 408, above.

[415]Former Yemenite silversmiths have described their work in their books, e.g., Kafih, *Jewish Life in Sanʿā*, pp. 190–192, 233–235, figs. 12, 24–28; Joseph Ḥubārāh, *Tribulations in Yemen and in Jerusalem* (Jerusalem, 1970), pp. 345–350 and passim (in Heb.). Y. Levi Naḥum, *Mitzfunot Yehūdē Tēmān* (Tel Aviv and Jaffa, 1962), pp. 58–62, figs. 6, 12–15 (all in Heb.).

[416]Pear, *kummathrā*, see App. D, n. 283, below. Pear-pins cost between 5 and 7, through 12 and 20 dinars (5: TS 8 J 5, f. 18d, l. 21 [dated 1157]; 7: ENA 2957, f. 32; 12: TS NS Box 324, f. 144, l. 6 [early thirteenth century]; 20: App. D, Doc. III, col. I, ll. 4–5).

[417]Amber apples in chains: see TS NS J 390, l. 5, App. D, Doc. X *e*, below. As solitaires: ENA 2747, f. l*v*, ll. 4–5; TS K 15, f. 79, col. I, l. 8. See also n. 497, below.

[418]Firkovitch II, 1700, f. 25*v*, l. 14 (1156): *zawj ḥilaq thūm*, costing 3 dinars; Bodl. MS Heb. f 56 (Cat. 2821, no. 16), f. 56, l. 17 (same price, 1186); *ibid.*, f. 55, l. 16 (same year, price 4 dinars). "Golden garlics," listed between a pair of pins and a bracelet: TS 10 J 21, f. 4a, l. 6 (ca. 1110). I suspect that what Higgins, *Greek and Roman Jewellery*, p. 51, tentatively describes as testicles were called by the artisans garlics.

[419]Pomegranates, *ramāmīn*, TS NS J 296 (right side) and TS Misc. Box 28, f. 51 (left side), ll. 5, 6, 10, see *Tarbiz*, 38 (1969), 397. Illustrations for the Oriental style in *EJ*, 15, between pp. 1260 and 1261, plates 4–5; for the North African, *ibid.*, pl. 3, and, more detailed, Eudel, *Bijoux*, p. 213. *Taboïm, Tepohim*, etc. is Heb. *tappūḥīm*, apples.

[420]Details in App. D, nn. 143 and 209.

[421]ENA 3030, f. 7, l. 5. The bride had a maidservant, and her deferred marriage gift amounted to 60 dinars.

[422]TS K 15, f. 111, col. I, l. 9.

[423]ENA NS 18, f. 29, l. 9, see *Med. Soc.*, III, 396, sec. 32, where I dated it ca. 1080, because the manuscript is written in the beautiful early style of Hillel b. Eli (dated documents 1066–1108). But the date 14[??] is visible, for which the earliest possible date is 1091. The number 30 after Jewelry, *ibid.*, should be deleted. The manuscript is too fragmentary to make any guess convincing.

[424]Bodl. MS Heb. f 56 (Cat. 2821, no. 16), f. 48, l. 10. Actually the manuscript has this: "A pair of marsīn pins [[gold-plated, 1]] golden, 4 dinars." This is what happened: the clerk assumed that the pins were made of a base metal and only plated with gold. He was informed otherwise and corrected the wording—and estimate—accordingly. For *marsīn* see Dozy, *Supplément* I, 582*a*.

[425]"Myrtle" pins: ENA NS 2, f. 25, l. 14; TS Arabic Box 4, f. 4, l. 3; TS NS J 414, l. 8, twice spelled without ' (and probably pronounced *marasīn*). *"Myrtle" rings:* TS 8 J 21, f. 23, l. 11. About the love of flowers see A, 5, n. 89, above.

[426]British Library, BM Or 5561 B, f. 2*v*, l. 9 (1164). TS K 15, f. 65, col. III, l. 12 (same time approximately, see *Med. Soc.*, III, 368, sec. 29).

[427]TS Arabic Box 4, f. 5, col. I, l. 9, given on deathbed to a female relative. This shows that the term was in living use and not a learned mistranslation; *ʿālam* means "eternity" in Aramaic, not in Arabic; Greek terms came into Arabic mostly via Aramaic.

[428]Birds on woodwork: *Med. Soc.*, II, 149. Figurines: App. D, nn. 97–98, 284, below. Pendant: n. 378, above.

[429]App. D, Doc. III, col. I, l. 5, *ṭawāwīs;* 7 dinars ("without pearls"): Firkovitch II, 1700, f. 27, l. 9, see text, introduced by n. 379, above; ENA 2957, f. 32 (1217); 8 dinars: TS K 25, f. 269, col. I, l. 3 (with pearls).

[430]Ar. *māsūr ṭāwusī,* TS NS J 231, col. II, l. 4 (1225).

[431]*EI*², III, 381 (Richard Ettingausen).

[423]TS 18 J 1, f. 26, l. 15, given as collateral (1160).

[433]PER H 22, l. 14 (1137). The festive first haircut was an ancient rite of passage among the Arabs and was done on the seventh day after birth; see *EI*², I, 337, s.v. "*ʿAkīkah.*" In late Judaism it was postponed until the boy was able to memorize some of the Hebrew benedictions, normally at the age of three (see the illustration, *EJ*, X 1357). The biblical authority for this was Deuteronomy 18:4, "give God the first of the fleece of your sheep," Israel being the sheep of God, e.g., Jeremiah 23:1. But this was late cabbalistic hermeneutics, although the custom itself was widespread. (My own golden locks—*o tempi passati*—cut on such an occasion, were treasured for decades). In Geniza times the first haircut was perhaps a mere family feast.

[434]TS 13 J 6, f. 9, col. I, l. 3 (thirteenth century). The undefined "pieces" looked perhaps like those in fig. 28 of Keene-Jenkins, *Djawhar.*

[435]The word *ṭārāt*, hoops, is written above the line, so that the text actually has this: *zawj ibar ṭārāt bi-shamsāt dhahab*, "a pair of hoop pins with gold 'suns', TS 13 J 3, f. 10, item III, l. 9. See n. 489, below.

[436]Firkovitch II, 1700, f. 27, l. 16. See translation on p. 203, above. Openwork: *mukharrama*, still used in this sense, see Wehr, *Modern Written Arabic*, p. 236*b*.

[437]TS 10 J 9, f. 24*v*, l. 10, *India Book* 224. Ben Yijū must have written this (and other) legal opinions in inland Yemen, because in Egypt he would not have permitted himself to assume prerogatives reserved for religious authorities. As I write these lines I have before me just such a delightful Yemenite *shamsa* bought from a village woman when she took it right off her forehead to show it to me.

[438]TS K 15, f. 65, col. III, l. 10. Bodl. MS Heb. f 56 (Cat. 2821, no. 16), f. 53, ll. 2–3 (1184): a pair of such pins costing 4 dinars. ENA 2957, f. 32, l. 6: valued at 7 dinars. A Sulaymān finger ring worth 3 dinars in TS 12.440, l. 11 (thirteenth century).

[439]Firkovitch II, 1700, f. 25, l. 12 (1156): "a pair of golden *ṭārāt* pins adorned with pearls, 30 dinars. TS K 15, f. 65, col. I, l. 9: three pairs of silver hoop pins. Bodl. MS

Heb. f 56 (Cat. 2821, no. 16), f. 47, l. 5: *zawj ibar ṭārāt majāmiᶜ*, "with compartments" (see App. D, n. 95, probably meaning: several hoops, one within the other). The term *ibar majāmiᶜ* (without *ṭārāt* and reported as missing) in ENA 2700, f. 33b, col. I, l. 3.

[440]Spoons, *malāᶜiq*, TS 8 J 9, f. 17, l. 4, and elsewhere. Small trays: *khūnjāt* (Persian, Dozy, *Supplément*, I, 414*b*); TS 24.9, l. 13. Compartments: see preceding note. Tambourines, *dufūf*: TS K 25, f. 269, col. I, l. 3 (with pearls costing 8 dinars). Pincers, *laqā'iṭ*: Bodl. MS Heb. f 56 (Cat. 2821, no. 16), f. 47, l. 4. Arrows, *nashāshīb*, in both gold, BM Or 5561 b, f. 3, l. 10, and silver, Firkovitch II, 1700, f. 27a, l. 15, and elsewhere. Clubs (or safety pins), *dabābīs*: Bodl. MS Heb. f. 56 (Cat. 2821, no. 16), f. 47, l. 6. (The same bride had pincer pins, see above in this note.) Shepherd's staff, *ᶜakākīz*: TS 8 J 5, f. 18d, l. 21 (1157) and common.

[441]Gold tubes: App. D, Doc. III, col. I, l. 13. See *ibid*, n. 92. Hair ornaments: Keene-Jenkins, *Djawhar*, fig. 13.

[442]Cups: App. D, Doc. IV, l. 7. Dervish cups, *kashkūlayn*: ENA NS 3 vellum, f. 18 (spelled *kshkwl*); *w* might designate either a long or a short *u*). According to Steingass, Persian-English Dictionary, p. 1033*b*, the beggar's cup was usually made in the form of a boat. I believe I have seen such an ornament, but do not remember where. Since *kashkūlayn* appears together with *barbakh*, see n. 464, below, I am not entirely sure whether or not real vessels are meant.

Stirrups, *zawj rukub mukallala*, adorned with pearls, worth 24 (actually 12) dinars, first item in a long, but only partly preserved trousseau list: TS 24.8, l. 15. L. 23 expressly states that the prices noted are twice the real value. In *Med. Soc.*, III, 408, sec. 233, the reader receives the erroneous impression that the fragmentary document contained no dowry at all, while *ibid.*, p. 455 n. 85, correctly notes a long trousseau list. *Ibid.*, p. 448 no. 33, I ascribed the document to the "late 13th century." Meanwhile, I found that the two signatories of this marriage contract also signed TS 13 J 2, f. 18, in Nov. 1337. Thus it is more likely that TS 24.8 was written during the first half of the fourteenth century, and *Med. Soc.*, III, 408 and 448, have to be corrected accordingly.

[443]App. D, X *c*, l. 6. The same contrasting pair *mushabbak-sādhaj* in ENA 2747, f. l*v*, l. 6; TS 12.530*v*, col. I, l. 21 (1105).

[444]E.g., an intersected, *mufaṣṣala*, amber necklace cost 20 dinars, a *sādhaj*, immediately following, 10 dinars: TS Arabic Box 4, f. 4, ll. 1–2.

[445]The terms *ṣāmit*, solid, and *manfūkh*, hollow, are mentioned together in TS 16.123, l. 10, where they follow the words "two pairs of *dumluj* bracelets," crossed out. But this deletion must have occurred after this orderly marriage contract (signed by seven gentlemen with good handwriting) had been finalized. For any change in a legal document must be noted at its end, but no correction is made. Edited first by S. Assaf and reedited, with many emendations, in Friedman, *Marriage*, II, no. 13, where the two terms mentioned are preferably translated as here.

It should be noted that for metals the Geniza uses *ṣāmit* throughout, and for clothing, *muṣmat*, where it means solid colored, as today.

[446]Exception: see preceding note. "Puffed up" *siwār* bracelets: a pair costing 12 dinars (TS 10 J 21, f. 4a, l. 2), another 13 1/2 dinars (Firkovitch II, 1700, f. 27, l. 13). A single bracelet worth 5 dinars: TS 13 J 6, f. 9*v*, l. 4 (all eleventh or twelfth century). A *manfūkh* copper vessel: ENA 1822, f. 46, l. 24 (a part of this document is translated in App. D, Doc. VIII.)

[447]Plated, *maṭlī ([bi-]dhahab)*, mostly said of pins: TS 10 J 21, f. 5, l. 7; TS 13 J 6, f. 9*v*, l. 7; Bodl. MS Heb. f 56 (Cat. 2821, no. 16), f. 48, l. 10. Of a *ḥadīda* bracelet: TS K 15, f. 79, col. I, l. 7. Silver as main material: Firkovitch II, 1700, f. 27, l. 15.

[448]PER H 22, l. 15 (1137): *khalākhil dhahab malwiyya*. TS K 15, f. 91, col. II, l. 16: *ḥadīda dhahab malwiyya* (approximately same time). ENA 2957, f. 32 (tiny fragment, 1217): basket's border, *ḥarf al-salla*.

[449]Filigree is still called *mushabbak* by the Jewish silversmiths from Yemen. But in Eudel, *Bijoux*, p. 127, the term has a different meaning. In all the examples noted, the filigree rings were of gold. An early case: Bodl. MS Heb. d 66 (Cat. 2878), f. 121*v*, l. 5 (Dec. 1027), ed. S. Assaf, *Tarbiz*, 9 (1938), 213, where *mshwbk* is a hebraized mushabbak, not a mistake for Heb. *meshubbaḥ* (valuable; they were not Ashkenazim). A later

one: Maimonides, *Responsa*, I, 141 (referring to Alexandria, 1201), where two filigree gold rings (and one silver ring) are described as Shīrāzī (made in, or in the style of, Shiraz, Iran).

[450]For vessels with filigree, see n. 536, below.

[451]Firkovitch, II, 1700, f. 24, l. 7 (see Doc. V); ibid., f. 25*v*, l. 5: *ibid.*, f. 27*v*, l. 13. See Keene-Jenkins, *Djawhar*, referring to Rosenberg, *Geschichte der Goldschmiedekunst auf technischer Grundlage* (Frankfurt, 1918), III, 96–104, Granulation.

[452]Higgins, *Greek and Roman Jewellery*, p. 28.

[453]Silver *dabla* finger ring with niello: TS K 15, f. 65, col. I, l. 11 (ca. 1160). Silver vessels: TS K 15, f. 99, col. I, l. 5 (early twelfth century), and the silver Torah ornaments, "pomegranates" and "crowns," TS NS J 296 (1159). Cf. M. Rosen-Ayalon, "A Silver Ring from Medieval Islamic Times," *Studies in Memory of Gaston Wiet*, ed. M. Rosen-Ayalon (Jerusalem, 1977), pp. 195–201 (twelfth century, niello work, engraved with Sura 112). The strange *al-ṣarmad* on p. 196 (for *al-ṣamad*, as in the Koran and the inscription) seems to be a mishap rather than a *varium lectionis*, as I had first thought.

[454]Higgins, *Greek and Roman Jewellery, p. 28*. The description of the Byzantine battle-ax is found in Ibn al-Zubayr, *Dhakhā'ir*, p. 63, ll. 6–7. Although the editor does not vocalize the term *mjry*, comment on it, or note it in his Index, this passage was of decisive importance for me; in Hebrew letters the word is written *mgry*. Heb. *g* stands for Ar. *gh* or *j*. For years I read the word as *maghrī*, fixed with glue, which seemed to make good sense, until the Arabic spelling in *Dhakhā'ir* taught me better. My assistant, Paula Sanders, provided me with another example from Arabic literature: Maqrīzī, *Khiṭaṭ*, I, 472, ll. 11–12, describing the figure of an elephant made of "kneaded" ambėr with large gems as eyes, each with a golden nail, "the black of which was treated," *mismār dhahab mujrā sawāduhu.*

[455]1117: Bodl. MS Heb. a 3 (Cat. 2873), f. 42, l. 19: *ḥadīda mujraya* (this is Middle, not classical, Arabic) *bi-sawād.* TS 10 J 21, f. 4a, l. 3: *thalāth ḥadā'id mujraya sawād*, 27 dinars. TS K 15, f. 79, col. I, l. 7: same expression.

The latest documents noting *mujrā* are those written by Mevōrākh b. Nathan, who was active until 1180, cf. *Med. Soc.*, II, 514, sec. 22 (where 1181 is to be corrected to 1180. The editor of the document on whom I relied had not paid attention to the month of the year 1180/1, which was Tishri, Sept.-Oct. 1180).

[456]As is evident from the preceding pages, earrings were of the greatest imaginable variety of materials and shapes, but they seem not to have been divided into fixed groups, as were armbands.

[457]App. D, Doc. III, col. I, l. 2, and col. II, ll. 1–3. A similar case in Bodl. MS Heb. a 3 (Cat. 2873), f. 42 (1117), l. 18: Gold section, a filigree *ʿiṣāba*, adorned (with pearls), 50 dinars. L. 20: Clothing section, a *farajiyya* (an open robe with wide sleeves) made of Dabīqī (linen) with gold threads, a white wimple with gold threads, and an *ʿiṣāba*, 50 dinars.

[458]See nn. 55–66, above.

[459]ULC Or 1080 J 49, col. I, l. 6 (App. D, Doc. IV): *mukammala*, which could mean "perfect" in the sense of excellent, or "supplemented," one or more missing parts having been replaced.

[460]Seven pieces: see preceding note, and TS 13 J 3, f. 10c, l. 8 (App. D, Doc. X *d*). Eleven parts: TS 13 J 22, f. 12*v*, l. 11 (deathbed declaration). The tiara of Moroccan Jewish women, shown in Jean Besancenot, *Bijoux arabes et berberes du Maroc* (Casablanca, 1953), pl. X, gives some idea of this type of the Geniza *ʿiṣāba*, as visualized above. I learned this detail from Y. K. Stillman, "The Costume of the Jewish woman in Morocco," in *Studies of Jewish Folklore*, ed. Frank Talmage (Cambridge, Mass., 1980), p. 373.

[461]App. D, Doc. III, col. I, l. 2. Doc. II, col. I, l. 3, with filigree; see n. 457 above. In addition to the latter and two other cases of an ʿiṣāba costing 50 dinars mentioned before, n. 459 (Doc. IV) and n. 460 (Doc. X *d*), a fourth, not described at all, but only heading a list of jewelry, is found in ENA 2808, f. 13a, l. 5, see *Med. Soc.*, III, 405, sec. 171 (ca. 1100).

[462]See n. 441, above.

[463]Stillman, *Palestinian Costume and Jewelry*, pp. 113 (Glossary) and 129 n. 43 (Notes). The section on hair ornaments, promised on p. 92, l. 8, seems to have been omitted by a mishap. I learned about it from Dr. Stillman's typescript, which she most kindly put at my disposal long before the book was printed.

[464]ENA NS 3 vellum, f. 18, see n. 442, above: *kashkūlayn wa-barbakh*, 6 dinars. TS 20.48, l. 32: listed together with a silver tray, 2 dinars. TS Arabic Box 4, f. 4*v*, l. 2: together with housewares here, probably not an ornament.

[465]Bodl. MS Heb. f 56 (Cat. 2821, no. 16), f. 48, l. 4 (1186): *khuyūṭ ḥarīr wa-ghairih*, 6 dinars. TS 24.15, l. 5: *khuyūṭ mudhahhaba lil-rās*, 1 dinar. TS 24.9, l. 17: *zawj khuyūṭ mudhahhaba*, 20 dinars. TS 13 J 6, f. 9*v*, col. I, l. 21: *khuyūṭ ḥarīr bi-fiḍḍa qaṣab maṭliyya*, 3 (dinars). TS 12.125*v*, l. 4: *ḥawā'ij khuyūṭ* (al-Maḥalla), 2 dinars.

[466]See *Med. Soc.*, III, 71. "Open hair on her shoulders" was such a common sign of virginity that little boys were lured by goodies to look at the bride, when she was solemnly conducted to the house of the groom. This was done so that when, later in life, she was suspected of premarital sex (as happened in the funny story told in *Med. Soc.*, III, 101), the boys, meanwhile grown up, were able to testify to the contrary. The custom was ancient, Mishna Ketubbot, 2:1. In Islamic times, I assume, even little girls always kept their hair covered by a cap, but certainly without "strings." The Jewish girls in Yemen wore caps in all photographs I have seen.

[467]*Khūṣa*: nn. 420–423; *kulband*: n. 386; *shamsa*: n. 437, above.

[468]Garlic: n. 418; houseleek: n. 427; cups and stirrups: n. 442, above.

[469]TS 12.530*v*, col. I, l. 20 (list of the belongings of a dead foreigner, 1105): *ḥalqatayn filfil liṭāf dhahab* (merchandise or worn by him?).

[470]*Mukhammas* worth 8 dinars: TS 24.16, l. 8 (ca. 1125). Wuḥsha's trousseau: ENA 2727, f. 8, ll. 9–10. Earrings willed to her brother: TS Arabic Box 4, f. 5, col. I, l. 5, see the preceding note.

[471]Solomon's ring: see n. 438, above. *Khamsa*: see *EI*², IV, 1009. The pendants in Keene-Jenkins, *Djawhar*, fig. 28, have five corners, but look rather like a floral design. Moreover, they are from Spain and late.

[472]Jerusalem: App. D, Doc. I. Damascus: TS 12.474, ll. 13–14. Tyre: TS 16.198, l. 9. Damsīs: PER H 24. Al-Maḥalla: TS 12.125*v*, l. 3 (worth 10 dinars), see n. 487, below. Other early, but fragmentary lists: ENA 2779, f. 3 (Friedman, *Marriage*, no. 25); TS 16.173, l. 8 (see *Med. Soc.*, III, 404, sec. 165); ENA 4100, f. 8 B (see *ibid.*, p. 403, sec. 151). One example from the thirteenth century: TS 13 J 6, f. 9*v*, l. 5. Used also in North Africa: see Eudel, *Bijoux*, p. 230, and, in particular, p. 120 (under *Lethrāk*).

[473]"Ribs": TS 12.474 (see preceding note), l. 13: *zawj tarākī aḍlāᶜ*. Repeated without *zawj* in next line. Weight: TS NS J 208, ll. 3–4.

[474]TS 12.12, l. 3: *zawj akhrāṣ muᶜanbara mukallala*. Cf. TS Arabic Box 4, f. 4, l. 1: *zawj hilaq ᶜanbarīniyya*.

[475]TS 12.119, l. 3: *zawj shunūf*, ed. Friedman, *Marriage*, no. 38, who quotes Maimonides' commentary on Mishna Toharot 11:9, ed. J. Qāfeḥ (Jerusalem, 1968), p. 120. See Stillman, *Palestinian Costume and Jewelry*, p. 103, s.v. "*shanf*," whose description is very close to that of Maimonides. The term *qurṭ*, so common today, seems to have had the general meaning of pendant in those days, see n. 529, below.

[476]Jenkins, *Fatimid Jewelry*, fig. 9.

[477]Bodl. MS Heb. f 56 (Cat. 2821), f. 53a (1184): *ibrat dhahab lil-ridā* (cloak).

[478]App. D, Doc. II, col. I, l. 12; Doc. IV, col. I, l. 9 (both dated 1146); Doc. V, l. 16 (1156); Doc. X *d* (1159). TS 20.8A, l. 6 (1155). TS 8 J 5, f. 18d, l. 22 (1157). The price of a regular pearl choker: 2–3 dinars; with gold spools 8 dinars (Doc. V).

[479]See n. 488, below.

[480]Damascus 959: Bodl. MS Heb. d 65 (Cat. 2877), f. 30, l. 12, see Friedman, *Marriage*, no. 18, about this widely discussed document. Beads, *ḥabba*, and "head" in TS 12.474 (also Damascus). Drops, *qiṭār*, in TS NS Box 323, f. 29, l. 13, ed. Friedman, *Marriage*, no. 23. In Mosseri A-52.1, l. 5, a poor woman had a gold *mikhnaqa*, see *Med. Soc.*, III, 399, sec. 88. The magnificent Hellenistic necklace on the colored plate opposite p. 168 in Higgins, *Greek and Roman Jewellery*, might provide an idea how the

best pieces of the medieval *mikhnaqa* looked (although there the little pendants are as in Yemenite silverwork, pears, not drops).

[481]TS 8 J 4, f. 16, l. 9 (Feb. 1100), given as security. TS 10 J 9, f. 24*v*, l. 10, see n. 437, above; Dozy, *Supplément*, I, 409*b*; Eudel, *Bijoux*, pp. 102–103.

[482]*Khaṣrayn*: ENA 3030, f. 7, l. 5. A silver ring, two *khūṣas* (see nn. 420–423, above) and two *khaṣr*s were valued, altogether, at only 1/2 dinar, while in ll. 1–3, a pair of *dumluj* bracelets cost 20 dinars, a single *siwār*, 12, and a pair of pins, 3. Yemenite girl with *subḥas* on her arms: Kafih, *Jewish Life in Sanᶜa*, fig. 12. Thus these *khaṣr*s probably were worth not more than 1 or 2 dirhems.

[483]See n. 434, above.

[484]Firkovitch II, 1700, f. 25*v*, l. 11, see *Med. Soc.*, III, 405, sec. 187.

[485]TS 20.8 A, l. 5, see *Med. Soc.*, III, 407, sec. 221.

[486]TS 12.125*v*, ll. 3–8. See nn. 465, 472, above, and 487, 488, below. For 12.125, *recto*, a letter, see *Med. Soc.*, III, 483 n. 44. "District judge" there refers to "the 'Court' [meaning judge] who has his permanent seat in al-Maḥalla," and is signed by ᶜAdāya (a very rare name) b. Peraḥyā, and a Peraḥyā, son of the late ᶜAdāya, signs TS NS Box 320, f. 17, dated 1158. This, besides the two scripts and other circumstances, assigns our list to the middle of the twelfth century.

[487]Aleppo: TS 16.107, see *Med. Soc.*, III, 111–112, and 408, sec. 236. Al-Maḥalla: TS 12.125*v*, l. 5. "Our friends from Aleppo": Dropsie 382; Friedman, *Marriage*, no. 25; ENA 2779, f. 3, l. 5.

[488]See App. D, n. 142. Prices of the *lāzam* varied. ENA 2808, f. 13, l. 7: 20 dinars; App. D, Doc. X *d*, l. 11: 7 dinars; TS K 25, f. 269, col. I, l. 2: 8 dinars (see *Med. Soc.*, III, 421, sec. 373); TS 8 J 5, f. 18 d, l. 22 (1157): 9 dinars; TS 12.125*v*, l. 9: 9 dinars; TS Arabic Box 4, f. 4, l. 1: 10 dinars; TS NS Box 324, f. 144: same; App. D, Doc. V, l. 11: same; ENA 2957, f. 32: 13 dinars. We cannot know whether the Geniza people said *lāzam* or *lāzim*, but since the word is never spelled *l'zym*, the former is likely.

[489]App. D, Doc. III, col. I, l. 3. Disk: *qurṣa* (noted only here). The word is regularly used for a round piece of bread. See C, 1, n. 131, below.

[490]The widow: ULC Or 1080 J 126, *recto*, l. 12.

[491]ENA 2743, f. 2a, ll. 7–9. Spools: *bakara*, as often.

[492]Firkovitch, II, 1700, f. 25*v*, l. 18: *katifiyya dhahab ᶜadad kharaz-hā al-dhahab 12, khārij ᶜan al-ᶜanbar*.

[493]TS 18 J 1, f. 26 (1160). See also Stillman, *Palestinian Costume and Jewelry*, pp. 94–95.

[494]TS 12.763, cf. *Med. Soc.*, III, 311 and n. 177. I have trouble with the price of that *qilāda*. It is 50 or 58, probably dirhems, and not dinars. Nowhere in the list of ornaments is gold or silver mentioned.

[495]Bodl. MS Heb. e 100, f. 59 (or 57), l. 4, a letter to the judge Elijah b. Zachariah (see the Index) from "The Lady" (*al-gevīrā*, Heb.)

[496]See n. 386, above. Gold grains: *ḥubūb*, Westminster College, Frag. Cairens. 120, l. 3.

[497]TS 20.25*v*, l. 8. Ascalon: Bodl. MS Heb. e 98, f. 60, ll. 2–5, ed. Friedman, *Marriage*, no. 52.

[498]The ubiquitous *maymūn*: App. D, Doc. II, col. I, l. 13; Doc. III, col. I, l. 11; Doc. IV, col. I, l. 10; Doc. V (twice); Doc. X *d*, col. I, l. 19. For amulet ornaments with other names cf., e.g., Stillman, *Palestinian Costume and Jewelry*, pp. 96–100.

[499]TS 28.6 C, l. 14. An illustration of the Yemenite *kitāb* in Kafih, *Jewish Life in Sanᶜa*, fig. 26. A filigree (or openwork) gold *taᶜwīdh* (a common Arabic word for amulet) cost 2 dinars at the sale of an outfit, TS K 25, f. 171, col. I, l. 2. The golden "Bible," with incised ornaments, *maṣḥaf dhahab manqūsh*, (TS NS J 414, l. 9, TS 24.9, l. 16) was different, see n. 528, below. A silver maṣḥaf is noted together with silver bells, *jalājil*, both destined for children: Dropsie 402, l. 6.

[500]Thirteen amber beads: ENA 2957, f. 32 (1217). Bodl. MS Heb. f 56 (Cat. 2821), f. 56*v*, l. 3 (1186): costing 10 dinars.

[501]E.g., Stillman, *Palestinian Costume and Jewelry*, p. 99; Kafih, *Jewish Life in Sanᶜa*, fig. 12.

[502]Dozy, *Supplément*, 180*a*. In medieval Islam carriages were not common, see *EI*², I, pp. 205–206, s.v. " ʿAdjala" (M. Rodinson).

[503]Sixty amber beads: TS Misc. Box 29, f. 29, l. 33, TS 24.8, l. 16. Seventy-two: TS 16.206, l. 13.

[504]TS 8 J 29, f. 7, ll. 2–4: *zawj damālij dhahab*, 15 dinars; *zawj aswira*, 15 dinars; *afrād* (singles, not a pair) *dastaynaq*, 15 dinars; *ibid.*, l. 7: *ḥadīda dhahab*, 3 dinars. For *siwār* and *dumluj* see Fraenkel, *Aramäische Fremdwörter*, p. 56.

[505]ENA 2727, f. 8 (Wuḥsha's trousseau), *dumluj, aswira, tastaynaq* (with *t* as first letter).

[506]See App. D, n. 28.

[507]See nn. 74–78, above, and TS 8 J 29, f. 15, l. 9 where it was worth 13 1/2 dirhems, far more than the other ornaments listed in that document.

[508]Eudel, *Bijoux*, pp. 64–66. When the India trader Ben Yijū, a Tunisian, gave his daughter as first and by far most precious item of her dowry a golden "ḥadīda" and again another one in gold, (see p. 203), he might have been following the usage of his native country.

Large ḥadīdas: Dropsie 333, see *Med. Soc.*, III, 400, sec. 100. Broad *ḥ.*: TS 10 J 21, f. 4a, l. 4.

[509]Lane, *Modern Egyptians*, pp. 572–573; Stillman, *Palestinian Costume and Jewelry*, pp. 100–103.

[510]Pearls: App. D, Doc. II, col. I, l. 10. Amber: ENA 2743, f. 2a, ll. 6–7. In the provincial town al-Maḥalla we find "a single pearl siwār": TS 12.125*v*, l. 5.

[511]See the paragraph ending with n. 452, above.

[512]Filigree: App. D, Doc. III, col. I, l. 9. "Beaded": see n. 451, above.

[513]Scorpion's tail: see n. 359, basket's border, n. 448, above.

[514]I prefer *dastaynaj* to *dastīnaj*, Dozy, *Supplément*, I, 442*a*, because it is always spelled with a *y* in the Geniza. The spelling with *t* as first letter is as common in the Geniza as that with *d*, similarly that with *q* at the end is as common as that with *j*. Lapis lazuli: TS 12.125*v*, l. 7.

[515]For these details see App. D, n. 172. When in ENA 2808, f. 13 a, a pair of *damālij* was valued at 30 dinars, it is likely that there, as often, the price was doubled in honor of the bride. The bride referred to in n. 361 above was a native of Alexandria, where they would inflate the prices four times the real value, but the contract was written in Fustat by the experienced clerk Hillel b. Eli.

[516]ENA NS 2, f. 25. In ULC Or 1080 J 55*v*, l. 4, a silver dumluj is sent from Alexandria to Barqa in eastern Libya.

[517]Examples: *nb'lh*, probably pronounced *nbēla*, mentioned between *dumlujayn* and *dastaynaq* in TS 20.6 (dated 1037), still used in Djerba and other parts of Tunisia for a large bracelet with geometrical and other designs: Eudel, *Bijoux*, p. 166. *Zaylaʿ*, denoting according to one ancient author, small cowry shells (see *Tāj al- ʿArūs*, V, 369) already occurs in Damascus in 933 and 956, also in Jerusalem and another place during the tenth century; but its exact character cannot be established with certainty; see Friedman, *Marriage*, nos. 18, 40, 53, and, in particular, no. 18, where the Geniza material on zaylaʿ is summarized. For the *tannūr* cuff see App. D, n. 71.

[518]King Saul: II Samuel 1:10. The Midianite nobles: Numbers 31:50. A silver *miʿdada* weighing 12 dirhems, approximately 40 grams: Justin G. Turner (private MS), G.-TB, ll. 4–8. Two others in silver: TS K 15, f. 65, col. I, l. 11; TS K 25, f. 171, col. I, ll. 5–6. Description not preserved: TS NS J 414, l. 11. A Yemenite blacksmith showed me an iron ring worn on his right upper arm, explaining that it added to the strength of the muscles (ca. 1930). Was this more than the magic power of iron? As far as they note the word at all, our dictionaries note *miʿḍad* in the masculine.

[519]See nn. 79–82, and 265 (*kummiyya*) above.

[520]1105: TS 12.530*v*, col. I, ll. 19 and 23, *shāhid dhahab* and *shāhid lūlū diqq*. 1106: TS 28.23, l. 5, *shāhid lūlū*, 1 dinar.

[521]See nn. 382–400, above.

[522]N. 385, above.

[523]F. Cantera Burgos and J. Millás Vallicrosa, *Las Inscripciones hebraicas de España*

(Madrid. 1956), pp. 376–377, cited in Schirmann, *Hebrew Poetry* (see n. 357, above), II, facing p. 560. TS K 15, f. 111, col. I, l. 7: *khātimayn dhahab mushabbak wa-khātimayn fiḍḍa*, 2 (dinars). Quarter dinar: TS NS J 231, col. II, ll. 4–5 (Sept. 1225).

[524]TS K 25, f. 269, col. I, l. 8 (early thirteenth century). One ring of gold and one of amber, together costing 1 dinar: TS 10 J 21, f. 5, l. 8 (same period).

[525]Dozy, *Supplément*, I, 424*a*, based on modern works (and also heard by me; perhaps less frequent in Palestine and Syria; not in Barthélemy, *Dictionnaire Arabe-Français*). TS 20.8 A, l. 6 (1155). Bodl. MS Heb. f 56 (Cat. 2821), f. 48, l. 11 (1186). Widow remarrying: TS 12.440 (late twelfth or early thirteenth century, see *Med. Soc.*, III, 400, sec. 98). Niello: see n. 453, above. A "pair" of golden *dablas*: TS NS J 306, l. 6.

[526]Anklets at the head of trousseau lists: see App. D, Doc. X *e*, end; TS 24.2, l. 7, one of the richest dowries, see *Med. Soc.*, III, 131 and n. 70, and 376, sec. 27. Valued at 25 dinars: TS 16.107 (Aleppo, 1107/8); 30 dinars: App. D, Doc. X *a*; 60 dinars or more: see nn. 362, 363, above. In other old marriage contracts: Bodl. MS Heb. a 3 (Cat. 2873), f. 39, l. 7; TS 20.25*v*, l. 7 (see *Med. Soc.*, III, 412, sec. 299); TS NS Box 320, f. 34, l. 7 (Karaite).

[527]Silver anklets: JNUL Heb 4 577/4, no. 98, l. 22, ed. Friedman, *Marriage*, no. 2.

[528]TS 8 J 17, f. 20*v*. The writer, Peraḥyā, it seems, was a member of the Ben Yijū family. Bible, *maṣḥaf*, designates not a book, for which the boy was too young, but an amulet in form of a book, which should remind him that soon he would start reading. The amulet *kitāb* was different. See n. 499, above.

[529]Grooming: *tantaqish, tatasarraḥ, tuqarriṭ* (from *qurṭ*, see n. 475, above), *tatalabbas, tatamashshā*: TS 8 J 24, f. 17*v*, ll. 20–21. Prices of mirrors: App. D, Doc. II, l. 11 (8 dinars); Doc. III, ll. 15 and 29; Doc. IV, l. 11; Doc. V, col. II, l. 7, and n. 147 (5 dinars); Doc. X *b*; Doc. X *d* (see n. 531, below); Doc. X *e* (see next note).

[530]*Muḥallāh bi-fiḍḍa*: TS NS J 390, l. 22 (Doc. X *e*), ENA NS 3, f. 26, l. 16, Friedman, *Marriage*, no. 1, where the Heb. word for silver is used. TS AS Box 146, f. 13: *bi-ḥilyat fiḍḍa* (in the hand of Nathan b. Samuel, *Med. Soc.*, II, 513, sec. 18). "Inlaid" translates *muk[h]awbaja*, a word I have never seen, but which must mean fixing in by hammering, whether we derive it from Ar. *khabaja*, to beat, or (preferably) from Persian *koba*, mallet. Found in TS Arabic Box 30, f. 201, l. 4. Since the Heb. letter *k* is not marked with a dot, it usually represents an Arabic *k*, not *kh*; cf. App. D, n. 266.

[531]TS 13 J 3, f. 10, item III, col. II, l. 4 (Doc. X *d*): *mir'āh mudawwara bi-ghaṭā fiḍḍa*. Firkovitch II, 1700, f. 27, l. 17: *mughashshā*. A "covered" *mughallaf*, mirror, "with a handle," *bi-yad* (ENA 1822, f. 57, l. 24) sent in a bundle consisting mostly of textiles (from Cairo) to Alexandria, might have been of the same type. Carried by Abu 'l-Surūr b. Sighmār for Abū ʿAlī b. al-Raqqī, both Maghribis (second half of eleventh century).

[532]Bodl. MS Heb. f 56 (Cat. 2821), f. 55, l. 3 (1186, very poor). TS 24.17, l. 23 (same time; poor scholar, see *Med. Soc.*, III, 113 and n. 70). Price range less than 1/2 to 1 dinar: PER H 20, l. 10; TS K 15, f. 65, col. II, TS K 25, f. 269, col. I.

[533]Bodl. MS Heb. e 100, f. 59, l. 3 (early thirteenth century). Silver vessels were exported in large quantities from Egypt to the Maghreb and to India. An example, below, for the former: against shipments of cheese, almonds, and saffron sent by Faraḥ (Joy) b. Joseph b. Faraḥ from Sicily and Tunisia to Egypt, Judah b. Manasse is asked to buy, among other things, for 200 dinars, "silver vessels, *maṣāgha*, such as a fine jewel box, *durj*, dessert bowls, *zabādī naqliyyāt*, small plates, a small tray, a sprinkler, small figurines, *quṭayʿāt*, and try to get them for the price of silver bars or less; but if you can get pieces of delicate, fine workmanship and the silver is shining (*durriyya*, pearl-like), buy them." TS 13 J 28, f. 2, ll. 29–31 (second half of eleventh century). India trade: *India Book* 1 and *passim*. See also n. 536, end, below, for the export of gold vessels from Cairo to Damascus.

[534]TS 16.181 d: *bayt ṭarā'if*. ENA NS 3, f. 24, l. 18, Friedman, *Marriage*, no. 1: 10 dinars (also called *bayt ṭarā'if*. *Durj*: TS 12.12, l. 4 (App. D, Doc. X *a*): 20 dinars. ENA 2727, f. 8, l. 16: 14 dinars. Bodl. MS Heb. a 3 (Cat. 2873), f. 42, l. 20 (1117): 8 dinars. Business letter: TS 13 J 28, f. 2, l. 29, see preceding note.

535Firkovitch II, 1700, f. 26, l. 2 (1156): 5 dinars. App. D, Doc. III, col. I, l. 31, Doc. II, col. I, l. 16.

536Dated 995: TS 16.70, l. 7. 1050: App. D, Doc. X *b*, ll. 7–8. 1063: TS 20.187. Tooth care: ENA 2738, f. 33 b, l. 18 (see *Med. Soc.*, III, 403, sec. 153).

The evasive general term *ḥuqq*, box, is listed in App. D, Doc. V (Firkovitch II, 1700, f. 25a, col. II, l. 4) under Copper, but is described as "for the jewelry" and costing 1 dinar. The Yemenite ḥuqq of the same price, appearing in TS 16.239 (early twelfth century) might have served the same purpose. We read about a crystal ḥuqq in ENA 4020, f. 36 (1155/6), and a silver one containing pearls, and buried, in ENA 4010, f. 1*v*, l. 12 (eleventh century). But a ḥuqq could be made also of wood, Bodl. MS Heb. a 3 (Cat. 2873), f. 40, l. 18 (1128), where it contains the bride's lingerie. On the other hand, sixty golden ḥuqq of topnotch quality were ordered in Cairo by a trader sojourning in Damascus, TS 13 J 15, f. 5, l. 12, trans. Goitein, *Letters*, p. 90. It is by no means sure that they served as jewel boxes.

537See *Med. Soc.*, III, 167, top. The letter cited, TS 13 J 8, f. 23, ll. 3–6, refers to a husband who complained that his recalcitrant wife neglected dressing her hair, applying kohl, and perfuming her body.

538Little amphoras: see App. D, n. 73. Marilyn Jenkins informs me that amphora-shaped Fatimid examples exist in bronze.

539*Mukḥula*, made of crystal: App. D, Doc. II, col. I, l. 15. With golden rim: Doc. IV, col. I, l. 14. Silver cover: TS Arabic Box 30, f. 201, col. I, l. 8. Made of silver: ENA 2727, f. 5; App. D, Doc. V, l. 18; in both cases costing 2 dinars. Adorned with silver: ENA NS 3, f. 26, l. 16; TS K 25, f. 269, col. I, l. 9. Two costing 1 1/2 dinars: Bodl. MS Heb. f 56 (Cat. 2821), f. 48, l. 12. Three crystal jars, worth 3 dinars: Firkovitch II, 1700, f. 27*v*, l. 3. Inventory: Dropsie 472, *India Book* 333. The word *mukḥula* came to mean jar or flask, in general, as in TS 24.37, ll. 29–30. A letter sent from Aden to Cairo in 1137, *India Book* 91: *mukḥulat misk*, a flask with musk.

540TS J 1, f. 29, col. I, l. 22 (Doc. III): *bāliẓiyya* (spelled *b'lṭyh*); see Dozy, *Supplément*, I, 112*b*: bulīẓa. TS K 15, f. 99, col. I, l. 16 (pawnbroker's notes, eleventh century?): *blṭyh* (no ') *billawr* a large crystal "ivory" (meaning: jar).

541Kohl stick made of crystal: App. D, Doc. IV, col. I, l. 15; of silver TS 24.15 (1125), l. 1; TS 8 J 29, f. 7, l. 9 (eleventh century), four valued at 1 dinar, etc. Lane, *Modern Egyptians*, p. 37, who notes only "*mirwed*," see n. 543, below.

542ENA 2700, f. 33b, ll. 5–6, a settlement listing on the left column pieces of the wife's outfit kept by the husband, and on the right side those not kept by him; among the latter, "a kohl stick on her cheek, earrings on her ears. . . ."

543*Mirwad* of silver, worth 1 dinar: TS NS 226, col. I, l. 10 (1244); TS 20.48, ll. 10–11 (also thirteenth century). Of silver: TS 20.33, l. 6 (ca. 1130); TS 13 J 6, f. 9*v*, col. I, l. 7 (ca. 1230). They were probably less elaborate than the one shown to Eudel, *Bijoux*, p. 158.

544See App. D, nn. 97 and 98, and ENA 2700, f. 33b (see n. 542, above), col. I, l. 7.

545Sitt al-Furs: TS 10 J 28, f. 9 (early twelfth century). Sitt Baghdād: TS 13 J 2, f. 14 (1106). About such names see *Med. Soc.*, III, 316. An unspecified number of *tamāthīl* valued at 5 dinars: Firkovitch II, 1700, f. 26a, l. 5 (1156); TS 24.9, ll. 19–20 (thirteenth century).

546Firkovitch II, 1700, f. 26a, l. 1: *musht fiḍḍa*, 1 dinar; TS NS J 306, l. 8: 2 dinars ("real value"); 4 dinars: App. D, Doc. III, col. I, l. 25. Karaite widow: TS NS J 86 (fragment). Ivory, *ʿāj*, comb: ENA 1822, f. 57, l. 26 (see n. 531, above).

547Letter to Alexandria, *funduq al-Qamra*: TS 10 J 12, f. 16, l. 12. Boxwood: *Maʿālim al-Qurba*, p. 91 of English summary. P. 226: *al-baqs* (or *buqs*) *al-rūmī*. European wines in Alexandria: see C, 2, n. 42, below.

548For "combing" flax: TS NS J 184, l. 14. "A box containing utensils for silk weavings, six combs . . .": TS NS Box [not: J] 184, f. 49, l. 6.

549See Krauss, *Talmudische Archäologie*, I, 233–244, cf. *Med. Soc.*, II, 261–272. Jewish ritual prescribes benediction over the enjoyment of scents just as over the taking of food.

550*Tāj al-ʿArūs*, VI, 110, explains *dāfa* as mixing medications or perfumes by the addition of water, and quotes pre-Islamic poets for this uncommon root, including one speaking of "musk mixed, *madwūf* (which is an entirely irregular form) with ambergris." On p. 112, last two lines, *Tāj* quotes an ancient author who notes that some people pronounce *dhāfa* instead. But even *Tāj* (eighteenth century), which notes many later usages, does not have the word *madāf*. Ashtor's spelling and translation in *Prix*, p. 370 n. 9, has to be discarded in view of the overwhelming testimony of the Geniza.

Dozy, *Supplément*, I, 476*a*, quoting al-Maqqarī, a seventeenth-century author, explains the word as a crystal box with compartments used for containing different types of perfumed oils. This definition is too specific and corresponds only to the object noted in App. D, Doc. III, col. I, l. 18, see App. D, nn. 95, 96.

551 See Krauss, *Talmudische Archäologie*, I, 243 (illustrations), 697 nn. 322, 323. Cf. also the four probes (*mīl, amyāl*) noted together in n. 541, above.

552 Silver *madāfs*: Bodl. MS Heb. f 56 (Cat. 2821), f. 47, l. 10: 1 dinar; App. D, Doc. V, l. 19: 2 dinars; Firkovitch II, 1700, f. 25*v*: 3 dinars (two others of the same price in the text above); TS 24.9: 5 dinars.

553 TS K 25, f. 42*v*, l. 2. The other half of this detailed trousseau list is preserved in TS Arabic Box 4, f. 4, often cited in this chapter.

554 1105: TS 12.530*v*, col. I, ll. 17–18; TS 16.70, l. 8 (995). Another from the twelfth century: ENA NS 7, f. 20 a. In the twelfth century the ointment jar was called *mud-huna*, in the earlier documents, as in our dictionaries, *mud-hun*. Labdanum or ladanum, Ar. *lādan*, is a fragrant oil, already used in ancient Babylonia (where it bore the same name). *Ghāliya*, "the precious one" is a mixture of perfumes, such as musk, amber, and civet, which was traded as a mixture; the business letters do not specify the ingredients of which it was composed.

555 Graham Hughes, *Jewelry* (London, 1966), p. 7.

556 For the relationship between silver and gold see nn. 372–376, above. The dying man's will: TS 20.99, ll. 15, 32.

C. FOOD AND DRINK

1. Food

1 TS 20.141, ll. 30–33, ed. Mann, II, 235. Baruch b. Isaac, the renowned rabbi of Aleppo, writes thus in spring 1094 about all his peers (*ki-sh'ar benē gīlī*, Heb.).

2 Noted both in classical collections and in the works of modern scholars, see M. Rodinson, "Ghidhā'," *EI*², II, 1066. Additional examples could be provided.

3 Ibn al-Mujāwir, *Ṣifat bilād al-Yemen*, ed. O. Löfgren, *Descriptio Arabiae Meridionalis* (Leiden, 1951), p. 36, ll. 16–17. The saying cited in n. 2, above, is quoted there in ll. 15–16. I am not sure that the explanation provided in Goitein, *Studies*, p. 251, holds water.

4 See E. Brauer, *Ethnologie der Jemenitischen Juden* (Heidelberg, 1934), p. 103, who emphasizes that *ḥarīsh* (with *ḥ*) is a similar, but quickly prepared, dish common among Muslims in Yemen. About the *harīsa* "hamburger" described in Islamic literary sources, see *Med. Soc.*, I, 115, and 424 n. 99. The story told here is alluded to *ibid.*, p. 72.

5 Al-Balādhurī, *Ansāb al-Ashrāf*, ed. M. Schloessinger and M. J. Kister (Jerusalem, 1971), IV a, 82. For parallels see *ibid.*, Annotations, p. 40, in n. *t*. Now see *Biblioteca Islamica* 28d, ed. I. ʿAbbās (Wiesbaden, 1979), pp. 98–99.

A similar story, in which an old Jewish convert to Islam recites a poem of his father and most offensively criticizes the gentle Muʿāwiya for having robbed ʿAlī, the Prophet's son-in-law, of the caliphate in T. Nöldeke, *Beiträge zur Kenntniss der Poesie der alten Araber* (Hannover, 1864), pp. 68–71 (from *Kitāb al-Aghānī*).

6 TS NS J 279, ll. 8–9. Honored also during the synagogue service: *Med. Soc.*, II, 162 and n. 26.

7 TS 10 J 13, f. 24, ll. 18–21. This item should be added to similar instances on voyages on the Nile described in *Med. Soc.*, I, 298. "I had hardly washed my hands

after eating," TS Arabic Box 18 (1), f. 10, was a way of saying "I had hardly completed my meal"; washing one's hands after a meal was a religious duty, BT Berakhot 53*b*.

[8]For instance, apples, as the fruit of a tree, take precedence over strawberries, the fruit of the soil. Moreover, the former are mentioned in the Bible, the latter are not, and so on.

[9]Cf. *Med. Soc.*, III, 166.

[10]Mishna Ketubbot 5:5.

[11]Proverbs 31, 10–31.

[12]Elizabeth Warnock Fernea, *Guests of the Sheik* (New York, N.Y., 1969), p. 101. Cf. Ghazālī, *Ihyā* (see n. 15, below), II, 5, l. 7: "The Prophet never criticized food. When he liked it, he ate it. When not, he left it."

[13]See Rodinson, *EI*[2], II, 1072; *The Fihrist of al-Nadīm: A Tenth-century Survey of Muslim Culture*, trans. Bayard Dodge (New York and London, 1970), II, 742. (None of the books mentioned there seems to have survived.) I have repeatedly asked my colleagues who work on the literary Geniza texts to watch for fragments of Judeo-Arabic cookbooks; for the time being, none has come to my attention.

[14]See now Albert Dietrich, *Medicinalia Arabica* (Göttingen, 1966), pp. 135–143, where a detailed analysis of an Istanbul manuscript of Isrā'īlī's *Kitāb al-Aghdhiyā'* is provided. About the author and this book, "probably the most comprehensive book on dietetics in Arabic," see Manfred Ullmann, *Die Medizin im Islam* (Leiden, 1970), p. 200.

[15]According to Maimonides, *Guide of the Perplexed*, III, 8 (trans. S. Pines [Chicago, 1963], p. 434), talk about food should be reduced to the necessary minimum. The rich talmudic literature on eating and table manners is not uniform. Although the frugal ways of the average Palestinian Jew formed the basis of the relevant rabbinical legislation, the reports about dinners on festive occasions (more than twenty such recurrent occasions are mentioned) clearly betray the influence of Roman and Persian models, see Krauss, *Talmudische Archäologie*, III, 26–63, especially 33, 35, 59, 61. The beautiful chapter on table manners and eating in general in Ghazālī's (d. 1111) *Iḥyā' ʿulūm al-dīn*, Revivification of Islam, Part II, ch. 1, repeatedly warns against adopting Persian customs, such as eating in silence; conviviality required talking, but, of course, about pious men and the like. Rabbi Yohanan's (third century) dictum "one does not talk during a meal" is a medical advice referring to the actual eating (BT Taʿanit 5*b*). "Saying a word of Torah at the table" was almost obligatory (Mishna Avot 3:3). The Yemenites call this *qishshūr*, combining, namely, the spiritual with the material, and often honor a boy with this beautification of the meal.

[16]Lane, *Modern Egyptians*, p. 151. TS 12.215, margin *qad ʿubil badanak* (voweled thus), a notable scolding his brother for carousing with the formidable general Fakhr al- ʿArab Nāṣir al-Dawla "day and night," at a time when the Sudanese and the Banū Qurra menaced Cairo in 1066–1067. *Ibn Mujalliḥ*, TS NS J 438, l. 20, ed. Gil, *Foundations*, p. 424 (ca. 1220). See Dozy, *Supplément*, I, 205*b*, and, in particular, *Munjid*, (a nineteenth-century Arabic dictionary), s.v. "*al-mujalliḥ al-akūl*."

[17]TS 12.3, see *Med. Soc.*, I, 50–51. Egyptian conviviality, *qad ṭāb lak mukhālāṭat al-miṣriyyīn wa-akl-hum wa-sharb-hum wa-laʿb-hum*: TS 18 J 2, f. 10, ed. Goitein, *Palestinian Jewry*, p. 266, 23–24.

[18]My translation of *ghadā'* as lunch, *Med. Soc.*, I, 87 and *passim*, is only approximate, as is evident from the discussion of the term in the text above. The two terms (*ghadā'* and *ʿashā'*) occur together, for instance, in TS K 15, f. 153, l. 6 (contract of partnership).

[19]Krauss, *Talmudische Archäologie*, III, 28–30; Lane, *Modern Egyptians*, p. 145. For medieval Western Europe: "Ideally it was considered that the first and principal[?] meal of the day was to be eaten at *none* [ninth hour after sunrise, noon] after many hours of hard and conscientious work," Henisch, *Fast and Feast*, p. 20.

The Sabbath was honored by the addition of a third meal in the late afternoon. (No reference to this in the Geniza. The "third meal" became popular later, when the Kabbala endowed it with a mystic halo.)

[20]The rich Geniza material about the ghadā' of workmen is conveniently assembled in Gil, *Foundations*, p. 550, s.v.

[21]See *Med. Soc.*, I, 114–115, Rodinson, *EI*², II, 1064.

[22]*Med. Soc.*, I, 95.

[23]Even a cantor—not a very profitable profession—is lauded for the variety of food on his table (and this in the address of a letter to him!), *le-mār Shemuel ha-ḥazzān asher ʿal shulḥānō kol māzōn* (Heb.), TS 10 J 13, f. 16. The Jewish judge of Palmyra (in the Syrian desert), writing to his opposite number in Aleppo, thanks him for having treated his son with all kinds of delicacies, *we-khol mīnē ʿiddūnīm he'eraḥtoh*(!). JTS Schechter Geniza 4, ed. S. Schechter, "Genizah MS," *A. Berliner Jubilee Volume* (Frankfurt, 1903), pp. 108–112, see Shaked, *Bibliography of Geniza Documents*, p. 49, no. 9. I have prepared an annotated translation of this interesting early eleventh-century letter, to be included in *Med. Soc.*, V (in preparation).

[24]"This is the way of the Torah: eat bread and salt, drink water in small measure, sleep on the floor, live a hard life, and toil with the Torah," Mishna Avot 6:4.

[25]Abraham Maimonides, *The Highways to Perfection*, II, 254, Ar. *anwāʿ al-ṭaʿām.*

[26]TS 12.244. *Med. Soc.*, II, 129, n. 24.

[27]Cf. an Easter Sunday meal in England in 1289/90, consisting of ten types of meat, eggs, cheese, and bread, Henisch, *Fast and Feast*, p. 53.

[28]*Alf Layla*, I, 79.

[29]The feast of (seven) weeks (after Passover), celebrated on two days, on this occasion a Friday and a Saturday. Instead of the warm and heavy *harīsa* (see n. 4, above) a cold dish was preferred on a hot Saturday in June. Household accounts connected with the Purim and Passover holidays are noted in TS Arabic Box 54, f. 56.

[30]Ar. *firākh*. But in a medical prescription: *al-ghadā' farrūj maslūq*, "food—a cooked chick."

[31]See Roden, *Middle Eastern Food*, p. 182. The Italian-Spanish name *sofrito* (lightly cooked), given by the author to this dish, seems to indicate that it is no less Mediterranean than Middle Eastern. Chard: Ar. *salq* or *silq*.

[32]TS NS J 437, written, it seems, by Solomon, the son of judge Elijah, at his best. The superscription does not express a morose mood, but the belief that any planning by a human being must bow to God's decree. The numbers are written in words with the exception of the item "fat tail," where Coptic numerals are used. One-sixth (a *dānaq*, see *Med. Soc.*, I, 359, used also for dirhems) was a common unit of account.

The cubeb, *Piper cubeba* L. (the Latin and English words are derived from the Arabic), a spicy fruit growing in southeastern Asia and, in dried form, serving as stimulant and diuretic, remained popular in the Near East well into the twentieth century, see Maimonides-Meyerhof, pp. 96–97, n. 194. Since it is listed here together with garlic it was probably used as a spice. Spelled *kbb*, not *kb'bh*, as usual.

[33]TS NS J 317. A partly faulty copy of the bill on one page is corrected on the reverse side. The ratio of the copper coin *fals* fluctuated between 24 and 48 fals to the dirhem, see *EI*², II, 769 (A. L. Udovitch). Here it is 1:48, a quarter dirhem contains 12 fals, a third, 16, an eighth, 6. Those who care to check will find that the clerk's arithmetic is correct.

[34]See *Med. Soc.*, II, 94 and the Index, and n. 32, above.

[35]A type of cucumber still consumed in Egypt and Palestine. It was identified by Jewish scholars of the Middle Ages (and modern scholars) with the biblical *qishshū* (Numbers 11:5), which the Children of Israel missed so much in the Sinai Desert after the Exodus, see Maimonides-Meyerhof, pp. 171–172, no. 343. Four *qudūr faqqūsiyya* (pots with faqqūs) were sent to Alexandria together with beans and *julubbān*, grass peas, from the countryside in INA D-55, f. 3, ll. 10–11.

[36]Text *hlwn*, Ar. *hilyawn* (vernacular *halyūn*), botanical name *Asparagus officinalis* L., a type of asparagus used for medicinal rather than culinary purposes, see Maimonides-Meyerhof, p. 55, no. 111.

[37]See *Med. Soc.*, III, 167 and n. 45.

[38]BM Or 10.599*v*. Friday begins on Thursday night, when the schoolmaster did his

shopping, cf. *Med. Soc.*, II, 188.

[39]A supervisor of a group of craftsmen or merchants recognized by the government, see *Med. Soc.*, I, 84; II, 479, sec. 24. I am inclined now to explain *al-ʿarīf al-shaykh Abū sijill* as "confirmed by the government."

[40]For fulling see B, n. 200, and the relevant text, above.

[41]Ar. *qulqās*. The thick, starchy root of this plant of large leaves is still eaten in Egypt and many other countries. It played a role similar to, but not as extended as, our potato.

[42]For *fals* see n. 33, above.

[43]Text: *hāja*, literally, "what is needed," My translation is a guess based on Yemenite *ḥawā'ij* (the plural) spices for the soup, cf. E. Brauer, *Ethnologie* (see n. 4, above), p. 104. I have little doubt that in Grohmann, *Einführung*, p. 155, bottom, where ḥawā'ij is mentioned between two meats, it means the same.

[44]The fals, which totaled only 1/12 dirhem, are not included.

[45]Since the total is 12 1/2 dirhems, these must be copper pennies.

[46]The bread was prepared at home and brought to a bakery for baking. Text: *khabīz khubz*, which is a vernacular form, see Dozy, *Supplément*, I, 348*b*.

[47]Drinking water was brought from the Nile.

[48]TS Arabic Box 30, f. 95*v*.

[49]See *Med. Soc.*, II, 513, sec. 17. The document of 1102: TS 8 J 4, f. 18c, ed. *JQR*, 66 (1976), 74–79, discussed in *Med. Soc.*, III, 190–191. The old man had difficulty in organizing our account. Mostly he writes the item first and the sum paid for it after, but not infrequently he reverses this order. The manuscript is damaged, especially in the concluding section listing the sums received for covering the expenditure.

[50]Oil for lighting purposes made mostly from the seeds of turnips and rapes (*Brassica napus*, a kind of turnip). The sick stranger was a scholar who wished to read during the long winter nights. See Gil, *Foundations*, pp. 178–179 n. 6, and pp. 97–99, where the types and quantities used for the illumination of synagogues are discussed.

[51]Text: *julāb* (arabicized Persian *gul-āb*) which, like its English derivative, julep, is a sweet drink often taken together with a medicine. To be differentiated, I believe, from *mā-ward* (Ar.), which also means rose water, a perfumed fluid with which the guests were sprinkled.

[52]Ar. *zubd* (not *zubda*, as usual). So also in ENA NS 2, f. 8*v*, l. 19.

[53]This was four times the quantity bought in the preceding document, see n. 47, above. No doubt, the water was kept in a separate jar destined for the patient.

[54]TS J 1, f. 26. Expenses for laundry: B, n. 200, end.

[55]See Ashtor, *Prix*, pp. 216–218, 367.

[56]ENA 2804, f. 7, Mann, II, 106–107 published the letter, but not the postscript. This was done by M. Gil, *Cathedra*, 8 (1978), 126–127, who also provided a facsimile. "Onion" means, of course, as the only additional food to bread. Onions, *bāṣēl*, and chicken, *tarnegōl* (probably pronounced thus) rhyme in Hebrew; moreover this is an allusion to a Talmudic saying: *ekhol bāṣēl we-shēv ba-ṣēl*, "eat onions and you will sit in the shade, but don't eat geese and chickens," that is, live frugally and you will have no troubles. BT Pesaḥim 114*a*.

[57]Nn. 1 and 2, above.

[58]Nehemiah 8:10. "Eat fat dishes, drink sweet juices, for this day is holy to our Lord, do not be grieved, for the joy of the Lord is your strength." Fatty food obviously was regarded as contributing to a joyous mood. "Fat" in biblical Hebrew means "the choice part." "The fat of the wine is the grain you give to God" (Numbers 18:12).

[59]BT Pesaḥim 114*a*, cf. n. 58, and the following nn. 60–62.

[60]BT ʿEruvin 55*b*, bottom. See Krauss, *Talmudische Archäologie*, I, 116–118, and preceding note.

[61]*Med. Soc.*, I, 119.

[62]C. Wissa Wassef, *Pratiques rituelles et alimentaires des Coptes* (Cairo 1971), pp. 430 ff., s.v. "aubergines," "colocases," "concombres," "corette potagère" (= mulūkhiya), "lentiles," "pois chiches," "radis (blancs)", and so on. I am grateful to

Paula Sanders, who drew my attention to this meritorious book.

[63]Ar. *nāranj*. In the 1920s still commonly used in Palestine. By now rare also in Egypt, see *ibid.*, p. 437, s.v. "oranges amères."

[64]Bodl. MS Heb. d 66 (Cat. 2878), f. 63*v*, top.

[65]Attention is drawn to E. Ashtor's detailed lists (which, naturally, can be expanded) of the prices of wheat and bread in Fatimid and Ayyubid times, derived from both the Geniza and Islamic sources, *Prix*, pp. 124–133. When not otherwise stated, the prices of wheat refer to *irdabbs*, those of bread to pounds.

[66]The literary sources mostly provide dates and thus form a most useful complement to the quotations of prices in the Geniza.

[67]About grain speculation (and government fighting it by price fixing) we read much in Arabic sources, but next to nothing in the Geniza because Jews, as a rule, were not active in the grain trade (except, perhaps, as small retailers). For this branch of business Jews lacked the necessary connections with the government officials who exercised control over Egypt's agriculture, see *Med. Soc.*, I, 211. Besides the source quoted *ibid.*, p. 452 n. 9 (TS 18 J 1, f. 9, see N. Golb, "Legal Documents from the Cairo Genizah," *Jewish Social Studies*, 20 [1958], 24, a story of grain speculation), a small Jewish rural dealer in wheat appears in TS 10 J 12, f. 3. He was in contact with the local *wālī*, police chief, and *ʿāmil*, finance director. A letter from al-Mahdiyya, Tunisia, TS 13 J 23, f. 14, ll. 18–20, mentions a Jew who had just returned from a journey and made a 100 percent profit in a grain deal. For the manifold disasters to which medieval Egyptian agriculture was exposed see Hassanein Rabie, "Some Technical Aspects of Agriculture in Medieval Egypt," *Islamic Middle East, 700–1900*, ed. A. L. Udovitch (Princeton, 1981) pp. 75–81.

[68]TS J 6, f. 4, ll. 3–8; TS 10 J 16, f. 15, ll. 23–24, *India Book* 222: *wa-lā tufrit fi 'l-qamḥ li'annoh aṣl min al-uṣūl*. Dropsie 395*v*, *margin*, ll. 4–5: *mā lī ʿindakum waṣiyya illa 'l-qamḥ wal- ʿanab*. TS NS J 327*v*, ll. 1–2: . . . *taqaddamt shary al-qamḥ wa-ja ʿalnāh fi 'l-azyār* [. . .] *fi 'l-shams fa-ṭammin qalbak*. For "the sun" see n. 70, below.

[69]"The privilege of eating good bread was jealously guarded and zealously angled for. . . . Large households, both lay and monastic, kept careful note of the grades of bread they used," Henisch, *Fast and Feast*, p. 157. The convert from Europe, referred to in n. 26, above, tells us that he was looking for tasty bread from the time he came to the land of Ishmael, but did not find any, until the woman to whom he wrote his Hebrew letter of thanks gave him some. About types of bread mentioned in the Geniza see n. 71. Deteriorated: TS 10 J 12, f. 3, namely, the wheat of the previous harvest and therefore worth only 0.4 dinars per irdabb at wholesale. Spoiled: TS Misc. Box 28, f. 155, ll. 8–10, *Nahray* 116. In Alexandria a storeroom belonging to Nahray b. Nissīm, Fustat, was opened and it was found that the wheat was spoiled, *talaf*; the writer asks for instructions on what to do with it.

[70]Jars, Ar. *azyār*. See n. 68, above. Uppermost floor, see A, 2, n. 183, above: the owner of the middle floor receives the right of storing six irdabbs of wheat together with their containers (the jars) on the upper story (belonging to his partner), as far as it is able to bear them. Sunny side or gallery: *mashraqa*, see Dozy, *Supplément*, I, 751*b*. The wife of Judah b. Moses Ibn Sighmār (see *Med. Soc.*, I, 158–159) writes to him from Cairo while he sojourned in Alexandria: "Our mashraqa was broken into, and two of the waybas which you bought for us were taken away, for the people perish now [by hunger]. It is now common that houses are broken into." We learn here also that each wayba was stored in a separate vessel. For the sunny side see also n. 68, above.

[71]Hinz, *Islamische Masse*, p. 39. The numbers were reached by computation and are approximate and provisional. For a more detailed discussion of the irdabb, which was already in use in Egypt before its conquest by Alexander the Great, see Grohmann, *Einführung*, pp. 156–160. Distribution of wheat, *Med. Soc.*, II, 129. Wheat was distributed on special occasions to enable poor people to make better bread than that available at the bazaar.

[72]TS 10 J 6, f. 4, l. 5. The approximate date of this calligraphic, but unfinished, letter (which, therefore, lacks the address) is derived from the repeated reference to

Abu 'l-Ṭāhir (b. Maḥfūẓ), the beadle, in connection with the Rayyis, namely, Abraham Maimonides. Abu 'l-Ṭāhir is mentioned in many documents between 1183 (TS K 3, f. 11*v*) and 1223 (TS NS J 375). Abraham Maimonides, who was only eighteen years old at the death of his father Moses (1204), took over fully as Head of the Jewish community only a few years later. Since the sender of the letter writes, "You may speak to the Rayyis in my name" (*verso*, l. 4), he must have been a person of some standing. He was perhaps a physician ("Your mother should not fast—as an expression of mourning for a dead—for this will impair her health"). Cf. also TS 12.243 *Nahray* 139: after having obtained, "traveling from one village to another" (l. 6), six irdabbs for his provision, *mūna*, in the countryside, he asks Nahray to get him "five or more" in the capital.

[73]TS 10 J 31, f. 13, ll. 14–16. The writer, Simḥa (Joy) Kohen (b. Solomon), appears in many letters, and, as first of five executors for an estate worth 2,000 dinars in Alexandria, 1201 (Abraham Maimuni, *Responsa*, p. 163) and was praised by the Spanish Hebrew poet Judah al-Ḥarīzī who visited the Mediterranean port around 1218, see *ibid.*, n. 8. A *ḥiml*, or camel load of flour, weighed 135 kg, see Hinz, *Masse*, p. 13, bottom; 405 kg of flour do not correspond exactly to 700 kg of wheat. But, naturally, much was lost in the processes of sieving and grinding.

The same number of ten irdabbs in n. 93, below; a letter from autumn 1200.

[74]TS Misc. Box 28, f. 72.

[75]See n. 70, above.

[76]TS 13 J 3, f. 3, ed. Goitein, "Wills and Deathbed Declarations from the Cairo Geniza," *Sefunot*, 8 (1964), 122–123.

[77]See *Med. Soc.*, III, 192, and 467 n. 150. Mevōrākh b. Nathan: ENA NS 19, f. 31, l. 15. Alexandria: INA D-55, f. 3, l. 20; see *Med. Soc.*, III, 194 and n. 164.

[78]TS 8 J 4, f. 18*c*, see *Med. Soc.*, III, 190–191, and 466 n. 145.

[79]ULC Or 1080 J 47. The husband had died on a voyage, and his brother freed his widow from the obligation of levirate marriage (about the latter see *Med. Soc.*, III, 210 ff.).

[80]TS 8 J 10, f. 17, see *Med. Soc.*, III, 191–192.

[81]See *ibid.*, II, 129.

[82]TS AS 152, f. 360, ed. Z. Falk, *Sinai*, 43 (1979), 147. The fragmentary document is in Hebrew. In reference to bread, the writer uses the Hebrew word *liṭrīn*, for meat the Arabic *raṭl* (both of which, like the English word for liter, are derived from Greek *litra*). Although different types of pounds were in use, even within Egypt, no such difference should be assumed here. We are faced, as in countless other cases, with the enervating "predilection for variety" indulged in by the medieval scribe, see *Med. Soc.*, II, 236–237. About Rūmī garments see B, nn. 307–311, above. Since this husband "maintained" his wife, her earnings belonged to him. (She probably earned something on the side for herself.)

[83]*Med. Soc.*, II, 126–129, 442 ff.

[84]The writer was a Maghrebi, who often used Abī instead of Abū as the standard form of the word.

[85]Abū Munajjā's story is told in *Med. Soc.*, II, 356, and 604 n. 36; III, 10–11. He was probably a Karaite (like his descendants), wherefore our writer, himself a Karaite was particularly interested in him.

[86]Mosseri L-197, ed. and trans. S. D. Goitein, *JQR*, 1983 (in press).

[87]Ar. *baytī* cannot mean home baked, since it was sold in the bazaar in commercial quantities. It was a slightly cheaper variety than the *sūqī* one.

[88]He means to say that had the prices remained as they were when the guest was with them, the family would not have been able to buy bread.

[89]The writer's wife and, most probably, the addressee's daughter. As the price of the tiara (see B, nn. 458–561, above) indicates, these were poor people.

[90]TS 10 J 17, f. 10, ll. 12–32, and margin. By an oversight, Ashtor, *Prix*, attributed the story told here to the Fayyūm oasis and town south of Cairo. But as the reader sees, this is a letter sent to the Fayyūm, not from there. Ashtor tentatively puts the account in the eleventh century. But the scribal hand, I believe, belongs to the

thirteenth. The person addressed is *al-sheykh al-Thiqa al-ṭabīb*, The Trusted, the Physician, an appellation that appeared at the end of the twelfth century and is frequent in documents of the thirteenth. The title *thiqat al-dawla*, Trusted by the Government, and the like are old; but the abbreviated form is late. Female names of the type Majdiyya are also late. The only dated document bearing that name known to me is from summer 1253, written in Baalbek, Lebanon (TS Misc. Box 29, f. 6).

Staying overnight: *yabāt*, becoming *bā'it*, day-old.

[91]TS 12.305*v*, ll. 7–12.

[92]ENA 19, f. 10, "written during the in-between holidays of Sukkot of *qs'* = 161." This is an abbreviated form of the date according to the Era of Creation, omitting the first three numerals *dtt* (4000, 400, 400 = 4800 + 161 = 4961). Between the opening and concluding holidays of Sukkot, the Feast of Tabernacles, on neither of which writing is permitted, there are five other days, on which, according to the prevailing opinion, writing is allowed; see App. D, n. 201. In Alexandria, which was dependent spiritually on both Palestine and Cairo, not only the Era of Creation but also that "of the Documents" was used in abbreviated forms for dating. Occasionally (but not here) it is doubtful how the numbers should be complemented.

Maimonides is simply referred to as a Rabbenū, ENA 19, f. 10*v*, l. 13: "Kindly convey my greetings and prayers to the *majlis* [reception hall] of our Master." Found also in contemporary letters. The identity is beyond doubt because the word is followed by the name R. Anatoli, who served around 1200 as spiritual leader of the Alexandrian community.

[93]See n. 73, above.

[94]Ar. *ṣaᶜīdī*, as opposed to *rīfī*. Fustat merchants, who were active in Upper Egypt in connection with the India trade also bought their wheat from there; see TS 10 J 16, f. 15, ll. 21–25 and margin, (*India Book* 222), and nn. 112 and 114, below.

[95]The grain stores were closed for fear of pillage. The little the merchants still had was hidden in their houses.

[96]Wholesale trade in wheat was conducted in hundreds of irdabbs. Thus one irdabb cost 2.25 dinars.

[97]Since 36 dirhems of low silver content were contained in a dinar, the price of six waybas (6 × 14) or an irdabb would amount to 2 1/3 dinars, an astonishingly slight difference between the wholesale and the retail price.

[98]Thus, the number of loaves to be had for 1 dirhem was one-fourth of the average and "steady" quantity of six loaves per dirhem reported from the capital in the preceding letter, nn. 87–90, above.

[99]Here follow notes about repairs in a synagogue financed by income from a *funduq* (see Index), which shows the writer as engaged in communal affairs, and a report about the dearth and brackishness of water in Alexandria, see A, 2, n. 115, above.

[100]The high rank of the Muslim would prevent his being robbed; moreover, the toll actually paid by him at the entrance to the city would be less than that imposed on the average traveler. In the later decades of the twelfth century (Ayyubid times) we often find Muslims transporting goods to Alexandrian Jews.

[101]Ar. *al-ᶜayn lahum*, which should not be translated here as "the evil eye."

[102]ENA NS 19, f. 10, ll. 10–20; *verso*, ll. 5–8.

[103]TS G 1, f. 1. (G is the manuscript mark for responsa, juris consults' answers to legal questions.)

[104]ENA NS 2, f. 40*v*, l. 17. Moses ha-Kohen (b. Ḥalfōn), who is addressed here with his five honorific titles. See *Med. Soc.*, II, 162.

[105]TS NS J 243, *India Book* 301. The supplier, Moses ha-Levi b. Nethanel "the sixth," is also well known from that period. I do not know why Ashtor, *Prix*, p. 127, put this document into the thirteenth century.

[106]TS 13 J 16, f. 19, l. 28, *Nahray* 224.

[107]TS 8 J 20, f. 2, margin. Not contained in Murad Michael's collection of Geniza texts referring to Nahray b. Nissīm, but he is mentioned in the letter.

[108]In view of Ashtor, *Prix*, p. 129, where beans appear to have been indefinitely less expensive than wheat, I explain *mithluh* as meaning "are equally high in price" (and

not that a wayba of beans cost 1 3/4 dinars).

[109]TS 10 J 19, f. 10, ll. 14–17.

[110]JNUL 10, ll. 10–11, and margin, Rosetta-*Rashīd*. The writer asks to send the wheat "with camels," meaning *not* by boat on the Nile (so that the grain should not be spoiled by water), although boat transport was probably cheaper.

[111]*Med. Soc.*, II, 438–440, to which ENA NS 22, f. 26 (a list of thirty-nine recipients of 1/2, 3/4, 1, 1 1/2 dirhems, respectively) and ENA 4010, f. 25*v* (in Arabic characters) may be added.

[112]TS Arabic Box 54, f. 93, l. 18, *India Book* 375. The recipient, Elazar b. Ismāᶜīl (Samuel), signed TS 13 J 1, f. 8, in 1033/4. Other personalities from this period, in particular, Abū Naṣr al-Tustarī, are mentioned. For *tillīs* see Hinz, *Masse*, pp. 51–52. The same price also in the fragmentary TS 6 J 3, f. 18, margin: "I was told that two waybas of wheat cost 1 dinar (= 1 irdabb, 3 dinars), and that our children are dying of hunger."

[113]Quoted by Ashtor, *Prix*, p. 125 according to C. H. Becker, *Beiträge zur Geschichte Ägyptens unter dem Islam* (Strassburg, 1902), I, 49.

[114]See n. 94, above.

[115]TS 13 J 18, f. 27, top, end. The Tunisian term *al-balad rākhī*, see n. 117, is used. Abū ᶜAlī b. ᶜImrān addresses his nephew Abū Mūsā Hārūn b. al-Muᶜallim Yaᶜqūb. The letter is analyzed in *Med. Soc.*, III, 34, and n. 2. Another letter by the same to the same in TS 8 J 17, f. 22. I ascribe them to the early eleventh century because of their script (the high and straight *l*s and the *b*s and *k*s with "crowns": very regular; in the style of the chancelleries of the Baghdad yeshivas.

[116]Mosseri L-52*v*, ll. 1–2, a letter addressed to Joseph Ibn ᶜAwkal, ed. S. D. Goitein, *Tarbiz*, 37 (1968), 50 (written in the 1020s or early 1030s). See *Med. Soc.*, I, 371, sec. 7. Ashtor, *Prix*, p. 125, first item, refers to the same text, included in my article, "The Exchange Rate of Gold and Silver Money . . . ," in *JESHO*, 8 (1965), 1–46, which was a blueprint for App. D in *Med. Soc.*, I.

[117]TS 13 J 15, f. 9, l. 14: "Balad Ifrīqiya balad *rākhī ᶜaẓīm*," trans. Goitein, *Letters*, p. 321. According to Hinz, *Masse*, p. 52, the Qayrawānesē thumn(a) contained 6.318 liters; thus 25 thumna would be approximately equivalent to 158 liters. The irdabb, we remember, contained about 90 liters.

I noted quite a number of prices of wheat from eleventh-century Tunisia. But in view of the many unsolved problems of measurements and weights of the period (see Idris, *Zirides*, pp. 647–651 and *passim*), I must leave this to specialists.

[118]DK XV*v*, l. 10. A detailed letter by Isḥāq b. Dā'ūd b. Sighmār, Fustat, to Makhlūf b. ᶜAzarya Bū Majjāna, temporarily in Jerusalem, with a note about military and political events at the time of the Sultan (Muᶜizz b. Bādis), and of Ben Hammād (1028–1054). The writer uses Maghrib, not Ifrīqiya. But the references to Ben Ḥammād ("with whom the Jews had it good") and "the Sultan who was not successful" (in Hebrew) in Msila, leave no doubt about the country meant (*ibid.*, ll. 12–15).

[119]Letter to Elijah: INA D-55, f. 3, ll. 12–14. An early period of judge Elijah's activities, when he occupied in Alexandria a position inherited from his father, is presupposed here, see *Med. Soc.*, II, 515, sec. 29. Therefore, the sum referred to cannot be "cut-up" dirhems, which appear in the Geniza only from the time of Sultan al-Kāmil (1218), see *ibid.*, I, 385.

The fugitive son: TS 10 J 14, f. 12, ll. 18–20. The full address is preserved in TS 10 J 13, f. 10: "To Fustat . . . to be delivered to the Rayyis (= physician) Abu 'l-Faraj, son of the Jewish judge of Alexandria." To the story told in *Med. Soc.*, II, 379, and the sources listed, *ibid.*, p. 610 n. 27, should be added. TS 12.415, a letter of Manṣūr b. Sālim to his fugitive son.

[120]Silk weaver in Aswān; TS 8 J 26, f. 18*v*, ll. 1–4. See *Med. Soc.*, II, 383 and n. 11. For the difference in price between good and mediocre wheat see n. 90, above.

[121]TS NS J 327*v*, l. 10, of lower fragment, and l. 1 of upper. The name of the sender of this tattered letter is complete in ENA 2805, f. 11 A: "Your disciple [rarely used in this correspondence] Hilāl b. Nissīm." Neither item is included in Murad Michael's collection of Nahray's correspondence. For putting wheat aside see n. 68, end, above.

[122]ULC Or 1080 J 71, ll. 4, 13–15, 16; *verso*, ll. 7–9 (trans. by me for publication). Lane-Poole, *History of Egypt*, p. 146: "A cake of bread was sold for 15 *D*., though an ardebb of corn could be bought for 100 *D*." This formulation seems to be incorrect. The first D is dirhem and the second dinār, and the relationship between bread and wheat was as expected. The "normal" price for an irdabb of wheat was 1 dinar, and that for a loaf of bread 1/6 dinar. Thus the prices here were 100 or 90 times higher, respectively. In our letter the price was 25–27 times higher than normal.

[123]ENA 2805, f. 9, ll. 20–22. Joseph b. Shemarya, the *dayyān* of Barqa, writes "to his brother" Nahray b. Nissīm. A passage from another letter of the same to the same, ENA 2805, f. 13, written on the very day when he set out for Barqa, is translated in *Med. Soc.*, II, 274, bottom. Since we read in the latter, ll. 16–22, that Nahray was about to leave for Jerusalem and also, *ibid.*, l. 13, that he is congratulated on having attained prosperity and high rank, we must be here in the early 1060s, that is, before 1071, when Jerusalem was taken by the Seljuks, but also shortly before 1065, when the years of famine started in Egypt.

[124]TS 10 J 15, f. 26, ll. 7–15. The cantor Isaac b. Ṣedāqā, who had been captured (by the Normans on the isle of Jerba in 1135, see *EI*², II, 459*a*, s.v. "Djarba"), sold to Egypt, and after having been ransomed there, returned to his native town of Tripoli, Libya, writes to his benefactor in Cairo. See *Med. Soc.*, III, 150 and n. 33. Tripoli was ruled at that time by two Bedouin factions, which were mostly at loggerheads with each other.

[125]TS 12.248, *Nahray* 75.

[126]The *qafīz* measure is regularly mentioned with reference to Tunisia, but sometimes also for Alexandria, which was partly dependent on the Maghreb for its supplies. The Qayrawān qafīz comprised 201,877 liters according to Hinz, *Masse*, p. 50 (which is based on Muqaddasi, p. 240, see, however, Grohmann, *Einführung*, p. 161).

[127]TS AS 147, f. 4.

[128]ENA NS 19, f. 31, l. 11. Cf. *Med. Soc.*, III, 467 n. 156, where 131 is a misprint for 31. The letter is addressed to the notable Thiqat al-Mulk, a government official, with whom Mevōrākh's family had close ties.

[129]TS 13 J 25, f. 2, ll. 14–16, 21 (a widow with children writes to her husband who had fled to Asyūṭ and left the family without support): "I had to leave a pawn with the *daqqāq* to get from him a bottle with flour—and this after the children had fasted three days and three nights."

[130]See nn. 73 and 127, above.

[131]Dropsie 472, *India Book* 333. Notes by the India trader Abraham Ben Yijū, after returning, with his Indian servant Bama, to Fustat. In addition to *khubz*, bread, he uses *raghīf*, literally, kneaded into a mass, and *qurṣ*, lit., a disk (which is the regular word for loaf in Yemen, where Ben Yijū sojourned for some years upon his return from India).

[132]TS 24.78, ll. 24–28, ed. S. D. Goitein, "The Tribulations of an Overseer of the Sultan's Ships," *H.A.R. Gibb Jubilee Volume*, ed. G. Makdisi (Leiden, 1965), pp. 274 and 279. For rice, see *Med. Soc.*, I, 119. It seems to have been a delicacy rather than regular food. A grocer orders for his store one hundred pounds of raisins, but only a wayba (ca. twenty-three pounds) of rice, TS 8 J 16, f. 19. Even for a Nagid rice was bought from a grocer in small quantities as were salt or apples, see n. 139, below.

[133]A similar observation was communicated to me by Professor A. L. Udovitch, derived from his fieldwork among the Jews of the island of Jerba (Djerba), Tunisia.

[134]Demetrios J. Constantelos, *Byzantine Philanthropy and Social Welfare* (New Brunswick, N.J. 1968), p. 128.

[135]*Med. Soc.*, II, 126.

[136]Roden, *Middle Eastern Food*, p. 284. When I arrived in Palestine in 1923, food was scarce and little variegated, but eggplant was offered—so the saying went—in seventy different dishes. When, two years later, I passed through Vienna, and was entertained by relatives in a plush restaurant, the first specialty with which I was expected to be surprised was—eggplant.

[137]Spelled *bwryq*, to be pronounced *burayq*, or perhaps, *burrayq*. Dozy, *Supplément*, I, 74*a*, does not vocalize the word, which is explained as *ḥabb qurṭum*, safflower seed. Safflower is used for coloring and flavoring dishes or soups, while the price indicated here—half a dirhem, for which one could have three to four pounds of bread—points to a more substantial vegetable.

[138]TS 13 J 25, f. 2, ll. 11–13. The letter was written by the recipient's son, but the speaker in most of it was his wife. Cf. n. 129, above. "Man, return to God," l. 9, that is, "you are a sinner," can be said by a wife, never by a son.

[139]TS 10 J 8, f. 7, l. 7. Together with rice, apples, chickens, salt, sesame oil, and other, partly effaced items. Early thirteenth century.

[140]Roden, *Middle Eastern Food*, p. 112, describes how the fellāḥīn women carry the *mulūkhiya* soup on their heads to the fields for the men to eat at noon. At dusk it is eaten again at home. Maimonides-Meyerhof, p. 113 n. 1, notes that the manuscript of the *Asmā al-ʿUqqār* (The Names of the Drogues) has only *al-baqla* the vegetable, and he, the editor, added *al-yahūdiyya*, the term still known in Egypt. It is possible, however, that the mulūkhiya, because of its popularity, was called "the vegetable" par excellence.

[141]N. 41, above. TS 16.232, l. 17, in a calligraphic but only partly preserved report about the recipient's sheep, colocasia, and *zarʿ*, grains.

[142]Chickpeas: see n. 48 (household account no. 4), above. Sesame-seed meal paste, *ṭaḥīna*, is noted in this account, TS NS Box 320, f. 19, of which only the lower part is preserved:

sumac	3/8 (dirhem)
ṭaḥīna	1/4
olive and sesame oil	3/4
salt	1/4
sesame oil	1 5/8
wood for fuel	1/4

Sumac is a brownish-red small fruit, which served in medicine as an astringent, and in the kitchen as a kind of gelatin and coloring. In Geniza times it was imported to Egypt from northern Syria.

In this, as in the first household account translated above, sesame oil appears twice. For each purpose for which the housewife needed it, she got the proper measure.

[143]Wissa Wassef, *Pratiques . . . alimentaires des Coptes* (see n. 62, above), pp. 402–407.

[144]Truffles, *kam'a*: TS 12.252, ll. 26–29. Jacob *he-ḥāvēr* (member of the Yeshiva-Academy), son of Joseph, President of the High Court, is addressed, see Mann, I, 37, who surmises that he moved from Fustat to Aleppo in the wake of al-Ḥākim's persecution of non-Muslims. The writer: *Misgavya* b. Moses. This is a pseudo-biblical name ("my stronghold is God," cf. Psalm 9:10), that is, formed like biblical names, but not found in the Bible, a rare case. Perhaps he was called Miskawayh-Mushkōe, like the famous Muslim writer (d. 1030), who was his contemporary. Misgavya is written with *samekh*, not *sīn*, which would have been proper.

[145]From al-Mahdiyya: TS 10 J 14, f. 20*v*, l. 4. The island: TS 13 J 26, f. 10. See Goitein, *Letters*, pp. 323–372, and, in particular, p. 325 n. 7. The seeds of this plant, becoming nettles after springtime, were used for medical purposes well into the twelfth century, Maimonides-Meyerhof, p. 11, no. 14.

[146]There was (and is) no absolute borderline between the medicinal and culinary use of plants. We remember that Isaac Isrā'īlī called his great pharmacopoeia "Book of Foodstuffs," n. 14, above, while Maimonides' "Book of Drugs" mentions many plants used as vegetables.

[147]Maqrīzī, *Khiṭaṭ*, I, 104–105. Apples and dates (*ruṭab*), 1,200 dinars; *dhabā'iḥ al-abqār* (beef), 1,000; same for cheese; *zarībat al-dhabīḥa*, the slaughtering pen (mutton), 700 dinars.

[148]*Med. Soc.*, I, 427 n. 40. Lane, *Modern Egyptians*, 480 and 485, has *nuql*, found also in the Geniza.

[149]When it is said of a man that he was seen in Cairo "carrying delicious things (*ḥamūdōt*, Heb.), two baskets with apricots," only fresh fruit can have been meant, Bodl. MS Heb. f 102, f. 52, l. 7, and *verso*, l. 1.

[150]See *Med. Soc.*, I, 424 n. 106. More could be added.

[151]*Qaṭā'ifī*, TS NS J 179, l. 6. See also S. D. Goitein, *JQR*, 49 (1958), 37 n. 5. Almond chewing gum: *ṣamgh lawz*, Gottheil-Worrell, XXXVII, p. 122, l. 38.

[152]ENA 1822, f. 92, dated 8th of II Jumādā (a Muslim month):

This is what Abū Saʿd bought in the store:

Rock sugar, *sukkar nabāt*	37 1/2 pounds	3 17/24 dinars
Hazelnuts	100 pounds	1 3/4 dinars
Sugar	340 pounds	15 1/4 dinars
Pomegranate seeds, *ḥabb rummān*	17 pounds	7/12 dinars
Sumac	20 pounds	16 [qirāṭs]
Raisins	20 pounds	13 [qirāṭs]
Pistachios	no weight	1/2 dinar
Raisins	[. . . . . .]	6 dirhems

The equipment of the store is his.

Also the price for banana leaves 1/4 dinar

Comments: Abū Saʿd admitted a partner to his store, bought from him the items listed here, while other items brought in by the partner and those possessed by Abū Saʿd before completed the stock of the partnership. This Abū Saʿd might well be identical with Abū Saʿd Khalaf b. Salāma (or Ḥalfōn b. Solomon, as he was called in Hebrew), mentioned in n. 132, above. From a huge document from March 1066, TS 20.83, we learn that he and a brother had been working in the caliphal mint. He came from a family of *sukkarīs*, or sugar merchants, see *Med. Soc.*, III, 14 and n. 86, and this store was probably one of several possessed by him, where the partner did the actual work.

For sumac see n. 143 above; of the price only *sṭ* is preserved. This writer spells the numbers 13–19 as they are pronounced today, namely with *ṭ* instead of *t*; thus siṭṭ[aʿshar is to be complemented, probably with qirāṭs, namely 16, which equals two-thirds of a dinar. When sent from Suwaydiyya in northern Syria, TS Arabic Box 18 (1), f. 164, ll. 8–10, one hundred pounds cost 5 dinars, thus twenty pounds would have been worth 1 dinar but this sumac was perhaps not fresh and of lower quality, see *Med. Soc.*, I, 213 and n. 16.

[153]TS 16.200, ed. D. Z. Baneth, *Asher Gulak and Samuel Klein Memorial Volume* (Jerusalem, 1942), pp. 50–56. The letter deals with philosophy. But when Maimonides and his descendants, who were physicians like him, were addressed in communal, religious, or philosophical matters, the writers could not often refrain themselves from squeezing in a request for medical advice.

[154]Black raisins for eating: BM Or 5566 B, f. 26, ll. 6–8, *Nahray* 141. "Making" raisins into beverages: TS 10 J 10, f. 29, ll. 10–11, *Nahray* 193.

[155]Besides the common words for dates, *tamr, balaḥ*, and *ruṭab*, literally, fresh dates, we find *busr*, unripe dates, sent by one grocer to another: Bodl. MS Heb. f 102, f. 29, l. 2; *ʿajwa*, pressed dates: TS Misc. Box 8, f. 2 (see Dozy, *Supplément*, I, 99*b*), and: *ibid.*, *tamr musqar ʿamal(!) al-Fayyūm*, "rich in sweet [literally, heated by the sun] honey, produced in the Fayyūm." Further details in *Med. Soc.*, I, 120–121. Transport from the country had its risks: "Send me two pots with *balaḥ*, but such that keep well, *yakūn fīhim muska*, until they arrive, for those that I received were spoiled and had become vinegar, *khall*, and I had to throw them away": TS AS 149, f. 10*v*, ll. 5–7.

[156]See n. 153, above. Dates from al-Fayyūm: TS 12.340, l. 8.

[157]See *EI*, IV, 550–551, s.v. "Sukkar" (J. Ruska; the article was written fifty years ago, but is still instructive); Andrew M. Watson, "A Medieval Green Revolution: New Crops and Farming Techniques in the Early Islamic World," in *The Islamic Middle East, 700–900*, ed. A. L. Udovitch (Princeton, 1981), pp. 29–58, esp. p. 49 n. 3; *Med. Soc.*, I, 125–126.

[158]See the quotation from the Book of Nehemiah in n. 58, above. Palestine was praised as the land of milk and honey, the latter word being understood in the wider sense of sweet foodstuff, including date honey, see Krauss, *Talmudische Archäologie*, II, 247, and 819 n. 785. The exile in Babylonia was regarded as a boon because of the abundance of date palms in that country, for sweetness is conducive to Torah, that is, study.

[159]For rock sugar, *nabāt* (the word is still in common use), see n. 152, above; for *qand* (from which our candy), and *qaṭāra*, sugar molasses, see *Med. Soc.*, I, 126 and nn. 78–83, and 463 n. 134. The documents quoted in the notes are from the eleventh through the thirteenth centuries. Molasses was not only traded in large quantities for the food industry, but bought from the grocer for the household, for instance, half a pound, Mosseri L-127.2, *India Book* 344*a*. The expression "*Miṣrī* sugar" (sent from Alexandria to Tunisia), in a business letter addressed to Joseph Ibn ʿAwkal around 1030, should be translated "Fustat sugar," for sugar was produced by Jews also in provincial towns such as al-Maḥalla, Minyat Ziftā, and Minyat Ashnā: TS 13 J 29, f. 2, l. 12, ed. S. D. Goitein, *Tarbiz*, 36 (1967), 384.

[160]See *Med. Soc.*, I, 125, and 429 nn. 70–77 (in n. 73, replace f. 29 with f. 19). Prices fluctuated between 2 5/6 dinars, see *ibid.*, p. 219, and 7 dinars: ENA 2805, f. 4 B, l. 12. "Brightens the eyes": cf. I Samuel 14:27–29.

[161]For oxymel, Ar. *sakanjabīn*, see *Med. Soc.*, II, 267, 268, 271.

[162]ENA 2808, f. 16a, ll. 10–13. The writer did not mention the melted butter, the *samna*, which was available everywhere. Very white: *ḥuwwārā*, see Frankel, *Aramäische Fremdwörter*, p. 32. In TS NS J 446, l. 15, a fragmented order, *daqq abyaḍ*, is used instead.

[163]*Med. Soc.*, II, 261–272, esp. pp. 269 ff. Orders: TS 8 J 25, f. 21, addressed to Abū Saʿīd al- ʿAfṣī, the gallnut dealer (family name), containing over thirty orders in small quantities. Inventory: ENA 4020, f. 60, of the *dayyān*, or Jewish judge, of Sanbuṭyā-Sumbāṭ, who earned most of his livelihood as a "perfumer" (autumn 1150).

[164]For almond chewing gum, see n. 151, above. Three ounces of pistachio gum, *ʿilk*, sent as a gift from Aden to India: TS 12.320*v*, l. 12 (*India Book* 51); half a pound: TS 10 J 12, f. 5, l. 10 (*ibid.* 53). See Maimonides-Meyerhof, no. 301.

[165]See *Med. Soc.*, II, 224 (bottom) 228. According to the biblical account, man was originally allowed to eat only plants and fruits. Permission to eat meat was granted after Noah had sacrificed some of the animals carried with him in the Ark (Genesis 1:29; 9:3). The eminent Bible scholar, Jehezkel Kaufmann, said that the sages of the Talmud had made the consumption of meat so difficult that if they had been given more time they would have ended up by making vegetarianism obligatory. (Kaufmann himself was a vegetarian.)

Just as the animal offered to God in the Temple had to be without blemish, thus meat consumed by man with God's blessing had to be "kosher," which means the same. The many rules defining this state of faultlessness gave rise to different interpretations, with the result that carcasses declared by one expert as "kosher" were prohibited for consumption by others. A long letter by the Rabbanites of Ramle, Palestine, to their brethren in Fustat exemplifies the troubles caused by such a situation, TS 20.19, ll. 30–49, ed. in Goitein, *Palestinian Jewry*, pp. 129–143. Other examples could be provided.

Karaites refrained from eating beef or mutton in Jerusalem, because no animal offerings could be made there after the Temple was destroyed, ULC Add 3430 (1028, a marriage contract, see App. D., Doc. I). An overscrupulous Karaite did not eat even fowl in the Holy City, ENA 3616, f. 9.

[166]When a husband allots his wife a pound of meat per week (see n. 82, above), and when even a communal slaughterer confines himself to this quantity (*Med. Soc.*, II, 227, bottom), clearly it was destined for two Sabbath meals of a small family.

[167]See Moshe Gil, who combined TS 13 J 13, f. 13, and TS 13 J 27, f. 5, in *Studies in [the] Geniza and Sepharadi Heritage, 1981*, p. 73, l. 14, where the old community official in charge of the slaughtering complains about the exacting sleepless Thursday nights (middle of eleventh century).

[168]TS 13 J 22, f. 14, ll. 16–19, *Nahray* 149. It was a time of anarchy and privation, when the al-Maḥalla community was unable to provide even bread for the poor, *ibid.*, l. 12.

[169]ULC Or 1080 J 82, l. 4, an account by Solomon b. ʿAzzūn for Faraḥ b. ʿAṭiyya lists among other items a *kharūf* costing 1 1/4 dinars. The account mentions Ẓāhiriyya dirhems and Nizāriyya dinars. Price of a pound of meat: see *Med. Soc.*, II, 227, bottom, and household account no. 2, n. 33, above. The probably Christian list of victuals from the ninth century discussed in C, 2, n. 33, below, notes three portions of meat each costing 1 dirhem, and one 20 1/3 dirhems. The latter was probably a lamb and the three others meats bought from the butcher, as here.

[170]Goitein, *Jemenica*, p. 5, no. 18. A devastating judgment about beef, *ibid.*, p. 140, no. 1044. See Mez, *Renaissance*, p. 430 (end of chap. 24).

[171]When a dish of goat's meat was praised at a dinner in *Alf layla*, I, 77, l. 12, "as good as in Yemen," probably the meat of a gelded buck was intended, still regarded as a delicacy in that country, see Goitein, *Jemenica*, p. 91, no. 608. (Jews were not permitted to eat such meat because of the blemish of castration, see n. 165, above.) Praise of Egyptian beef: Ibn Ẓahīra, *Faḍā'il*, pp. 134–135.

[172]TS NS J 458.

[173]"Red meat": Dozy, *Supplément*, I, 332*a*. For the *harīsa*, see n. 4, above.

[174]Infant: the weaned baby receives (the broth) of two chickens daily, see *Med. Soc.*, III, 194. Cooked, *maslūq*, chicken for the ill: TS 10 J 7, f. 27*v*, l. 11. A schoolmaster asks for help with the payment of the poll tax, for all his income from school fees was spent on chicken and medicine: Dropsie 410. Collection in a synagogue on Thursday morning to provide two chickens and bread for an old sick poor: TS 6 J 8, f. 4. See household account no. e, p. 232 above. In *Alf layla*, I, 81, l. 2, a soup concocted from four chickens was prepared for a man whose hand was cut off.

[175]See household account no. a, p. 230 and n. 31, above.

[176]Coops: *Med. Soc.*, I. 125 and n. 69. Pigeons: *al-ṭayr al-yamām*, TS AS 149, f. 10*v*, l. 4. Carrier pigeons: *Med. Soc.*, II, 85 and n. 88 (*ḥamām*). Pigeon racing, like all gambling, is prohibited by strict Islamic law. In Bukhara, I was told, even in modern times Jews risked grave danger because of indulging in this sport. About private messages sent with pigeons, see *Med. Soc.*, I, 291. For pigeons in Islam, see *EI*², III, 108–110 (F. Vire). The phrase, "I am like a pigeon whose wings have been clipped," TS 12.13, l. 1, is probably only a figure of speech and does not reflect any such practice.

[177]The omelette: TS 13 J 21, f. 29, ll. 20–22 and margin. Abū Zikrī Kohen: ENA 3971, f. 5. (In the early 1930s, I remember, one got a hundred ["second class"] eggs in the bazaar of Jerusalem for one shilling.) In this and similar cases, Abū Zikrī wrote: "Owed to . . . for . . . " whereas most of the eighty or so slips from his hand are orders: "Deliver to bearer. . . . " Therefore, I assume that in the former cases he did household shopping in person.

[178]Fish—a delight: see p. 234 and n. 64, revenue from—; p. 246 and n. 147, above.

[179]*Med. Soc.*, I, 430 n. 86.

[180]Text: *baṭārikh*. About the interesting history of this Greek-Coptic and then almost general Mediterranean word, see Dozy, *Supplément*, I, 94*a*.

[181]ENA NS 18, f. 6, ll. 6–11: The writer, calling himself Aaron, the ḥāvēr, son of Rabbi Ḥiyyā of blessed memory, was certainly not a "member," namely of the Jerusalem yeshiva (which, at that time, had its seat in Cairo), but the title ḥāvēr was merely honorific. Despite some mispellings his Hebrew was good enough for a fishmonger who had learned aspirations.

[182]See *Med. Soc.*, I, 46 (import from Sicily, Crete, and Rūm in general); p. 126 (local production and import from Palestine); p. 367, sec. 27 (partnership in cheesemaking); p. 428 n. 66 (types of local cheese); Goitein, *Letters*, p. 196 (sent to India). See Ashtor, *Prix*, Index, s.v. "fromage."

[183]The Jarwī pound is slightly heavier than the regular pound. At different times and places the weight differed.

[184]TS AS 147, f. 24. The first signatory is Zadok, son of the late physician, Samuel, probably of the Ibn al- ʿAmmānī family of Alexandria. Commuting: *mutaraddidīn*.

The molds were of many different sizes and weights. Egyptian countryside: *aryāf diyār miṣr.*

[185]TS 12.80, *India Book* 273 (Jan.–Feb. 1140). Some of the seven other letters of Abū ʿAlī to his brother also mention the cheese business.

[186]TS NS Box 320, f. 55, ll. 6–9, right half of a document dated 1156/7, which confirmed that a sale of eight molds was done in conformity with the ritual requirements.

[187]See n. 182, above.

[188]A. Harkavy, *Responsen der Geonim* (Berlin, 1887), p. 3, sec. 5. Each mold bore the stamp, *Berākhā*, Blessing, not a name, as the learned editor tentatively suggested, for a stamp was actually found which contained both this word (meaning the cheese is all right, you may say the blessing and eat it), and the name of the producer or trader, see M. Narkiss, "A Jewish Bread or Cheese Stamp of the Fatimid Period," *Bulletin of the Jewish Palestine Exploration Society*, 12 (1945/6), 62–74.

[189]Cf. TS Misc. Box 8, f. 66 (July 1150), a document about the subject with many details. Chicken: see n. 174, above.

[190]TS 13 J 9, f. 15. This information was given to me by Professor Meir Benayahu, who has made a special study of the late Mamluk and the Ottoman Geniza documents.

[191]*Med. Soc.*, II, 252. A photo of Maimonides' holograph is provided in *Med. Soc.*, I, following p. 20, illus. no. 7. The text is edited in *Tarbiz*, 32 (1962/3), 188.

[192]See *Med. Soc.*, I, 124.

[193]We read about the purchase (not yet carried out) of new bowls and cups for Passover, TS 8 J 15, f. 14, ll. 13–14, but not for a dairy department. Jerba: oral communication by A. L. Udovitch.

[194]For the prices see M. Gil, "Supplies of Oil in Medieval Egypt: A Geniza Study." *Journal of Near Eastern Studies*, 34 (1975), 67, esp. n. 36, and the references to Gil, *Foundations*, in n. 50, above.

[195]Abū Zikrī Kohen, representative of merchants in Fustat (see *Med. Soc.*, I, 241) buys it regularly together with hot, burning oil (for lighting): Mosseri L-76, slips 1 and 2; TS AS 145, f. 76.

[196]The "oil cruse," *kūz zayt*, usually brought in by a bride (see A, 5, n. 28), might have served people with limited means for both eating and lighting. In larger households the eating oil was probably kept in the measurements in which it was bought from time to time.

[197]See Andrew M. Watson, "A Medieval Green Revolution" (see n. 157, above), pp. 30–31.

2. Wine and other beverages

[1]See *EI*², IV, 659–660, s.v. "Karm" (viniculture, L. Bolens and Cl. Cahen); *ibid.*, pp. 994–998, s.v. "Khamr" (Juridical aspects, A. J. Wensinck; consumption, J. Sadan); pp. 998–1009, s.v. "Khamriyya" (wine songs; note the length of the article; J. E. Bencheikh). Cf. also J. Sadan, "Vin fait de civilisation," *Studies in Memory of Gaston Wiet*, ed. M. Rosen-Ayalon (Jerusalem, 1977), pp. 129–160.

[2]*Med. Soc.*, I, 122–123.

[3]Cairo, 1038: see R. Gottheil, "An Eleventh-Century Document Concerning a Cairo Synagogue," *JQR*, 19 (1907), 487. The document, which is not from the Geniza, is discussed in *Med. Soc.*, II, 243. Fustat, 1156: Firkovitch II, 1700, f. 18a, II: one-eighth of a house is bought in The Little Market of the Vizier on the Street of the Wine Sellers, *bi-darb al-nabbādhīn*. For the *suwayqat al-wazīr* see Casanova, *Reconstitution*, pp. 114–115, where the adjacent street is called al-Ṣayyādīn, Fishermen, who obviously replaced the Wine Sellers, whose status in Islam was, at best, suspect.

[4]Grohmann, *APEL*, I (1934), 254, no. 69, ll. 10 ff.

[5]TS 10 J 6, f. 4, ll. 6–7. See C, 1, n. 72, above.

[6]Maimonides, *Code*, book "Love" (of God), sec. "Benedictions," ch. 4:12. The sweet-smelling herbs, such as basil or mint, originally had the same purpose as the fumigators and fresheners discussed in A, 4, nn. 215 ff., above.

[7]I have not found this honorific title elsewhere. So the boon companion of our lover of wine must have been a quite exceptionally religious man. Ḥiyyā has an *h*, as last letter, not an Aleph, as usual. This is not a mistake. We find people signing their own name thus, e.g., *Ḥiyyāh* b. Meshullam (Jan. 1132, excellent script): TS 8 J 17, f. 19*d*.

[8]A Sabbath reading from the Prophets begins with the words "Let us go to Gilgal and renew there the Kingdom" (I Samuel 11:14). After the service, I imagine Rabbānā Ḥiyyā, while walking home with the writer of our note, said to him jokingly: "When shall we renew *our* kingdom," meaning: enjoy one another's company over a cup of wine, whereupon the latter made a remark which led to Ḥiyyā's promise. Soon an opportunity arose for a reminder.

[9]TS 8 J 22, f. 11. Painstakingly written in a beautiful hand. After bloodletting one drank red wine: "Red against red." See Krauss, *Talmudische Archäologie*, II, 241, for the ancient medical notion of fighting "the similar with the similar."

[10]Ar. *salīq*, see Dozy, *Supplément*, I, 676*a*. Years ago I took this word as Aramaic *selīq*, Finished, Farewell, said when one completed the study of a section of the Talmud on which occasion sometimes a festive dinner was given. But that dinner had another name.

[11]TS 10 J 7, f. 18. Two jars of wine sent to a junior business friend: *Med. Soc.*, I, 167, and n. 7. "Juglet" tries to translate *jurayra*.

[12]Partnership: JNUL, f. 83*v* (dated 1132), see *Med. Soc.*, I, 442 n. 18. Cooperation: Mosseri A-17, *ibid.*, n. 35. Heir: TS AS 155, f. 207, ed. Paul Fenton, "A New Fragment from the Responsa of Maimonides," *Tarbiz*, 49 (1980), 205–206.

[13]In addition to the fact that the kohl containers imitated the form of the amphora throughout the ages, see B, n. 538, and App. D, n. 73, undersea archaeology has revealed that Mediterranean ships from the High Middle Ages actually carried loads of amphoras. The measurements for the *jarra* found in papyri and Arabic literature are rare and differ so widely that they are practically useless, see Grohmann, *Einführung*, pp. 170–171, and n. 50, below.

[14]ULC Add 3413*v*, ll. 10–12. Postscript: Bodl. MS Heb. e 101, f. 16.

[15]ENA 1822, f. 59, ll. 10–14.

[16]TS 13 J 5, f. 3, item II, and *verso*, item I is dated June 1150: Most of the buyers were outsiders, several from al-Maḥalla, others from Tinnīs, Ashmūn, Sumbāṭ, one even from Ascalon, Palestine. When one of the buyers is called Son of the Woman from Fustat, he must also have been from a provincial town. A man simply referred to as Ṣāfī, who took part in four sales (col. I, 17, 23; II, 13, 17), was probably none other than the slave agent of the Head of the Yeshiva bearing that name, whose praiseworthy role in the case of an abandoned concubine is described in a document from the Sudanese port ʿAydhāb, trans. in Goitein, *Letters*, pp. 335–338. The *kutubī* who bought fifty jars, probably dealt in books of medicine, mathematics, philosophy, and the like. Hebrew books were sold by teachers, copyists, or court clerks. The market was too small for a Jewish kutubī, unless he traded in Arabic books, as in this century the late Isaac B. Yahuda, the brother of Professor A. S. Yahuda, whose collection of Muslim manuscripts is one of the treasures of the Library of Princeton University.

[17]Firkovitch II, 1700, f. 16a, item I: 350 clay ṭamāwiyas worth 0.2 dirhems each. For keeping this number in one's cellar, one received 1 dirhem per month (1156). A quantity worth 4 dirhems: TS NS J 78, see n. 31, below. Mevōrākh: ENA NS 19, f. 31, ll. 19–23. Ten pounds of silk: see *Med. Soc.*, I, 222.

[18]TS 13 J 30, f. 2.

[19]TS 24.25*v*, ll. 27–28. The Muslim years 558–559 (1162–1164) are referred to in this most important list of assets and liabilities, which is written on the reverse side of a document dated January 1149. (In the handlist of the Library it was dated 1091, because *shittīn* (60) was read to mean 2.) The list is often used in *Med. Soc.*, I; see I, 509.

[20]The term *laṭaf* for wine occurs in early Islamic literature, see Dozy, *Supplément*, II, 532*a*, bottom and *Bibliotheca Geographorum*, IV (Glossarium), 348, where *ʿushūr al-laṭaf*, tithes on sweets, is explained as *ḍarā'ib al-khamr*, taxes on wine.

[21]TS 12.587. The wine was found to be spoiled, *fāsid*, and the father of the young man returned the down payments, see *Med. Soc.*, I, 182 and n. 14. One sees that *jarra*

and *ṭamāwiya* were indiscriminately used together with either *nabīdh* or *laṭaf*. There was perhaps a difference only in the form of the two vessels.

[22]See H. Idris Bell, *Egypt from Alexander the Great to the Arab Conquest* (Oxford, 1948), pp. 46–47.

[23]TS Arabic Box 30, f. 84, nos. of order slips 3, 7, 19, *India Book* 137. The raisins might have been for eating or fruit juices, or both.

[24]TS NS J 321, f. 7a, *India Book* 316, trans. Goitein, *Letters*, p. 303.

[25]ENA 4100, f. 8. The agent: Abūn b. Ṣedāqā.

[26]When mentioned in a letter the month is usually followed by the wish: "May it be turned into happiness." See also *Med. Soc.*, III, 450 n. 82, for the weeks between Passover and Pentecost, as well as for the months of Tammuz and Av.

[27]See C. H. Roberts, *The Antinoopolis Papyri* (London, 1950), I, 96–99, no. 42. Antinoopolis was situated on the east bank of the Nile opposite Ashmūnayn, and served as the capital of a district.

[28]Cf. M. Ullmann, *Die Medizin im Islam* (Leiden, 1970), p. 168. See also n. 9, above.

[29]See nn. 16 and 18, above.

[30]TS 13 J 21, f. 17, trans. Goitein, "A Letter from Seleucia (Cilicia), Dated 31 July 1137," *Speculum*, 39 (1964), 300. Here I spelled *ṭimāya*, because I assumed (but did not say so) that the term was somehow derived from Greek *timē*, assessment, price. But nowhere is the word spelled with a *y* between *ṭ* and *m*. Barrel: *maṭar* (from the Greek word for measurement, from which our meter is derived).

[31]TS NS J 78.

[32]That is, for any quantity of ten or less jars the same tax had to be paid at wholesale. For this reason one tried to sell full units of ten, see n. 17, above.

[33]Grohmann, *Einführung*, p. 155, see C, 1, n. 169, above. The word for wine used: *nabīdh*. Eggs cost 1/24 dinar, equated by Grohmann with 1 dirhem, in ll. 4–5.

[34]ENA 2808, f. 49, the unsigned copy of a contract between the Rayyis Abu 'l-Bahā' and the Rayyis Abu 'l-ʿIzz. For cut-up dirhems appearing in the Geniza as legal tender during 1218–1225 see *Med. Soc.*, I, 385.

[35]TS 13 J 22, f. 22, ll. 8–12. In a letter, a son sends to his father a fulled *maqṭaʿ* cloth worth 49 dirhems and wishes to have for its price 150 jars (of what is not said, wine, oil, or other); if that sum were not sufficient, he would deliver the balance to the carrier: TS 12.345, ll. 18–23.

[36]TS Arabic Box 30, f. 177. The *lājiya*, pl. *lawāji*, has not been found by me anywhere else. It might have been derived from the Aramaic-Heb. *lōg* (not in Fraenkel, *Aramäische Fremdwörter*), which contained only the space for six eggs (Marcus Jastrow, *-Dictionary . . . of the Talmud . . .*, (New York, N.Y. 1950), II, 694; very common). "The small one," meaning probably having the form of a small *ṭamāwiya*.

[37]TS Arabic Box 18(1), f. 127. "Olive" *zatūna* (abbreviated from *zaytūna*), ll. 8, 15, 20. Underground storeroom: *maṭmūra*. The father and brother had pressed forty-two ṭamāwiyas, that is, had bought only minor quantities ready-made.

[38]Bodl. MS Heb. b 13, (Cat. 2834, no. 31) f. 50. The word translated as samples, *k(h)rwt(h)*, was certainly also a vessel, but I was unable to identify it. For another even more urgent entreaty to accept a gift of wine, see n. 10, above. Bouquet: *rā'iḥa*.

[39]TS NS J 183, dated Nov./Dec. 1240. For the office of superintendent see *Med. Soc.*, II, 77.

[40]Krauss, *Talmudische Archäologie*, II, 239–242.

[41]*Alf Layla* (The Arabian Nights), II, 438, l. 27 (in the story of Nūr al-Dīn): *khamr rūmī min mu ʿattaq al-khamr*.

[42]See Goitein, "The Tribulations of an Overseer of the Sultan's Ships," *Hamilton A. R. Gibb Jubilee Volume*, ed. G. Makdisi, (Leiden, 1968), pp. 270–284, esp. p. 282: four *qisṭs* of Rūmī wine (Greek *Xestos*, see Grohmann, *Einführung*, pp. 167–170) were worth 60 dirhems.

[43]TS 10 J 12, f. 16, l. 8. The *al-Qamra* was a predominantly Jewish neighborhood in Alexandria.

[44]Ar. *shayba*, lit. "the white hair of an old woman." Kinds of moss or fungus covering tree trunks, used in Egypt as yeast for making bread or, as we see here, otherwise as a

ferment. According to Maimonides-Meyerhof, p. 10, no. 11, at least eight kinds of lichen were available in the bazaars of Cairo.

[45]Ar. *qulfūniya* or *qalafūniya*, a resin extracted from a pine tree or a terebinth. The originally Greek word is derived from the town of Colophon on the west coast of Asia Minor, from where that resin was imported to Greece. When we find black colophony sent from Alexandria to Fustat, TS 12.263*v*, margin, it must have come to Egypt from Asia Minor or Greece. See Maimonides-Meyerhof, p. 176, no. 352.

[46]Ar. *tulayyis*, common in modern vernacular, for stopping an opening, Spiro, *Dictionary of Modern Arabic*, p. 398*b*; Barthélemy, *Dictionnaire arabe-français*, p. 771, crépir à la chaux (cover with chalk).

[47]ENA 2808, f. 22: *ṣifat nabīdh ṭayyib*.

[48]TS 13 J 18, f. 8, l. 34.

[49]"Exposed to the sun," *shamsī*, Maqrīzī, *Khiṭaṭ*, I, 44, bottom, Greek *heliaston*.

[50]None of the measurements tentatively cited by Grohmann, *Einführung*, pp. 170–171, tallies with the data provided in the Geniza. Hinz, *Islamische Masse*, does not list *jarra* at all. Our recipe, which prescribes an exact measurement for each ingredient, makes sense only when the main fluid with which they were mixed was also of a definite volume.

[51]About *dādhī* see the detailed discussion in Maimonides-Meyerhof, p. 46, no. 86. Wine made of that lichen alone: Ibn al-Mujāwir, *Descriptio Arabiae Meridionalis*, ed. O. Löfgren (Leiden 1951), I, 51.

[52]TS Arabic Box 43, f. 71, p. *c*, *India Book* 342*b*, written partly in Hebrew and partly in Arabic script. Mentions payments in the port of Aden and an order sent to Egypt, see B, n. 339, above.

[53]Grohmann, *APEL*, V, 154–155, with valuable explanations. Vendor of honey sherbet, *fuqqāʿī*: TS K 15, f. 50, B, col. II, l. 23 (1147); al-Mahdiyya: TS 13 J 29, f. 10, l. 15. *Fuqqāʿa* bottle: ULC Or 1080 J 111 (containing mercury); TS 10 J 18, f. 16, l. 10, *Nahray* 133 (honey). Prohibition: Josef van Ess, "Chiliastische Erwartungen . . .," *Abhandlungen der Heidelberger Akademie der Wissenschaften, Philos.-hist. Klasse* (Heidelberg, 1977), p. 11 n. 26.

[54]Maqrīzī, *Khiṭaṭ*, I, 368, ll. 11–12, reports that because of the popularity of the *mizr* beer made from wheat, the price of that grain was high.

[55]TS 18 J 3, f. 5, ed. Braslavsky, *Our Country*, p. 90. See *Med. Soc.*, I, 430 n. 87.

[56]Oxymel: See C, 1, n. 161, above. Plums: Ar. *(a)njāṣ*, which today means pear in Palestine and Syria, but in TS 12.24*v*, l. 4, must designate the plum, as in ancient Arabic poetry, see Fraenkel, *Aramäische Fremdwörter*, p. 291, bottom. Does one make fruit juice from pears? TS 12.24*v* discusses the various benedictions to be said over beverages other than wine. Several household lists noting beverages other than those summarized in *Med. Soc.*, II, 271, are preserved. Tamarind: TS 16.163*v*, l. 15: none of it is to be had in al-Mahdiyya. Asparagus: see C, 1, n. 36, above. Two pots with *sharāb safarjal* (both the Arabic and the English words come from the Greek) were left with many other things by the learned sharābī referred to in *Med. Soc.*, II, 264 and n. 22.

D. MOUNTS

[1]Cf. the role of the King's horse in the Book of Esther.

[2]The Rayyis [. . .] al-Dawla, probably a physician of distinction.

[3]Fakhr al-ʿArab (The Pride of the Bedouins) was the brother of Nāṣir al-Dawla b. Ḥamdān, about whom see Lane-Poole, *History of Egypt*, pp. 145 ff., and *Med. Soc.*, I, 310.

[4]Cash, Ar. *ʿayn*. A redundant long stroke and the mutilated first letter of the word betray the nervousness of the writer.

[5]TS 12.215, ll. 17–24, and margin.

[6]TS 13 J 28, f. 24. The buyer was probably a government official, or otherwise connected with it, e.g., as purveyor; therefore the sum was transferred monthly

(deducted from the buyer's salary or other payment due him) to the seller's banking account.

[7]Stables: A, 2, n. 160, and *passim*, above. Maidservant: *Med. Soc.*, I, 139 and *passim*. Silk: *ibid.*, p. 222 and n. 55.

[8]ENA 2738, f. 23. "Faḍl bought a he-ass."

[9]ENA 2808, f. 16, ll. 7–9, 14–17.

[10]TS Arabic Box 36, f. 119, l. 9. In Arabic characters, of course.

[11]TS 12.708, ll. 9–10: *jaḥsha ḥāmil.* Written in beautiful Heb. script.

[12] ULC Or 1080 J 138*v*, ll. 2–4 (1129). See *Med. Soc.*, I, 252 and n. 131.

[13]TS 18 J 4, f. 1, ll. 11–12. See *Med. Soc.*, II, 257 and n. 87.

[14]ULC Or 1080 J 89*v*, ll. 7–8, ed. J. Braslavi, *Eretz-Israel*, 5 (1958), 223, and J. Eliash in *Sefunot*, 2, (1958), 11. The reading of Braslavi is correct.

[15]TS NS J 7, *India Book* 206. Abū ʿAlī Ezekiel writes to his brother Ḥalfōn b. Nethanel. Unsaddled: *ʿury*. Outfit: *ʿudda.*

[16]TS NS J 27, l. 17 (1143); TS 20.187 (1083).

[17]TS 20.69, ll. 41–42, one of the more important business letters preserved. See *Med. Soc.*, I, 372–373, sec. 14, and B, nn. 229–230, above.

Cairo as provider of riding beasts: TS 10 J 31, f. 10*v*, ll. 12–13 (a note on the front page is dated 1215), a letter from Alexandria reports that a friend who had traveled to Miṣr and remained there for only one day had bought a mount in Giza, the well-known suburb on the western bank of the Nile, and had already arrived home riding it. He bought the animal in Giza to avoid crossing the Nile on his way back to Alexandria. An Alexandrian, who had to visit Cairo on a matter of inheritance at a time of great insecurity notes in a postscript on the top of his letter that he had bought four mounts in the capital and would either enter Alexandria with them or remain with them in Sanhūr, if crossing the gate was dangerous: ULC Or 1080 J 29 (ca. 1150).

[18]TS 12.655*v* (on *recto* a note mentioning the Nagid Abraham Maimonides [d. 1237]).

[19]TS 8 J 15, f. 25, ll. 9–13, four recommendations, among them "ask Musallām b. Ayyūb, he knows the reliable *ḥammārīn*." The letter is addressed to Abū Saʿīd Binyām (= Benjamin) al- ʿAfṣī (otherwise known, lived ca. 1100). Similar advice in TS 13 J 10, f. 13, l. 10 (written between 1031 and 1035), where, l. 4, also the muleteer Faraj is mentioned as charged with fetching parts of a Bible manuscript. A definite reference to a Jewish *mukārī* is found in TS NS Box 320, f. 7, l. 10 (1126), where a baby daughter of one is listed as having died in an outbreak of epidemics, see *Med. Soc.*, II, 140 and n. 7. For Jewish couriers cf. *Med. Soc.*, I, 285–286.

[20]TS Misc. Box 25, f. 20, a postscript to an order for medication sent to the capital Mad(h)kūr (a rare name) sends this message to Abu 'l-Karam.

[21]TS 13 J 21, f. 35 margin. Abū Naṣr al-Tustarī was the brother of Abū Saʿd, the vizier of the mother of the caliph al-Mustanṣir. The writer of our letter suggests to Abū Naṣr to give him 3 dirhems outright for the ride, and to ask his friends to contribute another 3 for provisions. This would sound odd if the Tustarī meant is he who was able to offer the caliph 200,000 dinars as his ransom, a sum corresponding to many millions of (1981) dollars. But the multimillionaires of dinars in the Geniza did not throw their dirhems around.

[22]TS 13 J 14, f. 23, ed. Mann, II, 113, with the emendations made in Reader's Guide, p. xxxi, bottom, where, however, some technical qualifications are necessary. The paper is torn away at the beginning of the line, not at its end. The missing part had run approximately like this: "*in ra'ā* ["If your highness thinks"] that a saddled mount, *bahīmat sarj*, should be sent to me, please do so."

[23]See *Med. Soc.*, II, 243.

[24]TS 8 J 31, f. 6. The saddling of the mount is a time-consuming affair. The story of a ride is mostly preceded in the Bible by a reference to the saddling, e.g., Genesis 22:3, Numbers 22:21, I Samuel 12:73, I Kings 2:40.

[25]See A, 3, nn. 67–69, above.

[26]See *Med. Soc.*, I, 214–217, esp. p. 217, top. Despite the natural assumption that a letter might be confined to the dealings between the writer and the recipient, it should

be noted that in most missives there are references to commercial transactions with other merchants. They acted not only in formal partnerships but as groups of business friends. The same was true in the India trade.

[27]*Ibid.*, I, 202–204. It should not be argued that people are reticent about their profits, but inclined to complain about losses. Troubling one's business friend with reports about one's losses was regarded as bad form. Misfortunes were reported when awareness of them was necessary for the proper conduct of reciprocal activities.

[28]*Ibid.*, I, 263–266. Here one must consider that dispositions of real estate and other arrangements about securing the rights and welfare of one's beloved were usually made long in advance of death. More about this in *Med. Soc.*, V, A, 3 (in preparation).

[29]TS Arabic Box 18(1), f. 155, see *Med. Soc.*, II, 417, sec. 24, and Gil, *Foundations*, pp. 77–79, 300–304.

[30]The list of long-lived buildings administered by the rabbinical community of Fustat, provided in *Med. Soc.*, II, 119–120, has been considerably enlarged by Gil, "Maintenance," p. 145.

[31]The Muslim who in Dec. 1032 rented a house in the Khawlān quarter (a Jewish neighborhood) from a Jew with the right to sublet it (which he certainly did) paid a yearly rent of 6 dinars, but the repairs were incumbent on the proprietor. See A, 3, n. 51, above.

[32]See App. A.

[33]In most Geniza documents dealing with real estate appear persons possessing shares in houses, not complete properties.

[34]See *Med. Soc.*, III, 363–422, Appendix, especially the Summary, pp. 418–422. The additional items on pp. 421–422 were added after the summary had been printed. Seventeen more cases were noted by me after the publication of the volume. The totals on p. 419 stand now as follows:

			Additional items	More cases	Totals
I	Destitute	57	1	4	62
II*a*	Poor	49	1	1	51
II*b*	Very Modest	67	1	2	70
II*c*	Modest	49	4	1	54
III*a*	Lower Middle Class	68	4	4	76
III*b*	Upper Middle Class	60	1	5	66
IV	Wealthy	16	—	—	16
	Total				395

[35]App. D, Doc. II, f. 47*v*, ll. 13–18. Joseph Lebdi acquires the mansion: TS 8 J 9, fs. 2–3, *India Book* 284. The romantic affair: after Joseph's death, his nephew, who liked his daughter, Sitt al-Ahl, could not visit the house anymore; therefore he asked for her hand. This happened when her brother, an India trader like his father, was out of the country. Sitt al-Ahl's mother wisely left the choice to her daughter, who agreed and was betrothed to her suitor: TS NS Box 184 (eight fragments selected from fragments nos. 58 to 98). When Sitt al-Ahl's brother, who obviously had a low opinion of his cousin, returned, he disapproved of his sister's choice and arranged a divorce (necessary after a betrothal, see *Med. Soc.*, III, 87–95); finally, in 1124, she married Abu 'l-Surūr (Joy), the perfumer, whom we find then as coproprietor of Joseph Lebdi's house together with Sitt al-Ahl's niece in App. D, Doc. II. See TS NS J 460. At the same time Sitt al-Ahl received another house from her brother (whether this was a sugar coating of the bitter pill of the divorce, is, of course, not evident from our documents).

I first got an inkling of Joseph Lebdi's attempts to acquire a house in Fustat while studying the Geniza fragments of the Library of the Alliance Israélite Universelle in Paris in summer 1950. TS NS J 460 (which I had seen, of course, more than once before), a fragment, was identified by me on July 2, 1981.

[36]For details see App. D, n. 168, above, and the references there.

[37]*Med. Soc.*, II, 91–143, 413–510.

APPENDIX D
Selected Documents on Clothing and Jewelry

Five Trousseau Lists. Introduction

[1]For the socioeconomic composition of the Geniza population, as far as evident from marriage documents, see *Med. Soc.*, III, 418–419, and D n. 34, above.

[2]About Nathan b. Samuel see *Med. Soc.*, II, 513, sec. 18, and ibid., III, 501–502 n. 96.

[3]D. H. Baneth, "A Doctor's Library in Egypt at the Time of Maimonides," *Tarbiz*, 30 (1961), 172 n. 6. See Ashtor, *Prix*, p. 567, s.v. "livres."

[4]TS 20.6 (Sept. 1037), ed. S. Assaf, *Tarbiz*, 9 (1938), 30–32, see Shaked, *Bibliography of Geniza Documents*, p. 72.

[5]A total of 120 dinars for bedding and housewares was not unusual for a middle-class outfit—provided it was considerably surpassed by jewelry and clothing, as, e.g., in Document II (342 dinars as against 140). Sahlān's comparatively small marriage gift also points to a union realized later in life.

[6]See, e.g., TS Misc. Box 29, f. 29, ed. Ashtor, *Mamluks*, III, 32–37: a very substantial ketubba totaling 560 nominal and 280 real dinars, has no items of furnishings or housewares. On the other hand, TS Arabic Box 4, f. 4, and TS K 25, f. 42, which together form perhaps the most detailed trousseau list of the thirteenth century, already comprise a number of the newfangled terms for garments, but possess also a remarkably rich assortment of copper and other housewares, perhaps the richest in the Geniza. Bedding is very poor, however, and represented only by the mattress-like *ṭarrāḥa*: there is not a single *martaba*, or sofa, an item rarely absent from a middle-class ketubba during the Fatimid period. Even the Karaite bride from Jerusalem, 1028, had two (Doc. I), while the rich bride (Doc. III) had five (in addition to other sitting and bedding facilities). Should we assume that sitting habits had changed and that the knee-high *martaba* had been replaced by the far lower *ṭarrāḥa* and the like? Compare Stillman, *The Jews of Arab Lands*, illus. 17, facing p. 316 (a kind of *ṭarrāḥa*), with illus. 19 (*martaba*, on which one would sit, not in the European way as did the nineteenth-century Jewish family depicted, but with the legs crossed). The *ṭarrāḥa* also replaces the *martaba* in other ketubbas from the Mamluk period, e.g., Ashtor, *Mamluks*, III, 68, 71.

[7]With the exception of TS Arabic Box 4, f. 4 and TS K 25, f. 42, see preceding note, where the value of the trousseau was estimated at 372 1/2 dinars, if my understanding of the various partial and final summaries is correct. Throughout the list Coptic numerals are used. Certain habits of their users were explained to me by Professors Bernard Goldstein and David Pingree, students of Arabic astronomy, where those numerals are in vogue.

[8]See *Med. Soc.*, II, 244, and the sources mentioned *ibid.*, p. 576 nn. 15–16.

[9]Lane-Poole, *History of Egypt*, pp. 171–173.

[10]For the year 1150 above, I noted twenty dated documents, including the draft of a petition to the Kurdish vizier and actual ruler of Egypt Ibn al-Salār al-Malik al- ʿĀdil, see *ibid.* In the complaint his justice is praised (indirectly, ll. 14–16, "the justice prevailing throughout the country in these flourishing days does not permit such oppression of your subjects"), but his murder in 1153 was as gruesome as his rule, TS 13 J 20, f. 5, see *Med. Soc.*, II, 353, and 604 n. 39.

[11]About the problem of inflated ketubba estimates see *Med. Soc.*, III, 126–130; about the practices of Nathan b. Samuel and his son Mevōrākh see *ibid.*, pp. 97–98, 364–369, 385–387. Data about them in *Med. Soc.*, II, 513 n. 18, 514 n. 22.

Document I

[12]The Hebrew part of this document (not the trousseau list, which is in Arabic, cf. above) has been repeatedly printed, see Shaked, *Bibliography of Geniza Documents*, p. 41, sec. 2. (At the time of the Hebrew publications the manuscript did not yet have the mark noted above). The full text is edited in my *Palestinian Jewry*, pp. 193–199.

[13]Chronicles 14:6, "Built"—they will have children, as in Ruth 4:11. Also in Rabbanite ketubbot.

[14]Isaiah 45:25.

[15]Ezra 6:14. See n. 13, above.

[16]The so-called Seleucid era (mostly named the Era of Documents), which began in September 312 B.C.

[17]The usual legal phrases by which a person takes upon himself an obligation toward another.

[18]The word means cypress.

[19]Jarīr was a famous Arab poet of the Umayyad period, who died around 728, that is three hundred years before the writing of this contract. It is a sign of the popularity of Arabic poetry that Jewish parents gave this name to a son.

[20]The same obligations are repeated in other words.

[21]This was obligatory among Karaites; with the Rabbanites twenty-five silver pieces were the gift due a virgin.

[22]In practice, the "additional" bridal gift was the main one.

[23]As in Malachi 2:14.

[24]Genesis 2:18.

[25]Genesis 3:16. From the husband love and affection, *ḥibba*, is expected; from the wife, love and considerateness, *ḥīsa*, a standard term in Karaite ketubbot.

[26]Not of her kin, since her father was not a Kohen. Probably a communal official, or otherwise a trustworthy person, who would count and lock away the silver pieces and be the legal representative who formally confirmed the conditions agreed upon before.

[27]Which was made, of course, prior to the wedding, and probably many months before.

[28]The *dastaynaq* (a Persian word), spelled also *tastaynaj*, as in Doc. V, l. 13, was a precious, broad wristband, often inlaid with pearls. Our women normally wear *one* bracelet of the same type; in Geniza times—as in those of the biblical patriarchs, see Genesis 24:22—invariably bracelets were worn in pairs, one of the same type on each arm. When only one was available (e.g., as reported in the Geniza, when a mother gave one to each of her two daughters) the list notes expressly: one *single* bracelet.

[29]The two missing superscriptions are taken from TS 16.80 (fragmentary), also Karaite and fairly contemporary with our ketubba; the bride was well-to-do. See n. 59, below.

[30]Literally, glassy cover, *qināᶜ zujājī* (*dj'ny* is a misprint). Their glass was mostly translucent, not transparent.

[31]The *miᶜjar*, or wimple, a turban-like cloth wound around the head and then flowing down over the body, was a main, and, as here, often the most costly part of the female dress. The term *ridawānī*, like a *ridā'*, or mantle, describes the wimple as particularly long and broad.

[32]The *ᶜaq(a)biyya* is very common in the Geniza, but I have not yet found it elsewhere. Dominique Chevalier, "Les tissus ikatés d'Alep et de Damas," *Syria*, 39 (1962), 310, gives *al- ᶜaqqābīyatayn* (spelled thus) the two green almonds, as the *color* of an *ikaté* textile. But, as is evident also from the example here, *ᶜaq(a)biyya* designates the form of a dress, not its color. I derive the word from *ᶜaqb*, heel, and explain it as a robe reaching down to the ground, unlike the usual dress, which exposed the lower end of the pants to the eye (as may be seen on thirteenth-century miniatures depicting both women and men. We have no earlier ones). The long dress, with the train on the ground, shows the woman as noble, that is, doing no manual work—a common

theme in Arabic poetry. The term is treated in Y. Stillman's article, "Libās," in *EI*[2] (forthcoming).

[33]The *mulā'a* was (and still is, see Stillman, "Female Attire," p. 57) worn as a cloak covering the woman's body while going out. At night, it served also as a blanket.

[34]Again, the rare *qinā*ᶜ is used; see n. 30, above.

[35]Ar. *wiqāya* (or *waqqāya*), literally, protective clothing, not found in other ketubbas, but mentioned in commercial correspondence.

[36]Rūmī, imported from Christian Europe, mostly southern Italy and Sicily. The *minshafa* (literally, towel) appears in numerous ketubbas at the very end, mostly close to the bureau containing the female "unmentionables." Sylvia Kedourie, on the basis of her knowledge of life in Jewish Baghdad, explained the term to me as bathrobe, worn when visiting the public bathhouse. See B, n. 311, above.

[37]*Lādh* was a red Chinese silk imitated in Sicily; see my paper "Two Arabic Textiles," *JESHO*, 19 (1975), 221–24.

[38]A dress of fine silk with sleeves, see *Med. Soc.*, I, 454 n. 53.

[39]Ar. *izār* designates the Jewish prayer mantle or anything like it.

[40]Ar. *sifl*, a loanword from Heb.-Aramaic *sefel*, see Fraenkel, *Aramäische Lehnwörter*, pp. 67–77.

[41]Defined by the classical Arab dictionaries as a basket, *quffa*, made of palm leaves containing a woman's perfumery and toilet utensils. This one was probably an imitation in brass; it is mentioned repeatedly. They also had baskets made of silver, TS 8 J 21, f. 4, l. 16.

[42]Used like soap for washing the body. It is found in almost every trousseau list.

[43]Such containers of perfumes, often made of silver, were intended to keep bad odors out of the house. They are rarely absent from a trousseau. The ginger vases used in England until the end of the eighteenth century (then made of porcelain) served the same purpose. Note the high price of this vase here.

[44]In almost all lists Bedding comes before Copper and is more valuable than the latter. Since the values are reversed here, the scribe also changed the usual sequence.

[45]A textile originally manufactured in Tabaristan, a province in northern Iran south of the Caspian sea. It was imitated in many places, especially in Ramle, Palestine.

[46]The Buzyōn, like the Ṭabarī, once was a very costly textile produced in northeastern Iran, see Serjeant, *Islamic Textiles*, pp. 15–16, and Friedman, *Marriage*, no. 5, l. 28 (where *Fizyōn*), but was later imitated and became available to the common people. In the marriage contract of Karīma b. ᶜAmmār (al-Wuḥsha, see *Med. Soc.*, III, 346–352), written around 1090, a Buzyōn *ṭarrāḥa* mattress (with its twȯ cushions), like here, cost 2 dinars. ENA 2727, f. 8, l. 18. The Karaite bride of TS 16.80, l. 8, had a Buzyōn pad, *barda*ᶜ*a*. Thus, this heavy textile was used for all types of bedding.

[47]Ar. *muḍarraba*, occurring also in the ketubba from Tyre, 1023, ed. Friedman, *Marriage*, no. 2.

[48]The actual grand total seems to be 70 1/2, not 61 1/2 dinars, but long experience has taught me that it is I, not the Geniza clerks, who make mistakes in additions. Here, something special might have happened. As often at weddings of people with little money, there was probably a squabble over the estimate, and finally an agreement about the total owed by the husband was reached.

[49]The dowry remains the property of the wife; the husband may use it with her consent.

[50]Rabbinical law was not as outspoken and liberal in this matter as the Karaite dispensation.

[51]Literally, her families, that is, from her father's side. Most of the Rabbanite Geniza marriage contracts have adopted the Palestinian custom that *one-half* of the dowry reverts to the wife's paternal family in case she has no child from the man she married. But this is not general rabbinical law.

[52]In theory, at least, the Karaites, like the Muslims, have no fixed calendar. As in ancient Israel, the new month was "declared," when the new moon was actually sighted, and a second Adar was intercalated when the grain in Israel had not greened

in time. The Geniza has preserved actual reports by Karaites about the greening of the ears, as well as a letter about a particularly pious Karaite who refrained in Jerusalem not only from beef and mutton, but also from chicken. (The Karaite calendar to this day differs from the Rabbanite. The Yom Kippur War was for them an Erev Yom Kippur war, for in 1973 their Day of Atonement fell one day later.) Any dispute arising in married life must be settled in a Jewish court.

[53]I take this as an abbreviation of *ṣ(ibbūr)*, meaning "ten men"; see S. D. Goitein, "The Hebrew Elements in the Vernacular of the Jews of Yemen" [Hebrew], *Lešonenu*, 3 (1931), 368. Reedited in *The Yemenites*, p. 27.

[54]Probably a variation of Zūṭā, Mr. Small.

[55]Here the word *ᶜēd*, witness, is omitted. I do not know how *Yḥy* pronounced his name.

[56]"Good tidings." This could also be read Bishr.

[57]Typical Arabic names such as ᶜOmar or ᶜAmr, or Jarīr (the grandfather of the bride, see n. 19 above), were common among Syro-Palestinian Jews.

[58]Because of the stream of pilgrims there was a very close connection between the Holy City and Sicily. Sicilian quarter dinars were almost the common currency of Jerusalem during the eleventh century. See also n. 36, above, about the term Rūmī.

[59]TS 16.80, see n. 29, above. Middle part of a huge document in early eleventh-century script, twenty lines, none completely preserved. *Rayyis*, Head, was an honorary title for a physician, namely head of a department in a hospital, *Med. Soc.*, II, 246. The girl was probably from a doctor's family.

Document II

[60]See n. 140, below. The socioeconomic background of this engagement contract is discussed in detail in *Med. Soc.*, III, 84–85.

[61]The first chapter of my *India Book* (in preparation) is dedicated to him.

[62]"Sprout," a messianic name; see Jeremiah 23:5.

[63]Heb. *marēnū we-rabbēnū*, our master and lord, originally (and here) preceding the name of a man with some learning but often simply meaning Mr.

[64]The gold pieces were deposited with a third party.

[65]When a person is obliged, for any reason, to take an oath, the opposing party might, under certain circumstances, impose on him an additional oath.

[66]See n. 51, above.

[67]See n. 17, above.

[68]A phrase commonly used, even when the woman concerned was well known to the judge or notary. Cf. *Med. Soc.*, III, 313–314.

[69]See n. 28, above.

[70]Ar. *mujrā sawād*; see Ibn Zubayr, *Dhakhā'ir*, p. 63, ll. 5–6. The same in Doc. III, l. 8 and Doc. V, l. 7. See B, nn. 452–455.

[71]As in Hebrew, *tannūr* means oven. The term has not yet been found elsewhere. Since it is mentioned between bracelets, I take it to be a cuff made of silver. The fem. *tannūra* is a piece of clothing, but not in the Geniza.

[72]"Auspicious," a very common ornament. The word was used also as a name. Maimonides' father was called thus.

[73]The nineteenth-century kohl containers in Egypt, Tunisia, and Algeria still had the form of a little amphora, as in ancient Egypt and Greece; see Lane, *Modern Egyptians* p. 38, and Eudel, *Bijoux* , pp. 138–139, 163.

[74]See n. 31, above.

[75]This garment is mentioned innumerable times in the Geniza, but as far as I can see, not in Arabic dictionaries. I derive jūkāniyya from jawkān, arabisized from Persian chawgān, the game of polo, the ball game played between riders on horseback. Polo players are frequently depicted on ceramics, metals, and miniatures, and it seems to me that the robe worn by them was shorter and occasionally plied, so as not to interfere with the polo stick. The tenth century "rustic" plate from the Hamburg Museum für Kunst und Gewerbe, reproduced in the admirable volume of D. and

J. Sourdel, *La Civilisation de l'Islam classique*, Paris 1968, opposite p. 381, no. 141, is an example. The robe has sleeves, like the jūkāniyya in the Geniza, but not long ones, as other robes, and uses a special form of fastening the edges of the garment, probably also for the safety and easy movement of the player. Thus this piece of clothing, special and elegant in form, was also practical for working women, which explains why jūkāniyyas were distributed to the poor and why they were so popular among women in general.

In vowelling jūkāniyya I followed Dozy, *Supplément*, I, 235b, who has jūkān, based on late medieval sources. This corresponds to the Geniza evidence, where only documents from the 13th century, such as TS 20.77, ll. 7–8 (1240), TS 24.9, ll. 20–32, or TS K 25.42, l. 8, spell the word without a *w*, that is, reflect a pronunciation even with a short *u*, *jukán* (also found in Dozy). The overwhelming majority of documents spell the word with *w*, that is, as *aw* or *ū*. The correspondence between literary sources and the Geniza confirms the derivation of the name (and probably form) of this most common garment from that worn at the polo game. See the paper noted in n. 37, above.

[76]Text *ksy* (*khṣy*). Reading and translation tentative. Since this common term is often mentioned together solely with a robe, it must designate a head cover. See Doc. V, *verso*, col. I, ll. 12 and 15.

[77]Cf. Steingass, *Persian-English Dictionary*, p. 430, *ḥamā'il*, necklace with flowers or small coins. Coins joined together to form an ornament have been preserved from the Fatimid period.

[78]Ar. *niqāb*, a face cover (with two holes for the eyes).

[79]Literally, "combined, connected," namely the two borders of the cloak.

[80]The trunk in which the wife's lingerie was kept. Found in most completely preserved lists.

[81]Ar. *ṣadr dībāj wa-mijnabayn*. The *majlis*, literally sitting room, main room of a house, was divided by a broad curtain, which was let down after the guests were seated. On both ends were narrow curtains through which attendants and latecomers moved. This arrangement is visible in many medieval illustrations, cf. e.g., Ettinghausen, *Arab Painting*, pp. 98, 99, 106, 107, 113, 121. Moses Maimonides had a servant described as *pardah-dār* (in Heb. characters: *prtd'r*), keeper of the curtain, usher, see TS 8 J 14, f. 18*v*, l. 12. Cf. A, 4, n. 77.

[82]The *maqṭaᶜ* is a piece of cloth large enough for one dress or robe and woven in a specific way, see Goitein, *Letters*, p. 134, and B, n. 206.

[83]Ar. *muzarra*, abbreviated from *muzarrara*, the buttoned one, known from literary sources as a bag held together by clamps fastened to buttons (button*holes* had not yet been invented in those days), see Dozy, *Supplément*, I, 584*a*. Common in the Geniza in the sense of a dressing gown made of heavy and costly materials, probably worn mostly in winter, which, in the sparingly heated rooms of Egypt, could be rather uncomfortable. The materials used for this gown were: brocade, as here, and below, Doc. III, col. III, l. 9; defined in ENA 2738, f. 33 b (*Med. Soc.*, III, 403, no. 153) as *European* brocade and costing there (as in Doc. III) 20 dinars; Qurqūbī, an originally *Iraqian* textile, TS 24.16, l. 11 (*Med. Soc.*, 407, no. 213), and TS K 15, f. 99, col. II, l. 24. Tustari, an originally *Iranian* heavy silk, TS 24.12, l. 9 (*Med. Soc.*, III, 414, no. 318), or *siglaton*, as below, Doc. III, col. III, l. 8. The unusually high amounts of money spent on the dressing gown by women (who could afford it) probably must be understood as an endeavor to appear well groomed in the intimate circumstances of nightly rest.

[84]Since Ṭabarī textiles were frequently imitated, see n. 45, above, a genuine Tabaristan was identified as such.

[85]Whether this common term designating a type of tapestry is derived from Persian *sūsan*, lily, or *sūzan*, needle, or was originally a place name, is not yet sure.

[86]Text: *mikhadd lil-khadd*, pillows for the cheek. In a society without chairs pillows were used all day long for reclining; sleeping pillows were often characterized as such. See p. 109 and A, 4 n. 2.

[87]See n. 42, above.

[88]Ar. *barniyyatayn*. This is strange. The *barniyya* was normally made of silver, as in

Doc. III, col. I, l. 31, and elsewhere, or of china, or of clay. Painted, *muṣabbagh*, vessels of this type were common.

[89]The pre-Islamic nucleus of the city of Fustat.

[90]The other half probably belonged to her brother (known from another source), wherefore the partner is not noted. Many Jews lived in the Mamṣūṣa.

Document III

[91]That is, ten disks of amber and five of gold on each side and one of gold forming the middle piece.

[92]Tubes: Ar. *qawādīs* (Greek *kados*), Dozy, *Supplément*, II, 314*b*. Probably hair ornaments, see B, n. 441, above. In Firkovitch II, 1700, f. 25*v*, l. 16, they were made of gold and pearls and cost 8 dinars. In TS 8 J 29, f. 15, l. 12, they were worth 3 dirhems and possibly made of copper.

[93]All these vessels were of silver or other precious materials.

[94]Ar. *zabdiyya*, still in common use.

[95]Text: *majmaʿ*, a utensil with compartments, also used at the visit to a bathhouse. See Dozy, *Supplément*, I, 217*a*, TS 10 J 10, f. 29, l. 14: *majmaʿ lil-ḥammām*.

[96]Ar. *madhāf*, a vessel for mixing ingredients of medicaments, food or makeup. See B, pp. 225–226 and nn. 550–553, above.

[97]The cock was perforated and contained a kohl stick. Many such figurines have been preserved.

[98]Ar. *sabʿ* (the same probably in Heb. *shevaʿ*. Be'er Shevaʿ: The Lion's Well). The lion, like the crystal cock in l. 23, was perforated and contained a needle, which served as an applicator.

[99]Ar. *jary al-qalam*. In calligraphic writing the lines ended with an elegant curve turning upward. This was imitated in textiles and, as I learned from pictures from Ṣaʿda in northern Yemen shown to me by Brinkley G. Messick III, also in architecture. This turning up of the left end of a line was common in documents from the Fatimid chancelleries and is found also in the Geniza as well as in present-day legal documents from Yemen. Ṣaʿda was an important center of book learning.

[100]This dress of European style is mentioned together either with a *thawb*, robe, or *jūkāniyya*, polo robe, or *ḥulla*, gala costume, and a cloak, or a wimple; see ll. 15–16, 21–22, and column III, 3–4. It must have been a garment of specific cut and should not be confused with the *mandīl Rūmī*, the Rūmī kerchief, found in countless ketubbas, see B, n. 309, above.

[101]*Makhtūma*, literally, bearing a seal, probably meaning an emblem, such as a goblet, a flower, an animal, or a geometrical design, such as the "knot based on an eight-pointed star" in Golombek-Gervers. "Tiraz Fabrics," p. 99, or perhaps even a Jewish symbol, see B, n. 349, above. Our bride had five makhtūmas, mostly made of costly materials such as siglaton, tabby, or brocade, the latter costing as much as 15 dinars (ll. 27–29, III, l. 2).

I am not sure that *ʿamal al-dār*, literally, made in the house, really means homemade. Perhaps it is abbreviated from *ʿamal dār al-ṭirāz*, made in the embroidery workshop (of the government). See B, n. 350, above.

[102]About this precious fabric of heavy damask see B, n. 195, above.

[103]Ar. *Al-Jazā'ir* became the name of the town of Algiers, called so after the islets near its coast. But I have little doubt that in the Geniza the word designates the Greek islands of the Aegean Sea. Cf. *EI*², s.v. "Djazā'ir-i Baḥr-i-Safīd."

[104]Ar. *bahā'ī*. This could be also a trade name, called so after the manufacturer, who bore the title Bahā' al-dawla, Luster of the state.

[105]Ar. *sāmān*, a fine reed growing in the Jordan valley near Beisan (Beth She'an); see Dozy, *Supplément*, s.v. "A Karaite ketubba," TS 12.658, l. 15 lists a mat made of this material.

[106]Ar. *khilāfī*, worthy of a caliph, big. Common. [As we say today "a king-size bed."—Paula Sanders.]

[107]Ar. *mudhayyal*, meaning, ornamental hems.

Document IV

[108]This name of the youngest son of biblical Judah (Genesis 38 and often) was popular in Geniza times. The corresponding Arabic name was (Abū) Sahl.

[109]His three titles in TS NS Box 246, f. 22, ll. 36–37, ed. N. Allony, *Sefunot*, 8 (1964), 132. Business partnership: TS 16.119, see *Med. Soc.*, III, 502.

[110]TS Misc. Box 24, 137, p. 4*v*, item I, ll. 4–5. The will, a draft, written by Mevōrākh b. Nathan, bears no date. But on the head of the same page Mevōrākh had entered a short note (on a debt to be paid in installments), dated 20 Shevat 1471 (Jan. 30, 1160). He then turned the sheet 90° to the right and used the extensive blank space available for writing Abu 'l-Ḥasan's will and a rider freeing his two maid-servants, see n. 121, below.

[111]Pins: ULC Or 1080 J 49, ll. 13–14. Collateral: *verso* ll. 11–12. Furnishings: *ibid.*, ll. 12–14.

[112]TS 10 J 28, f. 16, written by Mevōrākh b. Nathan.

[113]TS 16.239, l. 3, written by Ḥalfon b. Manasse in the later part of his activity as scribe (1100–1138), see *Med. Soc.*, I, 138 and 433. In 1146, Sitt al-Ḥasab had a maid with another name, see Doc. IV, *verso*, l. 15. The total of the dowry in TS 16.239 was only 183 dinars, but the items returned in the 1146 document add up to a far higher estimate. The name Lady Pride and Prudishness was also given to free women, see *Med. Soc.*, II, 432, sec. 162; III, 457 n. 12.

TS 16.239, although repeatedly referred to in *Med. Soc.*, I, is not included in *Med. Soc.*, III, where it should be entered on p. 414, as no. 324*a*.

[114]Bodl. MS Heb. d 66 (Cat. 2878), f. 77. She had claimed, among other matters, that he owed her 90 dirhems for rent.

[115]Auction, *al-nidā'*, (the crying out). This should not be taken to mean that the lady was present in the bazaar. The *munādī*, or market crier, had received definite instructions from her, see *Med. Soc.*, I, 161.

[116]Borders, *a ʿlām*, literally, signs, see Serjeant, *Islamic Textiles*, Index, s.v. "*ʿalam*" (sg.). Rows, *ṣaffayn*.

[117]Found in the Damascus ketubba of 933 (see n. 119 below) and in the late fourteenth-century marriage contract, edited in Ashtor, *Mamluks*, III, 32–37, see n. 119, below.

[118]See Stillman, "Female Attire," pp. 169–174, where the Geniza material is thoroughly discussed (with the spelling *mukallaf*). The ubiquitous *jūkāniyya* was also read by me originally as *jūkhāniyya* (with *kh*, not *k*), see *Med. Soc.*, II, 131, and later corrected in the article quoted in n. 37, above; see also n. 75 above.

[119]The new explanation was given in my edition of the Damascus ketubba of 933, see *Lešonenu*, 30 (1966), 203, first line. Ashtor, *Mamluks*, III, 35 n. 15, noting that *mukhlaf* could refer both to a head cover and a robe, seemingly implied that the term did not designate a specific garment, but in general a piece of clothing of a certain description, such as being patched. When TS 12.12, ll. 4–5 (see *Med. Soc.*, III, 375, no. 19) notes, however, "a white plain robe with gold threads, *its* wimple, and *its* mukhlaf" (and notes six other garments of that description), or when a legal document from the year 1162 speaks of "a blue gala costume consisting of a blue skullcap, a wimple, and a mukhlaf" (Bodl. MS Heb. d 66 [Cat. 2878], f. 77, ll. 14–15) the term must designate a particular garment, such as a patchwork cloak made not of one piece, but of different parts, probably also of different colors. See B, n. 348, above.

[120]Goitein, *Jemenica*, p. 150, no. 1182, with parallels.

[121]It is also remarkable that the brother, who clearly had no wife or child, granted liberty to his two maids in his will with the proviso that one of them, who had not yet reached maturity, should stay with his younger sister, until she came of age and could decide for herself whether to remain with her or accept liberty becoming a "Jewess": TS Misc. Box 24, f. 137, p. 4*v*, item I, ll. 12–end. His elder sister, Sitt al-Ḥasab, had manumitted a maid four years before, in 1157 (she was still alive when the brother made his will). Should we assume here a family tradition, which regarded the

emancipation of slaves as a deed of particular piety? On this problem see S. D. Goitein, "Human Rights in Jewish Life and Thought in the Middle Ages," *Essays on Human Rights*, ed. David Sidorsky (Philadelphia, 1979), pp. 251–254.

[122]The manuscript is disfigured by dark spots, and some words are effaced. Most of the objects listed have occurred on the preceding pages.

[123]Since the father was dead, another member of the ha-Levi family took care of Sitt al-Ḥasab's affairs, who probably was a mere teenager at that time. Her brother Abu 'l-Ḥasan was either himself too young, or abroad, probably the latter, see n. 131, below.

[124]Samuel b. Hananya, see n. 8, above. The text says not "Nagid" but "his Nagidship," *hadrat ha-negīdūth.*

[125]The professional judges, see nn. 136, 137, below. For the use of the term "Court" for judge see *Med. Soc.*, II, 314.

[126]Ar. *ku'us*, in the form of cups? Not noted elsewhere in the Geniza (but seen even today).

[127]Silver or copper covers are often listed in trousseaus without indication to which vessels they were attached, I assume, to glass or ceramics, which, because of their fragility, were not included in the "estimate" of a wife's outfit. The very extensive inventory of the estate of a seller of potions notes "five silver covers" (the only silver he had) "for the *khumsiyyāt*" (flasks of musk), TS NS J 27*v*, col. II b, l. 7 (dated 1143). Similarly, the four silver covers of Sitt al-Ḥasab probably were destined (or used) for flasks of perfumes and the like.

[128]This heading refers to both garments and bedding (which often were made of the same fabrics). The term *malbūs* (literally, what is worn) should be translated as textiles, just as Heb. *beged* in the Karaite ketubba, TS 16.80, l. 3, where we find the heading *bigdē malbūsh*, literally, clothes for wearing. See, however, Doc. V, below, where, as often, bedding, forms a separate section.

[129]Probably repeated erroneously.

[130]Objects like baskets, trays, or cooling jugs, were covered with kerchiefs, certainly embroidered, therefore, costly, see ll. 29 and 30.

[131]Probably given as collateral, when Sitt al-Ḥasab took a loan. Abu 'l-Faraj might have been the Christian friend of Abu 'l-Ḥasan (a government official, like himself), mentioned in his will (see n. 110, above), l. 9. He might have granted her a loan during Abu 'l-Ḥasan's absence.

[132]The paternal family, to which the young wife returned from the house of the husband. For the judge R. Ḥiyyā see n. 136, below.

[133]Perhaps a musical term, see Dozy, *Supplément*, I, 761*a*. About the names of maidservants see n. 166, below.

[134]Reading and meaning doubtful. Legal documents are normally signed by three, which number represents a Jewish court. David the Refugee, who was present, was invited by the judges to join them. The same person appears in TS 6 J 2, f. 5, l. 5, as witness.

Jewish history never lacks refugees, but I have not seen another refugee in the Geniza assuming this as a title with which to sign a document. I assume David was a refugee from the island of Jerba (off the coast of Tunisia), which was taken by the Normans in 1135, see Goitein, *Letters* p. 324 n. 1, *Med. Soc.*, III, 30 and 117, and 451 n. 96 (where TS 10 J 25, f. 26, should be read for 13 J 25, f. 26), references to "one of the captives from Jerba," who writes from Tunisia after having been ransomed in the capital of Egypt. David may also have come from Tripoli, Libya, which was ransacked by the Normans in June 1146, see Idris, *Zirides*, p. 351. Our document was written in September 1146, two months later.

[135]This blessing for a dead father, *mktm*, is known to me only from two other occurrences, TS 13 J 1, f. 21 (signed 1150) and Bodl. MS Heb. f 56 (Cat. 2821), f. 51 (signed 1185), both by one Berākhōt b. Japheth. The first two letters are, of course, *menūḥātō kāwōd*, Isaiah 11:10. The letters *tm* can be explained as acronyms in many ways, but none is known to me as traditional.

[136]The son and successor of Isaac b. Samuel ha-Sefaradi, see *Med. Soc.*, II, 513, sec. 19.

[137]See n. 11, above.

Document V

[138]This was the Arabic name under which the bridegroom was known. Bū stands for Abū. "Estimate *of*"—meaning made by. The bridegroom had to agree with the estimate of the experts, for he was responsible for the return or replacement of the items brought in.

[139]Unlike the deferred installment, which is "a debt," the immediate installment, like a gift, has to be delivered immediately, namely, at the time of the wedding.

[140]The "well-known" conditions are spelled out in the next ketubba, where, like here, the bride receives a marriage gift of 50 + 100 dinars and a comparably sumptuous dowry, but, in addition to the regular stipulations, imposes special conditions. The regular ones: the wife is trustworthy as regards the conduct of the household and any business done for the husband; no second wife for him; no maidservant disapproved by her; one-half of her dowry to be returned to her family in case she dies childless. The special conditions in the ketubba referred to: domicile in Fustat, *not* in Cairo; she is free to sell any part of her dowry to buy real estate. See also Doc. II and n. 60, above.

[141]See n. 70, above.

[142]Lāzam, not known to me from an Arab dictionary, but a common ornament of the Jewish woman of Yemen, where it is pronounced thus, like *khātam*, ring. It consists of rows of (gilt) silver beads and little sheets cut in different shapes and forming together a broad pendant decorating the upper chest. The *lāzam* should not be confused with the *labbāh*, made of rows of filigree work, the main ornament on the upper breast. The old hostess of the French Jewish explorer Joseph Halévy and his Yemenite companion Ḥayyīm Ḥabshūsh wore both a *lāzam* and a *labbāh*, see Goitein, *Travels in Yemen*, p. 108, l. 2, Engl. summary, p. 63.

The *lāzam* of Geniza times must have looked similar to that still worn by Yemenite Jewish women a generation ago, for in several trousseau lists it is described as consisting of five rows: TS 24.9, l. 12; TS 13 J 6, f. 9*v*, item I, l. 4; TS NS Box 324, f. 144, l. 6. In Firkovitch II, 1700, f. 27 a, l. 10, "a *lāzam*, not adorned with pearls" is listed, which shows that in Egypt (unlike Yemen, as far as I know) it normally had that additional ornament.

The term might have been connected with the *lāzma*, or curb chain of a horse, which was often decorated, see Eudel, *Bijoux*, p. 119. See B, n. 488.

[143]An imitation in silver or gold (mostly the former) of plaited palm leaves, probably for keeping the headgear in place. An inventory of objects belonging to a dead person lists "two *khūṣas* for women," which shows that this ornament was used also by men, probably for their turbans, TS NS J 184, ll. 9–10. See n. 209 below.

The addition here of the word black is redundant, for the term *mujrā* is an abbreviation of *mujrā sawād*, see n. 70, above.

[144]A circle with a dot in its center marks the transition from jewelry to another section, consisting of utensils made of precious materials and less valuable ornaments.

[145]Of slices of lemon and the like.

[146]Refers to the pair of gold pins mentioned in l. 9 above. The objects in ll. 2–3 were made of silver.

[147]The word regularly used by Geniza clerks, including Mevōrākh b. Nathan, for the ornamented mirror is *muḥallāt*, or other forms of this verb, see, e.g., above, Docs. II, l. 14, III, ll. 15 and 29; *muwashshā*, used here, must mean something special. It normally refers to a textile embellished by lively colors, but is said also of gold sewn on (not embroidered in) garments. See Serjeant, *Islamic Textiles*, XV-XVI, 76 a, bottom.

[148]During the estimate the price was upgraded. A big jump! See *verso*, col. II, ll. 3, 16; f. 25 a, col. I, ll. 12, 13, where similar changes occur.

[149]Originally the garments described in ll. 8–10 were evaluated as parts of a robe of

honor. After some discussion it was agreed that the robe was only a *jūkāniyya*, a shorter piece of clothing. In l. 2, above, there was a similar dispute about definition. The object was first described as a kerchief, then upgraded to a wimple. On the other hand, a kerchief of costly material naturally got a higher estimate than a wimple of a less valuable fabric, see ll. 9–10.

[150]See n. 76, above.

[151]See n. 37, above. The very low price of this piece makes it likely that this was not genuine Chinese silk, but a fabric imitated in the Mediterranean area.

[152]A kerchief kept in the sleeve, see B, nn. 72–74, above.

[153]Price reduced.

[154]A sarilike wrap. The word was originally written in the next line. Later it was decided that the bathrobe and the *fūṭa* together were worth only 1 dinar, whereupon the word *fūṭa* was squeezed in here.

[155]These kerchiefs were worn on the head above the skullcap and beneath the wimple (see Wahrmund, *Handwörterbuch*, I, 183*b*), but served also other purposes, such as covers for baskets (TS K 25, f. 269, col. I, l. 10) or cooling jugs (TS 20.8A, l. 10). Brides had them in considerable quantities like here; in one case twenty, costing 30 dinars: TS 24.9, l. 28. See also App. D., Doc. II, f. 47*a*, l. 35 (eight *bukhnuqs* for 6 dinars).

[156]Ar. *furush*, literally, (textiles) spread out, whether on structures serving as beds and/or sitting facilities, or on the ground as carpets, but including also hangings. In Doc. III, col. III, ll. 24–25, "bedding and hangings" are kept separate, but for *furush* is used another term, *busuṭ* (designating also specifically carpets).

[157]This is not an erroneous repetition. The long and comparatively high *martaba* stood at the "front", that is, the wall farthest away from the entrance to a room and was reserved for the host and his most honored guests. The two *ṭarrāḥas*, which were lower, were placed along the side walls and accommodated less prominent people. For a similar arrangement concerning curtains see n. 81, above.

[158]Deleted, because noted in l. 10, below.

[159]Ar. here and in the next ketubba in Mevōrākh's record book (Firkovitch II, 1700, f. 26 a, col. I, l. 3): *murāyash*; more common in the Geniza: *murayyash*, literally, feathered, decorated with sprigs made of costly materials, cf. Lane, *Modern Egyptians*, p. 568 (explanation of *reeshe*).

[160]The bed cover *liḥāf* was not a bedspread for the day, but served for nightly rest. Like here, it was often made of heavy material (brocade, as in Docs. I, near the end; II, l. 49; III, col. III, ll. 12–13, above) and lined, cf. TS K 15, f. 99, col. II, l. 21: "a small siglaton *liḥāf* with red lining."

Nūna, if my reading is correct, means fish, an appropriate ornament for the conjugal bed. But *nūna* designates a single fish, and, although Jonah's fish was a popular medieval ornament, I doubt that it is intended here.

[161]As the price indicates, "complete" probably includes the utensils regularly kept in such a box, see n. 163, below.

[162]Spain was a main exporter of fine copper ware in those days, see Doc. III, col. III, l. 27.

[163]The large box was noted in l. 20, and the small box was in the large one and included in its price, see n. 161, above, and Doc. III, col. III, l. 28: "a large box and a small box inside it."

[164]This is written in Aramaic, which seems to show that the entry "the bureau and its unmentionables [lingerie]" is pre-Islamic.

[165]Ar. *mujāwam*, derived from the Persian loanword *jām*, goblet. Norman Stillman, in his letter of April 20, 1980, informs me that the word in the description of a male robe occurs in Maqrīzī, *Khiṭaṭ* (Beirut, 1970), II, 129, as taken from a Fatimid source. The goblet was a very common heraldic emblem, and, thus, fits a male robe well. In the Geniza, however, the word is mostly used in the description of the female head cover *bukhnuq*, see n. 155, above. Thus another meaning of *jām*, glasslike, see Dozy, *Supplément*, I 168*b*, may be intended.

[166]Ar. *ʿūd al-zān*, see Maimonides-Meyerhof, p. 115, sec. 231. Wehr, *Modern Written*

Arabic, s.v. The maidservants often owed their names to the whims of their mistresses, cf. the names in *Med. Soc.*, I, 135–141, and n. 133, above.

[167]This backyard object was not in the place where the outfit was estimated and had, therefore, been forgotten. Women loved to dye their clothes at home, see *Med. Soc.*, II, 359–360.

[168]Amīn al-Dawla (Trusted Servant of the Government) was the honorary title of Abu 'l-Ḥasan, Sitt al-Riyāsa's brother. That the same person is first referred to as "her brother" and then solely with his honorary title is irritating to us, but was regarded as an elegant way of expression in those days, see *Med. Soc.*, II, 236–237. Here we learn that Abu 'l-Ḥasan, obviously, as his title implies, a well-to-do government official, had given his sister one-half of both a large and a small house confronting each other (thus described in his will) on the occasion of her wedding. Four years later, on his deathbed, see n. 110, above, he willed her the remaining halves.

Document VI

[169]Cf. Goitein, *Letters*, pp. 220–226, a husband out in the countries of the Indian ocean writing to his wife.

[170]*Med. Soc.*, III, 189–205, and, in particular, p. 200.

[171]Goitein, *Letters*, pp. 226 and 249–252.

[172]Ar. *dumluj*, a rigid bracelet mostly made of gold and in most ketubbot highly valued, e.g., a pair worth 15 dinars in Antonin 635, written in Tyre, Lebanon, 1054 (see Shaked, *Bibliography of Geniza Documents*, p. 167, re-edited by Friedman, *Marriage*, no. 29), l. 15, and in TS 8 J 29, f. 7, l. 2. (This document is not included in *Med. Soc.*, III, Appendix; it is detailed, but incomplete; the script points to the earlier part of the eleventh century.) A single dumluj worth 14 dinars in TS 13 J 3, f. 10c, col. I, l. 14 (1159, see *Med. Soc.*, III, 405, no. 170, and App. D, Doc X d). In the small town Damsīs, a pair was worth 3 dinars in 1083, PER H 24, see *Med. Soc.*, III, 388, sec. 7. Found in this form in ancient Arabic poetry, but dumluj is spelled here *dmlwj*, which is absolutely exceptional in the Geniza. The broker writes also *mwsthl* for *mustahill*, ll. 2, 4, etc. See B, n. 515, above.

[173]A grain, Ar. *ḥabba*, is 1/72 of a dinar. Since the loan given for a pawn was an approximate sum (and mostly smaller than the price of the object pawned), such precision is strange. The sums paid by the pawner were certainly given to her partly (or totally?) in promissory notes ("checks"). There was no coin of 1/72 dinar.

[174]Ar. *muzarra*, see n. 83, above. The Roman number after a Muslim month indicates its place in the Muslim year.

[175]Ar. *maṭraḥ* (from which English *mattress* is derived). As the material with which it was covered proves, the *maṭraḥ* was more than a mattress; it served as a bed.

[176]Ar. *ṭunfusa*, a common word for carpet in those days.

[177]A gown with sleeves.

[178]See n. 24, above. Maʿājir, spelled here wrongly *mʿjr*.

[179]Ar. *muṣmat*, of one color and without patterns. As the illustrations from medieval Muslim manuscripts show, their garments (also of men) were usually of several colors and different patterns. The trousseau lists normally note only one color or one pattern for a particular piece; they mean the *main* color or pattern by which a clothing or bedding could be identified.

[180]Ar. *maghsal*, destined for the washing of the hands by guests. Made of copper and sometimes of silver, as in TS 8 J 5, f.1, l. 19 (dated 1114), among the utensils left by a man from the noble Ben Naḥūm family. The unusually high price assigned to it here shows that this was an uncommon piece.

[181]Shawwāl was the tenth month of the year 441. Shaʿbān is the eighth month of the Muslim year. Thus here we are in 442.

[182]The "basket" was of silver and belonged to the wife's dressing table (for small utensils). This explains the high sum given for these items. A dinar was equal to 24 qīrāṭs.

[183]Most of a line is left blank; the broker remembered that there was another item, but did not find the relevant voucher.

[184]Ar. *ṭrḥh smn*, which stands for *ṭarrāḥah sāmān*. An object of the same type was evaluated in the trousseau list of the "rich bride" as being worth 3 dinars, see n. 105, above.

[185]Unnecessarily repeated.

[186]Ar. *mulā'a*, see n. 33, above, spelled here *mwlh*.

[187]There was still room on the page for about 10 lines, but the writer did not continue. He was confused, see nn. 183 and 185, above.

[188]Described in *Med Soc.*, II, 454, sec. 57 a. Edited in *Joshua Finkel Festschrift* (New York, N.Y., 1974), pp. 125–126.

[189]The costly *siglaton* textile, of which one effaced item was made, was used for both clothing and bedding, see B, n. 195, and here, n. 102, above.

[190]The date "First" is qualified by "during the first ten days of the month," meaning that the woman took her monthly alimony not on the New moon day, but a few days later. This dating after the three "decades" of a month was common in pre-Islamic Coptic as well as in the Muslim and Geniza documents.

[191]See n. 174, above.

[192]Cf. Ashtor, *Prix*, pp. 216–217, where 1 dinar per month is repeatedly assigned to middle-class women with one child (in the years 1066 and 1132, also 1151, where the number of children is not indicated). For the topic of allowances, see *Med. Soc.*, III, 191–200 (what absent husbands contributed to their families' maintenance) and D, Retrospective, above.

Document VII

[193]Examples in *Med. Soc.*, III, 243–244.

[194]Selected pieces: *ibid.*, p. 349, Assigning to heirs: *Sefunot*, 8 (1964), 116.

[195]TS 12.530, dated 2 Jan. 1105.

[196]TS 12.633. The left half of the document containing the name of the place where it was written is cut away and the remaining part is completely effaced so that, apart from the names at the beginning (of Ḥasan in TS 12.633, as here, in TS Misc. Box 25, f. 53, ll. 5 and 13, only Ḥ has been preserved), a few phrases, and part of the signatures, nothing can be read. The identity of the place name is established by the signatures of the court clerk She'ērīth b. Yākhīn (Remnant, son of Steadfast, Heb.) ha-Kohen and Shabbetay b. Abraham, the spiritual leader of the Jewish community in Minyat Ziftā, see *Med. Soc.*, II, 48–49; also ULC Add. 3423 (June 1175) and TS AS 147, f. 38 (June 1178).

[197]For instance, the very detailed inventory of the estate of Joseph b. Samuel of the noble Ben Naḥūm family taken on 11 August 1114, lists banker's and promissory notes, cash (in gold), silver vessels, jewelry, bars of precious materials, and two maid servants, but not a single piece of clothing. His widow testified that she had given all the jewelry contained in her trousseau to her daughter when she married her off to her son-in-law, who was present at the time of the stock taking, TS 8 J 5, f. 1, cf. *Med. Soc.*, I, 264.

[198]The presence of the widow on such occasions is attested in many Geniza texts. See also preceding note.

[199]See Mann, I, 244 (where 1711 is a misprint for 1171).

[200]See my article, " 'Ha-Rav'," *Tarbiz*, 45 (1976), 64–75, and its "Additions", *ibid.*, 46 (1977), 64–75.

[201]See on this question S. Assaf, *Gaonica* (Jerusalem, 1933), pp. 91–92, esp. p. 92 n. 1, and p. 97, where the Palestinian Gaon Solomon b. Judah (d. 1051) holds that writing and arranging a wedding on the "middle days" is not a deadly sin, but only contravenes the words of the sages, which might be disregarded in cases of emergency. The question was: What is urgent? Rabbi Yōm Tōv b. Abraham of Sevilla received permission to write down his *Novellae*, or new ideas, on the "middle days," because he might forget and thus "lose" them (ed. E. Hurvitz [Jerusalem, 1976], p. 3). A letter in which greetings to M. Maimonides are extended was written on the middle days of the Feast of Tabernacles (Sept.–Oct. 1200), ENA NS 19, f. 10*v*, ll. 10–15, see C, 1, n. 91, above.

[202]See the last section of our document (TS Misc. Box 25, f. 53, ll. 5–13).

[203]The second sheet, which clearly belongs to the same recordbook and is written up in full, contains seventeen lines.

[204]The document is in the hand of Mevōrākh b. Nathan, who for several decades served as clerk to the rabbinical court, see, for instance, Doc. V, written by him fourteen years prior to our record.

[205]ULC Or 1080 J 142, l. 8, where two *waṭās*, or sleeping carpets, are listed. "This bundle" refers to the third *waṭā*, which had been mentioned in the lost space on the lower part of the first page. *Verso*, l. 4, a fourth *waṭā* is introduced. This term stands for any facility on which one slept, but here, as often, it designates a sleeping carpet, which was rolled out on the floor and, when bundled up, could serve as a container of considerable size, cf. TS 8 J 24, f. 21, l. 7, trans. Goitein, *Letters*, p. 322: "I rolled out my *waṭā*, spread on it my bedding, and slept."

[206]Ar. *ifrīz*, pl. *farāwiz*, a loanword in classical Arabic (see Fraenkel, *Aramäische Fremdwörter*, p. 22) and still alive in the meaning of frieze (with which English word *ifrīz* might have a common origin) and the like. A look at the pictures of curtains in Ettinghausen, *Arab Painting*, pp. 98, 99, 106, 107, 113, 121, shows that on the top they had ornamental bands of different types, either sewn on them (as in pp. 106, 113, 121), or forming separate decorations, like valances.

[207]Ar. *qiṭʿa*, a decorative piece, mentioned here three times with the function of fastening the borders of a robe or cloak together, ll. 6, 12, 13, and three times as mere ornamentation, on a turban, l. 9, a shawl, l. 10, and a scarf, *verso*, l. 7.

[208]Ar. *sakākīn*, literally, knives, as decoration of a crested turban, see *Med. Soc.*, I, 419 n. 41, end. For illustrations of the pointed ribbons in which a turban might end, see Ettinghausen, *Arab Painting*, pp. 79 and 97.

[209]See n. 143, above. Blue might refer to semiprecious stones, used for the ornament, cf. B, n. 402, above.

[210]Just as the main room of the house had a center and two side curtains (see n. 81, above), a high and extended sitting facility on the wall most remote from the entrance, and lower and shorter ones on the side walls (see n. 157, above), thus one had a center carpet and lower runners on its side. See A, 4, nn. 81–84.

The carpet was white—one did not enter the *majlis* wearing shoes.

[211]Ar. *muzannar*, derived from *zunnār*, the girdle usually worn by Christians.

[212]Camphor-colored, that is, dark brown. The last ruler of Egypt before the Fatimid conquest was the Abyssinian slave Kāfūr Abu 'l-Misk, literally, Camphor father of Musk, both denoting that color. "Eye," a roundish ornament.

[213]Probably a carpet. Noted by me only here and in l. 11. May be derived from *qahramāna* (a female administrator of a princely household, being pronounced by Persians as *k*), or from *kahramān*, amber, a type of carpet originally known by that color, but later produced also in other colors.

[214]The Ar. root *lthm* designates a white material with which one covers his nose, mouth, and neck as a protection from dust.

[215]Ar. *ʿarḍī*, see B, nn. 16 and 331, above. Plain, *sādhij*, without patterns (which was uncommon).

[216]Ar. *ṭaraf*, from which *muṭraf*, the luxury garment par excellence of early Islamic times, is derived, see Doc. III, col. II, l. 8 above, where the edges are ornamented with gold threads.

[217]About this, originally Yemenite, type of clothing Ibn Abī d-Dunyā (d. 894) wrote in his *The Noble Qualities of Character*, ed. J. A. Bellamy (Wiesbaden, 1973), Arabic text, p. 92, l. 2: " 'Do you know what a *burda* is?' 'This is a *shamla* [large shawl, see B, n. 16] in which the decorative borders are woven in.' "

[218]The *muqaddar*, literally, a piece, whose measurements and value are determined, then "valuable," "large," was a type of male clothing, mentioned more than fifty times in the Geniza as handed out to community officials and others, but not yet found elsewhere as designating a garment. It was so common in Geniza times, that we even come upon a *muqaddarī*, or maker of muqaddars, *Med. Soc.*, II, 547 n. 28. About their distribution see *ibid.*, pp. 130–131; 448, sec. 33; 449, sec. 36, sixth paragraph (where, exceptionally, a woman was one of four recipients); 459 n. 71.

[219]This city in northern Iraq, which lent its name to English *muslin*, was famed as a textile center throughout Islamic history, see Serjeant, *Islamic Textiles*, pp. 38–39.

[220]The little yellow apples of the *mandragora* plant, which were regarded as an aphrodisiac (see Genesis 30:14–16, Song of Songs 7:14), appear repeatedly in the Geniza as a decorative pattern, e.g., *mukhlaf luffākha*, a mandrake-patterned patchwork cloth, *ʿarḍī luffākha*, a broad shawl of the same type, Bodl. MS Heb. f 56 (Cat. 2821) f. 48, ll. 3 and 13. Here, between *mandīl*, kerchief, and *luffākha* the word *sl'm* is written; *salām*, of course, means peace, greetings. The same combination "two *salām* kerchiefs" in TS K 25, f. 269, col. I, l. 27. Perhaps, originally a kerchief waved at a dance honoring the arrival of guests.

[221]Mentioned in l. 1, above.

[222]Ar. *mushāhar* (like this mostly in the Geniza) or *mushahhar* (e.g., TS 12.119, l. 4, ed. Friedman, *Marriage*, no. 38, or PER H 19, l. 11), see Dozy, *Supplément*, I, 795–796.

[223]Although the last sign of *jk'n'* cannot be distinguished from an *aleph*, no doubt a *yh* is intended in this as in the same word in the two next lines. Here, where Mevōrākh b. Nathan took an inventory at the very time when the objects to be noted were put into receptacles, he permitted himself abbreviations; in Doc. V, where he made a clean copy of an important "estimate," he wrote calligraphically. Princely fabric, Ar. *ṭarḥ al-imāra*, cf. Dozy, *Supplément*, II, 31*a*. The first letter of *'m'rh* is covered by a dark substance.

[224]Ar. *niqāb*, trans. above as face-cover for women. Here it designates a kind of hood attached to the burnoose, worn by men, cf. Stillman, "Female Attire," p. 175 n. 3 (based on Maghrebi sources).

[225]For *bukhnuq* see n. 155, above. Tinnīs linen: B, n. 121.

[226]Ar. *quwāra*, literally, scrap, something carved out, cut out, for instance, a round piece of cloth, especially for covering a table, Maqrīzī, *Khiṭaṭ*, I, 472, quoted by M. A. Marzouk, *History of Textile Industry in Alexandria* (Alexandria, 1955), p. 96, and found in this sense in ENA 1822, f. 57, l. 21, "a green *quwāra* for the table," sent from the Maghreb to Alexandria. Siglaton *quwāras* are mentioned early in the eleventh century, TS 12.12, l. 22; a Yemenite *quwāra* occurs together with other textiles from Yemen in a long trousseau list from the thirteenth century, TS K 25, f. 42, l. 10. In our document, where it contains clover, the translation "sachet" seems to be appropriate. The perfuming of clothing was almost obligatory. (See also *zanburiyya* for sachet: TS NSJ 390, last line.)

[227]Ar. *muzannar*, see n. 211, above, where the term describes a scarf.

[228]Ar. *zinjila*, pl. *zanājil*, as common in the Geniza as absent from dictionaries in this meaning of canister or the like, see A, 5. nn. 29–31.

[229]Ar. *zanfalīja* (of which Fraenkel, *Aramäische Fremdwörter*, p. 209, could not find the derivation), again a rare word, but common in the Geniza. The original meaning of slip case in TS 10 J 5, f. 15 (November 1021): a scribe undertakes to copy the books of Prophets and Hagiographs, to bind them, and to make slip cases for them. In the general sense of a container with a rigid cover: TS 16.32, l. 16 (also early eleventh century), where it is used for lingerie, that is, for textiles, as in our document; TS 12.520*v*, l. 9 (Jan. 1105, inventory of the estate of a foreigner), where it contains oil-painted wood, but is crossed out and replaced by *qimaṭra*, which Arabic word is derived from the Aramaic, as is well known from the Talmud, also with the original sense of a receptacle for books (BT Megilla 26*b*). In TS 10 J 11, f. 2, l. 5 the learned Nagid Mevōrākh b. Saʿadya is lauded as "a bookcase" with this Talmudic expression. See A, 4, n. 191, above. For another use of this word see n. 291, below.

[230]Ar. *marhamdān*, not found by me anywhere, but self-explanatory: *marham*, bandages (Ar.), *dān*, a Persian affix denoting a container.

[231]Since the word is clearly written and occurs also in l. 5, there can be no doubt about its reading; its meaning is defined by the addition "for kohl containers." This term should not be taken too narrowly. The physician kept in these containers the various ophthalmological medications. An ophthalmologist is called in Arabic *kaḥḥāl*, an applier of kohl.

[232]Ar. *marfaʿ*. This word has two entirely different meanings: (1) a container of water or other liquids, as in Doc. III, col. I, l. 16, above, often, as there, accompanied

by a cover and a ladle, a costly vessel, which, during meals, stood on the table like a tureen, and (2) a copper stand for cups or dishes used in the kitchen. See A, 5, nn. 63–69.

[233]Ar. *narjisiyya*. (Both the Arabic and English words are derived from the Greek.) The cup- or trumpet-like form of the narcissus flower easily lent itself to be used as a designation for a vessel. Found elsewhere in the Geniza as made either of silver or of brass, sometimes as having a cover (always needed as a protection against flies) or several of them brought in on a tray. They had also violet-shaped cups, *banafsajiyyāt*, but these were not as common as the narcissus-like ones. See A, 5, nn. 88–91.

[234]Ar. *dast*, as in Doc. III, col. 1, l. 34, where, for simplicity's sake, the translation "equipment for" was preferred.

[235]Not for cutting bread (it was "broken" or torn), but for cutting meat in the kitchen, often served as fillings for vegetables.

[236]No room for signatures and no need for them. This was the draft kept by the court and identified by the handwriting of Mevōrākh b. Nathan, the clerk.

Document VIII

[237]See *Med. Soc.*, II, 254–255, and *passim*.

[238]Ar. *qidam*, used in the sense of "antique" rather than "worn out."

[239]*Mulḥam*, a cloth whose warp is of silk and waft of cotton, see Kühnel-Bellinger, *Tiraz Fabrics*, p. 99 and *passim*. Common in the Geniza, especially in the early twelfth century.

[240]Ar. *busht* or *bisht*, a working dress made of brown wool, that is, retaining the natural color of that fabric, see Dozy, *Supplément*, I, 88*a*, probably connected with Persian *pūsh*, garment, and *pusht*, back. The inventory of the estate of a poor inner decorator contained, besides timber and marble slabs, only a *busht*, TS 8 J 4, f. 22, l. 9.

[241]Ar. *khalaq*.

[242]Ar. *malbūs*, simply "worn," without the connotation of being faded. The same Doc. II, margin I, l. 34, above.

[243]A gown into which the ornamental borders were woven, see n. 217, above.

[244]From Nūl, a place in southwest Morocco, not far from the Atlantic Ocean. Since we see here even a coppersmith in Fustat possessing two Nūlī *biqyārs*, it is no longer "strange" that the Sicilian geographer Idrīsī should refer to that place as one producing exquisite fabrics made of silk and linen, or silk and fine wool, Serjeant, *Islamic Textiles*, p. 185.

[245]Sūsī refers in the Geniza usually to the town of Sūsa in Tunisia. Here, I believe, the Sūs al-Aqṣā, the Moroccan province, whose womenfolk produced unsurpassed specialities, is intended, see Serjeant, *Islamic Textiles*, p. 189.

[246]Ar. *wa-khalwatoh*. I have not yet seen this word in the meaning of the container of a turban. It usually designates a small room into which one retires (today, for instance, a cabin).

[247]See B, n. 327, above.

[248]While on a trip to Spain, our coppersmith might have bought these robes for his own future use. One also carried textiles while transporting large quantities of other goods to use them to pay customs dues, when necessary, see Goitein, *Letters*, p. 184.

[249]It was common practice to pack objects (and not only fragile ones) in pillows or pieces of clothing, even pants. The two gowns had been destined to form part of the deceased man's burial attire, but had not been used for that purpose.

[250]The mats made of the reeds of ʿAbbadān in southern Iran, then renowned for its reeds, as it is now for its oil, usually appear in documents in pairs, since one slept on them. Our coppersmith was obviously not married.

[251]Pigeon races were a favorite sport, or, rather, pastime, see *Med. Soc.*, II, 85. The *zinjila* (see n. 228) contained food for the pigeons.

[252]These large jars for drinking water brought from the Nile, usually stood in the entrance hall of the ground floor. Since our coppersmith had no wife "to hand him a cup of water"—as the phrase went—he posited the jars on the second floor. The bucket in l. 34 was for well water used for washing, not for drinking.

Document IX

[253]Ar. *ḥuzza* (pl. *ḥuzaz*, TS 8 J 29, f. 7*v*, l. 4) originally the band that kept the underpants together, then used for the lower underwear in general. See B, n. 295, above.

[254]For the *tafṣīla* see *ibid.*, n. 222, above, and the comments below. It was sesame-colored, like that robe in l. 8, and perhaps worn together with it.

[255]Ar. *fātiḥī*, of light or faint color. Common in modern Arabic. Our thirteenth-century document is probably the oldest witness for this use. See ll. 6–8, 12.

[256]Made pure, meaning uniform in color. About this process see B, n. 199, above. The numeral above this item seems to be Heb. *r* with a dot, meaning *r(ubᶜ)*, a quarter.

[257]Red Indian silk, see *Med. Soc.*, I, 454 n. 53. When the shawl was made, two cubits of this material were not used.

[258]A Coptic numeral written beneath the upper part of the Hebrew section represents, it seems, the price for all the items of that part. The dealer, after having tentatively assigned prices for the first five items, suggested a lump sum for the entire group.

The Coptic fractions have different forms. I do not remember having seen the numeral after 8. The 1/2 in l. 1 of the text in Arabic script has the usual form. The sign for 1/2 above l. 3 is commonly used in Hebrew texts.

[259]Ar. *mulawwan*, see B, nn. 171 and 238, above.

[260]Ar. *ᶜimāma maḥshiyya*, see *ibid.*, n. 341, above.

[261]It is interesting that in TS NS Box 325, f. 13, the tafṣīla was sesame-colored as it is here and cost 42 dirhems, which corresponds to 1 dinar in our Hebrew text and the 42 dirhems in the Arabic.

[262]Cf. *Med. Soc.*, II, 94, and 542 n. 3 and III, 520 (Index, s.v. "Solomon b. Elijah").

[263]Ar. *farīda*, a precious pearl or gem set alone, or an outstanding middle piece of a necklace or shoulder band. The term *farīda*, used absolutely as here and in the next document translated (TS 20.7, l. 7) frequently occurs in classical Arabic literature, especially denoting a pearl of outstanding size and beauty, but is rarely used thus in the Geniza, see B, n. 398. It is more common in combination with the material from which it is made: An amber farīda with golden heads, 4 dinars, TS NS J 410, col. I, l. 8; made of silver, *ibid.*, l. 7; of gold, 5 dinars, TS K 15, f. 111, col. I, l. 5; of amber, 6 dinars, Bodl. MS Heb. a 3 (Cat. 2873), f. 42, l. 19 (dated 1117).

This term should not be confused with *farda*, single, as opposed to "a pair."

[264]Ar. *akhrāṣ muᶜanbara* (rare!) *mukallala*, see B, n. 405, above.

[265]Ar. *kummiyya* (not noted elsewhere), derived from *kumm*, sleeve. The ornamental stripe around the upper part of the sleeve, sometimes formed by pearls, see B, nn. 79–82, and n. 520, below.

[266]Text *krd'dy*. The reading is confirmed by TS AS 146, f. 7, *recto* and *verso*, dated June 6 and 7, 1082, respectively, where a married orphan receives an object bearing that name, which had been deposited with a third person. The word occurs there three times and a fourth time in Doc. X *e* (TS NS J 390, l. 6), below, so that there can be no doubt about its reading. The question is whether the Hebrew letter *k* represents Arabic *k* or *kh*, see the discussion of the term *mukhlaf*, above nn. 117–120, esp. n. 118. To the best of my knowledge there exists no Arabic or Persian word *krd'd*. *Khurdād* is the name of the third month of the Persian year, corresponding to May–June (details in *Wüstenfeld-Mahlersche Vergleichungs-Tabellen*, ed. B. Spuler [Wiesbaden, 1961], p. 46). Professor Jerome Clinton drew my attention to *Burhān Qāṭiᶜ* (Tehran, 1342/1963), II, 730, where the Khurdād is described as the month of "seeking a wife," or matchmaking. This would explain the name of the *khurdādī* as a traditional wedding present, although it does not help us to know its shape and specific purpose. When I was shown of late the illustration of one of four sides of a beautiful ivory box from an Islamic country with Hebrew good wishes for a wedding (as far as I know, still in private hands), it occurred to me that khurdādī might have been just the right name for such a jewelbox.

[267]Text *jān*, meaning soul and dear in Persian. This precious ornament was com-

mon in Geniza documents of the first half of the eleventh century, but disappears later entirely. In ENA NS 3, f. 24, l. 15, a gold *jān* is worth 25 dinars, see Friedman, *Marriage*, no. 1. Furthermore, TS 13 J 17, f. 14*v*, l. 1 (1030/1), see *Med. Soc.*, III, 182 and n. 110; TS 13 J 1, f. 12, l. 8 (1049), see *ibid.*, III, 183 and n. 118. In Al-Tanūkhī, *Nishwār al-Muḥāḍara* (Beirut, 1971), I, 272 n. 1, it is a common piece of jewelry possessed by the concubines of the narrator. (When he urgently needed money for an unforeseen demand, he asked them to deliver their *jāns* to him.) That happened in tenth-century Baghdad. Thus the *jān* obviously was an Eastern (Irani-Iraqi) ornament imported to Egypt by the many immigrants from that region, but later went out of fashion.

[268]The clerk used here the Aramaic word *ʿizq*, after he had written in the same line Arabic *khātam* for ring. Because of the religious significance of rings at the conclusion of a marriage, the Aramaic word perhaps lingered on in Jewish speech. In tenth-century marriage documents, where the trousseau lists are partly in Aramaic, *ʿizq*, of course, is constantly used.

[269]Ar. *maḍrab* (in the Geniza found by me only here), see Dozy, *Supplément*, II, 7, last item (taken from an Arabic-Spanish dictionary printed in Granada 1505), it is described as a glass vial. Here, too, the small vessel might have been made partly of glass (and only in part of silver).

[270]See *Med. Soc.*, III, 405, no. 181, where 50 + 40 is to be changed to 40 + 50.

[271]Flat or plain, Ar. *sādhija*. Here the clerk skipped over one word, probably a type of bracelet and not adorned with pearls or filigree. In the next two lines he wrote "rings" twice. In l. 5 earrings with pearls are noted.

[272]This shoulder band, *katifiyya* or *kitfiyya*, probably consisted of two interconnected chains, one having the gold apple and the other the gold "cherry plum," as its center piece. See n. 290, below, and B, nn. 489–492, above.

[273]A minor difficulty in the dating of this document must be clarified. Our record is item III of a series of five records written on six pages by the scribe Mevōrākh b. Nathan. Item II, which is written on the reverse side of item I, is clearly dated: "During the last ten days of the month Adar II of the year of the Documents 1470," which corresponds to March 11–20, 1159. The format of items I–II is smaller than that of the following pages. Item II is stuck to our document, which seems to show that they were preserved and later disposed of in the Geniza together. Our document bears no date, but its second page is found on a sheet containing items IV and V, in both of which the number 70 is written in an awkward way, possibly to be read as 60, "9th of Siwan," which would correspond to May 18, 1149. If this were true, the four pages of items III–V would be the oldest dated documents from Mevōrākh's hand, see *Med. Soc.*, II, 514, sec. 22. For the purpose of our study, it is irrelevant whether the date was 1159 or 1149.

[274]A tiara with the same number of pieces in Doc. IV, l. 6, above, see B, n. 460, above.

[275]About this ornament worn on the chest see n. 142, above.

[276]The same in Doc. IV, l. 9 and Doc. V, l. 16, above.

[277]See n. 141, above.

[278]See n. 143, above. The word *ḥadīda* was crossed out, because the scribe had overlooked the gold *khūṣa* palm leaf. The ḥadīda is properly listed in the next line. There was no similarity in form between the bracelet and the khūṣa ornament.

[279]Ar. *sharrāba* or *shurrāba*, pl. *sharārīb*. The tassel was probably formed by gold threads.

[280]Ar. *ṣʾfry*; the form *ṣāfirī*, although derived from *ṣfr*, yellow, is strange. Perhaps Ẓāfirī is meant, namely, gold coins with the name of the caliph al-Ẓāfir (ruled 1149–1154) ornamenting the pins, see Lane-Poole, *History of Egypt*, pp. 171–173.

[281]Ar. *madhāf*, see n. 96, and Doc. III, col. I, l. 20, above, where the same price is attached to it.

[282]See n. 145, above.

[283]Ar. *kummathrāʾiyya*, a flat piece of silver, having the outline of a pear; here not forming an ornament for a pin, as in Doc. II, col. I, l. 4, above, and in other Geniza

lists (cf. also Lane, *Modern Egyptians*, p. 574), but used for applying make-up. For *barniyya* see A, 4, n. 219, above.

[284]Perforated crystal figurines containing the kohl applicator as in nn. 97 and 98, above.

[285]The addition is exact, not rounded up or down.

[286]TS NS J 390, which is the major, but less well-preserved part of the manuscript, was copied by me in Cambridge, England, on Aug. 23, 1961, from the original. My intention then was to save of the New Series of documentary character (NS J) as much as possible, irrespective of the content. I copied TS 13 J 7, f. 8, in July 1977 from an excellent photostat because of my interest in the terms of material civilization occurring in it. That the two fragments belong together and form one complete document was realized only on Nov. 16, 1980, when I worked on this Appendix.

[287]According to my addition: 488. The parties might have agreed on a round sum.

[288]Ar. *raḥl*, literally, provisions for travel. The transition from "the mother's home" to that of the husband was indeed an arduous journey. For this term see App. C, above.

[289]Originally *tmnyn*, 80, was written, and the number was unsuccessfully tampered with. But there is no doubt about the correction intended, as the total of the estimate proves.

[290]Ar. *qilāda* (spelled here without *alif*), usually translated as necklace; but as the number of beads, the similarity with the *katifiyya* (see n. 272, above), and the meaning of the root (girding with a sword) seem to indicate, probably, some larger ornament is meant. Lane, *Modern Egyptians*, p. 572, describes it as "a long kind of necklace, reaching to the girdle." Similarly in Stillman, *Palestinian Costume*, p. 94. That even in ancient Arabia the *qilāda* must have been a very substantial piece may be deduced from this curious story told by Ibn Abī d-Dunya, *The Noble Qualities of Character*, ed. James A. Bellamy (Wiesbaden, 1973), p. 95, no. 343: when in the battle of Badr, the first fought in Islam, the husband of Muhammad's stepdaughter (who fought in the Meccan army) was taken prisoner, his wife sent the *qilāda* of her mother Khadīja (Muhammad's wife) as ransom for her husband. The Prophet recognized his wife's chain and sent it back together with the captive.

[291]See n. 266, above.

[292]Ar. *qimaṭra*, taken here, as in Doc. III, col. I, l. 28, above, as a jewel or scent box or case (so Steingass, *Persian-English Dictionary*, p. 988*b*) or the like. For another use of this Aramaic loanword see n. 229, above.

Index

NOTE: Because of the frequency of their occurrence, the following have not been indexed: Fustat, Islam, Jew[ish], Judaism, Muslim; Husband; Wife, Woman.

Compositor: Prestige Typography
Text: 10/12 Baskerville
Display: Baskerville
Printer: BookCrafters
Binder: BookCrafters